Faction Politics

Studies in International and Comparative Politics

PETER H. MERKL, SERIES EDITOR

Faction Politics:
Political Parties and Factionalism in Comparative Perspective

Frank P. Belloni
Dennis C. Beller
editors

ABC-Clio, Inc.

Santa Barbara, California
Oxford, England

Library of Congress Cataloging in Publication Data

Main entry under title:

Faction politics.

   (Studies in international and comparative politics; 11)
   Includes bibliographical references and index.
   1. Political parties—Addresses, essays, lectures.
2. Comparative government—Addresses, essays, lectures.
I. Belloni, Frank P. II. Beller, Dennis C.,
1934-   III. Series.
JF2011.F3   329'.02'09045   78-1524
ISBN 0-87436-248-2

American Bibliographical Center—Clio Press
Riviera Campus, 2040 A. P. S., Box 4397
Santa Barbara, California 93103

Clio Press, Ltd.
Woodside House, Hinksey Hill
Oxford OXI 5BE, England

Manufactured in the United States of America
First Printing
1 2 3 4 5 6 7 8 9 10

Contents

v

Part Four: Single-Party Systems

Part Five: Conclusion

Faction Politics

Part One
INTRODUCTION

1

The Study of Factions

DENNIS C. BELLER
FRANK P. BELLONI

The word *faction* is used frequently in the general sense of internal factions of an organization or group. Textbooks refer to factions in policy disputes, in political parties, and in various political organizations. The news media refer to factions in civil wars, in city politics, in Congress, and at the United Nations. The term is also used widely in nonpolitical contexts: we hear of factions in business corporations, churches, labor unions, clubs, and even families. But the word mostly connotes political competition and conflict, and so the concept of faction belongs primarily to the language of politics, where references to specific factions and to factionalism are common.

Despite the frequent use of these words, study of the politics of factionalism has not been highly developed. This is particularly so in the context of the large body of literature devoted to phenomena of organization and competition for power, where the major share of attention is given to political parties and interest groups. Definitions of factions vary widely, yet there tends to be general agreement that factions are not the same as parties or interest groups. Most commonly, factions are thought of as existing *within* interest groups or

This chapter is a revision of Frank P. Belloni and Dennis C. Beller, "The Study of Party Factions as Competitive Political Organizations," *Western Political Quarterly* 29, no. 4 (Dec. 1976): 531–49. Reprinted by permission of the publisher.

parties. In some countries intraparty factions are the most critical aspect of national politics; in others intraparty factions are at least politically significant. Since factions are relevant to the political processes of nearly all countries, the development of the study of factions is vitally important.

This book is an effort to develop such a study. It places factionalism in the foreground, and it treats the subject comparatively. It examines the theoretical questions involved in factions study and surveys factional case studies from around the world. Thus, this book has a dual purpose: to describe the factional political systems of fifteen countries and to analyze factions in broad and theoretical terms.

This chapter explores a traditional bias against factions, examines several questions recurring in earlier studies, and summarizes the case studies in this book.

The Traditional Bias Against Factions

Parties have received a lion's share of attention in the study of political competition. The significance traditionally attributed to political parties—and to a lesser extent to interest groups—as recognized organizations of political competition is partly due to the greater visibility of their structures and activities. Interest groups, and especially political parties, are more clearly evident and definable objects of study. The predominant attention given to parties also arises from the widespread idea that parties perform valid functions for the political system. Parties have achieved more legitimacy, although interest groups are also thought to play a positive role in the political process. Factions lack visible legitimacy.

The aura of legitimacy attached to party organizations and activities markedly contrasts with historical attitudes. When parties first emerged, in the eighteenth century, the reaction to all partisan groups was hostile. Opposition to parties was explicit and strong, and it reached a high point during the formative period of the American political system. The antipathy toward parties expressed by the American Founding Fathers is well known: parties were denounced for treasonable divisiveness and as sources of fanatical passions and violence; party spirit was viewed as the antithesis of public spirit. James Madison expressed his objections in his celebrated *Federalist*, no. 10, and George Washington warned against the evil of a creeping party spirit in his famous Farewell Address.[1] Parties were despised in Europe by those who witnessed their initial appearance.[2] Such attitudes were not confined to contemporaries of the emergence of parties; antiparty views persisted until the twentieth century, although many of the reasons for antipathy toward parties changed.[3]

When the politics of competitive partisan groups attracted hostile comments in the eighteenth century, little distinction was made between party and faction. The Founding Fathers used the two terms interchangeably, referring to them as a single phenomenon. Thus, Madison's strongly worded objection in *Federalist,* no. 10, referred both to faction and party, and in some cases used the phrase, "the spirit of party and faction." Washington's warning also referred alternately to party and faction. These men and their contemporaries used the terms *party politics* and *faction politics* as synonyms.[4]

Attitudes toward political parties have changed in modern times. Parties emerged and developed into distinct forms of political organization in the nineteenth and twentieth centuries; they appeared in more and more countries, and the notion of party outgrew earlier negative attitudes. Today parties are considered to be natural and proper parts of the political system. Parties have acquired legitimacy, and they are regarded as a necessity in most Western conceptions of democracy. As a result, parties have been given more objective consideration by political scientists, and the study of parties constitutes a subdiscipline with a large body of published books and studies. The significance of party politics in political science may be underscored by noting the status the concept of party system has achieved, along with its many subclassifications, such as two-party system, multiparty system, one-party dominant system.

There has been a parallel and more recent evolution of attitudes toward interest groups. Pressure groups evoked hostile reactions during the late nineteenth and early twentieth centuries. There was an almost universal tendency to doubt the propriety and morality of such inherently selfish groups. According to Samuel Eldersveld, leading scholar, "they [pressure groups] were considered, by scholars as well as muckrakers, as engaged in questionable goals. They were not considered as sanctioned by the community nor as having a legitimate regime status."[5]

In recent years, interest groups have come to be regarded as natural, generally useful, and essentially legitimate. This change has been slower in coming than the equivalent change in attitude toward political parties and is still in progress. In broad view, and particularly with the advent of pluralistic theories of politics and democracy, interest groups have acquired legitimacy both as elements of the political process and as valid objects of analytical study. The concept of interest group system has recently come into use, recalling the earlier adoption of the concept of party system.[6] The legitimization and rise in status of interest groups has also led to the development of a recognized area of study in political science, extensive research, and publication of many books and studies.

Factions have not acquired legitimacy. The consideration of factions is still inhibited by the values attached to antiquated conceptions of factionalism. The term *faction,* it has been observed, has been an "opprobrious epithet" in politics "since Roman days."[7] Conventional attitudes toward factions are based on values perpetuated since the early days when faction and party were associated with only negative values. A cursory examination of references in textbooks or newspapers confirms that the term *faction* continues to connote illegitimacy, if not malevolence and pathology. Factions tend to be viewed from the vantage point of parties—often to explain party weaknesses, disintegration of unity, corruption, and opportunism among party leaders. Competition between parties is often lauded for providing leadership and policy alternatives, but no such assessment is made of factional competition. Instead, factions are said to produce strife, leading to stresses and strains and other disorders of a malfunctioning organization.[8]

Even without those pejorative value judgments, factions are mostly considered to be insignificant and inherently temporary. They are treated as interesting curiosities or as dysfunctional aberrations that appear in times of controversy. These attitudes prevail even though factionalism may divide a party's elite into organized units, divide a party's general membership, and even divide the larger body of citizens who regularly identify with and vote for the party. In short, factions are not understood as political phenomena in their own terms.

Consequently, the study of factions has been relatively neglected. Biased perspectives have foreclosed studies in which factions are the explicit objects of inquiry. Thus, while political parties and interest groups are examined as discrete and functional parts of the political system, factions are not. Yet comparative studies indicate that it is as important to analyze factions as it is to examine parties. Without diminishing the importance of parties as competitive mechanisms, we must nevertheless recognize that factions may perform a role in structuring competition for political power equal to that of the party system. Indeed, the faction system may be prevalent in some countries. Yet because of intellectual and emotional biases, the reality of factional systems is often overlooked.

In short, there is no reason why politics should be studied only or even primarily from the perspective of a party or parties which happen to have internal factional divisions, any more than from the perspective of factions which happen to be contained within parties. The traditional antifaction bias must be overcome if we are to have a complete understanding of all political systems.

The Evolution of Faction Study

There is considerable disagreement on precisely what factions are and what they do. Most definitions tend to reflect the intellectual interests of their authors, and the range of definition extends beyond political science. The first studies of factionalism were made by social anthropologists interested in small-scale peasant communities in non-Western societies. That interest led to the development of a concept of faction as a common form of political organization in traditional village settings.[9] Anthropologists typically saw factions as groups which structured conflict within the village or community differently than the formal traditional organizations such as clans and lineages. Anthropologists described factions in terms of leaders, sometimes called patrons, plus a varied number of the leaders' personally acquired followers, sometimes called clients. Thus, anthropologists developed the concept of the patron-client or clientist relationship as a typical basis of faction organization.[10]

Harold Lasswell, a pioneering political scientist, defined faction as early as the 1930s,[11] but there were no serious studies of factionalism in political science until long after. The word either did not appear in political studies, or it was used casually in reference to wings of parties, in what was implicitly viewed as party pathology. One of the first students of political parties to give serious attention to factions was V. O. Key, Jr., in the 1950s.[12] Key's conception of faction focused on the phenomenon of a candidate's personal coterie and was particularly relevant in studying the primary election campaigns in so-called one-party American states. He used the idea of faction to explain politics in states where intraparty rivalry was the only form of political competition. Key found bifactionalism and multifactionalism to be two typical patterns in those states.

Key approached the study of factions in terms of the functions they performed in the political process. His basic concern was the potential impact of factions on democracy. He concluded that intraparty factions tended to perform the same political functions in one-party states that were performed by competing parties in other states. Following Key's analysis, Allan Sindler concluded that bifactional rivalry in one-party Louisiana could approximate a two-party system under the roof of the single dominant party.[13] Nevertheless, Key and Sindler agreed that factions are less democratic than parties. Key concluded that faction politics did not perform as well as party politics in democratic two-party states and that one-party states, even if factionalized, were decidedly undemocratic in contrast to competitive two-party states.

Factions were largely ignored by political scientists abroad, although Maurice Duverger mentioned factions in his comparative study of political parties in the 1950s.[14] The comparative and analytical study of factions per se was initiated by Raphael Zariski. In an article published in 1960, he suggested "the relevance of the party faction as an essential category" of political phenomena; this was the first conceptual treatment to offer hypotheses to explain factional politics in a comparative framework.[15] He examined structural aspects of factions, organization and duration, and he explored the self-awareness of faction members (faction cognition), their common underlying motivations (factional raison d'être), and the setting in which factions develop (the faction system). Zariski thus shifted the approach from function to structure and to the causes of faction. He presented a broader view from which to survey the phenomena of factionalism and the questions raised by faction study. Zariski thus took a major step in inaugurating the comparative study of factions.

Beginning in the 1960s, more studies of factions—including anthropological—appeared, some of which followed many of the lines suggested by Zariski, or developed new ones. Factions became for the first time a sustained concern of analysis in political studies—although still not always without the handicap of the traditional antifaction bias.

William N. Chambers developed a distinctive conception of faction in the 1960s. Chambers used the notion of faction to explain how modern political parties were born, conceiving of factions as preparties.[16] He studied the origin of parties in eighteenth- and nineteenth-century America, where he found political organizations were initially factional in form and later became parties. The parties thus evolved gradually out of factions. An organizational continuity linked the protoparty form of faction to the mature political form, the party. Thus Chambers contributed an essentially historical perspective, and in this respect his definition of faction was unique.

Richard Rose, a student of contemporary parties in Great Britain, made another important addition to faction study.[17] Rose's study separated faction from another type of intraparty formation, the tendency. He defined faction as an organizational unit of political competition, and tendency as a constellation of viewpoints and attitudes. Rose was concerned with intraparty organization, and he adopted a structural approach to faction. He used levels of organizational development to distinguish between tendency and faction, just as others have used the same type of structural criteria to distinguish between faction and party. In this view, only a group with real structural coherence should be regarded as a true faction. A similar view was expressed by Joseph Nyomarkay, who was interested in the factions of the German Nazi party.[18] Nyomarkay specified the distinction between factions and less well-organized wings within parties.

New anthropological studies of factions also appeared in the 1960s, some demonstrating that village factions may become inseparably related to political party factions. One of the first efforts conceptually to draw together the views of anthropologists and political scientists regarding factions was the work of Ralph W. Nicholas, an anthropologist and one of the first writers to acknowledge and reject the traditional bias against factions.[19] He used the concept of faction to explain the informal, personal clientist groupings of premodern communities. At the same time he extended his concept to include modern organizations. He suggested that factionalism in a traditional Indian village setting, for example, and factionalism in a modern Japanese political party, are variations of a single kind of political structure.

The question of function, first raised by Key, was explored further in a study of the Indian party system by Rajni Kothari, a political scientist who helped develop the concept of the dominant-party system.[20] He argued that a political system of one-party dominance is different from a one-party system; pressure is brought on the dominant party by opposition parties and by pressure groups, political notables, and factions of the dominant party. Kothari's study of the Indian Congress party of the 1960s was the basis for his conclusions that factional politics was a partial substitute for political party competition and a counterweight to the negative aspects of one-party politics. Kothari also suggested that intraparty factions in a dominant party may contribute to its continued dominance.

Finally, some writing has gone beyond factions, to faction systems. Norman Nicholson characterized faction systems as a distinctive "style of politics."[21] He postulated three basic types of faction systems, each unique as an arena and in terms of the typical structure of the factions in the system: first, factionalism in the small, homogeneous community of traditional villages; second, polycommunal factionalism in nationwide political organizations or political parties, with ethnically pluralistic local and communal groups; and third, hierarchical factionalism in highly centralized power structures such as national governments, bureaucracies, or national party elites. Generally, Nicholson's conception of faction corresponded to the patron-client model current among anthropologists.

The number of descriptive accounts of factionalism has grown in recent years, especially as some political systems have been recognized to be highly and permanently factionalized. Particular countries, such as Italy and Japan, where political systems are structured largely by a factionalized dominant party, prompt faction studies. Some studies show that factional politics make dominant-party systems more democratic; some studies disagree with this finding.[22] Other studies, concentrated in developing countries, particularly in Asia, have focused on the relationship of traditional village factionalism to modern urban political party factionalism, as postindependence parties extended their reach beyond the capital city into the countryside. Continued increase in the number of single-party and dominant-party political systems in the 1960s and 1970s raises a number of significant questions regarding factionalism.

Issues in the Study of Factions

Various concepts of faction have tended to reflect each individual author's interest in factionalism. Even so, a few basic categories of concern have recurred; these represent common intellectual issues in the study of factions. In general, three questions have dominated the analyses: How *structured* are factions? What are the *functions* of factions? What are the *causes* of factions?

Most writers touch upon structural analysis of factions. V. O. Key, despite his overriding concern with democratic functions, dealt with structure. However, his conclusions were negative and reflected his antifaction bias. Key's objective in studying faction structure was to demonstrate an inherent inferiority of factions in comparison to parties. Hence he emphasized the irregularity and discontinuity of faction organization. Like Key, Chambers described factions by contrasting them with parties. He described faction and party as extremes on a scale of organizational development. In this sense Chambers conceived of factions as structurally short-lived and of low visibility, unplanned and unconsciously constituted, with no stable ideology, heroes, or symbols.

Factions, in this conception, were embryonic parties in a historical context in which there were no political parties. Interpreted narrowly, Chambers's concept is only of historical interest. In a broader sense, however, his concept suggests a phase of party existence without reference to any particular time period or specific context. In these terms, even an intraparty faction may be a preparty. This is a likely conclusion when factions produce permanent schisms or when they secede from the parent party or are expelled. Moreover, if parties have had a preparty or faction phase, they may regress to this more primitive form. Such a notion was expressed by Giovanni Sartori, who conceived of factions as a stage of primitive partyness into which and out of which parties might move. It is a stage, he added, which parties would wish to avoid.[23]

There are several kinds of structural issues. One set of questions has to do with duration: Do factions last long—as long as parties? Another set of questions has to do with organization: How do institutions, leadership cadres, and communications develop in factions? Still other questions have to do with how formalized they become: Do factions have names, symbols, procedures, rules? Many of these issues were discussed by Zariski and other early faction scholars, especially when faction organization was viewed as less developed than party organization. Zariski raised other questions about structure, such as, How self-conscious are persons engaging in factional behavior (faction cognition)? He believed factions are comprised of self-conscious members; Chambers tended to view factions as unself-conscious, while Rose treated factions as clearly self-conscious groups. Finally, Zariski asked: why do factions exist? He suggested four raisons d'être of factions: shared values, shared strategies, socioeconomic affinities, and personal loyalties. The most common motivational issue raised by

other authors is the question whether factions are fundamentally ideological groups. Key and Chambers thought not, as did Nicholas and
most anthropologists. Rose and Nyomarkay disagreed, and Zariski was
open to both ideological and nonideological factions.

Key, Chambers, and Zariski were concerned mostly with the structural characteristics of factions in comparison to structural properties
of parties. Rose adopted a different perspective, distinguishing between highly organized intraparty factions and virtually unorganized
intraparty tendencies. Rose suggested that factions have certain structural properties: they express ideology; they have established leadership and cadres; they have technical expertise and communications
networks; they acquire and dispense resources; and they are self-consciously organized. In short, Rose concluded that factions are highly
structured, especially in comparison to tendencies. The point is an
important one; Zariski had made a similar observation—that there may
be many momentary constellations of internal groupings within parties, but only those that endure and develop real organizations and
self-consciousness qualify as factions. This distinction can be extended
to a wide range of contexts. It is possible, for example, that some of
the factions analyzed by Key would be classified by Rose as tendencies.
The preparty factions discussed in Chambers's growth theory of parties might be similarly distinguished. On the other hand, some of the
groups Rose identified as factions—especially Britain's Labour left—
come close to meeting Chambers's criteria for a political party.

Nicholas sought to transcend the gap between premodern village
factions and modern political parties by looking beyond specific structural properties, to develop general concepts about structure. Applying sociological and anthropological theory, he suggested that factions
were noncorporate groups. The corporate group concept, taken from
Max Weber, has been used extensively in anthropology. Nicholas contrasted factions with corporate groups, which meant contrast with both
clans and political parties. This contrast underlies the view that factions represent the patron-client model of group formation. This
model, also used more extensively in anthropology than in political
science, is part of anthropologists' extensive development of personal
factors in the structure of factions; it is, however, consistent with the
frequent characterization by political scientists of some factions as the
followings of party notables. In his consideration of arenas of factionalism, Nicholas suggested that any setting in which societal patterns
are weak or subject to change is inherently a faction-conducive political arena. Nicholas's concept of factional arenas thus bore the implicit
causal assertion that situations of societal change such as institutional
breakdown and weakened legitimacy tend to cause factionalized structuring of political conflict.

Structural questions dealing with the institutional setting of factionalism frequently become implicit inquiries into factional causation. Key was first to indicate that the nature of the party system can determine the characteristics of factions. He concluded that the more competitive the party system, the less will be the tendency toward factionalism in the competing parties, while the less competitive the party system (i.e., a one-party system), the greater will be the tendency toward factionalism in the main party. Thus Key is responsible for the suggestion that a prime cause of factionalism is a dominant or monopoly party. He also found that the direct primary electoral system is a contributing factor of factionalism.

Zariski developed his inquiry into the causes of faction by considering four possible causes: the electoral system, the party system, party structure, and social setting. He agreed that primary elections often foster factionalism. Zariski found that in European elections either where local party organizations are autonomous or where PR is coupled with voters' selecting among candidates (by means of preference voting), the use of PR electoral systems frequently encourages factionalism. He concluded that two-party systems are more likely to encourage intraparty bifactionalism than multifactionalism, and a multiparty system is more likely to encourage multifactionalism in parties. Zariski concurred with Duverger's view that a loosely structured party tends to contain more factions than a better-disciplined party, and he suggested that factions in loosely structured parties would tend more to be cliques or factions based on affinity. He hypothesized that factionalism, and especially multifactionalism of personal-clique-type factions, is more likely to occur in underdeveloped societies or in areas undergoing rapid social change.

Nyomarkay pointed out determining factors in the characteristics of the host party. He theorized that the nature of factionalism is conditioned by the nature of legitimacy of the organization in which the faction exists. He thus distinguished between factionalism in ideologically legitimized totalitarian (e.g., Communist) parties and factionalism in charismatically legitimized totalitarian parties (illustrated by the Nazi party). His concept implied that in any number of ways, characteristics of factions may be determined by characteristics of the organization of which the factions are a part.

The focus of inquiries into the causes of factions has been on the party system and on whether factionalism is intrinsically enhanced by a single-party or dominant-party system. This issue is inseparable from questions of function, the other major area of the study of factions. Those who have asked if one-partyism begets factionalism have implicitly asked if factions tend to express the political competition that is otherwise stifled by the minimizing or eliminating of other parties. This question was initially opened by Key—although he did not look at such questions other than through his concern for everyday American concepts of democracy in party politics. Nevertheless, he was responsible for the notion that factional competition within a dominant party might serve as a partial functional corrective for lack of party competition. His conclusion was that factions are functionally unsatisfactory for meeting the requisites of democracy and that they are internally undemocratic as well. Because he was oriented to contrast factions with parties, Key's negative conclusions about factions are meaningful primarily in the sense of the contrast he saw between the performance of democratic functions by parties and the performance of those functions by factions.

In the same line of analysis, Kothari found that factionalism is functional to a dominant party's maintenance of its own dominance, but he also concluded that factional political competition constitutes a democratic alternative to party politics in contexts in which a single party dominates or monopolizes the party system. Since Kothari's analysis of the special system of the Indian Congress party, other scholars have concurred in this thesis, on the basis of other dominant-party systems. Faction politics is not usually seen as an equivalent substitute for party politics; the argument generally is that factional politics produces more competition in a dominant-party political system than there would be if the dominant party had no internal factions. Finally, Nicholas implicitly saw factional politics as functionally adaptive, as one of the best or most natural ways in which conflict is structured and resolved under conditions of change. Factional politics are certainly better, he suggested, than other, more corporate forms of conflict organization. Thus, especially in institutionally unstructured circumstances, factionalism may be an adaptive mechanism in politics.

Conclusions

It is the argument of this book that factional politics is a neglected subject of study. The primary reason for this neglect is an inherited bias against faction—a traditional set of connotations of the word itself that are so negative that most serious study has been discouraged. Largely because of the neglect of faction, there is no consensus on precisely how to define the term. There have been many definitions given for faction. They involve significant differences which center on issues concerning the structure, the causes, and the functions of factions. Specifically, matters of structure include duration of factions, the levels and formalization of faction organization, the consciousness or cognition of faction members, continuity and cohesion of factions, factional raison d'être, the corporateness or noncorporateness of factions and the patron-client relationship basis of factions, and characteristics of the factional arena. Questions of function include whether factions articulate substantive issues and ideologies, the role of factions as campaign groups for leaders' candidacies, the articulating of concrete political interests by factions, whether factions can be substituted for parties, the democratic or undemocratic attributes of factions, the contributions of factions to system adaptability, and their contribution to the continuing dominance of a dominant party. Specific questions related to the causes of factions include the nature of the electoral system, the nature of the party system, structural characteristics of the host party, smallness of size of the host organization or arena, change or other environmental conditions, and conflict itself.

This book argues further that factional politics, despite confusion about its precise meaning, is a critical aspect of politics, a political phenomenon very much in need of explication in our total understanding of the political system. Most of the chapters that follow are case studies of countries whose political systems demonstrate exactly this point. In Chapter 2, Professor Zariski returns to many of the questions he raised in his inquiry of fifteen years ago. He reviews the product of those years relevant to the various propositions and hypotheses he advanced then and summarizes recent developments. Part Two presents case studies of factions in the national politics of five countries, all of which have in common the phenomenon of a dominant party. Part Three consists of seven case studies, covering eight countries, in each of which the political pattern is an alternation between or among two or several parties controlling the national government. Part Four examines case studies of two countries with single-party systems. Finally, in Part Five, we review the themes and considerations that emerge from these case studies and draw conclusions about factions and about the issues that confront the future study of factional politics.

NOTES

1. James Madison, *Federalist,* no. 10, in Benjamin F. Wright, ed., *The Federalist, by Alexander Hamilton, James Madison, and John Jay* (Cambridge: Harvard Univ. Press, Belknap Press, 1961), pp. 129–36; and George Washington, "Farewell Address," in James D. Richardson, comp., *A Compilation of the Messages and Papers of the Presidents, 1789–1902* (n.p.: Bureau of National Literature and Art, 1904), pp. 213–24. Professor Wright, in his volume, makes a good deal of the prevalence of this antiparty attitude among nearly everyone at the time of the founding of the union; see ibid., pp. 26–41. See also Austin Ranney, *Curing the Mischiefs of Faction* (Berkeley and Los Angeles: Univ. of California Press, 1975).

2. See J. A. W. Gunn, ed., *Factions No More: Attitudes of Party in Government and Opposition in Eighteenth-Century England* (London: Frank Cass, 1971).

3. Most of those who denounced parties and partisan politics and who were, like the Founding Fathers, contemporary with the emergence of parties did so because of the divisiveness and disunity, as they saw it, wrought by parties; parties were characterized as evil because self-interested divisions in society were evil. Thus, to a considerable extent, the arguments of the antiparty ideologues of the eighteenth century were implicitly directed against majority rule democracy, with which those writers associated parties. Later writers, largely of the nineteenth and early twentieth centuries, in contrast, valued majority rule democracy, and rejected parties because, as they saw it, parties distorted the processes and objectives of genuine democracy. To these muckrakers and reformers, parties were evil not because they tended toward democracy but because they corrupted democracy—they debased and compromised rule "by the people." For an extensive and comparative analysis of the evolution of attitudes toward party politics, see Austin Ranney and Willmore Kendall, *Democracy and the American Party System* (New York: Harcourt, Brace, 1956), pp. 116–54; and Frank P. Belloni and Dennis C. Beller, *Antipartyism: The Rejection of Competitive Party Politics and the Search for New Models* (forthcoming).

4. This interchangeability of party and faction has been widely noted: see, e.g., Wright, ed., *The Federalist,* pp. 33–37; Ranney, *Curing the Mischiefs of Faction,* p. 24; William Nisbet Chambers, *Political Parties in a New Nation: The American Experience, 1776–1809* (New York: Oxford Univ. Press, 1963), pp. 43–44; Ranney and Kendall, *Democracy and the American Party System,* pp. 126–29; and Dayton D. McKean, *Party and Pressure Politics* (Boston: Houghton Mifflin, 1949), p. 17.

5. Samuel J. Eldersveld, "American Interest Groups: A Survey of Research and Some Implications for Theory and Method," in Henry W. Ehrmann, ed., *Interest Groups on Four Continents* (Pittsburgh: Univ. of Pittsburgh Press, 1958), p. 183. Similar attitudes are reported in a variety of countries around the world, in the same volume.

6. "The interest group 'system' is with us whether we want it or not, and demands at least equal attention to the party system," declared Professor Ehrmann (ibid., p. 290). For an excellent review of the evolution of the inquiry into interest groups, see Eldersveld, "American Interest Groups," pp. 173–96.

7. Harold D. Lasswell, "Factions," *Encyclopedia of the Social Sciences,* 6:51. Lasswell himself adopted some of this opprobrium in the same article when he wrote, "a faction seems to subordinate the public good to private gain." Ibid., p. 51.

8. See, for example, "Appearance of Faction as a Sign of Dissolution of Party," in Anson Daniel Morse, *Parties and Party Leaders* (Boston: Marshall Jones Co., 1923), p. 44. Factionalism has been characterized as a particular type of "non-adaptive interpersonal conflict," arising from a complex "interaction of external stresses and internal strains." Bernard J. Siegel and Alan R. Beals, "Conflict and Factionalist Dispute," *Journal of the Royal Anthropological Institute* 90 (1960): 107–17.

9. Prominent among these are Robert Redfield, Raymond Firth, and others. See the citations to the works of these and other anthropologists in Ralph W. Nicholas, "Factions: A Comparative Analysis," in Michael Banton, ed., *Political Systems and the Distribution of Power*, Association of Social Anthropologists, Monograph no. 2 (London: Tavistock Publications, 1965), pp. 21–61; and Nicholas, "Segmentary Factional Political Systems," in Marc J. Swartz, Victor W. Turner, and Arthur Tuden, eds., *Political Anthropology* (Chicago: Aldine, 1966), pp. 49–59. As Nicholas notes, the use of the term *faction* by anthropologists goes back at least as far as the writings of Ralph Linton in the 1930s.

10. See George M. Foster, "The Dyadic Contract: A Model for the Social Structure of a Mexican Peasant Village," in Jack M. Potter, May N. Diaz, and George M. Foster, eds., *Peasant Society: A Reader* (Boston: Little, Brown, 1967), pp. 213–30; Jean Buxton, "The Mandari of the Southern Sudan," in John Middleton and David Tait, eds., *Tribes Without Rulers* (London: Routledge and Kegan Paul, 1958), pp. 67–96; Carl H. Landé, "Networks and Groups in Southeast Asia: Some Observations on the Group Theory of Politics," *American Political Science Review* 67, no. 1 (Mar. 1973): 103–27; and James C. Scott, "Patron-Client Politics and Political Change in Southeast Asia," *American Political Science Review* 66, no. 1 (Mar. 1972): 91–113.

11. Lasswell, "Factions."

12. V. O. Key, Jr., *Southern Politics in State and Nation* (New York: Alfred A. Knopf, 1949); Key, *American State Politics: An Introduction* (New York: Alfred A. Knopf, 1956); and Key, *Politics, Parties, and Pressure Groups* (New York: Thomas Y. Crowell, 1942). In fact, Key's elaborate analysis of factionalism in one-party states did not appear in *Politics, Parties, and Pressure Groups* until its 3d edition, 1952.

13. Allan P. Sindler, "Bifactional Rivalry as an Alternative to Two-Party Competition in Louisiana," *American Political Science Review* 49, no. 3 (Sept. 1955): 641–62; Sindler, *Huey Long's Louisiana: State Politics, 1920–1952* (Baltimore: Johns Hopkins Press, 1956); and Sindler, *Political Parties in the United States* (New York: St. Martin's Press, 1966).

14. Maurice Duverger, *Political Parties: Their Organization and Activity in the Modern State*, trans. Barbara and Robert North (New York: John Wiley and Sons, 1954). An American author who relied on the term *factions* to describe French parties during the Fourth Republic was Nathan Leites, *On the Game of Politics in France* (Stanford: Stanford Univ. Press, 1959).

15. Raphael Zariski, "Party Factions and Comparative Politics: Some Preliminary Observations," *Midwest Journal of Political Science* 4, no. 1 (Feb. 1960): 27–51.

16. William Nisbet Chambers, "Party Development and Party Action: The American Origins," *Journal of History and Theory* 3, no. 1 (1963): 91–120; Chambers, *Political Parties in a New Nation;* and Chambers, "Politics and Nation-Building in America," in Joseph LaPalombara and Myron Weiner, eds., *Political Parties and Political Development* (Princeton: Princeton Univ. Press, 1966), pp. 79–106. This preparty concept of factions may be found in other historically oriented studies: see, for example, S. B. Chrimes, "The Evolution of Parties and the Party System: Before 1600," in Sidney D. Bailey, ed., *Political Parties and the Party System in Great Britain* (New York: Praeger, 1952); and Ranney and Kendall, *Democracy and the American Party System*, pp. 83–115.

17. Richard Rose, "Parties, Factions, and Tendencies in Britain," *Political Studies* 12, no. 1 (Feb. 1964): 33–46.

18. Joseph L. Nyomarkay, "Factionalism in the Northern Socialist German Workers' Party, 1925–1926: The Myth and Reality of the 'Northern Faction,'" *Political Science Quarterly* 80 (Mar. 1965): 22–45.

19. Nicholas, "Factions;" and Nicholas, "Segmentary Factional Political Systems."

20. Rajni Kothari, "The Congress Party 'System' in India," *Asian Survey* 4 (Dec. 1964): 1161–74; and Kothari, *Politics in India* (Boston: Little, Brown, 1970), chs. 5, 8.

21. Norman K. Nicholson, "The Factional Model and the Study of Politics," *Comparative Political Studies* 5, no. 3 (Oct. 1972): 291–314.

22. See Hans H. Baerwald, "Factional Politics in Japan," *Current History* 46 (Apr. 1964): 225–29; George O. Totten and Tamio Kawakami, "The Functions of Factionalism in Japanese Politics," *Pacific Affairs* 38 (Summer 1965): 109–22; Michael Leiserson, "Factions and Coalitions in One-Party Japan: An Interpretation Based on the Theory of Games," *American Political Science Review* 62, no. 3 (Sept. 1968): 770–89; Raphael Zariski, "The Italian Socialist Party: A Case Study in Factional Conflict," *American Political Science Review* 56, no. 2 (June 1962): 373–90; Zariski, "Intra-Party Conflict in a Dominant Party: The Experience of the Italian Christian Democracy," *Journal of Politics* 27 (Feb. 1965): 3–34. That dominant-party factionalism tends to make the political system more democratic is found by Frank P. Belloni, "Politics in a Faction-Dominant System: Analysis of the Christian Democratic Party of Italy" (Ph.D. diss. Univ. of California, Los Angeles, 1972), chs. 5, 6. On factionalism in the dominant-party systems of India and Israel, see, for example, Mary Carras, *The Dynamics of Indian Political Factions* (London: Cambridge Univ. Press, 1972); and Efraim Torgovnik, "Election Issues and Interfactional Conflict Resolution in Israel," *Political Studies* 20, no. 1 (Mar. 1972): 79–96.

23. According to Sartori: "Parties in former times have been little more than factions: and this implies that they may well also relapse into something resembling a faction. In this sense, factionalism is the ever present temptation of a party system and its ever possible degeneration." Giovanni Sartori, "Tentative Framework for a Typology of Political Parties" (Draft paper for the Conference on Political Parties, Social Science Research Council, Rome, Jan. 1964).

2

Party Factions and Comparative Politics: Some Empirical Findings

Raphael Zariski

I wrote an exploratory article fifteen years ago which focused attention on factions as "forces which compete for the acquisition of influence over the principle institutions of intra-party government, over the formulation of party policy, and over the selection of party leaders and of party nominees for public office."[1] I noted that they were intraparty factional manifestations of pressure group activity; Catholic trade unionists within the Italian Christian Democratic party (DC) were cited as a case in point. However, I stressed that factions may also represent a broader range of interests and aspirations than pressure groups. Hence, I proposed that the party faction be treated "as an essential category in any behavioral approach to intra-party processes."

That article raised several general questions about the relationships between party factions and certain political and socioeconomic variables. Since then, numerous studies of party factions have been undertaken. This chapter examines the progress that empirical research has made in developing a theory of party factionalism. This summary emphasizes research on *party* factions, rather than on the village-level factionalism of interest to anthropologists,[2] and is limited to empirical studies *explicitly* concerned with factions and factionalism. Consequently, this survey does not treat all of the relevant research which has appeared since 1960 on factions.

There are numerous definitions of faction which reflect the peculiarities of various cultural contexts (Italian, Indian, British, etc.). Thus, an interest in Indian politics produced a definition of factions as "amorphous segments (factions) operating within a cultural context which places a high value on diffuse and unrestrained personal power and led by an elite whose orientations are self-centered and instrumental."[3] This definition is restrictive; e.g., it arbitrarily excludes ideology. Belloni and Beller have aptly summarized the variety of definitional approaches, noting that factions have been viewed as

> either groups of individuals who cluster around the personality of a great leader
> ... or groups of individuals who have some value—ideological, programmatic,
> economic—in common, which is the basis of their coming together in an orga-
> nized group, and without fundamental regard to who their leaders are.[4]

Cultural diversity has, so far, frustrated efforts to arrive at a single, commonly agreed-upon definition of faction, but it has provided useful definitional refinements. One contribution which helps accurately to describe faction is the concept of a clientele, i.e., the relationship of reciprocal obligation and service between a higher-status leader (or patron) and lower-status dependent followers (or clients).[5] This concept overlaps the concept of party faction, since clienteles operate within parties as well as in remote villages in tribal societies where there are no parties.

Richard Rose distinguishes between factions—groups of individuals organized in Parliament to promote a broad range of policies and objectives through conscious political activity, and tendencies—stable sets of attitudes which evoke support from issue to issue. For example, the Bevanites in the British Labour party are a faction, and right-wing conservatism is a tendency. Rose also notes that there are cross-party tendencies (e.g., the common reformist mood which joins left-wing Conservatives and right-wing Labourites).[6]

The definition of party faction is thus incomplete, but some progress has been made in clearing the ground. Concepts like clientele and the cross-party tendency help provide a firmer grasp of reality.

Structure of Factions

FACTIONAL ORGANIZATION, COHESION, AND CONTINUITY

There is disagreement about whether or not factions are well organized, cohesive, and durable, and each scholar bases his disagreement on the particular party system familiar to him. For example, British Labour party factions are disciplined, durable, and cohesive; Italian factions maintain liaison offices and press agencies and are regularly mentioned in the Italian press; but Burmese factions lack solidarity and stable membership and are unable to form and carry out plans efficiently.[7] These factional systems are not prototypical, but they do bias the researcher's outlook when research is based on the study of a single faction system.

There has been some empirical progress in theory-building in the study of factions. The propositions that have been developed concern the structure of individual party organizations, the electoral system, and the party system. Two points appear particularly promising to the development of a theory of party factions. First, several authors have noted the importance of cultural norms that affect the organization, cohesion, and durability of factions. Thus, Weiner notes that Indian leader-follower factions (not to be confused with the volatile Indian factional coalitions) are durable and stable because their members belong to tightly knit face-to-face groups closed to outsiders.[8] Similarly, suppressed antagonisms in Burmese villages may explain the lack of cohesiveness typical of Burmese village factions.[9] It is in this sense that Nicholson describes ways in which political culture provides a justification of factional behavior—a "factional ethic."[10]

Second, Sartori suggests that it may be feasible to develop some measurable indicators of factional continuity. He proposes that indexes of volatility and durability could be devised by counting the shifts of factional allegiance among national and provincial party leaders within a given time span, the duration of each faction in that time span, and the number of fusions and secessions each faction has experienced.[11] Such devices would be a major step in eliminating imprecision in our comparative analysis of factions.

FACTIONAL GOALS AND FACTIONAL RECRUITMENT

Most scholars tend to approach factional goals as being either primarily ideological and/or policy oriented or mainly based on the material interests of their leaders and members. Research has largely been concerned with classifying factions in a given political system under either of these two headings. British factions, for example, are generally described as ideological or policy oriented.[12] Conversely, Burmese factions and those in the Japanese Liberal Democratic party (LDP) are described as nonideological and oriented toward enhancing the prestige, power, and wealth of their members and leaders.[13] Factions in African single-party states have been described as personally loyal to local or regional leaders and not oriented to seek revisions in the policies of top party leadership.[14]

Other faction systems are less clearly characterized. Indian factions are described by Weiner as pursuing commonly held goals and values; their disputes center on ideological issues.[15] Nicholson and Brass, however, note that Indian factions seek power for the leaders and patronage for the followers.[16] In the Soviet Union, factions appear to be policy oriented; but professional interest, age, regional affiliation, and personal antagonism play a role, and some communist factional leaders adeptly shift their ideologies to fit the changing seasons.[17] Sartori divides Italian factions into factions of principle (ideological) and factions of convenience (opportunistic and power oriented) and hints that factions of principle tend to retain an external ideological guise while degenerating into factions of convenience.[18] Some writers claim that Italian factions reflect a medley of policy goals and personal and group drives;[19] others conclude that at least Italian Socialist factions are mainly ideological in character.[20]

Since classification is a prerequisite for theory-building, the empirical studies which describe and analyze factional goals perform a useful function. Some studies go deeper and emerge with tentative propositions. Thus Nicholson and Barnes point out that levels of education, levels of government, etc., can determine the salience of ideology for members of a faction. Nicholson indicates that national leaders are "more exposed to the normative pressure of nationalist ideology," while local leaders are more responsive to patronage.[21] Similarly, Barnes notes the relationship between educational levels and sensitivity to ideological issues: "Participation is also highly associated with ideological sensitivity, *but only for those with considerable education.*"[22] Thus, central-peripheral and educational stratifications affect factional goals.

The developing, testing, and qualifying of general propositions regarding factional goals is still in progress, and the basic problem of classification of goals remains. The impacts of a variety of environmental factors (the political system, the social structure, the geographic unit, the educational level, etc.) on factional goals have yet to be determined.

In the study of factional recruitment, several factors have been found to induce rank-and-file party members to join factions. Barnes suggests that "the more active, knowledgeable, issue-oriented, efficacious, urban, middle-class, and senior members of the party" are the most typical faction joiners, and that middle-class persons mostly join moderate factions.[23] Thus, political competence, urban-rural differences, class origin, and age influence the individual in joining a faction. Stern, Tarrow, and Williams, however, found very little relationship between personal factors and factional identifications, although the indicators used in that study may not be the best means for measuring the importance of personal factors.[24] Nevertheless, they have presented some evidence that personal factors are of relatively minor importance in determining who will join which faction.

Factions and the Host Party

The organizational structure of the host party (a party containing factions) can affect factionalism. Maurice Duverger analyzed Communist parties' prohibition of minority views and ban on "horizontal articulation" as effectively discouraging factionalism.[25] Recent research reconfirms this effect. Thus the Soviet Union's party apparatus penetrates all social structures and communications channels, making it hazardous for leaders of an opposition faction to seek support at provincial and local levels. As a result, factional struggles occur mainly at the top of the party hierarchy, in the Politburo and the Central Committee.[26] D'Amato's study of the Italian Communist party similarly notes that factions operate in a semiclandestine fashion, avoid proselytizing rank-and-file recruits, and concentrate on gaining key posts at the summit of the party organization. Factional strife among Communists in Italy is thus also confined to the top echelons.[27]

Organizational structure also affects factional systems in democratic parties. Several authors have indicated that decentralization tends to give free rein to factional activity in American parties.[28] Lack of central control over finances and campaign workers in the Italian Christian Democratic and the Japanese Liberal Democratic parties also tends to encourage proliferation of factions. Unions, corporations, farm organizations, and religious associations within such loosely structured parties may be closely identified with the party and still retain autonomy. Catchall party organizations thus encourage such groups to use financial power and activists to help politicians and factions sympathetic to their views. When a catchall party acquires significant patronage resources, a variety of factions of convenience will result.[29]

On the basis of the research to date, caucus-type parties (loosely organized parties of compromise that exist mainly to win elections) may be assumed to have more factions than branch-type parties (tightly organized and well-articulated parties of principle that seek to educate their members). Further, it may be assumed that factions in caucus-type parties are less ideological and policy oriented than factions in branch-type parties. The Italian and German Christian Democrats illustrate the caucus-type party in their internal factional systems. However, some doubt has been cast on the distinction between factions in caucus-type parties and factions in branch-type parties. The schism involving the branch-type Socialists and Social Democrats in Italy in 1969 split the "reunified" Socialist party, partly as a result of the struggle over patronage and power which the Social Democrats were clearly losing.[30] A recent study clearly demonstrates that the organization of the Argentine Socialists (also a branch-type party) created discontent among lower-level members who aspired to national leadership positions. That kind of frustration is heightened by electoral success of a party and helps to produce schism.[31] Thus, personal grievances and material ambitions tend to play an important role in the formation of factions and in the nature of factional conflict in either type of party.

What types of host party structural factors are most likely to foster intraparty democracy—measured in terms of open and free interfactional competition—is still not known. Barnes suggests certain factors that may influence such competition within the Italian Socialist party (PSI). (1) The PSI relies on volunteer party workers who are more strongly committed to internal party democracy than are professional party regulars. The volunteers are not readily subject to sanctions imposed by the national party leadership and are therefore a natural reservoir of opposition. (2) The party leadership cannot control all internal structures and communications channels. For example, leftist opposition factions in the PSI had their base of support in Communist-dominated labor unions associated with the PSI. (3) The party leadership in a democracy cannot prevent external communications from reaching party members. The PSI has its own official newspapers, but many Socialists in Arezzo Province read a Florentine conservative newspaper regularly. In short, the internal processes of a party like the PSI often fail to conform to the model of a branch-type party, which serves as an educational and communications sanctuary for its members, and intraparty opposition is the result.[32]

Factions and the Party System

FACTIONS AND THE ELECTORAL SYSTEM

The electoral system may also affect factionalism. V. O. Key, Jr., found that in one-party American states the direct primary encourages multifactionalism. Even in a two-party system, the direct primary may reduce the likelihood of orderly compromise of interfactional disputes, thus encouraging the growth of factions. It is sometimes supposed that proportional representation (PR) permits national party organizations to stamp out opposition factions and penalize legislators who violate party discipline. Yet the reverse may be the case. On the basis of the PR systems in Italy and in the French Fourth Republic, my earlier article suggested that

> when the unit of representation [i.e., the multimember district] is small in terms of population; when provincial or local party organizations enjoy an autonomy based on financial independence, socioeconomic diversity within the party ranks, or strong regional traditions; or when proportional representation is coupled with genuine provisions for preferential selection among candidates of the same party, minority factions may flourish despite the electoral law, and may even use the law to their own advantage.[33]

Recent research tends to confirm these generalizations. Obler's study of Belgium's PR electoral politics shows that national party leaders rarely intervene to block the renomination of incumbent members of Parliament who violate party discipline. Deviations are frequent, yet the mavericks remain unpunished. When national leaders do intervene in the local nominating process, it has nothing to do with internal discipline. Rather, it is usually to mediate disputes among local factions, *at their own request,* or to produce a balanced ticket which will appeal to a broader range of voters.[34]

This state of affairs results in some respects from factors like those quoted above: the spirit of local independence that prevails in Belgian politics; the socioeconomic and linguistic cleavages that divide the major Belgian parties into warring factions; and (shades of Key's *Southern Politics!*) the use by some Belgian parties of a form of direct primary —open to dues-paying party members—as a means of selecting candidates for Parliament. What is significant here is the mediating role of the central party organization in the PR system, and the ineffectiveness of PR in bringing about centralized dominance over factional opposition.

Other recent studies of the electoral system stress its tendency to stimulate factional activity or changes in factional strategy. For example, the growth of highly organized factions in Japan has been attributed partly to the adoption by the LDP of a new system for electing the party president by a vote of the LDP members in the Diet.[35] In addition, Japan's system for electing lower house Diet members from multimember districts, with each voter casting a single nontransferable vote, stimulates competition among LDP factions in each district.[36] Finally, in French politics, the adoption of a system for electing the president by popular vote contributed to the rise of a new Socialist party faction, dedicated to building a mass movement of the entire moderate left.[37]

The issue of the electoral system has generated the greatest controversy in Italy. Particularly provocative are the questions of whether PR augments the number of factions and the rise of factions of convenience as opposed to factions of principle. Sartori says yes on both counts and adds that the use of PR in intraparty elections has a much more significant effect on the multiplication of factions than does the use of PR in general elections.[38] Pasquino, Zincone, and Passigli argue instead that the intraparty electoral system may reflect, rather than condition, the balance of forces among party factions.[39]

Those who downgrade the significance of the electoral law in Italy have more evidence on their side. For instance, between 1954 and 1961—long before the Italian Christian Democrats adopted PR for intraparty elections—the number of factions in the DC was already increasing. Intraparty PR was adopted in 1964, yet by 1971 there were no more factions in the DC than there had been in 1964.[40] For this reason, D'Amato believes that the intraparty electoral system is less important for factionalism than the interparty general elections system.[41] Sartori and Lombardo, however, provide evidence that intra-

party PR leads to the emergence of factions of interest in place of
ideological factions. Thus, while the adoption of intraparty PR by the
DC in 1964 did not increase the *number* of factions, it did change their
character. [42]

There is general agreement among Italian scholars on one point.
Italy's system of allowing voters in general elections to write in the
names of the candidates of their preference on the party list for which
they have voted is regarded by virtually all observers as encouraging
factional activity.

One further question that has been explored is the impact of free
elections on factional activity in a society where free elections are an
innovation. An inauguration of free elections compels national parties
to establish a network of links reaching down to the local level, to
incorporate existing patron-client relationships in their organizations,
and thus to stimulate and subsidize factional activity. For an opposition
faction in a hostile village atmosphere this translates into encouragement and support from the national opposition party.[43] This involves
the institution of free (as opposed to ritualistic) elections, however,
rather than a specific type of electoral system.

FACTIONS AND THE NUMBER OF COMPETING PARTIES

The number of parties in the party system can have an effect on both
the number of intraparty factions and the ways in which those factions
resolve their disputes. According to Key, where a dominant party
encounters no meaningful opposition (e.g., in some Southern states in
America), a multifactionalism of personal cliques is likely to develop.
This appears to have held true for the Congress party in India, though
the evidence is not conclusive.[44]

In my earlier article, I suggested that a multiparty system is likely
to produce more than two factions in a given party, since there are
more alternatives in a multiparty system, and factions have less need
to compromise. Therefore, the price of intransigence and party split
is not as high as in a two-party system.[45] Conversely, in a two-party
system, there is more pressure on factions to compromise their differences rather than risk handing the next election to the opposition.
Also, in a two-party system the more limited range of strategic choices
confronting the party (i.e., absence of potential coalition partners) is
conducive to only bifactional divisions in parties.

These propositions have been tested several times, but the evidence is not supportive. For example, Barnes observes that in Arezzo
Province, Italy, where a multiparty system presents the members of a
party with numerous alternatives, the party leadership in order to
prevent secession must respect opposition factions. In other words,
there *is* some pressure to compromise in intraparty disputes.[46] Other
negative evidence is in Lanning's study of Latin American political

systems. He found that a two-party system can, under certain conditions, produce a multifactionalism of personal clienteles. This was the case in Colombia and Uruguay, where rigid two-party systems were superimposed on social structures marked by patron-client relationships.[47]

Lombardo argues that the Italian type of multiparty "polarized pluralism," with unacceptable antisystem parties at the extremes, tends to restrict the range of possible alternative coalitions. Moreover, the center-left (Christian Democratic-Socialist) coalition government formula further reduced the number of alternatives, yet this reduction in the range of alternatives did not significantly reduce the number of factions. Instead, it resulted in the replacement of ideological factions of principle by factions interested in power.[48]

Thus, there is a good deal of negative evidence on the proposition that a multiparty system makes for a broader range of alternatives, thereby encouraging multifactionalism, whereas a two-party system, by limiting the range of strategic choices, encourages bifactionalism. There is also some doubt about the related proposition that a multiparty system promotes intransigence in the settling of intraparty disputes, whereas a two-party system has the effect of imposing compromise. What seems to be at fault in these hypotheses is the assumption of a simplified relationship between only two variables (the faction system and the party system); this assumption ignores social and historical factors and other aspects of the political structure.

In a study of the Italian Christian Democratic party from 1946 to 1964, I concluded that dominant-party status increases the number of factions in the dominant party. I also argued that a dominant party tends to produce a faction system with the following characteristics: (1) its factions are based mainly on personalities rather than on principles; (2) distinctions among factions tend to be blurred; (3) faction leadership changes frequently, with many faction leaders migrating from one faction to another; and (4) factions are neither very cohesive nor long-lasting.[49] Some of these propositions have subsequently been challenged. For example, rather than continuing to increase indefinitely, the number of factions in the DC has actually diminished slightly since 1964. Another study concluded that ideology and principle, as well as personal ambitions and opportunism, can be the basis of dominant-party faction organization. It also found that some factions have endured for long periods of time—at least a quarter century in one case—albeit with changes in name. Furthermore, although faction membership in a dominant party changes over time, there is also likely to be a core of leaders and activists who remain committed to a particular faction throughout most or all of their political lives.[50]

Another question about dominant-party factionalism is whether the dominance of the host party serves not only to limit the multiplication of factions but also to discourage factions from breaking away from the parent party. In the case of the Italian Christian Democratic party, for example, Rizzi argues that DC factions have little, if anything, to gain by seceding.[51] Hence, while the leadership is reluctant to crack down on dissident factions, the factions in turn are restrained from leaving the party, as a consequence of a political situation which makes it unwise to leave the organizational boundaries of the dominant party. Weiner made the same point about the Indian Congress party: schisms were avoided partly because a dissident faction could only lose by seceding.[52]

FACTIONS AND THE STRENGTHS OF COMPETING PARTIES

The strengths of the various parties in a party system may influence any party's internal factionalism. In a study of the Italian Socialist party, I suggested that when a party has greater organizational strength (measured by number of members of the party's provincial branches) and greater electoral strength (popular vote), party members are more likely to support depolarizing (i.e., centrist) factions within the party. I also suggested that the moderate centrist faction would become weaker if rival outside parties became stronger.[53] In a subsequent study, Tarrow found only partial support for these propositions.[54]

Recently, we returned to these questions in a more systematic fashion.[55] For the most part, the hypotheses were confirmed—more so in some regions than in others. PSI organizational strength was fairly consistently related to depolarization in the PSI, and depolarizing tendencies within the PSI did vary inversely with a threatening political environment—with regional variations. Thus, generally speaking, the cliché that strength fosters moderation, while weakness breeds extremism, was confirmed—though not for all regions.

However, there is also contradictory evidence. In the Argentine Socialist party, as Wellhofer and Hennessey show, splits have usually followed electoral successes.

> That is, electoral success raises expectations concerning opportunities for advancement, while at the same time constraints on advancement serve to shatter such expectations and increase frustrations. This set of circumstances stimulates aspirants to use current ideological disputes within the party as instruments to create schisms.[56]

Brass attributed unbridled factionalism in the Indian Congress party to the absence of an external threat[57]—although by an external threat to the Congress Party he meant merely a party that could compete on equal terms, whereas an external threat to Italy's PSI was a hostile dominant party. Wilson found that in France growth of the dominant Gaullist party led to the emergence of a moderate depolarizing (i.e., centrist) faction in the Socialist party.[58] MacRae also concluded that there was no tendency for the left wing of the Socialist party in France to be stronger in areas where French conservatism was dominant.[59] Unlike in Italy, a threatening political environment did not breed polarization (increase in strength of extremist factions) in the French Socialist movement.

The difference here may lie in contrasts between the French and Italian conservative movements or in some feature of the local environment. Moreover, Communist dominance in a number of French constituencies (a threatening political environment to the Socialists) was usually not accompanied by the prevalence of the left-wing, pro-Communist (i.e., polarizing) faction in the French Socialist party. Stern, Tarrow, and Williams also reached conclusions at variance with my proposition regarding a threatening political climate in Italy: "The average Communist vote is lower in the provinces represented by our left-wing Socialists than in the provinces represented by the others."[60] Thus, many of the propositions I developed for Italy have been re-tested in France, Italy, and other countries, and found wanting.

There is other fragmentary evidence. For instance, Barnes cites the effect on factionalism of the size of the party organizational unit which is factionalized. He found that an opposition faction, whichever faction it might be, makes a much poorer showing in PSI party sections which have a smaller number of members. The reason had to do with the natural pressures toward conformity that operate on individuals in a small, intimate group. Only in a large, more impersonal organizational setting can the dissenters find the courage and self-confidence to stand up and be counted.[61] In a study of a sample of British constituencies, Janosik could find no confirmation for the hypotheses that personal factions are likely to prevail in constituencies where the Labour party is stronger, while ideological factions are likely to prevail in districts where Labour is weak.[62]

Despite their inconsistencies, these reports do amount to some beginning of progress toward theory-building about factionalism and the strengths of the parties. Many of the early hypotheses are not yet confirmed or disconfirmed. Several of them may require some modification to allow for the impact of regional traditions, and some may hold true for certain types of parties but not for others. Thus, for example, MacRae demonstrates how different French parties produced widely divergent factional alignments and alliance strategies in response to various types of political situations in their electoral constituencies.[63]

Factions and Society

FACTION AND THE SOCIOECONOMIC CONTEXT

There are several questions concerning the relationship between a faction system and the socioeconomic environment. For example, one might expect to find multifactionalism of personal cliques (i.e., clienteles) in preindustrial societies, where both trade and agriculture are relatively underdeveloped and where socioeconomic change has not yet brought about large-scale industrialization and widespread urbanization. Recent evidence from preindustrial societies in Latin America and Asia confirms that a low level of economic development usually coincides with systems of patron-client relationships. However, exceptions are found in a few underdeveloped societies, like Peru and Bolivia, where a major revolution by a class-based party laid the foundation for the politics of interest groups rather than clienteles.[64] Also, in some more highly developed societies like Colombia and Uruguay, a clientele system survives because a stable two-party system was imposed on a preexisting clientele structure, discouraging the formation of third parties and interest groups.

Evidence also indicates that scarcity makes the clientele system highly unstable by placing unusual "distributive" pressures on the central government, particularly in preindustrial societies where open elections enable clients to demand tangible rewards from patrons. With not enough resources to go around, patron-client groups tend to shift their party allegiances with considerable alacrity. This kind of distributive pressure is particularly heavy in less traditional areas like the Philippines, Indonesia, and Burma, where the ruling party is led by "new men" and relies on votes from uprooted populations. In Thailand, and formerly in Malaysia, traditional elites commanded more deference and were able to resist distributive pressures to a greater degree.[65]

Another issue is the relationship between the socioeconomic environment and the prevalence of moderate or depolarizing factions in a political party. In the article on Italian Socialist party factionalism, I hypothesized relationships between depolarizing tendencies in the PSI and industrialization and urbanization.[66] Those hypotheses have been discredited with the passage of time. MacRae found no consistent relationship between the factional allegiances of French deputies and socioeconomic characteristics of French constituencies, among all French parties except the Christian Democratic MRP.[67] Similarly, Tarrow found no relationship between local economic development and the dominance of depolarizing tendencies in Italian Socialist party provincial organizations.[68] Our reexamination of this problem even found a moderate inverse relationship in some regions.[69]

Social class, however, is a factor related to factionalism. Barnes shows that Italian Socialists who adhered to PSI factions were more educated and more urban and middle class in background than those who avoided factional identification. Also, those who had been brought up in middle-class families overwhelmingly favored depolarization.[70] Another study suggested that the reason Italian Socialists and Italian Christian Democrats have been so susceptible to ideological fragmentation is that their activists have been overwhelmingly middle class.[71] So socioeconomic factors appear to play a more important role at the level of the party elites and activists than at the constituency level.

Finally, the concept of factional arena is a way of differentiating socioeconomic milieus. Nicholson distinguishes among the "electoral arena of the village constituencies, the polycommunal factionalism of a national party organization, and the factions within the inner circles of party and government."[72] He found that as one moves from the local to the national level, governmental constraints on factions become greater. In other words, Nicholson cautions us that analysis of factions must proceed in terms of different levels of investigation. By the same token, analysis of factionalism must avoid oversimplified relationships between factions and the socioeconomic environment.

FUNCTIONAL UTILITY OF FACTIONS

Much of the discussion of the functions performed by party factions is strongly normative in tone. Those who approve of factions speak of their contributions to intraparty democracy, their recruitment of government and party leaders, and their linkage between various levels of the political system. Those who oppose them speak of their threats to party unity, their frequent tendency to engage in corrupt activities, their degeneration into mere veto groups, etc.[73]

Despite the moralizing, however, there have been a few empirical insights which touch upon significant aspects of factional performance. Brass points to two particularly useful roles played by factional coalitions in the Indian Congress party. First, by cutting across caste and communal divisions, they help reduce the danger that the Congress party might disintegrate into its component communal groups and castes. Second, they help to channel much of the potential hostility and conflict in the party; and by focusing on personal and material goals, they help to ward off a possible ideological split.[74]

Zincone, Fried, and Belloni and Beller stress useful integrative functions performed by factions. Factional coalitions can, in effect, cut across party lines and serve as bridges between mutually hostile parties. A right-wing Socialist faction, for instance, renders the Italian Socialist party more acceptable in the eyes of its Christian Democratic rivals. In a sense, the rigidity of the Italian multiparty system, with its polarized pluralism, has been broken down somewhat by the agile maneuvers of the factions.[75]

Finally, Milnor and Franklin present the idea that when parties have not yet taken a stand on issues, the factions can argue publicly until the government is ready to take a position. In the United States, however, factions cannot penetrate the presidency; consequently, a faction which has taken a strong public stand on an issue is not likely to influence the president. Ineffectiveness of this form of public opposition may tend to divorce policy deliberation from policy-making.[76] But the idea that factions may perform a valuable function in being freer to argue important public issues deserves further comparative study.

Conclusions

From this survey of studies of party factionalism since 1960, three general impressions bear emphasizing. First, it is evident that this promising field of political science is in a state of disarray. There is a lack of agreement on what factions *are*. Each country has its own variety of factional activity, and this inevitably shapes the concepts about factions of political scientists concerned with that country. In addition, empirical studies range from rigorous processing of quantitative data to informed but intuitive judgments. To be sure, many of the questions I have posed do not as yet lend themselves to quantitative analysis, or adequate indicators have not yet been devised. In any event, the overall impression is of the extreme variation in the literature on factions.

Second, empirical findings reported are often contradictory. Propositions which find confirmation in one social context are frequently contradicted in another. What is needed in the years ahead is a combination of intranation comparative studies of single countries together with cross-national investigations, to iron out the discrepancies and ambiguities such as I have described here. General propositions about factions can readily be formulated and preliminarily confirmed, but they need to be qualified and refined to account for deviant cases.

Finally, most of the analysis we have encountered here has been bivariate in form. An effort is needed to develop and test propositions involving more than one independent variable. The Wellhofer-Hennessey study is one example of the kind of payoff multivariate analysis can provide. The independent variables I have discussed do not begin to exhaust the field. It may be that we shall have to design more refined indicators to measure variables like socioeconomic development. Or it may be that we need more meaningful variables—such as perception of socioeconomic development.

To close this survey, I shall summarize the dozen most tenable and agreed-upon generalizations on factionalism that emerge from my analysis of the literature:

(1)   In the literature which deals with definitions of party fac-

tions, some empirically useful terms have been coined. These include *clientele, tendency,* and *cross-party tendency.*

(2)   In approaching factions from the point of view of their organization, cohesion, and continuity, several writers have stressed cultural norms as independent variables. Others have suggested more accurate indicators, such as indexes of volatility and durability.

(3)   In discussing factional goals, some scholars have stressed ideology or policy, while others have emphasized power and patronage.

(4)   There is limited evidence that personal factors play a relatively minor role in determining what kind of faction an individual will join. But affinity based on common social or geographic origins, common functions, or local or friendship groupings cannot be entirely ruled out as an independent variable on the basis of the evidence available.

(5)   Branch-type parties show considerable vulnerability to patronage considerations, which seem to be underlying factors provoking intraparty factional conflict. In this and other ways, their internal processes fail to live up to the standards postulated by Duverger.

(6)   There is evidence to confirm the hypothesis that depolarizing tendencies vary directly with the strength of the host party. Yet, a recent study shows electoral gains as contributing to schism in the Argentine Socialist party.

(7)   Under certain conditions, minority factions manage to maintain their autonomy under a PR system. There is, however, considerable disagreement over the relative importance of the electoral law—*inter*party or *intra*party—as an independent variable affecting factional behavior. Intraparty PR has a stronger impact than interparty PR on the character of factions, while interparty PR appears to increase the number of factions.

(8)   A dominant-party system and multiparty system both tend to encourage multifactionalism. Reducing the range of alternatives in a multiparty system characterized by polarized pluralism appears to result only in the replacement of factions of principle by power-oriented factions of convenience.

(9)   The hypothesis that depolarizing tendencies in a party are inversely related to a threatening political environment as measured by the strength of rival parties is partly confirmed for the Italian Socialist party. But, again, there is conflicting evidence from other party systems.

(10)   The prevalence of depolarizing tendencies in a party does not appear to be positively correlated to certain indicators of socioeconomic development, but it is positively related to *perceptions* of socioeconomic progress.

(11)   Factions perform a number of positive functions, such as easing communal and partisan tensions by cutting across communal lines and serving as bridges between parties.

(12)   Research on party factions needs to achieve greater coordination of goals and methods and a more imaginative search for appropriate independent variables.

These twelve points represent the conclusions and findings of social scientific research on party factions since my initial survey of a decade and a half ago. They reflect the beginnings of our accumulation of empirically based knowledge of factions and how factionalism interacts with various aspects of the political system. At the same time, they serve to suggest just how far social science has yet to go in the development of this field of study in the future.

NOTES

1. Raphael Zariski, "Party Factions and Comparative Politics: Some Preliminary Observations," *Midwest Journal of Political Science* 4, no. 1 (Feb. 1960): 19.

2. For analysis of the literature on this type of factionalism, see Norman K. Nicholson, "The Factional Model and the Study of Politics," *Comparative Political Studies* 5, no. 3 (Oct. 1962): 292–94.

3. Ibid., p. 292.

4. Frank P. Belloni and Dennis C. Beller, "The Study of Party Factions as Competitive Political Organizations," *Western Political Quarterly* 29, no. 4 (Dec. 1976): 544. A mixture of these two approaches, focusing on the leader-follower relationship but not excluding common interest, is to be found in Ralph W. Nicholas, "Factions: A Comparative Analysis," in Michael Banton, ed., *Political Systems and the Distribution of Power*, Association of Social Anthropologists, Monograph no. 2 (London: Tavistock Publications, 1965), pp. 27–29.

5. There is voluminous literature on clienteles. See, for example, James C. Scott, "Patron-Client Politics and Political Change in Southeast Asia," *American Political Science Review* 66, no. 1 (Mar. 1972): 91–113; René Lemarchand, "Political Clientelism and Ethnicity in Tropical Africa: Competing Solidarities in Nation-Building," *American Political Science Review* 66, no. 1 (Mar.1972): 68–90; John Duncan Powell, "Peasant Society and Clientelist Politics," *American Political Science Review* 64, no. 2 (June 1970): 411–25; and Carl H. Landé, *Leaders, Factions, and Parties: The Structure of Philippine Politics*, Monograph Series, no. 6 (New Haven: Yale Southeast Asia Studies, 1965).

6. Richard Rose, "Parties, Factions, and Tendencies in Britain," *Political Studies* 12, no. 1 (Feb. 1964): 37–42.

7. Ibid., p. 37; Luigi D'Amato, *Correnti di partito e partiti di correnti* (Milan: Giuffre, 1965), pp. v–vi, 96–98; Frank P. Belloni and Dennis C. Beller, "Faction Dominance in a Dominant-Party System: The Italian Case," *International Behavioural Scientist* 7, no. 3 (Sept. 1975): 15–16; and Melford E. Spiro, "Factionalism and Politics in Village Burma," in Marc J. Swartz, ed., *Local-Level Politics: Social and Cultural Perspectives* (Chicago: Aldine, 1968), pp. 415–20.

8. Myron Weiner, *Party Politics in India: The Development of a Multi-Party System* (Princeton: Princeton Univ. Press, 1957), pp. 237–39.

9. See Spiro, "Factionalism and Politics," pp. 414–44.

10. Nicholson, "The Factional Model and Politics," pp. 296–98, 301–03. We have already complained that Nicholson's view of factionalism is a bit restrictive. Possibly his fieldwork in India, where factions seem to be mainly concerned with power and patronage, has influenced his thinking. By the same token, this author finds himself taking the Italian factions as the proper models for the study of factional conflict and consequently attributing perhaps excessive weight to the ideological goals (or protestations) of factional leaders.

11. Giovanni Sartori, "Proporzionalismo, frazionismo, e crisi dei partiti," *Rivista Italiana di Scienza Politica* 1, no. 3 (Dec. 1971): 643–44.

12. See Rose, "Parties, Factions, and Tendencies," p. 37. See also Edward G. Janosik, *Constituency Labour Parties in Britain* (New York: Praeger, 1968), pp. 85–88.

13. See Spiro, "Factionalism and Politics," p. 415. On the Japanese LDP, see Nicholas, "Factions," pp. 26–27; Nathaniel B. Thayer, *How the Conservatives Rule Japan* (Princeton: Princeton Univ. Press, 1969), pp. 17–21; and Michael Leiserson, "Coalition Government in Japan," in Sven Groennings, E. W. Kelley, and Michael Leiserson, eds., *The Study of Coalition Behavior: Theoretical Perspectives and Cases from Four Continents* (New York: Holt, Rinehart, and Winston, 1970), pp. 82, 85, 99–100.

14. See William J. Foltz, "Political Opposition in Single-Party States of Tropical Africa," in Robert A. Dahl, ed., *Regimes and Oppositions* (New Haven and London: Yale Univ. Press, 1973), pp. 161–64.

15. Weiner, *Party Politics in India,* pp. 237, 246.

16. Nicholson, "The Factional Model and Politics," pp. 308–09; and Paul R. Brass, *Factional Politics in an Indian State: The Congress Party in Uttar Pradesh* (Berkeley and Los Angeles: Univ. of California Press, 1965), p. 238.

17. See Sidney I. Ploss, *Conflict and Decision-Making in Soviet Russia: A Case Study of Agricultural Policy 1953–1963* (Princeton: Princeton Univ. Press, 1965), pp. 278–81. See also Ghita Ionescu, *The Politics of the European Communist States* (New York: Praeger, 1967), pp. 227, 228, 269; and Frederick C. Barghoorn, "Factional, Sectoral, and Subversive Opposition in Soviet Politics," in Dahl, ed., *Regimes and Oppositions,* pp. 46–47.

18. Sartori, "Proporzionalismo, frazionismo, e crisi dei partiti," pp. 639, 644. For some empirical evidence backing his thesis in the case of the Italian Socialist party, see Felice Rizzi, "Dall' unificazione alla scissione socialista, 1966–1969," *Rivista Italiana di Scienza Politica* 3, no. 2 (Aug. 1973): 420–24.

19. Giovanna Zincone, "Accesso autonomo alle risorse: le determinanti del frazionismo," *Rivista Italiana di Scienza Politica* 2, no. 1 (Apr. 1972): 142; and Gianfranco Pasquino, "Le radici del frazionismo e il voto di preferenza," *Rivista Italiana di Scienza Politica* 2, no. 2 (Aug. 1972): 354.

20. Alan J. Stern, Sidney Tarrow, and Mary Frase Williams, "Factions and Opinion Groups in European Mass Parties: Some Evidence from a Study of Italian Socialist Activists," *Comparative Politics* 3, no. 4 (July 1971): 529–60; and Alberto Spreafico and Franco Cazzola, "Correnti di partito e processi di identificazione," in Alberto Spreafico, ed., *Ideologia e comportamento politico* (Milan: Communità, 1971), pp. 211–18.

21. Nicholson, "The Factional Model and Politics," p. 308. This point may help explain why Weiner's findings differ from Nicholson's.

22. Samuel H. Barnes, *Party Democracy: Politics in an Italian Socialist Federation* (New Haven and London: Yale Univ. Press, 1967), p. 165.

23. Ibid., pp. 111, 137–38.

24. Stern, Tarrow, and Williams, "Factions and Opinion Groups," pp. 535–36.

25. Maurice Duverger, *Political Parties: Their Organization and Activity in the Modern State,* trans. Barbara and Robert North (New York: John Wiley and Sons, 1954), pp. 47–50, 121–22, 174.

26. See Barghoorn, "Factional, Sectoral, and Subversive Opposition," pp. 40, 50. To be sure, there are some signs that these organizational restraints may be loosening. Barghoorn refers to "an increasing range of sites for oppositional activity" and to a wider distribution of power and influence (ibid., pp. 50–52). But so far there is little hard evidence that such activity is permitted at the lower levels of the party organization.

27. D'Amato, *Correnti di partito,* pp. 50–51, 71–86.

28. See especially V. O. Key, Jr., *Southern Politics in State and Nation* (New York: Alfred A. Knopf, 1949); and Key, *American State Politics: An Introduction* (New York: Alfred A. Knopf, 1956). See also the work of Allan P. Sindler, *Huey Long's Louisiana: State Politics, 1920–1952* (Baltimore: Johns Hopkins Press, 1956); Duane Lockard, *New England State Politics* (Princeton: Princeton Univ. Press, 1959); and John H. Fenton, *Midwest Politics* (New York: Holt, Rinehart, and Winston, 1966).

29. Sartori, "Proporzionalismo, frazionismo, e crisi dei partiti," pp. 640–41. On the role of Catholic Action and the Catholic trade unions in the factional struggle within the Italian Christian Democratic party, see Pasquino, "Le radici del frazionismo," pp. 364–68; and Zincone, "Accesso autonomo alle risorse," pp. 145–46, 150–52, 159. On the independent sources of financial support commanded by Japanese factions, see, for example, Hans H. Baerwald, "Factional Politics in Japan," *Current History,* no. 46 (Apr. 1964): 225–29.

30. Rizzi, "Dall' unificazione alla scissione socialista," pp. 422–24.

31. E. Spencer Wellhofer and Timothy M. Hennessey, "Political Party Development, Institutionalization, Leadership, Recruitment, and Behavior," *American Journal of Political Science* 18, no. 1 (Feb. 1974): 135–65.

32. Barnes, *Party Democracy*, pp. 227–28, 252–53.

33. Zariski, "Party Factions and Comparative Politics," p. 41.

34. Jeffrey Obler, "The Role of National Party Leaders in the Selection of Parliamentary Candidates: The Belgian Case," *Comparative Politics* 5, no. 2 (Jan. 1973): 157–84; esp. pp. 160–65, 168–69, 173–77, 180–84.

35. See Thayer, *How the Conservatives Rule Japan*, p. 21; and Michael Leiserson, "Factions and Coalitions in One-Party Japan: An Interpretation Based on the Theory of Games," *American Political Science Review* 62, no. 3 (Sept. 1968): 770.

36. Thayer, *How the Conservatives Rule Japan*, p. 21; and Baerwald, "Factional Politics in Japan," pp. 225–29.

37. Frank L. Wilson, *The French Democratic Left, 1963–1969: Toward a Modern Party System* (Stanford: Stanford Univ. Press, 1971), pp. 193–95.

38. Sartori, "Proporzionalismo, frazionismo, e crisi dei partiti," pp. 637–39, 646.

39. Pasquino, "Le radici del frazionismo," pp. 360, 363; and Zincone, "Accesso autonomo alle risorse," pp. 147–49. See also Stefano Passigli, "Proporzionalismo, frazionismo, e crisi dei partiti: quid prior?" *Rivista Italiana di Scienza Politica* 2, no. 1. (Apr. 1972): 135.

40. Pasquino, "Le radici del frazionismo," pp. 356–59.

41. D'Amato, *Correnti di partito*, pp. 99–100. On this point, he is at odds with Sartori.

42. Sartori, "Proporzionalismo, frazionismo, e crisi dei partiti," pp. 639–41. But see especially Antonio Lombardo, "Dal proporzionalismo intrapartitico al frazionismo eterodiretto," *Rivista Italiana di Scienza Politica* 2, no. 2 (Aug. 1972): 372–73, 379.

43. See Scott, "Patron-Client Politics," pp. 109–11; and Nicholson, "The Factional Model and Politics," pp. 307–09.

44. See Brass, *Factional Politics in an Indian State*, pp. 232–33; and B. D. Graham, "The Succession of Factional Systems in the Uttar Pradesh Congress Party, 1937–66," in Swartz, ed., *Local-Level Politics*, p. 356.

45. Zariski, "Party Factions and Comparative Politics," p. 43.

46. Barnes, *Party Democracy*, pp. 226–27.

47. Eldon Lanning, "A Typology of Latin American Political Systems," *Comparative Politics* 6, no. 3 (Apr. 1974): 385.

48. Lombardo, "Dal proporzionalismo intrapartitico al frazionismo eterodiretto," pp. 372–73, 378–79.

49. Raphael Zariski, "Intra-Party Conflict in a Dominant Party: The Experience of Italian Christian Democracy," *Journal of Politics* 27 (Feb. 1965): 3–34; esp. p. 33.

50. Frank P. Belloni, "Politics in a Faction-Dominant System: Analysis of the Christian Democratic Party of Italy" (Ph.D. diss., Univ. of California, Los Angeles, 1972).

51. Rizzi, "Dall' unificazione alla scissione socialista," pp. 422–23.

52. Weiner, *Party Politics in India*, pp. 242–44.

53. Raphael Zariski, "The Italian Socialist Party: A Case Study in Factional Conflict," *American Political Science Review* 56, no. 2 (June 1962): 383–85, 389.

54. Sidney Tarrow, "Economic Development and the Transformation of the Italian Party System," *Comparative Politics* 1, no. 2 (Jan. 1969): 169–75, 177–79.

55. Raphael Zariski and Susan Welch, "The Correlates of Intra-Party Depolarizing Tendencies in Italy: A Problem Revisited," *Comparative Politics* 7, no. 3 (Apr. 1975): 407–33.

56. Wellhofer and Hennessey, "Political Party Development," p. 144.

57. Brass, *Factional Politics in an Indian State*, pp. 232–33.

58. Wilson, *French Democratic Left*, pp. 193–95.

59. Duncan MacRae, Jr., *Parliament, Parties and Society in France, 1946–1958* (New York: St. Martin's Press, 1967), p. 292.

60. Stern, Tarrow, and Williams, "Factions and Opinion Groups," p. 545.

61. Barnes, *Party Democracy*, pp. 204–08.

62. Janosik, *Constituency Labour Parties*, pp. 97–99, 102–03.

63. MacRae, *Parliament, Parties and Society*, pp. 292–302.

64. See Lanning, "A Typology of Political Systems," pp. 388–89.

65. Ibid., p. 394; Graham, "Succession of Factional Systems," p. 356; and Scott, "Patron-Client Politics," pp. 111–13.

66. Zariski, "The Italian Socialist Party," pp. 383–87, 389–90. We have indicated elsewhere that the statistical methods we employed did not adequately test our propositions.

67. MacRae, *Parliament, Parties and Society,* pp. 290–302.

68. Tarrow, "Economic Development," pp. 164–69.

69. Zariski and Welch, "The Correlates of Depolarizing Tendencies," pp. 407–33.

70. Barnes, *Party Democracy,* pp. 107–08, 111, 137–38.

71. Stern, Tarrow, and Williams, "Factions and Opinion Groups," p. 558.

72. Nicholson, "The Factional Model and Politics," p. 310.

73. For a discussion of the functions of party factions, see Nicholson, "The Factional Model and Politics," pp. 309–10. See also Belloni and Beller, "Study of Party Factions," pp. 545–47.

74. Brass, *Factional Politics in an Indian State,* pp. 240–42.

75. Zincone, "Accesso autonomo alle risorse," p. 143; Robert C. Fried, *Planning the Eternal City: Roman Politics and Planning Since World War II* (New Haven and London: Yale Univ. Press, 1973), p. 208; and Belloni and Beller, "Study of Party Factions."

76. See Andrew J. Milnor and Mark N. Franklin, "Patterns of Opposition Behavior in Modern Legislatures," in Allan Kornberg, ed., *Legislatures in Comparative Perspective* (New York: David McKay Co., 1973), pp. 441–43.

Part Two
DOMINANT-PARTY SYSTEMS

In this section, party factions in five dominant-party political systems are described. Dominant-party systems are countries in which, although two or more parties engage in a competitive power struggle, one party, because its political strength is greater than that of its rivals, dominates the government. The dominance of one party does not mean there is no opposition: one or more other parties do compete with the dominant party. Because of the inequality of strength and resources between the opposition and the dominant party, however, the competition is ineffective in dislodging the dominant party from control of the government. Thus, dominance is not the result of the prohibition of opposition, as occurs in single-party systems; it is the result of the overwhelming and continuing success of the dominant force in the nation's political competition.

The dominant party does not necessarily have an absolute majority in the national parliament, nor a complete monopoly of the offices of government. It may or it may not; dominance can consist merely in the fact that the party consistently captures the largest share of the vote or of the representation in the parliament and consequently—in parliamentary constitutional regimes—is always the "anchor" party in every governing coalition. Besides its size and political strength, the position of the party on the political spectrum can also contribute to the likelihood that its plurality will result in dominance: a center position is more pivotal and increases the political weight of a large party. All of the dominant parties in these five countries have rivals both to their left and to their right.

Included in this section are chapters on two countries whose dominant party does consistently win overwhelming parliamentary majorities, and on three countries whose dominant party consistently wins, not majorities, but pluralities and consistently is the party from which most government ministers—including virtually always the prime minister—are drawn. In Chapter 3, Haruhiro Fukui analyzes factions in the Liberal Democratic party of Japan, which has always held the majority of representation in both houses of parliament, and in the Japan Socialist party, which has perennially been the opposition. In Italy the dominant party has been the Christian Democratic party, which has consistently won pluralities, not majorities, and has governed in coalition with other parties. In Chapter 4, Frank Belloni examines the faction system of the Christian Democrats and of the Italian Socialist party, for many years the opposition and in recent years the second largest party of government coalitions.

In Chapter 5, Myron Aronoff analyzes factions in the Israel Labor party, also a party holding parliamentary pluralities, not majorities, and a party which is the current form of a long history of forming, splitting, and remerging factions of Israel's political labor movement. In Chapter 6, Bruce Campbell and Sue Ellen Charlton examine factions in the dominant party of the French Fifth Republic, the Gaullist Union of Democrats for the Republic, which governs in coalition with smaller parties, and in the French Socialist party, the largest party of the opposition in France. In India, national politics has long been dominated by a single party, the Indian Congress party; the Congress party has monopolized national government, although it has governed in coalitions and has even been in the opposition in state governments in India. In Chapter 7, Norman Nicholson analyzes factions in the Congress party and the complex relations of national, state, and local party factions in India's federal system.

3

Japan: Factionalism in a Dominant-Party System

The Japanese political system dates from the end of World War II, when the American occupation forces wrote the Japanese Constitution, and from the evolution of Japan's political party system in the mid-1950s. For the past two decades, Japanese politics have been dominated by the Liberal Democratic party (LDP), formed by the merging of two conservative parties in 1955. Since then, the LDP has returned as the majority party in the Diet (parliament) in every election; every Japanese parliamentary government has been an LDP government; and every Japanese prime minister has been the LDP president. The opposition consists of one large and three small opposition parties: the Japan Socialist party (JSP), which has been the only sizable opposition; and the Japan Communist party (JCP), the Clean Government party (CGP), and the Democratic Socialist party (DSP), all three minor parties in terms of size of parliamentary representation.

Factionalism is prevalent in Japanese political parties, and textbooks on Japanese politics invariably treat it as a fundamental fact of political life in Japan. Burkes's standard textbook speaks of "a labyrinth of factions and counter-factions" in the ruling LDP and in the major opposition, the JSP.[1] Scalapino and Masumi, in their textbook, conclude that all Japanese parties are made up of factional coalitions or alliances. The authors define faction as the "primary unit" of Japanese politics and suggest that factional interest tends to take precedence over party interest, and even over national interest.[2] Ward found that both the LDP and JSP are factionalized and that the LDP is essentially "a loose coalition of factions united for purposes of campaign and legislative strategy, rather than a unified national party."[3] Ike, in his well-known textbook on Japanese politics concluded that both the LDP and JSP are "basically federations of factions."[4] Two books on the LDP have an entire chapter devoted to a detailed examination of LDP factions.[5] Thus there are numerous sources in English on factions in Japan's political parties, and there are many more in Japanese.

The reason for this concentration on factionalism in Japanese politics is that Japan's major parties have lasting, highly recognizable, and politically significant internal divisions. In the three small parties —the JCP, DSP, and CGP—intraparty divisions appear occasionally, while the LDP and the JSP are chronically faction ridden. Individual factions tend to fluctuate, and there may be anywhere from eight to a dozen factions in the LDP and from five to ten in the JSP at any given time. These groupings are widely known to the politically attentive public, and each faction is usually identified by the name of its leader. The factions are not defined by law—unlike the political parties—yet politicians, newspaper reporters, scholars, voters, and others generally understand references to factions without any need for clarification.[6] In short, political party factions are a widely recognized characteristic of contemporary Japanese politics.

Cultural and Institutional Background of Japanese Factionalism

Japan's political party factions are called *habatsu;* the root word *batsu* may be translated as "faction" in general. Faction in the generic sense refers to a wide range of social groups. Social anthropologist Chie Nakane argues that the entire social structure of Japan is characterized by the prevalence of vertically organized groups and that faction and factionalism are inherent in that structure.[7] In this view, factionalism in political parties only manifests a general and ubiquitous pattern of interpersonal relationships and group formations. Takeshi Ishida, a political scientist, explains the concept of faction in a similar vein. For Ishida, factions are found all over Japanese society; in modern Japan there are factions of government officials from particular provinces *(hanbatsu)*, of ultranationalist army and navy officers *(gunbatsu)*, of Imperial University of Tokyo alumni *(gakubatsu)*, and of wealthy and powerful businessmen and industrialists *(zaibatsu)*.[8]

Used in this general sense, faction is heavily traditional. Ishida explains:

Batsu (faction) means a private, informal group functioning in the field of public affairs. Such a group is held together by particularly intimate personal ties similar to those in primary groups in rural communities.

This group is characterized by a closed and exclusive unity oriented toward particularistic values, and often involves quasi-familistic relationships—paternalistic protection or patronage on the part of the leader, and dependence on the leader by the rank and file. This quasi-familistic relationship is often called the *oyabun-kobun* relationship (*oya* means parent and *ko* means child).[9]

Ishida identified conformity and competition as two basic forces in Japanese culture and argued that they are not mutually opposed, but rather, mutually reinforcing. Nakane focused on the vertical links among individuals as the basic pattern of social structure. These two propositions explain well the cultural matrix of faction in general and party factions in particular.

Nakane's model consists of a group in which members are positioned hierarchically in a rigid pyramid. At the top there is one leader. Immediately below him there are several senior members (subleaders) who are tied personally, emotively, and particularistically to the leader. Below each subleader are other members who are similarly tied to the subleader and, indirectly through him, to the top leader. Below these is a still lower layer of junior members with direct and personal ties binding them to the member immediately above and to several members immediately below, and so on. The only primary, direct, and viable interpersonal relationships are the vertical ties between any member and his immediate leader, and between any member and his immediate followers. Ties linking a member with others of equal or nearly equal status are either totally lacking or incidental and weak. Borrowing Nakane's illustration (with minor modification), this group structure looks like this:[10]

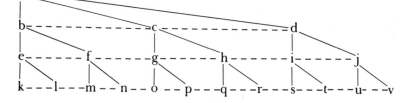

The leader (a) is personally and directly related to senior members (b), (c), and (d), who in turn are similarly related respectively to members (e) and (f), (g) and (h), and (i) and (j), and so on. On the other hand, the relationships between (a) and (e), (f), (g), etc. are indirect; those between (a) and (k), (l), (m), etc. are even more indirect. The lateral ties between (b), (c), and (d), or between (e), (f), (g), etc. are nonexistent or extremely weak. Actually, such relationships cannot be truly lateral, since each member's status in the hierarchy is determined by the closeness of his relationship to his immediate boss and through him to the bigger bosses in the hierarchy, ultimately to the top leader. As the figure above suggests, the psychological distances between (a) and (b) and between (a) and (c) are different; (b) is closer than (c) to their boss, while (c) is closer than (d). This means that (b) is higher in status than (c), and (c) higher than (d), in terms of the intragroup ranking system. Likewise, (e) is higher than (f), (f) is higher than (g), etc., and (k) is higher than (l), (l) than (m), etc. As Nakane points out, no two members can be of equal status in this type of group.

This structure is the context for Ishida's idea of simultaneous conformity and competition. A person's rise in power and prestige within a vertically organized group of this kind will depend on two factors: his personal relationship with his boss and his success in competing against others having a rank similar to his own for the boss's attention and favors. One is a function of the other. The system thus imposes conformity with values and goals of the leaders on the one hand, and intense competition among peer members on the other.

The model has several implications for political party factions. First, the model predicts that a group will require the presence of a particular individual who leads it. As a rule, this individual cannot be replaced by anyone else, since the ties which bind other members to him are personal and nontransferable. The departure or death of the leader will usually prove fatal to the solidarity and survival of the group.

Second, because a group is internally segmented it will be subject to divisive pressures generated and intensified by the competition among its members. In the illustration above, the entire group will be liable to divide itself into subgroups led by (b), (c), and (d) if (a)'s leadership is lost or substantially weakened for any reason. Each segment will tend to develop its own identity and viability strong enough to sustain it if the larger group should dissolve. In other words, each segment becomes a latent separate group.

Third, power will tend to be dispersed rather than concentrated in a group of this type. In order to keep the group together, the top leader has to rely on the loyalty and leadership of subleaders at the intermediate levels of the hierarchy. Without their support and cooperation he will not be able to mobilize effectively the entire membership; in fact, he will not be able even to get his messages through to those at the lower levels. The leader will tend to be attentive to the interests and opinions of the middle echelons. The typical Japanese leader is thus a sensitive organization man rather than a ruthless despot.

Finally, the vertical relationships sustaining such a group will tend to be based only implicitly and ambiguously on mutual benefits or rights. The sense of contractual relationship will be largely absent, and agreements on policy or programmatic issues will be largely irrelevant.

Factions in Japan's major political parties share the attributes of the general faction, but they are more explicit and more precisely defined structurally and functionally. Party factions fit the patterns of leader-follower interpersonal relations and vertical group formation of Nakane's analysis. They also exhibit the pattern of conformity and competition Ishida described, and as we shall see below, they confirm the predicted patterns of internal divisiveness. In short, both linguistically and sociologically, the *habatsu* (party faction) is a specific case of the generic category *batsu* (faction), exhibiting the latter's general characteristics but expressing more explicit structural and functional organization.

Nakane and Ishida distinguished between formal groups and informal groups, both of which are found in Japanese society. Formal groups are based on egalitarian, democratic, and universalistic principles; informal groups on traditionalistic principles. They believed that the former are alien to Japan's culture and values, and are therefore eroded, subverted, and subsumed by the latter, which are more congenial to the cultural values. This view echoes a widely held view of the process of Japanese modernization. A Kyoto University intellectual historian, Yuji Aida, has argued that in the actual functioning of Japanese society, it is not the formal groups and relationships but the "invisible," quasi-familistic groups that really matter.[11] To Nakane and Ishida, as much as to Aida, the somewhat surreptitious and subterranean world of such traditional groups and relationships is the more important of the two worlds in which contemporary Japanese live.

Both Nakane and Ishida sought basic principles of social organization that would explain the entire range of social processes in Japan. Thus Nakane's model of the typical Japanese small group is implicitly applicable to the total political system of modern Japan. According to the model, prewar Japan may be viewed as a gigantic pyramid, at the top of which sat the emperor. Like the small social groups discussed by Ishida and Aida, the large group Imperial Japan was also founded on quasi-familistic relationships, with the emperor playing as a surrogate father and all good Japanese subjects treated as loyal members of the family-nation, each positioned in their proper station in society's hierarchical order. The ties between the emperor (a) and leaders of the many social groups in the system—(b), (c), (d), etc.—were purely psychological and abstract. Yet these ties not only were real but were firm enough to sustain a legendary solidarity of the nation, until they suddenly and finally came unraveled with Japan's defeat in World War II. This was followed by a series of drastic changes in the framework of Japanese society and government. These changes in turn were the institutional context of contemporary Japanese party politics.

For present purposes, the most important of these changes was the status of the Diet in the distribution of political power in the system. In Imperial Japan all powers had been theoretically concentrated in the hands of the emperor, as the sacred and inviolable sovereign. In practice the emperor's powers were shared by several competing groups, such as the Meiji oligarchs and their successors, the military, the civil bureaucracy, and the hereditary aristocrats represented in the upper house (House of Peers) of the Imperial Diet. The lower house (House of Representatives) of the Diet was the only arena for action of political parties, but it was very narrowly restricted. However, in the new Constitution, drafted by General MacArthur's advisers, the National Diet was made "the highest organ of state power" and "the sole law-making organ." The prime minister and his cabinet became for the first time directly accountable to and controlled by the Diet. It was now the Diet, not the emperor, which would designate the prime minister; and the prime minister and a majority of cabinet ministers are now required to be members of the Diet.

These constitutional changes had far-reaching implications for postwar Japanese politics and for political parties. Premiership has now become the highest stake in the game of national politics, a stake within the range of any ambitious party politician, at least in theory. The approach to that highest seat of power is clearly marked and straightforward. Whoever controls a majority in the Diet (or at least in the lower house) is virtually assured of acceding to the premiership. Politicians harboring prime-ministerial ambitions now naturally seek control of a majority party or a majority coalition of parties in the Diet, in order to ride the parliamentary majority to the premiership.

In this process, winning the leadership of the majority party is the most critical step, rather than winning the formal election to premiership by the majority in the Diet. Because the LDP has dominated the Diet since the mid-1950s, the LDP presidency has become the ultimate focus of national power. Factionalism in the LDP has always revolved around the critical competition for the presidency of the party.

Conditions Contributing to and Inhibiting Factionalism

As I have described, chronic factionalism has been largely confined to Japan's two major parties, the LDP and JSP. Despite their mutual hostility, the LDP and the JSP share many important characteristics, including not only factionalism but some of its causes as well. Both parties came into existence with factionalism already built in. Each was formed in the 1950s as a merger of diverse political groups, often representing personal and ideological ties dating back to prewar days. For the LDP, the merger of the Liberals and the Democrats had been preceded by lengthy conflicts between prewar politicians and bureaucrats, many of whom had been removed from office during the Occupation, and those who had entered politics to fill the jobs vacated by the prewar men.[12]

For the JSP, the impact of divisions predating its merger was more extensive. The party was first formed in 1945 as a loose coalition of prewar socialist groups which had fought more among themselves than against authoritarian government in the 1920s and 1930s. Party leadership was split, reflecting divisions in the prewar labor movement.[13] The number of JSP leaders purged in the Occupation was relatively small, and old divisions continued until the party split into two separate parties in 1951. Four years later they reunited, but basic ideological and personality conflicts were never overcome. In 1960, over the issue of the U.S.-Japan Mutual Security Treaty, the extreme right-wing group bolted from the party and formed a separate party of its own, the DSP. Thus in both the LDP and the JSP, factionalism originated in premerger divisions.

The LDP and the JSP share at least two other important characteristics relevant to factionalism. One is their basic ideological orientations. Both are eclectic, tolerant, and inclusive, especially in comparison with the JCP and CGP—each in its own way ideologically puritanical, intolerant, and exclusive.[14] Although the JSP is often portrayed as an ideologically motivated radical party, it actually shares much more with the conservative LDP and differs more from the JCP, both in ideology and behavior. The JSP is officially committed, like the JCP, to the principle of "democratic centralism'" in making and enforcing decisions among its members. But the principle has not seriously inhibited factionalism, whereas the same principle has been used effectively, even ruthlessly, to root out intraparty dissidence in the JCP. The JSP, however, is notorious for its lack of a strong-handed party discipline. Such internal ideological tolerance encourages pluralistic tendencies and competition in both the JSP and LDP.

The other characteristic these parties share is their elitist, professional-politician-centered membership and organization. Despite its official emphasis on mass support and mass involvement, the JSP has not developed stable and effective local organization. The party's ties with its supporters are ephemeral and superficial. In the LDP, a general lack of a massive local-level party organization is matched by a lack of principled commitment to organization of the masses. This elitism tends to leave members of the parties' parliamentary contingents free to engage in the game of intraparty factional politics unrestrained by powerful grass-roots pressures.

Apart from these characteristics of political parties themselves, Japan's electoral system has also fostered party factions. Elections to the Japanese lower house are conducted under a multimember constituency system originally adopted in the 1920s as a device to enable each of the three parties then sharing power to win—or at least to hope to win—a seat in every constituency, and continued after World War II for similar reasons. Under the system, two, three, or four members are elected from each constituency to the House of Representatives. Consequently, two or more candidates from the major parties normally run in each district. These candidates compete with each other as well as with the candidates of rival parties.[15]

This system contributes prominently to the growth of factionalism in the two parties. An active member of the LDP's 1972 "mainstream" faction once declared that so long as he is forced to compete not only with opposition candidates but also with senior men from his own party, he needs the support of his faction simply to survive.[16] The support of a faction is highly important to an LDP candidate for campaign funds. It is perhaps even more critical for earning a nominee the official party endorsement, which often will make or break a candidate fighting in a competitive constituency. The impact of the electoral system is similar, but generally less decisive. This is not a difference in the nature of the impact, however, but reflects the fact that normally fewer JSP candidates than LDP candidates run in each constituency.

The most important factor contributing to the factionalism in the LDP and the JSP, however, has been the way desirable party, parliamentary, and, in the case of the LDP, cabinet and subcabinet jobs have been distributed within each party. For the LDP, virtual monopoly of appointive government jobs has served as a massive stimulus to factionalism. In the JSP's earlier days, ideology was the main cause of factionalism, but since about 1960, more pragmatic aspirations for control of the party apparatus have become at least as critical as ideology or policy considerations, if not more so. JSP factions have become progressively less distinguishable from their LDP counterparts in basic motivations and behavior, and it has become no longer possible to identify the factions of the JSP in terms of a simple ideological left-right dichotomy.[17]

The relationship between the distribution of posts and factionalism, however, has been most obvious in the LDP. The cycle of intraparty faction politics begins and ends with elections of the party president. Because whoever wins the support of a majority in the nation's legislature (or its lower house) is virtually assured of election to the premiership, and because the LDP has since its founding managed to control a majority of seats in both houses of the Diet, successive presidents of the LDP have automatically become successive prime ministers of Japan. LDP presidential elections are de facto elections for Japan's head of government, which raises the stakes and the heat of intraparty contests much higher than they would be if the two positions were not so joined. As LDP politicians themselves acknowledge, party presidential elections have become a major cause of factionalism in the party.[18]

In contrast to the two major parties, intraparty factionalism has been quite subdued in the three minor parties represented in the Japanese parliament. There are several factors which inhibit factionalism in these parties.

Although the DSP does not differ much from the JSP either in ideology or behavior, it is a much smaller party, roughly comparable to one of the major JSP factions in terms of its strength in the Diet. Actually, the DSP does appear to have been divided into protofactional groupings since the time when they bolted from the JSP in 1960. According to some accounts, these groupings were aligned in late 1968 roughly along mainstream-antimainstream lines, much like the factions in the LDP and the JSP.[19] The main condition inhibiting the growth of a more extreme factionalism in the DSP is its small size, and if it grows larger it will likely come to resemble the two major parties with internal factionalism.

The CGP and the JCP are rather different. Both are mass movement parties guided by an explicitly integrative ideology. Although CGP leaders would claim their autonomy from the militant Buddhist organization, the Sokagakkai, the two are in fact largely inseparable. Its relationship with the religious institution inhibits divisions in the CGP in two ways. First, the Sokagakkai is an authoritarian organization which imposes nearly complete doctrinal and programmatic conformity on its members, including especially those of its most visible and potentially most vulnerable organ, the CGP. Factionalism would be heretical and alien to the group's theory of organization. Second, the Sokagakkai provides its members with opportunities for gratification of aspirations for power and prestige. To some CGP politicians, posts in the party have a certain attraction; this group is small, and the number of attractively titled party positions is large enough to go around. For the rank-and-file CGP members the road to advancement lies not in the party but in the much larger Sokagakkai itself. Hence, factions are more likely to emerge in the larger organization of the Sokagakkai than within the CGP.

The JCP is a party even more ideologically oriented and more organizationally centralized than the CGP—although the Communist party is said to have become conspicuously less ideological and pragmatic in the past few years, and its recent successes in national and local elections are generally attributed largely to this shift of emphasis in programs and tactics. Despite this apparent softening of its public image, however, the JCP has not relaxed the legendary "iron discipline" of its democratic centralism. In its party constitution the JCP admonishes its faithful that "to . . . foster factions, or engage in sectarian activities, is to commit the worst crime against the party." In contrast to the JSP, the JCP leadership enforces its discipline without scruple. In short, the JCP offers a singularly inhospitable climate, ideologically and organizationally, to the rise of viable factional groupings. This does not mean that intraparty dissension is unknown in the JCP. On the contrary, the party has lived through a long series of bitter disputes and recriminations among its leaders. However, instead of resulting in lasting factions, dissident minorities have been expelled from party membership. The JCP has periodically purged its ranks of dissidents and thereby prevented the growth of internal factions.

General characteristics of culture do not by themselves explain the presence of factionalism in Japanese party politics. There have been specific conditions in the ideology, organization, membership, and environmental setting which have either encouraged or inhibited factionalism in each party. The impact of traditional culture and social structure emphasized by scholars like Ishida and Nakane does more to explain the *structural* attributes of Japanese party factions, whereas the current conditions contributing to factionalism do more to explain most of the important *functions* of LDP and JSP factions.

Structures and Functions of Japanese Factions

The factions of the LDP and the JSP have definite structural attributes, although their structure is rather simple, even primitive. To begin with, they have quite small memberships. It is difficult to estimate with precision the size of each faction. This is particularly the case with JSP factions, which include transitory affiliates among their members in the upper house and outside of parliament. In any event, no faction claims more than a hundred bona fide members; Table 1 shows the parliamentary membership of LDP and JSP factions (by 1974) as well below that number. Every LDP faction traditionally has a seniority-based list of members, according to the length of time each member has been affiliated with the group. This provides the faction with both a membership measurement and an internal rank order of personnel.

Largely due to this small size, the degree of internal diversification and specialization is limited. Typically, a faction has one or two specialists in each major policy area, parliamentary tacticians, accountants, and so on, but the lines of specialization are usually loose and flexible. Most factions, particularly of the LDP, handle considerable treasuries of their own, collected and disbursed for exclusively factional interests. Finally, many of the factions—again, particularly those of the LDP— maintain offices and meeting places in Tokyo office buildings or hotels, and periodically some factions hold "policy seminars" and "study sessions" at quiet suburban retreats.

Table 1. Estimated Strengths of LDP and JSP Diet Factions, 1974

LDP Factions	Lower House	Upper House	Total
Tanaka faction	47	46	93
Fukuda faction	56	28	84
Ohira faction	42	25	67
Miki faction	38	8	46
Nakasone faction	38	4	42
Shiina faction	17	2	19
Mizuta faction	13	3	16
Funada faction	8	4	12
Ishii faction	9	0	9
Unaffiliated members	11	7	18

JSP Factions	Lower House	Upper House	Total
Sasaki faction	28	17	45
Eda faction	30	4	34
Katsumata faction	26	4	30
Shakaishugi Kyokai	3	2	5
Kawakami faction	4	0	4
Ampo Daha Doshikai	2	0	2
Unaffiliated members	25*	35**	60

*Includes two members calling themselves Nomin Doshikai ("Friends of Farmers").
**Includes eleven members loosely grouped as Tokakai ("The Tenth Day Society").
Source: Mainichi Shimbun, July 15, 1974 (evening edition).

The degree of the institutionalization of LDP factions has been particularly noteworthy. Thayer refers to them as "formal political entities with a headquarters, regular meetings, a known membership, an established structure, and firm discipline."[20] Leiserson reported that within a few years of the formation of the party, LDP factions became entrenched and institutionalized:

> ... the factions became like army "divisions," headed by a "general" who was advised by his "General Staff." There were "line officers," fixed and known memberships, officers, publications, regular sources of funds, and so forth. In a word, the factions became institutionalized, and, because of that change, became able to perform some of the functions of parties in a coalition cabinet system of government.[21]

The part played by the personality of the leader is most significant in the political and social life of each faction. As their names imply, the factions usually have been formed by and for particular party bigwigs.

Often they are so heavily dependent on their leaders that when a
founder leaves or dies, a faction faces serious dangers of dissension
and fragmentation. This has been especially true of most LDP factions,
in which nonpersonal factors of cooperation and solidarity, such as
ideology and policy, are less significant even than in JSP factions. The
once-powerful factions led by such strong men as Kishi, Ono, and
Kono all split up on the leaders' retirement or death.[22]

However, splitting up has not meant complete disintegration. Of
the LDP factions in Table 1, all but the two still headed by their
original founders (the Miki and Ishii factions) are successors or segments of predecessor factions. Fukuda and Tanaka had been affiliated with former Prime Minister Sato. After Sato resigned from the
premiership in 1972, his faction split into the two fiercely competitive
rival factions, when Tanaka beat Fukuda for the LDP presidency and
the premiership. Fukuda remained Tanaka's formidable competitor,
and eventually succeeded in building his own majority. Ohira had once
been a trusted right-hand man of another former prime minister,
Ikeda. Following the latter's retirement in 1964, the faction's reins
passed first to the most senior among Ikeda's confidants, Maeo. But
Maeo never succeeded in establishing his authority or credibility as an
effective leader among the faction's important members. When he was
rebuffed in 1970 by Prime Minister Sato in his attempt to win a couple
of prime cabinet posts for the faction, Maeo had an intrafactional
rebellion on his hands and was forced to give up the position of faction
leader to Ohira. Ohira managed to keep the factional following together through his profitable friendship and cooperation with Prime
Minister Tanaka, which earned the faction some of the most desirable
party and government posts.[23] The succeeding prime minister, Miki,
headed an old faction which at various times over the years had aligned
with, and then broken with, Premiers Kishi, Ikeda, Sato, and Tanaka.
Miki's coalition, however, included at least nominally the support of
all LDP factions. Prime Minister Fukuda heads a faction once part of
the large Sato and Kishi factions.

The problem of leadership succession has been even more acute
for the smaller factions. The largest of these, the Nakasone faction, has
inherited half of the late Kono's factional following. But Nakasone's
position among the faction's senior members has been no more than
primus inter pares, and he has been constantly open to their challenge.
In the still smaller successor factions, led respectively by Shiina (Kishi's successor), Mizuta (Ono's successor), and Funada (Ono's successor), the leaders' efforts to make themselves acceptable to their
affiliates have often been frustrated by their inability to deliver enough
party and government posts. As a result, most of these small factions
are unable to act with unity either in a party presidential election or
during intraparty controversies over policy issues.

The experience of factions which have lost their original leaders thus suggests the validity of Nakane's model discussed in the opening section. The LDP factions are groups formed around particular individuals, rather than around ideologies or programs, and structured on the basis of chains of vertical ties. Their survival depends to a large extent on the strength of such ties. When these ties are severed by the departure or death of the leader, the groups become suddenly vulnerable to divisive tendencies inherent in their structure. There seem to be two reasons they do not fall apart completely and disintegrate into much smaller units or isolated individuals. For one thing, they are small enough not only for direct personal ties to grow between the leaders and all affiliates, including those at the lowest levels of the pyramid, but also for some horizontal ties to develop among members generally. Such horizontal ties are apparently extensive enough and durable enough to prevent a faction's total fragmentation on the departure of its original leader. For another thing, the seniority lists of the LDP factions mean that a member loses his seniority by transferring from one faction to another. This discourages frequent transfers among the factions and works against the total dissolution of a faction that suffers the loss of its leader.

The last point explains the strength and durability of LDP factions and contradicts the suggestion of fragility in Nakane's model. Over a period of about fifteen years, 1960 to 1975, most of the LDP factions of the late 1950s have undergone changes of leadership and splits. The once-powerful Kishi faction has become the Fukuda and the Shiina factions; the Ono faction, the Mizuta and the Funada factions; the Kono faction, the Nakasone faction and part of the Fukuda faction; and, finally, the Sato faction has become the Tanaka faction and part of the Fukuda faction. The Ikeda faction was passed to Maeo and to Ohira, as we have already seen. Only the Miki and the Ishii groups continue to be led by their leaders of the 1950s.

Despite all these changes, shifts in membership affiliations have been quite limited, other than shifts from an original to its successor faction. To illustrate longevity of faction affiliation, a count was made of the faction identifications of the most senior LDP parliamentarians. The LDP elected 271 members to the House of Representatives in the December 1972 general election. Of these, 124 had been returned in every lower house election since 1960 without interruption, and an additional 13 had been returned every time except once. Of the first group 98, or 80 percent, had never changed their factional affiliations during the same period, 25 had changed their affiliation once, and 1 had done so twice. Of the latter group 11, or 85 percent, had never shifted affiliations, while the remaining 2 had done so once.[24] This degree of constancy is remarkable.

JSP factions differ from LDP factions in several respects. They are relatively more concerned with issues of ideology and long-term policy. They contain, as a rule, more nonparliamentarian affiliates, and they are less stable in membership composition and patterns of leader-follower relationships. During the 1960s, the level of factional conflicts in the JSP increased substantially and, at the same time, the frequency of interfaction transfers and mergers and splits also increased. The largest factions—the left faction led by Sasaki, the right "structural reformist" faction led by Eda, and the middle-of-the-road Katsumata faction—were especially chaotic.[25] On the other hand, an increasing number of JSP parliamentarians tend to dissociate themselves from any of the factions. For the past several years, these unaligned have been about one-fourth of the JSP lower house members and about two-thirds of the JSP upper house members.[26] These may signal the gradual decline of the JSP factions, although hardly their demise.

Nevertheless, the structure of a large JSP faction closely resembles that of an LDP faction in its essentials. As Nakane's model predicts, it is based on and sustained mainly by intensely personal relationships between the leader and his followers. Ideology and policy are, of course, taken seriously in exchanges among faction theorists or tacticians. Yet, as participant-observer Kawakami (son of the late leader of a JSP faction) has pointed out, ideology, policy, and personality are often inseparable in JSP intraparty politics.[27] A JSP faction is almost as dependent on its particular leader as its LDP counterpart. When the leader leaves, the faction faces a crisis of survival and often goes through a period of severe instability and internal readjustment.

When we turn to the functions of the factions in the two parties, we find more striking similarities. For both parties, factionalism serves as the major mechanism for the allocation of important party and government jobs. Above all, faction competition structures the processes of choosing top party leadership. Because no faction in either party has become large enough to capture control of the party organization by itself, party elections are intense political rivalries aimed at building *coalitions* of factions. A party president or presidential aspirant is not only a faction leader, but is also leader of an ad hoc coalition of factions aligned with his own. The result in both parties has been successions of factional coalitions. Those which have gathered a majority of a party's votes have served as the mainstream, and most others have played the role of antimainstream or opposition; a few factions have avoided commitment to either side. Whenever there is a party presidential election, or other change of top party leadership, old coalitions are broken, and new mainstreams and antimainstreams are formed.

As I have indicated, politicking in LDP presidential elections is more intense than in the JSP because the LDP president virtually automatically becomes prime minister of Japan. The LDP had its first open presidential election in 1956; from that time until the end of 1974, there have been nine major faction alignments in the LDP, as shown in Table 2. Eligibility to run as a serious candidate in LDP presidential elections has been limited to those few powerful leaders who could at least hope to win the majority of votes necessary for election. The franchise in these elections is restricted by the party constitution to LDP members of both houses of the Diet plus one representative each from the forty-seven prefectural chapters of the party. Over the past fifteen years, the LDP has maintained a strength of around 290 seats in the House of Representatives (the lower house) and around 135 in the House of Councillors (the upper house). In order to win a party presidential election, a candidate would thus need about 235 votes. The best way to assure that many votes has been to organize and maintain as large and as stable a bloc of committed supporters as possible, well in advance of the election. Such blocs were the factions as they evolved in the first competitive election of this kind in 1956.

In fact, however, the largest of these factional vote-blocs has not built up a membership of more than about one hundred—around fifty LDP lower house members and another fifty upper house and prefectural chapter representatives combined.[28] Thus, building a coalition of factions around one's own bloc at the time of an election became the critical logistical operation for an LDP presidential aspirant heading a major faction. At each party presidential election, and occasionally at other times, coalitions are built, broken, and rebuilt. During such coalition-building, large amounts of cash freely change hands, personal loyalties are betrayed and promises broken, and all kinds of trickeries are resorted to.[29]

Any one of the LDP's three or four largest factions can hope to win presidential nomination for its own leader by building a factional coalition at the time of the election. The most common strategy used has been for two or three of them to reach agreement in advance, to the effect that they would join forces against a third or fourth candidate. The leader of one of them would win the presidency and would then share the remaining party and government posts with the collaborating factions. A presidential candidate must win a majority on the first ballot, or the first and second runners-up compete in a second ballot. In an election where more than two candidates compete, two or three large factions will collaborate to their mutual advantage in a flexible coalition arrangement. On the first ballot the leaders of all collaborating factions will run in competition with each other, as well as with noncollaborating candidates. If none of the candidates wins a majority and if only one of the leaders of the collaborating factions places either first or second on the first ballot, then the losers will

Table 2. LDP Diet Factions, 1956–1974

	Dates of Major Realignment							
April 1956	December 1956	January 1959	July 1960	July 1964	December 1966	October 1970	July 1972	December 1974
HATOYAMA	ISHIBASHI* (Hatoyama)**	KISHI	IKEDA	IKEDA	SATO	SATO	TANAKA (Sato)	MIKI
Ishii	Ishii	Kono	Fukuda-Kawashima (Kishi)	Kawashima (Fukuda-Kawashima)	Fukuda	Fukuda	Funada	Fukuda
Kishi	Ikeda (Yoshida)	Ono	Sato	Kono	Funada (Murakami-Funada)	Funada	Ishii	Funada
Matsumura	Matsumura	Sato		Miki	Ishii	Ishii	Miki	Ishii
Ono	Ono			Murakami-Funada (Ono)	Kawashima	Kawashima	Mizuta (Murakami)	Mizuta
					Mori (Kono)	Murakami	Nakasone	Nakasone
					Murakami (Murakami-Funada)	Nakasone	Ohira (Maco)	Ohira
						Sonoda (Mori)	Shiina (Kawashima)	Shiina
								Tanaka

Mainstream Majority Coalition

Table 2. LDP Diet Factions, 1956–1974 (cont.)

Yoshida	Kishi	Ikeda	Fujiyama (Kishi)	Fujiyama	Fujiyama	Fujiyama	Fukuda (Fukuda, Fujiyama, Murakami, Sato)
	Kono (Hatoyama)	Ishibashi	Ishii	Fukuda (Fukuda-Kawashima)	Miki	Maeo	
	Sato (Yoshida)	Ishii	Kono	Ishii	Maeo (Ikeda)	Miki	
		Matsumura	Miki (Matsumura, Ishibashi)	Sato	Nakasone (Kono)		
			Ono				

Mainstream

Antimainstream
Opposition and
Unaligned

* Presidential factions are capitalized.
** In parentheses are names of direct predecessor factions.
Sources: Asahi Shimbun, December 12, 1972; December 19, 1974.

59

"donate" their blocs of votes to the winning partner in accordance with the advance agreement. On the second ballot their combined strength can win them the party presidency even against a faction or a coalition of factions larger than any one of them separately.[30]

The absence of factions large enough to win a presidential election by themselves has made it meaningful, quite apart from reasons of incompatible ideologies or personalities, for the medium-sized and small factions to maintain themselves rather than disband and join larger ones. Under intense competition even the relatively small blocs of votes controlled by these factions often make an important difference in the outcome of the party presidential contest. This is particularly true because any faction leader's control of his faction members' votes is never complete, and some always go astray. This creates a situation of uncertainty sufficiently unsettling for leaders aspiring to the presidency to seek the last margin of security available. Smaller factions can offer such a margin and often are rewarded with a few lesser party or government posts.

Available for distribution to the winning coalition are some 120 directorships and chairmanships in each house of the Diet and, most important of all, the 21 cabinet ministerial portfolios and 24 parliamentary vice-ministerships. Of these, the highest stakes are the dozen top party posts, a few of the Diet chairmanships, and all of the cabinet portfolios.[31] As a rule, the most desirable among them, such as the party general secretaryship and the cabinet portfolios of Finance, Foreign Affairs, and International Trade and Industry, go to the faction led by the party president or a larger key faction in the mainstream coalition. This intraparty spoils system breeds and sustains LDP factions.

In the LDP, conventions regarding the distribution of major party and government posts are well defined and are observed with a high degree of consistency. The basic criteria used in termining the kind and number of cabinet posts allocated to each faction are the faction's size and its relationship to the prime minister's mainstream coalition. Of the 21 cabinet posts, 2 (the prime ministership and chief cabinet secretaryship) are excluded from general distribution; of the remaining 19, 2 go by custom to LDP members in the upper house and 17 to the LDP members of the lower house. Since there are about 280 LDP members in the lower house, a faction with 18 members in the lower house would qualify to receive at least 1 cabinet post on the principle of proportionate size alone. Whether it actually does or not depends on how cooperative it has been with the mainstream coalition and how it is likely to behave towards the mainstream in the future, especially in future presidential contests. This also depends on how rewarding or punishing its inclusion may be to others, i.e., how it may affect the behavior of other factions either in the mainstream coalition or in the antimainstream opposition.[32] These two basic criteria also apply, somewhat less rigidly, to appointments to other important party and government posts.

Since these posts are allocated on a faction basis rather than on an individual basis, up to a point it is left to each faction's leader to decide how to distribute its share of posts. Given the size of a politician's ambitions (and constituency pressures which nurture such ambitions), decisions relating to the interfaction allocation of the few posts are extremely sensitive. A wrong decision may cause sufficient frustration and resentment within a faction's ranks to threaten its survival as a united and competitive group. To hedge against such a risk, each faction develops a waiting list of candidates for appointment, based on seniority in terms of both Diet membership and affiliation with the faction or its leader. As I have pointed out, most LDP Diet members have been affiliated with the same factions ever since they were first elected to the Diet. Seniority in one sense is therefore a close approximation of seniority in the other sense in most cases. Some nonparliamentarians also enter the factions—usually LDP candidates in a general election or persons actively seeking the party's endorsement for their candidacy; such individuals are necessarily lowest in seniority.[33] So long as this principle of rewarding seniority is consistently adhered to, every member of a sufficiently large faction can expect eventually to rise to the top of the waiting list and to be appointed to a desirable party or government post, which will in turn guarantee his success in future Diet elections. Because of this, the system looks eminently fair and reasonable to most LDP politicians.

It is to the advantage of a leader to base his appointments on these carefully developed waiting lists. Difficulties arise when for tactical or other reasons a prime minister and his advisers refuse to respect recommendations based on a faction's priority list. The faction leader will resist the prime minister's "interference" in the internal affairs of his faction. However, there usually is not much the faction leader can do to change the party leader's mind, because the interference, if and when it happens, is most likely fully intended and deliberate. At the same time, because the interfactional power game in the LDP is so ruthless, a faction leader will often sacrifice an opportunity to win himself a desirable post out of concern for the internal harmony of his faction.

The struggle of the factions for leadership posts in the JSP is not as overt or as systematized as in the LDP. Except for a few special committee chairmanships in the Diet, none of the important public offices are available for distribution to the JSP. The potential stakes of JSP factionalism are limited to twenty or so party offices—all elective posts. Moreover, the mechanisms for electing these party officials are more complex than elections of LDP officers. The JSP Congress (which elects party officials) is attended by delegates appointed by the party's prefectural chapters, plus officials of the JSP national headquarters, and a limited number—about 10 percent of the total—of representatives from affiliated organizations. Members of the Diet receive no preferential treatment in this respect, and in fact, they are a minority among the voting delegates of the congress. For this reason, most of the JSP factions active in contests for party leadership positions have large numbers of nonparliamentarian members, and it is much harder for an outsider to identify the faction's actual membership strengths.[34]

Nevertheless, insofar as they do compete for these party posts, JSP factions' motivations and behavior are essentially the same as those of their LDP counterparts. JSP factions generally tend to be identified by the name of their faction leader—although there is a somewhat greater incidence among JSP factions of groups known by some descriptive title (usually of some policy or ideological content) rather than by someone's name. Although the JSP's factions normally sort themselves into a majority coalition and an opposition coalition, just as in the LDP, the JSP includes a greater number of factions not aligned with either the mainstream or the antimainstream. There have been eight major alignments in the JSP from 1955 to 1974, as shown in Table 3.

The involvement of factions in the allocation of JSP posts is as intense and conspicuous as in the LDP. In a way, it is even more dramatic, because elections to party office in the JSP take place at the annual party conference. The top stakes are the posts of chairman, vice-chairman and members of the Central Executive Committee, and general secretary. By convention, the chairman and the general secretary are chosen from two different factions. In the election of the Central Executive Committee, votes generally follow factional lines and, as a result, the committee's composition more or less accurately reflects the numerical balance among the major factions.[35] Because voting delegates to the JSP Conference include a large number of nonparliamentarian members, the Central Executive Committee also contains a substantial proportion of these; as of December 1973 they comprised nearly half of the committee. Many of these are only vaguely expected to be candidates in future Diet elections. Factional competition for party posts in the JSP thus involves nonparliamentarian members much more extensively than in the LDP, and the function of JSP factions in the distribution of offices is more diffuse within the party at large.

The factions perform several other important functions in both parties. I have already noted their involvement on behalf of their affiliates in headquarter's decisions on party endorsement of candidates in Diet elections. In published writings, this function has been emphasized particularly in discussions of LDP factions, but it is apparently just as important for JSP factions.[36] On the other hand, the role

Table 3. JSP Diet Factions, 1955–1974

	Dates of Major Realignment							
	October 1955	March 1960	March 1961	November 1962	May 1965	August 1967	December 1970	December 1974
Mainstream Coalition	Kawakami	Matsumoto (Kuroda, Suzuki)*	Kawakami	Eda (Suzuki)	*Heiwa Doshikai*	Eda	*Ampo Daha Doshikai* (*Heiwa Doshikai*)	*Ampo Daha Doshikai*
	Suzuki	Suzuki (Suzuki, Kuroda)	Suzuki	Kawakami	Sasaki	*Heiwa Doshikai*	Katsumata	Eda
				Wada		Katsumata (Wada)	Sasaki	Katsumata
						Kawakami	*Shakaishugi Kyokai* (Sasaki)	Kawakami
						Sasaki		Sasaki
								Shakaishugi Kyokai
Antimainstream Coalition and Unaligned	Kuroda	Kawakami (Kawakami, Nishio)	Matsumoto	*Heiwa Doshikai* (Matsumoto)	Eda		Eda	
	Matsumoto	Nomizo	Nomizo	Nomizo	Kawakami		Kawakami	
	Nishio	Wada	Wada	Sasaki (Suzuki)	Wada			
	Nomizo	DSP** (Kawakami, Nishio)						
	Wada							

* In parentheses are names of direct predecessor factions.
** Became a separate party in 1960.
Sources: *Asahi Shimbun*, December 12, 1972; December 19, 1974.

of the LDP factions as political fund raisers and funds distributors is hardly matched by the JSP factions. For Diet members of all parties, pressures for funds are great and constant, and rank-and-file Diet members do not have resources of their own with which to meet these financial demands. In most parties, members try to meet such needs with funds provided through the official party treasurers, supplemented by whatever they can raise from private sources. In the LDP, however, the factions function as an important additional source of funds. Their leaders are expected to collect sizable donations from their supporters and sympathizers—mainly business firms—and distribute them regularly and at the time of Diet elections.[37]

The factions may raise such funds through donations or in the form of loans. However, donations are supposed to be reported to the Interior minister twice a year and also before and after an election, and loans must presumably be repaid. Hence a popular alternative means of collecting contributions is in the form of memberships, since these do not have to be reported to the government or made public. Most donors, too, prefer anonymity, for understandable reasons. As a consequence, each LDP faction operates fund raising through one or more "research associations" founded on a membership subscription basis.[38] As much as half of the enormous amount of money collected and expended each year by the LDP and its members may be handled through such underground channels.

Indeed, the fund-raising capabilities of the factions are the basis of their viability as competitive groups. The official treasury of the LDP has been traditionally under the exclusive control of a very small group of mainstream leaders; in recent years access to party funds has been limited to a very few party officers—and for practical purposes, to the president alone. With this kind of exclusive control of party finances by the mainstream leaders, factions, especially those in antimainstream camps, would cease to function the moment they lost their own sources of funds. This helps explain why successive LDP presidents have self-righteously preached the need to eliminate factions for the sake of party unity, while antimainstream faction leaders have objected just as invariably.

Apart from performing these tangible functions, the factions also serve, like other types of small groups, to satisfy various psychological needs of their affiliates. For example, making available the use of comfortable offices in modern downtown office complexes or plush hotels in Tokyo, or the occasional meetings of "policy seminars" and "study sessions" at quiet retreats away from the noisy capital, can serve as strong material reinforcement to a politician's active adherence and participation in his faction. Moreover, to many politicians the personal friendships and comradery which grow out of such shared experiences become quite important.[39]

Impact of Factions on Japan's Political System

Among all social systems, political systems are relatively the most human-centered and most human-dependent, in the sense that they are bound and constrained less directly or critically by nonhuman factors such as physical environment—far less than, say, economic or technological systems. Compared to the latter, a political system is also more tolerant of and, at the same time, more sensitive to the play of idiosyncratic elements in human relations. In politics, much more than in economics or technology, the ideals and dreams, the passions and resentments, of individuals in power make an important difference. *Who* makes decisions? is the fundamental question to ask; *how* and *why* are often merely incidental to and derivative of that central question. Affecting the choice of society's rulers, political factions bear directly on this central problem of politics.

This truth assumes special poignancy for the political system of postwar Japan. The Diet, the highest lawmaking organ of the state, has been dominated continuously by Japan's conservative party, the LDP. Despite the general lack of unity in both the major parties, party discipline has been remarkably effective, to the point of being inflexible, in influencing parliamentary balloting. With few exceptions votes are cast both on the floor of the Diet and in its committees strictly along party lines. Under these circumstances, the will of the majority of the LDP, that is to say the will of the mainstream interfactional coalition, has been the will of the Diet. Faction politics in the ruling party have thus determined the performance and output of the Diet and, therefore, to a large extent, of Japanese government. This is the most general and important of the ways in which the party factions affect Japan's political system.

Beyond this general impact, the factions have affected the performance of the political system in numerous specific ways. I shall focus here on a few of the many consequences of Japan's political party factions. First, as I have suggested in previous work, the saliency of the LDP factions has created in the minds of politicians and voters alike an image of a quasi-multiparty system operating within the LDP and effectively replacing the five-party system as the main arena of competition for power.[40] When one LDP cabinet falls in the midst of an intense controversy over a policy issue, another LDP cabinet follows and carries on. In the process, only the mainstream factional coalition and the antimainstream factional coalition change places, and the dominance of the same conservative LDP government is perpetuated.

Since the LDP has maintained a majority in the Diet for the last twenty years, it might be argued that the rotation of the prime minister's office among the major LDP factions has been not only inevitable but justifiable. But factional rotation has considerably weakened the competitive party system by consolidating the LDP's monopoly of power. If there had not been the faction system in the LDP, especially the institutionalized system of competition between mainstream and antimainstream coalitions at any given time, an alternative to a discredited LDP cabinet would not have been sought so readily in another LDP cabinet. Because any cabinet represents not the LDP but the mainstream group in the LDP, and because any alternative represents merely the intraparty group that constitutes the opposition factional coalition, the significance of opposition parties as alternatives to existing governments is diminished.

Normally, discredited cabinets would dissolve the lower house of the Diet *before* taking controversial and unpopular policy decisions, rather than pass the buck to their intraparty critics *after* taking such decisions. In a Diet election called in the midst of an intense controversy—such as arose only once, over the revisions of the U.S.-Japan Mutual Security Treaty in 1960—while a decision is still pending, voters would return more opposition candidates. In practice, however, unpopular cabinets first resign, new antimainstream LDP cabinets form, the controversies blow over after the critical decisions have been railroaded through the Diet, and only then elections are called. Voters have thus merely voted to ratify the *change* from the previous cabinet to the new cabinet, thereby perpetuating LDP dominance. This is not to deny the range of policy commitments as well as ideological persuasions that the LDP represents, and the remarkable flexibility and adaptability that this heterogeneity affords the party. It is to argue, however, that the system of faction politics in the LDP has substantially reduced the level of genuine competition between the LDP and the opposition parties.

Second, factionalism in the two major parties has considerably weakened the authority and effectiveness of their leaders both as party officers and as public officials. The fact that important party and government jobs are distributed on the basis of factional interests and interfactional balances of power means that important positions are dispensed only marginally on the basis of individual merit. If the competent and skilled have been appointed or elected to appropriate posts, it is almost purely accidental. As I have indicated, the premium is on durability (seniority) and amiability rather than on functional skills or competence—especially in the LDP.

Furthermore, factional pressures for rapid turnover of high-ranking jobs have been so strong that tenures of offices have been very short. There is hardly enough time for cabinet ministers to get to know the structure, procedures, and psychology of the bureaucracy which they are supposed to lead and direct; as a result, the quality of work of an average Japanese cabinet is not very high. Moreover, because of pressures for appointments of as many LDP faction leaders as quickly as possible, it has become virtually impossible for a prime minister to recruit cabinet members from outside the relatively small group of LDP Diet members. The Constitution requires merely that a majority of cabinet members be from the Diet; in fact, until 1975, when a university academic was appointed minister of education, no one had been appointed from outside the faction leaders of the parliamentary party since the 1950s. The pool of talent and competence available for ministerial appointments is thus arbitrarily limited by faction politics. This also adversely affects the capability of the Japanese government.

Third, the factions have contributed to plutocratic tendencies in Japanese politics, particularly because the LDP's factions serve as major channels for the flow of political funds in the party. One could of course argue that politicians need money and would get it one way or another regardless of factions. Indeed, considering the exclusive mainstream control of the party treasury, one might even argue that the presence of the factions with independent sources of funds is essential to pluralism and intraparty democracy. Thus, if it were not for the active criticisms and competition of the antimainstream factions, a small mainstream oligarchy might become permanently entrenched as a new form of government dictatorship. In this perspective, the factions might be thought of as a bulwark of democratic politics in postwar Japan. If all the LDP factions but one, led by an incumbent president, were disbanded, the single faction might indeed be tempted and enabled to build itself up as a permanent mainstream in control of both party and government. In light of this, one could consider the enormous amounts of money which are annually raised and expended by the factions as a necessary price for the maintenance of democratic government under a de facto one-party dominant system.

I would argue, however, that had there been less money so readily available, Diet members and candidates would have been forced to depend less on the power of material incentives and more on better-developed policy programs, to win voter support and stay in power. For in effect, the factions have contributed to the vicious circle of the more money available, the more demands for more money, until the whole fabric of Japanese politics tends to become contaminated by the corrupting influence of plutocratic greed and bribery. It was charges of exactly this sort of abuse of power that brought down the Tanaka government in late 1974 and, indirectly, the Miki government two years later.

Last, the factions have interfered with rational decision-making in the formulation of policies. Policy issues often are pawns of the interfactional power struggle and become fouled up in the process of the ruthless pulling and hauling among the contending factions. Classic examples are the intraparty disputes over the peace settlement with the Soviet Union in the mid-1950s, the Police Duties Law revision in the late 1950s, and the normalization of diplomatic relations with the People's Republic of China in 1971–1972. Once a policy becomes a symbolic stake in an interfactional dispute, rational arguments become irrelevant and the real issue is buried under empty rhetoric. This is no less true in the JSP, as witnessed by the "structural reform" controversy between the right-wing Eda faction and the left-wing Sasaki faction in the early 1960s. As one expert on the JSP has concluded, "What the party calls its foreign policy is the outcome of an internal and often temporary factional compromise."[41]

The most important dimensions of the overall impact of the Japanese party factions, then, seem all to point in the same direction: reduction of the range of rational choice, whether in the election of high government officials or in the formulation and determination of important state policies. That is why many, both within and outside of the political parties, have called for a purge of the factions.[42] The early display of extreme factionalism in the LDP in the wake of the first party presidential election in 1956 alarmed the new president, Ishibashi, and the new general secretary, Miki, sufficiently to persuade them to call for an immediate end to all factional activities in the party. One year later, Ishibashi's successor, Kishi, spoke of the dissolution of factions as the "voice of heaven." In 1963 Miki took up the cause again, as chairman of the LDP Organization Research Committee, drafting a comprehensive plan for the "modernization" of the party structure, in order finally to bring the factions under control. Absolutely nothing came of any of these successive efforts.

Despite the discouraging record, however, in 1975 the party engaged in a new campaign to purge itself of factions. The election of the veteran antifaction crusader, Miki, to the party presidency renewed interest in a faction-busting campaign. Miki spoke out with a good deal of enthusiasm about the prospects of final success of the party's year-old antifaction campaign. But close study of the party's record suggests there was little prospect that he would succeed.

Thus, successive LDP presidents and their mainstream allies have many times called for the elimination of factions, and for obvious reasons: they were finally and exclusively in control of the party coffers. Get rid of the rival factions and they would monopolize more effectively all policy and personnel decision-making, both in the party and in the government. Precisely for the same reasons, they have met fierce opposition from their antimainstream critics and have retreated. There seems to be little reason to expect current leaders to succeed where their predecessors have invariably failed. The same thing may be said of current efforts in the JSP to purge the party of its own factions.

At least partly because the factions represent a basic pattern of Japanese social structure, as Nakane and Ishida and others have contended, the factions in the two major political parties of contemporary Japan appear to be here for a long time to come. Whether Japan's factions are peculiar to Japanese politics can perhaps be determined only from comparisons with faction systems in other cultures and political systems.

NOTES

1. Ardath W. Burkes, *The Government of Japan* (New York: Thomas Y. Crowell, 1961), pp. 81, 88.
2. Robert A. Scalapino and Junnosuke Masumi, *Parties and Politics in Contemporary Japan* (Berkeley and Los Angeles: Univ. of California Press, 1971), pp. 18–19, 54.
3. Robert E. Ward, *Japan's Political System* (Englewood Cliffs: Prentice-Hall, 1967), pp. 65, 68–69.
4. Nobutaka Ike, *Japanese Politics: Patron-Client Democracy* (New York: Alfred A. Knopf, 1972), pp. 81–83.
5. Nathaniel B. Thayer, *How the Conservatives Rule Japan* (Princeton: Princeton Univ. Press, 1969), ch. 2; and Haruhiro Fukui, *Party in Power* (Berkeley and Los Angeles: Univ. of California Press, 1970), ch. 5. Other studies include: Frank Langdon, *Politics in Japan* (Boston: Little, Brown, 1967), pp. 142–51; Lee W. Farnsworth, "Challenges to Factionalism in Japan's Liberal Democratic Party," *Asian Survey* 6 (Sept. 1966): 501–09; George O. Totten and Tamio Kawakami, "The Functions of Factionalism in Japanese Politics," *Pacific Affairs* 38 (Summer 1965): 109–22; and J. A. A. Stockwin, *The Japanese Socialist Party and Neutralism* (Melbourne: Melbourne Univ. Press, 1968).
6. The only exception is that references to parties and party politics in some localities rather than in national politics. In parts of Kyushu (in southern Japan), for example, the term *factions* refers to loose groupings dating back to the pre-Meiji (before 1867) feudal period. See Kanji Naito, "Kumamoto Niku" [Kumamoto second district], in Masao Soma, ed., *Nihon no So-Senkyo: 1969-nen* [General elections in Japan, 1969] (Tokyo: Mainichi Shimbunsha, 1970), pp. 361–73.
7. Chie Nakane, *Japanese Society* (Berkeley and Los Angeles: Univ. of California Press, 1970), ch. 2.
8. Takeshi Ishida, *Japanese Society* (New York: Random House, 1971), pp. 64–67.
9. Ibid., p. 64. See also Michiya Shinbori, *Gakubatsu* [Academic factions] (Tokyo: Fukumura, 1969), pp. 3–5.
10. Nakane, *Japanese Society*, p. 42, fig. 2.
11. Yuji Aida, *Nihon no Fudo to Bunka* [Japan's climate and culture] (Tokyo: Kadokawa Shoten, 1972), pp. 51–61.
12. Fukui, *Party in Power*, pp. 44–50; Yoshimasa Miyazaki, *Jitsuroku: Seikai Nijugonen* [Twenty-five years in the political world] (Tokyo: Yomiuri Shimbunsha, 1970), pp. 117–27.
13. Stockwin, *Japanese Socialist Party and Neutralism;* also Stockwin, "Faction and Ideology in Postwar Japanese Socialism," *Papers on Modern Japan*, ed. D. C. S. Sissons (Canberra: Australian National Univ., 1965), p. 37; and Masakichi Matsui, *Sengo Nihon Shakaito: Shiki* [Postwar Japanese Socialist party: a private history] (Tokyo: Jiyusha, 1972), pp. 17–18, 42–43.
14. For a supporting view, see Tamio Kawakami, *Gendai Seijika no Joken* [Conditions for a contemporary statesman] (Tokyo: Shunjasha, 1968), pp. 94–95, 133; Asahi Newspapers, Political Affairs Section, ed., *Seito to Habatsu* [Parties and factions] (Tokyo: Asahi Shimbunsha, 1968), pp. 235–72. For an opposing view which regards the LDP as

a party of patronage and the JSP as one of principle, see Ishida, *Japanese Society*, pp. 70, 72.

15. Thayer, *How the Conservatives Rule Japan*, pp. 35–39.
16. Hajime Ishii, "Hasso wo Daitenkan seyo," [Drastically change our way of thinking] in Shintaro Abe et al., *Jiminto Kaizo An* [A plan to reform the Liberal Democratic party] (Tokyo: Yomiuri Shimbunsha, 1972), pp. 48–49. See also Shintaro Abe, "Tetsugaku suru Seito e no Dappi" [Reform ourselves into a thinking party] in *Jiminto Kaizo An*, pp. 23–24; Kozo Watanabe, "Watakushi no Jiminto Kindaika Shiro" [My tentative plan for modernizing the LDP] in *Jiminto Kaizo An*, pp. 305–07; and Gerald L. Curtis, *Election Campaigning Japanese Style* (New York: Columbia Univ. Press, 1971), pp. 23–25, 30.
17. Stockwin, "Faction and Ideology in Postwar Japanese Socialism," pp. 45–46, 48; Tatsuo Nakano and Shigetaro Izuka, *Shakaito Minshato* [The JSP and the DSP] (Tokyo: Sekkasha, 1968), pp. 80, 86.
18. Toshiki Kaifu, "Omoiyari to Omoikiri no aru Seito ni" [Let us build a party of compassion and decision] in Abe et al., *Jiminto Kaizo An*, p. 87; Kazuho Tanigawa, "Sengo Choki Hoshuseiken no Shuen" [The end of permanent conservative rule in the postwar period] in Abe et al., *Jiminto Kaizo An*, p. 282.
19. Asahi Newspapers, Political Affairs Section, ed., *Seito to Habatsu*, pp. 112–13. See also Nakano and Izuka, *Shakaito Minshato*, pp. 250–56.
20. Thayer, *How the Conservatives Rule Japan*, p. 15.
21. Michael Leiserson, "Factions and Coalitions in One-Party Japan: An Interpretation Based on the Theory of Games," *American Political Science Review* 62, no. 3 (Sept. 1968): 771.
22. Fukui, *Party in Power*, pp. 110–11; Thayer, *How the Conservatives Rule Japan*, pp. 24–26.
23. See Isamu Togawa, *Soridaijin no Isu* [The prime minister's chair] (Tokyo: Futabasha, 1972), pp. 80–83; and Fumio Okamoto, *Sato Seiken* [The Sato government] (Tokyo: Hakuba Shuppan, 1972), pp. 280–82.
24. Calculated from membership lists in *Asahi Shimbun*, November 22, 1960; November 23, 1963; January 31, 1967; December 30, 1969; and December 12, 1972.
25. Matsui, *Sengo Nihon Shakaito*, pp. 171–76.
26. *Asahi Nenkan* [Asahi yearbook], 1974, p. 259.
27. Kawakami, *Gendai Seijika no Joken*, pp. 84–85.
28. For consecutive year-to-year tabulations of relevant figures, see Hans H. Baerwald, *Japan's Parliament: An Introduction* (New York: Cambridge Univ. Press, 1974), pp. 66–69, tabs. 11, 12.
29. For descriptive accounts, see Thayer, *How the Conservatives Rule Japan*, ch. 6; Asahi Newspapers, Political Affairs Section, ed., *Seito to Habatsu*, pp. 242–49.
30. On these procedures, see Fukui, *Party in Power*, p. 96.
31. For lists of these posts roughly ranked in order of their relative importance in factional competition, see Leiserson, "Factions and Coalitions," p. 778; and Fukui, *Party in Power*, p. 130.
32. For more simplistic views, see Leiserson, "Factions and Coalitions;" Asahi Shimbunsha, ed., *Jiminto: Hoshu Kenryoku no Kozo* [The LDP: the structure of conservative power] (Tokyo: Asahi Shimbunsha, 1970), p. 290.
33. For illustrations see Curtis, *Election Campaigning Japanese Style;* Masaya Ito, *Ikeda Hayato: Sono Sei to Shi* [Hayata Ikedo: his life and death] (Tokyo: Shiseido, 1966), p. 38.
34. See Nakano and Izuka, *Shakaito Minshato*, pp. 83–85.
35. For relevant comments, see Asahi Newspapers, Political Affairs Section, ed., *Seito to Habatsu*, pp. 81, 225; Miyazaki, *Jitsuroku*, pp. 299–300; and Fukuji Taguchi, ed., *Nihon Shakaito Ron* [On the Japan Socialist party] (Tokyo: Shin Nihon Shuppansha, 1969), pp. 9–13.
36. For example, see Asahi Newspapers, Political Affairs Section, ed., *Seito to Habatsu*, pp. 8, 274.
37. For details, see Thayer, *How the Conservatives Rule Japan*, pp. 26–31; Fukui, *Party in Power*, pp. 130–33.
38. Fukui, *Party in Power;* Asahi Newspapers, Political Affairs Section, ed., *Seito to Habatsu*, pp. 182–83.

39. These intangible functions, too, have been discussed in detail in various previous studies. See Fukui, *Party in Power,* p. 173; and Thayer, *How the Conservatives Rule Japan,* pp. 39–42.

40. Fukui, *Party in Power,* p. 138.

41. Stockwin, *Japanese Socialist Party and Neutralism,* p. 158. Cf. Fukui, *Party in Power,* pp. 135–36; and Leiserson "Factions and Coalitions," p. 770, fn. 3.

42. See especially Abe, p. 26; Kaifu, p. 87; Ichiro Ozawa, "Hoshu Seito no Taishitsu Kaizen Ron" [A view on the transformation of the Conservative party], in Abe, "Tetsugaku suru Seito e no Dappi," p. 173; Watanabe, "Watakushi no Jiminto Kindaika Shiro," pp. 297–98, 308; and Matsui, *Sengo Nihon Shakaito,* pp. 96–99, 102. See also Thayer, *How the Conservatives Rule Japan,* pp. 53–56.

4

Factionalism, the Party System, and Italian Politics

FRANK P. BELLONI

The purpose of this chapter is to explore the structure and role of factions in the Christian Democratic party (DC), the dominant party in the Italian political system, and in the Italian Socialist party (PSI), the Christian Democrats' major coalition partner during the 1960s and 1970s.

Factionalism has been a prominent feature of Italian political life for more than a quarter century. Italian parties are, in fact, structures within which the exercise of power is shared among organized factions, each of which may be an effective protagonist of power, not only within the individual party framework but also within the party system as a whole. A system such as this, in which parties are hosts to organized factions, produces a power equilibrium with distinctive characteristics. The fragmentation of parties, produced by the institutionalization of factions, diminishes the regulatory capacity of the party and elevates the faction to a salient position. So prevalent is factionalism that some scholars suggest it may be transforming not only the parties but the very character of the Italian competitive process. One of Italy's leading political scientists has concluded that the Italian system "has become a system of *sub-parties*," a system in which "the true operative units [of politics] are the factions."[1]

Much of the current literature on the Italian party system is concerned precisely with the consequences of the increasing fractionalization of the parties, and the shift from party to faction as the principal unit of competition. The proliferation of factions is seen as causing the party system to malfunction and the efficiency of government to decline. The difficulties experienced by Italy's governing structures in trying to cope with the problems of social and economic transformation during the past two decades are perceived as traceable to the factionalism of the governing parties. The argument is that factions have so exacerbated political problems, infusing them with subpartisan and opportunistic calculations, that policy-making processes have been practically immobilized. Finally, factions are charged with producing a situation in which the existence of any cabinet is in a continual state of doubt, thus diverting attention and energy away from the tasks of governing the country.

Although factions have developed in most Italian parties, several factors require focusing attention on the Christian Democrats and the Socialists. Not only have these two parties had the greatest number of factions, but their factions have achieved the highest levels of organizational development—particularly those of the DC. Despite the prohibition in the party's basic law against the forming of any internal "fractions" (*frazioni*), the DC is a party of vigorous factions. As a large and multiclass party, the DC inevitably has divisive tendencies; these divisions have become institutionalized as factions—called by the Italians *correnti* (literally, "currents"). The factions are quite developed organizationally, with names, internal hierarchies, and more or less routine procedures. Most have their own finances and their own press, and they usually reflect a distinct policy or ideological position in the DC. Factions in the PSI are not as developed organizationally; but they have many similar characteristics, and their mutual competition dominates intraparty politics almost as much as does that of the factions in the DC.

The factional systems of the DC and the PSI are especially important because of the governing role of these two parties. Again, this is particularly the case for the DC. Over the past thirty years, the DC has been the largest party in the country. Its continued strength at the polls and in the parliaments gives the party a position of political dominance. Given its dominant role, the emergence of a system of factions within the DC could not but have a critical impact on the operation of the political system. The impact of DC factionalism has been exacerbated, in turn, by the fact that after the DC, the party most highly factionalized is the PSI, which for the past decade and a half has been the DC's primary coalition partner. The Socialists, like the Christian Democrats, have been continuously torn by mutually competitive factions and, in addition, have suffered occasional splits in their movement—splits directly tied to factional divisions. Although the organizational structure of Socialist factions has not been as developed as that of DC factions, PSI factionalism remains important because of its impact on the stability and performance of Italian governments. The significance of Christian Democratic and Socialist factions will be clearer, however, if we examine the context in which they have emerged.

The Italian Party System

Italy is a classic example of a multiparty system. Since the party system stabilized itself shortly after the establishment of the republic in 1946, with only a couple of casualties, seven national parties have survived to today. These are, on the left, the Communists (PCI) and the Socialists (PSI); in the center (ranging from left to right), the Social Democrats (PSU, formerly PSDI), the Republicans (PRI), and the Christian Democrats (DC); and on the right, the Liberals (PLI) and the neofascist Italian Social movement (MSI). The latter incorporates the remnants of the Monarchist party (PDIUM), which after a number of changes since 1945 finally merged in 1972 with the MSI—although the MSI has recently been on the verge of a new split. One other casualty was the Italian Socialist Party of Proletarian Unity (PSIUP), the product of a Socialist split in 1964. Its life was terminated after eight years when the party dissolved itself in 1972, and most of its members joined the Communists. Completing the Italian party system are several prominent regional parties and a variety of local and other small groups of less significance.

While a variety of environmental factors have contributed to the survival of the Italian multiparty system, that survival appears to be clearly linked to the Italian electoral system of proportional representation (PR) and multimember districts. PR tends to translate voter choices into a distribution of seats in Parliament which closely reflects the relative voting strength of existing parties; it thus facilitates the survival of splinter parties. The electoral system also incorporates "preference voting": the voter, besides voting his party choice, votes his preference among those who are the candidates of his chosen party. The existence of preference voting means that besides the competition among the several parties, there is competition among nominees of a single party.

In addition to stability in the number and specific components of the party system, the level of support for parties has been relatively stable. The changes that have occurred have been incremental and gradual.[2] The Communists have enjoyed a growing base of voter support. In national elections, they have grown from 19 percent to 34 percent of the total vote during the period 1946–1968. The Socialists have won between 12 and 14 percent of the vote, although the party suffered a slight decline in 1968 after its short-lived merger with the Social Democrats. The Christian Democrats have loomed as the giant among the center parties, and Italy's largest party, with voting percentages hovering around the 40 percent mark. The remainder of the center is composed of the Social Democrats and the Republicans—small parties (especially the Republicans) which generally have polled less than 5 percent of the votes apiece. The right, the Italian Social movement and the Liberals, has generally attracted around 5 percent of the electorate.

By the mid-1970s some signs of change in this long-standing pattern became evident. In the 1972 parliamentary elections the PCI registered further gains over its 1968 position; even more significant advances were made in the regional and provincial elections of 1975 and in the parliamentary elections of 1976, making the Communist vote a very close rival to that of the DC. Specifically, in the 1976 voting the PCI captured 34 percent of the vote, while the DC vote was 39 percent. The Socialists secured 10 percent, while the small center parties, as well as the MSI on the right, suffered losses.

Multipartyism makes it exceedingly difficult to put together and sustain the parliamentary majorities upon which governments must rest. In a system in which more than a half dozen parties—ranging from the Communists and Socialists on the left, through several center parties, to the neofascists on the right—share the loyalties of the Italian electorate, parliamentary representation is considerably fragmented. Only in 1948 did a single party, the Christian Democrats, succeed in capturing a majority of parliamentary seats; even then, however, the leaders of the DC felt it expedient to form a coalition government. Since then, parliamentary majorities have been based on coalitions of parties not merely as a matter of political expediency but of necessity, as no party has ever received the requisite majority in Parliament.

As a consequence, Italy has become a leading case of chronic governmental instability. Since the fall of the fascist regime in 1943, as of 1976, Italy has had thirty-six governments, with the tenure of cabinets averaging only about ten months. Moreover, changes in governments are frequently attended by political crises—periods between the collapse of a government and formation of a new one; these have become increasingly lengthy.[3] During crisis periods, the political leaders tend to be preoccupied with the frenzy of activity associated with the search for a new government and the parliamentary majority to support it; the ongoing problems of the country, correspondingly, are neglected.

Yet the problem of governmental instability is due not simply to the multiparty character of the system. Additional complications arise from the existence of one or more parties on the political extremes which have been characterized as antisystem, and thus unacceptable as components of governing coalitions. At present the Communist party and the MSI continue to be viewed by many (though by no means all) as antisystem; until the early 1960s, this was the fate also of the Socialist party. The characterization of the Communists and the Socialists as antisystem began shortly after the founding of the republic, and was largely the result of a joint campaign of the Catholic church and the Christian Democratic party. They charged the PCI and the PSI with being incompatible with the democratic, parliamentary regime and hence unfit to participate in national governing coalitions on any terms.[4] Consequently, the PCI, even though the second largest party in the country, has been excluded from consideration as a potential component of any cabinet. Whether this policy of exclusion can be continued much longer is another matter. Given the new and more even distribution of power between the Communists and the Christian Democrats which has resulted from recent elections, and in light of the de facto dependence of the present DC cabinet upon the tacit parliamentary support of the PCI, it seems doubtful that the Communists can be kept out much longer. We shall return to this subject at a later point.

The exclusion of certain parties with sizable parliamentary contingents from participation in government coalitions has only added to the difficulties of creating and sustaining strong governments. Such exclusions have diminished by 30 to 40 percent the potential pool of parliamentary votes from which the necessary majority might be extracted. In the past, "governing parties" frequently sought to avoid even the uninvited votes of the antisystem parties in parliamentary voting on confidence in cabinets. Finally, within the diminished pool of potential governing parties, ideological differences exist which further hamper the formation of parliamentary coalitions and governing formulas.

Notwithstanding recent changes, the Italian party system has long been dominated by the Christian Democrats and the Communists. These two parties together have consistently commanded two-thirds of the total vote. Aided by their highly developed organizational apparatuses, they have penetrated deeply into Italian society and outdistanced all other parties. Yet the PCI and the DC have not been evenly matched; the latter has unquestionably been the most salient force in Italian political life since the fall of the fascist regime, and remains the leading party today despite recent PCI gains.

More important than differences of strength, however, are differences in governmental role. As a result of its continuing electoral lead, the DC has provided uninterruptedly the basic contingent of every government formed since 1946, and it has provided every Italian premier. The place of the DC in Italian political life has been so prominent for the past thirty years as to earn it the label of Italy's "dominant party." The PCI, in contrast, stigmatized as an antisystem party, has been formally excluded from any participation in the national executive since May 1947. Until 1962, Italy's third largest party, the PSI, was also excluded from the national executive branch because of its presumed antisystem character.

With two of the three largest parties for many years banned from an effective role in government coalitions, the business of governing the country has rested largely on the shoulders of the DC. At times the DC alone formed the government, with the agreement of one or more of the other center parties to provide parliamentary or "external" support; more often, the DC governed in direct coalition with one or more of these parties (the PSDI/PSU and the PRI; and even the center-right PLI), in what was known as the "democratic center" governing formula. This formula survived throughout most of the 1950s; as it grew weaker and more unstable with the gradual diminution of center party parliamentary strength and with the growing discord among the center parties, the DC began an agonizing search for a new formula —in the only direction in which it could realistically turn: to the left. Its search coincided with that of the PSI, which sought to detach itself from its association with the Communists and to carve out a more independent and influential role for socialism in Italian political life. The accommodation with the PSI by the DC—the "opening to the left" —produced the governing formula which prevailed during the decade of the 1960s.

It was by means of the center-left formula that the PSI was brought into the mainstream of national political life, as the PSI became a formal partner of the DC in 1963. (The price the PSI paid for becoming part of the DC-led cabinet was a fracture of the party; in early 1964 the Socialists' left-wing faction split from the PSI and formed the PSIUP.) Throughout the mid-1960s, governments rested on the DC-PSI alliance, frequently supplemented with participation by the other center parties. However, after suffering sizable losses in the 1968 elections, in the 1970s the PSI—or at least certain of its factions—has questioned the value of the center-left coalition formula. Some PSI factions have argued in favor of a new formula which would allow for formal participation by the Communists.

During both the 1972 and 1976 parliamentary elections, the PCI represented itself as a responsible party, totally dedicated to the democratic parliamentary system. Despite its role as the largest opposition party in Parliament, the PCI tacitly supported the DC cabinet of Premier Aldo Moro in the mid-1970s. The government has thus been dependent on the PCI for the passage of its legislation—the abstention of the Communists making it possible for the DC to secure voting majorities; and on PCI goodwill for maintaining a modicum of labor peace throughout the country.[5]

The prospect of eventual direct PCI participation in government is a matter of great concern for the DC and the PSI. The issue grows more significant with the diminishing prospect of securing an effective majority drawn from the center-left and in the face of growing economic and social crises. While government in Italy continues to be in the hands of the PSI and the still-dominant DC, their control is ever more conditioned by the posture of the PCI. The matter has engendered intense factional strife in both the PSI and the DC, and the actions of powerful intraparty factions are playing an ever more critical role in party policies.

The Christian Democratic Party and Its Collateral Organizations

The Christian Democratic party is what is often called a multiclass party—its members and supporters span the range of Italy's socioeconomic structure.[6] Over the years, the DC extended its reach deep into the administrative, judicial, and local political realms of the state, and into the economic and social fabric of the country. As a consequence of this penetration, the DC is closely tied to some of the most powerful social and economic interest groups in Italy, such as the business and financial communities, the large agricultural community, a significant portion of the labor movement, and above all, the Catholic church. The latter connection ties the DC to a vast network of church-related subsidiary and collateral organizations of Catholic workers, farmers, youth, women, professional groups, and others.[7]

Catholic Action and the Civic Committees

After World War II, when organizational resources were at a premium among political forces competing in the emerging political system, the DC drew heavily on the national organizations of the church to mobilize support against the Communists and Socialists. In particular, the DC relied on Catholic Action, the most overtly political of the church's lay organizations. Catholic Action directs the church's vast array of social, political, professional, and other organizations. With an aggregate membership in excess of three million, it is the largest mass political and social organization of Catholics and is one of the most significant forces in contemporary Italian politics.[8] More explicitly political are the Civic Committees, subsidiaries of Catholic Action. Based on the unit of the individual parish, the network of Civic Committees constitutes a nationwide body of cadres organized to serve as campaign workers and as a potent propaganda organization for the DC. Catholic Action and the Civic Committees have exerted influence within the party on the selection of DC candidates for office, the structuring of the preference votes of the voting faithful, and the naming of certain DC ministers in the government.[9] The Catholic Action organizations have provided special support to those leaders and factions within the DC most responsive to the church's concerns—predominantly factions of the DC's center and right wing. In the 1960s, however, the extent of Catholic Action involvement in the internal affairs of the party declined, in part because of a reorganization of the party and in part because the church has adopted a lower profile in DC affairs.

ACLI

The Christian Association of Italian Workers (ACLI) promotes church interests among the industrial working class. Created by Catholic Action, ACLI was assigned the function of upholding Catholicism among workers and, in the process, of counteracting Marxism. ACLI's task is thus simultaneously religious, social, and political. ACLI's membership of over one million overlaps significantly with DC party membership, and this has resulted in very close ties between ACLI and the party organization. The Christian Democrats in Parliament, for example, regularly include a group of MPs who are strictly identified as *Aclisti.* Most ACLI leaders, until the early 1960s, simultaneously held leadership posts in the DC party organization. This close intermingling of the association and the party has also involved ACLI in the politics of the DC's factions: *Aclisti* members of the DC have been associated primarily with the factions on the party's left.

CISL

The major Catholic organization of trade unionism proper is the Italian Confederation of Workers' Unions (CISL), with a membership of about two and a half million. CISL's ties with the DC have been very close. In past years a majority of CISL's national leaders have also held posts in the DC party apparatus and/or parliamentary party. And until recently, CISL members regularly and successfully competed for national offices of the DC. While CISL has been a big vote-getter for the Christian Democrats, its support has not been for the party as such, as much as for a faction (or factions) within the party that reflects CISL's interests. Because CISL members of Parliament could count on the preference votes of union members, their seats were relatively safe; thus they were largely freed of dependence on the party. CISL representatives in the DC have even constituted an organized left-wing faction themselves, in competition with other factions. However, in the 1960s the DC and CISL banned the simultaneous holding of national offices in both organizations. In the 1970s both ACLI and CISL have diminished their open political activity within the party, assuming more the role of pressure groups outside the DC; nevertheless, they continue to be a distinct presence within the DC and to be involved in its factional struggles.

COLDIRETTI

One of the most powerful interest groups in Italy is the National Confederation of Direct Cultivators, known in Italian as *Coltivatori Diretti,* or more simply, as *Coldiretti.* It represents the interests of some 80 percent of the owners of small and medium-sized farms; with a membership of about three and a half million, it is one of the most powerful interest associations in the country. In addition to seeking to protect the more tangible interests of its members, *Coldiretti* has assumed such general concerns as the "defense of democracy" and of private property, and has adopted a virulent anticommunism. The DC has been the principal recipient of *Coldiretti* political support, of enormous value in all of rural Italy, as well as the chief target of its political demands and pressures. It has enjoyed direct representation in the DC apparatus and in DC parliamentary contingents, as well as in all levels of government. *Coldiretti* is careful to discriminate in favor of its own sympathizers in the party;[10] it is thus automatically involved in intraparty politics in the DC, and it has tended to align itself with factions of the center and right against those of the left.

ENI AND OTHER GROUPS

There are numerous other organizations which also have or have had close relations with the DC. In the past, several large business confederations have been associated with the DC. These associations, firmly committed to private enterprise and a pro-Western foreign policy alignment, have been prominent supporters of the DC's right-wing factions. With the advent of the "opening to the left" of the 1960s, however, most of these organizations have withdrawn from active participation in DC affairs. More recently, an organization with influence in DC politics has been the National Hydrocarbons Trust (ENI). ENI is a large, powerful, and semiautonomous state conglomerate which oversees the planning and direction of many state industries. For the past two decades it has been an aggressive and effective actor in the pursuit of influence in Parliament, in the cabinets, and in the dominant party. It has an extensive system of public patronage, a large budget capable of disguising sizable direct and indirect financial contributions, and the power to shape opinion through its own mass circulation newspaper. To protect its position, ENI has actively involved itself in DC affairs; through cooperation with factions on the DC's left, ENI has affected the party's internal power structure, as well as its policies.

Catholic Action and the Civic Committees, ACLI, CISL, *Coldiretti,* and other interest groups are important collateral organizations whose interests result in a special relationship with the Christian Democratic party. Despite the closeness of the ties, however, they cannot be considered servants of the DC. They seek, by means of the preference vote and judicious use of their electoral resources, to secure the election of those DC candidates they have endorsed. More important, the collateral groups swing their support to (or away from) other candidates who are sympathetic to (or hostile toward) the group's interests. Hence, while the support of these collateral interest groups may redound somewhat to the benefit of the DC as a whole, the support of each one separately tends to be clearly earmarked for the faction or factions within the party whose policy positions are most closely in accord with its interests. Such groups thus constitute a major ingredient in the faction system of the DC.

Christian Democratic Factions

The DC has been factionalized since the party was founded; indeed, the roots of factionalism preceded its formation.[11] Throughout the 1940s and early 1950s, the party had an unquestioned leader, Alcide De Gasperi, who enjoyed the support of the great majority of the party's activists. However, there were other prominent leaders of the Christian Democratic party who had become heads of local clientelistic cliques in their home regions. Such groups within the DC were composed primarily of ambitious men whose devotion to their leader was more personal than anything else; leaders provided patronage and identity, followers provided factional strength. Leaders such as these were often referred to as "notables"; in its early years, the DC's internal structure was in large part that of a party of notables.

A few of these notables, who felt the urge to compete with De Gasperi over party policy and party leadership, sought to transform their personal followings into more regularized organizations. Thus, Giovanni Gronchi, a prewar Catholic labor leader, organized his following into a faction called *Politica Sociale* ("Social Policy"); another leader of the left, Giuseppe Dossetti, organized his supporters under the name of *Cronache Sociali* ("Social Chronicles"). Near the end of the 1940s, another group was organized on the party's right, and became known as the *Vespa,* after the place where its early meetings were held. Though De Gasperi eschewed faction formation and steadfastly refused to organize his group as a faction, his majority nonetheless came to be known as the *Centristi* ("Centrists"). Thus, during the late 1940s, the DC sorted itself into two distinct factions on the left, a large and unorganized *Centristi* majority, and a right-wing faction.

In the 1950s, a new intraparty majority was formed by Amintore Fanfani out of remnants of the *Cronache Sociali* faction, plus elements which had adhered to De Gasperi's center. Called the *Iniziativa Democratica* ("Democratic Initiative"), this grouping was given a very effective factional organization by Fanfani, and it rigorously controlled and extensively reorganized the party machinery throughout much of the 1950s. The labor wing of the party, or *Sindacalisti* ("Unionists"—largely the CISL members of the DC), was separately organized into a faction called *Forze Sociali* ("Social Forces"), under the leadership of Giulio Pastore. Farther on the party's left, a new group was organized, with collective leadership, and assumed the name *La Base* (loosely, "Rank and File"). On the right, a large right-wing faction, the *Primavera* ("Spring"), under the leadership of Giulio Andreotti, replaced the *Vespa.* Throughout most of the 1950s, this was the DC's internal political structure: the large *Iniziativa Democratica* majority faction controlling the party and straddling the area from left-center to right-center, the trade union and *Base* factions on its left and the *Primavera* on its right.

In 1959 the *Iniziativa Democratica* faction split and lost its majority. Control of the party eventually passed to one of its wings, which, together with some activists from the right, was reorganized as the *Dorotei* faction (named for one of its favorite meeting places), and led by Mariano Rumor. The *Dorotei* majority relied on its close association with a faction of the left-center, which was known only as the *Morotei*—the followers of Aldo Moro. Those loyal to Fanfani were reconstituted as the *Nuove Cronache* ("New Chronicles") faction, also known simply as the *Fanfaniani.* The trade union faction, led by Pastore and Carlo Donat-Cattin, was expanded to include the members of ACLI in the DC and was reformed under the name of *Rinnovamento Democratico* ("Democratic Renewal"). Thus, for much of the early 1960s, the majority faction was the combined *Morotei-Dorotei,* and the party's factional structure included the trade unionist and *Base* factions on the left, the independent *Nuove Cronache* of Fanfani, and a somewhat diminished *Primavera* on the right.

In the mid-1960s the two left-wing factions—the unionist *Rinnovamento* and the *Base*—merged to become the *Forze Nuove* ("New Forces") faction. On the party's right, a new group formed, under the leadership of Mario Scelba, called the *Centrismo Popolare* ("Popular Center") faction, which became the only right-wing faction after remnants of the *Primavera* integrated themselves into a new majority of the middle and late 1960s called the *Impegno Democratico* ("Democratic Commitment"). The *Impegno* majority was more of an interfaction alliance than an integrated faction. It gathered together Fanfani's faction, the *Morotei,* the *Dorotei* (by this time a heterogeneous collection of prominent moderates including Rumor, Emilio Colombo, and others), and remnants of Andreotti's *Primavera;* eventually Scelba's *Centrismo Popolare* also associated itself with the *Impegno Democratico.* By the end of the 1960s, the only factions not drawn into this alliance were the small *Amici di Taviani* ("Friends of Taviani") faction and the *Forze Nuove.*

In the 1970s the mergers of the 1960s split apart. The party's left faction split into its original components, the *Base* and the trade union group, the latter retaining the *Forze Nuove* title for itself. Also on the left was the *Morotei* faction, which reconstituted itself after the disintegration of the *Impegno* alliance. In the center, the former *Dorotei*, reorganized as the *Iniziativa Popolare* ("Popular Initiative") faction under the leadership of Rumor and his allies. The *Fanfaniani* were reformed under their pre-*Impegno* name of *Nuove Cronache* and were now located on the party's right-center, in terms of their policies. The right-wing regrouped under Andreotti and Colombo's leadership, and adopted for themselves the alliance-initiated title, *Impegno Democratico.* Finally, on the far right, a group was formed expressing a favorable disposition toward the neofascist MSI, under the name of *Forze Libere* ("Free Forces") and led by Scalfaro and Scelba.

As the foregoing discussion indicates, most factions are clearly identified with prominent party figures, and the core of faction membership is likely to be made up of the personal followers of such party notables. This does not mean, however, that faction support is limited to the followers of a specific notable, or to his home district. Most factions do enjoy particularly strong bases of support in certain regions; yet most factions tend to gather support in nearly all areas of the country. For example, *Iniziativa Democratica* created and sustained faction organizations in nearly every province in Italy.

Table 1 shows the factions as of the early 1970s, including their top leadership; their relative strength as reflected in the voting of the 1971 National Congress of the party; their strength in terms of number of faction exponents on the party's National Council, the number who were ministers in the cabinet, and the number who were government undersecretaries; and, finally, each faction's newspaper or newspapers. There were nine factions as of 1971: the trade unionist left *Forze Nuove,* led by Donat-Cattin; the ideological left *Base,* with collective leadership; a small *Nuova Sinistra* ("New Left") group; Moro's left-center *Morotei;* the center *Iniziativa Popolare* faction, led by Rumor; the Taviani group; the Fanfanian right-center *Nuove Cronache;* the right *Impegno Democratico,* led by Andreotti; and the Scelbian extreme right *Forze Libere.*

The DC's factions have been the primary basis of internal party politics. While the party's statute and bylaws define its "constitutional" procedures, in practice the party's internal processes have generated operational norms at considerable variance with the formal rules; several such operational characteristics of the party facilitate, if not encourage, intraparty factionalism. The most outstanding of these is the intraparty electoral system. At the DC's national congresses, the practice began early in the party's history of submitting rival "motions" of substantive policy to the congress for adoption as the party program.

Table 1. Strengths of Christian Democratic Factions, 1971

Faction Name	Faction Leaders	Percent Congress Votes	Seats on Nat'l Exec. Committee	Government Ministries	Government Under Secretaries	Faction Newspapers
Iniziativa Popolare	Rumor Piccoli	20.4	6	3	6	*Notizie Parlamentari*
Impegno Democratico	Andreotti Colombo	15.1	3	3	6	*Concretezza Impegno Democratico*
Nuove Cronache	Fanfani Forlani	17.4	6	2	5	—
Tavianei	Taviani	10.5	4	2	5	—
Morotei	Moro	13.4	4	1	4	*Progetto*
Base	De Mita Misasi	11.0	4	2	2	*Radar Politica*
Forze Nuove	Donat-Cattin	7.0	5	2	3	*Forze Nuove Sette Giorni*
Forze Libere	Scalforo Scelba	3.5	2	1	1	*Forze Libere*
Nuova Sinistra	Sullo	1.7	1	0	1	*Nuova Sinistra*

Source: Giovanni Sartori, "Proporzionalismo, frazionismo, e crisi dei partiti," *Rivista Italiana di Scienza Politica* 1, no. 3 (Dec. 1971): 650.

Each such motion was submitted jointly with a list of names of those who endorsed that motion's policy positions and who simultaneously sought election to the party's official executive body, the National Council, on that specific platform. On the basis of the votes received at the congress by each motion, seats were apportioned on the National Council to representatives of that motion's associated list. The tendency has been for these motion-lists to become identified with the organized factions. The factions structured the national intraparty competition for positions on the national party executive and were thereby further motivated to develop their organizational machinery.

In this way, the intraparty electoral competition, organized on the basis of the lists of candidates attached to policy motions, came to be tied to the internal factional rivalries of the DC. Initially, the candidates ran as unofficial nominees of each programmatic position competing for majority support at the congress. In 1964, however, the motion-list system, and thus the faction system, was given official sanction by the party Central Directorate, which adopted two new procedures which built factionalism into the DC's political processes. One was the procedure of requiring that only motion-lists could be submitted and that all nominees for the National Council had to attach themselves to one of the motions officially received by the directorate. Thus the highlight of every party congress comes in the voting on the motion-lists, by which the party chooses its majority platform and its majority National Council leadership. Every such motion-list, in effect, constitutes the ideology and the top leadership of a faction or a faction alliance. Seats on the National Council generally are filled either by direct proportional representation or by a modified version of it. The National Council, and thus the faction or faction alliance controlling the council majority, chooses the Central Directorate, which in turn selects the party's political secretary and his staff. Thus the battle of the motion-lists is the battle for control of the party.

Delegates to the National Congress are elected by the ninety-four provincial congresses, and delegations to the provincial congresses are elected by the party's thousands of sections (i.e., local) organizations. The second major procedural change adopted in 1964 was the requiring of the submission of motions to the Central Directorate prior to the convening of the provincial congresses. Thus the competition of the factions was moved directly to the local organizations, where faction leaders and activists campaigned arduously and, indeed, began to keep up year-round recruitment drives for potential adherents to their factions. Faction politics is now found in local ward and village organizations—the party sections—as well as in the provincial organizations and the national party apparatus. All national factions have a major interest in controlling as many of the party's provincial and local organizations as they can.

Once the struggle for position and influence over party policy thus became organized, the heyday of the individual notable came to an end and that of the organizational leader replaced it. For the past decade and a half the backing of an organized faction has been virtually essential for those who would pursue their interests within the framework of the DC. During these years the prize of the party political secretaryship, and that of premier in the Italian government, have gone to the prominent faction leaders—Fanfani, Rumor, Moro, Colombo, Andreotti, etc. Major shifts in party policy also require the kind of sustained organizational effort that a faction provides. The stakes in the struggle to influence party policy are high; their resolution is reflected ultimately in the governmental policies advanced by the DC, the dominant party in every Italian government.

All of these factions have had ideological orientations and policy positions which make possible reasonably clear distinctions among them. The factions have sorted themselves out fairly clearly, for example, on such major issues of DC policy as the center-left governing formula and the related issue of possible coalition with the PCI (or, for some, with the MSI) sometime in the future, the issue of trade union unity, the divorce issue, and the issue of the existence of the DC's faction system itself.[12] This can be illustrated with regard to the alliance question. With respect to the center-left governing formula and cooperation with the PSI in coalition cabinets, left-wing DC factions (*Base, Forze Nuove,* and *Morotei*) have been quite supportive. The party's center and center-right factions (the *Dorotei/Iniziativa Popolare, Nuove Cronache,* and *Primavera/Impegno Democratico*) generally have been less enthusiastic toward DC-PSI coalitions—although they have accepted them, and rather more disposed toward the classic "democratic center" governing formula (which would exclude the Socialists). The DC's extreme right, *Forze Libere,* is strongly opposed to DC-PSI coalitions.

Similar divisions separate the factions on the related issue of coalition with the Communists. The three left-wing factions of the DC have shown varying degrees of openness to the idea, with *Base* demonstrating the greatest enthusiasm. The moderately antileftist posture of the DC's center factions toward the PSI is accentuated, particularly among the Fanfanians *(Nuove Cronache),* with respect to the PCI. The extreme right of the DC is, of course, vigorously opposed to any alliance with the Communists, but is instead open to the idea of an alliance with the Liberals, and even with the Italian Social movement (the neofascists). With regard to the issue of unity in the trade union movement, *Forze Nuove, Base,* and the *Morotei* are in favor of it; the DC center factions are unenthusiastic; and the extreme right of the party is strongly opposed. On the issue of the "desirability" of the faction system within the DC, the highest levels of approval have been expressed by the party's left factions—*Base, Forze Nuove,* and *Morotei* (in that order); majorities of the members of center factions (*Iniziativa Popolare* and *Nuove Cronache*) accept the faction system without strong approval; a majority of the more conservative *Impegno* faction are opposed to factionalism; and the *Forze Libere* is virtually unanimously opposed to organized factions (in fact, its leader, Scelba, has become the principal opponent of the party's entire faction system).

Thus while factions were discernable from the early days of the DC—even prior to its founding—initially they were merely groups of DC militants who identified themselves with a particular prominent personality in the party, sometimes out of ideological predisposition but more often out of a careerist or clientelist followership. Within a decade, however, spurred by the irrepressible organizational talents of Fanfani, DC factions in the 1950s built solid organizational structures.

Further rigor in the organization of DC factions occurred in the 1960s, when the party, already divided internally by a de facto system of factional competition, acknowledged and sanctioned their existence. The decision to require early submission of lists of faction candidates for party offices, and to exclude all others, greatly stimulated the efforts of the DC elite to extend their separate factional machines into the thousands of local party sections. The transformation that resulted made the Christian Democratic party as much a congeries of contending factions as a party proper; and like a party, each of the factions engages in the business of nominating its candidates, campaigning in elections, dispensing patronage, and competing to acquire political power in ways otherwise quite like political parties.

Socialist Party Factions

Factions exist in several parties besides the DC: specifically in the PSI, the PSDI/PSU, the PRI, and the PLI. In fact, the only parties not significantly factionalized are those on the extremes of the political spectrum: the MSI and especially the PCI. Of the factionalized parties, the one—aside from the DC—of particular significance because of its size and its role in governments, is the PSI. The very position of the Socialists on the spectrum of Italian politics subjects them to strains which produce divisions. Ideologically and politically positioned between the PCI on its left and the DC on its right, the PSI is alternately pulled in one direction or the other—or simultaneously in both. The stress of conflicting orientations, over the alliance strategy issue especially, inevitably produces divisions, and occasionally a split, within the Socialist community.

The pattern of internal divisions and party splits was set early in the republic. In the first national election, the Socialists, then called the Italian Socialist Party of Proletarian Unity (the name subsequently adopted by the faction that split from the PSI in 1964), emerged as one of three roughly equal mass party movements (the other two being the DC and the PCI), and for a brief period was a component of a tripartite "national unity" government with the DC and the PCI. When Christian Democrats expelled both the Socialists and the Communists from the cabinet in 1947, the Socialists decided to ally with the PCI. This decision provoked the first major split among the Socialists. Rejecting the decision of the majority, a moderate, centrist-oriented faction, led by Giuseppe Saragat, split from the party and formed the Italian Social Democratic party (PSDI). The remainder of the old Socialist party, under the leadership of Pietro Nenni, reorganized itself under the name Italian Socialist party.

For several years the PSI remained closely aligned with the Communists in an alliance known as the Unity of Action Pact. In 1953, however, Nenni began to move the PSI away from its intimate connection with the PCI and toward a more autonomous role, a move which was to generate a major PSI faction—Nenni's—which came to be known as the *Autonomia* ("Autonomy") faction. The shift began with Nenni's proposal to establish a "Socialist alternative," and his decision that PSI candidates would run for office separately from Communists. In 1955 he called for a "dialogue" with the DC to seek a national alliance of Socialists and Catholics; and in 1956 he called for a reunification of the PSI with Saragat's Social Democrats. By 1957, the Nennian *Autonomia* faction had succeeded in persuading the party to accept an abrogation of the Unity of Action Pact with the PCI, and Socialist withdrawal from several Communist-led mass organizations.

The efforts of Nenni and the *Autonomisti* to diminish ties with the Communists stimulated considerable resistance within the PSI. The opposition organized into three factions—all to the left of *Autonomia*. One group was composed of the followers of Lelio Basso, who were sympathetic to a continuation of the PSI-PCI alliance; acquiring the name *Alternativa Democratica* ("Democratic Alternative"), this faction consisted of many party workers who had risen to power in the party during the phase of collaboration with the PCI, and who sought to continue the collaboration in order (partly) to protect their positions. A second opposition faction was the *Morandiani* (followers of Morandi) faction—composed of most of the party bureaucracy proper and consisting of those who were, even more stridently, supporters of a permanent Socialist alliance with the Communists. The third group was the *Carristi* faction—called "armored troops" as a nickname, a reference to their support of Soviet intervention in Hungary in 1956.

The ideological-political differentiation of these factions was sharpened in the struggle among PSI candidates for preference votes of Socialist voters in the 1958 parliamentary elections and in the post-election struggle for control of the PSI party apparatus at both the provincial and national levels. In the party's National Congress held in Naples in 1959, the party rank and file were presented, for the first time since 1949, with clear alternatives in the form of three distinct motions and slates of delegates: the Nennian *Autonomia,* the followers of Basso, and a *Sinistra* ("Left") faction formed by the merger of the *Morandiani* and the *Carristi.* Nenni succeeded in winning majority (58 percent) support for his "autonomist" line. However, the distribution of the remainder of the vote—33 percent for the *Sinistra* faction—indicated a growing polarization within the party. The remaining 9 percent went to the *Bassisti* (Basso's faction), which became dedicated to achieving a compromise which would avoid the extremes of the two larger factions and preserve party unity.

During the following two years, the internal struggle became increasingly sharp, as Nenni led the party further along the road towards cooperation with Italy's center parties. In late 1959, Nenni announced that the Socialists would support DC-led government measures which were harmonious with PSI goals; in 1960 the PSI abstained on the vote of confidence of the Fanfani (DC) cabinet, thus making it possible for Fanfani to win the required majority; and in 1961 the PSI agreed to enter into some center-left governments at the provincial and local levels, in coalition with center parties (while still continuing to work in coalition with the Communists in provinces where the left parties enjoyed a majority). These actions on the part of the autonomist leadership increased polarization in the party; at the 1961 party congress support for the *Sinistra* rose to 35 percent; the *Autonomisti,* on the other hand, was weakened slightly. Moreover, a subfaction concerned with the maintenance of party unity and under the leadership of Ricardo Lombardi crystallized within it. The *Lombardiani* faction adopted a more conciliatory stance toward the opposition factions on the left, and insisted—effectively—on their representation in the party's directorate.[13]

The effort of the *Autonomia* leadership to move the PSI out of alliance with the PCI and toward eventual collaboration with the DC thus stimulated an intense and increasingly organized resistance within the party. The several factions, in the pursuit of their respective interests in the intraparty struggle, all acquired fairly sophisticated organizational structures: each had its own newspaper or periodical, and each one capitalized on official party machinery if in the majority at the national or at the provincial level of party organization, or created their own organizational machinery and headquarters.[14] The faction system in the PSI, however, also had a clear ideological basis. The postures adopted by the several factions on the specific issues of alliances with the PCI, collaboration with the DC, and reunification with the PSDI, were consistently tied to general ideological orientations.

At the Socialists' Thirty-Fifth National Congress (1963), the *Autonomia* majority endorsed the center-left formula; the party prepared itself for direct participation in a center-left government, and in December of that year, the Socialists entered Aldo Moro's cabinet in the first coalition of the PSI with the DC. The *Sinistra* faction of the PSI refused to accept the party's decision to participate in a DC government and broke away, organizing itself into a separate party which took the old name of Italian Socialist Party of Proletarian Unity (PSIUP).[15] This split left the *Autonomia* faction with an overwhelming majority in the PSI.

A new phase of factional struggle developed within the PSI, however, over the issue of reunification with the Social Democrats, a move viewed by Nenni as a further step in his overall design of creating a "Socialist alternative" to both the Christian Democrats and the Communists. At the Thirty-Sixth National Congress (1965), the *Autonomia,* favoring immediate unification with the PSDI, won an 80 percent majority. However, a new left-wing faction emerged, this time led by Lombardi, which opposed immediate PSI-PSDI unification, and any further accommodation with the center in Italian politics. In an intermediary position, a new subfaction of the *Autonomia* emerged, led by Federico De Martino, which sought to postpone unification of the PSI and PSDI, and which simultaneously expressed reluctance towards a total break with the Communists. Pursuant to the decision of the congress, however, the PSI leadership formally "reunited" the party with the PSDI in 1966. The merged parties formed the Unified Socialist Party (PSU). By prearrangement the two components of the PSU maintained their separate party structures; these were to be dissolved after the 1968 joint National Congress, when an integral merger of leadership at both the national and provincial levels was to be effected.

In the parliamentary elections of 1968, the combined popular vote of the Socialist/Social Democratic list dropped by one-fourth of the aggregate vote polled by the two parties in the previous balloting. Most of the losses were clearly sustained by the PSI component of the new, merged PSU. Moreover, in 1968 virulent student and labor agitation broke out over much of Italy—agitation of a new type, arising outside of the traditional organizations of union and party, and aimed at total and revolutionary (rather than reformist or gradualist) objectives and employing extralegal and violent means. The heavy losses sustained by the Socialists in the 1968 elections and the public turbulence in the country had a dramatic effect on the new party: at the PSU National Congress of 1968, no less than five factions competed with one another.

Table 2 shows the strengths of the factions at the 1968 congress, in terms of congress votes and representation on the party Central Committee, and their leaders. The PSU factions are listed in order of their position along a right-left continuum, beginning with *Rinnovamento* on the right and moving to the *Sinistra* faction on the left.

Table 2. Strengths of Unified Socialist Party Factions, 1968

Faction Name	Faction Leaders	Percent Congress Votes*	Central Committee Seats	Percent Central Committee Seats
Rinnovamento	Tanassi	13.2	21	17.3
Autonomia	Nenni Mancini	34.3	43	35.5
Riscossa	De Martino	33.6	39	32.2
Impegno	Giolitti	5.2	7	5.8
Sinistra	Lombardi	7.3	11	9.1

*Total of Percent Congress Votes equals only 93.6 percent because a handful of votes were cast for candidates not identified with any faction.
Sources: For congress votes, Gianfranco Pasquino, "Le radici del frazionismo e il voto di preferenza," *Rivista Italiana di Scienza Politica* 2, no. 2 (Aug. 1972): 358; and for other figures, Felice Rizzi, "Dall' unificazione alla scissione socialista, 1966–1969," *Rivista Italiana di Scienza Politica* 3, no. 2 (Aug. 1973): 419.

The *Rinnovamento* ("Renewal") faction, led by Tanassi (Saragat's successor to leadership of the former Social Democrats) and composed almost exclusively of Social Democrats, was the third largest faction at the congress, and the most conservative of the Socialist groupings. Second on the right-to-left spectrum, and still the largest faction, was the *Autonomia,* led by Nenni and Mancini. This faction, composed of the *Nenniani,* along with the *Rinnovamento* faction, favored a complete break with the Communists within the trade union framework. In the middle of the PSU faction spectrum was the *Riscossa* faction, led by De Martino, and the second largest in the new party. It was composed of old-line Socialist (PSI) activists of the General Confederation of Italian Labor (CGIL), the large, Communist-dominated labor federation, and it, together with the left-oriented *Impegno* and *Sinistra* factions, opposed rupture with the PCI. The *Impegno* ("Commitment") faction, second from the left on the continuum, was composed of functionaries and technicians of public agencies and was led by Giolitti. Finally, on the party's far left was the *Sinistra* faction, led by Lombardi and composed largely of intellectuals and professionals of the Socialist movement.

The allocation of PSU Central Committee seats at the 1968 congress (Table 2) does much to explain the subsequent breakup of the newly reunified Socialist movement. The *Rinnovamento* faction—essentially the Social Democratic component of the PSU—was allotted only twenty-one seats, or 17 percent of the Central Committee representation. Prior to the 1968 congress, when the PSU still operated under the dual leadership arrangements effected at the time of unification, the PSDI component had enjoyed 50 percent of the total Central Committee seating, thus giving it parity with the larger PSI; in short, the PSDI component of the PSU's Central Committee had enjoyed considerable overrepresentation, given its actual strength within the framework of the merged party. However, in terms of *electoral* support the PSDI was relatively stronger: in the 1963 parliamentary elections and the 1964 provincial elections, the PSDI portion of the total electoral support for the yet-to-be-formed PSU was about 36 percent. In light of this, the *Rinnovamento* group complained bitterly that they were intolerably underrepresented in the post-1968 PSU Central Committee. But there was more to make *Rinnovamento* unhappy. At the national level, the *Rinnovamento* group was able to at least influence the central organs of decision-making by constituting part of the majority in the PSU's National Directorate; here it shared power with the *Autonomisti.* In the provincial and local party bodies, however, this same coalition arrangement was often not operable, and the *Rinnovamento* found itself in many areas excluded from local party executives, and thus cut off from decisions on appointments to posts in the *sottogoverno* ("subgovernment")—more aptly translated as the "spoils system."

The *Rinnovamento*'s unhappiness was not the only discontent expressed within the heart of the new party: De Martino's *Riscossa* faction, the largest after the *Autonomia,* became intransigently opposed to the policies and leadership of the party majority.

In 1969 the *Autonomia* was diminished in strength as a result of the formation and splitting away from the majority of a faction whose leader was Mancini. The Mancini split cost the *Autonomia-Rinnovamento* party coalition its Central Committee majority, and these two factions found themselves excluded from a new majority coalition composed of the *Manciniani,* De Martino's *Riscossa* faction, and Giolitti's *Impegno.* Exclusion from the majority at the national level was totally unacceptable to the Social Democratic *Rinnovamento,* and in that year they broke from the party, keeping for themselves the name of PSU. The Socialist component of the now ruptured PSU resumed their premerger name of PSI.

Since the breakup of the short-lived PSU, the faction system in the Socialist party (PSI) has resumed the pattern that had existed prior to its merger with the Social Democrats. On the eve of the 1972 elections, for example, the PSI was divided into five factions: the old *Autonomisti,* still led by Nenni; the De Martino faction, now consisting of a fusion of the former moderate *Riscossa* and Giolitti's left-oriented *Impegno;* the *Manciniani,* which initially formed within the *Autonomia* and then split off from it; the *Lombardiani,* or *Sinistra,* now in the role of the traditional left faction; and a Bertoldi group, which broke away from the *De Martiniani,* or *Riscossa,* faction and organized themselves into a separate faction devoted to the idea of including the Communists in future governing formulas.[16]

Italian Party Factions, Structural Features

Much of what we are about to say about factional organization is drawn from our knowledge of the factions in the DC, but is in most cases also applicable to factions in the PSI and other Italian parties. Organizational structure among Italian factions is in many respects remarkably developed, and includes formalized faction names, more or less distinct memberships, leadership cadres and chains of command, faction headquarters, communications networks including press organs, and faction finances.

Faction Name

In the DC, every major faction except the original De Gasperian majority self-consciously adopted its own name. The names were most often derived from the names of their faction newspapers; subsequently they attained semiofficial status as they appeared on the accredited motions of the party congresses. Names were generally chosen for political or inspirational connotations, e.g., Democratic Initiative, New Force, Democratic Renewal, etc., but in a few cases the names are more like nicknames, e.g., Vespa, Dorotei. In addition to their formalized names, most factions have also had a more informal but just as well-known name which is a derivative of the name of the faction leader. Thus the *Politica Sociali* was also known as the *Gronchiani* ("Gronchians"), the *Iniziativa Democratica* as the *Fanfaniani* ("Fanfanians"), the *Centrismo Popolare* as the *Scelbiani* ("Scelbians"), etc. In a few instances, factions were known only by their leader's name, as in the case of the *Morotei* faction.

MEMBERSHIP

No faction in any party has a "card-carrying member" concept of faction membership; rather, membership is composed of those who identify with the faction and accept its representation in the congresses and directive organs of the party. Its most committed and active members are its cadre and leaders at the various levels of the party's organization.

Actual size of faction membership is thus difficult to ascertain. DC factions have sometimes claimed their total "motion" vote in all the party as their membership. Thus, for example, at the Ninth National Congress (1964), motion no. 1, *Nuove Cronache,* accredited with a popular vote of 332,800, claimed that number as their membership; the party majority, motion no. 4, *Impegno Democratico,* had 724,600 votes which it claimed as members; etc. However, these are inflated figures, since the party membership was given no choice but to vote for one of the recognized motions. Generally about 10 percent of the full party membership are activists in party life, and the proportion is probably applicable to votes cast for the factions' motions.

At the same time, because a fundamental objective of the factions is to increase their numerical followings at the party's grass roots, factions are keenly interested in recruiting party members who will support their motions. In the DC considerable attention is paid to the compiling of lists of sympathizers among local rank and file in the party. Such lists are no doubt uneven in standards for identifying "members," and in any case are not made public. But participants have confirmed that such lists are kept.[17]

LEADERSHIP

Like membership, faction leadership is informally designated, yet precisely known by the participants. In most factions a single individual is recognized as the national leader, by faction members and nonmembers alike—and by the press. However, in some cases the leadership may be more collegial, as it has been to a certain extent in the DC's *Dorotei,* and even more so in the *Base.* The leader is generally flanked closely by other prominent figures in the faction, with whom he shares the job of leading the faction. Collectively these chief lieutenants and the top leader form a sort of "directive committee" of factional leadership, usually of about a half dozen or so. In addition, it is usually possible to identify a larger group of high-level faction functionaries who are the next echelon of leaders. The oligarchical character of factions' leadership cadres is reinforced by the durability of faction membership.

In the DC, the secretaryship—highest office in the party—is normally held by the leader of the party's current majority faction, and party vice-secretaryship and other secretariat staff positions have also gone to top leaders in the dominant faction. In 1965, however, four vice-secretaryships were created, one for each of the four major factions whose motion-lists had contested the National Council seats at the Ninth Congress. The practice of creating vice-secretaryships for each major faction was designed to maintain party unity, and clearly serves as recognition of faction leaders. A more formalized means of identifying faction leadership is the official motion of each faction presented at DC congresses, signed by the respective faction candidates for council seats. The names of the several most important leaders usually appear first, in rank order of leadership status in the faction; these are then followed by the larger number of remaining signers of the motion, all middle-echelon leaders of the faction and usually listed in alphabetical order.

In the provinces, the local counterparts of the national leaders of the various factions are also readily identified by party militants (and by the local press). Lower echelons of DC faction leaders include the party provincial secretaries, vice-secretaries and secretariat staffers, and members of the party provincial council or committee; they include also holders of such governmental positions as mayor and communal (town) councillor, and local government employees.

HEADQUARTERS

Though they are not lavish or prominent, the factions maintain some kind of headquarters, particularly for the national factional leadership. Some serve also as propaganda offices, but most often a headquarters facility is used for meetings of the faction leaders rather than as a place open to the public like the official party headquarters.[18] Often a faction headquarters comes to be the offices of the newspaper published by the faction, or, in the DC, the facilities of a collateral interest group with which the faction is closely associated. Often the group's leaders congregate in a private home or in the private office of one of their number.

In the case of the majority faction, however, offices and headquarters facilities of the party itself become available for use as the central rallying point for the faction—a distinct advantage for the majority. However, the national majority does not acquire all provincial and local offices of the party; peripheral offices become the facilities of the provincial or local majority, which may be a contingent of a faction in the minority at the party center. Major factions usually do maintain some sort of headquarters also at the provincial and local levels, though even more informally than at the national level.

PRESS

Over the years, factions have created a host of journals of news and commentary, to express their positions and to communicate with their adherents. Many of the papers have borne the same name as the faction itself, as shown in Table 1. The newspaper is at once the symbol of the faction, its official voice, a major means of recruiting new adherents, and its principal connection with those party members who come to form the rank-and-file supporters of the faction.[19] The paper gives voice to the faction's principles and ideas, and encourages other party members to join. It keeps its own supporters informed of its activities and successes, and engages in polemics with other factions in the party and with other parties or factions of other parties. The papers are published at various intervals—weekly, biweekly, monthly, or bimonthly—and not always on time; frequency of publication generally increases in the periods just prior to the holding of party congresses and during periods when the party is contemplating a major change in policy. Some factions also have their own press agencies, which gather information of importance to the faction and disseminate it to the independent press and to provincial publications.

DC factions also utilize the press and communications services of the DC's collateral organizations with which they are associated. The press organs of collateral interest groups become particularly active on behalf of certain factions during the party's congressional campaigns and in the elections for Parliament and for local government offices. Important also in the war of words are the official publications of the party itself. National publications reflect the prevailing views of the current majority faction, though they generally adhere to a policy of giving some expression to the views of minority factions as well. Factions in the minority nationally but in the majority in a provincial party organization will use the provincial party press in much the same manner as the national majority uses the national party press.

MEETINGS

Faction communications proceed not only through the faction press but also through faction meetings, parliamentary caucuses, and occasional special conventions; through the party congressional motions and speeches by faction leaders; and through primary communications such as face-to-face and telephone conversations, and private correspondence. Meetings are a continuous and ongoing component of the communications network of the factions. Faction meetings may be secret or publicized, depending largely on the possible advantages that the leadership sees in their disclosure. In general they are publicized, for such meetings become a part of the public side of the competition for prestige in the party: the more frequent the references in the press to meetings of the faction, the greater will be the impression of energy and activity on the part of the faction.

Meetings are also held frequently at provincial and local levels.[20] Provincial leaders frequently organize meetings which feature one of the leading national faction personalities. Such meetings are not only channels of national-local communication but serve to reinforce a sense of solidarity among the leaders and rank and file. Normally there is a close coordination of faction meetings at the national and provincial levels when decisions are being made—national meetings are followed by provincial and local meetings, to reduce possibilities of differences developing between the central and peripheral components of the faction.

FINANCES

Factiors, like other political organizations, are in need of financial resources to support their apparatus and activities. Generally, any position of official responsibility in government in which a faction leader has an activist "placed" may be a source of financial support for the faction, through the use of public moneys to support activities that are utilized for the faction's benefit. Thus mayors and town councillors, provincial government officeholders, ministers and under secretaries, and officials of national governmental and semigovernmental agencies, etc.—all are potential resources for factions. DC factions also rely on DC collateral organizations for direct and indirect financial support.

The ordinary party member who is an adherent of a faction is not generally relied on for financial support. A member's party dues, however, may indirectly contribute to the support of a faction, especially the faction in the majority. A majority faction is able to divert the financial resources of the party to its own advantage. It may hold meetings, for example, which are billed as official activities of the party but which are in fact activities of the dominant faction. Costs of faction activities thus borne by the party permit the faction to conserve whatever moneys it raises on its own. Where a faction is not in the majority, but controls important offices within the party, such as the DC's Press and Propaganda Office, similar advantages may exist. Fanfani, prior to having secured the majority in the national party, held hundreds of meetings and conducted other activities throughout the country at the expense of the DC. Although the official purpose of these was to build up the organization of the party proper and to increase its membership, in fact they contributed primarily to the development of the organization and membership of *Iniziativa Democratica.* Shortly afterward, the faction won control of the DC.

Finally, much about the financial resources of the factions is kept discreetly confidential. Any person or group donating money to a party may also be donating it to a faction. Italy has not had political contributions laws applicable to factions within a party, and such material support is treated as a private matter between donor and recipient. There is, however, a general awareness among most party activists, and in the press, of sources of financial support for various factions and their leaders. Allusions are made by participants, and by critics in the press, to anonymous benefactors.

Factions and the Political System

Factions are a part of the process of political competition. In Italian parties, factions exist because the bases for factionalism are present; because facilitating conditions, which foster factional development, are present; and because factors which tend to militate against or prevent factionalism are minimized or absent altogether. There is a good deal of discussion among Italian experts as to whether factions are based on clientelist or similar power phenomena, or on ideology. Sartori and several others discount the ideological significance of the factions and regard them not as groups "of principle," but as the degeneration of parties' internal dialectical processes.[21] Others argue that Italian factions are not purely personal power groups but that their bases are a combination of "notable" clientelism and ideological principle; and some place the stress on the ideological character of the factions.[22] In fact, in both the DC and the PSI, both ideology and clientelism are amply present as bases of factions.

In the DC the factions were given a massive organizational boost by the decisions of party leaders to acknowledge their existence and to permit the structuring of the party's internal political processes around their already developed patterns of competition. Such facilitative conditions in the DC have included intraparty proportional representation electoral mechanisms, the restricting of candidacies for party executive backers of national lists to elections in the party's provincial federations and local sections. Equivalent procedures in the PSI are not as dramatically favorable to factionalism but, in general, have tended to have the same effect. In addition, however, the electoral successes of the factions in both the DC and the PSI are closely tied to their use of the preference vote in parliamentary elections—the provision which permits Italian voters to express their preference for particular candidates among those on the list nominated by the party of their choice. Preference voting is manipulated by the factions and by the collateral interest groups which support various factions. Use of the preference vote has increased sharply among DC and PSI voters in direct relation to the increase in the degree of intraparty competition among organized factions in the two parties.[23]

Political differences in the PSU (the combined PSI-PSDI party) were not particularly greater than those which normally prevail in the DC, yet the DC has not suffered splits as a result of factionalism, while the PSU has—as has the PSIUP, in the 1940s. The difference is that Christian Democratic faction leaders and activists have been more sensitive to the fact that life *within* the party framework renders the most benefit to each individual faction; by remaining united to the DC, every faction of the party has a greater chance of sharing the perquisites of power than it would it it were to split off from the party. Therefore, DC factions, regardless of the distance which may separate them from one another, adapt themselves to coexistence and are capable of a united stance in the face of threats to their party. Of course, there are strong *dis*incentives to schism for the factions of the DC which are not, or are less, present for other parties; yet there *are* rewards for organized political competition as long as it is contained within the framework of the party and is not carried to the point of undermining the DC in its external competition with other parties. The dangers inherent in the failure to accommodate organized interests is illustrated, on the other hand, in the Socialist experience. Specifically, expulsion of the *Rinnovamento* faction from party executive bodies created intense fears among the members of this faction that they would no longer share in the distribution of *sottogoverno* perquisites, jobs in particular. Being a traditional "party of the government," the Social Democrats viewed threats to their anticipated share in the spoils system as more intolerable than the costs of rupture of the Socialist movement.

The pervasiveness of the Christian Democratic party's influence has permitted it to screen the flow of inputs into the government from all sources, and to have the overwhelming role in the allocation of political and economic rewards in Italian society. These rewards, in turn, have tended further to reinforce its position in the structures of the system. Though lacking absolute parliamentary majorities, the DC has been the party of relative but consistent dominance in Italian politics. Other parties in the system have had to content themselves with participation in the coalition mechanisms manipulated by Christian Democrats—providing, of course, that the "other" parties in question are not considered to be antisystem. Beyond this, other parties must seek to promote their goals through some kind of involvement in the intraparty politics of the dominant party.

The significance of Italy's pattern of power is that it has altered, at least partially, the character of the political struggle. In the absence of a politically "acceptable" opposition external to the DC and capable of substituting itself as the alternative to the governing party, the struggle for control of the national government has been displaced to a considerable extent from the interparty plane to the intraparty level of the DC. Since the governing majority in the DC has a determining role in the selection of governmental ministers, undersecretaries, etc., and ultimately in the formulation of the policies of the national government, the significance of its own intraparty competition is vastly enhanced relative to that of interparty competition. DC leaders have so regularly held corresponding leadership positions in the government that control of the party majority and the party machinery of the DC has been nearly synonymous with control of the Italian national government. In short, with the consolidation of DC power and without an effective alternative among the other parties, the DC has been the framework within which competition for control of the political system is concentrated.

Factions play several significant roles for the DC. They provide organizational channels through which are articulated the varied interests of the broad-ranging constituency of the DC. Each socioeconomic group represented by the DC—labor, industrialists, middle-class professionals, farmers, landlords, the clergy, etc.—is able to look upon one or more factions as representing its specific interests, in contradistinction to the interests of other groups within the society united in the DC.

Factions play another role for the party: through their struggle the party is continuously provided with structured political alternatives. Policies are constantly under fire—reviewed, discussed, debated; and at any given time, policy modifications and alternatives are being championed within the power centers of the DC by various factions. In the same way, party ideology is periodically under review and subject to alteration or refinement. The contending factions enable the DC to modify interpretations of party ideology when necessary by making alternatives available.

Provision of alternatives extends also to the element of party leadership. Factionalism becomes the regime of political competition through which leaders rise to the top—in the party and in the larger system. The overall power structure of the DC is polyarchical rather than monolithic; thus those faction leaders who control top positions in the party apparatus or government are always subject to challenge by ambitious leaders of other factions. The party is thus never without several alternate sets of contenders for its leadership. Such a system provides a proving ground for potential leaders, a context in which the skills of leadership are learned and tested in factions by those who would become the top leaders of the party. Furthermore, the provision by the factions of alternatives in policy, ideology, and leadership is the means for the provision of accountability within the party and, to some extent, within the system as a whole. A measure of accountability in DC politics results as a by-product of the public campaigns of the minority factions, those both to the left and the right of the majority.

Also, because the factions exist, all parties—from the PCI to the MSI—have available to them channels of access to influence at the seat of power. Such channels are more than mere points of contact; they are structured, semiformalized institutions within the dominant party. All groups which contend for power in Italy—parties, factions, interest groups—have an interest in becoming involved, directly or indirectly, in the factional intraparty struggles of the governing parties, especially those of the DC. Consequently, political forces external to the DC intervene in DC affairs either in cooperative or oppositional relationships with the various factions, often simultaneously cooperating with some and opposing others, as part of their participation in politics. And the DC lends itself particularly well to this process. The diversity of perspectives and interests reflected in the array of DC factions is such that the perspectives and interests of friendly or rival parties can usually find some kindred expression within the Christian Democratic faction system. The result is an overlapping of interests and views between left-wing factions in the DC and Italian left-wing parties; and between right-wing DC factions and right-wing parties.

The collaboration of non-DC elements with Christian Democratic factions occurs primarily (but by no means only) in the parliamentary arena. Here DC factions enter into agreements with other parties (or their factions) to support or oppose government legislation and to engage cooperatively in other kinds of parliamentary maneuverings. Such agreements include possible joint action on the critical matter of votes of confidence for new governments. Outside the parliamentary arena, other parties (and/or their factions) may involve themselves in the internal deliberations of the DC over the issue of governing formulas and other party policies. During DC party assemblies, proposals made by various Christian Democratic factions may be supported or opposed by other parties in the latter's own party presses or elsewhere, and these external interventions often become additional ingredients in the DC's considerations of such proposals. Furthermore, DC faction leaders may be expected to maintain close relations with leaders of other parties and to coordinate action on any mutual interests that might exist.

All parties are thus drawn toward the center, where government is monopolized, and on a patterned basis. Moderate left and moderate right parties, besides participating in coalition governments and parliamentary alliances with the DC, participate in the internal party politics of dominant party at the center. The extreme left and extreme right, too, participate at the intraparty level, and thereby have been less isolated, less excluded from the focus of governmental power than would appear to be the case given their antisystem characterization and persistent exclusion from national cabinets. Thus, an important consequence of the relations of other parties with the factions of the DC has been a reduction in the tendency toward polarization among Italian parties—the focus of so much commentary in the literature on Italian politics. The inevitable interpenetration among DC factions and neighboring parties has tended to blur the distinction between government and opposition, and to soften the rigidity of the antisystem characterization of the parties at the political extremes. This pattern of interaction between DC factions and other parties has contributed to the overall integration of the party spectrum in Italy.

In a political system in which the necessity of coalition governments makes political accountability very difficult, factions in the governing party—particularly its minority factions—can play a vital role. Given the dominant-party status of the DC, its minority factions have been as important in fulfilling the functions of a "loyal opposition" as the opposition parties themselves. The opposition internal to the Christian Democratic party may often be more effective in exposing an activity to a critical public light than the other parties, which may not be part of the government; even those parties which may be allied to the DC may not be as privy to what is happening as are the DC factions themselves. Thus, the factions of the DC, and especially the minority factions, have been a means of ensuring that the largest party in the country remains an open party, in which a broad spectrum of causes is defended. Moves by any set of DC party leaders in the direction of more unpopular policies or authoritarian methods of operation are kept in check and are likely to be the undoing of the leadership—as of Fanfani in 1959. Thus, factional competition has a democratic effect on the party. And, while the dominance of the faction system is in considerable measure a function of the relative dominance of the DC in Italian politics, at the same time the factions have imposed very real constraints on the DC, seriously conditioning its exercise of power. Although the DC faces external opposition—the increasingly formidable Communist party in particular—it also faces a fluctuating opposition that operates within its own party framework, and that is dispersed among several of its own factions. The consequences of this condition are a built-in check on the power of the government, a restraint on a party continuously in power. With the formal opposition dispersed among a multiplicity of parties ideologically at odds with each other, and with parts of it having been subject to a historic exclusion from participation in the national government, the internal constraint of the DC faction system has been of special significance.

Nevertheless, such democratic accountability through factional-ism appears to have been bought at the high price to the political system of chronic governmental instability. In the absence of a unified majority party, any organized unit whose support is required for the formation of a governing majority or its maintenance thereafter, and which is sufficiently unified to dispose of its votes in a cohesive manner, possesses what Sartori calls a "coalition potential" or "blackmail potential."[24] As long as the support of any one DC faction can make the difference between being or not being able to put together and maintain the requisite majority, then that faction possesses a determining influence, both over the DC and over any government the DC proposes to form or has formed. This difference is described by D'Amato as the "margin of security";[25] it might also be thought of as the "margin of insecurity." Every Christian Democratic faction constitutes a margin of insecurity for the DC, at least to the extent that each one is capable of threatening the life of a DC-led government. And, the existence in the PSI, or in any of the parties which might be included in a governing formula, of similar divisions organized by factions capable of operating independently of party discipline and control means that the vulnerability of governments is increased accordingly.

What this means is that the government's majority is subject to disintegration at any time by virtue of the withdrawal of support of a single faction whose voting strength is equal to the margin of security of the majority. The power of a faction, thus, becomes equal to the power of a disciplined party in a multiparty, parliamentary system. In short, control of the margin of security passes from the hands of the leadership of parties to those of faction leaderships. In Italian politics, this has led many to refer cynically to their system as *correntocrazia*, or "faction rule." Hence, if one can speak of rule by the oligarchies of parties—those required for the formation and maintenance of governing majorities—in a multiparty system, then one can speak also of rule by the oligarchies of factions in a system in which organized factions exercise a determining influence over the life and operation of parties and governments.

Conclusions

Since elections in a highly fragmented party system like Italy's do not produce the needed parliamentary majorities, the task of composing governments necessarily becomes a postelection operation. It is at this point that the power of the leaders of the organized political units which possess a coalition potential—whether these units be called parties or factions—is at its peak. In any party system lacking a majority party, and in which the parties are fragmented into organized factions, the principal unit of power becomes the organized faction. This is the case especially in Italy, since the range from which a majority may be generated is effectively limited by the exclusion of the Communist party, the system's second largest party, as a potential coalition unit. Operating within the constraints of this restricted potential heightens the influence of the factions. Where governments depend on the continued cooperation of organized units working together in a coalition framework, the units—whether they be parties or factions—are in a position to affect the operation and the very life of a government. Depending on the degree of cohesion of the units, the leadership of each is in a position to dispose of a certain number of votes: in short, to grant, withhold, or withdraw support.

Thus, in the case of a faction, its power becomes equivalent to that of a party on which a coalition government depends. Italian governments have usually been coalitions and have always depended on coalition support in Parliament. Thus, with the organization of ideological and interest differences into a system of competitive factions within Italy's governing party, with each faction in the system perceiving both the party and the government as means for achieving its own goals, it is hardly surprising that Italian governments are unstable: conflict among DC factions is the major cause of the short lives of cabinets, and of the crises that follow their failure. Since the inauguration of the republic, easily two-thirds of the government resignations have been attributable in whole or in large part to Christian Democratic factional strife,[26] and outsiders have again and again been moved to puzzle at "a political system in which the dominant party regularly destroys the Prime Ministers who have emanated from its ranks."[27]

DC factions constitute an almost self-contained system of organized competition for power in the Italian polity. This self-containment means that the factions compete for political power from a point of advantage, inasmuch as this faction system is housed within the acknowledged governing party. Thus Italy has a multiparty-multifaction competitive system—that is, a competitive system which brings together faction units and party units. Because of the predominating role of the DC among Italy's parties, the competitive faction system within the DC overshadows the competitive relations among the several parties.

The Christian Democratic faction system thus has acquired a salience in the Italian polity that warrants the kind of attention normally accorded only the party system itself. Party systems are the objects of attention precisely because parties are conceived of as the principal agents in the competitive struggle for control of government in democratically based political systems; yet in the Italian political system factions play a predominating role in the competitive process. Indeed, in the sense of actually winning power, the factions are the major contenders. In this strict sense, Italian governments may depend no more upon agreement among political parties for their support than they do upon agreement among factions within the DC. As the consent of factions is required to form governments, and as factions' support is essential to the maintenance of governments, it is the factions, rather than the parties, that are most often determining of the fate of governments in Italy. The party can do little more than officially express the agreement reached among its factions. Thus the crucial element of the Italian party system is not the competition among the array of units in its nominally multiparty structure, but the competition among the faction units in the unofficially permanent governing party. This is, in effect, a multiparty-multifaction political system.

NOTES

1. Giovanni Sartori, "Proporzionalismo, frazionismo, e crisi dei partiti," *Rivista Italiana di Scienza Politica* 1, no. 3 (Dec. 1971): 652.

2. See Frank P. Belloni, "Dislocation in the Italian Political System: An Analysis of the 1968 Parliamentary Elections," *Western Political Quarterly* 24, no. 1 (Mar. 1971): 114–35.

3. In the decade from 1950 to 1959, there were 150 crisis days, with the average crisis period lasting 15 days; from 1960 to 1969, 252 crisis days, with an average crisis period of 25 days; and from 1970 to the present, 350 crisis days, the average crisis lasting 58 days. See P. A. Allum, *Italy—Republic Without Government?* (New York: W. W. Norton, 1973), p. 118.

4. Whether the Italian Communist party is really antisystem is, of course, a matter of controversy. The antisystem thesis is illustrated by Giovanni Sartori, "European Political Parties: A Case of Polarized Pluralism," in Joseph LaPalombara and Myron Weiner, eds., *Political Parties and Political Development* (Princeton: Princeton Univ. Press, 1966). The contrary thesis is argued, for example, by Giorgio Galli and Alfonso Prandi, *Patterns of Political Participation in Italy* (New Haven: Yale Univ. Press, 1970), esp. chs. 6, 7.

5. The PCI reportedly voted against only 12 of the 76 government-sponsored bills in Parliament during the period of the Moro cabinet, which lasted from December 1974 to January 1976. Communist-led unions have deplored wildcat strikes and worked to avoid the kind of industrial warfare that could undermine the government. In considerable measure, the PCI contributed to the ability of the Moro cabinet to survive as long as it did. (Personal interview with the Washington correspondent of *Il Popolo*, the official newspaper of the Christian Democratic party, February 2, 1976.) Also see "Italy: Creeping Toward the Compromise," *Time* (Jan. 5, 1976): 50–51.

6. Leading studies of the Christian Democratic party include Richard Webster, *Christian Democracy in Italy, 1860–1960* (London: Oxford Univ. Press, 1962); Giorgio Galli, *Il bipartitismo imperfetto: Comunisti e Democristiani in Italia* (Bologna: Il Mulino, 1966); F. Magri, *La Democrazia Cristiana in Italia,* (Milan: La Fiaccola, 1954–1955), vol. 2; Giorgio Galli and P. Facchi, *La Sinistra Democristiana: storia e ideologia* (Milan: Feltrinelli Editori, 1962); Raphael Zariski, "Intra-Party Conflict in a Dominant Party: The Experience of Italian Christian Democracy," *Journal of Politics* 27 (Feb. 1965): 3–34; and Galli and Prandi, *Patterns of Political Participation.*

7. Although the precise nature of the relationships between the DC and each of these groups varies, the bonds of all of them with the party are sufficiently close to warrant their being described as *parentela* groups. For a discussion of *parentela* groups—and *clientela* groups, the type of relationship often characteristic of the tie between American governmental agencies and pressure groups—see Joseph LaPalombara, *Interest Groups in Italian Politics* (New Haven: Yale Univ. Press, 1964), chs. 8, 9. *Parentela* groups are discussed also in Agopyk Manoukian, ed., *La presenza sociale del PCI e della DC* (Bologna: Il Mulino, 1968).

8. In fact, according to one source, the level of political development of Catholics must be attributed more to the presence and activity of Catholic Action than to the DC.

Galli and Prandi, *Patterns of Political Participation,* pp. 175–76. See also Gianfranco Poggi, *Il clero di risèrva: studio sociologico sull'Azione Cattolica Italiana* (Milan: Feltrinelli Editori, 1963), esp. ch. 3.

9. See LaPalombara, *Interest Groups in Italian Politics,* pp. 336–37; Galli and Prandi, *Patterns of Political Participation,* pp. 176–77, 180–81; and Raphael Zariski, *Italy: The Politics of Uneven Development* (Hinsdale, Ill.: Dryden Press, 1972), pp. 115, 204, 220–22.

10. Allum, *Italy—Republic Without Government?,* pp. 98, 103. After urging its members to be "united and solid around the DC," it directs them to give their preference votes to the DC candidates "chosen and supported by our Confederation." *Coltivatori Diretti* 12, no. 6 (Mar. 1968): 155. See also LaPalombara, *Interest Groups in Italian Politics,* p. 245.

11. For a more detailed discussion of Christian Democratic factions, see Frank P. Belloni, "Politics in a Faction-Dominant System: An Analysis of the Christian Democratic Party of Italy" (Ph.D. diss., Univ. of California, Los Angeles, 1972).

12. See Robert Leonardi, "The Politics of Choice: An Inquiry into the Causes of Factionalism in the Italian Christian Democratic Party" (Ph.D. diss., Univ. of Illinois, 1973), ch. 6; and Leonardi, "Opinioni politiche delle correnti democristiane in Emilia-Romagna," *Rivista Italiana di Scienza Politica* 4, no. 1 (Mar. 1974): 287–307.

13. See Raphael Zariski, "The Italian Socialist Party: A Case Study in Factional Conflict," *American Political Science Review* 56, no. 2 (June 1962): 372–80. See also Gianfranco Pasquino, "Le radici del frazionismo e il voto di preferenza," *Rivista Italiana di Scienza Politica* 2, no. 2 (Aug. 1972): 353–68.

14. Zariski described the organizational structure of the factions at that time as comparable to "miniature parties." Each had its own publication—*Mondo Operaio* for the *Autonomia, Problemi del Socialismo* for the *Basso* faction, and *Mondo Nuovo* for the *Sinistra.* See Zariski, "Italian Socialist Party," p. 380.

15. Felice Rizzi, "Dall' unificazione alla scissione socialista, 1966–1969," *Rivista Italiana di Scienza Politica* 3, no. 2 (Aug. 1973): 407–24.

16. Franco Cazzola, "Partiti, correnti, e voto di preferenza," *Rivista Italiana di Scienza Politica* 2, no. 3 (Dec. 1972): 569–88.

17. According to a Christian Democratic provincial secretary (Venice Province), "Membership lists for the factions do exist. The leaders know with precision the number of followers of their faction. Although there is no formal membership card, one knows from the positions taken by individuals in the party assemblies or when they vote on motions what factions they adhere to." (Interview with Giorgio Longo, the then provincial secretary for Venice, June 1, 1968.) This fact was confirmed by other responsible party leaders, including Remo Gianelli, director of the editorial staff of *Politica,* press organ of the DC *Base* faction; interview, March 27, 1968.

18 Christian Democratic activists confirm that they exist, however: "The factions have their seats at the national level. *Forze Nuove* maintains its headquarters just in front of Montecitorio. It is also the seat of other activities. It is a cultural center and the seat of the [faction] weekly, *Sette Giorni,* which speaks for the *Forze Nuove.*" Interview with Ermanno Dossetti, then DC provincial secretary for Reggio Emilia, July 3, 1968.

19. Normally these papers are sent free of charge to those party members listed as adherents of the faction or thought to be sympathizers. Some faction papers, however, have elicited subscription payments from readers, usually nominal; such subscription fees serve to defray partially the costs of publication, but also involve an act of commitment on the part of the subscriber to the paper and, hence, to the faction which publishes it. In a few cases, the paper may be sold on the newsstands of cities and towns, especially in regions where the faction is at its strongest. When a faction can afford it, the paper may be sent unasked to larger numbers of party members—to spread the faction's message among those of other factional persuasions.

20. A concise description was given by the *Forze Nuove* leader in Modena:
Forze Nuove meets about once a month; last year we met about ten times. Rather than adhering to a fixed schedule, however, we meet every time it is necessary to make an important decision. As to the purpose, this varies with the political moment. Tomorrow, for example, we will discuss the position we must assume in the next elections. We always hold a series of meetings in anticipation of a forthcoming election.
Interview with Enrico Menziani, then provincial secretary for Modena, January 12, 1968.

21. Sartori, "Proporzionalismo, frazionismo, e crisi dei partiti;" Stefano Passigli, "Proporzionalismo, frazionismo, e crisi dei partiti: quid prior?" *Rivista Italiana di Scienza Politica* 2, no. 1 (Apr. 1972): 125–38.

22. Giovanna Zincone, "Accesso autonomo alle risorse: le determinanti del frazionismo," *Rivista Italiana di Scienza Politica* 2, no. 1 (Apr. 1972): 139–60; Alberto Spreafico and Franco Cazzola, "Correnti di partito e processi di identificazione," in Alberto Spreafico, ed., *Ideologia e comportamento politico* (Milan: Communità, 1971), pp. 211–18.

23. See especially, Cazzola, "Partiti, correnti, e voto di preferenza," pp. 580–88.

24. Sartori, "Proporzionalismo, frazionismo, e crisi dei partiti."

25. Luigi D'Amato, *L'Equilibrio in un sistema di partiti di correnti* (Rome: Edizioni di Scienza Sociali, 1966).

26. Belloni, "Politics in a Faction-Dominant System," ch. 6.

27. H. Stuart Hughes, *The United States and Italy* (Cambridge: Harvard Univ. Press, 1965), p. 212.

5

Fission and Fusion: The Politics of Factionalism in the Israel Labor Parties

MYRON J. ARONOFF

The Israeli political system has been characterized throughout its brief history by processes of fission and fusion, i.e., splitting apart and remerging of its political parties. In this chapter I shall analyze these processes, focusing on Israel's major labor parties and their factions. I shall explore the historical origins of factionalism in the labor parties of the prestate Jewish Yishuv in Palestine, and I shall relate the processes of fission and fusion to socioeconomic and political changes which have characterized the development of Israeli society. Thus, major characteristics of the political culture and institutional framework will be related to the nature of the factional system. The focus of the analysis will be on the structural and functional characteristics

My research on the Israel Labor party was conducted in two stages of fieldwork, September 1969 to July 1971, and November 1973 to April 1974, sponsored by the Social Science Research Council of the United Kingdom, and by the Ford Foundation and the Israel Foundation for Research Grants. I wish to express my gratitude to these institutions for the freedom they gave me to pursue my academic interests. I also wish to thank the many people in the Labor party whose generous help and cooperation made it possible for me to participate in and observe the internal life of the party. Finally, I wish to express my gratitude to my wife, Rita, and my colleagues, Joel Migdal, David Nachmias, and Jonathan Shapiro, whose careful reading of an earlier draft of this paper enabled me to clarify the presentation of my ideas.

of the factions in the Israel Labor party, and on their impact on political processes, especially the competitive process.

To begin the analysis, I consider certain basic elements in the conceptual framework within which the understanding of factions may proceed. I then set out the cultural and institutional framework—i.e., the arena in which factional politics takes place in Israel. This entails a brief description of several of the major characteristics of the political system, particularly those which have a bearing on the politics of factionalism. This is followed by a discussion of the major historical splits and mergers among the labor parties, without which it would be virtually impossible to understand contemporary factionalism in the United Israel Labor party. The major sections of the chapter then deal with the factional competition in the Israel Labor party from 1968 to 1973 and from 1973 to 1975. In the concluding section I discuss the application and utility of the initial conceptual framework, as an aid in explaining the factional process in the Israel Labor parties.

The Conceptual Framework

When examining the literature on factions, one cannot help being struck by the ambiguity of the concept, the lack of consensus, and even the contradictory definitions of factions. One of the most serious mistakes made by many using the concept is the categorization into dichotomous and mutually exclusive ideal types, contrasting factions with parties or other forms of political groups. I suggest that it would be more fruitful to think in terms of clusters of characteristics along a continuum; I shall illustrate with three of the clearest defining characteristics which seem to have gained the widest acceptance as factional criteria by those who have written on factions. There appears to be a consensus, first, that factions are subunits competing within a larger corporate political entity; second, that they are not themselves corporate units; and third, that they pursue particularistic interests generally viewed as selfish or against the common good. Other defining characteristics of factions, such as that they are leader-oriented, temporary, conflict groups, can be subsumed within the proposed framework for defining corporate characteristics and will be discussed in those terms.

Lasswell's definition of faction as "any constituent group of a larger unit which works for the advancement of particular persons or policies" seems to have gained some general acceptance in the literature.[1] Since social anthropologists and political scientists have studied factions at various levels within states, from local-level village factions to factions of national political parties, it is important to define the arenas within which the faction operates along a continuum of hierarchically arranged levels. For example, the Israel Labor party, which is subdivided into three major factions, is joined to another labor party

(Mapam) in an electoral alignment; the *Maarach* ("Alignment") competes with other parties on a joint electoral list, has joint consultative institutions, and is bound by joint coalition discipline. Within certain contexts each party, Labor and Mapam, could be viewed, according to the first of the three criteria, as factions within the Alignment. At the other end of the continuum, the three factions of the Labor party can be further broken down for the analysis of political networks, quasi-groups and action sets, and patron-client relationships.[2] (These concepts, like factions, are not without their ambiguities, and are equally in need of refinement.) Therefore, depending on the level of analysis, almost all of these units can be viewed as subunits of a larger whole. By emphasizing a hierarchical continuum one can bring out important differences between internal party factions and factional aspects of the independent parties within the Alignment, in specific contexts. This becomes clearer when we take into consideration the second criterion.

The noncorporate nature of factional structure is widely stressed in the literature. Factions are usually defined as leader-follower groups which are temporary; they are often seen as phenomena bridging the transition from traditional to modern party politics, or as bridges to other forms of transition in social change, such as the adaptation of immigrants to new environments.[3] Contrasting factions with political parties, Nicholas states that

> the party is a corporate group that continues whether or not a particular follower or a particular leader is present; a faction, by contrast, may disintegrate when the leader dies or ceases to exercise control over the political action of his followers. There is no jural rule of succession to factional leadership positions, though there may be regularities of practice in any arena.[4]

In fact, there are ample cases in the literature of factions exemplifying differing degrees of corporateness and longevity ranging from the highly temporary to those which have persisted for decades. Nevertheless, as Nicholas notes, that factions are noncorporate and impermanent does not mean that they may not last for a long time. Thus, it is necessary to find a way of resolving corporateness with reportedly "corporate" factions and factions found to have persisted over a long period of time.[5]

The first problem is to reach an agreed-upon definition of the term *corporate,* which was defined differently even by scholars like Weber, Maine, and Durkheim. I suggest the acceptance of Smith's definition of the properties of corporate groups as presumed perpetuity, boundedness, determinate membership, identity, autonomy, organization, procedure, and common affairs.[6] Rather than dichotomize these characteristics into mutually contradictory categories defining corporate and noncorporate, I suggest ranging them on a continuum. This would make possible the defining of groups ranging from those which maximize these features to those which least manifest such characteristics. This would enable us to deal with the placement of other properties which have been thought to characterize factions, such as the extent to which they are leader-oriented, the diverse principles through which factional supporters are recruited, the longevity of factions, the extent to which they are exhaustive, exclusive and functionally undifferentiated, and the extent to which conflict is essential to their existence.[7]

For example, of the last characteristic it has been widely argued that factions are "conflict groups." It seems likely that the less corporate a group, the greater the tendency to perpetuate itself through political strife. As one author has observed, "Continued conflict being a condition of survival for struggle groups, they must perpetually provoke it."[8] Whereas the institutionalized aspects of corporate groups tend to give them perpetuity even in the relative absence of strife, the noncorporate nature of loosely structured factions makes them even more dependent upon strife to maintain their identity and boundaries.[9]

This leads us directly to the third major characteristic of factions, their pursuit of particularistic interests. Firth defines factions as "groups or sections of a society in relations of opposition to one another, interested in promoting their own objects rather than those of society as a whole and often turbulent in their operations"; Pocock states that "the behavior of a faction is such that it attempts to bend the power and potentiality of the whole of which it is a part to its own particular interests and to dominate the other faction or factions which are similarly motivated."[10] Significantly, factions are similarly perceived in just these terms in the context of Israeli party culture. The word *siya* is used only to refer to a faction which has split off from the parent party, and is associated with the word *pilug* ("split"). Other words used in association with *siya* have definite negative connotations, e.g., *kantran* ("quarrelsome, pugnacious"), and *bogade* ("traitor, renegade"). When politicians refer to factions which have merged with and exist within the party, they refer to *chativa* ("group, section, bloc"), a much more neutral term. Israelis also refer to the factions by naming them as "the previous Mapai" or the "past Rafi."

Even though they use more neutral terms in referring to present factions, they all express the sentiment that factionalism is a negative phenomenon working against the unity and the general interests of the party as a whole. There is constant ritualistic expression of the desire for the rapid demise of the factions, particularly when a party split appears imminent, even by those who work hardest to maintain the factions and who have the most to gain through their perpetuation. While it is important to analyze the significance of conceptual systems in their specific political contexts, we must be careful to differentiate between the actors' values and conceptions and our own analytic framework. This is particularly important with regard to the so-called selfish behavior of factions.

I suggest that all political groups, including parties as well as factions, are by definition self-interested in the sense that they are competing for political power. All political groups must also articulate a conception of the general societal good, which is expressed through the biased frame of reference of the group's values and interests, because the political actors must legitimate their actions in the eyes of the public to which they appeal for support (and generally in their own eyes as well). Logically, if factions are competing within larger units, the larger unit represents a common good—if not through clearer articulation, at least through the fact of unity of the whole—and by their very competition, the subunits express more particularistic interests. Also the self-interest of factions is more obvious because their competition within the party or larger unit does not have to appeal to an "outside" public and therefore is usually a more blatant struggle for power, which is by its nature more difficult to clothe in ideology. I caution against the tendency to make ideal type distinctions between party and faction in terms of the party pursuing the general good and the faction pursuing selfish goals, but stress the need to focus analysis on the particular historical, cultural, and social contexts in which political groups manifest both types of behavior. I shall illustrate this in later sections of this chapter.

The Cultural and Institutional Framework

There is an old Jewish saying that for every two Jews there are at least three political points of view. The tendency of the Jewish people to divide themselves into competing political camps is amply illustrated throughout every stage of their history. A cursory look at the Bible reveals the difficulties Moses had with rebellious factions, the wars between the Jewish Kingdoms of Israel and Judah, and the fighting among Jewish factions within the walls of Jerusalem at the same time that the Jewish people were revolting against the might of the Roman Empire. Competing interpretations of the Jewish religion have occurred, from the rival schools of the followers of the famous Rabbis Hillel and Shamai, through the competition between the movements of the Haskala and Hasidism in eighteenth-century Eastern and Central Europe, to the present divisions between Reform, Conservative, and Orthodox Jewry.[11]

The most important institutional factor influencing the Israeli factional system is the electoral system, based on proportional representation within a single national electoral district. This system, which encourages a multiplicity of parties, frequently by the splitting off of sections of parties, has its historic origins in the earliest organizational meetings of the World Zionist Organization (WZO). Since the WZO needed to mobilize the widest possible support among world Jewry, and it lacked the resources and sanctions of a state, it sought to attain unity by allowing representation of all of the diverse views and interests of world Jewry which expressed themselves in many organizations, including factions and parties. Because the plurality electoral system leaves some groups unrepresented and involves a certain element of compulsion, and because the WZO's moral authority derived from its claim to represent all Jewry, it adopted proportional representation to ensure the inclusion and support of all groups. Once adopted, this system encouraged continued ideological diversification and the multiplicity of parties and factions. The same compelling need for unity led to the representation of minority parties not only on the Zionist Council and Executive but in the Zionist organization's bureaucracy as well.[12]

This framework was carried to Palestine by the pioneering settlers and was adopted for elections to the Histadrut (General Federation of Labor) and to the Elected Assembly in 1920. It was particularly well suited to the voluntary, nonsovereign nature of the political institutions of the Jewish Yishuv in Palestine, since it protected minority factions. The system assured all participants in coalitions their share of the spoils and resources of office. By 1948 the various parties were so well entrenched, each with its separate ideology, bureaucracy, affiliated institutions, patronage, and vested interests to protect, that it was natural that proportional representation was the system adopted for the elections to the Knesset (parliament). This helps explain why concerted attempts by no less a figure than David Ben-Gurion have failed to change the system.[13]

Observers have frequently commented on the intense ideological nature of Israeli politics, a characteristic obviously related to factionalism. Because the early Zionist institutions and those of the Jews in Palestine lacked territorial sovereignty and the regular means of coercion available to sovereign-state governments, and because they had to appeal to a widely scattered constituency, Zionists had to rely heavily on persuasion and moral pressure. There was a particularly important need for intensive ideological indoctrination of the pioneering settlers, who had to be motivated to endure great hardships and sacrifices during the colonization of the Yishuv. The Zionist parties were a product of the nineteenth and early twentieth centuries, and many of them arose in Eastern Europe and were influenced by the many progressive and radical ideologies popular at the time.

Many examples could be cited to illustrate the high degree to which political passions have been aroused at various stages of Israeli political history. For example, debates in the Elected Assembly between the leaders of the Socialist parties and Jabotinsky's Revisionist movement led to the outbreak of fistfights in the assembly itself. When the Kibbutz Hameuchad faction split away from Mapai and later merged with Hashomer Hazair to form Mapam, great ideological arguments which not infrequently ended up in physical fights raged on many kibbutzim and led to the separation of warring factions with barbed wire and to the expulsion of minorities from various kibbutzim. Many explosive issues, such as the German arms sales and German war reparations, caused volatile public debates and violent demonstrations among the parties and factions and in the general public. Various "affairs," such as the Kastner affair and the Lavon affair have embroiled top party leaders and the general public in major confrontations which have had far-ranging political ramifications

However, ideology increasingly has been reduced to a "ritual" role among Israeli party elites, and also has become less relevant among the general public. The changing role of ideology is related to major social, economic, and political changes that have characterized the dynamic development of Israeli society, in particular the increasing availability of and reliance on resources of power in the institutions of the state. Whereas ideology appears to have played an important role in the factional disputes of the earlier period, competition for power has been the more dominant characteristic of recent factional strife.[14]

Despite the major tradition of cultural divisiveness, institutionally the Israeli political system is characterized by a high degree of centralization of political power. The historical legacy of highly centralized colonial Ottoman and colonial British rule reinforced national unity and a highly centralized political system. The small size of the country reinforced the arguments of nationalistic leaders that local interests were parochial and detracted from national goals and interests. The fact that the parties of the right had strong local constituencies was an additional incentive for the labor leaders of the nationalist institutions to undermine local authority. In addition, the monopolization by the political leadership of the Jewish Agency, and later by the state, of the vast majority of national resources, especially contributions from abroad, enabled the continuation and consolidation of centralized power and control. Patterns of immigration were also under the control of the central government, and its creation of new settlements resulted in the control of remote towns by the center since the country's beginning.[15] Finally, the fact that Knesset members do not have local constituencies but are chosen by and are dependent upon national party leaders also contributes to the consolidation of power at the center. Although there have been signs of a trend toward greater local autonomy in recent years, the basic fact of overwhelming central domination has not changed significantly.

During its short history, Israeli society has experienced rapid development and growth, the absorption of waves of immigrants from diverse cultural backgrounds, the rapid expansion of the economic sector, and the successful defense of the country in several wars. In this context of rapid social change, all the major Israeli political parties from their beginnings have been characterized as movements, having provided a wide range of services not normally associated with political parties in Anglo-American tradition. The movement-type parties provided such services both because they were nonexistent in the prestate period and because they saw it as their task to cater to the social, cultural, and economic needs of their members. The parties founded agricultural settlements, industries, trade unions, newspapers, publishing houses, schools, youth movements, health clinics and hospitals, banks, insurance companies, housing projects, cultural centers, synagogues, sports clubs, and even paramilitary organizations. The Histadrut, established by the labor parties, and the parallel institutions established by other movements embody and symbolize the multiple extrapolitical roles of the parties as movements.

Since no single party has ever commanded a majority of the Knesset, government has been characterized by coalitions, bargaining, compromise of ideology and program, and divisions of spoils ranging from ministerial portfolios to the "rule" of various cities. However, since no coalition has ever been formed without the main labor party, Mapai (in its various forms), it has traditionally controlled the key ministerial portfolios and has been dominant in the government. Mapai's traditional coalition partner, the National Religious party (Mafdal) has participated in every government. Mapai has dominated Israeli politics since its formation in the 1930s. Throughout its past of dynamic changes and development, the political system has remained remarkably stable, in large part because the essentially conservative Israeli electorate has opted for the continuity of rule of a dominant party. Mapai comes very close to meeting Duverger's classic definition of a dominant party: "A party is dominant when it is identified with an epoch; when its doctrines, ideas, methods, its style, so to speak, coincide with those of the epoch. . . ."[16]

Stability notwithstanding, however, there have been several ramifications in the political system that are consequences of Israel's major socioeconomic changes. Most striking has been the decline in the ideological intensity of politics, already alluded to, and the decline in emphasis on ideals like voluntarism and egalitarianism which have been influenced by such general societal changes as mass immigration and rapid industrialization. The institutionalization by government ministries of functions formerly performed by party movements and their institutions, e.g., national defense, education, employment, housing, etc., has lessened the dependence of the citizens on the parties. This has been accompanied by a general decline in public involvement in political activities, a decline which has been particularly noticeable among youth—although there has been some reversal subsequent to the war of October 1973. The parties have not recruited significant numbers of young leaders into important national positions and have consequently had in many cases to turn to retired high-ranking military officers to fill top party leadership positions. The dominant position of the Labor party has been gradually eroded; this became serious in the 1965 election and reached a peak in the 1973 election, which resulted in a government coalition with a precariously narrow margin in the Knesset.

Fission and Fusion: The Historic Splits and Mergers

One of the main responses of the political system to societal changes has been the fission and fusion of parties and factions. Figure 1 graphically illustrates the splits and mergers of Israel's political labor movement. Two main labor parties of the Yishuv were founded in 1906. Hapoel Hazair was a purely Palestinian non-Marxist labor party influenced by A. C. Gordan's philosophy of "the religion of labor" and by the Russian Social Revolutionary party. Poelei Zion was founded as the Palestine branch of the European Socialist movement and was an orthodox Marxist party which stressed a platform uniting socialism and Zionism. These two parties both published journals and established institutions aimed at satisfying the economic and cultural needs of their members. In 1919, Poelei Zion, with the exception of its extreme left wing, united with nonpartisan workers to form Achdut Haavoda.[17] Achdut Haavoda and Hapoel Hazair jointly founded the Histadrut, in 1920, which assumed all of the economic and part of the cultural work of the two parties. Another organization, the Kibbutz Hameuchad movement (founded in 1927), through the wide scope of its voluntary activities at a critical stage in the development of the political and economic institutions of the Yishuv, gained access to positions of immense importance and power in these institutions. In 1930, Hapoel Hazair and Achdut Haavoda, the country's two major labor political organizations, merged to form Mapai, which dominated all of the major political institutions of the Yishuv, and which has remained the dominant political force in Israeli politics to the present.[18]

In the late 1930s and early 1940s a dissident faction within Mapai known as *Siya Bet* ("Faction B") formed around a group of members who constituted a majority of the Kibbutz Hameuchad movement. Siya Bet was based to a large extent on a younger generation of leaders and activists. Aside from their particular interests within the kibbutz movement, this faction was ideologically more favorably inclined to Marxism than was the majority of the party. They also opposed the majority position on the partition of Palestine. At the party conference in 1942 the majority supported Ben-Gurion's proposal to ban all internal fac-

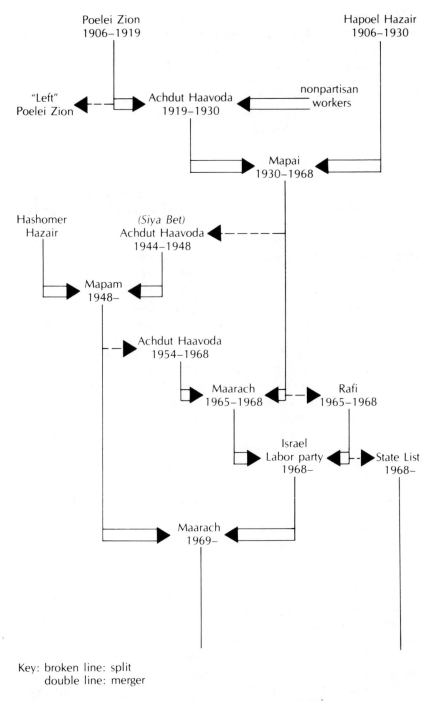

Poelei Zion
1906–1919

Hapoel Hazair
1906–1930

"Left"
Poelei Zion

Achdut Haavoda
1919–1930

nonpartisan
workers

Mapai
1930–1968

Hashomer
Hazair

(Siya Bet)
Achdut Haavoda
1944–1948

Mapam
1948–

Achdut Haavoda
1954–1968

Maarach
1965–1968

Rafi
1965–1968

Israel
Labor party
1968–

State List
1968–

Maarach
1969–

Key: broken line: split
     double line: merger

Figure 1. Splits and Mergers in Israel's Labor Parties

118

tional activity. Although this action was meant to avert a party split, it had the opposite effect. Siya Bet split off from Mapai in 1944 and reconstituted itself as Achdut Haavoda, taking with it the majority of the Kibbutz Hameuchad Federation (whereupon Mapai established Ichud Hakvutzot V'hakkibbutzim as its major settlement organization). The ideological overtones of the factional split in Mapai to a considerable extent reflected a dominant aspect of the political culture at that particular period in the development of the political system; yet the generational competition for leadership played at least as important a role in the factional struggles.

In 1948 this reconstituted Achdut Haavoda united with another group, Hashomer Hazair, to form the Marxist-oriented Mapam party, which provided Mapai with its major leftist opposition in the elections to the first Knesset. This merger lasted some six years, 1948 to 1954, during which time Mapam functioned as a two-faction party. The Achdut Haavoda faction of Mapam maintained its own kibbutz movement separate from that of its partner faction's Kibbutz Artzi movement. The former Achdut Haavoda faction became increasingly disenchanted with Mapam's pro-Soviet orientation, and split off in 1954, again reconstituting itself as the Achdut Haavoda party.

During the early 1950s a group of prominent Mapai members known as *Zeirim* ("Young Guards") began making public statements criticizing the lack of internal party democracy in decision-making. When they held a nationwide conference calling for a "movement of party regeneration," the party leadership, with the memory of the bitter split of Siya Bet still in their minds, feared the possibility of the new faction's following suit. The Zeirim faction was challenged by the Tel Aviv–based national party machine known as the *Gush* ("Bloc"). The tension between these two protagonists broke into conflict during the Eighth Mapai Conference, in 1956. The Zeirim succeeded in mobilizing majority support for a constitutional amendment whereby the party Central Committee would be composed of 123 members, two-thirds of whom would be elected by the branches and only one-third of whom would be appointed by a central nominating committee. This marked the only time in the history of Mapai (or of the Labor party later) that a majority recommendation of the standing committee was defeated on the floor of the conference. This victory was short-lived, however, as the Gush later succeeded in getting the Central Committee expanded to 196, with the addition of extra central appointments, thereby guaranteeing the continued domination of the party machine.

Although there were several important social and ideological views which differentiated the older generation of the Gush from the Zeirim faction, their struggle became primarily a contest for control of the party and succession to the top leadership. The men of the Gush, as a whole, had no marketable skills other than their political experience, which was vast. They had worked their way up from the bottom of the party and Histadrut hierarchy and were dependent upon their party jobs for their livelihoods. Zeirim members had better formal educations and were not willing to work their way up from the bottom. Since they had not served long political apprenticeships as their opponents of the Gush had done, they were unable to build strongly entrenched power bases in the party administration to rival that of the Gush. The Zeirim were known as *Bitzuistim* ("technocrats"—i.e., those who get things done efficiently), and they had little patience for the abstract, ideological hairsplitting of the older generation. They sharply criticized the old-style pioneering—symbolized by the Histadrut—for its inefficiency, and argued that the state should be the vanguard of pioneering. In the context of the state having incorporated into its jurisdiction the Defense Forces in 1948, the school systems in 1953, and the employment bureau in 1958, the call of leading Zeirim for nationalization of the Histadrut's health services precipitated a major conflict within the party over the boundaries of Histadrut and state jurisdiction.

The dominant factor of the factional struggle was succession to the top leadership of the party and the nation. Prime Minister David Ben-Gurion had been grooming a cadre of young protégés for cabinet posts, including Moshe Dayan, Shimone Peres, and others. This aroused the strong opposition of the Gush, leaders of the party and Histadrut bureaucracies, and particularly the secretary-general of the Histadrut, Pinchas Lavon, who had become embroiled in a bitter conflict with Dayan and Peres when Lavon was minister of defense (an episode which eventually became known as the Lavon affair).[19] This major power struggle involved not only deep personal antagonisms but intergenerational conflict, which manifested itself in conflicting organizational interests (i.e., state and Histadrut) and represented differences in style, values, and ideological positions.

The resignation of Ben-Gurion in 1963 brought in Levi Eshkol as prime minister, but raised the central question of who would succeed Eshkol. For the first time in Mapai history, a collective leadership emerged, with Levi Eshkol, Golda Meir, Pinchas Sapir, and others. They in turn gathered around them a group of top Mapai leaders, among whom the leaders of the Zeirim faction were not included. A crisis was precipitated by the opening of negotiations for an electoral alignment between Mapai and Achdut Haavoda. Mapai sought to increase its declining electoral strength and also hoped to obtain an absolute majority in the Knesset, to avoid their great dependence on coalition partners. However, an additional reason they sought a merger with Achdut Haavoda was to bring in a leadership group that would neutralize the influence of Dayan and the other young protégés of Ben-Gurion, whom the veteran leadership viewed as a threat to their continued dominant positions. The leaders of Achdut Haavoda—Yigal Allon and others—constituted a generation between the veteran Mapai leadership and the younger Ben-Gurion protégés, but were men who were ideologically much closer to the old pioneering values than were the younger proponents of statism. The Zeirim correctly perceived the alignment negotiations as a direct threat to their succession to highest political office.

Ben-Gurion openly opposed the terms of the alignment with Achdut Haavoda, especially Mapai's agreement to drop their proposals for electoral reform. The final showdown was fought out in the Tenth Party Conference in February 1965. On both major issues of the conference—the proposed *Maarach* ("Alignment") with Achdut Haavoda and an attempt by Ben-Gurion to reopen the Lavon affair—Eshkol and the party machine defeated Ben-Gurion by a majority of approximately 60 percent to 40 percent. When Eshkol was nominated as Mapai's candidate for prime minister in the forthcoming election, Ben-Gurion announced that he would form an opposition party list, called Rafi, and was joined by many of his loyal supporters, including Dayan and Peres. The results of the elections proved to be a decisive victory for Mapai under Eshkol's leadership. The Maarach gained 36.7 percent of the popular vote, to Rafi's 7.9 percent.

Unquestionably the most significant of several factors explaining the election results was the fact that as Ben-Gurion led his supporters out of Mapai and into Rafi, they left control of the vast party apparatus in the hands of Prime Minister Levi Eshkol, Golda Meir, and Pinchas Sapir. In addition, many of Ben-Gurion's sympathizers did not leave Mapai to join him in Rafi. Many were dependent upon the party or its related institutions for their livelihoods; others feared jeopardizing their political careers for what they viewed as a gamble. As Medding succinctly summarized the elections, "Organization triumphed over charisma and institutional power over prophetic morality."[20]

Less than three years after the 1965 split of Rafi and the alignment of Mapai and Achdut Haavoda as the Maarach, however, all three groups—Mapai, Achdut Haavoda, and Rafi—merged to form the present Israel Labor party, and thus ushered in a new period of party formation in Israeli politics. The Israel Labor party has remained dominant in Israel's party spectrum; but it has at the same time been the roof under which its three major factions compete and coexist. Finally, in 1969, the Labor party and Mapam formed an electoral alignment, again called the Maarach, which is still in force. These two parties have not completely merged. They have joint consultative institutions but otherwise maintain their own independent institutional structures.

I draw the reader's attention to the contrasting histories of the three constituent factions of the Israel Labor party. Poelei Zion existed for twenty-four years, from 1906 to 1930, including its phase as Achdut Haavoda, after 1919. In 1930 it merged with Hapoel Hazair, which also had a twenty-four-year history. The second Achdut Haavoda was independent during thirteen of the twenty-one years between its original split from Mapai and its realignment with it in 1965; the main body of Mapai continued to function as an independent party throughout the same period. Both maintained their independent institutiions during the period of their alignment in the Maarach. In sharp contrast to both, Rafi existed a brief two and a half years as an independent party. Their separate histories are important in explaining the nature of their relationships in the Israel Labor party.

Fusion: The Israel Labor Party, 1968–1973

The nature of the three labor parties' relationships during the years 1965–1968 had a particularly strong impact on the factional system in the newly merged Labor party. Mapai and Achdut Haavoda had become very close to one another. The alignment between them meant that they submitted a combined list of candidates to the Knesset, under the name Maarach. They were therefore automatically partners in the coalition government, and a very close working relationship developed among the top leaders of the cabinet. Although each party maintained its separate party institutions and kibbutz movements, they formed joint bodies of consultation which developed marked cooperation and convergence of views. A complete union of the two parties had not taken place only because of resistance from Achdut Haavoda's Kibbutz Hameuchad movement and from Mapai's elements sympathetic to Rafi.

In contrast, Rafi had become rather isolated. The full impact of Rafi's electoral failure in 1965 was particularly felt by its leaders, who were for the first time in their lives in the opposition. The fact that Rafi leadership spent most of its time in opposition, making bitter attacks on the Mapai leadership and government, was to affect relations between the Rafi and Mapai groups in the future Labor party. In addition, having left the vast apparatus of Mapai's bureaucracy and resources, Rafi's leaders had little more than their personal popularity and the appeal of their party platform. Moreover, Rafi never really made a serious effort to build a strong central apparatus or an extensive network of local branches.[21]

There were several initiatives, particularly from Mapai and Rafi activists in the kibbutz movement, to bring Rafi into a union with Mapai and Achdut Haavoda. In spite of the initial unwillingness on the part of the top Mapai leaders, events were soon to overtake them and their resistance to unification with Rafi. There was an increasing nationwide decline in Prime Minister Eshkol's prestige, which was linked to the serious economic recession and large-scale unemployment, the high rate of emigration (particularly among middle-class professionals), and the increasingly serious insecurity situation that came to a head in the crucial period before the war of June 1967.

During May 1967 tension mounted as the threat of war moved nearer. Two major partners in the government coalition, the National Religious party and the Independent Liberals, pressured Mapai for the inclusion of Rafi and Gahal (the major opposition party) in a government of national unity, and received support from Mapai leaders of the Haifa and Tel Aviv machines, and from other Rafi sympathizers within Mapai. Public opinion also played an important role at this juncture, one of the rare occasions on which public opinion has had an impact on Israeli politics. Led by the press, there was a wide public demand for Prime Minister Eshkol to relinquish the Defense Ministry to Moshe Dayan. Eshkol could no longer withstand such combined pressure, and finally was forced to invite Dayan into the government as minister of defense. Eshkol and other Mapai leaders never forgave the manner in which Dayan entered the cabinet under the pressure of a national crisis, and this was to affect their attitudes and actions toward Rafi when it reunited with them in the same party.

The merger that created the Israel Labor party, in January 1968, was preceded by intensive negotiations led by the Finance Minister Pinchas Sapir, who was to play a dominant role as the first secretary-general of the new united party. It was agreed in the negotiations that no open elections for party offices would be held, and no national party conference would be called, until after the 1969 national Knesset elections. Instead, it was agreed that the proportions of former party representation in the new party's elective institutions would be Mapai, 57.3 percent, and Achdut Haavoda and Rafi, 21.35 percent each. Thus the negotiations in effect resulted in a tripartite governance of the party, rather than a democratically chosen united party governance, at least for the first few years of the new party's life. The final agreement was unanimously accepted by Achdut Haavoda. Rafi split over the issue, approximately 60 percent favoring the merger and 40 percent opposing it; the majority, including Dayan and Shimone Peres, joined the Labor party, and the minority, led by the venerable David Ben-Gurion, established a new State List group.

The uniting of the three former parties, however, took place in the context of a major struggle for control of the new party. In this context, the "former Mapai," "former Achdut Haavoda," and "former Rafi" became the Mapai faction, the Achdut Haavoda faction, and the Rafi faction of the Labor party. Dayan, leader of Rafi and still minister of defense, urged his Rafi colleagues to fight to ensure that the next prime minister would not be Eshkol, and the next finance minister would not be Sapir. Achdut Haavoda made an equally outspoken bid for the succession to the premiership of its leading contender, Deputy Prime Minister Yigal Allon. The key to the resolution of this contest came to be Finance Minister and Mapai leader Sapir, who had chaired the tripartite negotiating committee which formulated the terms under which the three former parties were united.

Sapir temporarily resigned as finance minister to become the first secretary-general of the newly united party. As if in response to Dayan's challenge, Sapir succeeded in gaining a dominant position for the Mapai faction in the organizational machinery of the party. Sapir and Mapai successfully engineered a near-absolute takeover of the Labor party, its apparatus, and its enormous resources through expert use of traditional Mapai techniques of political manipulation, and by building a political machine based primarily on Mapai loyalists. These processes have had a major impact on the dynamics of factionalism in the Israel Labor party.

In 1968 and 1969 Sapir directed the massive organizational effort to mobilize the party—and his own political support within it. He directed the party's census and the party's membership drive, which enrolled 300,000 new members. Sapir maintained daily personal contact with the party central organization and the major branches, even when he was temporarily out of the country. He consolidated his alliances with important national and local leaders throughout the country. He used all of his considerable personal influence, for example, to gain renomination of his close friend and personal ally, Mayor Rabinovitz of Tel Aviv, thereby guaranteeing the continued loyal support of the Tel Aviv–based Gush. In several cases Sapir used his influence to prevent the nomination of candidates for mayorships, for example, who were known to be loyal to Rafi or to Dayan. Such intervention by Sapir on behalf of many local leaders who were his clients was general and effective, and it was through such personal intervention in party activity, virtually nationwide, that Sapir was able to build the Mapai faction machine in the Labor party.[22]

In the 1969 national parliamentary elections, Sapir personally organized and supervised the party's campaign. As one high-ranking party official summarized it, "Sapir ran the show." Sapir gained a predominant position in the selection of Mapai's allocation of Labor's candidates to the Knesset, and in the course of the campaign, he gained considerable influence with the entire Labor party contingent elected to seats in the Knesset.

Although after the 1969 Knesset campaign Sapir returned to his post of minister of finance and was replaced as secretary-general of the party by M. K. Arie "Lyova" Eliav, he in fact continued informally to dominate the party apparatus. Eliav, who had been among those who pressed for the inclusion of Rafi in the new Labor party, worked conscientiously for the unification of the party through close cooperation with deputies from the Rafi and Achdut Haavoda factions. At the same time, Sapir continued to work to undermine Rafi and members of the Mapai who were sympathizers of Rafi or of Dayan.

With the election to the Knesset over in the fall of 1969, the Labor party readied for its first national party conference, which was eventually held in April of 1971. Control of the first party conference was critical because the conference was to choose a new Central Committee—the first elective one. The Central Committee, as the largest permanent organ of the party, with several hundred members, would in turn elect the secretariat (of over one hundred members), and it would elect the smaller, thirty-three-member Leadership Bureau. Thus control of the conference would determine the distribution of power among the factions, not only on the Central Committee but on virtually all the party's national organs. The most important single variable determining the outcome of the party's elections of delegates to the conference was the fact that the organization apparatus which directed the election was under control of the top Mapai leadership. In spite of Secretary-General Eliav's sincere efforts to reconcile the party factions and to achieve genuine cooperation among them, the main efforts of the party apparatus, of which Eliav was not in control, were directed at the mobilization of the branches in support of Mapai faction (and Sapir-oriented) candidates. Moreover, in addition to the 2,206 delegates to the conference elected by the party branches, 735 delegates were "appointed" by a central nominations committee; an overwhelming majority of these delegates were Sapir loyalists, particularly from the Tel Aviv Gush. As a result of the Mapai machine, in short, Mapai and Sapir went into the conference with a significant majority of delegates on whom they could rely.

But the Mapai leaders did not rely solely on their majority in the national conference. The traditional means by which Mapai leaders maintained control of the old Mapai party and continue to dominate the Labor party has been small nominations committees. The nominations committees, appointed by the top party leadership, are charged formally with balancing the demands for representation of the various internal factions and interests in the party, and in fact with ensuring that those chosen are loyal to their patrons in the top leadership. The list, once compiled by the nominations committee, is submitted en bloc to the larger party institution which has the constitutional authority to make the nominations. This is always an essentially ceremonial vote: I am unable to find a single case in which the list proposed by a nominations committee was not accepted, either in the former Mapai party or in the Labor party.

Sapir's Mapai faction machine not only dominated the conference delegates, it also captured control, through its manipulation of nominations committees, of the conference's standing committee, which "ran" the conference. The standing committee drew up the new party constitution, formulated policy on a wide range of issues, struck from the conference agenda those controversial items which the top party leadership wished to prevent from being debated in the conference, and, most important, approved the composition of the new party Central Committee. The standing committee decided that the new Central Committee would be composed of 501 members, two-thirds to be elected by the branch caucuses of delegates to the party conference, and one-third to be selected by the central nominations committee. However, after the caucuses elected their Central Committee representatives, the nominations committee demanded and got permission to appoint an extra 100 places on an expanded Central Committee, bringing the nominations committee's appointments to 45 percent of the Central Committee membership.[23] This obviously increased the influence of the top party leaders of the three factions, who selected their own portions of the appointive seats. The total factional representation on the new Central Committee of 601 members was Mapai, 398; Achdut Haavoda, 115; and Rafi, 88—or approximately 66 percent for Mapai, 19 percent for Achdut Haavoda, and 15 percent for Rafi. The composition of the new party executive structure thus represented both a strengthening of the position of top party leaders of all three factions relative to regular party activists, and a strengthening of the Mapai faction relative to Achdut Haavoda, and especially relative to Rafi, over the 1968 formula.

Decline of the Labor Party Faction System in the Mid-1970s

The traumatic Yom Kippur War of October 1973 precipitated major changes in Israel's party system and in the Labor party's faction system. The war went badly for Israel, especially in its early stages, and the leadership of the Labor party bore the brunt of widespread and severe criticism for what was perceived as near-fatal errors in the preparation for and handling of the war. Criticism and demonstrations eventually brought down the government and led to a turnover in Labor party leadership. Ultimately, the aftermath of the war resulted in a major restructuring of the factional composition of the entire Labor party.

Following the conclusion of the war, as public criticism grew, internal party criticism grew also. Party conflicts centered on leadership—especially leadership in the government—and on policy. Many wanted Moshe Dayan's resignation as defense minister; some wanted the resignation of Prime Minister Golda Meir as well. In policy matters, party strongman Sapir sought a change in party policy on several fronts. At a private meeting of top party leaders in advance of the first party Central Committee meeting after the war, Sapir won agreement on his own "platform" in a compromise, which entailed his continued support for Meir's heading the government, and agreement not to reopen the party lists for candidates in the upcoming elections to the Knesset.

The Central Committee's meeting, in November 1973, was a stormy, day-and-night-long affair. There were attacks on and defenses of individual leaders, particularly Dayan. There was a confrontation over Sapir's platform, particularly with regard to its taking precedence over the party's previous policy, the Galili Statement (so named for its drafter, Yisrael Galili, a leader of the Achdut Haavoda faction). Factional competition played an important role in both personality and policy issues. Yigal Allon, the second-ranking leader of Achdut Haavoda and his faction's leading contender for the premiership, not only attacked Dayan but repudiated the Galili Statement. Dayan and Golda Meir supported the view that the Galili Statement remained in force as party policy; however, Meir did not defend Dayan against attacks on his mishandling of the war. In the end, the meeting avoided a showdown by contriving a ruling that each party member could follow his own interpretation of the status of the previous policy.

For the selection of the party's candidates for the 1973 Knesset elections, the leaders of the factions agreed among themselves to retain the same numerical positions on the party list that each faction had had in the 1969 election, and they also agreed that each faction would decide on its own candidates. This was a direct contradiction of the decision taken four years previously, that candidates would be elected by secret ballot on a nonfactional basis. When a rebellious member of the Central Committee challenged the legitimacy of the en bloc list submitted by the Mapai faction's nominating committee, basing her charges on the previous decision, she was rebuffed by the secretary-general, who claimed that the unification of the party had not progressed sufficiently to enable them to implement the prior decision and that "under the circumstances democracy can only work within the previous party factions."[24]

Thus leaders of all three factions were in agreement not to open the party's nominations for intraparty election but to keep candidate choice in the hands of the respective faction leaders. Galili of Achdut Haavoda, Meir of Mapai, and Dayan of Rafi were strongly in support of renewed party approval of the Galili Statement, while Sapir of Mapai and Allon of Achdut Haavoda supported the exclusive applicability of the Sapir platform. Dayan was defended by leaders of Rafi against the attacks of many leaders of Mapai and Achdut Haavoda, although some spokesmen of both groups, including Prime Minister Meir, attempted to remain neutral. These confrontations indicated a renewal of ideologically oriented policy goals, which became a part of the factional competition for power but which also led to alignments cutting across old factional divisions at the highest levels of party leadership.

In the Knesset elections, held in December 1973, the Labor party lost substantial voter support; although still by far the largest party, its parliamentary plurality diminished by enough seats that the coalition formula of the previous government would now not quite produce a majority. Golda Meir was given the presidential mandate to form a government; but this had now become an increasingly difficult charge, and in fact the country was in a government crisis for some nine weeks, from January to March 1974. The Labor party itself in those weeks moved perilously near to breakup. Dayan and Shimone Peres, the first and second leaders of Rafi, refused to join Meir's proposed minority government. They complained bitterly about the extreme criticisms of Dayan, which intensified in the early weeks of 1974, not only in the mass media but in internal party forums such as the party newspaper, *Ot.* In February 1974, it was Meir who became the most outspoken voice of growing fears that the party was headed for a split. Eventually she announced as her "final decision" that she was giving up her quest for the formation of a new government, and the crisis became a crisis of the country's dominant party as well.

In early March the Labor Central Committee held what some afterward called "one of the most fateful meetings in the history of the party"; factional strife brought the party to the brink of open rupture. Much of the bitterness of the rivalry among the factional leaders was brought out at the meeting. Sapir was accused by Rafi leaders of "working against Rafi" from the beginning, a charge which he went to great lengths to deny. Peres, the former communications minister, complained bitterly about his exclusion from the informal top circle of government ministers consulted prior to cabinet meetings. In a similar vein, Dayan complained: "Rafi does not want to exist. It does not have a newspaper [or] a kibbutz federation. . . . It exists because Mapai and Achdut Haavoda make it exist." In the end, the meeting concluded with an overwhelming reendorsement of Meir and her proposed government.

Afterward Golda Meir succeeded in establishing a minority government and held open the portfolios for Dayan and Peres, who later joined the government when a particularly serious military alert on the border with Syria justified their doing so "in the national interest." The report of the special commission appointed to investigate the conduct of the war led to the condemnation, and ultimate resignation, of high-ranking military personnel, but avoided the question of political responsibility of the minister of defense or the government. However, the criticisms and attacks on both Dayan and Meir—within the party and from increasingly organized public protest—intensified with the emergence of many new political protest groups. The mood in the party and in the public influenced Golda Meir finally to resign as prime minister in the spring of 1974.[25]

Meir's resignation resulted in the party's first open competitive election in the Central Committee, for selection of her successor as the party's choice for the premiership. The fact that the vote was an open one was a result of two things: Sapir's decision not to seek the position himself, and there being no other "natural" successor who enjoyed wide backing in the party and especially in Mapai. It is likely that if Sapir had wanted it, he could have gotten the nomination without an open vote. Many explanations have been suggested for his decision not to; his own stated reason was that it was time for a change. The other traditional contenders, Dayan of Rafi and Allon of Achdut Haavoda, had successfully neutralized each other through their long and bitter rivalry, and neither enjoyed the confidence of Mapai or a party majority. Other hopeful candidates who were Mapai men had all succeeded in the party as Sapir's "clients," and clientage means conformity to the wishes of the patron rather than independence and leadership capability.[26]

Instead, Sapir backed Yitzchak Rabin, who had successfully served as chief of staff of the Israel Defense Forces during the war of 1967, and had been an ambassador afterward, but who had not been active in party or factional politics. Sapir's backing won for Rabin the support of much of Mapai, and he was supported also by many of Achdut Haavoda's leaders. In the election, Rabin's competition came from Shimone Peres. Peres ran a very restrained and refined campaign—which contrasted sharply with the unofficial competition between Dayan and Allon over the years—and carried not only Rafi but a sizable portion of the Mapai leadership as well. Peres emerged from his defeat as the new leader of Rafi, and as a leader of considerable new standing in the party as a whole.

Sapir, who played the key role in the designation of Rabin as the party's successor to Golda Meir, refused to join Rabin's government and refrained from taking any more active behind-the-scenes roles in the party or the government. Rabin demonstrated considerable independence in forming his cabinet. Since he had never been formally affiliated with the Mapai faction, for the first time in the history of the independent State of Israel, the prime minister was not a member of Mapai. Although the Mapai faction was clearly represented in the cabinet, Mapai had lost several key ministerial posts.

Rabin moved the Labor party away from the factional structure which was built into it in 1968 and which almost brought the party to a breakup by 1973. Rabin built a new coalition based on the support of the major big-city machines, and was successful in working around and diminishing the significance of the once-established factions.

There were some efforts, by former Foreign Minister Abba Ebban with support from the indomitable Sapir, to reinvigorate Mapai as a structured faction and to regain its lost influence. The Rabin coalition, however, gained the support of Finance Minister Rabinovitz, who retained control of the major Tel Aviv party machine; of Labor Minister Baram, who dominated the Jerusalem organizations, and of Mayor Almogi of Haifa, who controlled the Haifa machine. This coalition succeeded in blocking the efforts to reconstitute the old Mapai faction.

The effort to abolish the old factions gained considerable support in the branches. At a meeting of the twelve largest branches (which have an absolute majority on all major national party institutions), a call was made for a "revolution from below," and a resolution passed to abolish the 1968 premerger factional divisions for the next internal party elections. The drive for Labor party unity had the support of the grass-roots membership in the branches. The new coalition had considerable success in efforts to free the party from the dominance of Sapir and his loyal devotees.

An at least partial consequence of the decline of the Labor party's factionalism is a tendency toward breakdown of the traditionally strong party discipline in voting in the Knesset, and the emergence of new, ideologically oriented factional groups among the party's Knesset members. A group of about twenty members of the Alignment (Maarach) of Labor and Mapam in the Knesset formed a leftist, "dovish" caucus, called the Free Platform, which met regularly and demonstratively abstained on motions sponsored by the government. An activist wing of Labor party Knesset members reacted by organizing their own caucus—named after the late Y. Tabinkin, a former leader of Achdut Haavoda, who was outspoken in his views that territories occupied after the 1967 war belonged to a historic "Greater Land of Israel." One prominent party leader, Knesset Finance Committee Chairman Yisrael Kargman, warned that "if this continues, our Knesset [Labor] group loses its value and meaning, especially when the others meet in caucus and decide on a common stand. . . . I have seen this process before, when Siya Bet first met to exchange views, until finally it voted itself out of the party."[27]

A more extreme manifestation of such developments was the exodus from the party of a few dissident members who formed a new political party of their own. Former Mapai Labor Knesset member Shulamit Aloni first established a "Civil Rights List" in the 1973 election and succeeded in winning three Knesset seats. Former secretary-general of the Labor party, M. K. Arie "Lyova" Eliav, also left the Labor party and, with Aloni and dissident leaders of other protest groups that emerged in the aftermath of the 1973 war, formed *Ya'ad* ("Goal"), a leftist party to be an alternative to the Labor party.

Conclusions

At the beginning of this chapter, I proposed to examine Israeli party factions' structures through an application of the concept of corporateness advanced by M. G. Smith, in which essential characteristics of corporateness are: boundedness, determinate membership, identity, organization, procedure, common affairs, autonomy, and presumed perpetuity.

Siya Bet originally was not a corporate group, being based to a large extent on a generational difference within Mapai. But it did express a comprehensive ideological orientation of its own in the form of a more Marxist interpretation of socialism, and it had specific national policies. Its major source of strength was the autonomous institutional framework of the Kibbutz Hameuchad movement in Mapai. As its struggle with the Mapai leadership intensified, the faction progressively acquired structural corporateness, chiefly by consolidating its organizational strength around the kibbutz movement, which provided it with sufficient autonomy eventually to leave Mapai altogether.

The 1948–1954 Mapam party existed entirely as a bifactional union, both factions retaining a distinctly corporate character and an independent resource base, each especially in the form of its separate kibbutz federation. Although ideological agreement was a factor in their merger, the differences in ideology were a factor in their split, and both the merger and the split immediately preceded major national election campaigns. Electoral strategy thus played an important, if not dominant, role in both decisions. The Mapam party of 1948–1954 therefore was a political marriage of convenience between two ideologically compatible and quite corporate partners, and it lasted only as long as it was deemed politically worthwhile for both.

The Zeirim, or Young Guards, who coalesced as a faction around David Ben-Gurion, were on the whole not a corporate group. Like Siya Bet, the Zeirim consisted largely of younger intraparty rivals of the established Mapai leadership. Although differences were expressed in style—i.e., "technocratic" youth vs. "machine"-type veteran professionals—and although they became involved in ideological debates, the dominant factor was the generational competition for succession to party and national leadership. The pattern of factional strife within Mapai had thus a distinctly noncorporate character in that it was based on the competition between a strong charismatic leader, Ben-Gurion, and the group led by Eshkol, which controlled the party machinery, and their respective followers. In 1965 much of this group seceded to form an independent party, Rafi, and thus to alter its structure as an autonomous group. Even as a separate party, however, Rafi failed to develop organizational structures and sophisticated procedures and was, as a party, an imperfectly corporate group at best.

The structural features of the three contemporary factions of the Israel Labor party differ significantly in corporate characteristics, as well as in the effects of these structural differences on factional competition. Table 1 summarizes the comparison of the corporate structural characteristics of the three constituent factions of the Labor party from 1968 to 1974.

Rafi was the least corporate of the three. The boundedness and degree to which membership could be identified was least clear in the Rafi faction. Not all of those who sympathized with Rafi's cause left Mapai when Rafi was formed as a splinter party; Rafi policy after it remerged with the Labor party was deliberately to perpetuate this lack of clarity of the identity of its membership. Thus, during the party census organized immediately after the merger, the Rafi leadership instructed its members and sympathizers not to answer the question which asked for former party affiliation. Their explanation was that they wished to avoid possible sanctions or discrimination against their members. Given the policies of the Sapir-dominated Mapai, this was not an unrealistic fear; it is also likely that Rafi leaders wished to avoid possible embarrassment from having it shown that their membership was considerably smaller than they had claimed.

Rafi was also organizationally the weakest of the three factions. Rafi never really organized a sound party apparatus during its two-and-a-half-year independent existence. It lacked the time, the resources, and the inclination to organize a national bureaucracy and a coordinated network of local branches. After the merger, Rafi's lead-

Table 1. Comparative Corporate Characteristics of Labor Factions, 1968–1974

	Faction		
Corporate Features	Rafi	Mapai	Achdut Haavoda
boundedness, determinate membership, identity	least clear	clear	clearest
organization	weakest	strong	strongest
procedure	ad hoc	informal regular	formal regular
common affairs	least comprehensive	comprehensive	most comprehensive
autonomy	through threat of split	through dominance	through independent institutions
presumed perpetuity	least likely	likely	most likely

ers, and particularly Dayan, showed no inclination to meet the challenge of engaging in practical political organization, at either the national or local level. During the factional competition from 1968 to 1971, the procedures, tactics, and style of Rafi were the least well organized and the most ad hoc of the three. Rafi ignored organization and, for its continued existence as a group, relied almost exclusively on the appeals of the personalities of its leaders and of its platforms. Their procedures were mainly confined to informal meetings among small groups of leaders, and irregular meetings of leaders and followers.

The common affairs of the Rafi faction consisted primarily of their shared loyalty to their charismatic former leader, David Ben-Gurion, and to their more recent leader, Moshe Dayan, who many perceived as charismatic. They shared policy views ranging from electoral reform to more conservative policies on social and economic matters, and more militant security and foreign policies. They also had ties of an elaborate network of patron-client relationships, which joined local-level activists to national leaders. Rafi had the least independent resources of all the factions; it had neither a kibbutz federation nor a newspaper of its own, nor any of the other institutional resources of the other two factions. The only patronage Rafi leaders could provide their followers was their small quota of memberships on party institutions.

The autonomy of Rafi was conditional, in that its existence was dependent on the actions of the other two factions, particularly Mapai. Rafi was successful in protecting its position and in gaining concessions by exploiting the ultimate threat of splitting off from the party. Finally, Rafi was the least corporate faction with regard to presumed perpetuity. Most of its leadership indicated that they desire integration within the party. It is likely that Rafi, as it existed in the past, will be no more—although it is also likely that certain personal ties and relationships among old Rafi members will continue to have an influence even in an integrated Labor party. If attempts to reconstitute the Mapai faction should succeed, then it is possible that the Rafi faction would reform or leave the party. In either case the long-term existence of Rafi as an active faction within the Labor party is unlikely.

The second "junior" partner of the Labor party, Achdut Haavoda, was clearly the most corporate of the three. The long history of independent existence of Achdut Haavoda produced a membership which was distinctly bounded and the identity of which could be easily determined. It had a well organized institutional framework, both in the form of its Kibbutz Hameuchad movement, which maintained its autonomy within the Labor party and in its local urban branches. Although the urban branches of Achdut Haavoda were integrated into the branches of the Labor party, they continued generally to maintain a sense of their separate identity and interests, and met regularly as factional caucuses to determine common policy.

Achdut Haavoda's shared common affairs included the most well-articulated ideology of the three factions, which was both more doctrinaire Socialist and more militant in security and foreign policy than the more pragmatic Mapai. Achdut Haavoda long had its own newspaper, which only fairly recently merged with that of the Histadrut. Achdut Haavoda also benefited from the special representation at the party conference and in other party institutions which is guaranteed to the members of kibbutzim in the Labor party. These autonomous institutions and resources gave Achdut Haavoda the greatest degree of corporateness among the three factions in the Labor party.

Given the fact that it manifested the most corporate structure and had the most independent institutions and resources, Achdut Haavoda is the most likely to perpetuate itself in its present form. Although there is some support among its leadership for a genuine integration within the Labor party, there is more resistance to that trend within the faction. Such resistance may slow down or even prevent the complete assimilation of the faction; nevertheless, there is no significant movement in the faction to split from the Labor party, and it is generally thought that such a move would be contrary to the interests of the Achdut Haavoda and of Labor as a whole. It is just as unlikely that it will split from the Labor party as it is that it will disappear within the Labor party.

The Mapai faction fit into an intermediate position between its two junior partners on a corporateness scale. The identity of its membership was generally clearly bounded, but the exact identity of former Mapai members who remained sympathetic toward Rafi was not always easy to determine. The core of the faction was originally a strong and well-organized, but informal, party machine, which was consolidated by Pinchas Sapir and finally dominated by him, until the party crisis in 1974. Mapai maintained its own kibbutz movement as the Labor party's and generally had use of party institutions, such as the party press, as its own. The faction evolved its own relatively well-institutionalized, though still semiformal, procedures in its organizational structure. Organizational and procedural distinctness was also characteristic of several of the city machines—particularly that of the Tel Aviv Gush—which, in effect, were subunits of the Mapai coalition.

Mapai's common affairs were primarily the elaborate network of patron-client relationships which successfully provided control of party institutions, and those of the Histadrut and other affiliated or party-dominated institutions—all of which provided control of the majority of the patronage positions of the many resources dominated by the party as a whole. In part, Mapai's lack of developed corporateness was a function of its partial indistinguishability, as the majority governance of the party, from the party itself. Mapai did not have autonomous institutions other than those of the Labor party, inasmuch as it successfully dominated the apparatus and institutions of the overall party through the political organization of Sapir's informal machine. Mapai in its earlier form will likely cease to exist in a united Labor party; but the possibility remains that Mapai will be reconstituted as a faction and again seek to dominate the party and thereby perpetuate the politics of factionalism in its traditional form.

Finally, it remains to consider some of the major functional and political consequences of the factional competition for the development of the party and for the political system generally. I have stressed the primary function of the factions for the mobilization of support in the competitive struggle for control of the party's central institutions. While factional affiliation played a dominant role in the competition for representation in these institutions, it played a relatively minor role in determining the stands of the participants in the debates in these institutions. This contrasts sharply with the earlier historical period, when ideological issues played a more important role in factional relationships, as well as with more recent times, when the old factional divisions based on former party affiliation appeared to be breaking down and new ideologically oriented factions were developing in the party caucus in the Knesset.

The major functions of the factions in the Labor party from its formation in 1968 to its crisis in 1974 were processing competition for representation in party institutions and for acquisition and distribution of power and resources, and providing the main channel of upward mobility in the networks of intrafactional patron-client relationships. The factional base together with the nominations system enabled the top factional leaders to renominate themselves, their protégés, and their clients to all important institutions. The retention of control of the party was the raison d'etre for the continuation of factional politics in the Labor party from 1968 to 1974, and retention of positions is the primary reason for resistance to the integration of the party.

Historically, such convenient techniques of control generally benefited the nation, because they contributed stability and continuity to a regime faced with enormous problems of national integration and development—e.g., the absorption of culturally diverse mass immigration, staggering problems of defense. The factional system performed another function for the highly pluralistic mass party, that of providing an additional institutional tie of loyalty which cut across other ethnic, geographic, and interest group ties. Factions thereby helped prevent possible polarization along any of these lines, and contributed to overall party cohesion.[28]

However, factionalism has not had an altogether beneficial impact on the party and the national political system. Factional splits in Mapai highlighted the absence of formal constitutional methods of leadership selection. The use of nominations committees in the absence of direct and open intraparty elections called into question the legitimacy of the party institutions, and left minority factions without any avenue of legitimate appeal to the party membership, or to the electorate, within the party framework. As Medding observed,

> While organizational strength was an advantage for Mapai, tight control by a small group neither directly chosen by nor responsible to the rank and file was a serious disadvantage because it intensified internal opposition that might have been muted by the existence of party bodies enjoying the unquestioned support of rank and file electoral choice and support.[29]

The continuation of these same procedures after the formation of the Israel Labor party was one of the primary factors which contributed to the perpetuation of factional competition within the party.

Moreover, to the extent that factional politics concentrated on competition for representation in party institutions, it largely detracted from recruitment on the basis of merit. Factional competition leads to bargaining for offices. Each faction attempts to maximize its own power and status at the expense of the others, not to find the most qualified party men to fill the jobs for which they are best suited. This has been abundantly illustrated in squabbling over ministerial portfolios and is indeed characteristic of local branch politics. Through the use of nominations committees, national and local patrons perpetuate themselves, their clients, and their allies in power without direct, open election. New or opposing groups have no avenue of direct appeal to the party membership or to the electorate, and internal opposition tends to become at first intensified, and then alienated and/or co-opted. This led to widespread feelings of political inefficacy among branch activists; the same thing is widely found among members of major national institutions and among party functionaries.[30] The fact that the top leadership had lost touch with the rank and file and with the general public was vividly demonstrated in the developments which followed the traumatic events of the October 1973 war. When the nation most needed dynamic leadership with fresh approaches to critical problems, the Labor party became embroiled in a major internal factional fight.

Factional strife directly contributed to the instability of Rabin's government. The government's shaky majority in the Knesset was under constant harassment by the coordinated efforts of all of the main parties of the opposition, and by the challenge of new Knesset factions which threatened to break down party discipline. Under such circumstances the government's future was constantly threatened—a most serious situation for a government which almost daily faced decisions which could mean the difference between war and peace. This negative impact of factionalism on the political system as a whole is of great significance: its short-term effects contribute to greater instability of the government. The long-range effects may well contribute to the renewal of ideological positions in party, which might result in a more vigorous commitment of party members to policies for resolving problems facing Israeli society—and/or to new splits in the party. Both are possible. An implication of this is that there are reciprocal relationships among the stages of mobilization of political support and the institutionalization of these relationships, and the changing role of ideology, its meaning and importance for the various actors in the political process, and its capacity to be effectively related to the major problems confronting the political institution in question. All aspects of these interrelated variables must be examined if we are to understand factional politics and its impact on the wider sociopolitical environment.

Factionalism in Israel's labor parties emerged as a fairly flexible means of routinizing relationships between latent groups with competing ideologies, interests, and styles within the larger institutional framework of the party. At different stages in the development of the political system, ideology has played a greater or lesser role in factional competition. When factional strife became almost exclusively a manifestation of a struggle for power and control of the party, its impact on the party and on the political system became increasingly negative. Whereas the various splits and mergers to a certain extent allowed for adaptation of the parties to general social changes, the failure of the factional competition to produce new policy alternatives in solution of new problems from the late fifties through the early sixties had serious ramifications which were manifest in the aftermath of the war in 1973. It may be that the moves to abolish the old factions, and newer ideologically oriented factional groupings in the party's caucuses, are manifestations of the adaptation of the party and its ideology to the new challenges of being out of power and of needing new policy alternatives to respond to a rapidly changing social reality, both internally and internationally. It is likely that factionalism in some form will continue to play an important role in this process.

NOTES

1. See Ralph W. Nicholas, "Factions: A Comparative Analysis," in Michael Banton, ed., *Political Systems and the Distribution of Power,* Association of Social Anthropologists, Monograph no. 2 (London: Tavistock Publications, 1965), pp. 21–61; Nicholas, "Segmentary Factional Political Systems," in Marc J. Swartz, Victor W. Turner, and Arthur Tuden, eds., *Political Anthropology* (Chicago: Aldine, 1966), pp. 49–59; and Nicholas, "Rules, Resources, and Political Activity," in Marc J. Swartz, ed., *Local-Level Politics: Social and Cultural Perspectives* (Chicago: Aldine, 1968), pp. 295–321; Burton Benedict, "Factionalism in Mauritian Villages," *British Journal of Sociology* 8 (1957): 328–42; and David Pocock, "The Bases of Faction in Gujerat," *British Journal of Sociology* 8 (1957): 295–306.

2. See J. A. Barnes, "Networks and Political Process," in Swartz, ed., *Local-Level Politics,* pp. 107–40; J. Clyde Mitchell, "The Concept of Social Networks," in J. Clyde Mitchell, ed., *Social Networks in Urban Situations* (Manchester: Manchester Univ. Press, 1969), pp. 1–50; Adrian Mayer, "The Significance of Quasi-Groups in the Study of Complex Societies," in Michael Banton, ed., *The Social Anthropology of Complex Societies* (London: Tavistock Publications, 1966), pp. 1–22; and James C. Scott, "Patron-Client Politics and Political Change in Southeast Asia," *American Political Science Review* 66, no. 1 (Mar. 1972): 91–113.

3. Moshe Shodeid, "Immigration and Factionalism: An Analysis of Factions in Rural Israeli Communities of Immigrants," *British Journal of Sociology* 19 (1968): 385–406.

4. Nicholas, "Segmentary Factional Political Systems," p. 57.

5. Cf. Frederick Barth, *Political Leadership Among Swat Pathans* (London: Univ. of London, Athlone Press, 1959).

6. M. G. Smith, "A Structural Approach to Comparative Politics," in David Easton, ed., *Varieties of Political Theory* (Englewood Cliffs: Prentice-Hall, 1966), p. 119.

7. Nicholas, "Segmentary Factional Political Systems;" Nicholas, "Factions," p. 27; and B. D. Graham, "The Succession of Factional Systems in the Uttar Pradesh Congress Party, 1937–66," in Swartz, ed., *Local-Level Politics,* pp. 323–60.

8. Lewis A. Coser, *The Functions of Social Conflict* (New York: The Free Press, 1964), p. 104.

9. Myron J. Aronoff, "Communal Cohesion Through Political Strife in an Israeli New Town," *Jewish Journal of Sociology* 25 (1973): 100–101.

10. Raymond Firth, "Introduction: Factions in Indian and Overseas Indian Societies," *British Journal of Sociology* 8 (1957): 292; and Pocock, "Bases of Faction in Gujerat," p. 296.

11. Jacob Katz, *Tradition and Crisis* (New York: The Free Press, 1961).

12. Ben Halpern, *The Idea of the Jewish State* (Cambridge: Harvard Univ. Press, 1961); and Walter Laquer, *A History of Zionism* (London: Weidenfeld and Nicolson, 1972).

13. Cf. Marver Bernstein, *The Politics of Israel* (Princeton: Princeton Univ. Press, 1957); Moshe Burnstein, *Self-Government of the Jews in Palestine Since 1900* (Tel Aviv: Hapoel Hazair, 1934); Oscar Kraines, *Government and Politics in Israel* (Boston: Houghton

Mifflin, 1961); Leonard Fein, *Politics in Israel* (Boston and Toronto: Little, Brown, 1967); Alan Arian, *Ideological Change in Israel* (Cleveland: Case Western Reserve Univ. Press, 1968); and Arian, *The Choosing People* (Cleveland: Case Western Reserve Univ. Press, 1973).

14. Myron J. Aronoff, "Party Center and Local Branch Relationships: The Israel Labor Party," in Alan Arian, ed., *The Elections in Israel—1969* (Jerusalem: Jerusalem Academic Press, 1972), pp. 150–83; and Aronoff, "Ritual in Consensual Power Relations: The Israel Labor Party," in S. Lee Seaton, ed., *Political Anthropology and the State* (Chicago: Aldine, 1976).

15. For an account of the effects of such centralization on a community which attempted to maintain independent local factions, see Myron J. Aronoff, *Frontiertown: The Politics of Community Building in Israel* (Manchester: Manchester Univ. Press; Jerusalem: Jerusalem Academic Press, 1974).

16. Maurice Duverger, *Political Parties: Their Organization and Activity in the Modern State*, trans. Barbara and Robert North (New York: John Wiley and Sons, 1954), p. 308.

17. Jonathan Shapiro, *The Organization of Power: The Formative Years of the Israeli Labor Party, 1919–1930* (Tel Aviv: Am Oved, forthcoming).

18. Peter Medding, *Mapai in Israel: Political Organization and Government in a New Society* (Cambridge: At the Univ. Press, 1972).

19. Amos Perlmuter, *Military and Politics in Israel* (New York: Praeger, 1969).

20. Medding, *Mapai in Israel*, p. 279.

21. In some cases local branches of Rafi had been legal factions created by local groups to compete in the national election campaign of 1965. See Aronoff, *Frontiertown.*

22. As one top party official explained to me, "Sapir was very interested in having his people as candidates rather than Dayan's boys or someone else's. Sapir talked to people and backed those he could trust." (Personal communication to the author.) See also Aronoff, "Party Center and Local Branch Relationships," pp. 150–83.

23. The process through which candidates are selected to major party institutions and to the Knesset is described in Aronoff, "Ritual in Consensual Power Relations," and Aronoff, "The Power of Nominations in the Israel Labor Party," in Alan Arian, ed., *The Elections in Israel—1973* (Jerusalem: Jerusalem Academic Press, 1975), p. 163.

24. Aronoff, "Power of Nominations," p. 163. Several high-ranking party officials expressed to me their feelings that through such behavior the party was committing suicide, and if drastic measures were not taken to alter the situation, not only would the government fall, but the public would surely vote the party out of power for the first time in the history of Israeli politics.

25. I have dealt with a more complete analysis of the implications of these events elsewhere. See Aronoff, *Ritual in Consensual Power Relationships: The Israel Labor Party, A Study in Political Anthropology* (Assen: Van Gorcum, forthcoming).

26. One of the results of Sapir's strong leadership has been a generation of party "leaders" who are adept at the game of political infighting, but who lack vision, ideas, and initiative and who are judged by their patrons among the older top leadership to be lacking in the qualities required to take the helm of the party and the nation. This is one of the main reasons why top party leaders have turned to the army to recruit candidates for high office in the party, in many cases in preference to those clients who have loyally served them, but who in doing so have not indicated ability, produced original ideas, taken independent actions, or made decisions. As one top leader said of a prominent potential candidate from Mapai for the premiership, "If he had only once said 'no' to Sapir, Sapir would have probably backed him for the Premiership."

27. Personal communication to the author.

28. For theoretical discussions of the role of cross-cutting ties contributing to social cohesion, see Georg Simmel, *Conflict and the Web of Group Affiliations*, trans. Kurt Wulff and Reinhard Bendix (New York: The Free Press, 1963); Coser, *Functions of Social Conflict;* Max Gluckman, *Custom and Conflict in Africa* (Oxford: Basil Blackwell and Mott, 1955); and Gluckman, *Politics, Law, and Ritual in Tribal Society* (Oxford: Basil Blackwell and Mott, 1965).

29. Medding, *Mapai in Israel*, p. 279.

30. Aronoff, "Ritual in Consensual Power Relations."

6

The Ambiguity of Faction: Fragmentation and Bipolarization in France

BRUCE A. CAMPBELL
SUE ELLEN M. CHARLTON

France is in a period of political flux. After the failure of the Fourth Republic and the subsequent Gaullist "breakthrough" of the 1960s, political competition became increasingly polarized between the left and the right. This bipolarization[1] was obvious in the highly contested legislative elections of 1973, the presidential election of 1974, and the municipal elections of 1977. Further verification of this basic trend can be seen in the overall direction of voting behavior and public opinion during the Fifth Republic.[2]

Factions have played a central though ambiguous role in the basic restructuring of political activity since 1958. French political culture has traditionally been fragmented by cleavages which dated, in some cases, from the French Revolution and the rise of industrialization. This fragmentation has long been an underlying cause of party factionalism. Various government institutions often further encouraged the development of factions. For example, in both the Third and the Fourth republics, parliamentary regimes with a weak executive, together with multiplicative electoral systems, supported both the proliferation of parties and intraparty factionalism. Under these circumstances, multipartyism and multifactionalism were often hard to distinguish.

In the Fifth Republic, both the structures and the functions of factions changed. As the following discussion stresses, the structure of factions ranged from formalized, ideological groups to amorphous leader-follower associations. Functionally, factions responded to the basic changes which produced the broad bipolarization in French politics. The result is some ambiguity in the role they played by the mid-1970s. On the one hand, factions made it possible for parties to broaden their base of appeal to a diverse constituency, and thus facilitated bipolar political competition. On the other hand, they continued to threaten the cohesion and stability of both the left and the right.

Factions in a Changing Political Context

FACTIONALISM AND FRAGMENTATION

French parties have traditionally been characterized as poorly organized, loosely structured, and inconstant—the chief exception being the Communist party. During the Third and Fourth republics, many parties underwent frequent splits, mergers, and reconstitutions; others, sometimes called "flash parties," emerged suddenly as major forces during an electoral campaign, only to fade away soon after. It was thus hardly surprising that many French parties could be identified as having two or more wings, sometimes ideological, sometimes representing interest groups, and sometimes purely power groups or followers of a particular leader. Such groups were known as *tendances.* At times, differing wings of parties competed with each other as much as with rival parties.

The best example of the coexistence of several factions within one party was the Socialist party (SFIO). The SFIO at various times had a "doctrinaire" *tendance,* a "progressive" *tendance,* and a "humanitarian" *tendance.* Formally, the SFIO prohibited organized factions, and such *tendances* among the Socialists were generally no more than leadership groups; however, Maurice Duverger has described how in the Third Republic factions in the Socialist party occasionally became highly organized, with distinct membership cards and their own newspapers.[3]

During the Fourth Republic the Socialist party sought to avoid organized factionalism, which was expressly forbidden in party statutes. Members were disciplined, and those who broke discipline—whether in parliamentary votes or in public criticism—were subject to sanctions, temporary suspension, or expulsion (as was the case for André Philip in 1957). Intraparty divisions generally were ad hoc and based on ideological differences with official party policy. At every party meeting, there were minority resolutions and positions, but it was rare that these led to polarization within the party. Generally the lines of majority-minority opinion overlapped from one issue to another. Only in two cases during the Fourth Republic were the issues of such virulence and the involvement of party activists of such magnitude as to threaten party unity: the issue of the European Defense Community, which the party weathered, and the combined crises of Algeria and de Gaulle. The second did produce a distinct minority faction, which split off from the party and eventually became the *Parti socialiste unifié* ("Unified Socialist party"—PSU).[4] Withal, internal divisions were largely unavoidable for the SFIO, given its own organizational and ideological heritage, and its strategic location on the political spectrum.

The picture of factionalism in the fragmented political system of the Third and Fourth republics is further complicated by the overlapping of faction and party. Some parties were little more than factions in general political or ideological tendency, while other parties were simply collections of factions, having little or no institutional structure beyond that of the constituent groups. In this respect multipartyism often was disguised multifactionalism.

This phenomenon was also seen in the instability and fluidity of center coalitions in the Fourth Republic, and even in the early Fifth Republic. Intraparty factions were frequently indistinguishable from interparty factions and tendencies, and largely accounted for the confusing array of political groupings during those periods. The full complexity of multifactionalism within the French center parties, and the number of parties and groups on both the right and the left, resulted in seemingly endless combinations of political forces, with little lasting solidarity. Party fragmentation contributed to cabinet instability, which in turn exacerbated party fragmentation. With coalition governments the rule, the multiparty system itself contributed to multifactionalism because of tactical competition and because of the ongoing tendency to resurrect and manipulate ideological differences. These conditions extended into the early years of the Fifth Republic. Consequently, factions were generally considered part of the debilitating instability which prevailed in France, especially during the 1950s.

More realistically, however, while factionalism appeared to be an undesirable characteristic of the political system from the standpoint of policy outputs, at the same time it probably prolonged the survival of that system. Until there occurred a basic evolution in the social and economic conditions which were the fundamental causes of political fragmentation, no other institutional structure was seriously conceivable. Thus, factional politics helped to hold together the fragmented political system of the Third and Fourth republics.

THE GAULLIST BREAKTHROUGH, 1958–1968

The usual image of the Fifth Republic is one of unchallenged Gaullist domination and an ineffective, divided opposition of the center and the left. In fact, however, the reality is considerably more complex than the image: there were many changes in political alignments between 1958 and 1977, both in the Gaullist movement and in the opposition parties. Some of these changes were the results of intraparty developments, some resulted from constitutional changes, and some were the consequences of the subtle socioeconomic and psychological developments which had begun even during the Fourth Republic.

The restructuring of the French political system occasioned by the de Gaulle presidency was the major factor in altering factional activity among political elites during the 1960s. Even so, the changing political conditions were relatively slow to make themselves felt both in interparty bargaining and in intraparty competition. For the non-Communist left, both tactical and ideological considerations inhibited rapid adaptation to the domination of the political system by the strong Gaullist movement. Gaullism had a profound effect on all French political parties. The success of the Gaullist movement was a challenge to the parties, which were compelled to adjust in order to compete in a newly structured political atmosphere where winning the majority was, after 1962, a prerequisite for a share of power.

Two distinct periods of de Gaulle's participation in the Fifth Republic are clearly distinguishable: 1958 to 1962, the onset of the Gaullist breakthrough, and 1962 to 1968, its consolidation. Initially, the political opposition to the Gaullists was confused and indecisive. Between 1958 and 1962 all French parties except the Gaullists, *l'Union pour la nouvelle République* ("Union for the New Republic"—UNR) plus the pro-Gaullist *Républicains indépendants* ("Independent Republicans—RI), and the Communists were badly divided by questions of the tactics and attitudes to be adopted toward the person of Charles de Gaulle.

The center parties (the center-right Independents, the Christian Democratic MRP, and the center-left Radicals) had been losing vigor since the 1950s. The inability of the center parties to define for themselves a viable role in the Fifth Republic was due partially to their internal structure and partially to their general loss of electoral support. Parties of notables and cadres, loosely organized and all with strong ties to the discredited Fourth Republic, were particularly prone to divisions in the face of a threatening political environment. Not so the Communists. Unhesitating in its opposition to de Gaulle, the Communist party (PCF) was the one French party with virtually no factionalism. The PCF prohibited factional activity and effectively banned "horizontal articulation" within its ranks. Such factional struggle as did exist was, to an extent even greater than found in other parties, an elite phenomenon.[5]

For the Socialists, the dilemma presented itself in a particularly sharp form. By the end of the Fourth Republic, the SFIO was badly on the defensive. Unable to compete with its Communist rival either in terms of party membership or of electoral strength, it retreated to outmoded Socialist slogans and political opportunism, while compromising its idelogical legitimacy with conservative policies.[6] The SFIO made possible the de Gaulle government that terminated the Fourth Republic in 1958, but the party subsequently split over the question of de Gaulle's investiture. Key members left the party in the summer and fall of 1958 to join the "new left" movement and the PSU.[7] While his party was dividing on the issue, party leader Guy Mollet and three other Socialist leaders remained in de Gaulle's cabinet until January 1959. But this opportunism failed to pay off, as the SFIO dropped from 93 seats to 44 seats in the National Assembly in the 1958 elections, the first of the Fifth Republic. Support for de Gaulle had not succeeded either in winning for the SFIO a place of influence with the government or in creating for the SFIO a role as the center of an effective opposition. On the contrary, it has simply accelerated division within party ranks.

The period from 1962 to 1968 was a time of the consolidation of the institutions of the Fifth Republic in France, and of de Gaulle's position in the republic. In those six years, with Gaullist strength flaunted in the referendum on the direct election of the president of the republic, the non-Gaullist parties sought to accommodate themselves to the new reality of a powerful president backed by a seemingly impenetrable majority in the National Assembly. The resolution of the Algerian conflict and the constitutional amendment for direct election of the president by universal suffrage changed the political calculations of the first years of the republic.

The emergence of a strong and united Gaullist party in the 1962 National Assembly elections resulted in further confusion of the non-Communist left and the center. The Gaullists had captured 213 seats; their closest rival, the SFIO, won 63. The Socialists had been slow to perceive the impact of a popularly elected president. Ultimately, however, it was precisely the necessity of finding a nationally acceptable candidate for the presidency which forced the SFIO to make a commitment with other parties to support a common candidate. When Socialist Gaston Defferre attempted his "Grand Federation" of the left and center in the mid-1960s, it did appear that a broad non-Communist opposition might be successful[8]

However, the minority which supported Defferre's presidential aspirations was not well defined within the SFIO. It was, for all intents and purposes, a center-left interparty *tendance.* One of the reasons for its eventual failure was precisely that it threatened the traditional party structures and elites, especially in the SFIO and the MRP. Ironically, the Defferre effort diminished factions within the Radical party, as members no longer had to choose between a coalition with the center or with the left. (When, years later, the Socialist-Communist coalition was sealed, one of the immediate casualties was the Radical party, which split openly over the question of signing the coalition *Programme Commun* ["Common Program"].) At the same time, Defferre's proposals tended to polarize the MRP, where many Christian Democrats had qualms about joining with a professed Marxist party. In other words, whether the SFIO chose to look left or right for its allies, it could not avoid further factionalizing the center. Likewise, whether the center parties or the Communist party put pressure on the Socialists, that pressure was conducive to intraparty divisions within the SFIO. Thus, in practice, Defferre's Grand Federation proved an impossibility. It was during this period, between 1962 and 1965, that it became clear that opposition politics would be a long-term feature of the Fifth Republic.

The Socialists' erosion of will persisted until 1969. Because the SFIO was organizationally weak—a weakness born of and further contributing to factionalism—it could not accept a unified strategy with the stronger Communist party. Most of those who strongly favored such a strategy had left the party over the Algerian crisis and Guy Mollet's support of de Gaulle. Consequently there was no faction which was both organizationally and ideologically prepared to take the initiative in coalition-building with the PCF. In effect, then, a further result of Gaullist domination was the preeminence of the moderate, depolarizing faction within the SFIO, particularly during 1962–1965.[9]

In mid-1965, however, when Defferre's effort to build his Grand Federation with the center failed, the initiative shifted to a faction preferring an SFIO-PCF alliance. François Mitterand, who was himself not an SFIO member, became for the first time the presidential candidate of the "united left." In 1966 the PCF and the SFIO reached an accord for mutual *désistement* ("withdrawal of candidates") on the second ballot of the 1967 parliamentary elections. Finally as the Socialists began to move away from the center and toward the left, a series of events took place which significantly altered the picture of French politics, and dramatically stepped up the restructuring of the French left and the emergence of the bipolar pattern of political competition.

FACTIONALISM AND BIPOLARIZATION

A new period of the Fifth Republic began with the watershed events of 1968 and 1969. In 1968 the country suffered massive civil disturbances and strikes, which were followed by new assembly elections; and in 1969 France was faced with a presidential ultimatum and resignation, then with presidential elections to replace de Gaulle. In this period the UNR was restructured, and there was a major reorganization of the non-Communist left. These developments opened a new period of political activity, with the fairly clear emergence of the bipolarization pattern. By the 1970s the French political system appeared to be moving toward "mature" status as an industrial democracy,[10] and a new importance had come to factions in building bridges among and within parties, and importance at least as great as they had had earlier in dividing parties.

The total reorganization of the Socialist party, beginning in 1969, was the spark for the political shifts which took place in the post–de Gaulle period. The new party took the name *Parti socialiste* ("Socialist Party"—PS) in 1971. Its organization made possible its alliance with the Communists, by committing itself to an all-out effort to expand and to enhance its national electoral appeal. One of the reorganizational devices chosen for that effort was factionalism. Factionalism in the new PS was part of the structural arrangements by which the party hoped to reinvigorate its membership and broaden its base, through the amalgamation of many independent Socialist groups. It signaled a tacit recognition of the polarization which was occurring in the French political system as a whole, and it was indicative of the commitment of party leaders to exploit bipolarity for the benefit of the Socialists and of the left in general.

According to the statutes adopted by the PS in 1971 at the Congress of Socialist Unity, at Épinay-sur-Seine, minority political views had the right to be proportionally represented in party congresses and in executive bodies at both the departmental and the national levels. Using the mechanism of proposing comprehensive policy resolutions which, if adopted, would define the official positions of the party, leaders of each political faction presented their resolutions to the departmental federations and sections prior to the convening of the national congress. The votes of delegates to the congress then represented the proportional strength of these factions within their departments. Candidates to party executive bodies were elected on the basis of the proportion of votes received by their resolutions. Any minority had to receive at least 5 percent of the total delegate vote to be represented in the executive bodies of the party.[11]

The congress at Épinay was the culmination of several years of efforts to bring together in one party all the parties and groups sharing similar ideologies and falling in the broad spectrum of social democracy. The original core membership of the PS came from the SFIO. Around it was grouped the *Convention des Institutions républicaines* ("Convention of Republican Institutions"—CIR), headed by François Mitterrand, and a plethora of study groups and political clubs. Not included were the extreme left—from the Maoists to the PSU—and the center-left, represented by the Radical Socialists. The structural task of the PS leadership was to hold together this diverse union, all the while strengthening the party's roots and creating a national image and

148   Bruce A. Campbell and Sue Ellen M. Charlton

membership competitive with that of the PCF.[12] It was assumed that
the role of organized minority political views within the party would
gradually become marginal, thus reducing the chance of sparking the
kinds of cleavages which had traditionally plagued the Socialist left. In
fact, the composition of minority factions changed after 1971, but they
continued to exist; and in the fall of 1974, the PS undertook still
another major campaign to enlarge its base—a campaign which, if
successful, would further contribute to the importance of intraparty
factions.

At Épinay, five of the general policy resolutions presented received sufficient votes for election of their supporters to the Executive
Committee of the party (see Table 1): one supported by Alain Savary
and Guy Mollet, which won twenty-eight of eighty-one Executive Committee seats; one represented by Jean Poperen (ten seats); one headed
by Pierre Mauroy and Gaston Defferre (twenty-three seats); the Mermaz-Pontillion resolution, which brough together Mitterand and CIR
leaders (thirteen seats); and the resolution of the *Centre d'études, de
recherches et d'éducation socialistes* (CERES) group. For the purposes of
determining both a viable Executive Committee majority and who
would be the titular head of the party, the factions coalesced around
two policy resolutions: one which came to be the party line (the official

Table 1. Factional Representation in Socialist Party Executive Bodies

Faction	Executive Committee	Secretariat
Épinay congress, 1971		
Mauroy-Defferre	23	3
Mermaz-Pontillion (with Mitterand)	13	5
CERES	7	2
majority total	43	10
Savary-Mollet	28	0
Poperen	10	0
minority total	38	0
total	81	10
Grenoble congress, 1973		
Mitterand (with Mauroy, Defferre, Savary, Mermaz, and Pontillion)	54	10
CERES	17	3
majority total	71	13
Bataille socialiste (Mollet, Fuzier)	6	0
Poperen	4	0
minority total	10	0
total	81	13

"Majority"), in the name of Mitterand, and the other (the official "Minority") in the name of Savary. The majority was thus formed by bringing together the Mauroy-Defferre group of former SFIO leaders, the Mermaz-Pontillion group and the CIR group, plus CERES. This Épinay majority gathered around the leadership of Mitterand, who became the party's first leader; on the Executive Committee, the majority controlled forty-three seats, and it dominated all ten of the positions on the party secretariat. The minority was composed of the Savary and Mollet and Poperen groups; it controlled thirty-eight Executive Committee seats, but was excluded from the secretariat by the majority. In fact, the difference between the majority and the minority was slight at the Épinay congress: while Mitterand became party secretary with majority support of the Executive Committee, his Majority represented only 48.5 percent of the Congress votes, over 46 percent for Savary's Minority.

The internal structure of the PS was thus marked by officially recognized factions. The reconciliation—or balancing—of these factions was the job of the first leader of the new party, François Mitterand. It was this structure that made the expanded PS possible, by amalgamating the most important parties and groups of the non-Communist left. The original factions represented different power bases, varying political priorities and tactics, and, in some cases, different ideological orientations. Of the ideological issues contributing to factionalism, the two most important were worker *autogestion* ("self-management") and foreign policy—specifically European integration.

At its second national congress, at Grenoble, in June 1973, four factions' spokesmen won representation on the party's Executive Committee: the core of the party leadership, including the Mitterand, Mauroy, Defferre, Savary, Mermaz, and Pontillion groups, winning fifty-four seats; CERES, winning seventeen seats and again joining with Mitterand in the party's official Majority, with a total of seventy-one seats; the Mollet and Fuzier groups, identified by the banner *Bataille socialiste,* winning six seats and joined in the official Minority by the Poperen group, with four seats. At the 1973 congress, Savary joined the Mitterand majority, while Mollet saw his influence reduced to a level of 5 percent or less of the congress votes—as did Poperen. At the same time, the coalition around Mitterand and the Majority had increased its strength in the party's representation tremendously, and even CERES had more than doubled its strength from 1971.

At the Grenoble congress, the secretariat was enlarged from ten to thirteen offices. While the composition of the Executive Committee followed closely the rule of proportional representation from the congresses, the secretariat was appointed by Mitterand, and included only leaders of the factions which had supported the majority motion.

The largest and most interesting of the minor factions in the PS was CERES. CERES originated in the 1960s, as a study group which brought together intellectuals and long-time party militants from the left, who were interested in exchanging ideas, plans, and strategies for uniting the left.[13] The "young Turks" of the reorganizing Socialists, they captured control of the Paris federation between 1969 and 1971 and, after Epinay, constituted the dynamic left wing of the PS.

While many Socialist leaders had long been associated with non-party clubs or study groups, generally these groups met so irregularly that they could not be categorized as intraparty pressure groups or organized factions at all. CERES was an exception. With a newsletter and a monthly journal of its own and a leadership drawn both from former SFIO and PSU members, its followers became so influential on the departmental level of the party organization that charges were raised that it constituted a "party within a party." From about 8 percent of the party delegates at Épinay, CERES grew to about 20 percent at Grenoble and 25 percent of the party delegates in 1975.

In October 1974, when the National Assize of Socialism was held to explore the possibility for an even more broadly based party, CERES served as a useful communication link with PSU representatives and with members of the *Confédération française démocratique du travail* ("Democratic Confederation of French Labor"—CFDT) trade union movement, who shared similar ideological interpretations of the necessity for worker *autogestion*.[14]

The existence of recognized factions within the PS constituted a potential threat to party unity, or at least an inherent source of weakness. The factions maneuvered for influence in party organization bodies and served as a continuous reminder of the potential for fragmentation. At the same time, however, the factions were a source of intraparty democracy. They ensured—as much as any party structure could ensure—a confrontation of theses and policies among party activists at the level of the national party federation and of the local party sections, as well as within the party's Executive Committee and other agencies.

Under the Fifth Republic, the term *Gaullism* implied a heterogeneity of parties, associated organizations, and small groups. When the umbrella party of Gaullism, the UNR, was created in October 1958, it institutionalized many of the sources of future factionalism within the party. The single unifying factor of these groups was a loyalty to the person of Charles de Gaulle and, in a less precise sense, to Gaullist ideals. The constituent groups of the UNR brought with them different organizational histories, diverse policy priorities, and, above all, conflicting personal loyalties—other than that to the General.[15] The

UNR's confederative effort presaged the similar experience within the Socialist party at the time of its 1969–1971 renaissance. Clientele politics and policy conflicts (notably over Algeria) defined UNR factions in much the same way that preexisting personal loyalties and ideological differences would draw factional lines in the PS a dozen years later. The result for the UNR was a two-year period of internal power struggles, from 1958 to 1960, with the old "historic Gaullists," who had personal ties with de Gaulle dating from World War II, dominating the party executive—men such as André Malraux, Michel Debré, Edmond Michelete, and Roger Frey.

The Gaullist party underwent several changes during the 1960s, changes which reduced the role of the first-generation Gaullists, but which did not eliminate their personal prestige within the party. The inherent contradictions within the party structure, which ultimately produced the factionalism of the early 1970s, persisted during this period. Until 1962, the old-guard Gaullists controlled the UNR executive. Gradually, after 1962, largely through a process of attrition, they became a minority.

During the years 1962 to 1968, internal politics in the UNR revolved around the question of "normalizing" Gaullism: institutionalizing the popular support for de Gaulle in the presidential elections and referenda into support for the UNR as a political party. In essence, this meant developing the party infrastructure, especially in regions where there was strong popular support for de Gaulle, and preparing the party for the post–de Gaulle era. In this effort, the UNR enjoyed a large measure of success. One study, for example, showed that the party was able to routinize the plebiscitarian mode of mobilization used by de Gaulle in the referenda: between 1962 and 1967 there was an increasing correlation between support for the Gaullist party and Gaullist support in the referenda and presidential elections.[16]

Partially because of its constituent groups and partially because of the *national* mystique of Gaullism, the UNR became a mass, voter-oriented party—a party designed on the one hand to legitimize the power of de Gaulle within the presidential system and, on the other, to serve as the instrument of transition when the General would be gone. Gaullists gradually responded to the slow coalition-building on the left, as the Socialists and Communists themselves were responding to Gaullist domination. Eschewing restrictive dogma, the moderate pragmatists within the party pushed for enlarging the UNR's electoral base and for strengthening its internal structures. They successfully engineered a merger of the UNR with a small, left-oriented, Gaullist labor group, the *Union démocratique du travail* (UDT). Their efforts were symbolized by the renaming of the party, first in 1967, and again in 1968, to *l'Union des démocrates pour la République* ("Union of Democrats for the Republic"—UDR).

While Gaullist leaders had been trying since 1962 to regularize their movement, and were partially successful by the later 1960s, the origins and the depth of the restructuring process became a subject of some debate. Jean Charlot, for example, argued that the UNR in the mid-1960s was still basically a group of ministers and a parliamentary assemblage which activated itself only at election time. According to his analysis, change came largely as the result of a conscious decision made at the November 1967 UNR party conference at Lille. The March 1967 parliamentary elections had brought home the necessity of adequately preparing the party for the post–de Gaulle period. As result, the party underwent major organizational change: it strengthened its regional links and inaugurated new communication channels designed to reinvigorate party activists.[17]

A second view held that the transformation of the parliamentary majority into a majority party was a more gradual process and was manifested in the 1967 elections. Between 1962 and 1967, the UNR had moved into de Gaulle's bastions in the rural northeast, inner west, and Massif Central. In this interpretation, the 1967 internal party changes were more properly regarded as after-the-fact adaptations to the new electoral situation.[18]

A third interpretation attributed the 1967 reorganization to the demands from within the Gaullist family for greater internal freedom of action in the movement. In addition, the party was responding to the demands of Valéry Giscard d'Estaing that the government modify the "blocked vote" rule, which obliged deputies to vote for or against an entire bill without considering it article by article. Giscard had made it clear that he wanted more influence for his Independent Republicans.[19] In this view, reorganization was designed to satisfy the complaints of some members within the party (notably the left wing), while also more clearly differentiating the UNR/UDR from its intramovement rivals.

Although this restructuring did, in some respects, contribute to intraparty democracy, it also encouraged further fragmentation, as it threatened both the power and ideology of the veterans. One result, for example, was the founding in 1969 of a new Gaullist association by Michel Debré, Pierre Messmer, and Louis Joxe, devoted to defending the spirit of "a precise image of France developed by General deGaulle. . . ."[20]

By the beginning of the current period of the Fifth Republic (post-1968), factionalism in the Gaullist movement had been somewhat clarified, if not diminished. The successor legitimacy of Georges Pompidou after 1969 was generally unchallenged, but under this symbol of Gaullist unity, the movement consisted of several levels: the majority coalition of Gaullist parties, dominated by the UDR and including Giscard's Independent Republicans and the *Centre démocratie et progrès* ("Democratic and Progressive Center"—CDP); *tendances* and factions within these parties, especially in the UDR; and numerous parallel organizations, from the *Nouvelle frontière* ("New Frontier"), representing leftist Gaullists, to special interest groups for youth and women.

The death of Georges Pompidou in 1974 and the resultant maneuvers within the Gaullist movement demonstrated the extent to which factionalism persisted. Long-time leaders and prominent personalities within the elite of the party cadre and within the parliamentary group consolidated their positions; several moved to bid for the presidency in the ensuing campaign. Personal differences were reinforced by the problem of tactics to be adopted regarding the presidential candidacy of Giscard. The numerous personal and tactical conflicts took place in the context of long-standing ideological differences among Gaullists. Organizationally, these many overlapping tendencies remained ill-defined, as there were no organizational provisions for proportional representation of factions in the governing bodies of the UDR comparable to those found in the Socialist party.

Table 2 illustrates these varied sources of factionalism in the UDR after the death of Pompidou. Many of the party's most outstanding factions were basically groups of followers of some half dozen or more prominent personalities within the party. A number of these had from time to time been prominent government ministers and several— Debré, Couve de Murville, Chaban-Delmas, and Messmer—had been premier. Besides the party's prominent personalities, there remained

Table 2. Sources of UDR Factionalism, 1974

I. *Personality—prominent party leaders*
Michel Debré
Pierre Messmer
Olivier Guichard
Maurice Couve de Murville
Jacques Chaban-Delmas
Edgar Faure

II. *Ideology—programmatic, ideological tendencies*
Gaullist traditionalism (Debré)
Gaullist "pragmatic" moderationism (Chaban-Delmas)
Gaullist leftism (Jean Charbonnel)

III. *Structure—potential UDR organizational bases*
party cadre (UDR secretary-general: Alexander Sanguinetti)
parliamentary group (*groupe* president: Claude Labbé)

IV. *Tactics—responses to Giscard candidacy and government*
active support (Jacques Chirac)
moderate cooperation
firm reserve (Charbonnel)

several ideological strains within Gaullism, which also formed the basis of poorly defined *tendances* in the UDR. These ranged from conservative Gaullist traditionalism and pragmatism (represented by Chaban-Delmas) to left-wing Gaullism. The left wing included intellectual leftists as well as labor-oriented leftists, such as remnants of the old UDT. Party organization provided little structural distinction for potential factions, because factional representation was not officially recognized within the party. Nonetheless, one could distinguish the organization cadre of the "regular" UDR, under the leadership of the then party secretary-general, Alexander Sanguinetti, from the UDR parliamentary *groupe,* under the presidency of Claude Labbé.

Finally, the experience of the party in the aftermath of Pompidou's death and during the presidential elections of 1974 illustrates the problem of tactical response to Giscard's successful bid to capture the leadership of the Gaullist movement. For the UDR, the development of its relationship with the RI was as important for internal UDR factionalism as the evolution of the Socialists' relations with the Communists was for internal factionalism in the Socialist party. Initially, a succession of hopeful "heirs apparent" to Pompidou surfaced in the UDR: Edgar Faure, Pierre Messmer, and finally, Jacques Chaban-Delmas. Giscard defeated them all by the end of the first round of presidential balloting, leaving the UDR torn between bitterness and the need to rally behind Giscard against the Socialist candidate, Mitterand, on the second ballot.

The divisions within the UDR continued as the victorious Giscard formed his government and invited many UDR leaders to accept cabinet posts. Tactical factionalism in the UDR caused by Giscard had not abated, with some Gaullists jumping at the opportunity to support the new president (led by Jacques Chirac, former minister of agriculture and Giscard's newly appointed premier); some willing to proffer moderate support and cooperation in the interest of the Gaullist cause; and some believing that the UDR should maintain its distance from the Giscard government. This last group included both those who, like Jean Charbonnel, feared that cooperation with the RI would pull the UDR farther to the right, and others who were simply bitter about the man who had defeated all the UDR candidates.[21]

The problem of the Giscard presidency exemplifies the effects of a threatening environment for the UDR. For the first time in the Fifth Republic, the president was not also the de facto head of the largest Gaullist party. The UDR was no longer *the* majority; it was the majority *within* the majority, and it became more important than ever to differentiate the UDR from the government.[22] While the ranks of UDR elites generally tended toward support of Giscard and the Chirac cabinet, much bitterness remained; later in 1974, divisions were reaffirmed in National Assembly debates on constitutional revision.[23] Moreover,

Charbonnel of the Gaullist left launched a major controversy by calling for depolarization and exploratory talks with the center and left;[24] meanwhile, party Secretary-General Sanguinetti was urging transformation of the UDR into a *rassemblement démocratique populaire* ("popular democratic rally").[25]

Sanguinetti's call for a transformed Gaullist movement produced no results in 1974. But by 1975, the inherent tension between the UDR and the RI surfaced again in a controversy over the government's economic and fiscal policies. After the two protagonists in the conflict, President Giscard (RI) and Prime Minister Chirac (UDR), failed to resolve their differences, Chirac resigned, in August 1976. Chirac subsequently devoted himself to consolidating his role as leader of a rejuvenated Gaullist movement. Clearly, his objective was to reverse the post-1974 situation when the UDR ceased to be, by itself, *the* majority and the sole claimant to legitimacy on the right. To realize this objective, Chirac used two tactics: reinvigoration of the party grass roots, and reduction of factionalism among the party elites. The symbol of this transformation was the renaming of the UDR to the *Rassemblement pour la République* ("Rally for the Republic"—RPR) in December 1976.

Chirac's determination to run against Giscard's candidate in the race for mayor of Paris in 1977 further clarified his strategy in the face of the increasing bipolarization of French politics, and the consequent competition for leadership of the divided right. Fundamental reorganization of the right, he maintained, was essential to prevent a leftist victory in the 1978 legislative elections. In view of the threat from the Union of the Left, the government's division and lack of direction would be an invitation to leftist victory. Under these circumstances, bipolarization meant that factionalism on the right would be disastrous. Only the new RPR, and specifically the leadership of Chirac, could forestall this eventuality.

Conclusions

The major restructuring of the French political system occasioned by the de Gaulle presidency was the most salient feature in the shift of factional activity during the 1960s. Nonetheless, changing political conditions were relatively slow to make themselves felt in interparty bargaining and intraparty competition. The case of the non-Communist left showed that both tactical and ideological considerations inhibited rapid adaptation to the domination of the political system by the strong Gaullist movement. Predictably, the shifts of opinion at the level of the mass electorate were even more tentative and subject to sudden reversals, such as in 1968. However, by the 1970s, the evidence was clear that the changing conditions which first made their appear-

ance during the Fourth Republic were contributing to a gradual bipolarization, which persisted, in spite of some shifts and reversals,
throughout the Fifth Republic. This bipolarization, in turn, was reflected in significant changes in party and factional politics.

On the left, efforts at consolidation by Socialists and Communists
began in earnest in 1967. The major reorganization of the Socialist
party, including an explicit "opening to the left," occurred at the
Épinay conference in 1971. This move was sealed by the *Programme
Commun* of 1972, and by the subsequent cooperation between the PS
and PCF in the parliamentary elections of 1973, the presidential campaign of 1974, and the municipal elections of 1977. These moves at
the elite level were related to both the growing strength of the left and
the increased willingness to bind old wounds.

Moreover, as we have seen, the factional structure facilitated the
very creation of the PS. This structure enabled the party to represent
much of the diversity of the non-Communist left; it acted as a mechanism through which additional groups could be brought into the fold;
and it was a vehicle for establishing ties with potential members or
allies outside of the party organization. Factions, in other words, while
indicative of the diversity of the constituent groups of the PS and of
the party's potential instability, were also a sign of its dynamism. They
permitted the party to enlarge its base and thereby strengthen itself
vis-à-vis the Communist party. At the same time, they both reflected
and contributed to the ongoing left-right polarization in French politics.

On the right, the situation was different: for the Gaullists the
problem was not to build a coalition but to keep one. Their watershed
year was 1958, when the accession of General de Gaulle to the presidency brought the majority coalition into being. As Wilson has noted,
however, this was not really a party but a social movement with a
charismatic leader.[26] The problem of building an institutional structure was not really confronted until 1967, when the threat of a united
left first materialized in an electoral coalition, and the prospect of de
Gaulle's ultimate departure loomed large. As we have seen, the Gaullist coalition consisted of numerous groups—at least three major ones
and several smaller ones, totaling perhaps thirty. The principal labor
of Georges Pompidou, both as prime minister and as president, was
to reform the party and create a structure which would bind together
all elements of the Gaullist movement. We have also seen that he was
not entirely successful. The party split over the 1972 referendum on
European integration, and, most obviously, the election of Giscard in
1974 handed the movement's most powerful office to the minority
Independent Republican faction.

The bipolarized political situation, however, forced the Gaullists
to emulate the Socialist rejuvenation of 1969–1971. In 1977, it was too

soon to tell if factionalism might serve the same creative function for the RPR that it had for the PS. Chirac's immediate concern, in fact, in forcing the renaming of the UDR and in pushing for party reorganization was to eliminate factionalism within the party. To this end, he skillfully exploited two external "enemies": Giscard on the right and the Communists on the left.

Contemporary French politics presents an unusual case in which factionalism has played several roles. Factions traditionally have both resulted from and contributed to France's multiparty structure, especially in the Third and Fourth republics. The Fifth Republic, however, has represented a political system in transition to a relatively polarized party structure. The system is based on a peculiar duality of parliamentary and presidential constitutional arrangements. Had the Constitution of the Fifth Republic been introduced in the absence of Charles de Gaulle and without the profound postwar economic and social changes which occurred in France, its impact undoubtedly would have been more limited than it was. But taken together, these changes produced a gradual, if erratic, movement toward bipolarization.

Under the new conditions of political competition in the Fifth Republic, factions have continued, but their purposes and source have changed somewhat. While factionalism persisted in its most traditional manner within the Gaullist movement, within the *Parti socialiste* it served increasingly as a bridge in the party's efforts to broaden its membership base. Factions were perceived as a way of both responding to and encouraging bipolarization.

It is perhaps ironic that, at least in the short run, Gaullist factionalism may facilitate realization of the Socialists' objectives. In the long run, however, any disintegration of the right, accompanied as it would be by at least a temporary resurgence of the center, might provoke dysfunctional factionalism within the PS, as conservative Socialists once again felt the attractions of the center's "siren song." Thus the picture is still hazy, even after nearly twenty years of the Fifth Republic. Nevertheless, for probably the first time since the founding of the Third Republic, factionalism has played a catalytic role in the evolution of new types of political competition in France.

The Fifth Republic is unique also in that factions have performed multiple roles and have taken multiple forms. Most writers have treated factions as subunits of existing political parties, whose major function is to compete for goals within the structure of the party. Seen in this way, factions can only lead to a breakdown of large parties, along the lines predicted by Riker.[27] Faction, in other words, is understood as leading to a splintering of political forces. To be sure, there is good reason to believe that such a dynamic exists in French politics today. The right, which de Gaulle cemented together through sheer willpower and the skillful use of political events, is today confronting this divisive tendency of faction.

There is quite another interpretation of the function of factions, however. William Chambers, a historian, takes the view that factions appear at a certain stage in the growth of a political party.[28] The faction is a "political embryo," an expression of like-mindedness which allows old divisions to be bridged and diverse groups to coalesce into the final party structure. On the French left, both the divisive function and the bridging function can be found. Factions within a party may make it easier or more difficult to engage in coalition-building with other parties. For example, factions within the Socialist party may weaken its internal structure, with the result that party leaders are less willing to make binding commitments with the stronger Communist party. On the other hand, a faction which crosses party lines may facilitate the recruitment of party members or even an amalgamation of two or more parties. As we have seen, the existence of the CERES faction within the Socialist party constituted a drawing card for the small Unified Socialist party (PSU).

In sum, the ambiguity of faction arises from the transitional nature of French politics. On the one hand, the institutions of the Fifth Republic, particularly that of a popularly elected and powerful president, have forced party leaders to recognize the benefits of broad and durable partisan coalitions. On the other hand, the quasi-parliamentary system still found in France continues to exacerbate the problem of legislative majorities and cabinet compositions. Even after the 1973 elections to the National Assembly, which revealed the continuing trend toward electoral polarization (further reinforced in the 1974 presidential election), it was clear that no single party could win a legislative majority. Hence, there is no assurance that the process of bipolarization is irreversible. Factionalism in the divisive sense remains an attractive alternative in legislative politics. However, the nature of faction is changing. Factions are less rooted in long-standing historical divisions in the political culture and are more responsive to different personal and organizational styles. Above all, factions are more responsive to the radically changed institutional structures and bipolarized political competion of the Fifth Republic. The power equation has changed and the cleavage structure has changed, leading to a reformulation of both the function and structure of faction in France.

NOTES

1. By *bipolarization* we do not mean radicalization. Rather the term refers simply to a movement away from a fragmentation of political power and toward a concentration into two broad poles, neither of which is necessarily at the end of any political continuum. If anything, this bipolarization has meant a deradicalization of French political competition, as we shall discuss.

2. Bruce A. Campbell, "On the Prospects of Polarization in the French Electorate," *Comparative Politics* 8, no. 2 (Jan. 1976): 272–90; and Campbell, "The Future of the Gaullist Majority: An Analysis of French Electoral Politics," *American Journal of Political Science* 18, no. 1 (Feb. 1974): 67–94.

3. Maurice Duverger, *Political Parties: Their Organization and Activity in the Modern State,* trans. Barbara and Robert North (New York: John Wiley and Sons, 1954), p. 120.

4. In neither case, however, was the dissidence unitary—i.e., the opposition to the secretary-general, Guy Mollet, was not homogeneous. Those who left the SFIO did so because of an accumulation of grievances over several years, and not all joined the PSU. Duncan MacRae, Jr., *Parliament, Parties and Society in France, 1946–1958* (New York: St. Martin's Press, 1967), pp. 290–91.

5. See Duverger, *Political Parties,* pp. 47–50, on vertical and horizontal links within parties. The two most complete sources on the internal structure and politics of the PCF are: Annie Kriegel, *Les Communistes français* (Paris: Editions du Seuil, 1970); and Ronald Tiersky, *Politely Awaiting the Revolution: French Communism 1920–1972* (New York: Columbia Univ. Press, 1973). François Fejtó has discussed some internal PCF changes contributing to greater diversity of opinion, although not factionalism: *The French Communist Party and the Crisis of International Communism* (Cambridge: MIT Press, 1967), pp. 165–76.

6. See the analysis by Charles A. Micaud in *Communism and the French Left* (New York: Praeger, 1963), pp. 200–15. Competition with the Communist party was all the more difficult because the PCF was not factionalized.

7. Most participated in the creation of the PSA (*Parti socialiste autonome*), forerunner of the PSU. Daniel Ligou, *Histoire de socialisme en France, 1871–1961* (Paris: Presses universitaires de France, 1962), pp. 625–26.

8. For a thorough discussion of Defferre's efforts, see Frank L. Wilson, *The French Democratic Left, 1963–1969: Toward a Modern Party System* (Stanford: Stanford Univ. Press, 1971), pp. 108–34.

9. Duncan MacRae has observed that during the Fourth Republic, Socialists tended to lean in the direction of the stronger neighboring party—e.g., a strong Communist organization in the district exerted an ideological appeal on Socialist deputies; where the Socialist and/or center influence was stronger, the attraction was to the right. Put differently, on the local level a threatening political environment did not encourage the emergence of an opposition faction within the SFIO. MacRae, *Parliament, Parties and Society in France,* pp. 292–93.

10. Harvey Waterman described this phenomenon as it developed during the 1960s in *Political Change in Contemporary France: The Politics of an Industrial Democracy* (Columbus, Ohio: Charles E. Merrill, 1969).

11. *Statuts (du Parti socialiste)*, supplement to *Bulletin socialiste*, no. 320 (Paris: Parti socialiste, 1971), arts. 15, 16.

12. An excellent analysis of the internal structure of the PS and the progress made in increasing its strength may be found in Vincent Wright and Howard Machin, "The French Socialist Party in 1973: Performance and Prospects," *Government and Opposition* 9, no. 2 (Spring 1974): 123–45.

13. "Le CERES qu'est-ce que c'est?" *Volonté socialiste* (Bulletin du CERES), no. 30 (Oct.–Nov. 1972): 1.

14. See the extensive discussion of the assize in *Le Monde*, Oct. 15, 1974.

15. Jean Charlot, *L'Union pour la nouvelle République: étude du pouvoir au sein d'un parti politique*, Cahiers de la Fondation nationale des Sciences politiques, no. 153 (Paris: Armand Colin, 1967), pp. 29–38.

16. David R. Cameron and Richard I. Hofferbert, "Continuity and Change in Gaullism: The General's Legacy," *American Journal of Political Science* 17, no. 1 (Feb. 1973): 77–98.

17. Jean Charlot, *The Gaullist Phenomenon: The Gaullist Movement in the Fifth Republic*, trans. Monica Charlot and Marianne Neighbor (London: George Allen and Unwin, 1974), pp. 92–95. Charlot also argues, however, that neither the UNR nor its successor, UDR, was able to win over local notables and build up a really strong national core of party activists (pp. 63–64). This problem was exacerbated by the fact that the UDR experienced a sudden influx of voters and members in reaction to 1968 events. This meant that the UDR was prone to comparatively unstructured factions fueled by personality differences.

18. Cameron and Hofferbert, "Continuity and Change in Gaullism," p. 94.

19. Lowell G. Noonan, *France: The Politics of Continuity in Change* (New York: Holt, Rinehart and Winston, 1970), pp. 223–24.

20. Charlot, *Gaullist Phenomenon*, p. 97.

21. See the description by two journalists of the traumatic weeks surrounding the death of Pompidou and Giscard's election: Michel Bassi and André Campana, *Le Grand tournoi: Naissance de la vie république* (Paris: Grasset, 1974), pp. 73–101.

22. The problem of differentiating the UDR as a political party from the government (and its policies) did not originate with Giscard's election. It was inherent in the construction of the UNR early in the Fifth Republic and in de Gaulle's refusal to engage in internal party and coalition matters. See Frank L. Wilson, "Gaullism without de Gaulle," *Western Political Quarterly* 26, no. 3 (Sept. 1973): 488–94.

23. *Le Monde*, Oct. 12, 1974, and *l'Express*, Oct. 21–27, 1974.

24. Cf. Charbonnel's interview with *Le Monde*, Sept. 5, 1974.

25. *Le Monde*, Aug. 2, 1974.

26. Wilson, "Gaullism without de Gaulle," p. 486.

27. William Riker, *The Theory of Political Coalitions* (New Haven: Yale Univ. Press, 1962).

28. William Nisbet Chambers, *Political Parties in a New Nation: The American Experience, 1776–1809* (New York: Oxford Univ. Press, 1963).

7

Factionalism and Public Policy in India: The Vertical Dimension

Norman K. Nicholson

Analysis of factionalism typically centers on the problems of gaining power—power in political parties, in bureaucracies, in businesses, in churches, in villages. Factionalism is usually viewed as a malady of the political order because it is divisive and because it is irrational in that it tends to cloud the clear presentation of political choices. The critical questions in the study of factionalism, therefore, have been, How does it originate? and What are the strategies for political success and survival in factional politics? The former is the concern of anthropological accounts of factionalism—anthropologists being alarmed at the dissolution of village societies.[1] The latter concern—survival strategies—has stimulated the interest of political scientists.[2]

However, the current factional literature fails to discuss the impact of factionalized political arenas on the process of decision-making and on policy outcomes. This is because analyses of factionalism remain within the confines of the particular party, bureaucracy, or legislature under examination, and seldom extend to the interaction of factionalism with its political environment. While anthropologists have found that factionalized villages appear to lose their capacity for collective action and that factional politicians have a great capacity for turning public goods into quasi-public goods which can be appropriated by specific individuals, political scientists, who study policy process in

order to illuminate the struggle for power, have not asked what effect
the factionalized power structure has on policy. We know little about
typical patterns of policy- and decision-making which emerge from
factionalized political arenas, and almost nothing about whether there
are comparable patterns in different political contexts in which factionalism appears.

This study, therefore, will examine how factionalism interacts with
other, more institutionalized elements of the political order in the
policy process. The emphasis will be on changes which occur in the
impact of factionalism as one moves vertically from the local to the
national level. The analysis is based on the argument that increasing
scale in society is directly related to greater differentiation of social
organization. More complex political arenas demand more abstract
"media of exchange" and more generalized value structures, which
effect alterations in the process of social change.[3] Differentiation is
likely to produce a more complex elite structure at the national level
with functionally specialized elites competing, if not for power, at least
for autonomy. The concomitant process of "generalization" is likely
to make possible longer-term commitments based on class rather than
individual benefits characteristic of the factional order. Scale, complexity, and generalization place strong environmental demands on
factional politicians to exceed the limitations of factional politics and
to deal in a more generally acceptable currency than the personalism
of factional competition.

This is not to suggest that factionalism is altered by increasing
social scale—quite the contrary. Factionalism is recognizable as a distinct phenomenon at all levels in the political system and arises from
analogous causes at all levels. What alters is the *impact* of factionalism
as institutional constraints on it alter, resources change, and the perspectives of politicians are affected by the differentiation and multiplication of political roles. This chapter will attempt to clarify the
impact of scale on the factionalized decision-making process in a single
country—India; nevertheless, the hypothesized relationships invite
comparison with other systems.

One may discern certain common elements of factional arenas
and of the factional style of politics, and construct an ideal type of
"pure" factional politics.[4] In constructing this model we must specify
the structural, behavioral, and normative components if we are to
provide a comprehensive analysis of the phenomenon.[5]

Descriptions of the structure of factional politics usually present
a picture of confusing and unstable sets of alliances among a variety
of small political groups. The large number and small size of these
groups are characteristics of factionalism. Factional competition requires a number of autonomous but socially equivalent groups in-
teracting in a bargaining style. Factional competition, however, is

oligopolistic and the number of competitors seldom becomes so numerous as to approximate pluralist models of group interaction. Rather, the factional arena is a narrow one, the cost of entry is high, and the risks are great. These characteristics are in part produced by the intensity and viciousness of factional politics, which persuade most people to avoid direct participation, and in part by the personalistic nature of factional leadership. The factional leader depends heavily on his own resources and his own intense political motivation to succeed in politics, and exploits relationships and obligations which apply to him as an individual rather than to any organization of which he is a part. Only a few, therefore, are in a position to contest for factional leadership. The majority rest content in their dependence on the oligarchs.

Personalism, together with a bargaining style of politics, also limits the size of factional groups. Communications are restricted by the predisposition toward personal linkages. Political payoffs are never to a class of beneficiaries, but become direct exchanges between a leader and client. In addition to this organizational limitation on size there is a limitation occasioned by the economics of bargaining politics. A bargaining and personalistic politics is not majoritarian in its orientation. On the contrary, the logic of the system demands that one maintain the *minimum* coalition necessary to retain a claim to power. The factional leader is forced to maintain a delicate balance between obligations and resources, and the limits on size become more compelling in conditions of acute scarcity and in small homogeneous arenas where the demands of clients are undifferentiated.

The behavioral component of the factional model is invariably stated as a highly self-centered and intense drive for personal power and position. This description is not unique to factional arenas, and corresponds closely to Harold Lasswell's classic description of political motivation in *Psychopathology and Politics.* [6] Lasswell's democratic politician, however, was described as displacing his private motivations onto public objects. In other words, the politician's personal drives became justified and shaped by the causes and issues he espoused. In factional politics, in contrast, such identification with broader interests and long-term commitments to causes are singularly lacking. Issues and causes become the weapons of personal advancement, not social constraints on political behavior.

Political actors generally give evidence of a much more complex and varied motivational structure than the above suggests. A distinction must be made, however, between the motivational structure of the central core of factional leaders and that of their clients on the periphery. Clients are motivated to enter factional politics for a variety of reasons. Some require protection; others wish to advance themselves or their community. Conversely, the factional leader, with an always unstable political base and suffering from the limited authority of his brokerage role, is constantly searching for the means to tie clients to his faction. Friends, business associates, clansmen, neighbors, fellow parishioners, all may contribute to the faction leader's resource base. It is seldom, however, that factional leaders confuse these diverse interests of their clients with their own desire for power. Flexibility, ruthlessness, and betrayal are the common coin of factional politics. The successful factional politician can seldom afford the embarrassment of unbreakable commitments or irreconcilable enemies.[7] It is precisely this flexibility of factional leaders that has led some students of political change to suggest that the factional style is actually functional adaptive behavior in the modernization process. It is the flexibility and selfishness of the factional leader that permits him to adjust his alliances to changing times and power structures. He cuts across traditional cleavages and loyalties, ignores existing prejudices, and lends his political support shamelessly to the most rewarding of available political causes.[8]

Bernard Siegel and Alan Beals trace the origins of factionalism in villages to outside stress and internal strains on local institutions.[9] Such stress and strain tend to weaken village institutions, which in turn weaken authority patterns and bring established norms into question. Factional conflict, therefore, is generally associated with a period of normative confusion within the community. Unless limited by rules of an institutional environment (e.g., fictive kinship, party, or bureaucracy) or by independent concentrations of power (especially superior authority), factional politics tends to become amoral in the midst of a general normative collapse. Self-interest triumphs because the moral order provides no alternative context for orienting oneself toward events. Traditional institutions no longer predictably control the environment, and political power becomes the key to prestige, wealth, or any other value a politician might pursue. Political survival, which is to say power, becomes the only meaningful outcome of social conflict.

If such amorality is merely a passing phase and if, as suggested above, factional politics may indeed be functional in a period of rapid change, then there is no need for concern about the consequences of such behavior. Unfortunately, we have considerable evidence that factionalism may become established within a political system with the evolution of a "factional ethic." Examples of such an ethic can be found in Edward Banfield's "amoral familism" or Manning Nash's "Pon."[10] A narrowly defined family interest or the self-evident superiority of those the gods have blessed with power may, over time, serve to justify factional behavior. It is this persistence of factionalism beyond brief transitional periods, its capacity to corrupt institutional norms and procedures, its contribution to a widespread cynicism regarding the political order, that makes factionalism of particular concern to students of public policy. It is when factionalism is established as a parameter of the decision-making process that we must treat it as something more than a limiting case of political disorganization or as the limit of rational politics. We must now examine it as an inherent component of a more complex system and explain its interaction with other elements of that system.

Factionalism and Public Policy at the Village Level

Almost any study of politics at the village level in India relies on two major variables to explain the structure of conflict—caste and faction. Of the two, caste appears to be the more basic because it represents a traditional and established basis of social cleavage within the village community. There are, of course, lines of economic cleavage within the village community, but generally these parallel the caste divisions so that, for most analyses, caste can operate as a surrogate variable for class, although the substitution is not perfect. Caste has been important over the years as a political force precisely because it provides a social grouping within which economic interest, ritual status, and kinship ties overlap, providing a strong objective basis for organization and mobilization by the caste elders or *panchayat* ("caste council"). Not surprisingly, therefore, both anthropologists studying local politics and political scientists working with aggregate data find caste a useful variable in their analysis.

The politics of the village has generally been controlled by the leaders of the dominant landholding caste in the region. The landlords combined economic power and social prestige to dominate the village *panchayat* and reinforced this local power through their control over the village's contacts with the outside world—namely, the government administration. The rural policies of the Indian National Congress party when it came to power in 1947 have served to remove the largest of these landlords, who had been favored by the British colonial administration as a means of controlling the countryside and of collecting taxes, but have still left power locally in the hands of a substantial class/caste of "middle farmers." Thus when Indira Gandhi's policies were directed toward improving the lot of the agricultural laborers of the "untouchable" castes, the farmers' opposition is both a defense of their economic interests and of their social status.

However, while caste frequently provides the social basis of political organization in India's villages, faction has increasingly become the mechanism for mobilizing that social base and for structuring the conflict. The reason for this lies in the contemporary stresses and strains which have weakened the authority structures of the village and destroyed many of its traditional institutions. The social policy of the Congress party for years has been directed toward the improvement of the status of the "weaker sections of the rural communities"—the untouchable laborers. Concomitant with this goal has been the desire to provide tenants with more secure claims to the land and gradually to reduce average farm size in the interest of producing a more egalitarian rural community. These policies have not been a great success; but they have succeeded in making traditional forms of economic dependence unenforceable in law, and they have created within the landholding castes considerable anxiety concerning their own security of tenure. Thus, landlords prefer short-term contractual agreements with laborers and other dependents, and are cautious about traditional forms which tend to connote the existence of established rights in land and shares of the produce on the part of clients.[11]

Reinforcing the impact of the new laws, the increasing commercialization of agriculture has made most traditional economic relationships irrelevant to the production process. The traditional village economy was largely introverted and subsistence-oriented. Now the "progressive" farmer looks to the outside market for inputs to improve his productivity, for credit to finance his operations, and for buyers for his produce.

The interests of both the rich and the poor, therefore, now extend beyond the confines of the village social order. The poor are encouraged to challenge that order, while the rich wish to free themselves from its constraints and to integrate themselves in the broader community. For many years now, villages have been unable to contain these conflicts and strains, and local authority has been weakened, community solidarity has declined, and factional conflict appears to have grown apace.[12]

Political changes since independence have furthered the development of factionalism by providing a new arena for factional conflict and new rewards for successful competition. In an effort to decentralize power, democratize the village, and restore the integrity of the village community, the Indian government instituted in the 1950s a system of rural cooperatives designed to benefit small farmers, and instituted in the early 1960s a system of local government *(Panchayati Raj).*[13] These *panchayats* were to have judicial, public service, and, most important, development functions.

The new *panchayats,* however, are not analogues of the old village *panchayats.* The old *panchayats* reflected the existing status system— power was a consequence of economic and social prestige. In the new *panchayats,* in contrast, power is typically the *means* to status. Political power becomes the mechanism of individual social mobility or of securing a share of the development resources flowing from the government. Control of local government, and the access to local administration which it provides, is now critical to the farming community, as the government administration controls more and more of the key inputs in agricultural production—water, credit, fertilizer, seed, equipment. It is somewhat doubtful if *panchayat* leaders ever spoke for the whole community, as some enthusiasts of the old order argue, but it is clear that now they speak for themselves and their supporters, and that elite competition to control resources and opportunities has increased.

In this struggle for power the interests of the landholding community are essentially similar, but conflicting because they compete for the limited available resources. The logical strategy in such circumstances is for leaders within the farming community to build factions by seeking alliances among laborers and artisans. These represent groups whose interests do not place them in competition for the same rewards sought by the landholders but whose votes, in the new system of elected local government, provide a useful resource in the political struggle. In short, factional organization permits the leader to cross traditional lines of cleavage in order to fabricate viable coalitions.[14]

These factional leaders, however, lack any real authority within the village, although they clearly have power. Neither the new system of election nor the uses of power once elected serves to legitimize local *panchayat* leadership. Nor has the factional style provided any stable means of linking power groups with leaders and parties. On the contrary, village alliances and majorities are in a constant state of flux as group leaders maneuver for advantage and status. What has emerged is a network of highly pragmatic dyadic relationships between high-caste factional leaders and a series of clients. The dyad survives on a direct exchange of benefits without reference to other members of the coalition. Commitments are limited. The faction represents the minimal organizational response to the problem of electoral politics at the village level.

In the working of the *panchayat,* factional politics is a reasonably efficient means of distributing scarcity. Factionalized elections at the village level provide a means of restricting access to public resources. More specifically, factional politics at the local level is functionally specialized to the needs of what Theodore Lowi has termed "distributive" politics.[15] Factional politics divides the rural community and tends to dissipate its demands for improvement in administrative services, the supply of inputs, alterations in government market regulations, or access to high-status jobs. The factional politician contents himself with winning a share of the available resources for his clients and a share of public offices for himself.

The unstable political base of the factional leader at the village level makes him highly dependent on his ability to assure the flow of public benefits from higher levels of government to his community, and also on his ability to manipulate government administrators who, in most cases, physically control the key resources. This, in turn, binds him to higher-level politicians at the state level who control both the distribution of benefits and the civil servants. The control of government resources is heavily bureaucratized, which is to say, hierarchically organized, and, in consequence, political power is similarly hierarchical within the Indian states.

The other major effect of the local politician's limited authority and weak political base has been the ineffectiveness of the *panchayats* in raising resources. Although conditions vary from state to state, all states provide *panchayats* with tax resources which are seldom exploited by local leaders. Available taxes are not utilized and even the collection of those imposed is frequently remiss. In consequence the *panchayat* leader becomes further dependent upon the state government, and his *panchayat's* resources and expenditure patterns are erratic over time. This inability or unwillingness to raise public resources and to produce public goods, it will be shown, is a direct consequence of the factional nature of village politics.

Parallel to these local governments, a system of multipurpose rural cooperatives was instituted to provide credit, inputs, and services to the farmers and, more generally, to strengthen the position of the farmer vis-à-vis the merchant community.

Cooperatives in the 1950s were expected to transform the socio-economic structure of India's countryside. The stated goal of the Congress party at that time was a "cooperative commonwealth." They have failed to live up to that expectation. In general, like the *panchayats,* the cooperatives serve as conduits for scarce benefits provided by the government. Also, like the *panchayats,* they have become the focus of factional struggle as factional bosses attempt to control cooperatives' resources to improve their own political base.

Both *panchayats* and cooperatives use external resources to sustain direct dyadic exchanges between factional leaders and clients. Neither institution has been effective in raising local resources or in improving the capacity of the village to produce public goods and services. The legitimacy of the *panchayat* or cooperative leader is generally insufficient to sustain a major extractive policy such as taxation or realization of unpaid cooperative loans. His dyadic exchanges simply cannot sustain the burden of such coercive policies. Furthermore, investment in public goods requires a long-term commitment of resources for future benefits. This is difficult in a factional system because trust in the ability of the leader to pay off is reduced by the highly fragmented, pragmatic, and unstable relationships between himself and his clients. The political economy of the factionalized village is very much a barter economy. Conversely, public goods, which by their nature are freely available to whole classes of citizens, are less useful to the factional politician precisely because he cannot control their distribution. Only if these goods can be "appropriated" by specific groups within the community in return for an immediate political payoff will these investments be useful.[16]

Thus, village factionalism in India has undermined the new local institutions in which the national leadership had placed so much hope. Barter agreements prevail over generalized payoffs and short-term advantage is preferred to long-term investment. Such a system is satisfactory for transmitting individual agricultural inputs to specific farmers, but it is ineffective in generating public resources or in encouraging collective action. When collective action has occurred, it has been initiated either by a small group of local elites for their own benefit or by higher-level authority.[17] For a variety of reasons, therefore, local leadership becomes dependent on higher-level authority, and it is this that explains the vertical factional linkages between the village and the national level which Paul Brass described as typical of Indian politics. The consequence of this is that interests remain fragmented and politics remains distributive.

Factionalism in State-Level Politics

Politics at the state level in India is primarily the politics of region and caste. Divisions among parties and within them commonly reflect, on the one hand, the differing power structures and political traditions of a state's several constituent regions and, on the other hand, the cross-regional aspirations of socially mobile caste groups challenging the status and dominance of the elites of the colonial regime or of the nationalist movement. Thus, state politics has both a vertical and a horizontal dimension.

India's states contain regions of vastly different ecological conditions, and the socioeconomic base of politics is correspondingly varied. Differing political traditions add yet another source of diversity because British authority extended unevenly throughout India, and the favored patterns of political settlement were altered considerably over the long period of imperial expansion. For these and other reasons, the nationalist movement, and hence the Congress party organization, also developed unevenly, and at independence, senior leaders were frequently concentrated in a few key districts in any given state. Regionalism, therefore, has been critical for the structure of Congress party politics.[18]

The support of state-level leaders in India bears a close resemblance to the "friends and neighbors" politics of South Carolina described by V. O. Key, Jr.[19] Ruling coalitions are created by aggregating the support of the several district bosses, and leadership is almost never based on broad mass support or even on a leader's identification with a dominant class interest. Rather, the road to top leadership is pursued by demonstrating skill in maintaining the uneasy coalition of regional segments within the party organization. Some leaders survive by acting as brokers. Others affect the stance of an impartial arbitrator. But each in his own way must confront the necessity of balancing regional demands for public office and resources, and these become the dominant issues in the formation of public policy. To put it another way, the dominant issues of state politics are similar to those of the village in being distributional (as opposed to extractive, redistributive, or structural), but differ in being geographical.

Caste plays an equally important role in both state and local politics in India, but in different forms. In state politics, caste has been transformed from a localized stratification system providing structure for economic and ritual relationships into a vehicle for class conflict and social mobility. The variety of these movements is great but the basic pattern has been common throughout the subcontinent. Urban commercial castes have challenged the domination of education and government jobs by high-caste, English-educated, urban groups; and to a very large extent the movement for the creation of linguistic states, where education and administration would be conducted in the vernacular, can be attributed to this demand. Cultivating castes have challenged the position of their higher-caste landlords with programs of land reform and tenancy regulation. More recently still, these same cultivating castes have followed the lead of the urban castes and demanded their share of access to the universities and administration. Untouchable landless laborers have been mobilized to assert their civil and economic rights vis-à-vis the cultivating castes. Since well before independence, casteism became an integral part of the Indian political process.

Unlike regional politics, which is contained within the confines of the patronage politics of the Congress party organization, caste politics is both a mass politics and a politics which attempts to expand the scope of participation and bring about major structural changes (land reform or states' reorganization) and a substantial redistribution of social benefits. A caste represents a broad stratum of society within a state, with objective interests in common, with established means of communication, with recognized leaders, and, increasingly, with an ideology of change. As such, casteism constitutes a major threat to the narrow, patronage politics of the factional order. Many of the more dramatic caste movements, such as the Maratha demand for a Maharashtra state or, in India's northwest, the growing awareness of the Jat community of their common interest as agriculturalists, have cut across party lines and seriously endangered the stability and integrity of the Congress party order.

Ultimately these intercaste conflicts reach the villages and engender conflict at that level, but it is important to recognize the origins of the conflict in the broader context of state politics. Furthermore, it is clear that these battles cannot be resolved at the local level. Major changes in the system of social stratification can only be accomplished with the active support of government and with the help of public resources. Given the nature of the Indian Constitution, this means through control of the state government.

Thus, the caste appeal appears in different forms. Within the broader scope of statewide politics, caste appeals become mass movements, the issues become widely redistributive, and group status becomes the currency of political exchange. Myron Weiner identified this tendency for mass movements to emerge in Indian politics and blamed it on the unresponsiveness of the civil service to group pressures.[20] An alternative explanation, however, is that the factional system cannot contain mass politics and must either fragment or localize the conflicts if it is to survive. Factional leaders do, in fact, respond by offering positions and patronage to *individual* caste leaders. This response frequently permits factional bosses to exploit caste vote-banks without at the same time fully acceding to the demand for structural change implied in the caste movement. This sometimes succeeds, but it is not at all common for state governments to collapse in the face of mass pressure. There is almost a regular cycle in state politics in which the removal of a strong leader, for whatever reasons, sparks factional instability, followed by increasing stagnation in the administrative services and decreasing responsiveness to mass protest, and culminating in the intervention of the prime minister and the fall of the state government. The recurrent instability of state governments is rooted in the incompatibility of factional structures with the increasing scale of political cleavage within the states.[21] We shall return to this point below.

Within the government itself factionalism has had a major impact on the processes of policy formation and implementation, and generally on the conduct of government business. The most basic political strategy in a heavily factionalized political order is to control strictly the flow of patronage and to prevent any situation developing in which the allocation of public resources could be placed in the hands of an opposition faction or under the control of some autonomous agency.[22] This strategic requirement has had its effect on the structure of ministries, on the relationships of politicians with technocrats and bureaucrats, and on the interaction of the state government with local governments.

In most Indian states the control of government departments has been fragmented in a multitude of ministries, both to prevent the aggregation of power by a potential rebel faction and also to provide as many political appointments as possible for paying off political debts. Conversely, it is common for the state leader and his most trusted colleagues to concentrate in their own hands key departments with coercive powers (e.g., police) or those with large amounts of public resources to distribute (e.g., cooperative banks). One finds in state cabinets, therefore, a plethora of small ministries whose configuration defies reason.

The fragmentation of ministerial responsibility and political rivalry among the ministers themselves enhance the coordinating role of the civil service. This, in turn, tends to magnify the administrative problems and complexities of development policy and, in consequence, to strengthen the already powerful tendencies within the Indian civil service to centralize decision-making hierarchically and to elevate the "generalist" (elite) civil servants over the technocrats.

The factional politician clearly cannot permit such increasing bureaucratic power to insulate allocative decisions from political interference. Such a concession would destroy the very basis of the political exchange on which the factional boss survives. The consequence is that party politicians continually attempt to interfere in administrative decisions, which is bad for administrative morale, and citizens have become increasingly convinced that governmental decisions are invariably partial and bureaucrats incorrigibly corrupt.

For their part, the bureaucrats are inclined to see the major problems of development policy not so much in the evils of political intervention but in the lack of political leadership. This is a position that has a good deal of truth in it, because the factionalism of state-level politics has made the political support for policy indecisive and erratic. Ruling coalitions are diffuse in terms of their component interests and are unstable as well. There is, in consequence, no clearly predominant coalition of interests which can give direction and support to policy over time. The success or failure of a program is determined not by the political power of the interest group it is designed to service, but by the extent and duration of the chief minister's personal enthusiasm for the project. The chief minister exploits any program for its immediate distributive benefits and then loses interest as its continuation demands a regular allocation of funds from the state budget. His interest is not in the maintenance of a service but in the direct political return from a group or region for which he has done a favor. In conditions of scarce resources and manpower, civil servants respond to such shifts in political attention quickly, and in the absence of a continuing pressure by organized interests, maintenance fails, infrastructure decays, and services suffer.

The impact of the factional system can also be seen in the evolution of local-state relationships. The result of the strong ideological predisposition of the Congress party for decentralization and local self-government was the introduction of local government institutions (Panchayati Raj); these institutions were no sooner established, however, than state governments began to reassert their administrative control over them. State political leaders were reluctant to lose control over the distribution of resources at the local level and, therefore, served to reinforce bureaucratic pressures for centralization. Thus, in spite of an ideological preference for decentralization and strong pragmatic reasons for doing so, state governments have declined to decentralize power either to local administrators or local governments. Although rural interests would clearly benefit from structural changes in district administration, including a larger role for the technicians, these reforms have been resisted by state governments. It is, of course, easy to see why the established, generalist civil service would resist these trends, but it is more difficult to explain why politicians from rural constituencies have not applied greater pressure for reform. We can only conclude that *both* the civil servant and the politician have an interest in retaining control of programs in their own hands. Both civil servant and politician have been inclined to resist the development of autonomous control over the distribution of public resources—be it technical control in the agriculture department, commercial in the cooperatives, or political in the *panchayats*. Factional politics has thus served to inhibit both administrative reform and any alteration in the balance of center-periphery power.

Yet, whatever its faults, the state civil service is not directly involved in the factional disputes of the Congress party organization and does not depend on the direct exchanges which sustain the factional politician. The civil service is a tenured, professional cadre which is reasonably well insulated from the vagaries of factional coalition-building. Thus, the civil servant has no particular reason for cooperating with the politician in servicing his factional clients; such cooperation is normally stimulated by the minister's role in personnel decisions. Civil service jobs are among the prize plums of socially mobile groups, and a great many officers owe their appointment or promotion to the intervention of a minister from their own community. An officer may be transferred to an onerous post or may be denied leave to accept a prestigious post in New Delhi or overseas. Such pressure plus the natural authority of ministerial rank provide valuable leverage to a minister. For the civil servant, however, acquiescence to political pressure is risky because opposition factions are quick to publicize irregularities. In consequence, there is a tendency for civil servants to attempt to neutralize distributional decisions by elevating the level of decision and by adopting excessively elaborate procedures. In effect, however, such techniques delay decisions and stifle initiative.

Perhaps the most general and successful bureaucratic response has been to develop some mechanistic distributional formula which can establish regional quotas. This has typically been done in fertilizer distribution where districts, blocks, and individual cooperative societies are given a quota on the basis of their reported crop patterns or previous year's use. In most cases, however, the allocative decisions are not "technical" but "arithmetic." Even when fertilizer is distributed according to crop pattern, which might appear technical, the formula is a rule of thumb and, of course, there is no guarantee that the fertilizer is actually used on the crops claimed. The value of the criterion is, then, administrative and not technical. This bureaucratic response may serve to contain factionalism in development decisions, but it does not alter the distributive character of the development decisions. The best defense against attack is to try to assure that resources are equitably distributed geographically—and, hence, not necessarily to maximize growth. The safest procedure is not to challenge existing patterns of distribution.

There is one other kind of constraint on factionalism which may be emerging. We have seen that in village politics the cooperatives were essential to the patronage politics of factional politicians; the same is true at the state level. However, there is some evidence that the cooperatives are capable of transforming amorphous factional divisions into political cleavages rooted firmly in economic class interests. In an exceptionally thorough and innovative study of factional politics in Maharashtra, Mary Carras has argued that the apparent randomness of factional alliances in that state masks a latent division within the community along the lines of economic interest and public philosophy.[23] More precisely, she suggests that factionalism increasingly divides the Congress party between cooperative-based politicians, whose constituency is the rural farm community, and urban politicians, whose base is the commercial castes. Factionalism tends to cloud this cleavage, but there are aggregate data to suggest that the division may become more manifest with further development of the rural economy.

In most states, however, it is not at all clear that the cooperatives either organize or represent farm interests effectively. After two decades of development it is still considered necessary to protect cooperatives from competition with the private trade. One would assume that after an initial period of uncertainty the cooperatives, by reason of the economies of scale and responsiveness to members' needs, would find it easy to compete with the private trade. Yet there are indications that they are not more efficient and do not necessarily provide better services.

Nevertheless, there has been an expansion of cooperative privileges—monopolies of input sales, transfer of some public functions, and exclusive rights to specified trade and manufacturing enterprises. Lax enforcement of loan repayments makes cooperative membership additionally attractive. The most obvious reason for this public generosity toward the cooperatives, given their poor performance, is that they are politically necessary to factional politicians. If cooperatives cannot attract members and if they do not control valuable resources, they are useless to the factional politician. In consequence, the rural politician cannot possibly permit the private trade to erode his political base. But if an increasingly commercial farm economy does bring discipline and professionalization to the cooperatives, we may well see, as Carras suggests, the more widespread appearance of a stable, structured exchange relationship between the political elite and a broad class of farm constituents.

To recapitulate briefly, the direct barter exchange characteristic of village-level politics in India is projected upward in the political system to the state level, where it generates a style of policy formation that is best labeled with Lowi's term, "distributive." The term implies a preference for policies characterized by a very remote likelihood of coercion and by an individualized orientation (i.e., the ability to transfer resources to specific individuals or groups). Lowi's argument is that distributive politics is "consensus" politics which avoids basic conflicts and structural changes within the policy while dissipating resources and control in the interest of bargains struck between politicians and clients. Any system of distributive politics relies on a source of resources outside the arena in question. In our case, although the bargains struck are parochial, the resources are generated in the urban sector. The mechanism linking the local exchanges to the state-level distributive programs is the factional network stretching vertically from the village to the state capital. In this connection, Lowi further argues that the public (or semipublic) agencies of distribution are often the most effective opponents of basic structural changes. The considerable opposition in India from the higher levels of the cooperative movement to the new national policies of encouraging an increasingly "capitalist" agriculture in the mid-sixties confirms this argument.[24]

The argument here is that distributive policies are very well suited to the needs of a factional political system and that support for development in India is commonly support for the distributive and promotional policies inherent in a basically permissive and mixed-economy approach to the task—not support for the structural reforms of the economy engendered in the concept. Nor is there much support at the state level for the politics of investment, which would remove resources from current consumption and transfer them to the public sector, presumably through taxation. Our argument is not the usual one that these policy failures reflect the vested interests of the larger landholders. On the contrary, the general weakness of state governments in formulating and implementing redistributive and regulatory policies has often harmed the farm community. Rather, to extend Lowi's argument slightly, it is suggested that factional politics makes it structurally difficult to adopt such policies.

Factionalism in National Politics

The amorphous factionalism which we find at the local and state levels in India persists in national politics as well. National party bosses with links to state and local factions complete the chain of dyadic relationships described by Paul Brass.[25] These factional divisions appear in the national Congress party organization, within the legislative party, and within the Council of Ministers. As at lower levels, the bases of factional alignments are diverse, including common regional origins, caste, personal friendships, similar institutional experiences (e.g., in trade unions or the Gandhian movement), and ideology. The respective factions are not coherent homogeneous groups, therefore, but conglomerates. Even the foundations of the factional leader's power vary. Some build on a firm base in a state party organization. Others operate entirely at the national level—aggregating dissidents within the Congress party in Parliament. In the past, though not recently, the trade unions have provided a factional base. Even a reputation for being a confidant of the prime minister can be conjured into a position of factional leadership on occasion.

The most striking thing about national-level factionalism in India is the fact that there is seldom any faction clearly in opposition to the prime minister. Only in the early fifties, when Sardar Patel was alive, and in the period between 1966 and 1969, when Indira Gandhi was consolidating her position, did opposition factions exist within the Congress party. In both cases splits in the party forced out the dissidents. In Delhi the struggles are not for leadership but for the ear of the leader. One may attack those close to the prime minister, but one does not back an alternative party leader. The pattern is a common enough one, familiar to students of personalist politics. The great strength of Indira Gandhi's position was that she was viewed as a party leader and not a faction leader; this insulated her from the uncertainties of factional coalition-building.

A second feature that distinguishes national from state-level factionalism is the tendency for the various national factions to group loosely around left-wing and right-wing poles. This should be taken to mean not that the party is basically divided on ideological lines but that the ideological symbols often provide a rallying point in national politics. Thus, in the decisions regarding the nationalization of the wholesale wheat trade, support or opposition for the policy was neither logically nor in practice a rightist or leftist stance.[26] Nevertheless, in spite of the actual complexity of the interests and issues involved, nationalization was largely discussed in ideological terms in New Delhi, and ideological interpretation of conflicts cannot be altogether dismissed. There has recently been an intense struggle within the Congress party between a small faction identified as the Socialist Forum, widely perceived as Marxist, and the Nehru Forum, a diverse ad hoc collection of groups believing that the prime minister had become too committed to confidants within the Socialist Forum. The nationalization of the wheat trade rapidly became a focus for the factional struggle and its failure became a major weapon in discrediting the Socialist Forum. Still, for most, the issue was not grain or ideology but access to the prime minister. Her solution was to abolish both forums, reshuffle her cabinet, and in no way to alter the generally erratic and ad hoc mode of making food policy decisions.

Neither ideological discipline nor personal commitment was characteristic of the participants in this ideological cleavage. Nor was there much congruity of interest in either coalition. Yet in spite of this, the participants invariably resorted to this basic left-right dichotomy to explain the situation and their position. Only after intensive questioning did it become clear how amorphous these coalitions really were. In fact, it was this very amorphousness of the coalitions, together with their scope, which forced the ideological jargon upon them. We have here an example of Parsons' concept of generalization. When a social system becomes more complex and increases in scale, he argues, ". . . its value pattern must be couched at a higher level of generality in order to legitimize the wider variety of goals and functions of its sub-units."[27] The ideological debate provides some normative structuring for the factional struggle and is useful in coalition building. The substance of the leftist or rightist position is not very stable, but for limited periods of time the label does provide direction and focus to the activities of the diverse factional groups.

A third feature of national level politics—in contrast to the pervasiveness of factionalism in the states—is that broad areas of government activity exist in Delhi which are fairly well insulated from factional politics. This process of insulation begins, as described above, with the prime minister. The prime minister is a leader with diffuse authority and, unlike most factional bosses, with widespread popular support. However much Prime Minister Gandhi may have dabbled in factional politics, therefore, it was evident even to her detractors that her status did not depend on the narrow calculus of factional coalition-building. This independence of the prime minister has its most immediate effect in recruitment to high office. In recruitment to the national Council of Ministers, during the period 1952–1967, a substantial portion of council members, at all ranks, were only marginally involved in Congress factional politics.[28] For 19 percent there was no evidence of factional activity at all. For another 30 percent the extent of the individual's involvement was that he was reported to be "connected" or "close" to some state or national faction leader. But, given the fact that these ministers had generally had no active role in their respective party organizations or in the politics of their states in general, this "closeness" meant nothing more than that they were known to the local party boss and not offensive to him. Hence they received the party ticket.

It is not only the prime minister, however, who is insulated from factionalism. Generally in India one can distinguish politicians who made their career in the party organization and those who came to prominence through their parliamentary activities. In addition, there is a group of ministers who are a bit of a puzzle in that they show no evidence of either experience and yet find appointment at all ranks within the council. These "uninvolved" ministers have constituted on the average about 25 percent of the council over the years.[29] Not surprisingly there is a high degree of overlap between the factionally neutral ministers and the "uninvolved." In short, nearly a quarter of the ministers are outside the factional network and have not followed career paths which would tend to involve them in it. If one adds to this a number of ministers with extensive parliamentary careers but who have been noticeably uninvolved in either the party organization or the Congress parliamentary party factional fights (averaging about 20 percent over the years), one has a group constituting over 40 percent of the entire council who appear to be outside the factional arena. Given the fact that it is in recruitment that factionalism is usually most virulent at lower levels, this is a surprising proportion.

The functions these individuals perform within the government explain their ability to rise independently of the party factions. They are invariably well educated, and most of them were recruited to the Council of Ministers to provide symbolic representation of regions, minority communities, or the intellectual and professional communities of India's major cities. Such symbolic representation also plays a role in state politics in that these ministers were originally provided tickets to fulfill the symbolic needs of a local organization, but they lacked the political weight to claim a place in the state cabinet. Instead, they were sent to Delhi, where they were accommodated by the prime minister. Leaders of marginal groups are in fact frequently courted by state bosses—Richard Sisson's study of Rajasthan, for example, documents the mobilization capacity of the Congress factional system[30]— but power at the state level is always in direct exchange for a specific bloc of votes which the marginal group politician can provide in a specific constituency. National recruitment, on the other hand, is sufficiently distant from the realities of local vote-getting that the individual's capacity to mobilize his community is hardly a consideration. Rather, his symbolic role is one of integration, not of mobilization.

On the scale of national politics, symbolic representation cannot be contained within the confines of factional dyads. The symbolic representative must be visible at the centers of power. His appeal must be broad, articulate, and open because he must reach out even beyond the normal factional networks. Furthermore, he must not merely represent his own community but must also embody the values of the "secular" Muslim, the educated tribesman, the nationalist Kashmiri, or the committed (as opposed to alienated) intellectual, etc. In the Parsonian schema this represents yet another example of generalization, and constitutes a dramatic advance on the dyadic exchanges of the factional order as an integrative device. This symbolic generalization depended for its success, however, on the power of the prime minister.

Thus, ideological labels have provided the beginnings of some systematic structuring of factional politics at the national level; and in addition, the power of the prime minister has contained factionalism in the recruitment process. The decision-making process is yet another constraint on the factional arena. Throughout the 1960s a substantial change took place in India's agricultural development policy which proved to have a momentous impact on a wide range of government activity. Administratively, the change began with the introduction in 1959 of the Ford Foundation's Intensive Agricultural District Program (IADP).[31] The Ford Foundation proposal was to select a limited number of highly favored districts with good growth potential for greatly concentrated investment to maximize food grain production. Politically, the most dramatic aspect of the program was the decision to concentrate investment in only a few districts. This was completely contrary to the existing policy which, in response to the realities of distributive rural politics, had attempted the widest possible application of government activities in the countryside. After ten years of experience with such distributive programs, it had become clear that government resources had been dissipated with no appreciable impact on agricultural production.

The IADP had to be adapted to the realities of state-level politics, however, first by permitting the state governments to select the six districts which would be favored—although the Ford Foundation closely monitored this process, and in at least one of the initial districts the state-level decision was reversed by the government of India on technical grounds. Second, resistance to concentrating resources was overcome by national financing of virtually all additional expenditure and a promise that the program would eventually be extended widely. Finally, as a concession to distributive politics, the government of India agreed to finance one project in every state, much beyond the six districts recommended by the Ford Foundation. With these minor adjustments, the financial autonomy of the central government (provided by the Ford Foundation) permitted the Ministry of Food and

Agriculture to bring about a concentration of administrative and financial resources in six selected districts and to establish in those districts a direct link to New Delhi, maintained by a steady stream of national-level administrators and technocrats. This direct link helped to insulate the projects from the vagaries of local politics and to sustain the interest of the state governments in the projects.[32]

Implicit in the new program, however, were a number of critical policy issues which received hardly any attention at the time. The most important of these was a shift from a policy of community development to one of agricultural development. Earlier programs had always aimed at the social and moral transformation of the village community and had placed primary emphasis on developing attitudes and institutions. The Ford Foundation approach, however, ultimately concentrated on the economic—i.e., production—side of the rural problem and furthermore tended to favor the larger farmer with resources to invest. This issue was in fact raised in the administration by the community development enthusiasts, but they had been discredited by previous failure, and there was a lack of public debate on the issue. Thus, a "capitalist" agriculture was born almost without public notice.

With the adoption of this policy, therefore, a substantial shift from "distributive" to "investment" politics took place; the direct administrative power of the central government in agriculture was, at least temporarily, increased.[33] Cooperative models of the rural community and broad questions of welfare were abandoned in favor of aggressively commercial agriculture—and all without a major factional battle. Two factors seem to have contributed to this result—the personal support of Prime Minister Nehru for the program, and the technical nature of the decision-making process. The director of the Ford Foundation had succeeded in bringing to the attention of Prime Minister Nehru early in 1959 what he considered an impending disaster in the imbalance of population growth and food production in India. He then received a mandate from Nehru to appoint an experts' committee to study the situation and make recommendations for its solution. The personal commitment of the prime minister, therefore, served to insulate the program from factional politicization within the party.

Even more important, the Ford team was a technicians' team. Unlike many policy committees set up in India that draw on the services of leading and vocal politicians, both the parameters and the details of the IADP were determined at the national level by technocrat and bureaucrat. The independence of the technocrats was largely established by the fact that they were foreign and on the Ford Foundation payroll—though over the years the indigenous technical staff has been increasingly strengthened within the Agriculture Ministry. Finally, farm interest groups are poorly articulated at the national level and cause little inconvenience.[34] Thus, once the initial concessions had been made to federalism—a district in each state—the Agriculture Ministry had a free hand.

The Agriculture Ministry is insulated from both faction and ideology most of the time, but more so in agricultural policy than in food policy. Although ideology has at times played a role in structuring broad factional conflict in the Congress party, I disagree with authors such as Francine Frankel who argue that ideology has had a systematic impact on agricultural policy formation.[35] Quite the reverse, agricultural policy is more typically dominated by ad hoc technical and administrative considerations than by a consistent ideological vector. The contrast between the politics of food policy and those of agricultural policy—of which the IADP experience is typical—is revealing. The IADP's basic program was worked out by the technicians and bureaucrats, the debate was nonideological, minimal concessions were made to the needs of distributive-federal politics, and the real issues were fiscal. Subsequently, the maldistribution of income brought about by the program and the strategy it entailed have been challenged in ideological terms; but the reaction developed within the civil service at least two years before it became a major political issue, and it is now clear that, after minimal concessions to redistribution, the technicians' preference for intensive investments has prevailed.

Food policy, in contrast, has always been a matter of intense public debate and scrutiny. Like land reform, food policy is comprised of redistributive issues—rationing, interstate movements of food, pricing, etc. Decisions in any of these areas involve obvious shifts in the burden of scarcity among large groups within the nation. Food decisions, therefore, have always been in the uneasy area between factional and mass politics. In the initial stages of a food crisis the inclination is to make the decisions within the context of the party organization, and these decisions reflect the needs and power of the state bosses.[36] As the crisis deepens, however, popular agitation spreads, and this is frequently used by faction leaders to pursue internecine struggles within the party. At this stage, careful administrative planning is often ignored at the cabinet level, and short-term political considerations prevail. Finally, if the crisis is sufficiently severe and the popular agitation continues, the top party leadership will intervene and return policy to administrative control. As at the state level, the national factional order is vulnerable to mass politics.

Thus, at both the state and national levels, factional politicians have a bias in favor of distributive politics, and tend to resist demands for structural changes. At the national level, however, the insulation of certain areas of decision-making from factional politics is possible and does permit more adequate responses to redistributional issues.

Conclusion

We began our discussion by noting that little attention has been given to the effect of increasing scale on factional politics. Our factional model suggested that factional politics is characteristic of small arenas and functions with a barter system of political exchange with extremely limited capacity. This raises the question of how a party system as heavily factionalized as the Indian can function effectively in a nation so diverse and complex.

The most important characteristic of Indian factionalism is that it is hierarchically ordered.[37] At each level, factional bosses depend on resources generated and disbursed to them by higher levels of government. The discipline of the Congress party organization, dating back to the independence movement, and the concentration of decision-making authority characteristic of India's cabinet system of government reinforce this hierarchy by concentrating control of those resources. The lack of any real autonomy on the part of "independent" agencies such as the cooperative banks or the Foodgrains Corporation, which play a key role in the rural economy, further strengthens the trend. The resources controlled by national leaders are usually more general—broad planning and budget allocations—but they also extend to the allocation of fertilizer, electric power, and prices for specific crops—vital to state politicians.

Prime ministers can exploit their position at the top of this factional hierarchy because they are to some extent independent of it. Intense factional negotiations surrounded the election of both Lal Bahadur Shastri and Indira Gandhi as prime ministers, but thereafter they shared some of the mass appeal and institutional authority which was characteristic of Jawaharlal Nehru. Ever since the days of Mahatma Gandhi's leadership, authority within the party has been centered in its leader, and the Congress party has never developed a tradition of collegial or collective decision-making. Whenever this leadership tradition has been challenged, the issue has been resolved in favor of the prime minister. Although there have been repeated attempts to strengthen the party organization and central control at lower levels, these have largely failed. The prime minister has sufficient autonomy at the national level to differentiate recruitment patterns, insulate the technocrats, and dominate the planning process.

There have been chief ministers who have achieved comparable status within their own states and have been able to contain the factional struggles. Such statesmen are almost invariably drawn into national politics, however, and their states return to factional disorder. These findings would tend to support observations on the crucial importance of the institutionalization of top leadership roles to the subsequent evolution of a new state.[38] In Nehru's case his insistence on maintaining a stance of issue-oriented politics and a highly ideological style of debate may have created, as some argue, a bifurcated political culture.[39] It also served symbolically to separate him from the political style of the Congress party machine.

We might have anticipated a greater role for the civil service in containing factionalism. At lower levels the stance of the civil service was typically, if often ineffectively, defensive. It does not appear to have been able to prevent the personalization of its own personnel decisions, let alone matters of public policy. The bureaucrats cannot, of course, be blamed for the weakness of political leadership, but neither have they been able to compensate for it or to counteract the basically distributive style of state and local politics. In fact, when administrative decisions have been free from factional corruption, the evidence is that it has been most often at the national level and is attributable to factors quite unrelated to Weberian norms of bureaucratic behavior.

Two of the factors we found which tended to insulate the national civil service from factional pressure were the nature of the decisions being made in the Food and Agriculture Ministry, and the structure of rural pressures and demands. These are, in fact, interrelated. National-level decision-making in agriculture centers on broad questions of strategy and regional allocations that are of little direct concern to the average farmer. The administration of the programs is usually under the control of the state governments, and it is here that the farmers concentrate their attention. In food grain pricing, in contrast, one would find much more farm interest and activity in New Delhi because this is a national responsibility and one which affects the farmer directly. Similarly, in ministries such as commerce and industry, where the national government directly allocates licenses and raw materials, factional intrusion resembles the factionalism common at the state level. In fact, those ministries are usually controlled by politicians heavily involved in the Congress party organization and factional networks.[40]

Even in food grain pricing, however, the farmer has difficulty in making his weight felt in New Delhi. The factional system works best at the local level, where individual deals are made for political support. At higher levels the farm interests tend to be diffused by the fragmented nature of factional power structures, and, with the exception of a few associations of cash crop producers, there are no really effective farm organizations at any level. Even the upward pressure on government procurement prices for food grains over the past few years can be attributed to the farmer only with some reservations. The pressure for higher prices has been applied through the factional chains reaching upward to New Delhi, and it has been the state chief ministers who provided the leverage. But the relative success of this leverage can be attributed not to the power of rural-based factions, but to the strategic situation of one or two chief ministers (Punjab and Haryana) who supply the bulk of the nation's grain stocks. These state bosses have been able to exploit the fact that without their cooperation no national food policy is possible. The weakness of the factional mechanism from the farmers' perspective is revealed, however, in the fact that the chief ministers have often been willing to compromise farm interests in support of their own personal advantage. The factional system itself short-circuits rural pressures.

Our model of factional politics identified three basic components—structure, behavioral tendencies, and normative orientations. Increasing scale affects each of these. The redistributive demands of broad-based caste movements pass quickly beyond the confines of dyadic factional exchanges. The diversity and complexity of the national community requires mechanisms of integration beyond that of the factional network. This is not to argue that the factional political order has been less effective than its enthusiasts have claimed, but it does mean that it has not been sufficient. The symbolic representation which we found in recruitment patterns of the Council of Ministers is illustrative of these alternative mechanisms. Caste conflict has been primarily centered at the state level in India, where it feeds factionalism and is imperfectly contained by factional politicians. The recurrent outbursts of caste and communal violence which have punctuated Indian political history are evidence of the limited effectiveness of these mechanisms. At the national level, however, leadership has been somewhat more successful in compensating for the fissiparous tendencies of diverse peoples. Recruitment patterns have provided physical mobility from parochial to national arenas, while linguistic states and special concessions to tribal areas have satisfied local minorities.[41] The prodigious efforts to achieve national integration are direct evidence that the boundaries of factional politics have been exceeded.

Ideology provides normative integration for these diverse groups operating at the national level. As such, ideological appeals are more abstract definitions of common interest than the narrow self-serving of factional exchanges, and tend to describe more generalized relationships which extend in time.[42] The normative constraints imposed by ideology are not overly impressive in Indian politics, but they are decidedly more compelling in national than in local politics.

Lastly, we may note implications for the motivational aspect of factional politics. No one would suggest that factional politicians in New Delhi are less self-serving than their associates at lower levels. Nevertheless, the diverse recruitment pattern at the national level does bring into positions of power many who have not entered politics through factional competition but have been recruited for their skills, professional prominence, or other nonpolitical considerations. The nature of national politics is also influenced by patterns of selection among the factional politicians themselves. It is difficult to succeed at the national level if one is identified too completely with any particular interest, region, or program. This is because national leaders play an important role in mediating in state factional disputes and resolving interstate conflicts. It is advantageous, therefore, for a national politician to cultivate an image of impartiality in policy decisions and the style of an elder statesman in intraparty disputes. In consequence, national leaders tend to lose their state factional base when they move to New Delhi and to alter their own perspectives.

The impact of scale on factionalism is, therefore, complex. It is limited by the personal orientations of top leaders and the diversity of national recruitment patterns. It is destabilized by mass movements and demands for structural change. Finally, it is simply transcended by normative patterns and functional responses necessitated by politics in an ethnically, culturally, and geographically diverse nation. It is this capacity to transcend the limits of factional politics that makes possible the "investment politics" characteristic of national policies. Conversely, it is the relatively more factionalized politics at the state level which encourages distributive politics and produces considerable governmental instability. One is tempted to argue, therefore, that many of the changes in political systems which theorists associate with modernization are instead the result of increasing scale of political organization and the concomitant of increasing political integration.[43]

In conclusion, we may hypothesize that in smaller nations factionalism might still persist in spite of extensive modernization. We may also suggest that one should not expect to see the replacement of factional-style politics by a more "modern" form, but rather the increasing restriction of factionalism to specific institutional environments and arenas.

NOTES

1. For example, Bernard J. Siegel and Alan R. Beals, "Conflict and Factionalist Dispute," *Journal of Royal Anthropological Institute* 90 (1960): 107–17; and Siegel and Beals, "Pervasive Factionalism," *American Anthropologist* 62 (1960): 394–417.

2. For example, B. D. Graham, "The Succession of Factional Systems in the Uttar Pradesh Congress Party, 1937–66," in Marc J. Swartz, ed., *Local-Level Politics: Social and Cultural Perspectives* (Chicago: Aldine, 1969), pp. 323–60; Nathan Leites, *On the Game of Politics in France* (Stanford: Stanford Univ. Press, 1959); V. O. Key, Jr., *Southern Politics in State and Nation* (New York: Alfred A. Knopf, 1949); and Zbigniew Brzezinski and Samuel P. Huntington, *Political Power: USA/USSR* (New York: Viking, 1965), pt. 2.

3. See Talcott Parsons, *Societies: Evolutionary and Comparative Perspectives* (Englewood Cliffs: Prentice-Hall, 1966), ch. 2; and Parsons, "On the Concept of Political Power," in *Politics and Social Structure* (New York: The Free Press, 1969), ch. 14.

4. I have already published elsewhere a summary of what is known about the nature of factionalism as a general phenomenon, and will present only an abbreviated description here. See Norman K. Nicholson, "The Factional Model and the Study of Politics," *Comparative Political Studies* 5, no. 3 (Oct. 1972): 291–314.

5. See David Apter, *The Politics of Modernization* (Chicago: Univ. of Chicago Press, 1965), ch. 1, for an example of a comparable analytical mode.

6. Harold D. Lasswell, *Psychopathology and Politics* (New York: Viking, 1960), pp. 183–84.

7. J. K. Campbell, *Honour, Family, and Patronage* (Oxford: Clarendon Press, 1964); and Ralph W. Nicholas, "Rules, Resources, and Political Activity," in Swartz, ed., *Local-Level Politics*, p. 301.

8. This argument is most thoroughly developed in Richard Sisson, *The Congress Party in Rajasthan* (Berkeley and Los Angeles: Univ. of California Press, 1972), esp. ch. 10. See also R. S. Khare, "Group Dynamics in a North Indian Village," *Human Organization* 21, no. 3 (Fall 1962): 209.

9. Siegel and Beals, "Conflict and Factionalist Dispute."

10. E. C. Banfield, *The Moral Basis of a Backward Society* (New York: The Free Press, 1958), ch. 5; Manning Nash, *The Golden Road to Modernity* (New York: John Wiley and Sons, 1965), p. 76.

11. Francine Frankel, *India's Green Revolution* (Princeton: Princeton Univ. Press, 1971), p. 197. See also Wolf Ladejinsky, *A Study of Tenorial Conditions in Package Districts* (New Delhi: Planning Commission, 1965).

12. The most comprehensive survey of the literature on caste and status conflict is David Mandelbaum, *Society in India* (Berkeley and Los Angeles: Univ. of California Press, 1970), esp. vol. 2, pts. 5, 6, 7.

13. On *Panchayati Raj,* see Iqbal Narain et al., *Panchayati Raj Administration* (New Delhi: Indian Institute of Public Administration, 1970); and S. C. Jain, *Community Development and Panchayati Raj* (Bombay: Allied, 1967).

14. George M. Foster, "The Dyadic Contract: A Model for the Social Structure of a Mexican Peasant Village," in Jack M. Potter, May N. Diaz, and George M. Foster, *Peasant Society: A Reader* (Boston: Little, Brown, 1967), pp. 213–30; Eric Wold, "Kinship,

Friendship, and Patron-Client Relations in Complex Societies," in Michael Banton, ed., *The Social Anthropology of Complex Societies* (London: Tavistock Publications, 1966), pp. 1–22; and James C. Scott, "Corruption, Machine Politics, and Political Change," *American Political Science Review* 63, no. 4 (Dec. 1969): 1142–58.

15. See Theodore Lowi, "Population Policies and the American Political System," in A. E. Kier Nash, ed., *Governance and Population: The Governmental Implications of Population Change*, vol. 4: *Research Reports* (Washington, D.C.: Government Printing Office, Commission on Population Growth and the American Future, 1972), pp. 283–300.

16. Norman K. Nicholson, *Panchayat Raj, Rural Development and the Political Economy of Village India*, occasional papers no. 1 (Ithaca: Cornell Univ., Center for International Studies, Rural Development Committee, 1973), pp. 48–49.

17. Theoretical treatment of this point can be found in Mancur Olson, *The Logic of Collective Action* (New York: Schocken Books, 1968), ch. 2.

18. Myron Weiner, ed., *State Politics in India* (Princeton: Princeton Univ. Press, 1968); and Robert Crane, ed., *Regions and Regionalism in South Asian Studies: An Exploratory Study*, Duke Univ. Program in Comparative Studies on South Asia Monograph Series, no. 5 (Durham, N.C.: Duke Univ. Program in Comparative Studies on South Asia, 1967).

19. Key, *Southern Politics*, ch. 7.

20. Myron Weiner, *The Politics of Scarcity* (Chicago: Univ. of Chicago Press, 1962), ch. 8.

21. The functional necessity for this balance of institutional and normative development with increasing scale is argued in Parsons, *Societies*, chs. 1, 2; S. N. Eisenstadt, *The Political Systems of Empires* (New York: The Free Press, 1963), ch. 2; Apter, *Politics of Modernization*, ch. 3; and Marion Levy, *Modernization and the Structure of Societies* (Princeton: Princeton Univ. Press, 1966), pt. 1.

22. Paul R. Brass, *Factional Politics in an Indian State* (Berkeley and Los Angeles: Univ. of California Press, 1965), ch. 10, esp. pp. 212–18.

23. Mary Carras, *The Dynamics of Indian Political Factions* (London: Cambridge Univ. Press, 1972).

24. This is based on interviews with key officials involved in both the initial decision-making which brought about the shift in the mid-sixties and also those who developed the more redistributive direction in 1969–1970.

25. Brass, *Factional Politics in an Indian State*, chs. 2, 3; see also Sisson, *Congress Party in Rajasthan*, chs. 5, 9.

26. See "Semantics of Foodgrains Trade Take-Over," *Economic and Political Weekly* (Mar. 3, 1973): 465–66; and "Hide and Seek on the Food Front," *Link* (Aug. 4, 1974): 9–14.

27. Parsons, *Societies*, p. 23.

28. Norman K. Nicholson, "Factionalism and the Indian Council of Ministers," *Journal of Commonwealth Political Studies* 10, no. 3 (Nov. 1972): 179–97.

29. Norman K. Nicholson, "Integrative Strategies of a National Elite: Career Patterns in the Indian Council of Ministers," *Comparative Politics* 7, no. 4 (July 1975): 533–58.

30. Sisson, *Congress Party in Rajasthan*, ch. 10.

31. *Report on India's Food Crisis and Steps to Meet It* (New Delhi: Government of India, Ministry of Food and Agriculture, 1959). Also see *Modernizing Indian Culture: Report on the Intensive Agricultural District Program (1960–68)* (New Delhi: Ministries of Food, Agriculture, Community Development and Cooperation, 1969), vol. 1, esp. chs. 2, 3; *Report of the Study Team on Agricultural Administration* (New Delhi: Administrative Reforms Commission, 1967); and V. Vemkatraman and John F. Kennedy, *Proposed Reorganization of Ludhiana IADP Functions* (New Delhi: Ford Foundation, 1966).

32. Norman K. Nicholson, *Rural Development Policy in India: Elite Differentiation and the Decision Making Process* (De Kalb: Northern Illinois Univ. Center for Governmental Studies, 1974), p. 62.

33. "Investment" politics is an adaptation of Lowi's "redistributive" politics in that the effect of the "redistribution" on investment decisions is to redistribute benefits in time by withdrawing them from current consumption and sinking them into capital. It also implies an increase of concentration of resources in contrast with "distributive" politics. Compare Nicholson, *Rural Development Policy in India*, pp. 5–13.

34. Weiner, *Politics of Scarcity,* ch. 6. Weiner's study is one of the few treatments of farm interest organization in India. The author's own work—still in progress—suggests, however, that national-level organizations of farmers have been ineffective and usually established to serve the political needs of food ministers, not the economic needs of farmers.

35. Francine Frankel, "Ideology and Politics in Economic Planning," *World Politics* 19, no. 4 (July 1967): 621–45.

36. Norman K. Nicholson, "Political Aspects of Indian Food Policy," *Pacific Affairs* 41 (Spring 1968): 34–50.

37. This contradicts earlier analysis of factionalism in India, such as that by Paul Brass; this can probably be attributed to the impact of development programs on political relationships.

38. Seymour Martin Lipset, *The First New Nation* (Garden City: Doubleday, Anchor, 1967).

39. See W. H. Morris-Jones, "India's Political Idioms," in C. H. Philips, ed., *Politics and Society in India* (New York: Praeger, 1962), pp. 133–54; Myron Weiner, "India: Two Political Cultures," in Lucian Pye and Sidney Verba, eds., *Political Culture and Political Development* (Princeton: Princeton Univ. Press, 1965), ch. 6.

40. Norman K. Nicholson, "Integrative Strategies of a National Elite."

41. Peter Blau presents a theoretical analysis of the integrative role of mobility in *Exchange and Power in Social Life* (New York: John Wiley and Sons, 1964), ch. 11.

42. This functional role of ideology is explored in Clifford Geertz, "Ideology as a Cultural System," in David Apter, ed., *Ideology and Discontent* (London: The Free Press, 1964), ch. 1.

43. Theoretical justification for this argument may be found in Eisenstadt, *Political Systems of Empires;* and Parsons, *Societies.* See also Parsons, "The Political Aspect of Social Structure and Process," in *Politics and Social Structure,* ch. 13.

Part Three
ALTERNATING-PARTY SYSTEMS

This section presents studies of factions in eight alternating-party political systems. Alternating-party systems are those in which several parties—at least two, often many more—maintain a continuous, effective competition for power, such that no one party manages to monopolize or dominate continuously the government and the national political processes. The relative long-term distribution of power among at least two of the contesting parties is sufficiently balanced to permit the prospect of either one gaining control of the government as a result of their competition. Although periods of dominance may be longer or shorter in the individual countries, the parties alternate their majorities or coalition majorities, and hence alternate control of the government.

Traditionally, alternating-party systems have been classified as two-party systems and multiparty systems. Two-party systems are those in which parliamentary majorities and control of government offices alternate back and forth between two parties, which thus dominate politics between them. Multiparty systems are those in which parliamentary representation and control of government offices alternate among numerous—three or more—parties, or, often, among shifting coalitions of several parties. Examples of both types are included in these chapters, although in several of the countries described

191

here, recent events have altered or abolished the political party systems.

The case studies in this section deal with five countries whose political systems are (or were) two-party systems, and three whose political systems are (or were) multiparty systems. In two of these eight countries, however, party politics have been abolished entirely, and in others it has been relegated to a marginal role. For these case studies the accounts are valuable as comparative analyses, though they no longer describe functioning political systems. Chapter 8, by K. G. Machado, presents an analysis of the changing faction system in the two-party system of the Philippines—a political system now defunct, since the suspension of constitutional government and of political parties in 1972. Colombia and Uruguay are both nominally two-party systems, and each has had periodic interludes of military or nonparty rule, in part as a response to the demands and pressures of modernization. In Chapter 9, Ronald McDonald contrasts the faction systems of Colombia and Uruguay, and the differences that have resulted from their different patterns of modernization.

In Chapter 10 the multiparty politics of West Germany, described by the author as a "party-state," is examined by Peter Merkl, who compares the factions within the major parties of the national party system, and nonpartisan factions of local-level politics in Germany. Bolivia has long had a multiparty system, with recurrent phases of popular party politics, interspersed with rule by military or civil-military regimes. In Chapter 11, Christopher Mitchell analyzes Bolivia's periodic phases of resurgent factionalism. A "classical" two-party system is that of Great Britain; in Chapter 12, Arthur Cyr examines the differences of factional divisions in Britain's Conservative and Labour parties. Chile is another country whose political party system is now defunct, since the overthrow of the government by the army, and the abolition of political parties, in 1973. The historical progression and demise of Chile's multiparty system is described in Chapter 13 by Jorge Nef, using factionalism to explain its evolution. Finally, in Chapter 14, Thomas Roback and Judson James analyze factionalism in the politics of the complex two-party system of the United States. They examine both historical and contemporary American factionalism, and compare intraparty divisions by faction and by tendency; and they consider factionalism's role in creating basic alterations in the two-party system itself.

8

Continuity and Change in Philippine Factionalism

K. G. MACHADO

Factionalism was long one of the most notable features of Philippine political life. Factional competition was the primary force underlying and giving shape to that country's political processes after elections were introduced and parties were organized under American colonial auspices early in this century. While key aspects of early Philippine factional processes underwent significant changes in succeeding years, the fundamental importance of factionalism remained undiminished until 1972. In that year, what had been one of the longest experiments with representative institutions in a new state was abruptly ended when the incumbent president, Ferdinand Marcos, declared martial law and systematically began construction of an authoritarian political system of uncertain duration. With the abolition of open political competition, the long-standing pattern of factional politics disappeared. Nevertheless, an understanding of that earlier pattern of politics is crucial to an understanding of Philippine political development.

This chapter describes the traditional pattern of Philippine factionalism, analyzes significant changes in that pattern in recent decades, explains the persistence of factionalism, and analyzes some aspects of the impact of factionalism on the course of Philippine political development. A brief discussion of factions and factionalism will help to place the Philippine case in comparative perspective. Only in such a perspective can analyses of specific cases improve understanding of factional politics in general.

Factions and Factionalism

Factions and factionalism may be found in any kind of organization (e.g., political, bureaucratic, academic). As we are concerned here with factions in political parties and factionalism in politics, this discussion will be confined to these types. Factions are groups within a party which have structure and purposes distinct from the formal structure and purposes of that party. They are distinguished by a lack of firm attachment to their parties, though there is some variation in this respect, ranging from a modest degree of attachment to virtually none. Factions seek to use their parties to advance their own purposes. They tend to place their purposes ahead of party purposes when these differ. Nonetheless, factions are less inclined in some cases than in others to abandon one party and ally with another. Factionalism is the process of conflict and alliance among factions within the same party, and among factions and groups outside their party. Such groups include bureaucratic agencies, interest groups, other political parties, or factions within any of these.

Factionalism is found in nearly all political systems, but there is considerable variation in how important it is in different systems. Factional conflict may be the dominant factor, an important factor, or a minor factor in political competition. There is also variation in the arenas of significant factional conflict in different political systems. Factional competition may be most marked at the national or the subnational level, or it may be equally prominent at both. Similarly, it may be most marked in legislative parties or in extralegislative party organization.

Party factions vary with respect to basis, degree, and permanence of organization. Faction organization may be based on different kinds of ties between members, such as kinship, patron-client relations, support for or opposition to specific leaders, common policy preferences, or ideological commitment. At one extreme, party factions may have very loose organization; at the other, they may have elaborate and well-defined organization. Party factions are frequently quite transient, lasting no longer than the career of a particular political leader, although sometimes they may exhibit a permanence or at least continuity beyond a single leader. Definitions of faction often include characteristics of *internal* organization. Factions are sometimes said to be distinguished by organization based on instrumental exchange relationships between leaders and followers, loose organization, and/or transient organization.[1] Factions may most usefully be distinguished, however, by their *external* relationship to the party with which they are associated, and internal organizational characteristics may more usefully be treated as variables for the classification of different types of factions.

The Traditional Pattern of Philippine Factionalism

At the outset, it will be worthwhile briefly to outline relevant features of Philippine political institutions.[2] Within a few years after the Philippines was taken from Spain by the United States in 1898, its new colonial rulers introduced rudimentary representative institutions at national and local levels. The franchise and the scope of authority of those institutions were gradually but continually expanded. In 1935, the Philippines acquired commonwealth status and became to a large extent internally self-governing. The Constitution adopted that year continued to be the fundamental law after the country became independent in 1946, and it remained in effect until replaced by the martial law regime.[3] During this period Philippine institutions were patterned largely on the American model. The governmental system was based on a separation of powers among a president, a two-house congress, and an independent judiciary.

At the same time, the Americans continued the Spanish pattern of centralized administration. Under the 1935 Constitution, the Philippines remained a unitary state. The country is divided into provinces, and provinces are divided into municipalities ("towns"). The latter are basic units of local government and are at the base of the national administrative structure. Outside the few urban centers, towns are comprised of a number of "barrios," or villages, and a "poblacion," or town proper. The poblacion is the site of a plaza surrounded by the public buildings, the main church, the homes of the leading families, and, depending on size, a central school and public market. In small towns, the poblacion may be comprised of little more than this; in larger ones, it may be a sizable urban center. In either case, the largest portion of a town's population resides in the barrios. The chief executives and governing bodies of the provinces (governors and boards) and of the towns (mayors and councils) were elected from the early years of this century, and those of the barrios (captains and councils) were elected from 1960. Within the centralized Philippine administrative system, however, the formal powers of local officials were limited. Political parties were organized early in this century.[4] The Nacionalista party (NP), formed in 1907, was predominant in the preindependence years. No single opposition party spanned that period, and all opposition parties were quite weak. The most intense competition in the preindependence years occurred in 1922 and 1934, when the NP briefly split into two national factions. The NP again divided into two national factions at the time of independence in 1946. In all three of these instances, the division of the NP was occasioned by a struggle for control of the party among top party leaders. The 1946 split became permanent, the breakaway faction assuming the name Liberal party (LP). From 1946 until the advent of martial law in 1972, the NP and the LP were the primary competitors in fourteen successive elections, seven national and seven local. While the NP had an edge in this competition, there was considerable alternation of power between the NP and LP, at all levels. Hence the Philippines gave the appearance of having a competitive two-party system after 1946. The two parties were identical in all important respects, however, and the dominant forces underlying political competition were conflicts between locally based factions associated with different parties, and conflicts among the locally based factions comprising each party.

The origin and development of factional politics in the Philippines has been extensively detailed by Carl Landé.[5] Philippine factionalism had its origins in local communities rather than in national politics. During the Spanish era, a common pattern developed in many towns, of competition for political influence between two or sometimes more groupings centered on leading families whose wealth and prestige were based on landownership. When elections were introduced, the new parties were, as Landé has shown, "organized upward, i.e., through the amalgamation into a nationwide alliance of numerous preexisting local political groups."[6] While acting as town branches of the parties, these groups were actually factions. Their structure and purposes were distinct from the formal structure and purposes of the parties with which they were associated, and their commitments to those parties were weak or nonexistent.

Town-based factions were not in any sense specialized political organizations. As Landé described them,

> local factions . . . possess a raison d'etre independent of the purposes of the national parties. . . . [They] have a range of concern and activity far exceeding the sphere of politics. . . . [They] serve as the nuclei for the organization of various local events of an ostensibly recreational nature which, organized and financed by members of the leading families of one or another faction, serve as vehicles in a continual contest for prestige in their community. . . . [In] election years . . . the competition which at other times appears to be mainly for prestige emerges as an openly political struggle. . . . [Elections] cannot be studied in isolation, as if factional competition in the elections were a distinct governmental-political process separable from the annual round of social and civic activity in the community.[7]

The structural origins of town factions were in extrapolitical forms of organization in the traditional social order rather than in the formal pattern of party organization. They did not come into being primarily for political purposes, and they engaged in many activities outside of politics. Town-based factions remained very much locally oriented. Local considerations were paramount in determining their actions in provincial and national as well as local political competitions. Landé said,

> the character of Philippine parties as a whole is determined more by local consid-
> erations than by national ones, i.e. the composition and structure of the national
> parties is affected to a greater extent by the composition and structure of their
> constituent local and provincial organizations than the reverse.[8]

For local faction members, factional loyalty took priority over party loyalty. Even though town faction leaders were linked to the national parties, the resources supporting their political activities were local in origin. This enhanced the political autonomy of town faction leaders. The strong local orientation of faction leaders inhibited the growth of the kind of firm and stable party loyalties that are important to the effective operation of a competitive party system.

Factionalism was pronounced throughout party organization. Alliances of town factions comprised provincial factions, which were often centered on a leading provincial family. Alliances of provincial factions comprised the national parties. Given the low level of party loyalty of town faction leaders, such alliances tended to be quite fluid. Faction leaders freely shifted their support from one party to another. The most durable basis of political competition in the Philippines was that between town factions associated with different parties. If one faction changed parties, for whatever reason, it was common for the competing town faction(s) to change also, effecting a reversal in party alignments between town factions. While in this manner perpetuating the traditional pattern of division in the towns, local factions were often found opposed to former allies, and allied with former opponents, in the alliances comprising the provincial and national party organizations.

Fluidity of party organization resulted in unstable legislative parties. Congressmen had their power base in alliances of town factions, and senators had theirs in nationwide alliances of provincial factions. If required by the exigencies of politics or if opportunities seemed better with another party, these politicians could and did easily change parties. Given this instability of legislative parties, the kind of intraparty factions found in Italy or Japan, more or less stable over time, were absent in the Philippines. The major divisions of the NP in 1922 and 1934 were of short duration, and division of the NP in 1946 presaged the emergence of a new party. Over the years, there were many factional alliances of legislators within the various parties, usually based on support for or opposition to particular party leaders, but these tended to be very transient. There were alliances of legislators that were relatively stable over time; but these were associated not with factions, but with specific economic interests, such as sugar production, and tended to cut across party lines.

The organizational center of the traditional local faction was normally a family, and kinship ties were the basic cement at the center of faction organization. Beyond this, personal loyalty and mutual obligation growing out of the exchange of favors between unequals, that is, patron-client relationships, were the primary ties binding the heads of lesser families at the periphery to the faction's leaders. Landé found that

> the typical local faction . . . is a loose combination of a number of . . . family constellations with a rather large and prosperous family constellation at its core and smaller or less prosperous ones at its periphery. Within each family constellation, a strong web of kinship ties binds related families together into a cohesive group. Between the allied constellations of the faction, a smaller number of dyadic ties—more commonly ties of marriage, compadre ties, or ties of patronship and clientship rather than ties of blood—create a lesser bond.[9]

There was, then, a basic instability in the composition of traditional factions, particularly at the periphery. Nonetheless, there tended to be considerable continuity of the leading families at the centers of the competing local factions in most towns. In many cases, the same family provided leadership for a faction over several successive generations.

There were important variations in the size, homogeneity, and cohesiveness of the families at the centers of traditional factions. Because the Philippine kinship system is bilateral (that is, paternal and maternal relationships are equally important), because relationships to the second or third degree are normally recognized, and because the country's birthrate is very high, Filipinos normally are close to quite large numbers of relatives. A rural person might easily recognize as many as two hundred blood relatives. Politicians attempted to recognize and maintain ties with as many relatives as possible. Smaller old leading families of rural towns were often fairly homogeneous, being comprised primarily of prominent, poblacion-dwelling members. Larger leading families also often included some poorer, barrio-dwelling members. Among such families, heads of the more prominent branches took the lead in politics. Generally, the Philippine family tends to demand a deep loyalty from its members. In many cases, families at the center of traditional factions were closely united in politics. In larger extended families, not all relatives were likely to be included among one's political allies. Where intermarriage between members of competing families was common, divisions within families over politics were particularly likely. In some cases, competing factions even centered on different, but usually not close, branches of the same large family.

Traditional factions tended to be virtually identical in socioeconomic composition. Landé said that the "membership of a typical faction, being bound not by categorical ties but by a network of individual dyadic relationships, . . . will usually be a cross-section of the community."[10] The relative portions of members from different sectors of the community, however, changed over time. At the outset of American rule, the franchise was restricted by property and literacy qualifications to those leading families who had been prominent during the Spanish era. Hence, factional competition was confined to the more prosperous poblacion-dwelling families. With the broadening of the franchise in 1916, leading families at the center of these factions began attempting to mobilize barrio voters, but really large-scale involvement of the latter in town politics did not begin until after independence.

Changing Aspects of Philippine Factionalism

In some areas of the Philippines, the traditional pattern of factionalism had been undergoing significant changes for several decades.[11] These were in the organization of local factions and the nature of their leadership, and in the relationship between local factions and provincial and national party leadership. There, changes began as early as the 1930s in some areas and became widespread in the years after independence.

Where change was taking place, local factions lost many traditional organizational features and were transformed into specialized political machines. The new variant of the local faction was not a family-centerd organization but an electoral organization centered on an individual leader and a hierarchy of followers that had been built specifically for political purposes. The new faction was a machine, an organization devoted primarily to the political support of its leader and the maintenance of its members through the distribution of immediate concrete and individual rewards to them. New faction leaders might still have drawn important support from their families. The family was still often a significant component of the new faction, but it was no longer the core. That position was filled by a specialist organization whose primary reason for being was the mobilization of political support for its leaders.

An associated change in faction organization was that kinship ties became less important, and instrumental relationships became more important ingredients of the cement binding the central element of the faction. Kinship ties were reduced in importance because the family had ceased to be the central element, and patron-client ties were correspondingly increased. The patron-client relationship is an "instrumental friendship" based on reciprocal exchange between more and less powerful persons.[12] In this exchange, the more powerful provides security and personal rewards, and the less powerful provides services and support. Such ties often existed between members of the central family constellation and the heads of families at the periphery, and between various faction members and their nonkin followers in traditional factions. In the new faction, however, the core organization itself was based largely on patron-client ties rather than on kinship.

Faction organization also became more transient. The decline in importance of the family at the center of new factions meant a decline in the continuity of factions from generation to generation. While traditional factions were somewhat unstable, they had considerable continuity at the center. In the new factions, it was more likely that when the political career of the faction leader came to an end, the faction would disintegrate or undergo major changes in composition.

Whether local factions adhered more to the traditional pattern or the new pattern in other organizational respects, they all tended to be more inclusive than the traditional factions of preindependence years. For with the rapid expansion of mass electoral participation after 1946, all factions developed larger followings in the barrios.

In many cases, these organizational changes were associated with changes in the nature of faction leadership and leader-follower relationships. There was a tendency for notables from old leading families to be replaced in positions of town political leadership by upwardly mobile "new men" from small farming, fishing, and business families and other more humble backgrounds. For such leaders, participation in factional competition was not an avocation intended to reinforce their already high prestige in the community as it was for most traditional faction leaders. For "new men" (and some traditional faction leaders as well), politics became a career intended to provide a livelihood or to protect or advance a basic source of livelihood. For followers, support of a new faction was less an act of obligation to family or an act of deference to a social superior, and was more a means of acquiring small but immediate payoffs of various kinds.

In recent decades there was also an increase in the importance of provincial and national considerations, and a decline in the importance of local considerations in shaping the faction's character and its political actions in all arenas. While this was true for both traditional and new factions, it was more true of the latter. Local considerations were still of considerable importance, but faction leaders had less overwhelmingly local orientations than they had once had. This development was associated with a growing reliance by local factions, particularly new ones, on resources provided by politicians in higher arenas in exchange for their turning out voters on behalf of the latter. Increasingly, provincial and national political considerations shaped the actions of town faction leaders in those arenas as well as in the local arena itself.

Changes in local factionalism are partially explained by the impact of increasingly intense national political competition in rural communities and growing mass electoral participation after independence. Beyond this, the emergence of "new men" and professionals in local politics and the changing organizational aspects of factions were interrelated. These changes were not uniform throughout the Philippines, and were more likely to develop under some conditions than others. Such changes had been more likely to occur where, in both the town and the province of which it was a part, first, the level of social mobilization was comparatively high, and, second, the concentration of landownership was comparatively low. Areas of higher social mobilization are areas directly within the orbit of Manila (roughly a 100-mile radius), other urban centers, and immediately adjacent areas in the rest of the country, and, to some extent, the larger towns (e.g., provincial capitals). Within these areas, change was more pronounced in places where landholding was less concentrated.

More intense national political competition resulted in growing demands by national politicians that as many rural voters as possible be turned out on their behalf and thus resulted in a corresponding infusion of external resources into provinces and local communities to support such efforts. Such demands created the need for professional politicians in rural towns, thus necessitating new criteria for recruitment to positions of leadership in areas of comparatively high social mobilization and low concentration of landownership. These new criteria included the kinds of organizational skills and personal qualities which, along with necessary resources, were required to develop and maintain an extensive network of close personal ties. These ties were essential in securing the support of large numbers of voters. In areas of lower social mobilization and higher concentration of landownership, by contrast, criteria for recruitment had changed less, as the ties of prominent families still sufficed to a greater extent in building political support. In any case, application of the new criteria increasingly opened positions of leadership to a broader sector of the population in rural communities, resulting in the recruitment of many "new men." Because they lacked the kind of family prominence and ties that would assure their position of leadership in the town even when out of office, "new men" had more compelling reasons than notables from old leading families to make a career of officeholding once they became officials.

The impact of more intense national political competition in rural communities had likewise been partially responsible for eroding the traditional pattern of factionalism and stimulating organizational change in local factions. Scott has advanced a persuasive explanation for the emergence of machines in societies in the early stages of modernization that fits the Philippine case very well.[13] He argues that the

machine is the product of competitive, mass participation politics under conditions in which political loyalties based on traditional patterns
of deference in rural society are breaking down as a consequence of
rapid social change, but have yet to be replaced by broader loyalties
based on civic consciousness, and in which poverty is widespread.
Competitive political organizations will seek support by attempting to
meet the growing but still particularistic demands of their family and
community-oriented political followers. In the areas of the Philippines
where the level of social mobilization is comparatively high, social
change has been most disruptive and traditional patterns of deference
have been most weakened. And the latter are weakest in areas where
the concentration of landownership is also comparatively low. Correspondingly, these are areas in which popular demands have most rapidly grown or been stimulated by the actions of politicians, albeit such
demands are still essentially personal in nature. Successful efforts to
turn voters out on a large scale under these conditions required that
political leaders meet such demands insofar as possible, and that they
organize machines to that end.

The changing pattern of factionalism and organizational adaptation to these general conditions were consequences of choices made
by local political leaders. Local leaders who were "new men" made
choices and took actions conducive to such changes more often than
those who were from old leading families. They were less likely than
men from old leading families to have either the family connections or
the motivation necessary to perpetuate established patterns of factional politics. National and provincial politicians had increasing need
for allies in the towns who could mobilize large numbers of voters, and
their control of governmental resources put them in a position to
provide strong incentives for local leaders to become their allies. The
only way in which "new men" could develop the base of power requisite to political survival was to build a machine, as they lacked the kind
of local resources useful in political organization enjoyed by men from
families of prestige and wealth. They had to depend on newly available
external resources to do this.

As a consequence of these changes, Philippine political parties
became alliances of local factions that differed in important respects.
In some towns, factions were still basically traditional in form; in others, they were machines; and in still others, they were in a process of
transition. Some of the differences between such factions, which have
only been described in general terms, will now be illustrated by comparison of a representative example of a machine and of a traditional
faction. These are the dominant machine in the capital of Batangas
Province, Batangas City, and the dominant traditional faction in a
small town in Capiz Province, Dumalag. This comparison will focus on
the leadership and organization of these two factions and the relation

of the faction leaders to provincial and national parties as they were in 1970.[14]

Machine and Traditional Faction: A Comparison of Cases

Batangas and Capiz provinces, and the specific towns under consideration here, felt, to approximately the same extent, the impact of increasingly intense national political competition and the influence of rising electoral participation, but they are characterized by differing socioeconomic conditions of the sort associated with the contrasting types of faction. Conditions in Batangas Province and in its capital city are those associated with the emergence of "new men" in local politics and the organization of machines, while those in Capiz Province and Dumalag are the conditions associated with the traditional factions. Batangas Province is near Manila and is very much in the orbit of the political, cultural, and economic center of the country. Capiz is on the western Visayan island of Panay and is some distance from any urban center of national importance. The level of social mobilization, as indicated by the possibility that people will be exposed to various modernizing influences, is considerably higher in Batangas than in Capiz. And concentration of landownership is considerably higher in Capiz than it is Batangas.[15]

Batangas City is a comparatively large provincial town about ten kilometers south of Manila. In 1970, the total population was nearly 110,000, with around 18,000 persons resident in the poblacion.[16] The poblacion is highly urbanized. Batangas City is the provincial capital and the site of both provincial government and numerous branch offices of national government agencies. It is a regionally important business and commercial center. Some heavy industry and much light and cottage industry are located in the town. Batangas City is also a regionally important transportation and communications hub and educational center. Buses travel between the town and Manila with great frequency. Though the poblacion is extensively urbanized, the population as a whole is still predominantly rural. Less than one-third of the total population, however, is actually engaged in farming; the tenancy rate is very low, with only about one-tenth of the total population resident on tenant farms. Many persons living in the barrios are employees of the government or of private firms in the poblacion, engaged in cottage industry and the marketing of its products, or fishermen.

Dumalag, by contrast, is a small farming town in the hills of Capiz. It is some forty-five kilometers inland from the provincial capital on the coast. The population in 1970 was about 18,000, with 2,600 persons resident in the poblacion. The small poblacion is the site of the plaza, the church, the municipal hall, the market, a vocational high school, a few small shops, and the homes of the residents. There is also a small sugar central, which employs around four hundred persons, near the poblacion. Dumalag is on a main cross-island road linking the provincial capital of Capiz with that of a neighboring province. Buses pass through the town several times a day. Dumalag is primarily an agricultural cummunity, nearly 60 percent of the population being engaged in farming. The tenancy rate is also quite high, 40 percent of the town's population being residents of tenant farms.

PATTERNS OF FACTIONALISM

The pattern of factionalism in Batangas City has undergone considerable change in recent decades, while that in Dumalag has remained largely traditional. Early in this century, Batangas City politics was dominated by the town's wealthiest and most prominent landowning families. Most of their land was in neighboring farming communities, as there were few large landholdings in Batangas City. Hence these families lacked one of the more enduring bases of traditional power—the sure votes of large numbers of tenants—enjoyed by their counterparts in Dumalag and in many other Philippine towns. Town politics was initially the exclusive preserve of those leading families which were, in shifting combinations, at the center of contending factions. Batangas City politics was very competitive, but competition was not based on any long and consistent line of division. A stable, clearly defined pattern of traditional factional competition of the sort found in Dumalag and many other Philippine towns never developed in Batangas City.

As early as the 1920s, "new men" began to enter Batangas City politics. In the 1930s, competing town factions began to assume some of the characteristics of machines. The powers of the old leading families began a slow decline during these years. Family members gradually withdrew from electoral competition, though their support long continued to be of major importance to the "new men" entering politics. This pattern continued into the early postindependence years. In the 1950s, the old leading families ceased to exert any decisive influence in Batangas City politics. From then on, competing factions in the town's politics were all under the leadership of "new men." Under the auspices of the latest of these "new men" to assume leadership in Batangas City, Pedro Tolentino, a specialized political machine established what was to be long-term dominance in the mid-1950s. As late as 1970, there were some traditional vestiges in the pattern of factionalism in the town. Despite the fact that it was led by "new men," the chief opposition to the dominant Tolentino faction resembled a traditional family-centered faction in many respects.

Pedro Tolentino was first elected mayor of Batangas City in 1955 and was in his fourth term in 1970. He was from a barrio family of modest circumstances. He completed teacher training on a government scholarship, prospered in a successful business venture during the World War II Japanese Occupation, and later in his career he studied law on a part-time basis and passed the bar. He entered politics and was elected to the town council immediately after the war, and he built a significant following before running for mayor. After 1955, he began expanding the machine that was at the center of his faction. He did this primarily through establishment of a townwide network of personal supporters. He tied the latter to himself through judicious dispensation of patronage, project support, and personal favors. Mayor Tolentino's faction included several components, but it was clear that his personal organization provided the consistent hard core of support that had been the primary basis of his political dominance in Batangas City.

In contrast to Batangas City, a fairly stable, clear-cut, and quite intense pattern of bifactional competition involving two leading families had persisted in Dumalag from the early years of this century to 1970. One faction had been centered on the Frial family and the other on the interrelated Castro and Advincula families. Both families had large landholdings and many tenants. The division between these families had its roots in the late Spanish period, and, with the introduction of elections in 1907, it became the primary basis of political competition in the town. Every mayor except two since 1907 had been an immediate member of one of these families. The Castro/Advincula faction was dominant in Dumalag politics until 1931, but the Frial faction had controlled the town administration without interruption since that date.

The mayor of Dumalag in 1970 was Conrado Salcedo, a retired medical doctor and sugar planter. He had long been politically influential in the town, but he had not run for or held town office prior to his election as mayor. Like Mayor Tolentino, he was first elected in 1955 and was in his fourth term in 1970. The bases of his faction's power were family ties and landlord-tenant ties. His grandfather was the progenitor of the Frial family, and his father and two uncles were former mayors of the town. Most of the key leaders of the faction were his relatives. And in 1970, nearly half of the productive land in the town was owned by various branches of the Frial family. There were other components of the Frial faction, most important the owners of the sugar central and their employees, but the family was at the center.

Despite the extended dominance of first one and then the other of the two families, Dumalag factions had always been quite competitive. In conformity with the traditional pattern, factional competition still extended far beyond the political sphere and was clearly manifested in most other aspects of the community's social life. The two families were approximately equal in strength, and the owners of the sugar central held the balance of power between them. The latter had been with the Frial faction since 1947, guaranteeing Frial dominance of the town. Had it not been for the unique role of the sugar central, Damalag politics would have been in most respects a textbook model of the traditional pattern of factionalism described by Landé.

FACTION ORGANIZATION

Some Batangas City politicians had developed specialized political organizations in the prewar years, but Mayor Tolentino's organization was more formalized, more elaborate, and more extensive than any of those. It was representative of the machines that had emerged in many Philippine towns. His organization included a large portion of the other elected town officials and of the barrio officials. In 1970, eight of the other nine elected town officials were formally allied with the mayor, and he enjoyed the support of about two-thirds of the eighty-two barrio captains. In most barrios where he did not have the support of the barrio captain, he had other *liders* (persons who mobilize voters for a candidate), who were in some cases barrio councillors. Under the chairmanship of the mayor, these persons constituted the Batangas City chapter of the Nacionalista party. In Batangas City, there was considerable coincidence between the mayor's faction, the town political party, and government organization.

Town officials affiliated with the mayor's faction all had some kind of independent base of support. Possession of such support was a prerequisite for inclusion on the slate of NP candidates for town office. Three of the councillors aligned with the mayor were attorneys and were "well known" because their profession permitted them to provide free services to a great many people. Another had for over twenty years been a registrar of a local college that specialized in teacher training, and most of her students were from the barrios. Hence she was "well known" among barrio teachers, who often had considerable influence. Another, who had no regular occupation, devoted nearly all his time to cultivating his personal following. For example, he spent many mornings at the municipal hall greeting people and accompanying them to the administrative officials with whom they had business, and he spent much time at the provincial hospital commiserating with patients and their relatives. Such town officials had built followings of their own. They could then offer the support of their followers for the mayor's candidacy in exchange for his support of their candidacies in his bailiwicks.

The mayor's most important supporters were clearly his barrio *liders.* There were at least one or two and in some cases several such *liders* in nearly all barrios. Many of these were men with whom Tolentino had been closely associated sincè early in his political career. Some of the strongest barrio captains could easily deliver one hundred or more votes for the mayor. These men were, then, the backbone of the mayor's organization and played the most critical role in mobilizing voters on his behalf.

Mayor Tolentino's organization was activated as a political party only at election time, that is, for a few months every other year. Despite this, it had to be maintained regularly to ensure its effective functioning at those times. It was held together primarily by personal ties built on mutual exchanges of an instrumental nature. The mayor dispensed projects and personal favors to and through the members of his organization. He was the town official to whom barrio captains had to look for project assistance, as he had a decisive say in the allocation of local funds. He was the town official with the most influence in higher echelons of government, and he could thus make the most effective representations for outside financing of projects. Similarly, he had an important say in city appointments, though he shared this with a key congressman from the province and the governor in the case of appointments to top posts. In return for his considerations, the members of the mayor's organization mobilized voters on his behalf and otherwise gave him their political support when called upon to do so.

It was clear that most of the mayor's barrio *liders* regarded themselves as simply his personal followers and had little sense of being affiliated with the Nacionalista party as a distinct organization. The instrumental and personal nature of the relationship that existed between Mayor Tolentino and his barrio *liders* is well illustrated by the following very characteristic comment of one barrio captain. When asked if he was a *lider* for the NP or for the mayor personally, he told me,

I work for the mayor as a person, not because he is with the NP, and I don't choose any candidates by the party they are with, but for their personal qualities. It is individuals, not parties, that help the barrio.

The highly personal nature of leadership in the faction meant that it could not be transferred to another person. Hence the faction and the Batangas City NP had no basis for organizational continuity beyond the mayor's political career.

Mayor Tolentino estimated that his personal organization mobilized at least half of the votes that he received. There were several other components of his faction. The members of his family, which was quite large, were concentrated in six barrios. These constituted a stronghold that he carried overwhelmingly at election time, and that accounted for close to 20 percent of his total vote. He attended to the needs of these barrios very well. His home barrio was the site of the first barrio high school in the city. In any case, family ties were important in the support that he received from people in this area. He said that the remainder of his support, about 30 percent of his votes, came from a variety of followers, such as compadres, beneficiaries of small favors, city employees, and families with whose heads he was more or less allied.

In Dumalag, both factions still largely fit the traditional pattern of organization. As in most Philippine towns, they had by 1970 become more inclusive than in earlier decades as a result of the growth of electoral participation. They were, however, still centered on extended leading families. The Frial family, at the center of the dominant faction, was actually comparatively small by Philippine standards. Nonetheless, it controlled a majority of votes in seven of the town's eighteen barrios and provided much of the top leadership for the faction's electoral organization. The remainder of the leadership was provided by the heads of allied families and the owners of the sugar central.

Heads of the Frial family's branches and heads of allied families were responsible for mobilizing voters in their own domains. These were areas where their relatives lived and/or where they owned land and could count on their tenant's votes. This family-based electoral organization was loosely coordinated by the mayor. Mayor Salcedo gave me a detailed description of this faction's electoral organization:

> The family heads that make up the coalition that is the party are responsible for getting out the vote in their respective domains. The big family heads include seven Frials, four Fuertes, three Frios, the Faldoneas, and the Grinos. [The owner of the sugar central is also part of the organization.] Each holds sway in a different area. . . . Then the candidates for the Vice Mayor and Council, nine in all, are each assigned to two barrios. They may or may not belong to one of these big family groups. If they do, they will work along with their family. If they do not, they will assist them in getting out the vote, but it is the big families of landholders who have the decisive influence with the voters. [There are also] the Barrio Captains, if they are with us, or if not, other barrio *liders*. . . . These are mostly all men [owing their allegiance to] the big families. Below that, barrio *liders* have contact with their relatives and sub*liders.*

Some of the other families mentioned by the mayor as being at the center of the faction were also related to the Frials.

Unlike Mayor Tolentino, whose major strength lay in a townwide network of loyal barrio *liders,* Mayor Salcedo and his predecessors had traditionally relied on the heads of the Frial family branches and of allied families to mobilize voters through their respective *liders.* These were often their *encargados* ("overseers") or trusted tenants. This meant that *liders* owing first allegiance to the mayor were concentrated in his own bailiwick and that his ties with barrio *liders* outside this area were only indirect. As a consequence of the very close competition in town elections, Mayor Salcedo and the leaders of the opposing faction had become heavily involved in the elections of barrio captains in the late 1960s. In this way, the mayor seemed to be developing more direct ties with *liders* throughout the town. Given the power of the landlords, however, it would have been difficult for the mayor to exercise much influence outside his family's bailiwick if his wishes had run counter to those of the landlords in those areas.

Kinship ties and landlord-tenant relations were the major factor in voter mobilization for the Frial faction. For those at the center of the faction, family ties were paramount. The need for expansion since independence meant that the heads of smaller barrio families and smaller landlords had been recruited into the faction, and their support had been secured partially by instrumental inducements. Their followers were, however, like those of the heads of the central families, mobilized largely on the basis of family ties and landlord-tenant relationships. The comments of one barrio *lider* associated with the Frial faction were indicative of this and of the absence of any meaningful partisan commitment. He said:

> I am the only *lider* here. . . . In this barrio there are only [a few] voters, and most of them are my relatives. I tell them who to vote for and they just follow me. I am LP, but I have my sister campaign for the NP to try to make everybody happy. It is best to be on good terms with both parties. . . . Even though my sister sort of campaigns for the NP for that reason, she and the others vote LP with me.

This *lider*'s support for the faction was based primarily on instrumental considerations, but the support he received was based largely on family ties. Dumalag landlords expected a traditional kind of deference from their tenants, and the votes of many of the latter were still mobilized for the faction on that basis. Because of the closeness and the growing intensity of competition in the town, however, cash and coercion were increasingly being used to maintain tenant electoral support.

The constellation of families at the center of the Frial faction was able to secure the votes of about one-third of the Dumalag electorate. The owners of the sugar central, who had been associated with the Frial faction since 1947, were able to secure another 15 to 20 percent of the votes in the town. These were primarily the votes of their tenants and of their employees at the central. The central owners were members of the town's traditional leadership stratum, but because of the nature of their business, they were less concerned with local politics than with forging useful alliances with national politicians. That concern made them key participants in Dumalag politics, as they wished to be able to mobilize as much support as possible for favored national politicians. In any case, their support was crucial to the mayor.

FACTIONS AND PARTIES

Before the war, nearly all the leaders of contending factions in Batangas City were nominally Nacionalistas, but they had limited connections with the national party. With the postindependence organization of the Liberal party, the consequent development of more consistently structured partisan competition in national politics, and the growth of local demands that could only be met with provincial and national resources, the need for town officials to establish ties with the national parties had grown. Mayor Tolentino was the first Batangas City executive to concentrate on forging such links. He assiduously cultivated ties with key leaders of the dominant provincial and national NP. After his first election as mayor in 1955, which he had contested as an independent candidate, he was accepted as an ally by the province's key congressman and powerful governor, who were both with the NP. As a founder and first president of the Municipal Mayor's League of the Philippines in the late 1950s, he had established good relations with the late NP President Garcia. And in 1970, he was a member of the NP's National Directorate.

Mayor Tolentino's long-standing ties with the NP had not been translated into the kind of firm and dependable sense of affiliation that would ensure consistency of association with that party. In 1969, in fact, he made a serious threat to seek the LP nomination for Congress in the district containing Batangas City. He did this in the context of a dispute with the provincial governor over whether the town was to become a chartered city. This was of considerable importance to both parties, because a town gains substantial resources at the expense of the province upon becoming a city. Tolentino indicated that he fully intended to carry out his threat if the governor did not relent. Because the nature of the national Philippine party system did not encourage or reward consistency in affiliation, Mayor Tolentino's commitment to the NP was as firm and dependable as could have been expected. It was also clear that it could easily have changed under a number of conditions.

In Dumalag, the Frials were originally associated with the opposition to the dominant family in Capiz and the Nacionalista party with which the latter was associated during the early years of this century. In the late 1920s, the Frials associated with the NP following the marriage of a family member to an immediate member of the dominant provincial family. This association was the key to their assumption of political control in the town after 1931. The primary political figure in the dominant Capiz Province family was Manuel Roxas, the founder of the Liberal party and first president of the independent Republic of the Philippines. Maintaining their alliance with Roxas, the Frials affiliated with his new LP in 1946. This began a long-standing Frial association with the LP. Correspondingly, they had been closely tied to the congressional representative who since 1946 had represented the district containing Dumalag as an LP congressman.

It was clear that the Frial's long association with the LP had not produced strong commitment to the party. This was demonstrated in 1969. The congressman from their district joined the NP when he failed to secure the LP nomination for president that year. At the same time, the dominant provincial family was still united behind a prominent member who was president of the national LP. The immediate result of the congressman's change of party was a division in the Frial faction's leadership. Mayor Salcedo, who was most dependent on the congressman for access to provincial and national resources, changed to the NP along with some other faction leaders. Others would not change. This was not because they were committed to the LP but because they were unwilling to cooperate with their traditional opponents in the town in support of the NP slate. In 1970, it seemed improbable that the division in the Frial family would persist. It was widely thought that while some Frials might be able to work with the Castro/Advincula faction in national politics, there was no way they could join in support of common candidates for town office. It was believed that the Frials would be reunited at the next local election, either as Liberals, regardless of the congressman's wishes, or as Nacionalistas, if the opposing faction should realign with the LP. In either case, their decision would not be based on partisan commitment.

Continuities in Philippine Factionalism

The emphasis here on changes in local political leadership and organization should not obscure the high degree of continuity that existed in Philippine party politics up to 1972. Factionalism had not been diminished in the least prior to the declaration of martial law. The new machines were as much factions as the more traditional, family-centered groups. Structurally, the machines had become somewhat less distinct from formal party organization than the traditional factions had been. But their purposes remained as distinct as ever; they were much more oriented to their own perpetuation and advancement than to party purposes. Because they were centered on individual leaders rather than families, machine-type factions had less organizational continuity than many traditional factions. This made it impossible for them to become party branches of enduring reliability for either party. More important, machine leaders had no greater stability of commitment to a national party than traditional faction leaders had. While increasing reliance on national resources reduced the autonomy of the leaders of factions of both types, making it harder for them to pursue their own ends, it did not increase their loyalty to either party. Until 1972, there had been little change in most fundamental aspects of Philippine party politics, which were to a large degree shaped by the factional basis of the parties. Whether the changes under way in local factionalism might eventually have contributed to important changes in the working of the party system can only be the subject of speculation under current conditions.

The persistence of factionalism in the Philippines was a result of factors that inhibited local factions from developing lasting and consistent associations with national parties and thus becoming real party branches, only some of the more important of which can be examined here. The family-centered organization of traditional factions assured that they would command the first loyalties of their members, and their deep roots in the social fabric of rural communities assured that they would be primarily locally oriented. This orientation was reinforced by the competitive aspects of traditional factionalism, which were so heavily invested with elements of prestige and other extrapolitical considerations. There were probably no conditions under which traditional factions could have become basic units of stable national parties. To the extent that local political organizations were still of this type, then, the persistence of factionalism was to be expected.

While the "new men" who had organized machines were not as inhibited by inherent structural constraints from developing stable associations with national parties as the heads of traditional factions, they did not do so. The interaction of the demands placed on machine leaders by their constituents and the inducements held out to them by competing national and provincial politicians discouraged such associations. And basic characteristics of the parties and the political system further encouraged factionalism.

Constituent demands on machine leaders were very heavy. Given the low level of civic consciousness in the rural Philippines, such demands were almost exclusively immediate and either personal or community centered. They had at least partially to be met if local leaders were to maintain their followings. They could only be met through good connections with the powerful and access to extralocal resources, not through efforts to promote general policy. This gave machine leaders strong incentive to make the best alliances they could with national and provincial leaders in order to secure such connections and resources. At the same time, national and provincial politicians were in strong competition to forge alliances with local leaders in order to maximize their support. They employed only political criteria in distributing the resources at their command, rewarding allies and punishing opponents. And, given the highly centralized administrative system in the Philippines, this gave them great leverage in dealing with local leaders. Under these conditions, machine leaders had strong incentives to make and break alliances with national and provincial politicians quite freely, depending on where the best opportunities were to be found at any given time. Morevoer, in the context of a society that lacked good economic opportunities for the provincial middle class, these kinds of conditions made politics one of the more attractive potential routes to economic advancement in the larger provincial towns. This tended to attract growing numbers of political entrepreneurs into local competition and thereby to increase the tendency to factionalism.[17]

Basic characteristics of the Philippine parties and political system further encouraged factionalism. The original organization of Philippine parties around traditional factions meant that the parties were virtually identical in their socioeconomic composition and in their highly conservative orientation. The replacement of traditional factions by machines in the structure of the parties in some areas did not alter this. The kind of popular demands made of politicians did not force them to adopt policy stances or ideological positions that would have encouraged differentiation of the parties. Moreover, the interests of the small group of nationally powerful persons had long been well served by the issueless, personalistic politics that prevailed in the Philippines because it ensured that no serious challenges to the status quo would be expressed through the parties. Hence national leaders of real influence had no interest in making the kinds of serious appeals to the powerless or taking the kinds of direct initiatives that would have been necessary conditions for diversification of the parties. Given the identical nature of the two parties, there was no incentive for leaders at any level to develop strong attachments to one or the other of them, especially since all leaders had strong motivation to be alert to possibilities for making more advantageous alliances.

Factionalism and Philippine Political Development

Philippine political parties were important instruments of integration in the political system until September 1972. While the two major parties were individually quite unstable, the party system had deep roots in rural society. These characteristics of the party system were due largely to the fact that the parties were comprised of locally based factions. The family-centered factions were still deeply embedded in the social fabric of smaller and more traditional communities, while the emergence of machines was a more or less successful organizational adaptation to changing conditions in some areas. The links between the leaders of these local factions and provincial and national leaders through the parties clearly bridged the "elite-mass gap" that is often quite broad and only weakly bridged in many developing countries. The parties, then, contributed to Philippine political stability over an extended period of time.

While Philippine parties may have been comparatively effective instruments of political integration, they had many weaknesses that were impediments to democratic development. And these weaknesses were largely a consequence of factionalism. As noted, factionalism inhibited the growth of party competition along lines of economic cleavages and of stable party loyalties. The parties were too unstable to be effective instruments for the operation and management of government. The extreme reliance placed on patronage and political criteria in resource allocation as a means of building support in the absence of partisan loyalties inhibited rational administration. The bureaucracy was swollen, incompetent, and very expensive to maintain, and administrative actions were, in any case, inevitably based on political considerations. The parties' approach to building support made it unnecessary for them to provide any clear sense of direction with respect to governmental policy, and there was no other source of such direction within the political system.

Two additional weaknesses of the faction-based party system were becoming increasingly apparent in the period prior to the declaration of martial law. First, factional politics could not accommodate the demands of persons concerned with fundamental change in the distribution of values in the society. Growing numbers of such persons were found among the middle class in Manila and other cities, among peasants in areas traditionally marked by agrarian unrest, and among the Muslim minority in Mindanao. This was reflected in growing civil strife in Manila, and peasant dissidence in some areas. Second, what Scott has called the "inflationary character of patron-client democracy"[18] was increasingly afflicting the Philippines. This was shown clearly in 1969, when expenditures for the reelection bid of President Marcos were so great as to be a major factor leading to the 1970 devaluation of the peso. More seriously, such activities had long diverted resources from more productive efforts. The costs of factional party politics appeared to be reaching limits imposed by the Philippine economy.

A major weakness of the Philippine political system, revealed by the ease with which Marcos assumed complete control in 1972, was its vulnerability to a centrally directed coup. While in no way providing a complete explanation of this vulnerability or of the coup, some aspects of factional politics stressed here help to explain both. First, given the pattern of popular interests and loyalties underlying factional politics, perpetuation of representative institutions was almost exclusively contingent on the support of only the very small top leadership stratum. This proved to be an element of great fragility in the system when the strongest of those top leaders decided to bring it to an end. Second, the growing centralization of power and declining autonomy of local faction leaders, reflected in the increasing dependence of the latter on central resources, facilitated this kind of action. Finally, weaknesses already identified along with many others, such as massive corruption and endemic violence, provided a rationale for decisive, even though authoritarian, action that gave the appearance of being change oriented. It should be noted in this connection that while Philippine factional politics had numerous and serious faults, it is not at all certain that the country's major social and economic problems can or will be dealt with any better under authoritarian dispensation.

Finally, from a comparative perspective, there are both similarities and differences between the pattern of factionalism in the Philippines and patterns of factionalism in other political systems. By way of conclusion, it will be useful to point to a few of these and to suggest where one may look for their explanations. Internal organization and leader-follower relationships in Philippine factions, particularly those of the patron-client-based machines, were quite similar to those found in other predominantly rural societies which have been similarly disrupted by modernizing forces (e.g., India), or in societies where a feudal heritage is still strong (e.g., Japan). As in other societies where factionalism is a major factor in political competition (e.g., Italy, Japan, India), factionalism in the Philippines had adverse consequences for party stability. This was, however, manifested in the Philippines in its most acute form, because Philippine factions had no attachment to their parties at all. In more socioeconomically and ideologically diverse societies where there are substantial differences between parties (e.g., Italy, Japan), factions could not as freely abandon one party and associate with another as they could in the Philippines, where the parties were identical in all important respects. The most distinctive feature of Philippine factionalism was that it was constituted of primarily locally based groups, rather than of diverse but relatively stable groups in the parties' legislative contingents, as is the case in most other factional political systems. This distinctive characteristic reflected the specific historical origins of Philippine parties and the lack of differences between them. The greater degree of stability of composition of legislative parties that accompanies real differences between them is probably necessary for the formation of relatively stable legislative party factions. In any case, comparative study of many faction systems should suggest other factors and more complete explanations of various patterns of factionalism.

NOTES

1. In defining a political faction, some social anthropologists stress internal organizational features. F. G. Bailey, *Stratagems and Spoils: A Social Anthropology of Politics* (New York: Schocken Books, 1969), pp. 51–55, stresses the transactional nature of leader-follower relations in factions. Ralph W. Nicholas, "Factions: A Comparative Analysis," in Michael Banton, ed., *Political Systems and the Distribution of Power*, Association of Social Anthropologists, Monograph no. 2 (London: Tavistock Publications, 1965), emphasizes the nonpermanent nature of faction organization and the diverse nature of leader-follower relationships. Many political scientists stress that factions, as opposed to parties, are loosely organized and lack continuous organization. See, for example, William Nisbet Chambers, *Political Parties in a New Nation: The American Experience, 1776–1809* (New York: Oxford Univ. Press, 1963), pp. 45–48.

2. A useful standard source on Philippine government and politics is: O. D. Corpuz, *The Philippines* (Englewood Cliffs: Prentice-Hall, 1965).

3. Although adoption of a new charter was being considered by an elected constitutional convention prior to the declaration of martial law, the 1935 Constitution was essentially replaced by fiat of President Marcos in 1973.

4. On the evolution of Philippine parties, see Dapan Liang, *Philippine Parties and Politics*, rev. ed. (San Francisco: Gladstone, 1970).

5. His standard treatment of the development of factionalism in the Philippines is Carl H. Landé, *Leaders, Factions, and Parties: The Structure of Philippine Politics*, Monograph Series, no. 6 (New Haven: Yale Southeast Asia Studies, 1965). The following analysis of traditional factionalism follows that of Landé closely.

6. Ibid., p. 4.

7. Ibid., pp. 14–15.

8. Ibid., p. 5.

9. Ibid., p. 17.

10. Ibid., p. 18.

11. The following argument has been elaborated in my "Changing Aspects of Factionalism in Philippine Local Politics," *Asian Survey* 11 (Dec. 1971): 1182–99; and my "Changing Patterns of Leadership Recruitment and the Emergence of the Professional Politician in Philippine Local Politics," in Ben Kerkvliet, ed., *Political Change in The Philippines: Studies of Local Politics Prior to Martial Law* (Honolulu: Univ. Press of Hawaii, 1974), pp. 77–129.

12. The nature of patron-client ties and the variation in affective and instrumental relationships within such ties are analyzed by James C. Scott, "Patron-Client Politics and Political Change in Southeast Asia," *American Political Science Review* 66, no. 1 (Mar. 1972): 91–113.

13. James C. Scott, "Corruption, Machine Politics, and Political Change," *American Political Science Review* 63, no. 4 (Dec. 1969): 1142–58.

14. The descriptions that follow here are based on my own fieldwork in the two provinces in 1969 and 1970. These two cases are introduced here for the purpose of illustration. I have presented a systematic comparison of six cases and survey data in support of the argument given here in my two articles cited in note 11. For a more

detailed case study which focuses on the transformation of one faction during this century, see my "From Traditional Faction to Machine: Changing Patterns of Political Leadership and Organization in the Rural Philippines," *Journal of Asian Studies* 33 (Aug. 1974): 523–47.

15. Social mobilization is here assessed as each province's ranking on five indicators: literacy, percent of work force in nonagricultural occupations, urbanization, numbers of motor vehicles, and homes with radios; each was assumed to be related to the possibility that people will be exposed to various modernizing influences. Concentration of landownership is here assessed as the percentage of the total population residing on tenant farms; this was relevant because it showed the portion of the population (and of voters) directly subject to the influence of landlords at election time.

16. The data cited in this and the following paragraph are from Bureau of Census and Statistics, *Census of the Philippines-1960* (Manila: Republic of the Philippines, Bureau of Census and Statistics, 1963).

17. This argument is made and demonstrated in Thomas Nowak, "Class and Clientelist Systems in the Philippines: The Basis for Instability" (Ph.D. diss., Cornell Univ., 1974).

18. Scott, "Patron-Client Politics and Political Change in Southeast Asia," p. 111.

9

Party Factions and Modernization: A Comparative Analysis of Colombia and Uruguay

RONALD H. McDONALD

Colombia and Uruguay share one political characteristic uncommon among Latin American nations. They have sustained for most of the present century functioning two-party systems. In both party systems, the two major parties emerged after independence in the early nineteenth century and corresponded to the "liberal-conservative" division common then in most of Latin America. In addition to this bipartisan division, politics in both of these countries has been complicated by the competitive interaction of intraparty factions. It is my intention here to identify the factions which have produced factional politics in these two countries, and to compare the consequences of their separate histories of factionalism. The inquiry will be guided by the hypothesis that the particular character of factional development in each nation was partly a response to their respective experiences in modernization—a blending of the personalistic politics of a traditional society and the bureaucratic party politics of a modern state.[1]

Despite the similarity of their party systems, Colombia and Uruguay differ in many respects. Perhaps most important are the differences in their levels of modernization and the periods during which each experienced high rates of social mobilization and economic development.[2] Uruguay is a small, highly urban, semi-industrialized, and socially advanced nation, which reached high levels of social mobilization and bureaucratization of its society early in the twentieth century. Its income distribution and class structure are among Latin America's most equalized, and its level of educational attainment one of the highest in the region.[3] Colombia is much larger in population, predominantly rural but rapidly urbanizing. It is socially rigid and stratified, unequal in income distribution and class, and limited in educational opportunities and attainment. Economic modernization has been largely an experience of the last generation.[4] Finally, Uruguay's population is European by origin, while Colombia's is a mixture of various combinations of immigrant and indigenous peoples.

Although the functioning and implications of factional politics have been different in each country, there have been some common experiences. While politics remained without serious strain, factions contributed to political stability by assisting the two parties' mutual interaction—in one case, through interparty faction coalitions—and by allowing personalistic politics ample scope for political competition without upsetting the basic structure of the party system in either country. Under conditions of stress, however, rather than neutralizing party factions in both cases have contributed to systemic paralysis amid public violence, and ultimately in each case to an unprecedented military intervention.

Factions and Modernization

While a concern with party factions involves many important questions, the issue of how factions' evolution is affected by the level and rate of modernization is most important here, as our concern is with two *transitional,* rather than traditional or modern, countries. Although much emphasis has been given in recent years to modernization as an orientation for comparative politics, the general concept is not new to political science. Its origins, in fact, can be found in the writings of Max Weber, whose ideas were transmitted through Talcott Parsons and others to more recent theorists, like Samuel Huntington, Fred Riggs, and David Apter.[5] The modernization concept is relevant to Latin America, since most of its countries can be classified as transitional, a mixture of traditional and modern, or as what Riggs calls "prismatic societies."[6] And it has special relevance for this chapter, as it is my contention that factions evolved and were sustained in Uruguay and Colombia largely, if not solely, in response to conditions generated by modernization.

Weber views bureaucratization as a consequence of what now is commonly called modernization. Bureaucratization is a process which continues as society and culture become more complicated and specialized; "bureaucracy," he says, "offers attitudes demanded by the external apparatus of modern culture in the most favorable combination."[7] Weber sees bureaucracy as the rationalization, specialization, and persistence of organizations designed to perform important social functions. While he is concerned only with administrative organizations, his idea need not be so limited: bureaucratization—the legitimization of organizations—is essentially what Huntington defines as institutionalization, i.e., ". . . a process whereby organizations and procedures acquire value and stability."[8]

Weber shows a remarkable sensitivity to the processes implied in the transformation from traditional to modern society. He believes that bureaucratic structures emerge only ". . . on the basis of a leveling of economic and social differences . . .," since the "propertyless masses especially are not served by a formal 'equality before the law.' "[9] He argues that bureaucratic organizations will not naturally emerge in traditional societies because they are biased toward specific classes which are not in a majority, and the values which sustain bureaucratic organizations—in Huntington's terms, values which permit them to institutionalize—presume some degree of socioeconomic leveling as society becomes more complex and specialized. Socioeconomic leveling occurred relatively early in Uruguay's national development, permitting political institutionalization and stabilization in its party factions and other political and governmental structures. The leveling process has not yet occurred in Colombia, with the result that its parties and factions are predominantly elitist and personalistic, rather than bureaucratized.

Huntington views political parties specifically as the most critical organizations to emerge with modernization. This is because to the extent that parties become institutionalized, they can absorb and channel in socially acceptable ways the increasing levels of political participation which generally arise with the social imbalances characteristic of modernization. He argues that

> . . . societies which have created large-scale modern political institutions with the capability of handling much more extensive political participation than exists at present are presumptively stable, [while] . . . societies where participation already exceeds institutionalization are, clearly, unstable.[10]

The normal experience for transitional countries, as Huntington and others suggest, is for the forces of change imposed on traditional societies to stimulate social mobilization, which, Huntington argues, if not matched by economic development and mobility opportunities, increases participation. The latter, unless within the context of increasing institutionalization, is destabilizing.

In Uruguay and Colombia, as a consequence of the issues generated by the independence movement in the early nineteenth century, strong party identities and allegiances preceded growth in social mobilization and preceded both the institutionalization of party structures and popular electoral participation. These identifications developed early after independence; leadership and expression of party interests were left to elites and individual leaders who, in traditional ways, provoked and rallied their followers to action in their causes—and, in extreme cases, to violence. The consequences during the nineteenth century were periodic instability and "party"-oriented civil wars.[11] In both countries, factions permitted strong personal allegiances to find expression within the general framework of two-party cultures, without prompting the formation of new party alternatives. Party heritages persisted as ambitious leaders fought for control of the party banner. In Uruguay, rapid social mobilization, largely through immigration and economic development, encouraged leaders to accept a partial socioeconomic leveling of their society and institutionalization of party structures while still accommodating the traditionalism of personalistic politics.[12]

As different as their experiences were, there are common components and sequences in Uruguay and Colombia. In both countries, the two-party systems conform to what Riggs sees as a characteristic of transitional societies: the blending of *personalistic* politics, represented particularly by party factions, and *bureaucratic* politics, represented by institutionalizing party organizations. Party factions permit the release of traditional political pressures through personalistically differentiated factions that coexist with more modern, institutionalizing structures. Factions became a principal political loyalty in each case, but in Uruguay they became institutionalized, bureaucratized, and partly contained, following the early and rapid social mobilization of its population. Uruguayan elites agreed among themselves to divide political hegemony spatially between parties and to restrain party conflict, and, at the same time, to permit and to control factions. Uruguay thus protected national party structures through legal controls which gave formal identity and security to factions but which also set limits on factional behavior, so as not to destroy the viability of the larger party units.[13]

In Colombia, on the other hand, factions remained ad hoc and uninstitutionalized, which encouraged alliances between factions of different parties. Ad hoc factionalism also invited political violence, as social mobilization increased in the absence of increasing institutionalization. Colombian parties can be seen as products of factional activity; until recently, parties, except as party-label identifications, did not exist beyond the voluntary associations of factions and their leaders. As a consequence, interparty factional coalitions have been easier and more common in Colombia, particularly during the period from 1958 to 1972. In more bureaucratized Uruguay, by contrast, intraparty factional coalitions have been more common, and interparty factional coalitions exceptional.

In both countries factional leaders have been the principal contenders for the highest elective office, the presidency. It is too simple to conclude that factions in either country are merely followings of ambitious politicians coveting the presidency, for there has been sufficient stability in many factions to permit alternation in leadership over the years. It is true, however, that once becoming a faction leader, one almost automatically is, in each system, a presidential contender. There have been presidents who had not been faction leaders, but they reached the presidency only with the support of faction leaders.

The most severe crisis of modernization for both countries occurred as a result of social mobilization, which gave the party of urban residents increasing control over national political life by virtue of their higher level of mobilization and their support of modernizing elites—the Colorados in Uruguay, the Liberals in Colombia—making each the stronger, politically dominant party in its nation. This growing dominance by urban-based, modernizing elites challenged the rural-based, traditional parties—the Blancos in Uruguay, the Conservatives in Colombia—and promoted extended periods of sociopolitical violence, climaxing in Uruguay during the last decades of the nineteenth century, and in Colombia from the mid-1940s to the late 1950s. This stage created in each society a "politics of confrontation" organized around two political parties. Its resolution in Uruguay was facilitated by the willingness and ability of dominant party elites to enter into political agreements with the opposition, dividing power on a spatial basis; in Colombia, a temporary resolution was achieved through a constitutional coalition which divided and alternated national power.[14]

The resolution in Colombia was only partial, however, because socioeconomic leveling did not occur, and party structures did not significantly institutionalize or adequately contain competitive political activity. Intraparty factional rivalry over the issue of leveling often exceeded interparty rivalry, and Colombian interparty factional coalitions have been common. Recent economic development and the first major threat from a third party apparently have persuaded many Colombian leaders of the eventuality of some socioeconomic leveling, and Colombia may now be responding to political forces experienced in Uruguay over a half century ago. The Uruguayan system survived within the context of high social mobilization as long as economic development and "mass satisfaction" remained high. After 1953 in Uruguay, however, economic stagnation and decay, and growing polarization of the society on new class, generational, and political lines, produced new factional alliances, growing intraparty factional hostility, gradual deinstitutionalization of the traditional party structures, and ultimately military intervention.[15]

The Evolution of Colombian Party Factions

Following independence in 1819, the issues which divided Colombian party elites were formidable. Conservatives sought centralized government and close ties between church and state, and advocated interests of the then-dominant rural elites. Liberals wanted decentralization and federalism, and separation of church and state, and increasingly promoted the interests of urban areas.[16] Both parties, however, existed in the context of a traditional society, lacked organizational and bureaucratic structures, and depended upon shifting coalitions among national leaders—for personal, tactical, and only occasionally ideological considerations.

Economic regionalization and limited communications in the context of geographical isolation combined to promote strong local identities and loyalties, and stimulated political machines which often viewed any strong central government as a threat to their survival.[17] Even the Conservatives, who in principle advocated strong central government, periodically sought and utilized decentralization as a way of wresting control of one or more states from Liberal machines. While there was in the aggregate a national two-party system, each party specialized in specific, territorially defined and delimited areas. These machines might dominate an entire state—there were twenty-one states in 1851—but generally their control was even more localized.[18] Within the traditional plantation economy and social system, an individual landowner could decide the political orientation of his family and all those whose welfare came under his control—often including adjoining communities which were socially or economically dependent upon him. Party identification and factional support developed both personal and regional bases as a result of this checkered pattern.

Moreover, popular electoral participation was severely restricted in nineteenth-century Colombia, except for a few years following the 1853 Constitution, when the country briefly experimented with a broadened franchise. Government officials were either elected indirectly, or states were left to decide for themselves who could participate, which in most instances meant few.[19] The numerical strength of a party's mass support was thus unrelated to the outcome of party competition, since elections were at best highly exclusive rituals. In spite of this, however, party awareness and identification was fairly broad based and strong by the middle of the nineteenth century.[20] The socioeconomic basis for party leadership was upper class, but competing elites could provoke widespread support for their political and philosophical crusades among the unenfranchised masses. This traditional nineteenth-century basis of national party politics continued until the 1930s, despite increasing signs of change.

By the middle of the nineteenth century the pattern of factional politics had also been set and included periodic interparty coalitions. Besides the tendency for localism to engender personalistic and regional factions, each party also tended toward division between "hard-liners" and "moderates," a division which came to form a major basis of the evolving factions. When hard-liners gained control of one or both parties, the result was political polarization and civil strife. As moderates gained control, sometimes within the framework of an interparty coalition between them, the result would be conciliation and so-called regimes of national unity.

In the late 1870s, the Liberal party had split over the presidential candidacies of two of its leaders. One, representing a faction known as Independent Liberals, formed a coalition with Conservatives and took power from the other Liberal faction, known as the Radical Liberals. Within a few years, however, disenchantment with the new regime induced most Independents to return to unity with the Radicals and to confrontation with Conservatives. Following a disastrous civil war (1899–1901), which cost at least one hundred thousand lives, Conservatives regained control over the army and the ballot boxes, and acquired a hegemony which lasted until the 1930 presidential election.

By 1930, important social changes were occurring in Colombia which, reinforced by the worldwide depression, returned the Liberals to power after almost thirty years of opposition. The peaceful change from Conservatives to Liberals was no small accomplishment in the historical context of Colombian politics, and was facilitated by the willingness of many Conservatives to accept the moderate Liberal, Enrique Olaya, who had been elected; Olaya reciprocated by calling for a "national government" and dividing cabinet positions equally between the two parties.[21]

Besides the national economic crises brought on by the depression, however, Colombia was also experiencing rapid social changes in this period.[22] These changes caused strains on society that produced serious political crises, polarization and radicalization of factional politics, and ultimately were to result in a sustained period of widespread violence climaxing in military intervention in 1953. Growing social mobilization in the twentieth century, moreover, was accompanied in Colombia by the gradual extension of the franchise. With the brief exception noted above, elections in the nineteenth century remained indirect rather than direct, and enfranchisement remained limited to literate males who could meet property requirements, effectively precluding any translation of mass political support into political power through electoral processes. Some reforms were introduced beginning in 1910, and a limited proportional representation was inaugurated in the 1920s; however, it wasn't until 1936 that both literacy and property qualifications for voting in national elections were removed. Women were not enfranchised until 1954.[23]

The possibility of popular control over party elites in Colombia thus came long after the reality of party awareness and mass identification, and it came within the context of growing social mobilization. By the late 1930s, the Colombian masses at least in principle were able to use parties as a check on national political elites, in contrast to the traditional system in which elites used parties to provoke the masses into actions supportive of their respective interests. The congruence of these two basic changes in Colombian political life was the beginning of modern politics in that country, and its principal consequence was the rebalancing of party and of factional power.[24]

The mold of modern party factions was also set by the late 1930s. Factional leadership, as one might expect in so lately a traditional society as Colombia, had familial dimensions, with at least one personalistic faction of each party persisting through a second generation and into the present. More important, however, each party had acquired more or less permanent divisions of "moderates" versus "radicals." The 1930 Conservative defeat divided their party leadership, producing new personal loyalties and somewhat vaguely defined ideological, philosophical, and policy rationalizations for them. Within a decade it was clear to most Conservative leaders that their party had been not merely defeated but reduced to a permanent minority status in their country. Liberals, meanwhile, divided over what to do once in power, especially in relation to those issues identified with socioeconomic leveling. Olaya, despite his verbal overtures for change, remained a moderate, and did little to upset the traditional elites on whose support his regime was based, or to respond to those seeking reforms. However, his successor, in 1934, the more radical Liberal Alfonso López Pumarejo, appealed to the emerging middle class and to the working class.

The contest between moderate and radical Liberals became the principal division within the party ranks, and in national politics. López, ineligible constitutionally to seek a second term, was succeeded in 1938 by a moderate Liberal, Eduardo Santos, a business-oriented leader who, like Olaya, took Conservatives into his government. The radical Liberal López won a second term in 1942, facing, however, a congress dominated by opposition moderate Liberals and Conservatives. His administration was racked by personal scandal and corruption, providing his enemies with sufficient ammunition to force his early resignation, in 1945. He was succeeded for the remainder of his term by the *designado*, Alberto Lleras Camargo, a moderate Liberal who proclaimed a "National Unity" government comprised equally of Liberals and Conservatives.

The successor to López as leader of the radical Liberals was Jorge Eliécer Gaitán, a charismatic reformist who, as Robert Dix correctly observes, was "the only Colombian to have attained major political stature by challenging the position of the elites and appealing to the Colombian masses."[25] In the 1946 election, Gaitán ran for the presidency against another Liberal, Gabriel Turbay, and against the Conservative candidate, Mario Ospina Pérez. The split in the Liberal vote elected Ospina; shortly after the election Turbay died, leaving Gaitán the undisputed leader of the Liberal party. Gaitán, clearly prepared to run in 1950, was assassinated by a fanatic in 1948, precipitating what came to be known as the *bogotazo,* a spontaneous outbreak of urban violence which left the capital city of Bogotá looking like a city under siege. The *bogotazo* signaled the beginning of an extended period of rural and urban sociopolitical violence known as *La Violencia,* a complex experience which profoundly shook the foundations of Colombian society.[26]

In 1946, the new Conservative president, Ospina, tried at first to continue the moderate Liberal Lleras Camargo's National Unity government; in the first two years of his presidency, Ospina appointed more Liberal cabinet ministers than Conservatives. But the assassination of Gaitán in 1948 reversed this, and Liberals refused increasingly to participate in the government. By the 1950 elections, Liberals refused to even compete against what they saw as an increasingly dictatorial Conservative regime. With the growing violence and the constitutional inability of Ospina to seek a second term, leadership of the Conservatives fell to Laureano Gómez and his extremist faction. Gómez won the presidency in an unopposed election, and his regime rapidly deteriorated and repression of individual liberties became widespread. Alienating all Liberals and many Conservatives, Gómez was eventually deposed by a military coup led by General Gustavo Rojas Pinilla. General Rojas tried to install a Peron-type dictatorship in Colombia, but was himself deposed in 1957 after a period of continuing violence and growing dissatisfaction with his regime.

The deposing of Rojas was facilitated by an agreement between two exiled political leaders, the moderate Liberal Lleras Camargo and Laureano Gómez of the Conservatives. Upon their return to Colombia, a plebiscite on their agreement was held in 1957, which established the *Frente de Transformación Nacional* (FTN), inaugurating for a period lasting until 1974 alternation of the presidency between Liberals and Conservatives and parity between the two parties in congressional, departmental, and governmental offices. In the Conservative party, Laureano Gómez, who had helped to bring about the FTN, reversed his position when the moderate Ospina faction won a superior position to the Laureanista faction in the 1958 congressional elections (conducted without separate lists), while Ospina, at first opposed to the FTN, embraced and supported it.

The FTN period, from 1958 to 1974, was one of increased factional politics. Despite the FTN arrangements between the parties, factions remained free to compete among themselves for available elective positions, and interparty coalitions of factions for and against the national unity governments emerged. The FTN period was thus also one of increased interparty factional coalitions. Those factions supporting the FTN were generally united, those opposing the FTN were not. The FTN was able to function effectively as an interparty factional coalition because the two dominant factions in each party were the politically moderate ones, differentiated ideologically only to a small degree, and sharing real political and financial interests in Colombian development.

The factions supporting the FTN were the moderate *Oficialista* Liberals and *Unionista* Conservatives; those opposing the FTN were the more radical *Movimiento Revolucionario Liberal*—("Liberal Revolutionary Movement"—MRL) and the *Doctrinarios* Conservatives. There were other small and transient factions periodically emerging in both parties during the FTN, but with the exception of one, ANAPO, which appeared in the latter 1960s, they were small, usually quite local in influence, and purely personalistic. The strengths of the major factions of the FTN period, as indicated by percent of the total popular vote in national elections, are shown in Table 1.

Each of these principal factions was highly personalistic, although different ideological orientations were usually attributed to them by their leaders and followers. The Official Liberals were led by Alberto Lleras Camargo and by his cousin, Carlos Lleras Restrepo, both of

Table 1. Strengths of Colombian Factions as Percent of
Popular Vote in Congressional Elections, 1958–1972

Year	LIBERAL				CONSERVATIVE				ANAPO	All Other Parties
	Official	MRL	ANAPO-L	Other	Unionista	Doctrinarios	ANAPO-C	Other		
1958	58		—	—	42	—	—	—	—	—
1960	43	11	—	4	22	17	—	2	—	—
1962	34	19	—	—	26	16	4	—	—	—
1964	33	17	2	1	35	—	12	—	—	—
1966	38	13	3	1	16	12	15	2	—	—
1968	47	2	3	1	23	—	14	8	—	—
1970	26	—	14	11	15	—	19	13	3	2
1972	16	17	—	12	30	—	—	1	19	3

Source: Adapted from Republica de Colombia, Departamento Administrativo Nacional de Estadística (DANE), *Resultados electorales Frente Nacional, 1958–1972* (Bogotá, 1972), p. 43.

whom served a turn as president (Carlos Lleras from 1958 to 1962, and Alberto Lleras from 1966 to 1970). They were political moderates, committed to a broad program of economic development and some socioeconomic leveling. The Unionist Conservatives were led primarily by the moderate Mario Opsina Pérez.

The opposition MRL Liberals, under the leadership of López-Michelsen (son of former President López), generally were considered to be more ideological, but the movement was essentially personalistic and geographically localized, and was unable to draw support from the lower classes toward whom its appeals were directed. Small in size, the faction never seriously competed with the majority Liberal faction. After a serious setback in the 1968 congressional elections, López-Michelsen joined the Lleras cabinet. The major opposition faction of the Conservative party, known sometimes as the Doctrinarios, was also known as the Laureanistas while under the leadership of Laureano Gómez and later, after Laureano's death, as the Alvaristas under the leadership of his son Álvaro. The faction was generally considered to be the more conservative faction of the party, although its campaign appeals were personalistic and its legislative policies were decided by political exigencies and by the personal ambition of its leaders.

By the mid-1960s a new force emerged, as former dictator Rojas Pinilla, assisted by his daughter Maria Eugenia, who had gained election as a senator, announced the formation of ANAPO, the acronym for National Popular Alliance. ANAPO was clearly rooted in the personality of its leader and his Peronista-styled appeals for mass support. The group submitted faction lists under both the traditional party labels, but most of its votes came from Conservatives. ANAPO presented itself as "the opposition," claiming that other national leaders were all part of the same oligarchy and that no real alternatives existed; in a period when Liberals and Conservatives were often cooperating under the FTN, the charge was not implausible. In 1966, when under the FTN agreement a Liberal would have to be elected, ANAPO found an almost unknown politician who had been officially registered as a Liberal to run as its candidate, with Rojas conspicuously standing in the wings. In 1968, ANAPO picked up strength in the congressional elections to the point that the FTN could no longer muster the required two-thirds vote in the legislature for important legislation. In 1970, Rojas (identified as a Conservative by party affiliation) ran against the FTN-supported Conservative candidate, moderate Misael Pastrana, and almost won; many Colombians are convinced that he did win, since Pastrana's final vote was only slightly greater than Rojas's.[27]

The nearly successful challenge of the two-party system by ANAPO had important repercussions for the traditional elites as the period of the FTN agreement drew to a close. Álvaro Gómez of the radical Conservative faction and López-Michelsen of the radical Liberal faction both conspicuously moderated their positions prior to the 1974 presidential elections, and won nomination by their respective parties in the first contest held after the FTN expired. ANAPO, for the first time operating as a third party rather than as two factions, nominated Maria Eugenia. However, as a third party it could no longer employ traditional Liberal and Conservative sympathies to increase its vote. López won the presidency with a clear majority, and ANAPO was badly beaten, leaving the two traditional parties each at least temporarily internally united and moderate, a consequence of the external challenge by ANAPO.

The Evolution of Uruguayan Party Factions

Following independence in 1825, Uruguayans, like Colombians, divided over basic issues, including centralization. In 1830 a Constitution modeled after that of the United States was adopted, and a centralist, General Fructuoso Rivera, was installed as president. The opposition, including leaders who had helped win the nation's independence, led a revolt against Rivera and government centralization, and installed a federalist, General Manuel Oribe, as president. Rivera's followers then provoked a new revolt, which led to fifteen years of civil war—the *Guerra Grande*—in which many foreign powers intervened. Oribe's followers, supported by landowners, merchants, and high clergy, were identified by the white hatbands they wore in battle, and became known as the Blancos. Rivera's followers, supported by middle-class liberals, were identified by red hatbands and became known as Colorados.[28] The two opposing forces signed a pact in 1851, but it was a short-lived peace. General Venancio Flores (Colorado) assumed power for four years but was then overthrown by Oribe, who retained power for the next ten years. In 1865, when Flores recaptured the presidency with the aid of the Brazilians, neighboring Paraguay came to the aid of the Blancos; the Colorados thereupon added Argentina to their alliance. The Colorados, with Argentine and Brazilian assistance, soundly defeated Paraguay and the Blanco forces in the War of the Triple Alliance.

In an effort to terminate the civil wars, the Colorados appeased the Blancos by giving them control over four interior provinces, and a five hundred thousand peso indemnity. The four provinces became the stronghold of Blanco power and economic interest. In return for this security, the Blancos in effect surrendered national power to the Colorados for nearly a century: although regular elections were soon held, it was ninety-three years before the Blancos could regain control over the nation at the polls.[29]

The Colorados ruled without serious challenge for the rest of the nineteenth century through a series of dictators, most of them from the military. But fundamental changes were beginning to occur in Uruguay. Refrigerated ships by the 1870s encouraged a national economic boom by the export of fresh meat and by-products to Europe. Immigrants poured into Montevideo from Europe's troubled cities, swelling the ranks of the already urban-based Colorado party. In 1876 the country established an ambitious system of free, public education modeled after that of the United States; Uruguay was one of only three nations in Latin America to do so.[30] The influence of the church was contained, and electoral suffrage was broadly extended. Blanco-inspired strife prompted a "New Party Pact" in 1897, which made further concessions to the "opposition" Blancos, by then officially known as the National party. The concessions included hegemony over six instead of four provinces and a new electoral law which guaranteed minority representation in the senate. The gesture avoided another civil war with the Blancos, who were becoming increasingly aware that they could not hope to defeat the Colorados through the ballot box.

In 1903 Uruguayans elected a new Colorado president, José Batlle, one of the most important twentieth-century leaders in the Western hemisphere. Batlle served twice as president (1903–1907, 1911–1915) and had a lasting impact on national life.[31] Above all, he was a consummate politician, one who could communicate his ideas enthusiastically to his countrymen. Looking at Latin America's and his own nation's nineteenth-century history, he saw two causes for perpetual political instability: chronic party warfare and gross inequalities rooted in economic and social classes. Batlle wanted to eliminate both these evils and thereby achieve political stability.

To eliminate social and economic inequalities, Batlle called for a vast system of social welfare, including public health care, expanded education, retirement, and industrialization designed to service the consumption and employment needs of an urban middle class—the principal source of his party's support. His plans, even by European standards, were visionary. To contain party warfare, he proposed the elimination of the presidency—which he viewed as a threat to representative institutions in Latin America, and the way in which ambitious men established dictatorships.[32] He established in 1918 a system of proportional representation, which legally recognized the legitimacy of parties and factions (officially termed *lemas* and *sub-lemas* respectively.[33]

Uruguay's Batlle-inspired electoral system borrows many devices commonly employed in European proportional representation systems, yet it also responds to traditional Uruguayan party politics and, specifically, subsidizes the two major parties. Party activity and elections are regulated by the Electoral Court, comprised of nine members elected by the legislature, five candidates being selected for their presumed impartiality and four selected as party representatives, two from the largest faction of the leading party and two from the largest faction of the second party. The Electoral Court administers elections and campaigns, adjudicates disputes, and allocates campaign funds afterwards, proportional to party and faction voting percentages.

Voting is by closed-list ballots, printed and distributed by the factions according to government specifications and identified officially as numbered *listas* ("lists"). Seats are allocated by a modified version of the d'Hondt formula, which essentially allows a primary election within a general election. To determine who will be seated, all votes for all factions *(sub-lemas)* within a party *(lema)* are totaled, and the number of seats assigned to parties is proportional to their share of the total vote. Election of specific individuals is determined proportionately according to each faction's share of the total party vote, utilizing the rank listing of candidates on the closed ballot. A vote for any party's faction helps the party as a whole. Campaigning is entirely at the level of the factions, and all those of the same party share the same *lema* colors in their literature and ballots (red for the Colorados, blue for the Blancos, etc.).

The effect of this system, despite proportional representation, is to reward the strong and restrain the weak, in both representation and campaign reimbursement afterward. Hence, new or small parties, perhaps more politically equivalent to the major parties' important factions, must compete for seats and funds with the two major parties. It could also be argued that, to some extent, the system specifically helps the Colorado party maintain its dominant position, and, accordingly, places Colorado factions in a more favorable position to win seats than Blanco factions.

Factions are numerous and fluctuate enormously from one election to another. An ambitious or popular politician may start his own for the purpose of gaining office, by grafting on to his specific office list (senate or chamber) candidates for other offices from another list, forming in effect a kind of intraparty alliance. Parties in principle can decide whether or not to permit a new faction, but in fact few are ever denied the right to participate, for to the extent that they do attract votes, however many, the entire party benefits. All lists are numbered separately for each administrative department in the nation where different candidates are running.

The quantity of lists for any election can easily rise to over one hundred nationally, although many are "related" because the presidency and the senate are elected from a national constituency, and the same names appear on all lists endorsing those candidates. None of the numerous factions is particularly distinguishable from another, except that each one represents the followers, supporters, and alliances of a single politician. The *sub-lemas* persist as long as their principal leader does, and differ ideologically to the extent and in the ways that individual leaders do. One of the most remarkable qualities of the

Uruguayan electoral system is that not only does it provide a simultaneous primary and general election, but it allows for endless personalization of the campaigns without challenging the viability of the two traditional parties—indeed, it reinforces them.[34]

In the twentieth century Uruguay achieved and sustained a high level of political institutionalization, bureaucratization, and stability. By the time of Batlle's death in 1929, Uruguayan politics had been drastically transformed. Civil strife had been replaced by electoral politics. Industrialization and prosperity were increasing through nationally controlled and subsidized ventures. Political parties, once merely loose bands of armed men possessing deep hatred and identifying with ill-defined causes, had become bureaucratized and demilitarized local and national organizations. Well-defined and protected factions were becoming vehicles for ambitious leaders, and competition within parties was often as significant as between parties.

Despite the institutionalization of Uruguayan politics and government, however, Batlle himself exemplified the traditional role of the strong party leader, and he stimulated a counterpart in the National party, Luis Alberto de Herrera. So strong and so personal was the leadership of these men over their parties that factions arose in each opposed to them; and under the new 1918 Constitution, factions were formally recognized and empowered to compete electorally against the men they opposed. The Colorado party by 1930 was divided between the Batllistas, those who even without their leader carried on his programs, traditions, and symbols, and the Independent Colorados, opposed to *Batllismo*. In the National party there were Herrera and his followers, and opposed to him, the Independent Nationals. These factions by and large were not ideologically differentiated or divided primarily on policy questions, but over questions of leadership.

In the twenty-year period 1930–1950 factions multiplied, and some acquired more ideological orientations. In 1932, women were enfranchised, and the country could be said to have reached a level of social mobilization equivalent to many modern European nations. By the early 1950s, a shaky alliance between the orthodox Batllistas, led by José's two sons Lorenzo and César Batlle Pacheco, who controlled their father's famous newspaper *El Día,* and the supporters of Blanco leader Herrera pushed through a constitutional reform abolishing the presidency and instituting a nine-man collegiate executive.[35] This diluted national leadership at a time of worsening long-term economic problems. The Colorados remained divided between two principal factions—List 14, led by the Batlle Pacheco brothers, and List 15, led by former president Luis Batlle Berres, a nephew of José Batlle.

The Blancos continued to be divided between the supporters of Herrera and the so-called orthodox Blancos, who made coalitions among several factions within their party to balance the stronger faction. By the mid-1950s, a new faction appeared, led by Benito Nardone, a self-styled champion of the rural poor whose authoritarian and fascist inclinations put him on the party's extreme right. The combination of worsening economic conditions, unsatisfactory national leadership under the Colorado-controlled collegiate executive, and increasing factional divisions in the Colorado party which were, with the appearance of leftist Zelmar Michelini's List 99 beginning to acquire significant ideological dimension, resulted in the downfall of the century-old Colorado domination of national government. The Blancos swept the election of 1958, winning national power, including six

Table 2. Uruguayan Parties, Factions, and Candidates in Montevideo Department, 1966

Party (lema) and Faction (sub-lema)	Presidential and Vice-Presidential Candidates*
Partido Colorado (Colorado party)	
List 15: *Unidad y Reforma* ("Unity and Reform")	Jorge Batlle Julio Lacarte Muro
List 123: *Unión Colorado y Batllista* ("Colorado and Batllist Union")	Oscar Gestido Jorge Pacheco Areco
List 515: *Frente Colorado de Unidad* ("Colorado United Front")	Oscar Gestido Jorge Pacheco Areco
List 99: *Evolución y Gobierno del Pueblo* ("Evolution and Government of the People")	Zelmar Michelini Aquiles Lanza
List 315: *Antorcha de Batlle* ("Torch of Batlle")	Amilcar Vasconcellos Renán Rodriguez
Lista 10 ("List 10")	Justino Jimenez de Arechaga Nilo Berchesi
Partido Nacional (National party)	
Unión Blanca Democrática ("Blanco Democratic Union")	Alberto Gallinal Juan Pedro Zaballos
Herrerista Ortodoxo ("Orthodox Herreraists")	Alberto Heber Nicolas Storace Arrosa
Movimiento Popular Nacionalista ("Nationalist Popular Movement")	Martín Echegoyen Dardo Ortíz
Azul y Blanco ("Blue and White")	Victor Haedo General Mattos
Partido Democrático Cristiano (Christian Democratic party)	Adolfo Gelsi Miguel Saralegui
Movimiento Cívico Cristiano (Christian Civic movement)	Chiarino Venancio Flores
Frente Izquierda de Libertad—Fidel (Leftist Freedom Front)	Aguirre Gonzalez Pastorino
Unión Popular (Popular Union)	Enrique Erro Marino

*Some of the candidates' names are incomplete. The many available sources on Uruguayan elections tend not to identify minor parties' candidates beyond last names. The incompleteness is unfortunate but unavoidable.

of the nine collegiate executive seats, for the first time in the twentieth century—though Herrera, shortly before he was able to assume office, died.

In the last few years, deeply rooted economic disequilibriums have generated a long-term process of decay.[36] Political leaders could not or would not make unpopular decisions, and public confidence in national institutions declined. The presidential and congressional elections of 1966 and 1971 saw a continuation of traditional politics. Factions formed around traditional leaders competing for the presidency and the senate, often making intraparty coalitions and cross-endorsing other lists' candidates for other offices. With the possible exception of Michelini's leftist List 99 in the Colorado party, none of the factions of the two traditional parties acquired a clear ideological position or generated new alternatives to solve the growing national crisis. The major national factions operating in the department of Montevideo are identified in Table 2 for the 1966 election. There were additional lists available for each party, with various cross-endorsements, but these were the principal ones.

While the established parties and factions were continuing traditional politics, conditions throughout the country generally declined to the point of provoking radical responses. A violent and notoriously skillful urban guerrilla movement appeared, known as the Tupamaros. As a political protest movement emulating Chilean counterparts, a Marxist-dominated interparty coalition was created as a "third force" *(Frente Amplio)* for the 1971 elections, and it received the endorsement of several factions of the traditional parties.[37] National political paralysis extended into almost all areas, from continuing economic stagnation to unabated urban violence. In a gradual, almost step-like process, the traditionally neutral military increased its influence over national institutions, leaders, and policy, until by 1973 the government was military in all but name.

Factional Structures and Organizations

The influence of modernization on Colombian and Uruguayan party factions is nowhere more apparent than in their organization. Colombia's parties do have official organizations, and although there are signs that these are becoming more important, historically they have had little to do with the functioning of the parties. The principal bonds between party leaders at different levels and the electorate are personal ones. Likewise, the principal divisions between party leaders which produce factions are primarily, if not exclusively, personal animosities and conflicting ambitions. Factions have never been well organized in Colombia, being instead loose and shifting groups of congressional and local leaders, a series of often complex patron-client relationships. When structure was required, as, for example, in an electoral campaign, it was either bought outright by hiring semiprofessional campaign workers or co-opted at local levels through government, business, and social elites.

All this existed within a framework of traditional party loyalties and allegiances, which permitted voters to change factional allegiance by different list voting without violating their party loyalties. Particularly during the 1958–1972 FTN period, the alternatives on key issues—such as support for the FTN itself—were to be found within each party as well as between the parties. Even the third party movement (ANAPO), which tried to challenge the traditional parties, operated from its inception in the early 1960s until the end of the FTN (1974) within the legal framework of the two traditional parties, drawing most of its support as a list of the Conservative party.

By contrast, Uruguayan parties were uncommonly well organized, exhibiting a kind of political bureaucratization in which the keystone was the faction. These factions were organized in Montevideo on a neighborhood basis, through a vast network of political "clubs" which served as direct links for neighborhoods between elected officials and the voters—like a kind of ombudsman between the voter and the vast, often impenetrable administrative bureaucracy which affected almost everyone's life.[38] Unlike comparable experiences in United States cities with political machines, Uruguayan neighborhoods had competing clubs representing different factions and different parties. There was a mutual advantage to the politician—particularly the faction leaders—and to the voter in this arrangement. The politician had a regular source of organizational support when required for campaigning, and in return for his allegiance, a voter known through the club to be loyal to a particular faction could, to the extent at least of his support, gain access to political favors.

The system worked remarkably well until about ten years ago; it encouraged factions within a party to limit intraparty competition to reasonable bounds because the electoral system rewarded all in the form of party representation for the vote given to anyone of them. Intraparty competition and divisions between factions and their leaders were most visible during campaigning, as each tried to maximize their share of the party's representation, but there were no electoral rewards for crossing party lines, and it rarely occurred. Unlike Colombia, where dissident factions from both major parties often formed a legislative alliance to oppose the factions supporting the regime, there were no such permanent divisions in the Uruguayan congress. Individual members could cross party lines in voting, as they do in many countries, but it was an ad hoc process.

The Uruguayan system was based on an implicit assumption that the basic political questions in the nation concerned distribution of goods and services in an affluent economy, not an unreasonable assumption a half century ago, when the institutions were evolving; the final collapse of the system is perhaps as much as anything tied to the changing reality of economic stagnation and decline, and an inability of the party system to shift from allocational decisions to developmental ones. The lack of constraining structure in Colombia during the FTN, on the other hand, permitted development-oriented factions in each party to work together without making serious concessions to those who might seek a redistribution of wealth in a highly unequal society—such as the MRL faction of the Liberal party, at least in its earlier days, and ANAPO, which almost captured the presidency in 1970 with the appeal of its image as friend of the poor and the disadvantaged.

The institutionalization of the Uruguayan factions was further reinforced by the identification of newspapers directly with factions and leaders. The tradition was started by Batlle himself, and opposition factions had to accept the practice of aligning themselves with newspapers opposing Batlle in order to survive against so formidable a figure as Batlle and his newspaper *El Día.* Thus, newspaper owners and journalists have often played key roles in the leadership structures of factions in Uruguay; conversely, faction leaders have regularly been recruited by newspapers as columnists and spokesmen for their viewpoint. In Colombia, newspapers are identified with parties—indeed, several key political figures have founded or owned newspapers; nevertheless, Colombian newspapers have been somewhat less important in mobilizing support than in Uruguay. The difference is attributable in part to the fact that Montevideo's daily newspapers are for all practical purposes national ones read throughout the country, whereas Bogotá's daily newspapers, while distributed elsewhere, have strong competitors in regional cities and cannot exercise as strong an influence nationally. Even more important in explaining the difference is the fact that most Colombians don't read newspapers, because they are either illiterate or too poor to afford one, while newspaper consumption is high in Uruguay.

Considerable differentiation can be found in the socioeconomic bases of factional affiliation in Colombia. On the basis of survey data collected in Bogotá prior to the 1970 presidential election, the Liberal and Conservative factions supportive of the FTN (*Oficialista* and *Unionista*) drew heaviest from the upper classes and least from the lower classes.[39] The more radical Alvarista and ANAPO factions, on the other hand, drew significantly more from lower classes and less from upper classes. Lower-class affiliation is not concentrated within any single party. While it is more apparent proportionately in some Conservative party factions than in Liberal party factions, the total size of the former is much smaller. When factional affiliation is viewed relative to the educational level attained by adherents, similar patterns are found. Adherents to the MRL and Alvarista factions show higher educational attainment than those in the ANAPO factions. Data are not available for comparison with Uruguay, although it is unlikely that either class or educational attainment is important in distinguishing factional affiliation, since the differences are far less pronounced in the society.

The Consequences of Factional Politics in Colombia and Uruguay

We originally questioned why factions came to play so prominent a role in Colombian and Uruguayan party politics and whether the evolution of factions might be linked to modernization. Specifically, we asked how, almost uniquely in Latin America, pressures for increased participation coming from social mobilization were channelled into multipyling factions of two parties rather than, as has often occurred in proportional representation systems, into multiplying parties drawing upon socially mobilizing elements of societies.

There are some parallels in the experiences of the two countries. Both nations had mass-party identifications before the onset of modern politics, of the bureaucratization of party organizations, or of mass electoral participation. As social mobilization began, the franchise was slowly extended, and broader participation became possible. The argument is often made that two-party systems tend to arise as a consequence of single-member districts and majority or plurality electoral systems. But both Colombia and Uruguay have multimember districts and proportional representation, which permitted factions a degree of political—and in Uruguay legal—autonomy, and which encouraged the growth of factional rather than central party organizations.[40]

The eventual electoral dominance of a stronger over a weaker party and the traditionalism of party identification combined to make it easier for persons to shift factional loyalties within their party than to cross party lines. The specific electoral system adopted in Uruguay protected the integrity of factions, discouraged interparty factional coalitions, and encouraged intraparty coalitions among factions. Curiously, the legal regulations adopted from 1958 to 1974 under the FTN in Colombia seem to have had, probably unintentionally, the opposite effects, encouraging interparty and discouraging intraparty, factional coalitions. Both nations formally discouraged the emergence of small or third parties; Uruguay by making small groups, political equivalents to *sub-lemas,* compete electorally for representation with *lemas,* and Colombia by the party alternation agreement requiring that only Conservatives and Liberals could hold office. Still, third forces did emerge in both nations. ANAPO in Colombia submitted lists on both the Liberal and Conservative party labels. The *Frente Amplio* in Uruguay in the 1970s, under conditions of extreme economic and social tensions, has aggregated disenchanted factions from both traditional parties and other small groups into a single front, a severe challenge to the traditional institutional system.

Historically, factions in both nations were largely the result of personalistic followings rather than ideological or policy differences of individual leaders. However, in Uruguay the higher level of party bureaucratization restrained the electoral and congressional behavior of leaders. The dominant party in each country was particularly susceptible to division over questions prompted by their incumbency. The most common question was: Who would hold what power, when, and for how long? In Colombia, the divisions also concerned issues of how much and how fast socioeconomic leveling should be induced into the society; these issues profoundly divided the Liberal party between supporters of the López and Gaitán radical faction, and the more orthodox Liberal faction. Uruguay's Colorados split over Batlle's visionary program of socioeconomic welfare, as well as his personal control over the party, and in the past decade became increasingly polarized on issues of how to restore economic development and eliminate political terrorism.

As long as the traditional levels of influence could be maintained in Uruguay, the system of factional politics was a stabilizing influence on the society. It held the two traditional parties together in the face of strong personal rivalries; it set limits on the ability of the dominant party to overwhelm the minority party; and it created a system of incentives for each party's factions to cooperate after an election, while not forcing individual factional leaders to conform to central decision-making by the party. The elections permitted the voter simultaneous primary and general elections and, through factional organizations, more or less regular communications channels to the national leadership. Yet in the context of worsening national problems, this same stabilization created a political paralysis, making it almost impossible for Uruguayan leaders to make unpopular or difficult decisions. Thus as conditions became politically unstable, faction politics not only did not foster stability but contributed to the stress conditions and ultimately to military intervention—in Colombia in 1953 following a period of rapid social mobilization, and in Uruguay in 1973 following tensions generated by economic decay within the context of high social mobilization and thwarted expectations.

The special arrangement in Colombia under the FTN accomplished its basic goal of forcing a degree of cooperation between moderate factions of the traditional parties, but it also encouraged more radical factions led by those opposed to the FTN's policies. The apparent growth in voter dissatisfaction with the moderate factions that controlled the FTN governments may have been little more than the influence of this unusual electoral arrangement, which permitted voters to express disenchantment without violating traditional party loyalties.

The Colombian and Uruguayan experiences should, at the very least, suggest some caution in the traditional interpretations of behavior in two-party systems and factional politics. Proportional representation, it should be clear by now, does not necessarily encourage or produce proliferation of political parties. The presence of party factions may serve the same purpose and, through specific legal controls and incentives, may be encouraged to do so. Two-party systems are not necessarily more stable or more likely to promote moderate policy alternatives. At various times historically the Colombian and Uruguayan experience has been one of polarization and paralysis resulting from two-party intransigence. Factions, in both instances, have occasionally diverted and limited interparty rivalry, allowing new structures and identities to emerge with the mobilization of new elements into the societies. Finally, Colombian and Uruguayan factions have permitted a blending of personal and bureaucratic party politics in societies which were themselves changing from traditional to modern.

The Colombian and Uruguayan experiences are different, and for Latin America, exceptional. But in each instance, the origin and evolution of party factions can be seen to be a natural, perhaps spontaneous response to the influence and crises of modernization.

NOTES

1. The concept of modernization used here is from Samuel P. Huntington, *Political Order in Changing Societies* (New Haven: Yale Univ. Press, 1968), p. 32; see also Daniel Lerner, *The Passing of Traditional Society* (Glencoe, Ill.: The Free Press, 1958), p. 438; and Fred W. Riggs, *Administration in Developing Countries* (Boston: Houghton Mifflin, 1964), pp. 27–49.

2. Deutsch describes social mobilization as a process through which "major clusters of old social, economic and psychological commitments are eroded or broken and people become available for new patterns of socialization and behavior." Karl W. Deutsch, "Social Mobilization and Political Development," *American Political Science Review* 55, no. 3 (Sept. 1961): 494.

3. Uruguay has not been well researched in recent years; dated but useful surveys include Russell H. Fitzgibbon, *Uruguay, Portrait of a Democracy* (New Brunswick: Rutgers Univ. Press, 1954); Phillip B. Taylor, *Government and Politics in Uruguay* Tulane Studies in Political Science no. 7 (New Orleans: Tulane Univ., Department of Political Science, 1960); Taylor, "Interests and Institutional Dysfunction in Uruguay," *American Political Science Review* 58, no. 1 (Mar. 1964): 62–74; and Nester Campiglia, *Los grupos de presión y el proceso político* (Montevideo: Ediciones Arca, 1969).

4. Colombia has generated much interest in contemporary social science; see Robert H. Dix, *Colombia: The Political Dimensions of Change* (New Haven: Yale Univ. Press, 1967); Vernon L. Fluharty, *Dance of the Millions* (Pittsburgh: Univ. of Pittsburgh Press, 1957); James L. Payne, *Patterns of Conflict in Colombia* (New Haven: Yale Univ. Press, 1968); and Francisco Leal Buitrago, *Análisis histórico del desarrollo político nacional, 1930–1970* (Bogotá: Tercer Mundo, 1973).

5. Besides works mentioned above by Huntington, Riggs, and Lerner, see Talcott Parsons, *Essays in Sociological Theory*, rev. ed. (Glencoe, Ill.: The Free Press, 1954), pp. 142–44, 239; and S. N. Eisenstadt, "Institutionalization and Change," *American Sociological Review* 24 (Apr. 1964): 235–47.

6. Riggs, *Administration in Developing Countries*, pp. 27–31.

7. Max Weber, *From Max Weber: Essays in Sociology*, trans. Hans Gerth and C. Wright Mills (New York: Oxford Univ. Press, 1946), p. 216.

8. Huntington, *Political Order in Changing Societies*, p. 12.

9. Weber, *From Max Weber*, p. 224.

10. Huntington, *Political Order in Changing Societies*, p. 398.

11. For further discussion of the nineteenth century, see Jesús Maria Henao and Gerardo Arrubla, *History of Colombia*, trans. J. Fred Rippy (Chapel Hill: Univ. of North Carolina Press, 1938); and Rafael Azula Barrera, *De la revolución al ordén nuevo: proceso y drama de un puebla* (Bogotá: Editorial Kelly, 1956).

12. Simon G. Hanson, *Utopia in Uruguay* (New York: Oxford Univ. Press, 1938), gives an excellent account of Uruguay during its period of rapid modernization.

13. Phillip B. Taylor, "The Electoral System in Uruguay," *Journal of Politics* 17 (Feb. 1955): 19–42.

14. Dix, *Colombia*, pp. 129–36.

241

15. Ronald H. McDonald, "Rise of Military Politics in Uruguay," *Inter-American Economic Affairs* 28 (Spring 1975): 25–43.

16. This is a considerable oversimplification; see Milton Puentes, *Historia del Partido Liberal Colombiano*, 2d ed. (Bogotá: Editorial Prag, 1961), pp. 125–40.

17. William Marion Gibson, *The Constitutions of Colombia* (Durham, N.C.: Duke Univ. Press, 1948), pp. 306–10.

18. A study of electoral politics of this period can be found in David Bushnell, "Voter Participation in the Colombian Election of 1856," *Hispanic-American Historical Review* 51 (May 1971): 237–49.

19. Dix, *Colombia*, pp. 184–88.

20. Helen Delpar, "Aspects of Liberal Factionalism in Colombia, 1875–1885," *Hispanic-American Historical Review* 51 (May 1971): 251.

21. Buitrago, *Análisis historico del desarrollo político nacional*, pp. 306–09; see also Buitrago, *Estudio del comportamiento legislativo en Colombia* (Bogotá: Tercer Mundo, 1973), pp. 307–10.

22. The best indicators available for this period suggest significant and rapid social mobilization, in terms of growth in urbanization, literacy, employment in nonprimary sectors of the economy, communications, and educational attainment. See J. Mark Ruhl, "The Influence of Social Mobilization on Latin American Military Intervention" (Ph.D. diss., Syracuse Univ., 1975).

23. Literacy and property qualifications for municipal and local elections, however, had been removed in the nineteenth century. See Dix, *Colombia*, p. 185.

24. See "Two-Party Competitive Systems: Colombia, Uruguay, and Honduras," chapter 4 of Ronald H. McDonald, *Party Systems and Elections in Latin America* (Chicago: Markham, 1971), esp. pp. 178–98.

25. McDonald, *Party Systems and Elections in Latin America*, p. 108; see also Antonio Garcia, *Gaitán y el problema de la Revolución Colombiana* (Bogotá: Artes Graficas, 1955); and Jorge Eliécer Gaitán, *Las Ideas Socialistas en Colombia* (Bogotá: Editorial America Libre, 1963).

26. *La Violencia* has been extensively studied; see Orlando Fals Borda and Eduardo Umana Luna, *La violencia en Colombia: estudio de un proceso social* (Bogotá: Tres Mundos, 1963); R. S. Weinert, "Violence in Pre-Modern Societies, the Case of Rural Colombia," *American Political Science Review* 60, no. 2 (June 1966): 340–47; and R. C. Williamson, "Toward a Theory of Political Violence: The Case of Rural Colombia," *Western Political Quarterly* 18, no. 1 (Mar. 1965): 35–44.

27. Judith Talbot Campos and John F. McCamant, *Cleavage Shift in Colombia: Analysis of the 1970 Elections*, Comparative Politics Series, vol. 3 (Beverly Hills: Sage Publications, 1972), pp. 34–41. ANAPO ran its own separate list in 1970, as well as its Liberal and Conservative lists, evidently anticipating operating entirely independently by 1972. It became officially a separate, "third" party on June 31, 1971.

28. See Juan E. Pivel Deveto, *Historia de la Republica Oriental del Uruguay* (Montevideo: R. Artagaveytia, 1945); Pivel Deveto, *Historia de los partidos políticos en el Uruguay* (Montevideo: Tipografia Atlántica, 1942); and Mauricio Schurmann Pacheco, *Historia del Uruguay* (Montevideo: A. Monteverde, 1956).

29. Fitzgibbon *Uruguay, Portrait of a Democracy*, p. 142.

30. The other two were Argentina and Chile. See Telmo Manacorda, *José Pedro Varela* (Montevideo: Consejo Nacional de Enseñanza, 1949); also Fitzgibbon, *Uruguay, Portrait of a Democracy*, pp. 198–212.

31. See Milton I. Vanger, *José Batlle y Ordóñez of Uruguay, the Creator of His Times, 1902–1907* (Cambridge: Harvard Univ. Press, 1963).

32. Fitzgibbon, *Uruguay, Portrait of a Democracy*, pp. 122–36.

33. Taylor, "Electoral System in Uruguay," pp. 19–25.

24. See McDonald, "Two-Party Competitive Systems," esp. pp. 198–214.

35. The first experiment with the semicollegiate executive is reviewed by Goran G. Lindahl, *Uruguay's New Path: A Study of Politics during the First Colegiado, 1919–1933* (Stockholm: Institute of Ibero-American Studies, 1962); also, Milton I. Vanger, "Uruguay Introduces Government by Committee," *American Political Science Review* 48, no. 2 (June 1954): 500–13.

36. Herman E. Daly, "The Uruguayan Economy: Its Basic Nature and Current Problems," *Journal of Inter-American Studies* 7 (July 1965): 316–30; David C. Redding,

"The Economic Decline of Uruguay," *Inter-American Economic Affairs* 20 (Spring 1967): 55–72; Arturo C. Prozecanski, "Uruguay's Continuing Dilemma," *Current History* 66 (Jan. 1974): 28–30, 38–39.

37. Ronald H. McDonald, "Electoral Politics and Uruguayan Political Decay," *Inter-American Economic Affairs* 26 (Summer 1972): 25–45.

38. One of the few to discuss these organizations is Campiglia, *Los grupos de presión y el proceso político*, pp. 199–201.

39. Ronald H. McDonald and J. Mark Ruhl, "Attitudinal and Social Bases of Electoral Participation and Party Affiliation in Bogotá, Colombia," (unpublished paper).

40. Dix also notices this paradox, *Colombia*, p. 188.

10

Factionalism:
The Limits of the West German Party-State

PETER H. MERKL

"Parliamentary democracy is party democracy," wrote West German Interior Minister Gerhard Schröder on the occasion of preparing a major bill regulating political parties in 1957. "It is [only] through the parties that the people express the popular will. Political ideas and strivings that are not taken up by the parties stand little chance of being articulated as the state decides its policy."[1] The term *party-state (Parteienstaat)*, derived from German constitutional jurisprudence, refers to the monopoly of decision-making power implicitly granted to German parties under the Weimar Republic, and made explicit under the Bonn Constitution (Article 21 of the Basic Law). Thus, now well-established political-constitutional norms make the West German parties the mechanisms through which popular will is expressed in the governing institutions, and through which interests that seek representation are channeled. The strength and dominance of the political parties in the German system had of course already been well established in the Bonn Republic and in its predecessor, the Weimar Republic. Yet there is an irony in the minister's statement because there have indeed been "political strivings" of factions both within the parties and outside the parties that frequently get their way in spite of the carefully regulated decision-making procedures of the German party-state.

Unlike the founders of the diffident Weimar Republic, those of the Federal Republic firmly put their trust into party government without any reservations about the practical monopoly of the party-state on policy, personnel, and power. The dominant position of the major parties today, the Social Democrats (SPD), Christian Democrats (CDU/CSU), and Free Democrats (FDP), naturally raises questions of oligarchy and influence with regard to their internal decision-making structure, their relation to factions within and interest groups outside, and their accountability to the electorate at large.

West German parties differ considerably in their internal structure and character. The SPD has the most explicitly "democratic" structure for its 820,000 (1971) members, a pyramid of levels the lower levels of which elect and hold responsible the higher levels of delegates and leaders. Within this kind of structure, a faction such as the Young Socialists is most likely to operate chiefly at the local level. Large outside organizations of overlapping membership such as the Trade Union Federation (DGB), on the other hand, can be effective at all levels and especially at the very top if they make a serious and concerted effort. The CDU/CSU, by way of contrast, is a pluralistic party in which special organizations for labor, industry, the *Mittelstand* ("handicraft, small business"), local government personnel, women, youth, and refugees may play a prominent factional role. Their membership is not restricted to party members, and therefore the door is open to interest group activities. The SPD generally seeks to avoid such "corporatist" organizations (except for youth) but has factory committees, working committees of lawyers, doctors and pharmacists, etc., which somewhat resemble the CDU/CSU components but are not nearly so important. The FDP, finally, is a loosely knit party of notables with only two special organizations, for youth and for women. Its individualistic style of representation, of course, also lends itself to the formation of factions as well as clienteles. Taken together, the 1.3 million members of the three parties probably include no more than 15 percent (or about two hundred thousand) regularly participating activists. Until recently, local meetings have rarely been occasions of intense debate on personnel or issues. Even the more carefully provided devices for intraparty democracy, of course, give little assurance for overcoming the oligarchic tendencies of large bureaucratic organizations.

Factions are likely to form at whichever level they can, but most of all at the local level. They receive less attention there than when they involve the federal leadership of a party or, most important, officers of the federal government. We shall attempt to review, briefly, some of the more notorious incidents of factionalism at the highest level during the past quarter century and give examples of leadership factions, policy factions, and cross-party factions in the Bonn Republic before taking a closer look at the local level.

Factions in the Party-State

MULTIPARTYISM AND FACTIONS

In the multiparty Weimar Republic, excesses of intraparty factionalism, party splits, and the notorious *Querverbindungen* ("cross-party factions") seriously weakened the stability of the party system until its final collapse in 1933. Despite this fragmented pedigree, the Federal Republic has been considerably more cohesive and has grown more so since its multiparty beginnings in 1949. Yet, here too, factional politics has tended to emerge, giving expression to the divisions and social heterogeneity of contemporary Germany. Factional politics afflicts especially and notoriously whatever parties happen to be in power. And, as we shall see below, there is also a pervasive fabric of local nonpartisan factions at the smallest local government level, where the party-state seems unable to maintain control.

At the outset of the Bonn Republic, there was a noticeable trend toward proliferation of parties. In addition to the three major West German parties of today, the first West German Bundestag included five small parties, the Communists (KPD); the states'-rights Bavaria party (BP); the chiefly Lower Saxonian German party (DP); the Catholic Center party (Z), which had refused to join the CDU/CSU; a demagogic movement from Munich, the Economic Reconstruction Union (WAV); as well as three small splinter groups. There was also a noticeable trend toward multipartyism at the state level which cost the major parties dearly, while regional movements, refugee parties, and right-wing organizations made inroads everywhere. Two of the major parties themselves were still laboring under the strain of their relatively recent formation or unification. The Christian Democrats represented a union of the bulk of the old Catholic Center party with conservative Protestants and other bourgeois elements without a political home. The adherence of the Protestants and of certain regional blocs was often in doubt until the CDU finally settled down to a rather decentralized "federal" system which allowed for a kind of symbiosis with the DP in Lower Saxony and accepted the autonomy of the Bavarian CSU within the party.[2] The FDP likewise embodied very considerable heterogeneity since it first united two traditional strands of German liberalism in 1948. To this day, differences between states where the FDP has a dominant tradition of nineteenth-century economic liberalism and those where it has a tradition of cultural liberalism, especially in the south, are much of the basis of FDP factionalism.[3]

LEADERSHIP FACTIONS IN THE CDU/CSU

The prodigious growth of the CDU/CSU vote under Konrad Adenauer in the 1950s progressively reduced the number of West German parties to the present three. This consolidation was achieved both by the workings of the electoral law, which decreed a minimal popular vote of 5 percent as the threshold of representation, and by the spectacular economic growth which integrated refugees and other victims of the effects of World War II into West German society and eventually into the major parties. This process produced factionalization of the small coalition parties of the CDU/CSU which Adenauer had taken into his cabinets. One by one, first the Refugee party (BHE), then the FDP, and finally the DP were split each into a ministerial faction consisting of some cabinet ministers and their friends, and a protesting rump party in the Bundestag. The ministerial faction was usually induced to join the CDU, while the rump group found itself stripped of campaign funds, and declined. Only the FDP managed to survive this treatment, while its ministerial faction, under the name of Free People's party (FVP), slowly sank into oblivion.

No sooner had Chancellor Adenauer reached the peak of his consolidated power than cracks began to show in this imposing edifice. Following the Christian Democratic electoral victory of 1957—the first time any German party had polled a clear majority of the popular vote —many of the party and in its bourgeois coalition partners began to suggest that the octogenarian chancellor should be replaced. The free-trading FDP, and important parts of the CDU and of the CSU in particular, wanted to promote Ludwig Erhard, the popular architect of the so-called economic miracle, as his successor. In 1959, Adenauer attempted to outflank Erhard's bid through some constitutional manipulation involving his own candidacy for the figurehead federal presidency, which was to be built up along the lines of De Gaulle's office in the Fifth Republic of France. Adenauer would have permitted Erhard to become chancellor without really turning over control to him. Eventually Adenauer dropped the scheme amid outspoken criticism in the press and among the parties. His critics in the FDP and CDU and in the CSU formed a cross-party faction called the *Fronde,* which worked for his replacement by Erhard.

The election campaign of 1961 not only brought the succession crisis in the CDU to a head, it also revealed the complex factional interplay both within the CDU and between CDU groups and other bourgeois parties, such as the FDP. Owing to its decentralized structure, the CDU/CSU had formed an equilibrating system of a number of distinct and relatively autonomous groups held together by a modicum of consensus on Christian Democracy and by the tangible advantage of party unity. An elaborate system of party committees on several levels, moreover, channeled the programmatic and policy demands of such groups as labor, industry, handicraft and small business, refugees, local government officials, women, youth groups, etc., through various party committees on social policy, economics, the *Mittelstand,* agriculture, communal policy, and others, as the route to the party's policy-making apparatus. Thus a web of factional associations ranging from the Catholic labor organizations to business, farmers', women's, and youth organizations tied the party to all kinds of groups and social forces of West German society.[4]

As chancellor, Adenauer had always refrained from commitment to any one of these policy-related factions, and had instead played the role of broker among the contending factional groups. But once his leadership was threatened, he was not above manipulating the factional system in his defense. When the FDP promised in the campaign that it would topple Adenauer, it counted on the assurances of Erhard, Gerstenmaier (a prominent Protestant CDU leader), Strauss (the CSU chairman), and a group of CDU deputies from Hamburg. But the labor wing of the CDU/CSU, in exchange for certain concessions, threw its support behind Adenauer. He then invited the SPD leadership for discussions of foreign policy, which was generally understood as his exploration of an alternative coalition, and industry promptly put pressure on the FDP not to drive Adenauer into the arms of the SPD. Ultimately, the CDU/CSU resolved to retain the Old Man as chancellor for two more years, while the FDP had to beat a humiliating retreat to its old role as his coalition partner.[5]

Adenauer's final resignation and replacement by Chancellor Erhard in 1963, however, was not the end of the leadership crisis for the CDU/CSU. Many leaders had seen in Erhard merely a temporary solution prior to their own push for the top position. The most important of these rivalries among leadership factions in the mid-sixties was between Gerhard Schröder and Franz-Josef Strauss. Strauss, the strongman of West German defense, had made a comeback after the devastating *Spiegel* affair of 1962, secure in the knowledge that his Bavarian CSU was an indispensable power base in any CDU/CSU government. His personal ambition soon became identified with a foreign policy faction, the so-called German Gaullists, who shared De Gaulle's doubts that America would really risk its cities in a nuclear showdown with the Soviets over Berlin or West Germany.

Schröder, the foreign minister in the Erhard post-Adenauer era, was pursuing an "Atlanticist" foreign policy that was more strongly anti-Gaullist than Strauss was anti-American. His factional following comprised the majority of the CDU, but was probably more inspired by a dislike for Strauss than by a desire to elevate Schröder to the chancellorship. There were many confrontations and bitter recriminations between the Gaullists and the Atlanticists, which eventually evolved into Strauss's struggle for a German nuclear weapons role against the *Ostpolitik* of Willy Brandt.[6] At best, these were leadership factions with only modest commitments to specific policies.

POLICY FACTIONALISM IN THE SPD

The other major party, the SPD, was seemingly spared much of the bitterness of factional strife in the first twenty years of the Federal Republic. Nevertheless, there was hardly an absence of disagreements or of recognizable groupings—in spite of the well-established tradition of Socialist solidarity. In the immediate postwar years there had been several major disputes over such issues as relations with the Communists and the future of Germany. In the mid-fifties, after the death of the charismatic SPD leader Kurt Schumacher (1952), there were factional groups that vociferously attempted to change the course he had established. Other groups became intensely involved in the street campaign against German rearmament and Germany's role in NATO. They were not about to follow willingly when the party did change its course and adopted a positive stance toward German defense and the Western alliance. From the time of the great turning point for the postwar SPD—the Bad Godesberg Conference of 1959—there continued to be a substantial minority that was against abandoning the traditional Marxist ideology and class character of the party and that expressed its dismay again and again about the new course of the party under Herbert Wehner and Willy Brandt. After the 1961 campaign, for example, the irreconcilables as well as many young Socialists angrily protested the "apolitical" new style of campaigning of Brandt and the seeming turn of the party from issues to personalities.[7] In 1966, again, a chorus of opposition arose within the party against the decision of the leadership to enter a "grand coalition" with the CDU/CSU.

A major basis of faction formation in the SPD has always been the large number of trade union (DGB) members among the SPD members and deputies. This led to tension at times of disagreement between party goals and trade union goals, such as during the compromises of the grand coalition, and in fact resulted in the organization of trade union committees at all levels of the SPD. The DGB thus hoped to achieve leverage on all issues relevant to the unions. When the formation of an intraparty faction did not produce the desired results, it was left with the only alternative of pursuing its goals "outside and over the heads of the party." Nevertheless, none of these factional struggles and protests drew even a fraction of the public attention devoted since 1969 to the Young Socialists.

The Youth Movement and Factions

YOUTH FACTIONS IN THE MAJOR PARTIES

All three of the major parties have so-called youth sections: the SPD, the *Jusos* ("Young Socialists"); the CDU/CSU, the Young Union (JU); and the FDP, the Young Democrats (DJD). These youth sections generally include all party members below a certain age. Jusos claims some

250,000 SPD members, though in fact probably no more than 40,000 are actively identified with the organization.[8] The CDU Young Union had a reported 120,000 members in 1966 (exclusive of Bavaria) of whom 40,000 were not CDU members, an indication that the JU is meant, among other things, as a CDU recruiting device. The DJD is an entirely separate organization of some 25,000, although they frequently belong to the FDP as well. In addition to these youth organizations, all three parties have maintained university student groups, which often have feuded with the parent party—even before the years of the upheaval at the universities. The most notable of these groups was the Social Democratic Students (SDS), which was expelled from the SPD in 1961; the SDS was followed by the Social Democratic University Federation (SHB), which developed a similarly radical posture toward the parent SPD, and which has been threatened and censured by the SPD several times over the years.[9] The CDU and FDP have not been much happier with their university groups. Below the university level there are further partisan youth groups, such as the Social Democratic *Falken* ("Falcons") and more recently, a Christian Democratic High School Student Union.

Initially, following the Nazi debacle, there had been a deeply disillusioned youth generation that wanted nothing to do with political activity of any sort. Dubbed "the skeptical generation" by German sociologists, they were conspicuous by their failure to join any partisan group. In the mid-sixties, however, an entirely new youth generation with pronounced political interests grew up, through the secondary school *(Gymnasium)* level and into the universities. Conspicuously well informed about politics and of an activist temper, they were an unprecedented generational challenge to their elders.[10]

This generational wave first crested outside the established parties and their youth sections, in the Extraparliamentary Opposition (APO) to the grand coalition of CDU/CSU and SPD (1966–1969) in Bonn.[11] The student revolt, too, during its peak years 1967–1969, tended to prefer the political *Groupuscules* and mass confrontations of the campus to the established parties. Unlike the American student rebellion, however, the German student movement had at its core considerable numbers of ideologically committed young people who were determined to "change the system" along lines spelled out by a group of young Marxist theoreticians, such as Rudi Dutschke, Wolfgang Lefevre, and Hans-Jürgen Krahl. APO militants, and student rebels generally, protested a variety of causes, from Vietnam and Third World issues to higher education reform and the democratization, or "deauthorization," of West German society from top to bottom.

In 1969 the grand coalition, the raison d'etre of the APO, came to an end. It was replaced with the reform coalition of SPD and FDP under Willy Brandt, who promised to tackle all kinds of domestic reforms and to establish better relations with the eastern neighbors of the Federal Republic. Although neither Brandt nor the FDP leaders had ever been spared the wrath of APO and student confrontationists, their ascent to power became the signal for the more reform-minded of the rebels to crowd into the established parties at the local level, followed by scores of new recruits who had been too young to be very active before 1970.[12]

The established parties were more willing to co-opt their youthful erstwhile critics. They hoped to infuse their own tired, aging ranks with new blood and to benefit from the boundless energy and new ideas of the young; at the same time they expected thereby to sap the strength of the youth rebellion against the system.[13] Universities, publishing houses, television, the press, and local governments all followed by hiring large numbers of new leftists who were still bent on their "long march through the institutions of West German society." Within a remarkably short time, the young rebels of APO and the student movement were successful in penetrating crucial sectors of West German society and in becoming prominent factions in the parties and among the party leadership.

Their triumph was not limited to the SPD. The Young Democrats had long been in rebellion against its parent FDP, especially in response to the challenge of the grand coalition of 1966 and after some involvement with APO and the student movement. Some state associations of the DJD openly split into "social liberal" loyalists and a "radical democratic" opposition. The latter considered themselves to be to the left even of the SPD, and liked to spike their circulars with new left slogans such as *Venceremos* and expressions of sympathy for Swedish or Yugoslav types of socialism. They too have followed a strategy of joining the FDP in order to reform the system from within, and the FDP has encouraged them as long as they agree to describe their goals not as "anticapitalistic" but as "the transformation of the system *(system-überwindend)."* Finally, by 1972, even the Young Union had abandoned its loyal conservative stance and started an emphatic push to turn the CDU/CSU into a reformist, program-oriented party. It would be an exaggeration to characterize the JU as young people bent on "transforming the system from within" rather than as well-meaning technocrats or moral traditionalists; nevertheless, the CDU/CSU on the whole has also tended to encourage and promote even its critics in the JU, if only to keep pace with the headlong rush of the SPD and FDP into the future.[14]

THE ROLE OF THE YOUNG SOCIALISTS

The most spectacular role of all the youth factions remained that of the Young Socialists. Until 1970, in spite of their growing power in many localities, their strategy had not been worked out much beyond a desire to turn the external opposition of APO and student revolt into an internal opposition. There had been demonstrative gestures of repudiation of SPD leadership, and a radical critique of SPD policies, ever since the Jusos congress of 1969 in Munich. The critique was aimed at the whole complex of ideas and policies which since the Bad Godesberg Program have led the SPD toward becoming a "people's party," and to seek common ground and cooperation with the other major parties. Jusos yearned to rekindle the working-class militancy of the early Social Democrats of the nineteenth century. Their policies were addressed mostly to the transformation of the economic system, especially by taxation and control of financial forces, and to the democratization of society by means of education reform, with a new, militant version of labor codetermination. To gain leverage for their "system-transforming reforms," they employed the "double strategy" of boring from within the party while mobilizing a socialistic consciousness in the people through special grievance campaigns. Communist (DKP) allies have been welcome to the Jusos as they had never been to the post-1945 SPD.

Their work at the base of the party consisted of a major effort to contest nominations to party and elective offices, and of endless "debates of principles" in which the old party stalwarts found themselves upstaged. Given their early encouragement of the Jusos, the established local and regional SPD leadership was rudely surprised when in district after district it was challenged, publicly attacked, and, in many cases, ousted in disgrace. By 1974, the Jusos had made spectacular inroads in many areas beyond traditionally left-wing districts like South Hesse and Schleswig-Holstein. Only the top leadership groups and most incumbents in legislatures and city councils survived the onslaught at the base of the party. In some cases, Jusos factions have striven to subordinate elective mandates to the orders of the party apparatus which they had already captured. At the federal level, SPD leaders Brandt and Schmidt tried to maintain a delicate balance between the pressure of the left-wing Jusos on the one hand and their economically conservative coalition partner, the FDP, on the other.

To complicate the factions picture further, the Jusos, like other militant political youth organizations before them, repeatedly change their thrust and repudiate their own antecedents and former leaders. They have thus tended to generate their own factions, which differ sharply on policies and strategies. At their Hanover Congress of 1971, there were four distinctive Jusos factions: (1) the *Stamokap* group, whose theory of "state monopoly capitalism" and propensity for alliances with the DKP stem from the old Social Democratic University Federation, especially in Hamburg and Berlin; (2) the "nonrevisionists" from Hanover and Göttingen, who particularly opposed the politics of accommodation of the SPD; (3) the more practical-minded group of "ethical socialists" from Schleswig-Holstein; and, (4) the majority group under Juso Chairman Wolfgang Roth, who aimed at "structural, anticapitalistic reforms" that take into account the depoliticized state of mind of the West German populace after decades of prosperity, consumerism, and Cold War.[15]

Three years and several congresses later, at the Jusos' Munich Congress of 1974, Roth's reformist faction barely squeaked by with its plank on economic policy. The enlarged *Stamokap* faction elected a representative onto the six-member council. Roth's successor found it necessary to play the broker's conciliatory role among the centrifugal forces at work. Observers predicted that the Jusos were more likely to debate each other into oblivion than to constitute a threat to the system.

The intense factionalism within the SPD is showing signs of taking its political toll. There has been an unbroken string of electoral defeats for the SPD in state and local elections since the SPD victory in the federal elections of 1972. In some cases voters' fear of the "red menace" is undeniably a major cause. In state elections in November 1974, for example, the voters of Munich and Frankfurt, both traditionally SPD cities, went out of their way to vote down every one of the local SPD candidates for the state diet in favor of candidates of the CDU/CSU. The Munich SPD had not only controlled all these seats before, but it had been the scene of a particularly successful Jusos takeover which led to the withdrawal of the incumbent from the mayoral race of 1972. Frankfurt's situation was similar in that there was constant agitation that the public associated with the extreme left. Given the popular mood of fear of inflation, left-wing terrorism, and economic crisis, the Jusos had evidently made it nearly impossible for the SPD to achieve a majority in a federal election.

The Nonpartisan Local Faction

Factionalism is nowhere more ever present than at the local level. A thorough study of factionalism in the German Federal Republic should really start at the local level, both in and outside the major parties, and work up to the higher party levels, where factions are more likely to draw attention.[16] It must suffice here at least to look at local factional phenomena outside the parties.

NONPARTISAN LOCAL FACTIONS IN BAVARIA AND HESSE

Wasserburg is a small (7,000 inhabitants) town in Bavaria whose walls rise steeply from the bend of the Inn River where it has nestled for nearly eight hundred years. In the 1972 reorganization of Bavarian counties, this proud town was stripped of its role as the county *(Kreis)* seat and became merely another small town in a corner of an enlarged *Kreis,* Rosenheim. The rest of the old *Kreis* Wasserburg was merged with another neighboring *Kreis* so that the new county boundary now separates the town from much of its historic hinterland. This humiliating experience at the hands of a Christian Democratic (CSU) state government caused six of the seven CSU city councilmen to resign from the party and, together with other independent elements, to form a nonpartisan bloc called the *Wasserburger Block.* Very instrumental in the formation of the new local faction were three local notables, a hotel owner, a transportation business owner, and the scion of another old Wasserburg family. A person entering the heart of the old town can hardly miss the gilded wrought iron trade signs of the hotel or the transportation firm.

Thus a faction was born of local spite against the machinations of the larger parties.[17] The *Block* soon organized an angry, well-attended protest rally in Wasserburg, and sent a large delegation to complain in person to the minister president (state chief executive) in Munich. They then put up an independent mayoral candidate and a full slate of city council candidates at the next election. Their choice for mayor, a well-educated but unknown former county administrator, and six of their twenty council candidates, won office. The *Block* then formed a coalition with other minority elements and proceeded to govern the town.

This *Wasserburger Block* is typical of nonpartisan factions in small towns and communes in areas of West Germany where the major political parties hold sway in the federal parliament (Bundestag), state diets (Landtag), and bigger cities. In the 1950s, these nonpartisan blocs and "voters' associations" were regarded with great suspicion because they tended in some cases to be fronts for outlawed neo-Nazi or Communist groups. Much of the German literature on local factions, in fact, questions their legality or constitutionality.[18]

At first glance, these factions look like a kind of local multiparty-ism. An excellent study of nonpartisan factions in the state of Hesse reports an extraordinary variety of groups and group labels in the first communal elections (1946) there, mostly reflecting partisan groups of the Weimar era.[19] Others bore names like the Bourgeois and Peasant party, the Refugee and Evacuee Association, or the Democratic Bloc. At the level of the county diets (Kreistage), 3 percent of the seats, and in towns and communes subordinate to the counties, 16 percent of the seats went to groups other than the Social Democrats, Christian Democrats, Free Democrats, or Communists. While some of the revived Weimar groups soon joined one or the other of these major parties, many nonpartisan factions remained independently prominent in town politics. Larger cities which had not had much of the phenomenon initially, experienced it in the 1950s: the Free Voters Group polled

9.8 percent in Darmstadt, two "independent" or "suprapartisan" voters' associations received 9.6 percent and 8.4 percent in Marburg; even Kassel and Wiesbaden had some nonpartisan factions. Their slogans tended to emphasize the *Mittelstand* and to advocate a "depoliticization of the communes," or to appeal to the special interests of refugees, wounded veterans, or temporarily disadvantaged former Nazi-era civil servants.

Most of these local factions in Hesse were not neo-Nazi front organizations like the National Voters Association of neighboring Hanover or the Free Voters Association of Pyrmont. Neither were they Communist cover organizations like the Stuttgart Voters Union.[20] Rather, most reflected the traditional bourgeois distrust of the political parties in nonpartisan issues of local politics. They frequently attacked special interests and "political egotism" at the same time that they served local handicraft and small business interests with obvious zeal. The Hessian study concluded its survey with a typology which distinguishes six types of nonpartisan factions: (a) groups articulating interests of persons claiming damages from the war or denazification trials; (b) *Mittelstand* groups such as small business or handicrafters eager to coalesce with other parties; (c) antisocialist blocs, often including other organized groups; (d) fronts for the extreme right or left; (e) short-lived associations of existing public interest groups such as housewives associations; and (f) protest slates against a government, especially involving appointed persons in prominent local office.[21]

In the late 1950s, while most of the smaller political parties at the federal level were being swallowed up by Konrad Adenauer's successful drive for a majority, the two largest parties, SPD and CDU/CSU, also strove to field more candidates in the small Hessian towns and communes below the *Kreis* level. Nevertheless, between 40 and 50 percent of the vote at that level, and a good two-thirds of the council seats, were claimed by the nonpartisan factions and their allies, leaving the rest to the major parties. The strength of the nonpartisan vote varied considerably from *Kreis* to *Kreis*. It was highest in the areas with the largest percentage (21 to 42 percent) employed in agriculture and where the population was dispersed in small communes. Communes of less than fifteen hundred were in fact nearly always dominated by a nonpartisan faction or two, and in the smallest communes there was often only one united ticket put together in an open town meeting. Sometimes a "peasants' bloc" was competing with a "bourgeois bloc."[22] On the other hand, in communes of over five thousand the nonpartisan factions' share of the seats dropped off to about one-fourth, and in those of over twenty-five thousand, to one-eighth of the seats.

NONPARTISAN LOCAL FACTIONS IN OTHER STATES

What has been true of the state of Hesse also applies to other states of the Federal Republic, in varying degrees. Baden-Württemberg, Rhineland-Palatinate, Lower Saxony, and Bavaria rather resemble Hesse in their dispersion of population and in the dominant role played by local factions in the smaller communes. Though the nonpartisan factions were said to be declining in some areas, communal elections in 1972 in Bavaria, for example, showed clearly that they were still going strong in others. In the twenty-five larger cities of the state, the major parties captured about 93.9 percent of the seats, a picture not unlike the Bundestag and the state diets of West Germany in the same year, where they held a near-monopoly of representation.[23] They did nearly as well in the *Kreis* diets, where their combined total was 81.5 percent of the seats. But in the small towns and rural communes, the major parties received no more than 28 percent of the seats.[24] The nonpartisan factions, by contrast, held 38.8 percent. Another 14.4 percent were joint tickets, which reflects the tendency of local party politicians, especially of the CSU, to run under a nonpartisan label rather than their own.

The 38.8 percent of seats for the nonpartisan factions in the smaller Bavarian communes in 1972 can be compared to 40.9 percent in 1966, and 40.2 percent in 1960. This is hardly a story of steep decline, although communal reorganzation of the state is likely to reduce the role of the nonpartisan factions by increasing the size and reducing the numbers of the smaller communes. Their proportions of communal council seats are matched by the role of nonpartisan factions in electing mayors: in 1960, 34.9 percent, and in 1966, 36.2 percent of the mayors (mostly honorary) represented such factions.

Table 1. Local Government Legislative Seats Held by Parties and
Nonparty Factions in Bavaria, 1972

	Independent Cities (25)	*Kreis* Diets (71)	Local Communes (4,381)	All Units
CSU	44.4%	49.1%	15.9%	16.6%
SPD	46.7	31.7	12.0	12.8
FDP	2.8	0.7	0.1	0.2
small parties	0.4	0.3	0.1	0.1
joint tickets	1.1	5.0	14.4	14.0
nonpartisan	4.6	13.2	38.8	38.1
no ticket	—	—	18.7	18.2
	100%	100%	100%	100%

There is a clear relationship between community size and the role of nonpartisan factions in electing the mayors of smaller communes.[25] The very smallest communes get along mostly without either parties or nonpartisan factions. Communes of between two hundred and three thousand inhabitants depend rather heavily on the factions. In larger communes, especially of about one thousand inhabitants or more, parties and joint tickets, especially CSU coalitions, play an increasingly important role, and in towns with a population of two thousand or more, parties and joint tickets approach a dominant role.[26] There is also a shift from small town CSU and CSU-coalition mayors toward mayors of the SPD and its coalitions in communities of about five thousand or more, a trend that becomes a Social Democratic near-monopoly among the large cities and metropolises of West Germany.

Comparisons among all the German states are made difficult by the considerable differences in electoral laws and other factors.[27] The city states of Hamburg, Bremen, and Berlin have no comparable phenomena. In the more heavily industrial and urbanized states, North Rhine-Westphalia and Saar, the major parties get a lion's share of the votes in communal elections: 95.3 percent of North Rhine-Westphalia voters chose the big parties and a mere 4.7 percent the nonpartisan factions. In the Saar it was 82.9 percent and 9.9 percent, respectively. Table 2 shows that the nonpartisan factions and other deviations from the party-state have been most prominent in Bavaria and Baden-Württemberg, but that Hesse, Schleswig-Holstein, and Lower Saxony, despite a high major-party vote, were not far behind in nonparty seats.

Table 2. Communal Legislative Seats Held by Parties and Nonparty Factions in Several German States

	Bavaria (1966)	Bad.-Wttbg. (1971)	Hesse (1968)	Low. Sax. (1968)	Schlsw-H. (1970)	Rhine-Pl. (1969)	N. Rh.-W. (1969)	Saar (1968)
major parties	24.0%*	27.7%	40.8%	53.1%	47.0%	26.0%	94.2%	78.3%
nonparty factions	40.1	37.7	58.3	44.5	52.3	34.7	5.7	12.5
joint tickets	11.3	2.2	—	—	—	—	—	—
no ticket	25.1	32.3	—	—	—	39.3	—	7.1

*The statistics of Table 2 have been adjusted for distortions.

In Schleswig-Holstein, the nonparty factions constituted 35 percent of the seats in communes of between 750 and 2,000, 75.5 percent in communes of under 750, and over 90 percent in communes of under 200 inhabitants.[28] Schleswig-Holstein is roughly between Hesse and Lower Saxony in this respect. The incidence of nonpartisan blocs on communes under 2,000 seems just as high in Schleswig-Holstein, Lower Saxony, Baden-Württemberg, and Rhineland-Palatinate as in Bavaria. In Rhineland-Palatinate, moreover, there is direct election without benefit of ticket, which accounts for 95.6 percent of the seats in communes of below 150, and 75.5 percent in those of between 150 and 500 persons. On communes with between 500 and 1,000 inhabitants, no-ticket candidates share the stage with the nonpartisan factions, which in turn share it equally with the major parties in communes of between 1,000 and 3,000. In towns of above 3,000, the parties receive more than three-fourths of the seats.

Conclusions

Factionalism has been part of the German multiparty system throughout the Bonn Republic, and during the Weimar Republic before it. West Germany's major parties, the CDU/CSU and SPD, have their own histories of internal faction politics, histories further complicated by the factional developments of the youth movement in politics in the 1960s. At the same time, factionalism has been endemic at the local government level, not only in the parties, but most prominently in the form of local nonpartisan factions.

The existence of these factions at the smallest local level in the Federal Republic is of considerable significance. The most patent reason for local nonpartisan factionalism may be in the proportion of numbers: of some 24,500 communes in 1967, 21,000 had below 2,000 inhabitants and their total population constituted only about one-fifth (12.5 million) of the West German population. The major parties have tended to concentrate their activities in the cities. Their estimated 200,000 party activists may simply not suffice to field candidates for all these small local positions. The local party organizations, in fact, number only about 10,000 for each party. While the Federal Republic may indeed be a party-state at the federal, state, and city levels, the parties have evidently not yet succeeded in penetrating completely the small town and rural scene.

On the other hand, the nonpartisan factions also constitute an expression of traditional antiparty sentiment, of resentment against the complex, large organizations and their "out-of-town" leadership. Local government elections boast the highest electoral participation rates in the country. The nonparty factions reflect not only local, personality-based politics as opposed to the regional and national concern of the parties. They also symbolize the small town and rural belief in the wholeness and peace of the parochial world, far from the "dirty politics" and the institutionalized conflicts of the party system. It is not by accident that many of these factions call themselves by names such as Unpolitical Voters Association, Unity, Common Good, Justice, Village Peace, or Concordia, not unlike the names of traditional singing clubs, and that their names nearly always invoke the name of their town or village.

The small town or rural voter tends to be conservative and to have a genuine aversion to political parties that threaten to carry their conflicts into his small world. His isolated social world is, of course, not really free of social tension and cleavages. Quite the contrary may be true, but it is far more vulnerable to explicit sociopolitical conflict than, say, a differentiated, metropolitan environment. Hence this rural conservatism, with its myth of the peaceful village community, may well serve to protect the society and its patterns of social control and of traditional deference to the rich and the powerful.[29]

Some commentators have also pointed to the antiparty tradition of Prussian conservatism and to old corporatist *(Ständisch)* notions among the small town and rural citizenry. The nonpartisan factions, among other things, help to facilitate representation, and even political change, with a minimum of conflict. In many cases, they may serve as a safety valve for the parties and their manipulations. They are often wide open to the articulation of new interests through them. They frequently force the parties to listen to local grievances. On the other hand, they also have a way of becoming party-like, or of joining with parties themselves, once they are continuously competing with the long-lived, well-established major parties. Thus they may become agents of social transition and change as well as vehicles of representation that are congenial to the small town and rural environment. Finally, as a political environment, these small communes are nearly all slated for extinction by the communal reorganization measures which have established a minimal community size varying between 5,000 and 8,000 inhabitants in the several states. When the smaller communes go, most of the nonpartisan factions will probably disappear also.

Party factions, however, are likely to remain. National party factions have varied from the personal following of Konrad Adenauer and the competing leadership factions of the CDU and CSU to the regional and policy-related factions of FDP and SPD, and to the youth sections of the three major parties and the shadings from multipartyism to internal factions of the major parties at local, state, and federal levels of government. The proverbial spirit of faction, it appears, is present in the politics of every community, party, elected assembly, or election to an important post. Factions form wherever individuals or groups combine to gain political control of a community, however it may be defined. They are the very life of competitive politics, and the higher the political stakes, the more factions compete for them. If a party is in power, if an election is likely, or if benefits are to be derived from control, there is something to gain by acting in concert, certainly more than among those out of power. Parties themselves are really factions that have become institutionalized and, perhaps, domesticated over time.

Before we begin to attach the term *faction* to any and all political combinations, however, we must remember that a term can have analytical value only so long as it does not become too inclusive. As an analytical tool, the term *faction* should probably be used rather restrictively. It should always be related explicitly to a particular arena such as a small town electorate, a city council or legislature, or a local organization or representative body of a party. It may be a good idea also to restrict the term to conspiring collectivities who know each other rather than to whole social classes or rather indirect or speculative links.[30] And a faction should always be related to a set of goals such as political control of the arena, winning the next election, defending vital interests, or achieving a certain policy outcome.

NOTES

1. Gerhard Schröder, "Preface," *Rechtliche Ordnung des Parteiwesens*, Federal Ministry of the Interior (Frankfurt: Metzner, 1957). See also Peter H. Merkl, "Party Government in the Bonn Republic," in Elke Frank, ed., *Law-Makers in the Modern World* (Englewood Cliffs: Prentice-Hall, 1966).

2. For details, see Heino Kaack, *Geschichte und Struktur des deutschen Parteiensystems* (Opladen: Westdeutscher Verlag, 1971), pp. 199–218.

3. Factionalism in the FDP erupted especially over the state coalitions of the FDP with the SPD in the south, and in the debate on the attempts of the FDP of North Rhine-Westphalia and Hesse to found a nationalistic mass movement, in the early 1950s.

4. For details, see especially Gerhard Schulz, "Die Organisationsstruktur der CDU," in *Zeitschrift für Politik* 3 (1956): 161; and Schulz, "Die CDU-Merkmale ihres Aufbaus," in Max Gustav Lange, ed., *Parteien in der Bundesrepublik* (Stuttgart: Ringverlag, 1955), p. 143.

5. Peter H. Merkl, "Equilibrium, Structure of Interests, and Leadership: Adenauer's Survival as Chancellor," *American Political Science Review* 56, no. 3(Sept. 1962): 638–49.

6. See Peter H. Merkl, *German Foreign Policies, West and East: On the Threshold of a New European Era* (Santa Barbara: ABC-Clio, 1974), pp. 105–25. Strauss's personal following in the seventies has been rivaled by leadership factions gathering behind Rainer Barzel and Helmut Kohl.

7. On the right and left wings of the SPD in the 1950s, see Peter H. Merkl, *Germany: Yesterday and Tomorrow* (New York: Oxford Univ. Press, 1965), pp. 314–21.

8. See Helmut Bilstein et al., *Jungsozialisten—Junge Union—Jungdemokraten* (Opladen: Leske Verlag, 1972), pp. 15–23.

9. See Ossip K. Flechtheim, ed., *Dokumente zur parteipolitischen Entwicklung in Deutschland seit 1945* (Berlin: Wendler, 1966), 5:302–17; and Flechtheim, ed., *Die Parteien in der Bundesrepublik Deutschland* (Hamburg: Hoffman and Campe, 1973), pp. 500–502.

10. See, for example, the research of Peter Menacher on fifteen-year-olds in Bavarian *Mittelschule* classes, in *Jugendliche und Parteien* (Munich: Olzog, 1971).

11. On the APO, see Kurt L. Shell, "Extraparliamentary Opposition in Postwar Germany," *Comparative Politics* 2, no. 4 (July 1970):653–80.

12. There were also those whose opposition on principle kept them from working within the system; other terrorist elements which have meanwhile gone their own way; and others who went instead to the newly established Communist party.

13. This author was given a revealing glimpse of these motive forces at work in the town of Fribourg, where the local SPD minority had long suffered from a dearth of university-trained personnel for public office. In 1969, the old party stalwarts were happy to accept substantial numbers of students and recent university graduates and, in fact, conferred all kinds of offices and career opportunities upon them. Their enthusiasm soon gave way to deep dismay, however, when the young recruits proved to be not only arrogant and abrasive in public debate, but in many cases unabashed careerists who seemed to be using the Fribourg SPD merely as a stepping-stone to regional and federal careers.

14. See Jürgen Kunze, "Die Jungdemokraten zwischen Liberalismus und Sozialismus," in Jürgen Dittberner and Rolf Ebbinghausen, eds., Parteiensystem in der Legitimitätskrise (Opladen: Westdeutscher Verlag, 1972), pp. 307–26; Ulrich Grasser, "Die CDU und die Junge Union," in Dittberner and Ebbinghausen, eds., Parteiensystem in der Legitimitätskrise, pp. 41–67.

15. See Volker Mase and Peter Miller, "Die Jungsozialisten in der SPD," in Dittberner and Ebbinghausen, eds., Parteiensystem in der Legitimitätskrise, pp. 280–89.

16. There is a penetrating analysis of SPD factionalism in West Berlin which covers twenty-five years and no less than seven "alternations of power" among the factions. Joachin Raschke, Innerparteiliche Opposition: die Linke in der Berliner SPD (Hamburg: Hoffman and Campe, 1974).

17. The Social Democrat mayor and councilmen for reasons of their own chose not to make an issue of the damage to civic pride.

18. The Basic Law (Art. 21) accords political parties a privileged role; not until 1961 did the Federal Constitutional Court finally declare the nonpartisan blocs to be perfectly legal and constitutional. See, for example, Werner Grundmann, Die Rathausparteien, Göttinger Rechtswissenschaftliche Studien, vol. 31 (Göttingen: Schwartz, 1960); Arnold Köttgen, "Parteibegriff und Gemeindewahlrecht," Deutsches Verwaltungsblatt (1958), p. 593; and Köttgen et al., Rechtliche Ordnung des Parteiwesens, Bericht der vom Bundesminister des Inneren eingesetzten Parteienrechtskommission (Frankfurt: Metzner, 1957), pp. 135–39.

19. Vera Rüdiger, Die Kommunalen Wählervereinigungen in Hessen (Meisenheim: Hain, 1966), pp. 2–75.

20. See Günther Rabus, "Kommunale Wählervereinigungen als Ersatzorganisationen verfassungswidriger politischer Parteien," Archiv des öffentlichen Rechts 80(1954): 203–11; and Wilhelm Henrichs, "Kommunale Splintergruppen und Parteiengesetz," Kommunalpolitische Blätter (1953), pp. 103–206.

21. Rüdiger, Die Kommunalen Wählervereinigungen in Hessen, pp. 76–88.

22. Rüdiger, Die Kommunalen Wählervereinigungen in Hessen, pp. 90–115. See also Bernhard Vogel, "Die Unabhängigen in den Kommunalwahlen westdeutscher Länder" (Ph.D. diss., Univ. of Heidelberg, 1960), who stresses the role of local notables and local opposition to the ticket presented by the dominant major party in an area.

23. The only state diet seat not held by the SPD, CDU/CSU, or FDP in 1972 was a seat held by the South Schleswig Voters Association (SSW), a Danish minority group. (Data courtesy of the Bavarian Ministry of the Interior.)

24. It is worth noting that electoral participation in communal elections was remarkably high at this level, 80.8 percent of eligible voters, as compared to 68.2 percent in the independent cities.

25. Kommunalwahlen in Bayern, Mar. 13, 1966, and Mar. 8, 1970 (Munich: Bayerisches Statistisches Landesant, 1970), pp. 40, 49, 75.

26. If we distinguish the mayors of independent cities and of Kreis seats from the rest of the salaried and nonsalaried mayors, the nonpartisan bloc candidates turn out to be most heavily concentrated among the nonsalaried, honorary mayors, where they constitute 38.3 percent; another 34 percent were elected without a formal ticket. The city and county seat mayors have hardly any nonpartisan sponsors; of the salaried small town mayors, only 27.8 percent are bloc candidates, and 2.2 percent are no-ticket candidates. Verzeichnis der Oberbürgermeister, Landräte und ersten Burgermeister in Bayern (Munich: Bayerisches Statistisches Landesant, 1973), p. 7.

27. The communal electoral law of Lower Saxony, for example, allows voters a choice between a few names or, if they cannot identify the names, a list. Characteristically, the number of voters choosing the list declines with community size from 40 percent in communes over twenty thousand to a mere 4.2 percent in those below five hundred.

28. Die Kreis-und Gemeindewahl, Apr. 26, 1970, in Schleswig-Holstein, Statistisches Landesant Schleswig-Holstein, Kiel (1970), p. 14. Compare Heino Kaack, "Parteien und Wählergemeinschaften auf kommunaler Ebene," in Heinz Rausch and Theo Stammen, ed., Aspekte und Probleme der Kommunalpolitik (Munich: Voegel, 1972), pp. 138–50.

29. On the nature of small town and rural notables, see also Ulrich Matthee, "Elitenbildung in der Kommunalen Politik" (Ph.D. diss., Univ. of Kiel, 1967). Matthee found the notables to be distinguished by their length of residence, family tradition, or size of property in rural Schleswig-Holstein.

30. This would not preclude "federations" of like-minded factions, or the growth of a legislative faction from representatives elected by like-minded factions in many separate communities. Knowing one another need not be face to face, but it does require a sense of community and a network of communication such as certain large organizations may provide.

11

Factionalism and Political Change in Bolivia

CHRISTOPHER MITCHELL

During the past forty years, the greatest upswings of factionalism in Bolivian political movements have tended to come when those movements were isolated from rank-and-file support. Factionalism has engaged primarily the political elite and has tended to intensify when—for one reason or another—a segment of that elite has found itself without firm popular backing. In this chapter, I describe the association between nonpopular politics and factionalism in Bolivia during three recent particularly factionalized periods. I also speculate on functions factionalism may perform in more basic processes of political change in Bolivia.

Factionalism here means a condition of deep structural division within a single ideological movement or tendency. This division may take the form of organized subunits within a political party, or of many rival parties within a given ideological movement. This is a broad definition of factionalism, but it seems to better describe Bolivian conditions than more restrictive definitions which have been offered.[1]

Though factionalism in Bolivia may take the form of multiple political parties, multipartyism and factionalism are not necessarily identical. Bolivia has had a multiparty system for the past fifty years, and in many cases these parties have each represented diverse doctrinal persuasions. Only when multiple political parties divide a single ideological movement would the term *factionalism* apply.

In the latter instance, division within parties and division among parties tend to occur together and to become, for practical purposes, almost indistinguishable. Mutually hostile subunits within a given party may elect to stay within a very loose confederation, or they may set themselves up as formally separate parties. These new parties, in turn, may further subdivide or may recombine into multiparty "fronts" or even into new parties. Thus, rigid distinctions between intraparty and interparty division don't seem helpful in discussing these cases. Instead, I stress the existence of fragmentation—whatever particular form it may take—within a given political movement.

A number of different motives may lead to such division, though the movement which is fragmented was originally based on ideology. Factional leaders may be guided by personal rivalries, regional disputes, and splits within transnational political movements, as well as by important disagreements over doctrine. Indeed, doctrine often plays a very small role, though efforts are almost always made to defend factionalism on ideological grounds.

Bolivian factions tend to be loosely structured. Leaders' powers, while considerable, are seldom formalized, and membership (even at the upper levels) is often subject to rapid change. Complex hierarchies and organization plans, in the few cases where they exist, are generally irrelevant to the haphazard and personalistic way most factions make decisions. This looseness of organization helps blur the distinction between a faction within a party and a separate "independent" party.

Finally, distinguishing the periods of intense factionalism in Bolivia is to some extent a matter of judgment. Factionalism at some level has been part of Bolivian politics during the whole period (1934–1974) which this chapter examines. The direct participants in factional disputes also almost invariably have been members of the political elite, as is true in most countries. I will analyze in detail only what seem to be the upswings of factionalism, the periods when division was especially bitter and had a marked influence on later events. These periods also seem, I argue, to be ones in which the political movement involved was particularly isolated from popular support. There have been three highly factionalized eras.

First, during the late 1930s, the Bolivian left was deeply divided by a factionalism which was primarily ideological. Many small parties and segments within parties debated how Bolivia's working class might gain and use political power, though the workers themselves did not yet see the parties as their instruments. This left-wing factionalism diminished after 1941 as a few of the radical parties gained sizable followings and less popular rivals disappeared.

In the years 1956–1964, a second factional upswing took place, this time largely from personal motives and within a single centrist political party. The ruling *Movimiento Nacionalista Revolucionario* ("Nationalist Revolutionary Movement"—MNR) felt itself forced in 1956 to take highly unpopular economic steps which alienated large groups of former supporters. Largely cut off from their former popular involvements, the MNR leaders intensified old intraparty divisions and created new ones. This bitter MNR factionalism contributed to the party's overthrow by the military in 1964.

A third period of factional activity came in 1969–1971, again within the Bolivian left and again primarily motivated by ideological issues. A series of "nationalist" and/or "Socialist" military governments, which tended to be friendly or tolerant toward the left, held power. A confusing array of rival "new left" and "old left" parties fought over many of the same issues that had dominated politics thirty years earlier. The distance which separated the left from large-scale popular support was revealed, however, by the bloody success of a repressive right-wing military *golpe* in August 1971. In exile, the left has tended to consolidate during the succeeding years.

As I describe these three Bolivian cases of factionalism in detail, it may be useful to have two basic questions in mind. First, what were the principal motivations behind factional activity in each case—personality, religion, ideology? And second, what were the factions' attitudes toward possible or eventual popular backing—were they basically seeking such support, or the reverse? When we begin to see a pattern in the answers to these questions, it will be possible to comment on factionalism's possible role in Bolivian political change.

Factionalism of the Left, 1934–1941

During the 1930s Bolivia's traditional, narrowly based political system was rapidly losing all legitimacy. The economy, dominated by the export of tin ore, had been severely hurt by the world depression; as in other Latin American countries, trade income, taxes, and employment all declined sharply. But the Bolivian regime compounded these difficulties by stumbling into and through a bloody border conflict with Paraguay. During the three-year Chaco War (1932–1935), political and military mismanagement was evident on almost every hand. The army could not be supplied, even minimally, in the remote Bolivian southeast; its training and organization were seldom a match for the Paraguayans'; and there were frequent disagreements over strategy between President Daniel Salamanca and his generals. By the war's end, these weaknesses had contributed to the loss of the area in dispute, and to the death of more than fifty thousand Bolivian soldiers.

Under these circumstances, it became more and more difficult to sustain the legitimacy of a political system which excluded from voting (through a literacy test) nearly 90 percent of Bolivia's four million people. Three traditional parties, based in the very small middle and upper classes, had dominated national politics since 1900: the *Liberales,* the *Republicanos Genuinos,* and the *Republicanos Saavedristas.* Their professed doctrines basically reflected the liberal constitutional ideas of nineteenth-century America and England: limited government, democratic popular expression within a system of orderly competition, guarantees for free enterprise, etc. They had never seriously tried to tamper with the economic and political power of the three large tin mine entrepeneurs (Aramayo, Hochschild, and Patiño), or with the system of plantations and rural servitude that gave Bolivia (along with Chile) the most unequal landholding system in the world.

With their governing abilities largely discredited by the conduct of the war, the traditional parties drew together and abandoned what had at times been a bitter mutual rivalry. The general interests—which these parties shared—of the middle and upper classes were now at stake, and by 1939 the three groups had formed an alliance, called the *Concordancia,* to defend those interests. The threat to them came from discontented, and largely disenfranchised, workers' groups, and from critical middle-class intellectuals.[2]

But by the time of their alliance, however, these "democratic-liberal" parties had already lost effective political power to the army, which had taken over the government fully by 1936. The most innovative and active civilian political tendencies were the left and center-left, where a great many diverse new groups burst into politics during and immediately after the Chaco War. These organizations, which variously termed themselves "parties," "cells," or "groups," shared a number of characteristics. They were small, with at most a few hundred members each, and more usually a few dozen. Their leaders were usually young members of the upper middle classes—often aged between twenty and thirty—who had not been active in the traditional parties. And, most of the new groups drew on some variant or interpretation of Socialist thought for offering their plan for Bolivian political modernization.[3]

Many of the groups making up the left were also very loosely organized, with rapidly shifting leaderships and goals. Division often appeared within a new organization, which might then split into several parties or groups; these in turn might continue independently or merge with other groups into a new front or party. Leftist politicians often transferred their activities rapidly from one party to another. In short, the Bolivian left and center-left were thoroughly factionalized, with between five and fifteen competing groups at any given time in the late 1930s.

A good example of these factional disputes—atypical only because it had some roots in the pre-Chaco period—is the fate of the *Partido Nacionalista* (PN). Organized in 1926 as a support to then President

Hernando Siles, the PN combined older traditional politicians (including Luis Fernando Guachalla, Enrique Finot, and Rafael Taborga) with young student leaders and intellectuals (most important, Enrique Baldivieso, José Tamayo, Augusto Céspedes, and Carlos Montenegro). In 1935 the Nationalists held their first post-Chaco convention, and the party's younger and more radical elements immediately seceded, forming the *Célula Socialista Revolucionaria*. The more traditional PN elements disbanded. The *Célula*, with a very moderate Socialist program, rapidly set about recruiting allies on the left. It absorbed the *Bloque Intelectual "Avance,"* and much of the group known as *Acción Socialista Beta Gama,* though some more radical members of the latter remained independent as the *Bloque Socialista de Izquierda.*

The new alliance growing out of the *Célula Socialista Revolucionaria* took the name *Partido Socialista* (PS) in early 1936. Led by Baldivieso, Montenegro, Tamayo, Luís Iturralde Chinel, and Alberto Mendoza López, as well as some labor leaders, the PS supported the army in its May 1936 takeover of power. The party received two ministries, but Baldivieso quickly came under intraparty attack for having allied the *Partido Socialista* with the remnants of the traditional Saavedra Republicans. When the army ousted all parties from cabinet participation in June 1936, the PS rapidly disappeared, leaving behind only its newspaper, *La Calle.* Edited by Montenegro and Céspedes, the paper became a political success, and its writers helped form and publicize the *Movimiento Nacionalista Revolucionario* in 1941.[4]

Few of these small groups had national networks of chapters (the *Socialistas* had branches for a short time, and a brief effort was made in 1937 to set up a nationwide, government-sponsored *Partido Socialista de Estado*).[5] Instead, they were usually small circles of political activists in the capital or in individual provincial cities. Some new parties offered candidates in the periodic elections, but none expended much energy appealing to a still very restricted electorate.

The newly active elite groupings and parties were much more concerned with debating the ways in which massive political participation might *ideally* be stimulated. Though small and drawn largely from the social elite, the post-Chaco leftist groups favored the expansion of politics to include large numbers of workers and even peasants excluded by the traditional system. Not yet really competing for this new support, they debated both how mass support should be sought and what strategy should guide its use in building a stronger and more just Bolivia.

The motives behind leftist factional divisions in the 1930s were thus primarily ideological. Though personality certainly played an independent role occasionally, more usually ideas or ideological commitments cast personalities in one competing group or another. By the late 1930s, the terms of the ideological debate among leftist factions were becoming better defined, as a half dozen more durable parties emerged from the welter of post-Chaco groups and cells.

In the most moderate Socialist position, the *Partido Socialista* called for an important governmental role in the economy, including creation of state industries, public participation in tin mine profits, and nationalization of oil and gold deposits. But the PS also advocated increased foreign investment in the exploitation of other natural resources. While they offered plans for better labor legislation, health benefits, and education, the *Socialistas* had no program for land reform.[6]

To the left of the PS, in both basic doctrine and policy proposals, was the *Partido de la Izquierda Revolucionaria* (PIR). The PIR was based on the *Grupo de Izquierda* in the provincial city of Cochabamba, and was led by José Antonio Arze and Ricardo Anaya. Formally organized in 1940, it combined *indigenista* ideas with a Moscow-line gradualist communism. It proposed full nationalization of the mines, railroads, and petroleum industry, centralized economic planning, and—most radical for the period—thorough agrarian reform. But the party believed that proletarian power could not triumph immediately, and would have to wait for middle-class democracy to present its inevitable contradictions.[7]

A more radical position favoring proletarian power was taken by the *Partido Obrero Revolucionario* (POR), which had a tenuous existence in the 1930s but which was to increase in power during the two succeeding decades. The POR was founded at Córdoba, Argentina, in 1934 by a group of leftists exiled during the Chaco War. It was revived in Bolivia in October 1938, and a major split immediately appeared within it. A faction led by Tristán Marof argued that the party should have strong discipline but should welcome Socialist-inclined members of all classes into its ranks. The (less numerous) followers of José Aguirre Gainsborg, much influenced by the ideas of Leon Trotsky, argued that the POR should concentrate on the proletariat as the most committed revolutionary class. The flavor of this ideological debate is conveyed by the Gainsborg group's account of it:

> In the first days of October of this year [1938], the POR held its first conference in the city of La Paz, in order to solve an important problem: whether the POR should continue existing as a revolutionary class party, or whether on the contrary it should organize itself in such a way that all sorts of careerists and those who support any form of socialism (be it reformist, petty-bourgeois, or whatever) would be able to enter. . . .[8]

The *Marofistas* withdrew from the POR during this first conference, creating the *Partido Socialista Obrero de Bolivia*. This group rapidly declined due to poor internal coordination and overdependence on

Marof, while the POR gradually gained strength. Though crippled by Gainsborg's death immediately following the split, the Trotskyite POR gained a considerable following among the mine workers in the 1940s, and influenced government policy-making after 1952.

Standing somewhat outside this leftist ideological debate, and with a program which was vague in part because of its great internal diversity, was the *Movimiento Nacionalista Revolucionario*. The leaders who organized the MNR in 1941 ranged from leftists such as Walter Guevara Arze and Hernán Siles Zuazo (Siles had belonged to the old *Beta Gama* with Aguirre Gainsborg), through moderate Socialists like Victor Paz Estenssoro, to the pro-German and antisemitic group which ran *La Calle* (Céspedes and José Cuadros Quiroga). Cuadros Quiroga drew up the party's first statement of principles, which included only vague provisions: "Against false democracy which sells out the nation; Against pseudo-socialism; For the consolidation of the state and the security of the homeland; For the economic liberation and sovereignty of the Bolivian people; With the Nationalist Revolutionary Movement."[9] Nevertheless, the MNR kept its internal uncertainties and disagreements from leading to serious secessions, and by the late 1940s the party had adopted a variety of Marof's basic organizational idea as its own strategy. It brought together a mass following made up of many small interest groups, cutting across class lines. The party's philosophy and strategy were certainly not classically leftist, but were labeled instead "revolutionary nationalism." What this alliance lacked in coherence it temporarily made up in sheer numbers, and the MNR won unprecedented national power in the 1952 revolution. Borrowing parts of its governmental program from the PIR and POR, the MNR was able to rule until 1964.

Factionalism on the Bolivian left and center-left declined sharply at the beginning of the 1940s, as the surviving leftist parties began earnestly to seek popular support in a variety of ways. The PIR did well in the 1940 presidential elections, and gained the support of a multiunion labor organization, the *Confederación Sindical de Trabajadores de Bolivia*. The MNR allied itself with discontented younger army officers, and participated in the government of Colonel Gualberto Villarroel (1943–1946). While in the Villarroel cabinet, the party began to cultivate labor and peasant support, and after Villarroel's overthrow, its mass backing came to outnumber that of the PIR. The POR, true to its ideology, worked primarily among labor unions, particularly the miners. With a numerically small but strategically placed following in the tin industry, and a reputation for incorruptibility, the POR survived into the 1970s.

Most leftist factions of the 1930s, in short, were partisans of mass politics; they sought widespread popular participation for the political system and strong popular backing for themselves. The strength of

this opinion favoring greater participation is indicated in a statement
made by Ricardo Anaya (PIR) during a parliamentary debate in 1944:

> Democracy . . . is an effective government of the majority, if not of the totality,
> and it is informed by the principle of equality. . . . Those of us who are democrats
> pursue an effective government of the majority and even the dictatorship of the
> proletariat. . . . Being a dictatorship of the majority, such a system is much more
> democratic than the effective dictatorship of the bourgeoisie, which is lyrically
> termed democracy.[10]

Though the leftist groups had had little popular backing during the
1930s, that period of factional debate and rapid organizational rise and
fall had served an important purpose. It had allowed the innovative
younger leaders in Bolivian politics to try out new ideas, if only in the
forum of ideological controversy. Very rapidly, the de facto political
relevance of working-class and peasant groups was overwhelming the
de jure limits on political participation; how this participation was to
be channeled was the principal topic of debate. Practical tests of different parties' organizing strategies came in the 1940s. But the factionalism of the 1930s had provided a forum in which those strategies could
be discussed, winnowed, and refined.

Factionalism within a Populist Party: The MNR, 1956–1964

One of the major issues in the leftist debate of the 1930s was whether
one social class or several should be mobilized in support of a Socialist
government. The MNR chose the latter course, and between 1946 and
1952 assembled a huge coalition of small discontented middle-class
and worker groups. After leading these groups in the 1952 revolution,
during which the regular army's crack units were routed, the MNR
acquired massive peasant support as well. the MNR's revolutionary
policy steps included the nationalization of Bolivia's principal tin enterprises (October 1952), sweeping and rapid land reform (August
1953), and—in recognition of the changes in participation patterns
which had brought it to power—the institution of universal adult suffrage (July 1952).

But the insistent demands of the MNR's enormous following, both
for resources and for power, put great strain on the nation's economy
and on the MNR's capacity to make enforceable decisions. Administrative decentralization and labor union power contributed to very rapid
monetary inflation, in which living costs were multiplied twenty-two
times between 1952 and 1956. Food became scarce, and crucial sup-
plies had to be sought from United States surplus stocks. By 1956, the
MNR leaders' fears—that the revolution was becoming completely
incoherent due to interest group power—coincided with pressures
from the United States and the International Monetary Fund to the
effect that economic "order" was needed before any further aid could

be supplied. In December of that year, a very stringent economic stabilization program was instituted by President Hernán Siles Zuazo. Though this set of decrees ended most urban food shortages, and effectively raised or stabilized the living standards of some labor and most middle-class groups, it also alienated important sources of MNR popular support. The mine workers' real wages dropped, and many fruitful sources of middle-class profit and corruption ran dry.[11]

In order to give his administration enough independence to carry the stabilization program through, Siles felt it necessary to reduce radically the participation of social pressure groups in policy-making. Until 1956, some of the cabinet's most powerful members had represented the nation's major labor unions, a system officially termed *co-gobierno*. The railroad workers controlled the Ministry of Public Works, the mine workers the Ministry of Mines, and the factory workers "received" the Ministry of Labor. Siles soon ended this system, replacing group representatives with technicians or politicians unaffiliated with labor.

In thus turning away from close involvement with its social bases, particularly the labor movement, the MNR abandoned the form of mass participation which had been crucial to its success. Unlike the factions of the 1930s, the MNR continued to roll up huge popular votes, with nearly a million supporters in 1960 and 1964. But voting was much less important to the MNR's hold on its following than the sense of direct representation which most pro-MNR groups had felt before 1956 and which they lost during the stabilization crisis.

The steps taken by Siles confronted MNR politicians with the problem of how to protect and promote their political careers now that power was not primarily weighed in terms of the size of one's popular following. Their solution—a makeshift one, to be sure—was to group themselves into elite factions which could compete for government jobs and for power. Ever since the party's founding, MNR leaders had differed over some points of party strategy and government policy. But these disagreements had been kept relatively informal, and few politicians had had to choose sides with any finality. After 1956, intra-MNR factions became much more formal, and their competition much more bitter.

Ideology played a relatively minor role in the motives of these factions, in part because new ideologies stood little chance of being implemented as long as the centrist MNR ruled. The union-affiliated leftist faction, for example, recognized that the unions alone did not form a popular base large enough to support a workable government. Although, as one observer noted, "each faction *(sector)* has put on certain ideological clothing in order to justify its existence," the basic goals were employment and power, and the basic organizing theme was a leader's personality.[12]

The largest and most durable of the factions, the *Sector de Izquierda* ("Leftist Sector"—SI) was organized around Juan Lechín, leader of the mine workers and of the new national labor confederation. It represented the interests of labor-affiliated MNR leaders whose influence had been reduced by stabilization. Declaring themselves further on the right of the party and opposing the *Lechinistas* were the followers of Walter Guevara Arze, calling themselves the *MNR Auténtico*. Guevara, who served as Siles' minister of government and foreign minister, tended to attract the MNR's older and more "gradualist" leaders. In 1961, Aníbal Aguilar Peñarrieta and Edil Sandóval Morón organized the so-called *Sector Socialista*, which, despite its name, was basically concerned with representing jobholders who had lost power at the end of Siles' term in 1960. Also in the early 1960s, a group called *Bloque de Defensa del MNR*, made up of followers of Siles and representatives of other factions, was organized to oppose Victor Paz Estenssoro's renomination for president in 1964.[13]

At times the MNR group which happened to control the presidency found it useful to sponsor factions within the party. Thus Siles, while president, encouraged the creation of *Izquierda Nacional del MNR*, a short-lived faction led by Jorge Alderete Rosales, Julio Ponce de León, and Edil Sandóval Morón. *Izquierda Nacional* criticized the Lechín group and was the immediate stimulus to the formation of the *Sector de Izquierda*.[14] A half decade later, Paz Estenssoro discreetly sponsored the Sector Pazestenssorista, as a prop to his own try for reelection.

Several of the major MNR factions—the *Izquierdistas*, the *Auténticos*, and the *Socialistas*—were quite formally organized. They had membership lists and membership cards, and they participated as units in local party leadership elections.[15] In addition to their names, some had symbols: one can still see, painted on walls in La Paz, the elephant design that was the symbol of the *Socialistas*.

The tactics used by the MNR factions, in competing with one another and with the government, were varied. If a faction had representatives in Parliament, opponents could often be harassed in debates and through interpellations of cabinet members. The *Sector de Izquierda* frequently used parliamentary weapons against Siles, though the president retaliated through his influence over parliamentary nomination. The factions also controlled votes in the party's quadrennial conventions, which could be used as bargaining weapons. In 1960, to cite a case, the *Pazestenssoristas* and the *Lechinistas* combined to block the plans of Guevara (possibly backed by Siles) to win the presidential nomination. Very often, the factions competed through a "war of manifestos" in the newspapers. One or more factions, for example, might refuse to participate in elections for a local MNR leader, charging that the voting was rigged by their opponents and demanding that the central party secretariat supervise the election. Their opponents would of course vigorously deny any irregularity, and long negotiations would be necessary to reach a multifaction compromise.[16]

The basic idea behind these factional maneuvers was clear: to threaten the party's national image of unity and competence so long as a faction's demands were not met. Publicized disruption was the factions' chief weapon, and the desire to preserve a unified appearance was the MNR government's chief motive in trying to satisfy the party's disgruntled factions. Such conflict itself of course tended to discredit the party. It was also very difficult to stop, in part because few factions had or sought very large popular followings. Factional strife was primarily a war of publicity (where it is hard to tell who has won), not a war of votes (where it is quite easy to know the winner).

Only the *Sector de Izquierda* had large or reliable mass backing. It could count on many of Bolivia's tin miners, and it also had the support of some peasant leaders in Achacachi, near La Paz. But even the *Izquierdistas*, at their first national conference, in October 1962, drew only 22 percent of their delegates from the mining areas as compared with 44 percent from the capital city and department of La Paz.[17] This social isolation of the ruling party is well described in a letter which, though written in 1966, applies to conditions since about 1958. An MNR activist in La Paz wrote to an exiled party leader:

> We are involved, as you will see, in a "personalist" dispute which can bring no benefit to the MNR. The presence of some discommodes others, and the attacks are reciprocal and permanent. . . .
> This dispute, in addition, has broken out only at the leadership level, because among the rank-and-file, as has been shown, there is no division. . . . We, the leaders, are presenting a sad spectacle which contrasts with the firmness and the revolutionary strength of the poor people—the workers and the peasants.[18]

The personalistic roots of MNR factionalism, as well as its weakening effects on party unity, can be seen in the way factions seceded to form new parties. In 1959, the *Auténticos* left the party when it became clear that Guevara would not get other factions' backing in his try for the 1960 presidential nomination.[19] The *Lechinistas* decided to remain in the party, winning the 1960 vice-presidential nomination for their chief, while Paz Estenssoro headed the ticket. Lechín was waiting for 1964 and was even willing, in order to gain the presidential nomination, to support a number of policies which labor disliked. Paz Estenssoro, however, decided to seek reelection, a move which provoked first the angry opposition of the *Izquierdistas*, and later their secession, to form the *Partido Revolucionario de la Izquierda Nacionalista* (PRIN) in 1963.[20] MNR factions only formed separate parties when leaders' personal ambitions were blocked.

An important long-range effect of MNR factionalism was the discrediting of the party in the eyes of competing urban power groups, particularly the army. Over nearly eight years, the *Movimiento* came to be thought of as constantly squabbling, unmanageable, unpredictable, and weak. Divisions among MNR leaders thus encouraged the party's opponents—and also increased their numbers, as an occasional faction formally withdrew from the MNR. By 1964, the "loyal" MNR really consisted of only Paz Estenssoro and his factional followers. In an atmosphere of general popular apathy, an army *golpe* exiled Paz Estenssoro in November of that year. The Guevara and Siles followers, together with the PRIN, supported the military takeover, but the army viewed all the MNR factions with distaste. Within a year, Lechín, Siles, and former Vice-President Ñulfo Chávez had been exiled, and only Guevara, with a new group called the *Partido Revolucionario Auténtico* (PRA), continued in the good graces of the new Bolivian government.

In the years since 1964, the MNR has continued to be nonpopular and deeply factionalized. The PRA and PRIN never rejoined the party; disputes within the MNR have usually centered on personalities, with an occasional bitter disagreement over tactics. In the late 1960s, the party included: (1) the Victor Andrade faction, a small group of older leaders which posed no serious challenge to the Barrientos government and which was permitted to use the official MNR symbols and name in the 1966 elections; (2) the *Movimiento Revolucionario Pazestenssorista* (MRP), a group of younger leaders headed by Jaime Arellano—running as, in effect, a separate party, the MRP did well in mining areas and elected a senator and a deputy in 1966; (3) the *MNR Unificado*, headed by Ronant Monje Roca, a very loose group which was numerically the largest but which was itself divided; and (4) the *MNR Alderete*, a small leftist organization led by Jorge Alderete Rosales, which had some strength among university students in La Paz. Only the *Unificado*, of these groups, had Paz Estenssoro's blessing.[21]

MNR factionalism was the form which political competition took within a party which had decided to abandon the mass involvement of populist politics. Unlike the leftist factionalism of the 1930s, it did not afford a forum in which new ideas could be developed, in preparation for later popular political mobilization. Instead, it was a sterile and hard-to-resolve conflict among politicians who were often, when all was said and done, afraid of their own constituents. If the MNR's factionalism had any function for the political system, it was to underscore the failure of multigroup populism as a formula under which mass participation and stable government could be reconciled in Bolivia.

Factionalism of the Left: The 1970s

In September 1969, General Alfredo Ovando Candia carried out a coup d'etat which triggered, among other effects, an increase in Bolivian political factionalism. Ovando announced himself as opposing many policies followed by the military (in power since 1964), including encouragement of foreign investment, opposition to labor organizations and demands, and surveillance and repression of political opponents. Though he himself had helped plan and carry out these conservative measures for five years, Ovando sought to legitimize his takeover by adopting a new ideological line. Proclaiming his regime as "revolutionary nationalist," the new president quickly repealed several repressive laws, permitted labor unions to reorganize, and nationalized the holdings of the Bolivian Gulf Oil Company, an arm of the U.S. Gulf firm. The general's tactical switch was motivated in part by a desire to broaden the military government's base of popular support. Though Bolivia's peasants, and especially Bolivia's workers, had been denied any effective power by Barrientos, their political relevance had never fallen to pre–Chaco War levels.[22]

The coming to power of Ovando intensified factionalism within Bolivia's centrist or nationalist political parties, as they debated how to handle the army's move into what had been their ideological territory. Soon after the September coup, a faction of the MNR (led by Alderete) and a dissident group within *Falange* formed *Frente Nacional de Izquierda*. The *Frente* announced that it supported Ovando and hoped to enter his government. The same day, an identically named front was created by the Christian Democratic party (PDC—a *tercerista* organization whose ideas resembled those of Frei's PDC in Chile) and a non-Trotskyite faction led by Guillermo Aponte within Lechín's PRIN. The factions making up these *frentes* represented "collaborationist" opinion within the centrist parties, but they were not able to pressure the larger segments within their parties into supporting Ovando.[23]

But it was on the left that factionalism particularly blossomed during the early 1970s. This ferment appeared in different forms: as divisions within existing parties; as multiparty competition; and as the creation of new small leftist parties. The leftist political debate, encouraged by the relaxation of police action and by the regime's doctrinal vagueness, was primarily ideological. *Socialism* became the nation's leading political catchword, and a lively, hard-fought discussion raged over what the term meant and how it should be put into practice in Bolivia.[24]

Sometimes factions within older centrist parties would rebel and move to the left. Within the Christian Democrats, a group calling itself the *PDC Revolucionario* (PDCR) appeared. Jorge Ríos Dalenz, the PDCR's leader, announced:

> There is an ideological crisis because, unlike the old guard of the PDC, the party's youth accepts all scientific contributions in its ideological conformation. This includes, of course, the great Marxist contribution which, combined with Christian humanism, we believe to be the most relevant body of thought in the world.[25]

The PDCR, which withdrew from its parent organization, called for a mass-based Socialist government. Its program urged "development by a non-capitalist route," and an initially mixed economy. The government, rather than basing itself on a revolutionary elite, should be "highly democratic . . . national and popular . . ., with the working class at its vanguard, allied with the peasants, urban petty bourgeoisie, revolutionary intellectuals and marginal people."[26]

Bolivia's established leftist parties also took part in the emerging debate. The two Communist parties, Moscow-line and Peking-line, rehearsed their familiar disagreements, which were extended to include their attitudes toward military reformism. The *Muscovitas* argued for a "popular anti-imperialist government" which would arrive, however, only at a "properly conditioned moment." Meanwhile, they announced that they would support "all conduct which attacks the interests and positions of imperialism," while retaining the right to criticize the military government fully.[27]

The *Pekineses* responded caustically that only a "people's revolutionary war" could bring about Bolivia's liberation from imperialist domination. While "only a broad front of classes and forces effectively interested in the process of liberation" could carry out a revolution, that front would have to be "under the direction and hegemony of the working class." The pro-Mao Communists also rejected the Ovando government as only superficially reformist: "We all know that Siracusa [the US ambassador] and Ovando are the same thing, since both are united to oppress this country.[28]

The *Partido Obrero Revolucionario* led by Guillermo Lora basically agreed with the Peking-line Communist party. Revolutionary leadership would have to come from the working class; "the formula of 'a popular anti-imperialist government' (which social class will dominate and direct this conglomerate of classes?) is reactionary in historical perspective. . . ." Though Lora could not foresee precisely what form of "direct action" the necessary revolution would take, he believed it "evident that there is no room for the peaceful or parliamentary transformation of the country. . . . We will expell the military government from the Palacio Quemado [Government Palace]. . . ."[29]

New parties were also formed on the left, particularly during the year-long rule of Ovando's self-proclaimed "Socialist" successor, General Juan José Torres (1970–1971). A new *Partido Socialista* (PS) was founded, led by Mario Miranda Pacheco and Marcelo Quiroga Santa Cruz. The program of the new PS was vague—demanding, in its words, a powerful movement of popular anti-imperialist unity, directed by the working class, which would end foreign power and internal reaction.

Far to the left of the *Socialistas,* the *Ejército de Liberación Nacional* (ELN) became active during 1970 and 1971. The Peredo brothers,

"Inti," "Chato," and "Coco," kept alive the guerrilla organization which Ché Guevara had led in 1966–1967. In December 1969, they carried out a daring daylight robbery in La Paz, and in July 1970, the ELN launched a new guerrilla effort near Teoponte in northeast Bolivia. With recruits drawn largely from Bolivian student leaders, the Teoponte guerrillas were easily defeated militarily. But the Teoponte fighters won major popular sympathy in the cities. Though Ovando promised amnesty, those who surrendered in the face of jungle hardships were systematically tortured and executed by the army. In part because of the fighters' social prominence, as well as their revolutionary ideals, the ELN martyrs gained a far larger popular following than Guevara's guerrilla group had. In 1971, the ELN turned to urban "armed propaganda" and terrorism in support of its thesis of immediate violent revolution; these tactics lost it a good deal of popular support.[30]

Finally, new activity was shown by a group of progressive Catholic priests, *Iglesia y Sociedad en América Latina* (ISAL)/Bolivia, led by Mauricio Lefebvre, Pedro Negre, and José Prats. ISAL advocated the "Paulo Freire method" of "conscientization": activist education in social awareness, which, they argued, would lead to revolutionary mass insurrection. An early pronouncement of ISAL gives an indication both of its doctrine and of the excessive abstraction by which the Bolivian left of the early 1970s was plagued:

> What matters in a dialectical and dynamic historical process is not that the vanguard . . . make theoretical statements, but that it *interpret* correctly the concrete historical reality of the moment and *utilize* correctly the forces which are part of it, even without knowing the theory. Or, as PAULO FREIRE would say: [one needs] critical insertion in the transformative reality-action, in contraposition to the mere *understanding* of reality (nature, society, and the men mediated by these forces).[31]

The factionalized forces of the Bolivian left under Ovando and Torres were obviously preoccupied with the question of how large groups of participants were to assert their power in Bolivian politics and provide the motor for socialism. Ideological debates centered on precisely which class or group was preeminently revolutionary, what sort of alliance should develop around that class, and how strong revolutionary party leadership should be. Generally, the *Pekineses* and the POR argued for working-class hegemony and tight party structures, while the *Socialistas,* PDCR, *Muscovitas,* and PRIN called for looser multiclass alliances against imperialism. But the leftist factions and miniparties had, as yet, very little direct support of their own. The PRIN, which gave Torres "support combined with criticism," could still count on mine worker backing, and the Communists had small networks of urban *militantes,* but the other parties had not yet mobilized an active public base. When, during Torres' tenure in office, the Popular Assembly was organized to represent union and *campesino* ("peasant") forces as well as the ideological left, the unionists resisted what they regarded as the provocative tactics and ideas of the leftist parties. The unionists feared that Torres might be replaced by a reactionary military junta before effective leftist mobilization could be started.[32]

As matters turned out, both the ideological left and the unionists were partly right. Thoroughly frightened by the rhetoric and publicity skills of the leftist factions, the most conservative forces in the Bolivian military united to defend themselves. When a right-wing coup was launched in Santa Cruz in August 1971, the lack of organized mass leftist support became tragically clear. Without a determined, armed, and disciplined popular backing, the forces of the left were crushed in three days of almost hopeless fighting.

Since 1971, the Bolivian left has been persecuted within the country, forced to operate largely from exile, and badly hurt by Chilean repression following the 1973 anti-Allende coup. In the face of these hardships, left-wing factional competition has diminished. *Frente Revolucionario Anti-imperialista,* bringing together parties which had supported the Popular Assembly, was formed in Santiago, and it cooperated with the PRIN and with the *MNR de Izquierda* of Hernán Siles Zuazo. Former President Torres, in 1973–1974, set up the similar *Alianza de la Izquierda Nacional,* and in May 1974, the leftist opposition forces were bolstered by the vigorous anti-Banzer attitude of the PRA and the *tercerista* PDC.[33] However, unable to operate and organize freely within Bolivia, the leftist groups still basically were an elite force not able to seriously threaten Banzer. In late 1973, he was able to cancel promised national elections without any important leftist challenge.

Like the leftist factionalism of thirty-five years earlier, the divisions of the 1970s served largely as a debate over political values and strategies. With centrist nationalism discredited, factionalist competition expressed the uncertainty of new and old leaders over what form of socialism should replace it. But the left-wing debate had at least two weaknesses, along with its innovative qualities. It was highly formalistic, reviewing almost for form's sake many issues which had been flayed in the debates of the 1930s. And, relatedly, the leftist forces moved too slowly from the stage of planning to actually securing a mass following. At least temporarily, the left was deprived of the chance to remedy these problems by the army's brutal preemption of political power.

Popular Participation and the Functions of Factionalism

In reviewing Bolivia's recent experiences of intense party factionalism, I have argued that this form of political division tends to coincide with periods of nonpopular politics. The movements most prone to bitter factionalism seem to be those which lack regular and at least somewhat organized and intense involvement with rank-and-file social support. Few of the leftist parties of the 1930s and 1970s had secure popular followings, and the MNR in the mid-1950s had abandoned interest group representation, a vital form of participation during the party's earlier development.

Bolivian factionalized movements appear to fight over different things, and their main motives for competition seem to be linked to their attitudes toward mass political participation. Movements which favor the expansion of political participation appear to divide internally over issues of ideology and values: what groups should be appealed to, and what policy aims the new participation should serve. The many center-left and leftist leaders of the post-Chaco period were basically rival ideologues, sometimes devoting their whole political careers to beliefs which only a few faithful followers shared. The bitter intraleft debates of the Ovando and Torres years were in part recriminations over the past, but largely the clashes of differing plans for the future.

At least one movement, on the other hand, which had come to *fear* the power of mass participation—the MNR of the 1950s—developed a factionalism which was largely grounded on personal rivalries. Behind the ideological protestations of the MNR's rival groups lay a jockeying for power among leaders and the *camarillas* ("cliques"). Leftists and rightists alike within the MNR were willing to sacrifice or postpone the achievement of the "ideals" as long as their personal positions seemed secure. When these were threatened, however, the factional leaders withdrew from the party or encouraged, directly or indirectly, its military overthrow in 1964.

This pattern of relationships is in some ways an encouraging one, to an observer concerned with the strength and justice of the Bolivian polity. Factionalism may not be, in all cases, merely a set of sterile and divisive squabbles. On the contrary, it may serve as a period of intellectual testing among the advocates of popular mobilization, a period free of mass involvement after which the surviving plans may be tried out. The views of some political scientists suggest that this sort of sequential tackling of political problems would assist political modernization —in Bolivia and elsewhere. Dankwart Rustow and Lucian Pye, for example, have argued that it is difficult (even if common) to have to undertake different aspects of political modernization simultaneously.[34] The influx of mass participation might well put especially great strain on a political system which had not benefited from factionalism and was still preoccupied with basic issues of political philosophy or organization.

But Bolivia's three cases of factionalism also suggest caution and indicate that factionalism's function is qualified and limited by at least one important factor: the *content* of the mobilizational ideology which a factional struggle produces. That ideology may or may not be able, in the long run, to reconcile mass participation with governmental strength and coherence. The MNR's formula of populistic nationalism was able to do this only up to a point, and by 1956 the party's strategy no longer stressed participation. The various Socialist doctrines of leftist factions in the 1970s rather quickly provoked massive repression, without firmly harnessing mass support. When a mobilizational movement cannot fully reconcile participation and order, that movement may well be stillborn or may decline into an unproductive factionalism based on personalities.

NOTES

1. Richard Rose, for example, analyzing British political parties, views factions as exclusively intraparty units; Joseph L. Nyomarkay, studying Nazi factions, suggests that factions must be intraparty, relatively well organized, and issue oriented. This research, along with that of other students of factionalism, is cited and discussed in Frank P. Belloni and Dennis C. Beller, "The Study of Party Factions as Competitive Political Organizations," *Western Political Quarterly* 29, no. 4 (Dec. 1976): 531–49. Andrew J. Nathan, basing his model on politics in the early Republic of China, defines a faction as "a functionally specific, self-conscious, relatively persistent non-corporate political conflict structure." (Nathan, "Factionalism in Chinese Politics: The Case of the Cultural Revolution" [Paper prepared for the Annual Meeting, American Political Science Association, Chicago, Sept. 1971], p. 3.) An interesting aspect of this definition is that it does not restrict factionalism to conflict within a party. Factionalism seems not to lend itself to useful *general* definition. Political scientists have tended to define it in terms of its particular manifestation in the country or period they were concerned with. My working definition—which makes no claims to be generalizable—follows this pattern.

2. See Herbert S. Klein, *Parties and Political Change in Bolivia 1880–1952* (Cambridge: At the Univ. Press, 1969), p. 306. For a Marxist critique of the traditional parties' programs, see José Antonio Arze, "Necesidad de un programa basada en el estudio de la realidad nacional," in Guillermo Lora, ed., *Documentos políticos de Bolivia* (La Paz and Cochabamba: Los Amigos del Libro, 1970), pp. 417–23.

3. Few important groups appeared on the right during the 1930s and early 1940s, if one excepts the short-lived pro-German tendency within the MNR. The most important anti-Communist grouping was *Falange Socialista Boliviana,* founded in 1937. For ideological statements issued by *Falange,* see the reference work edited by Mario Rolón Anaya, *Política y partidos en Bolivia* (La Paz: Juventud, 1966), pp. 241–67. A conservative and *indigenista* organization known as *Pachakutismo,* led by Fernando Diaz de Medina, appeared in the late 1940s, but was soon dissolved. Diaz de Medina later became chief political adviser and speechwriter to President René Barrientos.

4. Klein, *Parties and Political Change in Bolivia,* pp. 92–95, 209–17, 228–39. On the *Partido Nacionalista*'s founding and internal division, see also the account by one of its founders: Augusto Céspedes, *El dictador suicida (40 anos de historia de Bolivia),* 2d ed. (La Paz: Juventud, 1968), pp. 88–90.

5. See Klein, *Parties and Political Change in Bolivia,* pp. 263–64.

6. Ibid., pp. 215–16; see also pp. 233–34 for the more moderate statement of Baldivieso on taking office as foreign minister in 1936.

7. Ricardo Anaya, "Democracia y revolución," excerpted in Lora, ed., *Documentos políticos de Bolivia,* pp. 338–43, and Rolón Anaya, ed., *Política y partidos en Bolivia,* pp. 403–20.

8. "Nota explicatoria de la segunda conferencia del POR," Faction statement of Dec. 1938, reprinted in Rolón Anaya, ed., *Política y partidos en Bolivia,* pp. 369–70. Also Klein, *Parties and Political Change in Bolivia,* pp. 195, 295–98.

9. "MNR: bases y principios de acción immediata," excerpted in Rolón Anaya, ed., *Política y partidos en Bolivia,* pp. 273–75.

10. Ricardo Anaya, "Democracia y revolución," p. 426.

11. On the stabilization and the political steps which accompanied it, see George Jackson Eder, *Inflation and Development in Latin America* (Ann Arbor: Univ. of Michigan, Graduate School of Business, 1968); and James M. Malloy, *Bolivia: The Uncompleted Revolution* (Pittsburgh: Univ. of Pittsburgh Press, 1970).

12. Oscar Barbery Justiniano, "Lo que debemos hacer," pamphlet (Santa Cruz: n.p., n.d., published in January 1964 but written July 1963), pp. 22–23.

13. On the formation of the *Sector de Izquierda*, see *El Diario* (La Paz), June 23, 1958. On that of the *Socialistas*, see ibid., May 18, 1961. On the *Bloque de Defensa*, a highly biased but still useful source is Luís Antezana, "Por qué cayó el MNR?" pamphlet (Cochabamba: privately printed, 1967).

14. The founding documents and declarations of *Izquierda Nacional* were published in *El Diario*, Mar. 23, 1957. They called for the strengthening of "party government" and placing "the Single Command of the forces of the National Revolution in the MNR National Political Committee," which was controlled by Siles.

15. For a photocopy of an *MNR Auténtico* membership card, see *El Diario*, Sep. 26, 1959.

16. An election for leaders of *comandos zonales* (the smallest party unit) in La Paz in 1963 ran into this sort of problem. A full description of this case (which was by no means unique) is given in an unpublished report from the election supervisor to President Paz Estenssoro, dated Apr. 17, 1963. This report is in a private collection of MNR documents in La Paz.

17. On peasant backing for the SI, see *El Diario*, Feb. 24, 1961; on the national conference, see ibid., Oct. 27, 1962.

18. This letter, dated Jan. 14, 1966, is in a private collection in La Paz.

19. For the *Auténticos'* first declaration of principles, see Lora, ed., *Documentos políticos de Bolivia*, pp. 180–224. The new *Partido Revolucionario Auténtico* (PRA) had few followers but an active career. It supported the overthrow of Paz Estenssoro in 1964, and participated in several of the Barrientos cabinets (1966–1969). It opposed the government of President Hugo Banzer.

20. Lechín, in breaking openly with Paz Estenssoro and the MNR, charged the president with full responsibility for MNR factionalism:

He [Paz Estenssoro] was the first to argue the need for leadership groupings, which later became factions and which provoke party division. It was Dr. Paz Estenssoro, not I, not Guevara, not Siles. But, naturally, since we were all ingenuous we did not understand what political maneuvering was. . . .

El Diario, Dec. 7, 1963.

21. See the *Andradistas'* program, "Manifiesto a la nación y a la militancia del MNR," mimeographed (La Paz, 1968); the MRP's "Declaración de principios," *Presencia*, May 18, 1966; the *Unificados'* printed occasional La Paz newspaper *El Intrasigente*, various issues in 1966; and the *Alderetistas'* 1969 statement, "MNR—manifiesto a los trabajadores y pueblo de Bolivia," mimeographed pamphlet (La Paz). This factional lineup changed with Paz Estenssoro's decision to support the 1971 military coup against "Socialist" President Juan José Torres. Siles opposed this alliance with a conservative army group and with *Falange Socialista Boliviana*, and set up the *MNR de Izquierda* in Santiago, Chile. In November 1973, Paz Estenssoro announced the MNR's withdrawal from Banzer's government over the issue of canceled national elections, and the following year he was exiled to Paraguay.

22. The Ovando government's first stagements were published in a pamphlet, "Por qué? para qué—documentos del gobierno revolucionario de Bolivia" (La Paz: Ministerio de Informaciones, Sept. 1969). Excerpts from Ovando's early speeches are available in Alfredo Ovando Candia, *El pensamiento de la revolución* (La Paz: Ministerio de Informaciones, Dec. 1969).

23. The formation of the two *frentes* is reported in *Presencia*, Nov. 25, 1969. Though they never played any major political role, the centrist debate which the *frentes* symbolized did have important consequences. In an action reminiscent of the traditional parties' agglutination in the 1930s, the two major centrist parties (MNR and *Falange*) abandoned thirty years of rivalry to support the right-wing Banzar coup in August 1971.

24. See *El pensamiento político boliviano después de la nacionalización del petróleo* (Cochabamba: Federación Universitaria Local, 1970). Another useful collection of party views on the meaning of socialism appeared in *Presencia*, Aug. 6, 1971.

25. *Hoy* (La Paz), Oct. 15, 1969.

26. Jorge Ríos Dalenz, "Hacia el socialismo por una vía no capitalista," in *El pensamiento político boliviano*, pp. 182–83. Ríos Dalenz, a political refugee in Chile, was killed during the official terror there after September 11, 1973.

27. Jorge Kolle Cueto, "El reformismo no puede sustituir a la revolución," in *El pensamiento político boliviano*, pp. 154, 159–160.

28. Oscar Zamora Medinacelli, "Guerra popular: único camino para la liberación nacional," in *El pensamiento político boliviano*, pp. 110–15, 125.

29. See Lora's statement on the meaning of socialism, *Presencia*, Aug. 6, 1971.

30. On the ELN, see Carlos Maria Gutiérrez, "Informe sobre la guerrilla boliviana," originally published in *Marcha* (Montevideo) and reprinted in *Temas Sociales* (La Paz), no. 5 (Mar. 1970): 115–25. On the Teoponte guerrillas, see the collection of documents and diaries edited by Hugo Assmann, *Teoponte: una experiencia guerrillera* (Oruro: Centro "Desarrollo Integral" [CEDI], 1971). Some excerpts from the very moving Teoponte diaries are available in English in Alistair Horne, *Small Earthquake in Chile: Allende's South America* (New York: Viking, 1972), pp. 259–86.

31. Iglesia y Sociedad en América Latina (ISAL), "¿Cuáles deben ser las características de la vanguardia en América Latina?" (Aug. 1969), in *Temas Sociales*, no. 4 (Nov. 1969): 145–46 (emphases in the original). See also *Presencia*, Aug. 6, 1971. Mauricio Lefebvre was killed while trying to rescue one of the wounded during the resistance to the Banzar coup in late August 1971.

32. On political parties' lack of popular bases, see Alfonso Camacho, "La transformación política en Bolivia," in Centro "Desarrollo Integral," ed., *La Transformación actual en América Latina y en Bolivia* (Oruro: CEDI, 1971), p. 158.

33. See *Latin America* (London), Jan. 26, 1973; July 13, 1973; Jan. 11, 1974; May 31, 1974; and June 14, 1974.

34. See Dankwart A. Rustow, *A World of Nations* (Washington, D.C.: Brookings Institution, 1967), and Lucian Pye, *Aspects of Political Development* (Boston: Little, Brown, 1966). This is of course a widely held view in the literature on political modernization and development.

12

Cleavages in British Politics

ARTHUR CYR

This chapter discusses the concept of political faction in terms of British politics. In common usage, the word *faction* describes a wide range of conflicts within political parties, governments, and other organizations. It has been employed as well to characterize more general tensions within a nation or part of a nation. There is a strong pejorative connotation to the word, with the implication that those who adhere to a faction are rigid and unbending in their beliefs, willing to threaten the destruction of party or government because of a particular disagreement. Consequently, there is a tendency to use it to refer to many types of divisive and destructive political activities. In this line of thinking, parties become factions when critics regard them as promoting unhealthy trends.

In the latter part of the eighteenth century, before political parties in their modern forms existed, party was literally synonymous with faction, and statesmen—such as George Washington, in his often-cited Farewell Address—argued that the growth of parties in the republic could only serve to destroy its fragile unity. The general negative perspective on factions has persisted. In modern times there has been a tendency among students of comparative politics to regard two-party systems as more desirable than multiparty systems because they allegedly foster consensus and discourage politics from degenerating into "factional" disputes among many small, narrowly based parties.[1]

While *factionalism* occurs in many contexts, usually the term is used to describe tensions within rather than between political parties, and that is the sense in which it is employed in this chapter. The analysis which follows discusses internal conflicts of the two main British political parties, the Conservatives and Labour, in terms of Richard Rose's important analysis.

Factions and Tendencies

In one sense at least, it is particularly unusual in the British context to concentrate upon factions rather than parties as the basis for analysis. Many—though by no means all—scholars who have studied British politics have stressed the stability of the two-party system and the strength of party discipline and unity. In consequence, factionalism has not received primary attention. To some extent, this reflects the general bias among political scientists toward focus on parties rather than factions.

At the same time, this general point about factions should not be exaggerated. A number of political scientists who have studied British political parties have made informed and insightful comments on factions. The work of Samuel Beer, Leon Epstein, Robert McKenzie, and Robert Jackson may be cited along with that of a number of others. The point is not that factionalism has been ignored; rather, it has generally been examined from a focus which emphasizes political parties. One scholar, however, who has engaged in explicit analysis of factions in British political parties is Richard Rose, in an article first published in 1964, and several times reprinted.[2] Although his conclusions about the factional differences between the two major parties in many ways reflect those of other political scientists who have studied them, Rose is singled out because he has studied factions from a perspective which attempts to go beyond the customary concentration on parties.

A basic distinction in Rose's essay is between a *faction* and a *tendency* in parties. The initial conceptual division was made by Samuel Beer, but Rose deserves credit for refining and developing the two concepts in applying them to British politics. A faction is defined as an organized group within a larger political party, made up of people who are self-conscious of this role and recognized by others as comprising a separate formation. Members of a faction may or may not follow a particular leader. They are committed to an ideology, defined as a structured and codified set of beliefs about politics. In consequence, an important goal of political factions is to gain victories for the policy positions which proceed from ideology.

Because the purpose of factions is practical influence and policy success within the party and broader political systems, it is important for them to have adherents within the parliamentary party, especially since bureaucrats in the party administrative headquarters, for reasons of both professionalism and self-preservation, tend to be neutral on controversial questions. In order to maintain momentum and coordination, and give coherence to policy and strategy, factions build formal membership organizations and communications networks, and have some interest in use of technical expertise to press favored positions and arguments. These features, in turn, provide structural bases and supports for factions. The existence of a visibly organized, coherent structure, which continues over time, enables factions to socialize their members and helps to promote unity. It is much more difficult to break away from a faction than from a looser, ad hoc coalition.[3]

A tendency, on the other hand, refers to just such a loose, informal, and flexible sort of association over particular issues. Instead of a continuing group of activists committed to certain specified principles, a tendency is related to more general biases, opinions, and beliefs concerning politics and public policy. Actual divisions and cleavages among partisans shift and change with the issue at hand, as groups break apart and recombine. As Rose puts it, a tendency refers to ". . . a stable set of attitudes, rather than a stable group of politicians."[4]

Rose also identifies a third general position of party activists— *nonalignment.* This refers not to styles of political activism but to more general partisan identification. Those who are nonaligned are committed to very general sentiments in favor of one party and against the other, unrelated to positions on particular policy issues. Party members occupying this category represent potential supporters who may join and tip the balance in favor of one competing faction or tendency.

As Rose notes, these categories are more analytical than empirical. That is, in reality party life is made up of complex, shifting combinations of groups and individuals. The purpose of these categories is not to represent fully the patterns of intraparty conflict but rather to outline main sources of division in pristine form, and to penetrate the familiar approach of concentrating on parties at the expense of concentration on parties' internal cleavages.[5]

Cleavages in the Major Parties

A basic conclusion of Rose's analysis is that the Conservative party has been characterized by tendencies, and the Labour party by factions. While clearly there are tensions among the Conservatives, and sections of the party may be divided very generally and assigned to different parts of the political spectrum, such conflict has lacked the predictability, the ideological overtones, and the organizational bases which would justify concluding that those involved were divided into factions. True to the definition of tendencies, activists move and shift over time, depending upon the issue at hand. It is not possible to identify, beyond these general biases, the specific characteristics of factions. Rose describes the main tendencies within the party as "reaction, defense of the status quo, amelioration and reform." The Labour party, by contrast, has been dominated by factions rather than tendencies. Within the party, political cleavages have been much more sharply defined.

Rose's essay successfully employs the concepts of faction and tendency to make explicit and to expand upon an important difference between the two major parties. Other political scientists have made the point that Labour has been more characterized by factionalism than the Conservative party; Rose's contribution is the precision of his conceptual distinction.[6]

Tendencies in the Conservative Party

First, concerning the Tories, Rose provides a useful definition of tendencies, though with no real empirical elaboration beyond a formal listing of categories from reaction to reform. In this connection, it is useful to consider a recent review by Beer of especially serious disagreements within the Conservative parliamentary party in recent years. In the mid-1950s, the Tory government compromised plans to cut back a subsidy for the whitefish industry. This was a direct result of pressure from back-benchers representing constituencies with significant dependence on fishing. Conservative MPs not only met with the minister principally involved, they also threatened to go to the extreme length of voting against their own party. Faced with this sort of hostility, the government agreed to maintain the subsidy at higher levels than originally proposed.

In 1957, similar sorts of opposition from the Conservative back-benchers persuaded the government to abandon a plan to allow the Central Electricity Authority to make its own electrical equipment, and to ease readjustment problems of poorer tenants resulting from implementation of a significant rents decontrol bill. In the former case, resistance to official policy was centered among MPs associated with the utilities industries. Yet another example during the same period involves a government effort to have retail stores close earlier in the day. The Labour party backed the measure, along with the large national interest groups representing owners, managers, and workers in the retail sectors of the economy. Nevertheless, small shopkeepers, viewing the legislation as a threat to their livelihood, mounted a campaign against the proposal and effectively linked themselves with Conservatives on the back-benches of Parliament. The alliance proved strong and determined enough to bring an end to this governmental initiative.

The most serious such conflict in the Conservative party since World War II took place in 1964 over the Resale Price Maintenance Bill. Resale price maintenance refers to the practice in which retailers are forced by their suppliers to refrain from selling goods below a minimum price. Various commercial interest groups which are powerful within the Conservative party opposed prohibition of this practice, and successfully frustrated for over a decade any efforts to weaken or end it. While the party leadership ultimately was successful in compelling the parliamentary rank and file to accept abolition, this occurred only after a long controversy and the granting of some concessions. Moreover, it was not until Edward Heath, an especially determined individual, became head of the Board of Trade in 1964 that it proved possible to force through a bill that brought an end to this restraint on the market.[7]

Several characteristics of these conflicts are useful to a discussion of divisions within the Conservative party and of the reasons why Tory divisions are classed as tendencies and not factions. First, they consisted of ad hoc alliances of MPs gathered together on a particular issue, having at times strong ties to constituency associations and economic interest groups, without the formal organization and continuity over time characteristic of factions. The division over resale price maintenance was comparatively long term, but the opposing sides within the party did not form factions in the sense in which we have defined the term.

Second, while these conflicts obviously had doctrinal overtones and implications, they were focused upon very specific—at times quite technical—economic policy issues. They therefore are not directly congruent with the broad ideological perspectives characteristic of factions.

Finally, in part again because the issues are mainly technical, it is not easy to divide partisans along a spectrum running from reaction to reform. The end of resale price maintenance, with its indirect subsidy for large firms, or taking steps to ease the readjustment problems of poor tenants, might be termed victories for reform elements. With other issues, however, the relationship between abstract categories and actual intraparty differences is not so clear. For example, is it reform or reaction to end the whitefish subsidy? Promoting freer competition might be labeled reform, but threatening the livelihood of vulnerable fishing villages could be termed reaction.

In summary, discussion of important specific conflicts among Conservatives illustrates the limitations of describing tendencies in terms of abstract attitudinal categories without supplementing the outline through examination of specific examples of conflict.

Factions in the Labour Party

In moving to the Labour party, our attention shifts to intraparty factions. Political scientists generally agree that there has been an especially important internal cleavage between an organized left faction, with which other activists within the party have allied on particular issues, and a more general and amorphous majority of party moderates. Rose appears to accept this distinction, in such statements as:

> The Labour left as a faction shares a desire to transform Britain into a completely socialist society, and the need to act together . . . in attacking the leaders of the Labour moderates. The persistence of left factions from generation to generation shows the deep roots of the left in the Labour Party.

Nevertheless, he does not maintain a focus on this important cleavage, or develop any extensive comparison between the left and the moderates.[8]

The Labour left finds structure and coherence, properties of factions, in a number of ways. There is an ideology, in that faction members are clearly committed to achieving very thorough Socialist reforms. This is to be done through strict implementation of the comprehensive domestic program adopted by the party in 1918, *Labour and the New Social Order*. Policy goals, which have been quite consistent over time, involve substantial nationalization of the means of production, combined with very heavy taxes on the wealthy sectors of the population. In the past, the Labour left was also committed in foreign affairs to a policy of unilateral nuclear disarmament and neutrality, meaning specifically, independence from the United States and the rest of NATO.[9]

Aside from ideology, the Labour left has had a number of other sources of unity. For years after World War II, and especially from 1951, Aneurin Bevan was generally viewed as the leader of the left wing of the party. His reconciliation with moderate leaders in 1957 over the issue of nuclear disarmament was a major blow to the faction. Additionally, the left has sources of coherence in an established communications network, and the use of cadres to mobilize support. Publications such as the *New Left Review* and the *Tribune,* and the organized "Tribune group" in Parliament are prominent in filling these roles. The left's unity, however, should not be exaggerated. Rose aptly describes it as "notoriously schismatic," echoing the observations of other analysts. Nevertheless, the left has maintained overall unity, particularly on issues such as those cited above, which have pitted it directly against party moderates.[10]

The Labour party moderates, by contrast, have lacked the developed factional characteristics of the left. Party parliamentary leaders in the past have generally been identified with moderate positions, and have spent considerable time trying to mobilize coalitions at annual conferences and in Parliament to resist challenges from the left. The task has been made difficult by the fact that the moderates, though normally in the majority on most issues, have not had clear-cut ideological or inclusive organizational bases.

The trade union movement has been a very important factor in conflict between left and moderates. The unions are enormously influential within the party, providing significant financial and organizational support. They elect twelve of a total of twenty-nine members of the National Executive Committee, the party governing council, and strongly influence the selection of six others. The unions sponsor and provide financial support to a number of parliamentary candidates, most of whom contest pro-Labour seats. Also, because of the system whereby union members are counted automatically as party members, trade union leaders control "bloc votes" which amount to about 88 percent of the delegates at the annual party conference.[11]

In the past, the largest unions could usually be counted upon to support moderate party leaders and provide an important source of strength for the antileft coalition. Between 1948 and 1950, Clement Attlee's Labour government was able to implement a successful wage restraint policy primarily because support was provided by powerful and influential trade union leaders. Between 1951 and 1964, when Labour was in opposition, both the annual assembly and parliamentary party experienced severe conflict between the left and moderates. The left normally controlled about one-quarter of the parliamentary party, though this rose to about half on some issues.

The important trade union elements throughout this period were vital—directly in assembly votes, more indirectly within Parliament— in enabling the moderates to maintain control of party policy. The unions do not uniformly agree among themselves, and they lack the codified ideology of the left. At the same time, however, their structured organizations, close links to one another, communications capabilities, and human and financial resources give them at least some of the qualities of a party faction.[12]

Here again, consideration of Rose's discussion of intraparty cleavage results in a difference in emphasis rather than real disagreement. Rose properly stresses the factional character of conflict within the Labour party. At the same time, his analysis might have been expanded through greater emphasis on the basic cleavage between left and moderates in the party and the important role of the trade unions.

Cleavages in the 1960s and 1970s

Rose's basic distinction between factions and tendencies was accurate and useful at the time when he wrote, and events since then have generally confirmed his analysis of the differences between the dominant patterns of cleavage in the two major parties. The Labour party remains factional, though the issues which are emphasized and the structural components of the left have changed. As for the Conservatives, because of issues now prominent in British politics, one might have expected right-wing factionalism within the party; this, however, has not developed.

Britain has experienced a variety of very serious international and domestic problems over the last decade. It is reasonable to assume that many members of the Conservative party are especially nationalistic and strongly inclined toward authoritarian responses to developments viewed as weakening the nation. Moreover, until recently the far right viewpoint within the Conservative party had a prominent, articulate, and—according to public opinion polls—very popular spokesman in Enoch Powell. Therefore, success for a right-wing faction within the party might lead to victory for the party within the country as well.[13]

Nevertheless, the Conservative party has not developed a right-wing counterpart to the Labour left, despite some sporadic attempts. The members of the party's Monday Club have tried to do so, but have lacked the visibility and force of the Tribune group. Enoch Powell in the late 1960s became increasingly critical of the Tory party leadership, especially on the topic of nonwhite immigrants in Britain, but was unable to mobilize a faction. Rather, his increasingly direct and blunt criticism of the hierarchy rendered him more and more isolated within the party. In 1968, the party leader, Edward Heath, dismissed him as chief opposition spokesman on defense matters. In 1974, Powell refused to run as a regular Conservative in his English constituency, and instead was elected as an Ulster Unionist in Northern Ireland. He remains highly prominent, but also very peripheral within the party.

Various factors contributed to Powell's fate. Doubtless his failure in the challenge to the party leadership reflects in part tactical clumsiness in intraparty maneuver. Nevertheless, he also faced the barrier that direct, dramatic head-on confrontations with the leadership by dissident individuals and groups are not in tune with Tory style. The Powell case demonstrates that the Conservative party is hardly without internal tension and disagreements, yet the methods by which the party conflicts are expressed have not led to clear factional cleavages.

The basic factional character of Labour party cleavages also has not changed over the last decade, confirming the observations of Rose and others about the importance of the left within the party. Members of the left still consider themselves an organized faction, and are viewed as such by others. The Tribune group appears to be an even more important source of unity and cohesion. This reflects the fact that a strong leader of the stature of Bevan has still not emerged to assume personal direction of left-wing efforts. Anthony Wedgwood-Benn has obviously aspired to be Bevan's successor. However, he has not yet been able to establish the same sort of influence and prestige either among his factional colleagues or within the party as a whole. Moreover, the decisive national referendum majority in favor of remaining within the Common Market was, nevertheless, a serious personal defeat for him.[14]

At the same time, changes in the nature of political issues in Britain have had an effect on Labour's intraparty conflicts. Earlier foreign policy themes have not been stressed in recent years. The issue of Common Market membership aroused many members of the left, but it is arguable that this is as much a domestic as a foreign policy subject. The shift to focus on domestic concerns doubtless reflects Britain's decline as an international power. The earlier debates within the Labour party occurred at a time when it was easier to regard Britain as roughly on a par with the United States and the Soviet Union in international prestige, commitments, and influence, and, indeed, Britain played a major role in world politics in the period immediately after World War II. The situation is quite different today.[15]

There has also been an important structural shift in the composition of the left and moderate sections of the party, with implications for policy. Since the mid-1960s, some powerful trade unions have changed allegiance from the moderate coalition to the left faction. There was a hint of things to come in the late 1950s, when Frank Cousins, leader of the Transport and General Workers Union (TGWU), the largest union in Britain, joined with the Labour left to defeat the party leadership's nuclear weapons policy at the 1960 Labour conference. Though Gaitskell and the Labour moderates were able to reverse the defeat the following year, they did so only with very extensive effort.[16] By the late 1960s, two very powerful unions, the TGWU under Jack Jones and the Amalgamated Engineering and Foundryworkers Union (AEU) under Hugh Scanlon, plus several smaller unions, became firmly aligned with the Labour left on economic policy, especially concerning wages and industrial relations.

This development appears to reflect a very substantial change in union members' attitudes, in contrast to the earlier union movement toward the left. There is no indication that Cousins and other union leaders who adopted unilateralist positions represented rank-and-file sentiments. Rather, the circumstances of normal union selection processes simply put into power men who coincidentally happened to be sympathetic to the foreign policy of the left. On the other hand, the evidence is that the recent trade union shifts have been the result of growing militancy on wages and related industrial issues among union members. There has been a significant increase in the number of strikes at the individual plant level in Britain recently, and even militant national union leaders often appear moderate in comparison with local shop stewards.[17]

This realignment has an important, possibly decisive, bearing on the balance of political forces in the Labour party. In the past, predominately moderate party leaders could rely upon strong union support most of the time; the present situation is much more uncertain. The TGWU and AEU together control two million of the slightly over six million votes cast at annual Labour conferences. Therefore, alignment of these two unions with a few others could easily create a left-wing majority. The party's National Executive Committee has already moved noticeably further to the left. Trade unions are also becoming more powerful within the party as a whole, thanks to the falloff in individual party memberships in recent years, and to the current serious financial crisis. Consequently, it is quite possible that there may eventually develop a dominance of the Labour party by the new alliance between the unions and the left faction. So far, however, this has not happened; rather, there is a much closer and more equal division of forces than before between the left and moderates.[18]

Nevertheless, the power of this new alliance to frustrate policy initiatives has already been demonstrated to an impressive degree. In order to try to cope with a worsening inflation, Prime Minister Wilson in 1969 put forward a proposal for labor reforms, including a twenty-eight-day cooling-off period for unofficial strikes, to be enforced with financial sanctions for noncompliance. The Trades Union Congress immediately demanded that the proposed legislation be dropped. It proved impossible in Parliament to keep the party together in favor of the proposed reforms; indeed, the majority of Labour MPs moved to oppose them. This in turn led to major defections within the cabinet, virtually isolating Mr. Wilson. In the face of this resistance, he relented.[19]

The new intraparty balance of forces puts a significant strain on leaders. Qualities of conciliation and compromise, an ability to patch up differences and opposing points of view, have always been required in the party, but the roughly even balance between the left faction and the moderates makes them especially important now to the maintenance of unity. Harold Wilson seems to have been well suited for such a role. Initially on the left of the party, he later moved easily to the center. Changing positions on the Common Market and income policy questions has been symptomatic of his general approach to controversial issues. Wilson's readiness to accommodate various groups within the party worked to blur the basic division between the left factions and the moderates, as well as other lesser divisions which occasionally arise. It is likely that precisely this sort of highly flexible political leadership is necessary in the present period of fairly even divisions within the Labour party.[20]

One more point should be made concerning the organizational implications of the recent changes in power balances within the Labour party. Earlier, it was noted that nonaligned partisans may play a significant role in deciding intraparty disputes. However, the extremely significant shift in the relationship of forces which has occurred in the Labour party in recent years has not primarily involved nonaligned partisans, but rather the realignment of significant memberships of trade unions from moderate to left. In effect, on important economic and other policy issues, two of the most highly organized sections of the party—the left faction and the unions—have partially overlapped. The fact that unions are represented within the party as large blocs of conference votes has made the transition both easy to carry out and immediately effective in terms of impact.

Bases of Factions and Tendencies

It is possible to make another general observation concerning Rose's essay, beyond the specific points already raised. While the definition of tendencies and factions is handled with precision, the discussion never addresses the question of why the dominant internal cleavages of the two parties have been so different in character, or the question of why they have not destroyed party unity, especially in the case of Labour. An effort to address these points requires putting cleavages and tendencies into the more general contexts of party philosophies and styles of operation.

The Conservative party is often described with justification as the oldest political party in the world. Its roots may be traced back through three centuries of political development in Britain. During this period, the nature of political competition has changed, parties have become much more formally organized and central to political processes, and various groups and parties in opposition to the Conservatives have come and gone. The Tories have moved and changed with the times in such a way that it has been possible to avoid the defeats and decay which have undermined and destroyed other parties. By contrast, the old Whigs evolved into a very new formation, the Liberal party, and the Liberals were in turn replaced by the Labour party in the first part of this century.

A central feature of Toryism therefore is adaptability. The party's doctrinal base, reflecting this point, consists of general beliefs and attitudes rather than an elaborate ideology. Toryism is usually understood to include nationalism and the more specific firm respect for the institution of the monarchy, belief in hierarchy rather than equality

and in the greater fitness of certain sectors of the social order to
undertake governmental responsibilities. Beyond these general attitudes, there is a flexibility to the party's approach to politics which has
enabled it to survive various transformations in the size and composition of the electorate, the structure of government, and the scope of
public policy. To quote Samuel Beer:

> ... the term ideological can be applied to the Conservatives in only the most
> tenuous sense. An array of diverse and contradictory perspectives inhibits simple
> theoretical formulations and purposes. ... In any case it is not accurate to think
> of the Conservatives as nothing more than the party of the status quo. On the
> contrary, they have often been the agents of modernization.

It was a Conservative leader, Peel, who brought the Corn Laws to an
end in 1846. Under Disraeli, the party implemented a range of significant social reforms. More recently, the Tories have both enlarged the
welfare state and strengthened the role of government in planning and
managing the economy.[21]

Belief in hierarchy is reflected not only in association of the party
with the monarchy and the notion of a governing class, but very explicitly in the power and importance given the party leader. Thanks to
Tory theory, the leader is automatically in a position of great influence
and leverage. While consultation takes place within the party, particularly among the other powerful figures in the actual or shadow cabinet,
in a basic sense he (or, now, she) is the dominant figure. In recent
years, the process of leadership selection in the party has become more
open, formal, and democratic. Previously, it involved at most close
discussions among the monarch, the retiring leader, and a few very
senior members of the party. Now, however, the leader is elected by
the parliamentary party. Nevertheless, while this reform signals a
somewhat more open and egalitarian spirit in the party, it hardly spells
the end of very old, powerfully rooted Tory notions of hierarchy and
inequality.[22]

In contrast to the Conservatives, the Labour party is much more
formally and explicitly committed to solidarity and a type of internal
party democracy. Traditions and history help to maintain the cohesion
of the Conservative party; Socialist doctrine does the same for Labour.
Labour's constitution commits the party to a specific program of reform, and defines party conflict in class terms. Following from this,
there is a strong commitment to establishing the working class in
power. Socialist theory, as it has developed within and influenced
Labour circles, explicitly recognizes two main classes and holds that
the interests of the working class are directly represented in the party
program. The program, in turn, is further refined and made operational through resolutions of the annual party conference. As this

implies, the leader is considerably more restricted than in the Conservative party. He does not stand alone, symbolically or actually, but rather is a member of, and works generally within, the National Executive Committee.[23]

These differences in philosophy and approach to party governance influence internal conflicts. In both parties, there are broadly accepted ideas about the nature of partisanship which promote cohesion, restraining particular groups from breaking away. Tory notions, while not formally elaborated in a written constitution, have an impact in forming the tone and style of party activity. Internal disagreements are not eliminated, but they are muted by Tory beliefs in hierarchy and deference toward authority.

Labour, on the other hand, has a much more clear-cut conception of the opposition party as being composed of class enemies. It is not surprising that Labour's internal splits have been very sharp, given the party's more democratic ethos. In this connection, the party commitment to an explicit, structured ideology provides two important influences on internal cleavages. First, it encourages a separation between those who are primarily concerned with doctrinal purity (the left), and others who are interested in compromising doctrine in order to gain electoral victories.

Second, however, party ideology, especially one so strongly committed to class conflict, encourages overall unity in the face of the enemy, even when internal divisions are severe. In conclusion, the Conservative party has had less structured and sharply defined guiding ideas and internal cleavages; the Labour party has experienced more serious, continuing internal division, but has a firm inclusive ideological shell. Ideological solidarity helps Labour resist pressures from within; strains inside Tory ranks have generally been weaker, reflecting a different party ethos.

Cleavages and Parties in Britain

It is especially instructive to consider British politics from the viewpoint of cleavages within the two major parties, given the natural inclination to emphasize other characteristics—the division between the parties, and the apparent strength of formal party discipline in Parliament. Focusing on intraparty cleavages provides a balancing perspective, directing attention to the complexity of internal conflict and the differences between the parties in ethos and structure.

Intraparty cleavages, whether factions or tendencies, perform a variety of important functions. They represent different constituencies within a single party, providing influence on leaders during periods between elections. While party leaders technically have considerable authority to enforce discipline, the situation in reality within each party is not a simple one of direct control from the top, but rather involves a constant process of give and take, mutual interaction and influence between members and leaders. As Beer observes concerning the parliamentary parties: "On few generalizations do former Ministers agree more than on their report of the constant, anxious and even deferential attention Cabinets give to the opinions of their back-benchers."[24]

As noted earlier, internal divisions in both parties have had important impacts on policy outcomes. On this theme, they can have influence not only through controversies which actually occur but also through party leaders' anticipation of potential intraparty opposition to policy proposals. Additionally, intraparty cleavages may undercut very directly the main division between Conservatives and Labour by joining partisans of both parties on specific issues. For example, the issue of continued membership in the Common Market created an important national cleavage which cut across party lines.

A final source of cleavage in British politics which should be mentioned results from the recent growth in support for third parties—the Scottish and Welsh nationalists and the Liberals. Not only does this development complicate cleavage patterns between British parties, it carries implications for intraparty divisions as well. Internal cleavages of the Conservative and Labour parties in the past have been restrained not only by doctrinal influence but also by structural considerations. The comparatively even balance between the two parties in popular support has meant that an open break from one of them by a dissident group could easily lead to victory for the other side. These assumptions are now open to question. Increasing numbers of activists, and voters, are indicating that neither of the major parties provides the most attractive choice for them. If present tendencies toward greater strength of third parties and general political independence continue, this could result in significant alterations within the two major parties.[25]

With the weakening of the basic cleavage between Tories and Labour, maintenance of party unity will probably become much more difficult. In a situation resembling a flexible multiparty system, breaking away from one would have less impact than in a rigid competition between two parties roughly equal in size. There would be less direct trade-off between the fortunes of Tory and Labour. Internal divisions may therefore become markedly more significant and provide a greater challenge to the maintenance of unity within the two main parties. Our analysis of factions and tendencies encourages the conclusion that this would probably be more significant for the Labour party than for the Conservatives.

Intraparty cleavages are therefore unlikely to decline in importance in the future. As we have seen, focused examination within the

Conservative and Labour parties highlights differences between them, but also makes clear that both are characterized by significant internal divisions. While the degree to which unfolding changes will alter the British party system is not yet clear, it is obvious that the rigid party bipolarity of the postwar period is breaking down. As a result, intra-party divisions, whether tendencies or factions, may become stronger and more significant to British politics, and hence to the analysis of varied forms of cleavage and political competition.

NOTES

1. For a useful general discussion on party and faction, see Carl J. Friedrich, *Constitutional Government and Democracy* (Waltham, Mass.: Blaisdell Publishing, 1950), pp. 410, 420.

2. Richard Rose, "Parties, Factions, and Tendencies in Britain," *Political Studies* 12, no. 1 (Feb. 1964), reprinted in Rose, ed., *Studies in British Politics* (London: Macmillan, 1966), pp. 314–29. See also Samuel H. Beer, *The British Political System* (New York: Random House, 1974); Beer, *British Politics in the Collectivist Age* (New York: Alfred A. Knopf, 1967); Leon D. Epstein, *British Politics in the Suez Crisis* (Urbana: Univ. of Illinois Press, 1964); Epstein, *Political Parties in Western Democracies* (New York: Praeger, 1967); Robert Jackson, *Rebels and Whips* (London: Macmillan, 1968); and Robert T. McKenzie, *British Political Parties*, 2d ed. (New York: Praeger, 1964).

3. Rose, "Parties, Factions, and Tendencies in Britain," pp. 318–19.

4. Ibid., p. 319–20.

5. Ibid., p. 320.

6. See, for example, the discussion by Beer, *British Politics in the Collectivist Age*, p. 220, on Labour factionalism in the early 1950s, and on Tory policy development during the same period. Ibid., p. 308.

7. Beer, *The British Political System*, pp. 122–24.

8. Rose, "Parties, Factions, and Tendencies in Britain," p. 323. It should be stressed that no normative implication is intended by use of the word *moderates*. Leon Epstein discusses this point in "Organizational Policy Making: British Labour Revisited," unpublished paper, 1974, pp. 1–2.

9. Beer, *British Politics in the Collectivist Age* p. 138; Jackson, *Rebels and Whips*, p. 47.

10. Rose, "Parties, Factions, and Tendencies in Britain," pp. 321–24.

11. Epstein, "Organizational Policy Making," pp. 8, 11.

12. Beer, *British Politics in the Collectivist Age*, p. 223.

13. Anthony King, "The Election That Everyone Lost," in Howard Penniman, ed., *Britain at the Polls: The Parliamentary Elections of 1974* (Washington, D.C.: American Enterprise Institute, 1975), p. 19.

14. *Economist* (London), June 14, 1975.

15. Among various studies of British foreign policy since World War II, one of the most significant is Kenneth Waltz, *Foreign Policy and Democratic Politics* (Boston: Little, Brown, 1967).

16. Beer, *British Politics in the Collectivist Age*, p. 226.

17. The role of shop stewards is discussed at length in the Donovan Report, *Royal Commission on Trade Unions and Employers' Associations, 1965–1968*, Cmnd. *3623, (London: HMSO, 1968),* esp. ch. 3.

18. Epstein, "Organizational Policy Making," pp. 7–9, 11. In 1973, the National Executive Committee developed a party program which involved very substantial nationalization. The program was partially adopted at the party conference soon after.

19. Beer, *The British Political System*, pp. 125–27.

20. See the comments of Anthony King, "The Election that Someone Won—More or Less," in Penniman, ed., *Britain at the Polls*, p. 179.

302

21. Beer, *The British Political System*, p. 179.

22. Concerning recent leadership selection in the Conservative party, see *Economist*, Feb. 1, 1975, pp. 11, 19–21.

23. Beer, *British Politics in the Collectivist Age*, ch. 5, concerning the development of Socialist theory within the Labour party.

24. Beer, *The British Political System*, p. 121.

25. See ibid., ch. 11, on the growth in strength of third parties, and the related development of increasing volatility generally within the electorate. The combined Conservative/Labour vote in general elections has declined from a peak of 96.6 percent in 1951, to 75.4 percent in October 1974.

13

Factionalism and Political Stalemate: Chilean Politics, 1920–1970

Jorge Nef

Studies of Chilean party and group politics are not scarce; nevertheless, despite wide acknowledgment by analysts that groups, cliques, and factions have played a significant role in the country's political life, specific studies of factionalism in Chile are rare.[1]

The term *facción* is rarely used in Chile's political language. Expressions such as *línea* ("line"), *corriente* ("current"), *ala* ("wing"), *tendencia* ("tendency"), *sector* ("sector"), or even *matiz* ("shade") are more commonly used when factional groups in the country's political brokerage structure are described. Unlike Uruguay, where the *lemas* and *sub-lemas* have been the institutional expression of party factions, Chile exhibited relatively little stability and formalization of factionalism. Factionalism in the Chilean context has meant lines, currents, wings, tendencies, sectors, or shades within the structures of relatively institutionalized political brokers, including political parties, interest groups, elites, officialdoms, and the like. However, while their presence is by no means limited to political parties, most often factions have been associated with parties and intraparty aligments.

Factionalism has existed in Chile since the 1920s. It has contributed to the maintenance of political stalemate; at the same time, it helped unleash forces which in the long run were highly dysfunctional for the maintenance of a pluralistic political system. The forms of extreme authoritarianism and incipient fascism in today's Chile are partially rooted in the way in which factional brokerage was structured and operated in earlier times. Not that Chilean fascism can be exclusively explained as a result of the country's internal developments: external factors, too, played a decisive role in bringing down the Chilean democratic system.[2] However, this chapter concentrates on internal conditions—conditions which facilitated both intervention and the military coup.

Traditional Chilean Politics: Stalemated Class Brokerage

The interplay of social, political, and economic forces in Chile's development has resulted in three mutually reinforcing contradictions. First is that of stagnant and unevenly developed economic capabilities, unable to keep pace with an increasingly socially mobile population with growing aspirations. The result has been what some have called a "revolution of rising frustrations."[3] The second contradiction is that between an increasingly parasitic and internationally dependent elite and a large and increasingly mobilized mass.[4] Under conditions of economic stagnation, social conflict has become highly polarized— Chile came to be a form of "polarized pluralism"[5]—resulting in an erosion of elite legitimacy. The third contradiction is that between the formality of sovereignty and the reality of dependence. Chile, like most of Latin America, has experienced a form of satellite development, reflecting a semicolonial status.[6]

In the context of these contradictions, Chile's options for processing conflict through the polity have been limited. There has been diminished possibility of a consensual-incremental mode of conflict resolution—i.e., a social "truce" based on compromise—and a revolutionary breakthrough has remained objectively unlikely. Consequently, Chile's political alternatives tended toward either stalemate or repression. So long as social mobilization and mass political participation were kept at what the elites considered a tolerable level, class conflict could be institutionalized in the political order through mechanisms of parliamentary democracy.[7] The result was a kind of perpetual political draw, or stalemate, at the price of a persistent inflationary spiral. Ultimately, when mass mobilization—traditionally one of the safety valves of inflationary politics—generated its own contradictions, by making it possible for nonelites to gain political control through "respectable" mechanisms such as the ballot box, repression became the new political arrangement for perpetuating the existing socioeconomic order. Thus in general terms the Chilean political system between the 1920s and the 1970s was one in which non-decision and continuous political deadlock contributed to only minor substantive rearrangements of the social forces competing for their share of society's values, as most of the political struggle was diluted in bureaucratic procedures. Once the legal stalemate was exhausted as a device to keep intact the socioeconomic status quo, the military stepped in, and stalemate was replaced by repression in the coup of 1973.

Political party forces in Chile have long been distinctly aligned into three conventional blocs: the right, the left, and center. For Chile's political party system, the pattern of traditional politics resulted in a situation in which a centrist party or group of centrist parties dominated the political scene. In the culturally and structurally fragmented Chilean political system, polarization had contributed to the preeminence of the center as the primary locus of the political struggle. Although the center did have control of the bureaucratic apparatus, the strength of the center was not so much a function of its possession of independent bases of power in wealth, numbers, militancy, organization, etc., as it was its unique position in a polarized society and its functional relationship with the traditional elites. Lacking a major power base of its own, the center generally played broker between the right and working-class organizations. It was thus the favorable position of the center that made it decisive both as a component of any political alliance, either rightist or leftist, and as a necessary intermediary between the upper strata and the populous working classes. Since 1938, the middle sectors have been the principal rulers of the political arena. In practically all governmental coalitions in one way or another the center was the main force; middle-class forces became the "center of gravity" in Chilean politics, and for a number of years molded the rules of the political game to fit their own interests.

However, the existence of such a center did not favor a centripetal leadership in the political process. The center became not only the reflection of a polarized society but a "feedback" of the centrifugal tendencies which prevail in the system: hence the center was both consequence and cause of polarity.[8] The limited possibility of the right and the left for governing explains the prevailing irresponsible opposition and overall ideological, nonpragmatic pattern in Chile's political competition. The decline in the number of small parties, in favor of fewer, larger ones, contributed to an increase in the ideological distance between the principal axes of the system. The exaggerated promise was instituted as a rule of the game: those who did not have to deliver on their promises were in good positions to make inflated promises. The notorious growth of the center since the 1940s was largely a reflection of the stronger polarity of the party system.

The prime trait of this centrist dominance was immobilism. Under conditions of policy deadlock, a great gap developed between the real capacity of the polity to satisfy demands and symbolic satisfaction of these demands. Inflation of values thus became endemic in the political process. It constituted a sort of accommodation to conflicting demands and resulted in the draw which in the short run gave the illusion of some kind of gain. In this situation, real change could occur only as a response to changes in the system of capabilities of the society that did not alter the status quo regarding the distribution of output—such as in periods of "bonanza" in copper production, foreign exchange, or even loans. As a result, in a pattern of circular causation, demands were presented in an apocalyptic way and in terms of absolute-value orietation.

In one expert's analysis, in Chile's spiraling inflation, the behavior of the various political groups was a sort of latent violence which materialized when demands for additional money income were not resisted immediately and in an open and violent way, but instead were indirectly opposed after a time by similar demands on the part of other groups.[9] Inflation thus became a means for the coexistence of various actors whose feelings were not conflictive enough to fight a civil war over the distribution of the social product, yet who were not sufficiently cooperative to agree to divide this product among all of them. These mechanisms of conflict resolution resulted in a situation in which the most common outcome of the sociopolitical process was continuous stalemate. Straightforward dissent, face-to-face relations, overt agreement, and compromise were strenuously avoided, and indirectness prevailed. In this view, inflation is a social substitute for civil war, which makes the players

> maintain a militant and hostile stance while playing an elaborate, largely non-violent game in which everybody wins sham victories. The result is, of course, that nothing is resolved—no one has attained his objectives except the perhaps not important one of gratifying his hostility. The realization of having been cheated by inflation may then heighten bitterness and hostility.[10]

In general, the structure of political agents in Chile tends to reflect the class structure of society. Because of this, and because Chilean political brokers are mutually entangled, it is more meaningful to focus on the structures of mediation as a set of factional clusters normally representing class aspirations than to focus on each agent to be studied as a separate entity. Thus we shall examine Chilean politics and factionalism with reference to the major sociopolitical sectors: the right, the left, and the center.

The Right

POLITICS OF THE RIGHT IN CHILE

The major parties of the right in Chile have been, since the nineteenth century, the Conservative party and the Liberal party, or, since the two merged in 1965, the National party. These parties represented the interests of the old families of the landowning aristocracy, and the

owners of commerce, industry, and banking: the undisputed "aristocratic" elite. What the aristocratic class lacked in numbers, it more
than made up for in wealth and skills of political organization. The
business elements are organized into a number of associations, the five
most important of which are united in a national umbrella organization, the National Confederation of Production and Commerce. The
real locus of power of the Chilean right has been not so much in the
National party as in the confederation. Its members' networks of financial, technical, social, and personal interrelations provided the basis of
a powerful political force, enhanced by its members' traditional access
to all levels of government and by its control of mass media.[11]

No formal relation has existed between the confederation and the
National party, or other parties. Individual member organizations of
the confederation have had links with parties—not only with those of
the right but also with center parties—but formal party ties have been
avoided by the confederation itself. Nevertheless, informal links between the confederation and the National party have been strong and
lasting. Such links include both ideological ties and ties of overlapping
memberships. One observer has concluded that the confederation has
been such a highly political organization that it questioned "the validity of the political parties as the only organizations" for representing
the electorate.[12] Thus politics in Chile must be viewed in the context
of a highly articulate and very powerful conservative sector, whose
stakes in national commercial and political issues are extremely high,
and whose domination of the political right and of much of the nation's
political resources (and whose strong ties to foreign financial and
political interests) make it a most formidable force.

The right experienced a serious decline in voter support after the
1950s and became reactionary. The decline progressed rapidly during
the presidency of Jorge Alessandri and culminated in the 1964 collapse
of the Democratic Front—an uneven coalition of the Conservative and
Liberal parties with the Radical party of the Chilean center.[13] These
uneasy allies suffered electoral defeat in 1965, when Eduardo Frei of
the centrist Christian Democratic party (PDC) won the presidency with
the help of the left. As agrarian reform, tax reform, and other social
reforms were implemented by the Frei government, the Nationals
grew increasingly bitter, reacting to what they called an attack on
Chile's basic institutions. In part, the militancy of the right in the late
1960s was the result of more aggressive leadership, less inclined to
accept the rules of the parliamentary game; and in part, rightist impa-
tience was caused by the realization that with broadened political participation resulting from reforms, the chances of a victory by the left
were inevitably growing. Eventually the fear—and ultimately the fact
—of a leftist electoral victory in the 1970 presidential election forced
the right not only to close ranks but also to look desperately for

solutions outside party politics. Thus the party system ceased to function, and the military took over. After the coup, and with the subsequent suppression of political parties, the confederation has been in full operation under the junta and has become the nucleus of Chile's new "corporatist" structure.

FACTIONALISM ON THE CHILEAN RIGHT

To a great extent the origins of the entirety of Chile's multiparty system can be traced to the country's historic Conservative and Liberal parties. Intraelite factionalism manifested in successive splits from these old parties created the "rainbow" configuration which characterized Chile's party politics after the 1860s. In the nineteenth century, the Liberal party (and an early National party) separated from the Conservatives; the Radical party (later a major party of the center) emerged as a splinter group from the Liberals. The entire first half of the twentieth century was characterized by intraelite struggles as the parties divided and subdivided, resulting in the myriad of mostly small conservative and liberal parties which existed by the middle of the twentieth century.

In the 1950s, this trend of the right toward fission diminished and reversed itself. This began with the consolidation of several conservative groups into a single party—the third United Conservative party—in the 1957 parliamentary election; and culminated when the Conservatives and Liberals came together to form the National party, in 1965. The trend toward fusion, characteristic of much of Chilean politics since mid-century, seems to have been forced upon the right by its sheer need for survival.

Simultaneous with its decline in voter support since the 1950s, the right has been experiencing an increase in internal solidarity and apparent absence of internal factionalism. A shrinking electoral base, both in relative and absolute numbers, has increased party unity and has contributed to the apparent elimination of internal factionalism. At the same time, the National party since the late 1960s began moving away from exclusive concentration on elections and toward consolidation of its informal bonds with the business sector—and in particular with the National Confederation of Production and Commerce.

The consolidation of the right was given impetus not only by its own decline but by the growing militance and the growing popular support for the left and the center-left. The consolidation of the right was also encouraged by the emergence of highly militant groups outside the confines of the National party, such as the archconservative *Fiducia* group (named for the Society for the Defense of Property, Family, and Tradition—similar to groups that had been organized in Brazil during the Goulart government and that played a significant role in its overthrow). Another such extremist organization, after 1970, was the neo-Nazi Fatherland and Freedom Nationalist Front (FNPL, better known as *Patria y Libertad*.[14] Double memberships between the Nationals and the FNPL, and between the latter and the confederation, facilitated both vertical and horizontal communications within the increasingly integrated, and increasingly reactionary, Chilean right.

Consolidation on the right had even extended beyond the right proper, and into the center. With the growing polarization between the leftist government of Allende and the opposition parties, all anti-Allende parties moved toward a system of defensive alliances: from short-lived and sporadic congressional actions to the formal structure of the *Confederación de la Democracia* ("Confederation of Democracy"—CODE), created in 1972. CODE was essentially an alliance between aristocratic and business-oriented rightists represented by the National party, and petty-bourgeois elements clustered around the centrist parties like the Christian Democrats and splinter groups from the Radical party. Despite its limited original intent to provide an oppositionist electoral basis for the 1973 elections, CODE went far beyond mere electoral politics. Late in 1972 it threw its support to a business- and professional-inspired "middle class strike" that brought the country to a virtual standstill, in protest of the socialization policies of the Allende government. Although CODE fell short of the electoral goal advocated by its extreme elements—to obtain over 66 percent of the seats in Congress and thus to have the capability of impeaching Allende—it polled more than half of the popular vote. It also was instrumental in articulating the "legitimate" political arena in a rigid anti-Allende stand which facilitated the military coup in 1973.

In sum, in the Chilean right, internal fractures were hardly visible at the time of the coup and the setting aside of party politics. Today the organized forces of the right are the only ones tolerated by the regime and allowed to operate, largely because of the right's functioning through an organization claiming not to be a political entity—something the officers of the army relate to, as they also think of themselves as having no political aims. Consequently, the right today remains the most priviledged sector of Chilean society, and stands second only to the military among those who have the most to lose, should the order of things be rearranged. And thus far, at least, the right appears to be a highly integrated, united, and unfactionalized political force.

The Left

POLITICS OF THE CHILEAN LEFT

The left parties are principally the Socialist party and the Communist party, though there are some minor parties, particularly splinter groups of the Socialists. Left parties in Chile are associated with the bulk of the labor movement; here again, a substantial correspondence exists between class and party. The greatest strength of both the Communist and Socialist parties, in terms of party memberships and electoral support, has always been from the labor unions, and particularly from the national Workers' Central Union (CUT).[15] Historically it is difficult to separate early Chilean leftism from Chile's early labor movement. During the initial stages of the labor struggle, the traditional parties—Conservative, Liberal, and Radical—remained almost completely indifferent to the working class, and the labor movement turned to revolutionary militancy. In the 1910s the young Labor Federation of Chile formed the Socialist Workers party, which adopted Marxist ideology; in the 1920s this organization became the Communist party of Chile, joining the Third International. In the 1930s the Communist party divided into Stalinists and Trotskyites, the latter leaving the party and joining with other radical groups to form the Socialist party; in recent decades, splits from the Socialists have formed a Popular Socialist Union (USP) and the left Revolutionary Movement (MIR).

The Communist party of Chile (PCCH) has been the most cohesive and articulate of the parties of Chile's Left; it is one of the best organized Communist parties in Latin America, with the strongest ties with the working class. At the same time, the PCCH has been quite unrevolutionary and, although totalitarian in internal organization, has been highly flexible and accomodating with non-Marxists. The PCCH has followed the Moscow line of peaceful coexistence—that is, struggle within legality. It has demonstrated considerable ability to compromise and has been very effective in relating to its grass roots in the unions and in urban neighborhoods and the universities. Internally, recruitment and promotion have been bureaucratic and slow, with requirements of at least ten years' service to the party before anyone may be considered for a position of prominence and responsibility.[16]

Chilean Socialists have been the most radical and revolutionist partly because the original influence of the Trotskyites was predominant. The ideology of Chilean socialism has been less articulate and less stable than that of the Communists: Socialists have variously been militant anti-Communists, Titoists, and Castroites, and the only constant element has been their fervent, highly anti-American, Latin American nationalism. At the same time, they have been pragmatic and have exhibited a capacity to adhere to the rules of the traditional political game and to moderate to a great degree some of their radical postures.

There have been two Socialist parties since the 1970s. Allende's Socialist party (PS) was the larger and more moderate of the two. The PS espoused alliance with other popular forces, especially the Communists, and toleration of "bourgeois-democratic" parliamentary government. The other group, Raúl Ampuero's small but important Popular Socialist Union took a more radical stand, opposing a "front" of leftist parties. Also, in the 1960s a group of militants in Concepción Province abandoned the PS and founded the Left Revolutionary Movement. The MIR grew by adding disenchanted splinter groups of the Socialists, and by 1966 was quite institutionalized, as the first "significant violent anti-parliamentary leftist movement since the early 1930s."[17] Finally, also, the left in Chile has periodically been shaped by major alliances and coalitions. Socialists created a popular front with the Communists in 1952; and in 1957 the Socialists of both Allende's and Ampuero's factions joined with the Communists in the Popular Action Front (FRAP), which lasted throughout the 1960s. In 1969 the broad Popular Unity (UP) front was formed, including the Allende Socialists, the Communists, most of the former centrist Radical party, and the new Unitary Popular Action Movement (MAPU), a highly dynamic splinter group from the centrist Christian Democrats. The UP was the movement backing Allende's presidency, from his electoral victory in 1970 until the coup in 1973.

FACTIONALISM ON THE LEFT

The labor movement itself has had a serious problem of internal fragmentation and infighting. Early unionism saw confrontations among Communists, anarchists, and *mutualistas* (a type of "co-op" or mutual-benefit guild movement) in which the first eventually got the upper hand. In the 1930s, the vicious fight between Trotskyite and Stalinist Communists split and weakened labor organizational strength, and throughout the 1940s the labor movement was split into many antagonistic factions. Often violent confrontations between Socialist and Communist labor organizations further sharpened the divisions in the labor movement. Only when the CUT was created in the 1950s was there a beginning of real labor unity.

There were other aspects of the fragmented state of organized labor. One was that despite the CUT's overwhelming Marxist-Leninist orientation, non-Marxist groups were also represented in it.[18] Another element of labor disunity was that in organizational terms the CUT, unlike the right's National Confederation of Production and Commerce, was poorly integrated, due in no small part to labor legislation designed to fragment union strength. The CUT was not a uniting of "peak" labor organizations, but rather in some cases controlled, and in some cases was controlled by, individual unions of the highly fragmented universe of *sindicators*—one per firm, as required by law.[19]

Despite its strongly authoritarian pyramidal structure and democratic centralism, even the Chilean Communist party has had divisiveness and factionalism. The sources of conflict in the PCCH are mainly the ideological rifts in the global Communist movement, and not political conditions specifically Chilean. With the violent struggle between Stalinists and Trotskyites in the 1930s two Communist parties—or factions—existed for a time, until the Trotskyites merged with the Socialists. During the Communists' period of clandestine activity (especially under the harsh repression between 1947 and 1949, when scores of party members were sent to detainment centers), new splits emerged. The most serious was between those who advocated armed resistance and terrorism, and those who sought to influence other, non-Communist, legal parties. Eventually party unity was maintained, and the action-oriented dissidents were purged.

The repression of the 1940s gave the Communists a great organizational and ideological strength which allowed them to survive subsequent internal rebellions. In the 1960s, with the Sino-Soviet split, a pro-China faction emerged, known as the *Espartaco* ("Spartacan") group, and was expelled from the party. In defiance of the PCCH Central Committee's line of "struggle within legality," dissident factions of the party's youth formed microparties, like the Revolutionary Communist party (PCR) and the Marxist Revolutionary Vanguard (VRM). Parts of the PCR and VRM ultimately fused, along with the *Espartaco* group, in the MIR, which then had become the rallying point for most noncomformist Marxist revolutionaries, leaving the PCCH a relatively more unified party. By the time of the UP coalition, the Communists undoubtedly were the best organized and most coherent force backing the Allende administration. Despite the continuing existence within the party of *obrerista* ("workers") and intellectuals sectors, these groups did not materialize into significant political factions, and the PCCH remained a relatively unfactionalized party—due in considerable measure to purges and the discipline of democratic centralism.

Historically, Socialists have been plagued by internal conflicts and quarreling factions. In its very origins the party was a fusion of many dissimilar groups, its history forever affected by its acceptance of the Trotskyites after their purging from the Communists.[20] As tensions in Socialists' relations with Communists mounted, intra-Socialist fragmentation grew. With the outlawing of the Communist party in 1947, one segment of the Socialist party thought it opportune to take revenge and collaborate with the anti-Communist government. This dominant faction became the Socialist party of Chile (PSCH). The other—rebel—faction, led by Ampuero and Allende, opposed collaboration and generated their own organization, the Popular Socialist party (PSP).

Cooperation between the two rebel Socialist leaders, however, did not last; Allende quit the Popular Socialists and returned to the Socialist party of Chile; he then managed to create the People's Front with support from the outlawed Communists, and ran as a candidate of the People's Front in the 1952 presidential election. Later, with the creation of the broader Popular Action Front in 1957, the two Socialist parties merged again in the Socialist party. FRAP provided a framework for electoral coordination, but old rivalries and factions remained. Although FRAP increased its strength in the elections of 1958 and 1964, it did so at the cost of further compromising the Socialists' autonomous revolutionism and alienating the Ampuero segment of the party, which came to oppose electoral alliances. When the strategy of expanding the FRAP into a broader coalition of Popular Unity was undertaken, the Ampuero segment again abandoned the PS, forming the Popular Socialist Union. Even after Allende's and the UP's victory in 1970, the USP remained aloof from the coalition and from Allende's government.

The most important split in the ranks of the Socialists was that of the radical faction which left the party to form the Left Revolutionary Movement. The existence of the MIR has been a source of factionalism for Socialists ever since. One faction (Allende's), made up of the PS's most conspicuous old-timers, opposed the MIR and adhered to constitutional parliamentarianism and "the legal way." Its opponents referred to this group as *los guatones,* or "the fat cats." The other faction, called by their more moderate adversaries *los guatapiqueros,* or "the firecracker-throwers," was led by Senator Carlos Altamirano and was openly supportive of MIR's policies and actions.

Although the leftist parties created workable coalitions among themselves, these alliances were far from highly cohesive or stable. The UP, which included the PS except for the Ampuero faction, the PCCH, the bulk of the Radical party, and smaller groups like the Independent Popular Action (API), the Social Democratic party (PSD), and the dynamic MAPU group that seceded from the Christian Democrats, succeeded in 1970 in bringing Salvador Allende to the presidency, and received almost one-half the popular votes in subsequent municipal and congressional elections.

Ideologically, the major characteristic of the Communists and the Socialists as the primary partners of the coalition was Marxism as the basic source of doctrinal inspiration. However, these two major parties were not merely divided by temporary or superficial issues, as was the case with the Conservatives and Liberals on the right. The left is conditioned by having suffered the continuous and frequently violent warfare between Communists and Socialists throughout the 1930s, 1940s, and much of the 1950s. Other groups in the UP were quite different from one another. Some very small parties in the UP, for

example, were either personalistic or ad hoc organizations, legacies
from earlier extremes of multipartyism in Chile representing very narrow sectors of society. The Radicals, a middle-class and quite nonideological party, represented traditional white-collar and public employee
sectors of the population, and vaguely espoused "state socialism." The
MAPU, highly doctrinaire and elitist, articulated a determined an-
ticapitalist view which attempted to incorporate both Christian and
Marxist humanism. Although speaking on behalf of the working class,
MAPU had no significant popular base, as had the Communists and
Socialists.

Despite the fact that Socialists and Communists were the leading
forces in the UP, Allende's personality and leadership came to be the
major factors in molding the coalition and in keeping it together.
Popular Unity gradually became more associated with Allende than
with any party or group; this was a decisive factor both for eliciting
support for the government outside the parties joined by the coalition,
and for keeping the alliance together in spite of dissensions and rivalries. Nevertheless, on the whole the *Unidad Popular* was not a highly
coherent political force. It was largely an umbrella organization for
mobilizing electoral support. Despite its continuous backing of governmental initiatives, the UP, as a bloc of parliamentary forces, left a
great deal to be desired—due both to its minority status and its general
lack of structural coherence. As a functional governmental and policy-
making coalition, moreover, it was utterly ineffective. Plagued by internal party fragmentation and intraparty conflicts, it was characterized
by immobility and inability to produce consistent policy on anything
except the more general principles. Its greatest limitation, however,
was as a mechanism for mobilizing mass support beyond electoral
politics—a task which the UP leadership neither wanted nor was prepared to undertake.

The Center

CENTER POLITICS IN CHILE

The center, representing the salaried employee segments of society,
has been a dependent sector, as a result of accelerated urbanization
and bureaucratization and not of wealth distribution. The middle class
is not cohesive, or even homogeneous; actually the "middle class" is
complex and fluid in Chilean society. It is made up of very dissimilar
social segments, from blue-collar laborers who "made it" into the
employee sector, to bourgeois types hoping to be accepted into the
ranks of the aristocracy, to declining aristocrats. The characteristics
that make middle-class Chileans distinguishable from the upper and
lower classes are their deep-seated feeling, not of solidarity, but of

being "neither-nor" in relation to the other classes, and their almost desperate concern for maintaining social status.[21] Ideologically, the center became a staunch defender of the status quo and an ally of the right, adopting patrician "establishment" values. Most recently, since the early 1970s, the middle classes have come to represent mutations of such values as constitutionalism and law and order, which, out of fear, ultimately supported the abandonment of the constitutional system. The middle class has also been the source of a significant amount of generalized political alienation, from the early 1930s Chilean Nazi movement to the Agrarian Labor party (PAL), formed by Ibáñez in the late 1940s. The ideological strain they represented remained; many of these "corporatist"-oriented factions have constituted a basis of civilian support for the military dictatorship.

The two main center parties are the anticlerical, bureaucracy-based, and pragmatic Radical party and the very anti-Radical, Catholic-oriented, and reformist Christian Democratic party. The Radical party, along with the Conservatives and Liberals, is one of the oldest Chilean political organizations—originally created in the nineteenth century from a splinter group of the historic Liberal party. Chilean radicalism was influenced by the French and Italian Radical parties; like them, it represented parliamentarian, pragmatic, and evolutionist liberal values. Once a defender of laissez-faire, radicalism moved toward the advocacy of a mild welfare state; its most permanent doctrinal feature has been a profound anticlericalism.

Radicals played a crucial role in Chilean politics and government from the 1920s until their electoral decline in the 1950s and 1960s. Radicals joined the Alessandri administration in establishing the coalition with Conservatives and Liberals known as the Democratic Front. The front proved to be a disaster, as the coalition collapsed, leaving Radicals with only dismay and frustration, and no popular support. By the 1960s the PR was identified with bureaucratic irresponsibility, inefficiency, and corruption; the prestige that the party had once enjoyed had faded away, and its patronage, through the public services, was coming to an end. Its decline was accompanied by the rise of the Christian Democrats, who increasingly were perceived by the middle class as a "safety shield" against Marxism.

The Christian Democratic party originated as splinter group from the Conservative Youth, in the 1930s, with the name of National Falange. The Falange was originally a confessional (Catholic church–oriented) organization and was authoritarian, with corporatist, even semifascist, overtones.[22] In the 1940s and 1950s, the party became a more genuinely pluralistic movement, even trying its hand at labor organizing; in 1957 it was formally instituted as the Christian Democratic party. It absorbed other groups, including some leftist intellectuals, who helped provide a more secular ideological base, thereby removing strong confessional overtones and making the PDC more of a center-left party.

Since the mid-1960s, as "the malaise of the middle strata" grew, the PDC gained the support of most middle-class elements. The PDC claimed to be a "polyclassist" nationalist movement and sought to take advantage of growing fears of an extreme leftist revolutionary movement. The party emboldened its inroads into labor organization and was successful in areas long neglected by established unions, such as among *campesinos* ("peasants") and *pobladores* ("the urban poor"). Even segments of the right, once the shaky Democratic Front collapsed, turned to the PDC. The PDC's success was thus extremely fast. Sub-rosa American and West German financial support, coupled with help from the Chilean right, contributed to its meteoric rise. In a very short time the PDC had become the leading political force in the country, its candidate, Eduardo Frei, winning the presidential election in 1964. On the heels of its dramatic successes, however, the PDC began experiencing setbacks, and in 1970 lost the presidency to the UP.

FACTIONS IN CHILE'S CENTER PARTIES

Since the 1940s, the Radical party has had an internal division between a right and a left wing. Even before that, intraparty distinctions existed in the PR: in the 1880s a *mutualista* faction emerged—later splitting from it to form the Democratic party—and in the early 1900s, rival laissez-faire and state-interventionist factions developed. After the party's formal advent to power during the Popular Front (1939), a sharp bifactional division developed between rightist leadership and the more progressive and populistic elements in the party.

Alignments of these two factions with interest groups outside the party heightened the division. The party's right wingers were either associated with business organizations or occupied high positions in the foreign copper concerns, while the left wing was usually identified with white-collar labor organizations. Co-optation of high-ranking bureaucrats into the country's socioeconomic elites facilitated the perpetuation of a rightist Radical party leadership. Moreover, the Radicals were an individualistic party, not exhibiting much teamwork or centralized decision-making. The party's open structure, coexisting with its rather oligarchic leadership, made internal fragmentation not only possible but often inevitable.

After Frei's election and the collapse of the Democratic Front, the Radicals were even more sharply divided, the right wing pushing for an alliance with the National party, and the left wing supporting a coalition with FRAP. As the party's popular following of the past vanished, the internal struggle between these factions grew in intensity. the explosion came when the tiny *cenista*—the leadership faction on the party's National Executive Council (CEN), which until 1969 held the party together—could no longer maintain its neutrality, and moved to the left. A minority faction, those opposed to entente with the left, broke with the PR and created the Radical Democratic party (PRD) in 1969. These Radical Democrats rallied much of the PR's right wing; it espoused a McCarthyist anti-Communism.

The majority remained as an uneven amalgam of *guatemaltecos* (originally, those disgusted over U.S. intervention in Guatemala in 1954; later, any left-leaning party member), nostalgic old-timers of the Popular Front era, and a number of opportunists. This was the PR that joined the Communists and Socialists in the UP. After the UP's victory in 1970, these Radicals did quite well, being alloted three major ministries in Allende's government. In 1971, one faction sought an even greater share of the spoils for their role in providing respectability to the UP; other factions increasingly resented the role the party was playing in a thoroughly Marxist government coalition, and accused the CEN of *entreguismo* ("surrender to the enemy"). This group of discontented Radicals split from both the UP and the PR, becoming known as the Party of the Radical Left (PIR). With an acrimonious critique of Allende's government, the PIR moved toward convergence with the National/Christian Democratic opposition to the UP.

Thus, by the time of the demise of the constitutional republic in 1973, the degree of internal fragmentation in the Radicals had reached its peak. Had it not been outlawed by the military along with the rest of Chile's political parties, it is likely that desertion and disintegration would have put an end to the party. A microcosm of stalemate politics, the Radicals lasted as long as institutionalized class struggle was able to endure.

At the very time of its dramatic successes, centrifugal forces had been set in motion in the Christian Democratic party. In its too accelerated expansion, a superficial integration of dissimilar elements and expectations within a single political organization had generated the basis for fragmentation. An insightful observer noted that

> the PDC includes members of several religions as well as atheists. There are workers, peasants, industrialists, and intellectuals within the ranks, and economic views of members range from Marxism to Christian-inspired socialism to new capitalism. At times the PDC resembles a debating society more than a political party.[23]

Two years after the party's advent to national power, its popular decline began, showing up in diminishing popular support in 1967 municipal and 1969 congressional elections; ultimately its internal divisions led to the split of the *Rebelde* ("Rebel") faction and to their subsequent creation of MAPU.

The PDC contained structural and ideological contradictions which in its rapid ascent to power it could not consolidate into one operating ideology and program. An underlying division between authoritarian-corporatist and democratic-populist factions was overlaid by strained relations between the party's organizational leadership and the *Freista* team. Frei's "official" (government) faction grew impatient to subordinate the party to the government and to gain complete control of the party machinery.

While the corporatists viewed "pluralism" from the status quo perspective of a pyramidal and organic society controlled from the top, the populists regarded pluralism as active participation in decision-making by all sectors of society, including the underprivileged ones. *Tercerista* ("Third Force") and *Rebelde* factions—mostly younger elements, intellectuals, and PDC grass-roots organizations—represented the populistic tendency. The older members of the party, like the old Falangists (with certain notable exceptions), the former Agrarian Laborites, and the government "team," representing the corporatist approach, gained control of the party in 1969, precipitating a split in the party which gave rise to MAPU, led by Jacques Chonchol and prominent PDC Rebels. Many important clientele organizations left and followed MAPU.[24] The split between *Rebeldes* and *Oficialistas* meant the loss to the PDC of a large segment of the Youth Organization and the Student Federation of Chile; thus the PDC's influence on the student movement, after a decade of undisputed control, vanished almost overnight.

Increasingly in control of the Frei machine, the PDC moved farther to the right during the UP era, and established a "tactical alliance" with the National party and the Radical Democrats; the remaining populistic elements in the party then left in protest of this alliance. This faction, known as the Christian Left, eventually joined the UP, part of it also going into MAPU. The old guard finally was left alone in absolute control of the PDC organization. These "hard-liners" embarked on a conspiratorial strategy and helped pave the way for the military coup. At first the PDC extended its respectability to the revolt, though not fully to the repression which followed, for the soldiers demonstrated almost as great a contempt for Christian Democrats as for the left. The PDC eventually disintegrated into multiple acrimonious factions, with at least one of them supporting the junta. The Frei faction, while justifying the coup, complained of abuses of power and humbly begged for a return to "constitutionalism." Other factions have been openly critical of the coup, and their leaders have chosen the road to exile. Even in the unlikely event that the country returned to constitutional rule, it is unlikely that the Christian Democratic party would exist as a viable political force.

Conclusions

PATTERNS OF FACTIONAL POLITICS

The general pattern of Chilean party politics over the past fifty years has been one of continuous factional splits and mergers. By and large, factions have resulted in formal secessions from existing parties and in the subsequent creation of new parties. The development of Chile's multiparty system has been the outgrowth of a series of historical schisms, as shown in the diagram below. The Conservative Party (PC) was founded in 1830; the Liberal party (PL) was formed as a breakaway faction in 1854. Another early breakaway faction of the PC was the early National party (PN), which existed until 1920. The Radical party (PR) originated as a breakaway faction of the Liberals in 1863; the Democratic party (PD) split off from the Radicals in 1884. In 1912 the Socialist Workers party (POS) split off from the PD; the POS in 1923 became the Communist party of Chile (PCCH). In 1930 the Agrarian party (PA) developed from a faction of the Liberals and became the Agrarian Labor party (PAL) in 1949. The Socialist party (PS) was formed in 1932, in large part out of the Trotskyite faction expelled from the PCCH. At about the same time the National Falange party (PFN) was formed as a breakaway faction from the Conservatives, in 1935. The Socialist party of Chile (PSCH) and the Popular Socialist party (PSP) emerged in 1947 from two major factions of the PS; these remerged in the PS in 1957. In 1957 also the Christian Democratic party (PDC) was formed out of the PFN. The Movement of the Revolutionary Left (MIR) was formed in 1963 as a split-off faction of the Socialists. In 1965 the modern National party (PN) was formed as a merger of the historic PC and PL. The Popular Socialist Union (USP), formed in 1968, was another former Socialist faction; while the Radical Democratic party (PRD) was formed in 1969 from a faction of the Radicals. Unitary Popular Action Movement (MAPU) also created in 1969, was formed from a factional split-off from the Christian Democrats.

The the same time, despite a growing propensity for fragmentation, since the 1950s Chilean politics shows a marked tendency toward the regrouping of political brokers into large and entangled blocs—*alianzas, frentes,* or *confederaciónes*—roughly along class lines. Such a trend, while reducing the number of small ad hoc and personalistic parties, tended to increase the overall polarity of the system, or at least to reinforce ongoing polarization. The emergence of large blocs, moreover, did not mean an overall decrease of party factionalism, nor result in a lessening of the system's propensity to fragment. It rather meant the formation of broad and mutually antagonistic conglomerates (such as UP and CODE) of internally factionalized political forces.

This pattern—growing internal fragmentation accompanied by a trend toward the creation of broad, entangled, class-based alliances—

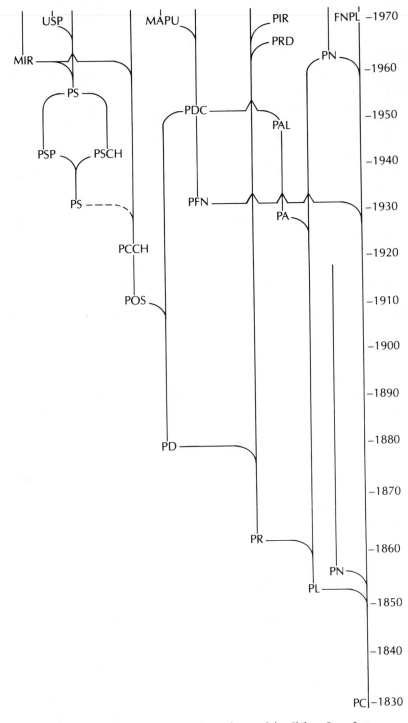

Diagram 1. Parties and Factions in the Evolution of the Chilean Party System

can be most clearly seen in the case of the left since 1957, with first the FRAP and later the short-lived UP. On the right since the 1950s, in contrast, while there was also a consolidation trend ultimately resulting in the creation of the National party in 1965, internal factionalism apparently diminished. Concentration and cohesion were accomplished as relative electoral support for the right parties dwindled; thus, diminishing popular support seems to have contributed to the withering away of intraparty and intraclass factional cleavages.

The center parties, in turn, have followed a factionalism pattern similar to that of the left. While, with expanding political participation, the relative share of electoral support going to the centrist parties generally increased (as did that going to the left), internal factionalism grew. A basic characteristic of both center parties—Radicals (since the 1950s) and Christian Democrats (since 1967)—was that an acute process of internal polarization and factionalization was taking place. Unlike either the traditional right or the left, the parties of the center after the 1950s could not constitute broad, class-based coalitions (and any coalition of the rigidly anticlerical PR and the once-confessional PDC was ruled out by both parties from the outset). Moreover, the PDC, by assimilating smaller groups into its structure, began to resemble a factional coalition itself.

Furthermore, the formulation of blocs of the right or the left precluded the center from using the pragmatic strategy of shifting alliances it followed at the time of Radical dominance, from 1938 to 1952. Although the Christian Democrats were able to abjure alliances briefly, from 1964 to 1970, toward the end of the Frei administration the need for outside support became evident—and this need then became a further fragmenting factor itself. The party split: a majority of the leadership chose the right, while much of the party grass roots moved left. The Radicals experienced a similar schism, when their party leadership elected to enter the UP.

In the universe of Chilean multiparty politics which existed until 1973, only one major party outside the right apparently escaped internal disintegration—the Communist party. The Communists' successful avoidance of serious factionalism appears to have largely been due to its unique structural arrangements, based on "democratic centralism." Through it, the PCCH has been able to maintain great unity while other parties were dividing and subdividing.

CONSEQUENCES OF FACTIONALISM

An overall analysis of Chilean politics indicates that the general impact of factionalism in the country's political life has been diverse, depending on the level of the system one examines and the changing nature of the system's internal constraints and contradictions. When traditional Chilean politics had still a fairly clear flavor of "gentlemen's politics" and the relevant strata of the population were relatively few, factionalism within the elite facilitated the maintenance of systemic stability and a modicum of what has been called "oligarchical pluralism." Once middle-class control changed from a buffer-like contention of lower-class demands (and participation) to polarized pluralism, the functions of factionalism were drastically altered. In the context of broadened participation, factionalism ceased to be the result of divergent intraelite viewpoints and became the consequences of conflicting demands from different social strata.

Factionalism thus was inseparably linked to cultural and structural fragmentation, and its increasingly probable outcome was a mixture of political immobility or stalemate, and instability. For as long as the rapidly fragmenting middle classes were capable of moving through alternative "legitimate" solutions (e.g., Radical party dominance, *Ibañismo*, the rise of the PDC), with the alliance of a shrinking oligarchy, instability remained latent, but at the cost of political effectiveness. Moreover, systemic constraints resulting from Chile's dependence on foreign aid and markets, coupled with an increased degree of transnational integration of crucial segments of the elite—such as the officer corps and the business community—severely limited Chile's real autonomy and reinforced the institutionalization of ineffectiveness.

The stalemate solution was exhausted and overplayed in Chile by 1973. Popular mobilization had already surpassed the ability of the institutional left to channel it. Neither did the left seem willing or able —internally fragmented as it was—to change the "rules of the game" and transform stalemate into a revolutionary solution.

Traditional centrist politics, on the other hand, with its emphasis on form and procedure rather than on substance, could not rapidly come to terms with a process of basic grass-roots democratization that the country was undergoing. The mobilization of peasants, shantytown dwellers, and in general the large mass of urban poor was more than party politics could absorb without producing a drastic overhaul of Chile's entire structure of socioeconomic inequalities. Polarization of the system in this case did not end in a pattern of weak centrist dominance, as existed until 1970. On the contrary, the cumulative feedback of extreme polarity in 1972–1973 produced an even greater fragmentation of the middle-class-based PDC, and a displacement to the right. Extremist groups at both ends of the spectrum, in the form of the FNPL and the MIR—in part a reflection of an increasingly intensified, yet deadlocked, political struggle—furthered the polarization.

The high degree of factional fragmentation existing in the centrist parties not only made impossible the centripetal integration of the polity but, more important, gave the upper hand to those middle-class sectors whose alienation from politics was extreme. These elements, represented by the thoroughly middle-class "professional" officer corps (although not limited exclusively to it), stepped in when the traditional brokers were too fragmented and stalemated to produce a solution to Chile's social crisis.

This bloody eruption gave birth to one of the most repressive regimes in contemporary Latin America—surprisingly, in a country with a long reputation for democratic stability.[25] The coup of September 1973 changed most of the conventional generalizations and myths about Chilean democracy, party competition, factionalism, consensus, etc., into a matter of political archaeology. Among a great many facets of this complex and dramatic phenomenon, factionalism in Chilean politics is one of the critical elements in an understanding of at least this part of the world contemporary scene.

NOTES

1. A notable exception is the article by George W. Grayson, Jr., "Chile's Christian Democratic Party: Power, Factions, and Ideology," *Review of Politics* 31, no. 2 (Apr. 1969): 147–71. For general studies in Chilean politics, see Federico Gil, *Los partidos políticos Chilenos* (Buenos Aires: Depalma, 1962); and Gil, *The Political System of Chile* (Boston: Houghton Mifflin, 1966); also Ernest Halperin, *Nationalism and Communism in Chile* (Austin: Univ. of Texas Press, 1970); and James Petras, *Politics and Social Forces in Chilean Development* (Berkeley and Los Angeles: Univ. of California Press, 1969).

2. Cf. *Time* (Sept. 30, 1974), pp. 20–28; *El Sol de México*, Nov. 16, 1974; *Los Documentos secretos de la ITT* (Santiago, 1972). For a comprehensive analysis of the coup, see *Latin American Perspectives* 1, no. 2 (Summer 1974), entire issue.

3. Osvaldo Sunkel, "Change and Frustration in Chile," in Claudio Véliz, ed., *Obstacles to Change in Latin America* (New York: Oxford Univ. Press, 1965), pp. 116–44.

4. Cf. Stanislav Andreski, *Parasitism and Subversion: The Case of Latin America* (New York: Pantheon Books, 1966).

5. Giovanni Sartori, "European Political Parties: A Case of Polarized Pluralism," in Joseph LaPalombara and Myron Weiner, eds., *Political Parties and Political Development* (Princeton: Princeton Univ. Press, 1966), pp. 3–42.

6. See, among others, Osvaldo Sunkel, "Capitalismo transnacional y desintegración nacional en América Latina," *Estudios Internacionales*, 4, no. 16 (Jan.-Mar. 1971): 3–61; and Andre Gunder Frank, *Capitalism and Underdevelopment in Latin America: Historical Studies of Chile and Brazil* (New York: Monthly Review Press, 1969), pp. 1–115.

7. Cf. Norbert Lechner, *La Democracia en Chile* (Buenos Aires: Signos, 1970), pp. 61–66.

8. Rafael López, "El Sistema de partidos en Chile: un caso de pluralismo extremo," mimeographed (Santiago: Instituto de Organización y Administración [INSORA], 1968), p. 3. This is a paraphrasing of Sartori's analysis, "European Political Parties," applied to Chile.

9. Albert O. Hirschman, "Alternatives to Revolution," in Laura Randall, ed., *Economic Development: Evolution or Revolution?* (Boston: D. C. Heath, 1964), p. 84. See also Hirschman, *Journeys Toward Progress* (New York: Twentieth Century Fund, 1963), pp. 202–09.

10. Hirschman, *Journeys Toward Progress*, p. 223. See also Win Crowther, "Political Bargaining, Inflation, and Industrialization in Chile," unpublished paper (Berkeley: Univ. of California, Dept. of Political Science, 1970), p. 5; and Alfred Stepan, "Political Development Theory: The Latin American Experience," *Journal of International Affairs* 20, no. 2 (1966): 225.

11. For analysis of the Chilean right, see Frederick B. Pike, *Chile and the United States, 1880–1962: The Emergence of Chile's Social Crisis and the Challenge to United States Diplomacy* (Notre Dame: Notre Dame Univ. Press, 1963); and Constantine C. Menges, "Public Policy and Organized Business in Chile," *Journal of International Affairs* 20, no. 2 (1966): 343–65.

12. David Cusak and Jorge Nef, "Interacción entre el sector público y los agents mediadores en el sistema político Chileno," mimeographed (Santiago: INSORA, 1968),

p. 68. See also Petras, *Politics and Social Forces in Chilean Development*, pp. 53, 68–72; and Kalmzn H. Silvert, *The Conflict Society: Reaction and Revolution in Latin America* (New York: American Universities Field Staff, 1966), p. 234.

13. On the Democratic Front, see Frederick M. Nunn, "Chile's Government in Perspective: Political Change or More of the Same?" *Inter-American Economic Affairs* 20 (Spring 1967): 74–75.

14. See H. E. Bicheno, "Antiparliamentary Themes in Chilean History: 1920–1970," *Government and Opposition* 7, no. 3 (Summer 1972): 187.

15. S. Fanny Simon, "Anarchist and Anarcho-syndicalism in South America," *Hispanic-American Historical Review* 26 (Feb. 1946): 52–53; cf. Tomás Moulian, *Estudio sobre Chile* (Santiago: Orbe, 1965), pp. 23–26; also Cusak and Nef, "Interacción entre el sector público y los agents mediadores," p. 65. CUT represented over 70 percent of the country's unions, including all the largest and most important ones.

16. Gil, *The Political System of Chile*, pp. 280–81; also Germán Urzúa, *Los partidos políticos Chelenos* (Santiago: Editorial Juridica, 1968), p. 30. See also W. Raymond Duncan and James Nelson Goodsell, *The Quest for Change in Latin America* (New York: Oxford Univ. Press, 1971), pp. 456–57.

17. Bicheno, "Antiparliamentary Themes in Chilean History," p. 386. In spite of its success, the MIR was not without internal schisms. Several small ultraleftist groups resented its "indirect" and "defensive" revolutionary tactics, based on raising the level of political consciousness of the lower classes, and abandoned MIR. Some of these were to engage in acts of terrorism; the Peoples' Organized Vanguard, for example, claimed credit for the assassination of former Minister Edmundo Pérez Zujovick in 1971.

18. In 1968, out of twenty-nine national councilmen in CUT's congress, fourteen members belonged to the Communist party, seven to the Socialists, three to the Christian Democrats, two to the Radicals, and one to the Popular Socialist Union. *El Siglo* (Santiago), no. 25 (1968): 7. Also see Jorge Barría, *Breve historia del sindicalismo Chileno* (Santiago: INSORA, 1967); and Manuel Barrera, *Tres experiencias de participación de las organizaciones empresariales y sindicales en la planificación en Chile* (Santiago: INSORA, 1968). (The affiliations of the remaining two councilmen were not given in *El Siglo.*)

19. These important individual unions were largely those which had been able to integrate their constituents on a wider basis, such as the Copper Workers' Union, the Municipal Laborers' Union, and, to a lesser extent, certain white-collar organizations of the public sector (e.g., the civil servants' and teachers' unions). However, the latter were more oriented to middle-class interests, and maintained greater affinities with Radicals or Christian Democrats.

20. Jack Ray Thomas, "The Socialist Republic of Chile," *Journal of Inter-American Studies* 6 (Apr. 1964): 203–20; and Thomas, "The Evolution of a Chilean Socialist: Marmaduke Grove," *Hispanic-American Historical Review* 47 (Feb. 1967): 22–37.

21. On the Chilean middle classes, see Petras, *Politics and Social Forces in Chilean Development*, pp. 132–36; Moulian, *Estudio Sobre Chile*, pp. 41–43; John Johnson, *Political Change in Latin America: The Emergence of the Middle Sectors* (Stanford: Stanford Univ. Press, 1958), pp. 77–93; and Pike, *Chile and the United States*, pp. 285–87. See also Carlos Neely, *Cambios políticos para el desarrollo* (Santiago: Editorial Universitaria, 1968); the author argues that the Chilean middle class has been mostly an artifical creation of the oligarchy to establish a buffer class between them and the *rotos* ("reds"), and has only contributed to social parasitism and stagnation.

22. See Sergio Gilisasti Tagle, *Partidos políticos Chilenos*, 2d ed. (Santiago: Editorial Nascimiento, 1969), pp. 199–204; also Gil, *Political System of Chile*, pp. 267–68, and footnote 37.

23. Grayson, "Chile's Christian Democratic Party," pp. 150–53.

24. These included groups such as Conchol's Institute of Agrarian Development, and the *Promoción Popular*, a semiofficial agency created to organize slum-dwellers into grass-roots organizations. Some, like the latter, had been highly controversial not only as national policy but also within the PDC.

25. Martin C. Needler, "Population Development and Socioeconomic Development: The Case of Latin America," *American Political Science Review* 6Z, no. 3 (Sept. 1968): 889–97; also Phillips Cutwright, "National Political Development: Measurement and Analysis," *American Sociological Review* 28 (Apr. 1963): 253–64; and Russell H. Fitzgibbon, "Measuring Democratic Change in Latin America," *Journal of Politics* 29 (Feb.

1967): 129–66. On the coup and the repression, see in the *Le Monde* section of the *Manchester Guardian* (weekly), articles by Marcel Niedergang (Oct. 13, 1973) and Philippe Labreveux (Jan. 5 and 12, 1974); also E. Bradford Burns, "Reform Gunned Down: The True Verdict on Allende," *Nation* (Oct. 29, 1973); and Lawrence Littwin, *Latin America: Catholicism and Class Conflict* (Encino: Dickenson Publishing, 1974), pp. 122–27.

14

Party Factions in the United States

THOMAS H. ROBACK
JUDSON L. JAMES

Party factions in the United States share the basic structural problems of American political parties themselves. The decentralization of the government structure, the decline of patronage and other material rewards, and the low public esteem for party organizations cause both political parties and factions within them to be fragmented, loosely coordinated, understaffed, and limited in influence. Moreover, analyzing party factions in the United States poses a different set of issues than those characteristic of more ideological party systems. Since the party factions are less frequently and consistently organizationally developed, the evidence necessary for analysis is more elusive and diverse in sources and character. Tracing these issues involves consideration of changing patterns of factionalism over time, the classification of different types of factions, and analysis of the functions and consequences of factions for the party system.

The Development of Party Factions in the United States

Political parties in the United States do not currently possess many examples of highly developed factions. But the relative absence of this type of party faction does not eliminate the value of considering party factions as an analytic category in American politics. The diverse patterns of factional behavior over the history of the United States are

329

illustrative of a number of important points that can be applied to the study of the American political system and to comparative political systems as well.

In analyzing party factions in the United States, we can link two conceptions of factions that often seem to be alternative rather than compatible ideas. These are factions as a developmental stage in party history, and factions as ongoing entities within an existing party system. Factions in the contemporary setting can be seen not merely as extensions of preparty factions, but also as transitions to postparty factions, and as alternative forms of competition within parties.

EARLY AMERICAN FACTIONS

In the United States, as was true in many Western European countries, factions arose first as precursors to the development of political parties.[1] Factions emerged in the eighteenth century as a rudimentary intermediate political institution that attempted to provide continuing links between people and their government. As the notion of democratic responsibility began to influence the organization of political processes, these informally structured factions initially formed around an important political personality, influential family, major office-holder, or perhaps a regional economic interest. These factions differed from earlier political groupings because the existence of elections and representative assemblies created new arenas of competition and demanded new organizational weapons to mobilize a broader range of participants. Intrigues around the monarch or the principal national officials now needed some degree of popular support and ratification. Influencing the election of legislators required constituency organization of at least local notables and elites even if suffrage was narrowly defined.[2] The growing capacity of legislatures to influence the operations of government required organizing their operation and coordinating the tactics of supporters within the legislatures.

In the history of American and Western European political parties, one can trace the combination of many factions into larger and more comprehensive political organizations as democratic political competition demanded more consistent and broader ranges of political participation. More and more individuals in each constituency had to be reached. Competition for control of national policy made formation of nationwide coalitions before elections advisable for electoral success. In the United States, the broad political consensus, the single-member district, and competition for the office of the president provided exceptionally strong pressures on regional factions to combine into one or two national parties, and worked against the survival of political parties based on single factions.[3]

In the early stages (the 1790s), the pattern of competition varied from state to state.[4] In Boston, the Caucus Club would meet in advance of town elections; or in New York, the leading families, the Schuylers, the Livingstons, and the Clintons competed on the basis of their social standing and vast landholdings, much like nobility in England. The combinations were often transitory and based on the personal attributes of the families involved. Without organizational stability or loyalties, the participants were free to depart for new coalitions at any time.

But the intensifying conflict between Alexander Hamilton, John Adams, and the Federalists on one side, and Thomas Jefferson, James Madison, and the Republicans on the other replaced the unstructured political competition.[5] Hamilton began by developing the first nationwide faction, linking together by correspondence the potential Federalist elites in each state. Madison countered by organizing an opposition faction in the House of Representatives. As a consequence, both sides reached out to contest congressional and state legislative elections, the latter being the key to victory in the Electoral College and the capture of the presidency. The need to contest for the presidency combined the constituency and state organizations into the major national parties.

Once political parties began to develop, factions developed in three different directions. One pattern has already been described, the generalization and combination of factions to provide collectivities large enough and diverse enough to compete nationally amid a diverse electorate and in diverse constituencies. Factions with well-defined interests and attitudes, on the other hand, evolved toward interest group organizations and competed in the political process by maximizing intensity of their support and access through the variety of tactics of pressure group politics. But the development of two distinct kinds of political organizations, political parties and interest groups, both of which provide links between the general public and the governmental process, should not obscure the persistence of factions within political parties as a third and continuing category of factional activity.

Factionalism persisted within political parties, retaining many of the characteristics that it had previously exhibited with different forms and consequences in the preparty stage. Factions continued to have cadres, an internal communications system, rewards, and offices, all of which had helped to maintain preparty factions. However, factions were in a different situation once the party system was established. Previously, factions were relatively unconstrained in their competition as far as potential alliances and available tactics were concerned. Within political parties, factions were defined more by the party's constituencies, constituents' interests, and issue bases. Competition was constrained by party rules and the need to unite in the general election. But even after the Republican party was established, Jefferson and Madison had to deal with difficult factional leaders such as Aaron

Burr in New York and John Randolph in Virginia. When the Federalist party declined, the various Republican party factions were no longer constrained by general election competition, and internal conflict tore the Republican party apart and destroyed it within a few years.

As political parties stabilized as continuing mechanisms in the political process, factions became a means by which the prizes attainable through political parties were distributed and fought over. The earliest factions within ongoing political parties closely resembled the factions in the preparty stage, being organized around important political families or individual leaders. But with the development of the spoils system and the politics of patronage in the early nineteenth century, political machines developed in individual communities and to a partial extent on a statewide basis.

POLITICAL MACHINES

From the second third of the nineteenth century through the first third of the twentieth century, the patronage system and the numerous political machines provided the principal basis for factional politics.[6] Patronage quickly generated defined systems of distribution for these rewards, and an organized competition for them in the form of the convention system. The machine, the characteristic political party organization of this period, provided a way of maintaining cadres, an internal communications system, and consistent rewards for factional participation.[7]

The patronage-based political machine had exceptional durability and effectiveness as a party faction in the United States. Its comprehensiveness was based on the utilization of party workers in each precinct. This enabled it to contest nominations and general elections at any time and for any office without the initial mobilization effort which constituted such a formidable hurdle for sporadic challengers of its dominance. This cadre of workers was disciplined and rewarded by the patronage of jobs, favorable treatment by government agencies, and campaign expense money. These same resources were used by the cadres to gain loyal voters for the organization. These loyal supporters and active precinct workers would, especially with typically low voting turnouts, control the nominations of the major parties and thereby control access to public office and the resulting government policies and employment.

The vertical structure of the political machine paralleled the combination of voting precincts into wards and districts. Because they combined and controlled the efforts of the individual precinct workers, ward or district leaders (the second level of the organization) were also critical intermediaries in the process of distributing rewards and providing communications in both directions between the machine bosses and the rank-and-file precinct workers. Patronage and related rewards provided the glue to hold together a political machine as a continuing political faction. It provided the necessary incentives to recruit workers, and it established an effective leadership structure, a reason for continuing activity, and a task-oriented internal communication pattern.

The decentralization of American governmental structure provided a base for a political machine in each community, county, and state. The relatively higher government employment and less restrictive civil service practices of state and local governments meant that national political machines and national patronage-based factions were very unlikely and very unstable. No temporary national party leader could provide rewards that competed successfully with those available to more permanent state and local party leaders. State and local leaders could offer jobs, while national leaders could offer only a few prestigious positions, which were not very relevant to rank-and-file party workers. Since political machines never became nationwide or comprehensive and the existence of spoils provided a basis for conflict within the party, the existence of a party machine usually carried with it the possibility of contending alternative factions either in other parts of the state or even as divisions within the political machine of any given community.[8] For example, a minority faction opposing the majority Democratic machine faction in the city of Baltimore could sustain itself by allying itself to the statewide organization of the governor of Maryland and receiving patronage from it.

As machine politics began to break down in the middle of the twentieth century, the factional nature of the intraparty competition began to weaken. The institution of the direct primary and other electoral reforms weakened its role in intraparty competition. Civil service reform and national government assumption of many social services cut away both cadres and rewards to distribute. The decline of large-scale European immigration in the 1920s began to cut away the most dependent sectors of the electoral base of the organization. The decay of party organization and factions based on patronage politics led to the decline in the coherence and effectiveness of party factions, since they lost their major institutional prop for continuity.[9]

Although patronage-based factions have largely disappeared, or declined drastically, in American politics, they do persist in some traditional areas of American politics. Today's descendants of political machines typically are in areas either suffering long-term economic depression or containing a large proportion of recently arrived, low status, minority group members. Individuals in these areas still create a demand for low-paying government jobs, which is the basis for machine activity. The remaining party machines in the areas least affected by civil service reform provoke some factional politics as a necessary basis for competition against them.

In Southern states, where both patronage and traditional personality and familial politics are still possible, there are some examples of persisting factions. The supporters and opponents of Huey Long and his family in Louisiana politics provided well-defined factional competition within the Democratic party of that state for many years. Aided by the election procedures, candidates for county and local office could affiliate with the statewide campaigns of gubernatorial candidates within Democratic primaries. This way, the primaries became similar to general elections because the gubernatorial tickets with their local allies provided the major alternatives available to most voters for most offices, just as the party label does in competitive general elections. Unlike the typical, unstructured, "every man for himself" primaries elsewhere, the Louisiana voter could vote for an entire ticket gathered around one or another statewide campaign in the primary.

This ticket system was dependent on the special provisions of Louisiana election law, plus the exceptional impact of Huey Long as a political leader and his polarization of political opinion and choices in Louisiana. The groups which supported or opposed Long comprise a vivid example of party conflict that derived from the mixture of personalism and populism that characterized this era of Louisiana politics. From his unsuccessful race for governor in 1924 until his assassination in 1935, the Kingfish was the embodiment of Southern factional politics in American political lore. His eventual dictatorial control of the Democratic party and the state political system grew out of the seamy political climate in Louisiana and Long's role as champion of the common man against the "sinister" financial interests that controlled the Democratic party machine.

Long waged war against what he considered the evils of an entrenched faction in the Louisiana Democratic party that was controlled by the New Orleans machine and was beholden to powerful business and financial interests. Key points out that these included "the mercantile, financial, and shipping interests of New Orleans . . . sugar growers . . . cotton planters of the Red and Mississippi Rivers . . . the lumber industry . . . oil . . . add to all these the railroads and gas and electrical utilities, and you have elements susceptible of combination into a powerful political bloc.[10] This moralistic approach to politics was successful in attracting lower-class workers and farmers to Long's faction and was based on what Key called the "hell-of-a-fellow" syndrome. This pertains to an earthy, often profane, always disrespectful ridicule of middle- and upper-class politicians and interests. These two factions—the "nicer" people and the organizations of a succession of Longs—conducted factional conflict through campaigns that often resembled great moral dramas. Against rough tactics on the hustings, the middle-class respectable candidate became the helpless object of merciless attacks by the hell-of-a-fellow supporters of the Long family.

For example, Earl Long described his 1940 opponent Sam Jones as "high hat Sam, the High Society Kid, the High-Kicking, High and Mighty Snide Sam, the guy that pumps perfume under his arms."[11]

Southern political history is full of both populist and traditional appeals that evolved into factions of the machine variety. The Talmadges in Georgia, Bilbo in Mississippi, the Byrds in Virginia, and "Kissin' Jim" Folsom in Alabama also represent this type of factional organization. But even these conspicuous examples of factional politics in recent American political history have substantially declined and been eroded by more modern, national bases of political conflict.[12]

Instead of the traditional working-class machines, today we have what has been called middle-class, "country-club" machines that are fueled by preferments in contract allocation, influence peddling, and other forms of indirect material reward, and that have replaced the direct patronage machine. Cases of graft, kickbacks, and other criminal activity still occur (as witnessed by the circumstances surrounding Spiro Agnew's resignation) and constitute a more sophisticated form of what often took place under traditional machine politics.[13] However, it is interesting to note that Chicago Democratic organization precinct captains still consider the distribution of free garbage cans to be a valuable means of reaching Chicago voters.

The decline of the political machine as a basis for factions within American political parties did not lead to the substitution of another broad basis for political factions. The decentralization of political parties in the American political system limits the relative formalization of factions beyond face-to-face legislative groups without the material incentives which made political machine-based factions possible. Instead, there is a trend toward the development of various kinds of "tendencies" rather than factions.

Intraparty Competition by Tendencies

Classification of American party factions is problematical for two major reasons: first, because of the general definitional fuzziness and lack of consensus over the proper focus and range of the faction concept; and second, because of the nonprogrammatic nature of the American two-party system which has provided an infertile ground for the type of issue cleavages that have spawned factions in many other more programmatic, multi-party systems. However, a preliminary "mapping" of American party factions is possible, and several concepts discussed earlier provide a vehicle for classification.

Internal group competition and conflict in American parties can be classified according to two major types—tendencies and factions. In conformity to Rose's seminal notion, tendencies refer to less structured, less stable, and less enduring patterns of internal party competition.[14] In discussing tendencies and party divisions in Great Britain, Rose points out that

> Adherents are often not self-consciously organized in support of a single policy and they do not expect, nor are they expected, to continue to operate as a group supporting the same tendency through a period of time. For instance, many M.P.s will at some time or another show support for a reform tendency . . . but this will not make them all members of a reform faction, supporting a *wide* range of changes. In so far as an electoral party is primarily characterized by factionalism, then cleavages within the party tend to be stable and follow predictable lines. In so far as groups of politicians do not self-consciously band together, then party divisions are less fluid and less easy to anticipate.[15]

In the American political system, party divisions are becoming increasingly expressed as tendencies. The variety of tendencies within American political parties form a set of overlapping rather than exclusive categories. One variety, "ideological" tendencies, is manifested by amorphous group affiliation that consists of attitudinal identification with political symbols, principles, or personalities, i.e., ideological "wings" of parties that have no continuing structures of communication and mobilization and have no organizational basis by which to wage battle with other wings of the party. Another category can be called "electoral" tendencies, where like-minded individuals band together in nomination and campaign situations to support particular candidates who may or may not possess a particular ideological identity. These manifestations of personalism as politics are temporary and usually provide no basis for continuing factional activity after the election.

These tendencies in place of factions as a basis for competition within parties have also been described by one set of writers on American politics as examples of "feudal" politics.[16] The campaign organizations of individual candidates for elective office provide the factions that might exist within the political party and disappear after the campaign concludes. Competition is individualistic and not organizational, with no continuing lines of conflict. The candidate, his or her staff, and active supporters contend with other candidates, their staffs, and supporters, just as rival barons warred with each other in the feudal days of weak kings in the Middle Ages.

The best examples of the importance of tendencies can be seen in recent campaigns for the presidency.[17] Senator Barry Goldwater in 1964, Senator Eugene McCarthy in 1968, and Senator George McGovern in 1972 were all political figures around whom a variety of like-minded individuals, bound together by ideology or a related set of issues, provided the basis for a very severe and extensive intraparty conflict. In each case, the tendency (or movement, as one might call it) sought out and adopted the candidate. The supporters of each candidate were not tied together initially by any form of factional organization though they maintained some kind of organization for the duration of that campaign. After the campaign ended, the adherents of the individual candidates moved on to the campaigns of other candidates. The campaign structure disappeared and little or no basis or a continuing faction remained.

Typically, in campaigns within state and local parties, the candidate has to create an organization for the campaign, and officials who are in office maintain incipient campaign organizations for future use.[18] These campaign organizations, or provisional campaign organizations, become the basis of what are often called factions within American political parties. The principal elected officials have sufficiently extensive personal organizations and continuing political activities that they constitute a close approximation of political factions on a continuing basis. This is why many writers talk about the personalization of factions or about factions as defined by a leader-follower relationship. The leader-follower relationship is probably important only where in fact the faction has less formalization and less effectiveness. This is closer to a tendency or faction of a preparty phase, than to what is meant by a faction in a more formal sense. For example, the Kennedy brothers of Massachusetts have had personal organizations which provided an electoral tendency based on specific campaigns and candidates rather than on general ideology or a specific wing of the Democratic party.

TENDENCIES IN THE AMERICAN SOUTH

Tendencies are often closely linked to political culture and may vary in intensity and substance depending on regional and subcultural context.[19] Traditionalistic Democratic politics in the South is a case in point, especially when the growth of competition from Republicans is taken into account. The aristocratic, hierarchical politics as practiced by state party organizations often controlled by small cliques, courthouse "gangs" or individual personalities has given way to new ideologically based or mixed leader-ideology-based tendencies that have brought about new styles of political and partisan identifications and activism.[20] Thus Key's notion of Southern factionalism was based on factions that were often merely loose followings of particular candidates whose appeal was based on personalism and family or geographical ties.

With the emergence of the "New South," two ideologically based tendencies have emerged. One variety reflects a new commerce-oriented, middle-class type of activism that is competing with Elazar's "plantation type," and can be called the "new right." Such Southern Republicans and Democrats have rejected "classical" conservative principles and embraced the primacy of economic and political security by means of political privilege and cozy relationships between business and government through subsidies for oil, construction, textile, and defense industries. Laissez-faire capitalism is an artifact in this context, and ideological tendencies have manifested themselves in competition with the more traditional Southern party organizations over the last thirty years.[21] These changes have been accompanied by the development of competitive Republican state parties that have been anxious to capitalize on conservative discontent among Democrats. Often this results in internecine warfare between moderate and conservative wings of the GOP over the role that converted Democrats should play within the party. For example, in Virginia, the splintering of the Byrd organization, coupled with the perception of the national Democratic party as liberal on economics and race, has provided prominent converts to the Republican party.

Another type of evolving tendency in the American South that has had substantial partisan cleavage potential is mass-based and deals with salient social issues upon which leadership can capitalize. The Wallace phenomenon in the South and in other regions combines both personalism and ideological intensity in a curious chemical mixture that has been quite successful. It is important to recognize the extent to which the attractiveness of the Wallace candidacies represents an electoral tendency within a segment of the mass membership of the Democratic party and among the public at large. Wallace was able to articulate social and economic positions related to disaffection and alienation from governmental solutions to controversial problems of the 1960s and 1970s. While his effect on the organizational operation and control of the national Democratic party was negligible, his secondary influence on the ideological positions of major Democratic candidates and the policies of officeholders and organizational leaders was quite real. The Wallace movement articulated positions on issues related to law and order, foreign policy aggressiveness, federal policies in school integration, and economic inequities related to social welfare and taxation policies, positions that were co-opted in varying degrees by the major presidential candidates in both 1968 and 1972, and in 1976. While racial hostility lay at the core of a segment of Wallace support, his appeal had broadened by 1968 to include traditional Democratic voters who felt that their party and government no longer had their best interests at heart. Lipset explains the Wallace popularity outside the South in terms of a feeling of "relative deprivation," in which blue-collar workers felt that their social and economic advancement was not keeping up with the advancement of white-collar classes.[22] Wallace has tapped several raw nerves of public discontent in periods of political and economic turmoil, and his doing so influenced changes in the electoral strategies and ideological directions of both major parties.

On the national level, electoral tendencies as expressed in ideological form were operational in the presidential candidacies of Barry Goldwater, Eugene McCarthy, and George McGovern. In each of these cases, a combination of personalism and ideological identity provided a nucleus around which like-minded adherents could cluster. Such tendencies were often categorized as "amateur movements" because they were often supported by people who had no prior political experience in parties or campaigns. The common denominator that helped unite such groups was a focus on ideological principles and policy programs as reasons for political activity. Party organizations were seen as means by which elected officials could implement a particular set of policies after the election. The initial impetus for each of the above-mentioned candidacies rested upon a feeling of ideological identification with positions on certain issues that were considered salient.

In the case of the Goldwater campaign in 1964, the perception of the personal characteristics of the candidate himself as a man of integrity, honesty, and "principle" also played a part in generating support.[23] Indeed, the attitude of "purism" as opposed to the compromising, "win at any cost" attitude of regular party professionals is another major characteristic of such tendencies. The McCarthy candidacy usually is associated only with opposition to the Vietnam War, but it attracted a diverse following because of the remote, symbolic nature of McCarthy's appeal. Voters with often very different ideological beliefs projected onto McCarthy those needs, fears, or characteristics that the individual wanted or needed to find in a leader. He was the recipient of a "protest" vote that was both antiestablishment and based on moral dissatisfaction with the political system. Although it was not the same tendency that developed around Wallace in 1968, McCarthy tapped another tendency that provided enough organized energy for a strong presidential bid.[24] The McGovern campaign could be called a legatee of the earlier McCarthy and Robert Kennedy tendencies, but it had a more homogeneous ideological following that captured the nomination while deeply dividing the Democratic party. The results of the new rules and procedures for selecting delegates to the national convention caused many regular party leaders and interest groups to feel antagonistic toward McGovern's candidacy in the general election. Despite rifts between the McGovern organization and organized labor and regular party professionals, the McGovern candidacy represented an electoral tendency in the Democratic party that developed an effective organization around which particular ideological groups could cluster.

This pattern of linking a particular candidate's campaign organization with an ideological mood constitutes the most prevalent form of tendency in recent American politics. Especially during primary campaigns, such ideological movements evolve into highly organized factions designed to facilitate electoral victory. However, these amateur ideological groups usually continue to play critical roles even when sophisticated campaign techniques are implemented. Since these ideological disciples constitute cadres that can do the necessary campaign work that the understaffed regular party organization can no longer do, they acquire influence disproportionate to their actual numbers. The low-turnout primaries are particularly vulnerable to the impact of intense activity by the ideologically committed few. As witness to this proposition, consider how busloads of students provided the critical impetus for the McCarthy and McGovern campaigns in the New Hampshire Democratic presidential primary in 1968 and 1972, respectively. In both cases the front-runner (Lyndon Johnson and Edmund Muskie) was undone by the lack of intense activists doing their door-to-door campaigning.

Intraparty Competition by Factions

Party factions have several distinct properties that differentiate them from tendencies. Factions should approach the minimal characteristics of a rudimentary organization and possess (1) explicit consensually shared major goals; (2) a formal structure of authority that facilitates the activities of a cadre; (3) technical expertise to aid in the mobilization of support; (4) temporal durability; (5) internal and external communications networks; (6) an incentive system to reward members and sympathizers; and (7) a group or ideology around which the motives of often diverse types of activists can cohere and through which factional goals can be developed and pursued. The critical distinctions between factions and tendencies are in the development of cadres and an internal communications network that sustains the faction over time. A faction is marked by a persistent organizational structure (formal or informal), and a tendency is only momentarily organized, if at all.

The general decline of party organization in the twentieth century has also limited the likelihood of stable factional activity. The limited rewards available to cadres, the personalization of political campaigning, and the fragmentation of partisan participation caused by progressive reforms, especially civil service and the direct primary, all combine to make factions difficult to organize and sustain. The growth of independent voting and ticket-splitting has also contributed to an environment not conducive to factional development. The decentralization of government structure and the separation of branches of government have continued to provide some potential for party factions by maintaining sufficient institutional basis for ongoing, *geographically* based political cleavages. The major alternative basis of constructing factions comes from participation of some interest groups within the party structure. When the group has a strong partisan identification and an extensive membership—labor unions, for example—it can become an important component in a tendency, like the New Deal Coalition within the Democratic party. But the group interest usually precludes submersion into an ongoing faction or complete identification with a particular party. Interest groups are more likely to support a specific candidate or associate generally with one wing or tendency within the party.

LEGISLATIVE FACTIONS

The principal identifiable factions found in political parties in the United States today are either legislatively based or ideological intraparty organizations. Legislative factions often are based on ideology or specific coalitions of interest groups, although both characteristics are usually also closely related to and expressed through geographical cleavages. It is important to differentiate between such factional entities in terms of governmental level. Because regularized communications, organizational control, and consensus on goals all tend to decrease the further one ascends the governmental ladder, factional activity tends to show considerable variation on all these elements, depending on whether one is looking at local, state, or national legislative factions.

At the national level, one of the most enduring and important factional phenomena in the American Congress has been the Conservative Coalition. Since the time of Franklin Roosevelt, this alliance has existed between conservative Republicans and conservative Democrats, mostly from the South. This cross-party coalition translated ideological legislative factions into a powerful force for congressional policy-making. The nonprogrammatic, decentralized character of the American party system is reflected in the Congress, where party discipline gives way to compromise, defections, and cross-party coalition formation. Manley points out that the Conservative Coalition has had varying degrees of success in influencing policy. For example, it has dominated national policy-making by passing conservative legislation and stalemating liberal bills (80th Congress, 1947–1948), while at other times it has had little effect on blocking sweeping legislation extending the scope of federal intervention in the nation's life (89th Congress, 1965–1966).[25]

There has been some controversy over the actual "existence" of the coalition because of the informal nature of its factional interaction in the House and Senate. The coalition has operated in a subtle fashion with almost no evidence of formal organizational structure. Manley points out that

> Simple policy agreement may be the single most important element holding the Conservative Coalition together, but the claim that the Coalition is no more than an accidental meeting of minds is excessive. There is substantial evidence of joint planning on the part of coalition leaders and ... a number of cases of overt bipartisan cooperation. . . . The fact that no regular formal caucuses of conservatives are held, and the fact that Republicans sometimes vote with Northern Democrats against Southern Democrats, are insufficient to support the claim that the Coalition is many times a consciously designed force in the legislative process. . . .[26]

Several of the leaders of the coalition during the 1950s and 1960s have given testimony to its existence and mode of operation. Representative Howard W. ("Judge") Smith (D.-Virginia), a powerful figure in House appropriations struggles during the 1950s and 1960s, observed that

> Our group—we called it our group for want of a better term—was fighting appropriations. We did not meet publicly. The meetings were not formal. Our group met in one building, and the conservative Republicans in another, on different issues. Then Eugene Cox, Bill Colmer or I would go over to speak with the Republicans, or the Republican leaders might come to see us. It was very informal. A coalition did exist in legislation, but we met in small groups.[27]

While the Conservative Coalition is a unique case in that it relies on cross-party cooperation and has no formal structure, it nonetheless meets the requirements of a legislative faction because of the close communication and concerted action between its voting members and their staffs.

Other legislative factions at the national level include the liberal House Democratic Study Group and the Republican Senate and House "Wednesday Clubs." Named for the day on which it meets, the Wednesday Club represents a faction that attempts to offset total conservative domination of the Republican party. One of its most recent activities was lobbying with former President Ford on behalf of retaining Vice-President Nelson A. Rockefeller on the GOP ticket in 1976. Senators Clifford Case, Jacob Javits, and Charles Percy expressed concern over their perception of Ford administration favoritism toward the conservative wing of the party that is centered in the smaller states. The 1972 Republican National Convention witnessed an open struggle between a faction of delegates from the larger states, with heavy electoral votes, and the smaller states, over delegate apportionment. The Wednesday Club openly articulated its belief that since its fourteen members represented 162 out of 270 electoral voted needed for election, the state parties and urban constituencies it represented ought to have had greater imput into President Ford's reelection strategy and national party policy for 1976.

The communications opportunities are more constant at local and state party levels, and, therefore, the instance of party faction formation and continuing activity is considerably greater within local and state party organizations. Particularly àt the state level, the divisions between party organizations based in major metropolitan areas and those elsewhere in the state, between distinct regions within the state, between legislators representing safe seats and those from marginal districts, and between legislative groups supporting and opposing the governor, all have durable bases of support in local party organizations. These bases allow such groupings to approach the status of factions with cadres, internal communications patterns and rewards based on protection, and extension of persistent interests underlying the groupings. Nearly all states have a long history of factional activity based on these geographical cleavages. They were present during the period of patronage politics, when they reinforced machine factions, and they have persisted after the decline of patronage resources and political machines. These geographical cleavage factions are most notable and effective in state legislatures where the considerable potential for internal communication and rewards is especially suitable for sustaining factional politics on a continuing basis. In local government, similar opportunities exist to a lesser degree, with the high likelihood of less continuity and less formal organization.

The most common expression of geographical cleavages in state legislative activity is the conflict between the biggest city in the state and the rest of the state: Chicago and downstate Illinois; New York City and upstate New York; or Atlanta and rural Georgia. Based on different social and interest groups, the legislators are divided not only on a partisan basis but also within parties. The long-standing conflict between relatively rural Democrats from downstate Illinois and Chicago Democrats selected by the Cook County machine of Mayor Richard Daley led to prolonged balloting in early 1975, when they failed to agree on a party choice for Speaker of the General Assembly (the lower house of the state legislature). The resulting deadlock over what is usually a strict party-line vote paralyzed the Illinois legislature for more than a month. These conflicts are usually much less obvious, but are a general feature in state legislative politics, and enter into the resolution of many issues.

Representation by geographical district heightens legislative sensitivity to interests that are concentrated in specific constituencies. Since the common characteristics of rural districts are likely to enter into many legislative issues, the rural legislators are likely to interact so frequently with each other that continuing communication and organization (formal or informal) will be natural and rational. As members of such a faction, the rewards of joint action (maximizing their voting power) will reinforce continued participation. Similar factions will develop among other legislators whose interests coincide with those of specific legislators over a large range of issues. Geographical cleavages are most likely because they are a shorthand expression of typical clusters of issues, and not because geography is always a dominant factor.

IDEOLOGICAL FACTIONS

Another type of American intraparty faction deals with the achievement of ideological policy objectives by means of party reform and regeneration. This category of extralegal organizations often has an intelligentsia at its core and closely approximates our concept of faction. The "amateur" club movements of the twentieth century waged internecine warfare with "professionals" in regular party organizations and placed a much higher emphasis on political issues than did the "regulars."[28] The club movement was an instrument for both local electoral objectives and ideological programs and its achievements in New York, Wisconsin, and California deserve mention.

The New York Democratic Reform Clubs had a highly developed organizational structure built to destroy the Tammany Hall machine, and they attracted a highly educated, upper-status type of party activist. These organizations attempted to replace the cadre structure of the regular party with a club membership that would appeal to the interests of young, idealistic reformers. Their memberships were usually motivated by a set of liberal policy goals and directed toward breaking the hierarchical authority of "bosses" by instituting intraparty democracy. The club movement was opposed to the personal and ethnic material rewards of traditional party politics and sought to reorient the direction of the party organization toward ideological issues and principles. They were able to offer candidates and periodically win control of segments of the Democratic organization in New York City.

The Wisconsin Voluntary Organizations developed as a conservative Republican splinter group during the 1920s. Sorauf points out that the conservative wing always lost in primaries to the LaFollette progressive wing, so it formed a separate, extralegal party organization to represent its ideology and support its candidates in the primary.[29] When the progressives formed their own state party in the 1930s, the "regular" Republicans found it easier to operate through voluntary organizations than through the carefully regulated statutory organization. The Democrats did the same thing in the 1940s and 1950s, and at present both parties operate through these separate voluntary organizations, which parallel—county organization for county organization —the regular party structure. The voluntary organizations, bolstered by membership organizations in many counties of the state, hold the major substance of party power. By the late 1950s the two parties' voluntary organizations had enrolled some twenty thousand dues-paying members, most of them in urban areas.

The California Clubs developed in the 1930s, when liberal Republicans founded the California Republican Assembly to revive the faltering Republican party. A conservative competitor, the United Republicans of California, sprang up in the early 1960s to oppose the liberals of the CRA, and conservatives captured the CRA just a short time later. In 1965 the liberal Republicans started a new set of organizations, the California Republican League. Among California Democrats, the liberal California Democratic Clubs were founded in 1953 by remnants of Adlai Stevenson supporters, and the CDC organization has become a major faction within the state party.

Other examples of extralegal organizations that have the potential to engage in ideological factional activity are the various Democratic and Republican auxiliaries. These are primarily state-level women's and youth organizations that have united into national federations having close ties to the official state and national party committees. Groups such as Young Democrats, College Republicans, and the Federation of Republican Women retain independent status but very rarely create overt factional conflict. However, the youth groups provide arenas for internal ideological battles of contending factional groups in the regular party. The election of officers at state youth group conventions often are contested along bitter ideological lines that involve conflict between factions and lead to the creation of elaborate coalitions. Friction between senior party organizations and youth auxiliaries is not uncommon and usually stems from a combination of youthful exuberance and lack of communication. The women's groups usually maintain a more conformist position with the regular party that includes fund raising and unglamorous campaign work such as canvassing, telephoning, and grass-roots organizational chores. However, in presidential years, militant women's rights groups have been formed in both parties to press for issues favorable to the women's movement.

Regional organizations of party officials and officeholders recently have begun to develop and to hold periodic conferences. In the South, the Southern Republicans Conference has been especially active. It provides a platform for prominent national Republicans, offers workshops on campaign organization, and discusses issues of regional concern. A similar pair of organizations has grown around state governors. Republican governors were especially active immediately following Goldwater's defeat in 1964 and established a full-time Washington office with financial assistance from the Republican National Committee. Of late, with the increase in their number, a similar attempt by Democratic governors to play a role in the Democratic National Committee has developed. They have used their conferences to articulate state and metropolitan problems and to complain of presidential and congressional party insensitivity to the gubernatorial presence in the ruling circles of the party. These organizations help to provide a barometer by which to measure the ideological balance of power within both parties, and they help to identify important political issues.

The policy-making bodies of the national committees themselves have reflected intraparty factional divisions in their deliberations. For example, the Democratic Policy Council was established by the Democratic National Committee in 1969 to replace the old Democratic Advisory Council. The latter group was formed in 1956 by liberal Stevenson Democrats to prevent the senators and representatives of the "congressional party" from controlling the national Democratic party. The Policy Council (DPC) was established to develop programs on major issues and generally took traditional liberal positions. Sorauf describes how its traditional liberalism met with protests from former supporters of the McCarthy and Robert Kennedy campaigns who represented a new left wing of the party, and who were able to gain increased representation. He adds that

> their supporters generally intend them to prevent the party's congressional party from acting as the only spokesman of the opposition party. That desire to compete with the congressional party stems from disapproval of the relative conservatism of the party's congressmen. Second, groups such as the DPC are intended as the opposition party's mechanism for opposing the president's policies.[30]

Formal organizations like the DPC are internal ideological voices and tend to function as continuous platform committees that reflect the views of ideological factions within American parties.

On the Republican side, there are numerous examples of factional activity that are characterized by ideological intensity, durable organizational structure, and communications networks that provide both internal control and external propaganda potential. The persistence of well-structured and relatively consistent alignments of state delegations to Republican national conventions since 1940 with either conservative or moderate-to-liberal presidential candidates argues that these ideological tendencies approach factional status.[31]

Numerous organizations within the Republican party have contributed to and reflect this ideological polarization. On the GOP left, the Ripon Society is a lonely but notable example.[32] Although GOP conservatives perceive Ripon as a collection of button-down Abbie Hoffmans, their general approach to political change is rather mild and not radical in the new left sense of the term. Ripon was patterned after the highly successful Bow group in the British Conservative party and continues to pamphleteer and urge a broad-based pluralistic Republican party that is not dominated by conservative dogma. Named for the city in Wisconsin that claims to be the birthplace of the Republican party, the society is mostly composed of young Eastern academic and professional activists whose work is scholarly and directed toward broadening the ideological and social base of the Republican party.

Republicans for Progress was another organization of the GOP center-left that developed as an outgrowth of the Committee to Support Moderate Republicans, which was set up to funnel money to anti-Goldwater candidates.[33] RFP primarily functioned as a research agency and fund-raising organization for liberal Republican candidates. The web of interlocking affiliations of RFP is interesting. For example, in 1955–1956 it gave $18,000 to the Committee for Republican Research, whose function in turn was to underwrite a staff for the group of liberal Republican congressmen in the Wednesday Club.

Other moderate GOP organizations developed in the early 1960s to oppose the candidacy of Barry Goldwater. The All-Republican Conference met in Gettysburg at the farm of General Eisenhower, its honorary chairman. They developed several working committees to develop issues and candidates that moderate Republicans could support. After Goldwater's defeat, a similar organization of Republican leaders was established, called the Republican Coordinating Committee. The Republican Wednesday Club and the Republican congressional leadership in both houses appear to be the current major spokesmen for Republican moderates.

On the opposite end of the ideological spectrum, several groups continue to raise money for the support of conservative candidates. United Republicans of America and the American Conservative Union (ACU) are political education and action groups that serve as Republican ideological factions.[34] The ACU in the mid-1960s was led by Congressman John Ashbrook, who steered the financially plagued ACU into a close alliance with another nonpartisan conservative group, Young Americans for Freedom.

The development of these formal intraparty ideological organizations suggests that a potential substitute to the old-style patronage factional system is a more comprehensive organization of ideological factions focused on specific groups concerned with maintaining certain ideological tendencies. The persistent cleavage between liberal Democrats and other Democrats, and the high probability that the ideologically motivated will participate in politics, provide a basis for a communications system among like-minded activists which could give more shape and definition to a tendency and make it something approaching a faction. For example, the previously mentioned Democratic Study Group within the U.S. Congress and a fund-raising organization, the National Committee for an Effective Congress, perform these two functions to some degree.[35] Similarly, the recently active Committee on Conservative Alternatives can help to give more coherence, more effective communication, and more sense of definition and belonging to a conservative faction within the Republican party. Such developments are very rudimentary presently and have only begun to be studied, but constitute a promising line of development.

Factions as Agents of Third Parties and Realignments

A final way to view American party factions concerns their role in the evolutionary patterns associated with historical instances of party realignments. The factors affecting the perpetuation of two-partyism are well known, but their relationship to mature varieties of factionalism that have realigning potential need to be made explicit. The single-member district–plurality election rule, the necessity of forming national coalitions in competition for the presidency, partisan loyalty and direct party primaries, and the myriad statutory barriers related to ballot laws, filing deadlines, and petition requirements all make the growth potential of factional parties rather limited.[36] However, significant party realignments and third parties have periodically occurred in American history. Unlike the minor national or local factions and parties, this type of disturbance in normal two-party patterns is identifiable by its wide voter appeal and its ability to cleave the constituencies of the two major parties.[37]

Issues framed in moral dimensions that can be exploited and articulated by zealous leaders often provide the initial source of such factional developments. Such factional activists choose to support a position in defiance of regular party leadership, and at the expense of party unity. The developmental sequence portrayed in the following diagram depicts an ideal model of the stages of such potent factional activity at the national level:

salient issues	party	party	minor or major
and interests	tendency	faction	third party
articulated and	develops	develops	activity and
aggregated			possible realignment

The preconditions for this type of factional development are periods of intense issue cleavage resulting from severe political crisis and stress. Such salient issues and their entrepreneurial leaders develop followings within existing parties that surface as tendencies. Ideological wings of parties and electoral organizations based on mixtures of issues and personalism are manifested in this preinstitutionalization stage.

The passage of these party tendencies into the faction stage depends on the intensity, duration of commitment, and leadership skills of the dissidents. If the type of issue flares briefly, subsides, is unable to overcome the straddling efforts of regular party centrists, and is unable to sustain a division in public opinion, then major party disruption is averted. However, if issue saliency continues to grow, and voters revise their perceptions of the core meanings attached to the parties, and as tendencies become institutionalized as minority factions with organizational structure, the possibility of more permanent party divisions emerges.

This pattern has been operative at several points in American political history and has resulted in important alterations in the party system.[38] The realignment of the 1850s provides a classic example of how intense factional activity can bring about such significant party change. The slavery issue had polarized the nation and cut squarely across the two major parties that existed at that time, the Democrats and Whigs. These polar political forces began to cleave the major parties as the presidential election campaign of 1848 began. By the election of 1860, slavery had hardened the factionalism within the Democratic party, leading to the nomination of candidates from its Northern and Southern wings, and allowing Lincoln and the Republicans to rise from obscurity to the presidency in four short years.

However, severe political crisis need not always lead to the type of major party factionalization described above. An alternative is the splintering from the parties of tendency groups which, along with independents, become susceptible to the appeals of a personality or ideology organized within a transitory third party. In such a situation, no organized intraparty factions need occur among activists or leaders for fundamental shifts in mass voting to take place. The American Independent party (AIP) and George Wallace in 1968 fit such a description. National preoccupation with race relations, Vietnam, and law and order had divided the parties and electorate and created an intense minority that was "hawkish" on both Vietnam and domestic issues. While the Democratic and Republican parties occupied the center on these issues, Wallace was able to appeal to many voters who were overwhelmingly committed to an extremely punitive minority position on Vietnam, race, and crime. The sharp increase in the number of independent voters in America increases the possibility that ideological factionalism may express itself in temporary third-party movements in future periods of political and social unrest.

American party history contains a large number of minor ideologically based third parties that never were capable of having a major impact on elections. Such parties often perform a factional role and function as propaganda disseminators, and often act as a temporary base for both nonpartisan ideological interest groups and disenchanted major party activists. Competitive, ideological warfare characterizes such parties.

Ideologues who feel disenchanted about ever achieving control in the Democratic or Republican parties may prefer to participate in the long-standing minor parties. Parties such as the Socialist party and its various spin-offs, and the New York Liberal and Conservative parties, are examples of homogeneous, ideological parties that continue to thrive on emotional, moralistic crusades. The problem faced by such parties is that they constantly risk being overshadowed by the existing ideological wings in the major parties. Thayer points out this problem as it was experienced by New York Liberal party:

> the Liberals . . . are always haunted by the specter that, were there no Liberal party at all, most of the faithful would vote liberal Democratic anyway. This explains why the party feels it very important to maintain the image of a pure, mildly crusading organization because, without it, no one could tell the difference between a Liberal and a Democrat. Secondly, the Reform Democrats, those hardy souls who always seem to be battling Carmine DeSapio . . . are rivals to the Liberal party. If these people can accomplish the necessary purification of the Democratic party, the reasoning goes, then there is no need for the Liberals. This development has created the ludicrous situation in which two reform groups are battling each other for survival.[39]

Such a pattern is characteristic of minor American third parties due to the consensual, pluralistic character of the major parties. Internal tolerance of ideological heterogeneity and temporary exit and reentry activity often preclude the organizational alienation that can lead to intense factional politics and permanent third party formation.

Conclusions

Factions in the United States have developed concurrently with democratic institutions, mass participation, and the structural attributes that maintain a two-party system. Factions emerged in the eighteenth century as intermediate linkage devices that often were based on familistic, sectional, or philosophical differences. As organized parties took form, factions became constrained by the narrowing effects of special interests and constituencies which they identified with and represented. Competition between the major parties maintained some measure of cohesion in the nineteenth century, but factional divisions frequently surfaced and altered both the parties themselves and their bases of support. The development of the spoils system, patronage, and political machines provided a way to maintain factional structures through a reward system. Upon the demise of machines, patronage-based factions only continued in areas of economic depression or where particular institutional arrangements or leadership styles encouraged them (e.g., Louisiana, Chicago, Jersey City). The decentralization of American parties and their nonprogrammatic nature have not provided an environment for the type of doctrinaire ideological factions that are tendencies in many countries in Western Europe.

Two varieties of factional activity exist: tendencies and factions. Tendencies are less structured, less stable, and less enduring patterns of internal party competition and are classified according to two attributes: electoral and ideological. The most common tendencies are candidate-centered party organizations that wage political battle and then usually disintegrate. Often such tendencies have ideological roots because they represent various ideological wings of the party. Tendencies often are linked to political subculture and vary by region, state, or locality. The linking of a candidate's campaign organization with an ideological mood constitutes the most common form of tendency in current American politics.

Intraparty factions have a higher degree of organizational structure and a cadre that persists over time. The principal factions found today are either legislative or ideological and vary according to level of government and geographical region. Reform groups and club movements in many states provide numerous examples of U.S. factions. Party auxiliaries, regional organizations of officeholders, and various ideologically based committees and organizations constitute another set of factions that operate either within or outside the legal party apparatus.

American party factions also have played a historical role as important agents in the creation of third parties and major party realignments. In periods of intense political crisis, tendencies and factions frequently surface and lead to party divisions and realignments and third party formation. The contemporary Wallace movement has generally operated outside the organizational factions in the major parties.

Formal party factions in the United States do not exist in the same manner as they do in other political systems. Since the pluralistic American parties are not heavily ideological or representative of a single interest, it is difficult for them to sustain rigid factionalism over long periods of time. Increasing educational levels and distrust of government by the American public have created a loss of acceptance of party labels as cues to political participation. Unquestioning party loyalty has given way to independence and discrimination in choosing among issues and candidates. Since the American two-party system requires a politics of low intensity and pragmatic consensus in order to form winning electoral coalitions, it appears that the major sources of factionalism currently are tangential to the parties. The number of independent candidacies and ideological or issue movements has grown substantially over the last decade, and Sorauf points out that "all of these nonparty organizations will reflect and embrace the new ideological politics in a way the parties never could. . . . Amateur voluntary organizations within the parties are probably less vital and influential today than they were in the 1950s. Issue-oriented and ideological activists increasingly turn outside the party."[40] Even McGovern's capture of the Democratic party from 1968 to 1972 was a tendency phenomenon rather than a bona fide faction struggle. The

McGovern forces' success was achieved outside the regular party and the pluralistic, heterogeneous nature of the Democratic party could not support intense, highly structured, organizational factionalism.

What appears to be taking place in this context of party decline is the ascendance of electoral tendencies as a major vehicle by which parties contest their internal conflict. The "new" electoral politics of personalism, media, and the manipulation of short-term issues has replaced traditional party politics in many locales. Party politics may increasingly resemble the previously mentioned one-party factionalism and personalism characterizing the American South in the 1940s and 1950s. In this environment, traditional party organizations merely act as props for the media, and campaign "factional" organizations treat the party organizations as a facade that must be worn. Under the present party system, even when a particular ideological wing takes control of the party machinery, its purism and intensity become diluted as pragmatism and "professionalism" reassert themselves and factional identity gives way to consensus politics.

The 1976 Jimmy Carter campaign is a good example of an electoral tendency that successfully mastered the new party rules and limited factional conflict. President Carter's strategy of running in all the primaries and in caucus states where proportional representation was in effect allowed him to operate outside the divisions caused by state party factionalism. His early primary success attracted maximum media exposure that built momentum and eventually drew in diverse party factions and tendencies whose common denominator was a preference for a winning candidate in the general election.

The creation of factional parties, according to the Western European model, might only take place if a major party reidentified with one dominant ideology could create such an environment for change. Thus, Burnham suggests that perhaps America is moving toward an alignment of the poor and the advantaged against the middle strata;[41] Rusher sees a realignment taking place that results in a conservative party representing "producers" (middle-class managers, blue-collar workers, farmers, etc.) and a liberal party of "consumers" (the poor, academics, bureaucrats, mass media sector, foundations, etc.).[42] However, if the parties have declined beyond a certain point, such realignments may be impossible and electoral tendencies might continue to grow in importance.

Perhaps a hybrid form of American party faction is developing without detection. The great complexity of the American political system makes any plotting of institutional shifts extremely difficult. The evolution of certain ideologically based electoral tendencies could lead to their institution as structured organizations within the parties. The recent growth of ideological participation and conflict within the major parties could significantly improve the environment for the development of party factions. Certainly some of the evidence summarized above supports the plausibility of such a trend. The role of ideological organizations as nuclei within tendencies, the increase of ideological incentives to partisan and factional participation, and factional conflict as a stage in party realignment provide a fertile environment for a type of American party faction that has both a clear ideological identity and the capacity to compromise for party survival.

NOTES

1. Austin Ranney and Willmore Kendall, *Democracy and the American Party System* (New York: Harcourt, Brace, 1956), pp. 88–89; and George B. Adams, *Constitutional History of England* (New York: Holt, Rinehart and Winston, 1934), pp. 334–37, discuss this transition.

2. See Ranney and Kendall, *Democracy and the American Party System*, ch. 5; and William Nisbet Chambers, *Political Parties in a New Nation: The American Experience, 1776–1809* (New York: Oxford Univ. Press, 1963).

3. Among the many places this argument is summarized is Judson L. James, *American Political Parties in Transition* (New York: Harper and Row, 1974), pp. 34–40.

4. Chambers, *Political Parties in a New Nation*, pp. 4–5.

5. Ibid., ch. 2–4.

6. James, *American Political Parties in Transition*, pp. 73–81.

7. Frank R. Kent, *The Great Game of Politics* (New York: Doubleday, Doran, 1935), provides an excellent description of the characteristics and operation of the political machine based on patronage.

8. Ibid., pp. 24–27, is a representative description of the political machine-faction relationship.

9. Frank J. Sorauf, "The Silent Revolution in Patronage," *Public Administrative Review* 20, no. 1 (Winter 1960): 28–34.

10. V. O. Key, Jr., *Southern Politics in State and Nation* (New York: Alfred A. Knopf, 1949), p. 159.

11. Harnett T. Kane, *Louisiana Hayride* (New York: William Morrow and Co., 1941), p. 434.

12. Allan P. Sindler, "Bifactional Rivalry as an Alternative to Two-Party Competition in Louisiana," *American Political Science Review* 49, no. 3 (Sept. 1955): 641–62.

13. See Raymond Wolfinger, "Why Political Machines Have Not Withered Away and Other Revisionist Thoughts," *Journal of Politics* 34 (May 1972): 365–98.

14. Richard Rose, "Parties, Factions, and Tendencies in Great Britain," *Political Studies* 12, no. 1 (Feb. 1964): 31–46.

15. Ibid., p. 107 (emphasis added).

16. Lewis Chester, Godfrey Hodgson, and Bruce Page, *An American Melodrama: The Presidential Campaign of 1968* (New York: Dell, 1969), pp. 421–23.

17. Ibid.; John H. Kessel, *The Goldwater Coalition* (Indianapolis: Bobbs-Merrill, 1968); Theodore H. White, *The Making of the President, 1964* (New York: Atheneum, 1965); and Denis G. Sullivan et al., *The Politics of Representation* (New York: St. Martin's Press, 1974).

18. This argument is more fully developed by Joseph A. Schlesinger in his article, "Political Party Organizations," in James E. March, ed., *Handbook of Organizations* (Chicago: Rand-McNally, 1965), pp., 764–801; see also March, *Ambition and Politics* (Chicago: Rand-McNally, 1966).

19. Daniel J. Elazar, *American Federalism*, 2d ed. (New York: Thomas Y. Crowell, 1972), ch. 4.

20. V. O. Key, Jr., *Southern Politics*, ch. 14.

21. See Ibid., ch. 13; also John C. Topping, Jr., John R. Lazarek, and William H. Linder, *Southern Republicanism and the New South* (Cambridge, Mass.: Ripon Society, 1966); and Ripon Society, *Jaws of Victory* (Boston: Little, Brown, 1974), pp. 288–95.

22. Seymour Martin Lipset and Earl Raab, "The Wallace Whitelash," *Trans-action* 7 (Dec. 1969): 23–35.

23. See Aaron Wildavsky, "The Goldwater Phenomenon: Purists, Politicians and the Two-Party System," *Review of Politics* 27, no. 3 (July 1965): 386–413.

24. For a psychological interpretation of the motivations of McCarthy supporters, see Steven R. Brown and John D. Ellithorp, "Emotional Experience in Political Groups: The Case of the McCarthy Phenomenon," *American Political Science Review* 64, no. 2 (June 1970): 349–68.

25. See John F. Manley, "The Conservative Coalition in Congress," *American Behavioral Scientist* 17 (Nov.–Dec. 1973): 223–47.

26. Ibid., p. 231.

27. Quoted in ibid., pp. 231–32.

28. See James Q. Qilson, *The Amateur Democrat* (Chicago: Univ. of Chicago Press, 1962); Francis Carney, *The Rise of Democratic Clubs in California* (New York: McGraw-Hill, 1960); Leon D. Epstein, *Politics in Wisconsin* (Madison: Univ. of Wisconsin Press, 1958); and Thomas H. Roback, "Amateurs and Professionals: Delegates to the 1972 Republican National Convention," *Journal of Politics* 37 (May 1975): 436–68.

29. Frank J. Sorauf, *Party Politics in America* (Boston: Little, Brown, 1972), p. 79. See also Epstein, *Politics in Wisconsin*, pp. 80–81.

30. Sorauf, *Party Politics in America*, p. 31.

31. The continuity in Republican factionalism is documented by Frank J. Munger and James Blackhurst, "Factionalism in the National Conventions, 1940–1964: An Analysis of Ideological Consistency in State Delegation Voting," *Journal of Politics* 27 (May 1965): 375–94.

32. See the discussion in Stephan Hess and David S. Broder, *The Republican Establishment* (New York: Harper and Row, 1967), pp. 68–70. See also Ripon Society, *Jaws of Victory.*

33. See Hess and Broder, *The Republican Establishment,* pp. 71–73.

34. Ibid., pp. 76–77.

35. See Harry M. Scoble, "Political Money: A Study of Contributors to the National Committee for an Effective Congress," *Midwest Journal of Political Science* 7, no. 3 (Aug. 1963): 229–53.

36. For a more complete discussion of these factors, see Douglas W. Rae, *The Political Consequences of Electoral Laws* (New Haven: Yale Univ. Press, 1967), ch. 5.

37. Major faction-based realignments occurred in the 1850s, 1890s, and 1930s, and minor realignments in several other periods. Mazmanian points out that the average third-party vote cast for the presidency equaled 5.6 percent of the total popular vote. Ten parties have surpassed that average in eight elections extending from the Anti-Mason party of 1832 to the American Independent party of 1968. See Daniel A. Mazmanian, *Third Parties in Presidential Elections* (Washington, D.C.: Brookings Institution, 1974), pp. 4–5.

38. For a detailed discussion of these variables and outcomes, see James L. Sundquist, *Dynamics of the Party System* (Washington, D.C.: Brookings Institution, 1973), pp. 16–35.

39. George Thayer, *The Farther Shores of Politics* (New York: Simon and Schuster, 1968), pp. 454–55.

40. Sorauf, *Party Politics in America*, p. 418.

41. Walter Dean Burnham, *Critical Elections and the Mainsprings of American Politics* (New York: Norton, 1970), pp. 137–40.

42. William A. Rusher, *The Making of the New Majority Party* (New York: Sheed and Ward, 1975).

Part Four
Single-Party Systems

In this section, studies of factions in two single-party political systems are presented. Single-party systems are those in which one party claims a moral and/or legal monopoly of political representation and political activity. No other party is permitted to compete with the exclusive party, which, through its control of the government and its enforcement machinery, either lawfully forbids or effectively prevents any rivals from competing politically. In short, organized political *competition* with the exclusive party is prohibited. The basic characteristic of a single-party system is this absence of any organized party competition, and of *any* organized opposition; in contrast to the dominant-party system, the single-party system is characterized by a dominating party which eliminates its competition.

The claim of the exclusive party in a single-party system to a monopoly of power and governmental office has its limits. Institutions and groups do exist and possess organization, and may be expected either to compete for control of the exclusive party from within, as they do for example in Communist China; or, if outside the party, they may resist the monopolistic orientation of the exclusive party to the extent that they can, as they did in the regime of Franco Spain. Thus, prohibitions notwithstanding, organized interests exist even in single-party systems, and compete for control of the dominant party's drive for supremacy and exclusiveness in the system.

In the single-party systems of these case studies, the exclusive parties are Marxist-Leninist—i.e., Communist—parties. Communist parties have unique forms of factionalism because of their extraordinary ideological as well as political determination to prohibit development of intraparty groups, which is part of what makes them "authoritarian" regimes. The two chapters in this section include factional analyses of authoritarian single-party systems of the Soviet Union and the People's Republic of China. In Chapter 15, Carl Linden analyzes the intraparty factional pattern in the Communist party regime of the U.S.S.R., and in those of Communist countries generally, drawing comparisons among varied examples of a consistent Communist pattern of factionalism. In Chapter 16, Andrew Nathan reviews in detail a model of the faction as a special type of group formation, together with the major distinctive characteristics of factional behavior. He then builds a deductive argument that factionalism is a plausible explanation for elite politics in China on the grounds of the circumstantial evidence of the behavior of the Chinese elite.

15

Opposition and Faction in Communist Party Leaderships

CARL A. LINDEN

A paradox immediately strikes the observer of the history of the modern Communist movement and the internal politics of the Communist parties. The movement was founded on the conviction that worldwide revolution was assured by a proletariat forged into a massive and seamless instrument of political and class coercion. This Herculean task was to be achieved in Lenin's conception by a single-minded leadership of Communists unified and armed for action by the Marxists' science of society and revolution. Yet, despite the notable successes of Leninist Marxists as engineers of power, Communist leaderships have in practice been plagued from their inception by a chronic splitting tendency within their ranks. In fact, Marx's opening line in the first chapter of the *Communist Manifesto* may be parodied and applied to the history of Marxist politics so as to read: "The inner-history of all hitherto societies of Marxists is a history of factional struggle." Cycles of schism, reformation, and renewed schism have followed one upon another.

A HISTORY OF FACTIONAL STRUGGLE

Marx and his followers fought fiercely against the anticentrist Proudhonists and anarchists, among others, for the leadership of the First International until that association of revolutionists broke down under

361

the strain of the conflict. The Second International, formed after Marx's death, became the arena of combat between evolutionary and revolutionary Marxist Socialists. A house divided against itself, it too collapsed, at the outbreak of World War I, when conflict between revolutionary and national loyalties pulled it apart.

Lenin, who assisted in the work of destruction of the Second International, picked up the pieces to build the Third International of Marxist parties. It was the most fateful of attempts at reformation of the Marxist movement for the politics of the modern world as a whole. The Bolshevik faction Lenin formed in Russia before World War I and the breakaway factions in the European Social Democratic parties which accepted his lead provided the nucleus of the new International and were the forebears of today's Communist parties.

The Leninist branch of political Marxism, as distinguished from Marxist schools of social and economic theory, has been animated by a creed of political and ideological monolithism far exceeding the solidarist notions of other Marxist parties. Nonetheless, Communist parties have been periodically shaken by internecine factional conflicts, ranging from the Stalin-Trotsky fight for Lenin's mantle after the latter's death, to today's conflict between the Soviet and Chinese Communist party-states. The patterns of factional conflict in and among the parties display striking similarities. While these patterns have sources in Marxism itself, their specific features can be found in Lenin's founding model of the Communist party and party-state.

Lenin saw himself as the savior of the revolutionary soul of Marxism. He engaged in constant polemics against proclaimed revisionists of Marxist teaching, like Eduard Bernstein in German Social Democracy. Through a succession of splits he forced in Russian Marxism, he produced a kind of purified remnant of professionalized revolutionists. His concept of the new party is contained in his well-known pamphlet *What Is to Be Done?*, his polemic against all who in his lights blunted the revolutionary thrust of Marxism.

In *What Is to Be Done?* Marxist theory is presented as a credo of action not subject to debate in its fundamentals. While put forward as truths of science, those fundamentals in Leninism are endowed with the sacred aura of truths of faith. Lenin later offered his following a new dispensation in his work *Imperialism,* his comprehensive and refurbished explanation of the twentieth century.

Marxist economic theory was increasingly interpreted by leaders in the mainstream of the European and Russian Marxist movements as justifying gradualist or phased approaches to political change. Social Democracy found new opportunity in winning power through constitutional rather than violent means in the increasingly democratic nation-states of Western Europe of the late nineteenth and early twentieth centuries. In *Imperialism* Lenin salvaged the determinist elements

of Marxist economic doctrine in a new interpretation of world developments, of imminent rather than delayed or moderated revolutionary
change. Lenin defined a new "imperialist" stage of wars among capitalist states. World War I to him marked the development of a new
stage and the disruption of capitalist systems by self-destructive conflict. Such conflict, according to Lenin, opened the way for the worldwide Communist-led revolution. Lenin's concept of the party and the
revolution taken together provided the basis for Lenin's formation of
a new "vanguard" to preside over the Marxist revolution in the twentieth century.

Lenin's concept of the Marxist revolutionary party marked a great
divide in the practice of modern Western politics. Though it logically
applied and extended certain political notions of radical minorities of
the modern West, it profoundly departed from the mainstream of
Western parliamentary and democratic constitutionalism in Europe
and the United States. It laid the foundation of the intramural politics
of the movement of Communist parties, and still explains the inner
political life of those parties.

LENIN VERSUS MADISON ON FACTION

The Leninist view of internal party politics can be usefully placed in
bold relief by comparing the views of Lenin and James Madison on the
question of factionalism. Just as Lenin was the theorist and founder of
the modern Communist party movement, James Madison occupies a
similar, if not so lonely, place in the theory and practice of pluralist
constitutional democracy in the modern world.

Both Lenin and Madison focused their attention on the problem
of faction in politics and how to deal with its destructive potential in
political groups. Lenin in founding the Soviet Communist party and
the Soviet one-party state sought to cure the "mischiefs of faction" by
means Madison rejected in his famous essay on faction in *Federalist,* no.
10. Lenin sought to remove the causes rather than to control the
effects of faction. Madison sought the reverse and recommended the
proposed American Constitution as a specific prescription for limiting
the destructive effects of faction in the United States. Madison's characterization of the methods for removing the causes of faction in
politics can be paraphrased to describe Lenin's approach. Lenin, and
most of those following in his stead, worked to destroy "the liberty
essential to the existence of factions" in the party and party-state. They
have rather sought to give every member of the party "the same opinions, the same passions, and the same interests."

On one point Lenin and Madison generally agree—the term *faction* retains the original and defining sense which once was a common-
place of political discourse. The term is not simply a synonym for any
and all partisan groups in a political community as it is often used

today, but in its specific sense refers only to partisan groups whose purposes or deliberate actions injure the common good or interests of society as a whole or violate justice due to members of the society. However, Madison refers the common good or interest—and justice for the citizen—to the existing political community; Lenin transfers and attaches these ends, ultimately to the future revolution and the Communist community to which it is to give birth, and mediately to the agencies of the revolution— the party and the party-state.

The basic difference between Lenin and Madison resides ultimately in their view of human nature. For Madison, as will be recalled, the latent causes of faction are "sown in the nature of man," in his fallible reason and the consequent diversity of opinion among men, and the peculiar ties between his opinions and his passions which his egoism and self-love can produce. Moreover, for Madison, the diversity in men's abilities and talents—the gifts of human nature are not equally distributed among men— is a constant source of divisions and distinctions in society. Of the divisions and differentiations resulting from such causes, according to Madison, some are essential to society, some superficial or frivolous, and some register man's proclivity to fall into mutual enmity or to oppress each other instead of cooperating for a common good.

For Lenin, following Marx, not human nature but class society is the sole source of faction among men. Men in history are corrupted by class conflict where politics is a question of "who dominates whom," in Lenin's phrase. Man's nature, which only will be fully unfolded in its true form in postrevolutionary society, is innocent of blame. Class society in Marx and Lenin is inevitably the arena of conflicts. By definition these conflicts are factional conflicts—each class seeking through political struggle to enforce its own interest against the social interest of the whole. The factional character of classes applies also to the proletarian class, which in Marxist terms has no interest in preserving the society of which it is a part. Rather the proletarian class, once conscious of its interest, organizes itself into a "political party," according to both Marx and Lenin, dedicated to destroying and replacing it with a new society. Though destined to destruction, the internal differentiation of class society is an outcome of the division of labor which the historical and collective development of mankind's productive powers requires. This development of man's collective powers, from Lenin's Marxist view, entails the stunting of the individual faculties of the working class in cog-like factory production. Under capitalism—the epitome of the class stage of human society—society for Lenin is divided into master and slave classes beneath its differentiated external structures.

For Madison *political* liberty—freedom of speech, assembly, the franchise, etc.—while necessary to faction, is also essential to political life and to the release of the human powers and talents which contribute to the well-being of society. *Political* freedom for Lenin does not extend beyond, and is focused in, the party member's voluntary submission to the cause of revolution and to its agency, the party.

Where Madison viewed as impracticable any attempt to give all members of a political society the same opinions, passions, and interests, Lenin never doubted, first, that the formation of an indivisible elitist association of like-minded militants was practical, and second, that a similar like-mindedness could in turn be extended to the party membership and ultimately to the postrevolutionary society at large. The first goal Madison would have allowed was quite possible, since zealous partisans have often manifested such qualities of like-mindedness, but only temporarily; the second for Madison was both impractical and undesirable. Marxist theory here serves Lenin as the basis of the like-mindedness of the party membership and as a "science" of revolutionary action and basis of common policy.

In the Madisonian view political leadership should aim through constitutional structuring at making it difficult for a group with genuinely factional motives to win a stable and lasting majority necessary for enforcing its will on political society as a whole. The Communist party for Lenin, on the other hand, is designed as the minority spearhead of the proletarian party, which, as earlier indicated, is properly a faction in a world of class society even in Marxist lights. The party's professed function is winning supremacy and domination over capitalist and other classes through the institution of a political dictatorship. The latter, in turn, is to serve as the bridge to the classless society. However, in the long view for either Marx or Lenin, no group of "true" revolutionaries *within* the party itself and the party-state can be a faction in the ultimate sense. From the perspective of the future revolution, the Communists, in both Marx's view and Lenin's, stand outside and above all political parties and factions.

Yet, for Lenin, the party is never free of the menace of corruption through infection from the universal faction-class struggles in the surrounding world as seen in the Marxist analysis. Moreover, out of his own experience in the quasi-conspiratorial revolutionary politics of an authoritarian Tsarist Russia, he was disposed to see the enemy always at the gates ready to enter through the slightest fissure in the party's ranks, first secretly then openly, and to strike at its heart.

The Framework of Communist Factionalism

THE LENINIST IDEOLOGICAL TRADITION

It is within the framework of Lenin's concept of the monolithic party institution that the various factors which have produced factionalism and conflict in Communist parties have operated. Within this framework cleavages in Communist parties to this day have assumed patterns which have been variations on a theme. The attitude of collective party leaders is a kind of unity-of-opposites, combining a passion for unity with an acute sense of the potential for division among themselves.

Since the notion of a "loyal opposition" has little standing in party tradition, the dividing line between permissible intraparty debate and factional activity remains obscure. How is an element of the party to be judged as factional, i.e., in opposition to the interests of the revolution or the party? In theory, it is through a collective judgment of the party that the element is guilty of doctrinal error or deviation, or by the very fact that the element has formed itself into a group in opposition to established policy. The latter criterion was formally instituted in the Soviet party's statutes at the Tenth Party Congress in 1921 following the Kronstadt sailors' revolt against Bolshevik rule. It has since been formally adopted by virtually all other Communist parties. Nonetheless, in practice, the line between acceptable criticism and factional opposition has been drawn by the victors after a kind of behind-the-scenes trial by battle within the narrow circle of the leading group of a party.

The judgment and condemnation of the defeated as factionalists become the prerogative of the leader of the group winning a decisive ascendancy in the struggle. Much as Robespierre assumed the role of judge of the public virtue or corruption of his fellow revolutionaries in the French Revolution, so Lenin, Stalin, and Mao became judges and disposers of those charged with ideological and factional deviation within their own parties. The notion that all serious conflict in party ranks must be a manifestation of the outside class conflicts intruding into the party, together with the absence of the idea of a permissible circulation of leaders from incumbency to loyal opposition and vice versa, inevitably makes the struggle for control of the party apparatus and organizational structure crucial for contenders for leadership. In his conflict with Stalin, Trotsky gave classic and succinct expression to the dilemma of a party leader without portfolio taking a critical stance against the incumbents: he complained that he found himself in a logically impossible position, since one cannot be "right against the party."

Instances in practice within individual parties of relaxation of the dogma outlawing faction have been not only rare but tenuous, as in the case of the Yugoslav party's relative internal liberalization after Tito's assertion of independence from Moscow; or else relaxation has been short-lived, as in Mao Tse-tung's let-one-hundred-flowers-bloom policy of 1957. The liberalized party regimes of Imre Nagy in Hungary in 1956 and of Dubček in Czechoslovakia in 1968 were cut short by Soviet armed intervention. In the Eastern European party-states, the winning of some measure of autonomy from Moscow in the post-Stalin era has not necessarily led to greater tolerance of freer play of conflicting forces within the party. Neither Rumania's independent foreign policy nor Kádár's economic reform policy has been accompanied by relaxation of the proscription of faction or political activity outside the party. Even in the Yugoslav party, where real though limited elbowroom for a play of conflicting political elements has been permitted, the Leninist dogmas against political pluralism inside and outside the party are being reasserted as Tito's leadership and life come inevitably to a close.

In practice though not in theory, the great breach in the proscription of faction has occurred *among* rather than *within* the parties since World War II. The so-called condition of polycentrism among today's parties indeed deeply affects the internal politics and factional struggles inside the parties both in and out of power. Despite temporary compromises and accommodations among the parties at meetings and conferences over the years, there likewise has been no effective collective effort to devise a new model or "constitution" to bring the conflicts among Communist parties under control. Polycentrism is primarily a condition issuing from factional power politics and not the name of a deliberate long-term policy arising out of collective statesmanship among the parties. This phenomenon—in contrast to the practice of parliamentary or constitutional-democratic policies—continues to reveal the strength of the antipathy to oppositional politics in the Leninist tradition. That tradition finds great difficulty accepting the notion either that any conflict of groups in Communist party politics can be in itself legitimate or that *both* adversaries in a serious debate can be loyal to the party as an institution.

The antipluralism of the Leninist tradition, however, has not prevented factionalism from being a way of life within and among party leaderships. That tradition seems only to have lent a kind of repressed intensity to the conflicts that arise in the normal course of affairs among political men. In the absence of institutionalized methods for resolving conflicts and despite the bureaucratic structuring of party apparatus, the party's leading circle is a kind of no-man's-land where few internal inhibitions or external restraints operate upon the antagonists in political struggle. Nonetheless, so long as a factional struggle has not reached a culmination, the participants observe a taboo against direct public revelation of their dispute and sustain the image of a unified and indivisible leadership.

The larger constituency of party-state functionaries does receive signs and signals of the conflict from the combatants in the inner circle. Each contender in the conflict seeks to persuade the larger constituency of its cause through indirect communication within party channels and in the party press.[1] The manipulation of symbols of rank and prestige among the leaders, broad or unspecified allusions to the dangers of error or deviation, and tendentious variation of ideological or policy formulas are the familiar stock-in-trade of factional communication to the politically sensitized outside the inner arena of conflict. Something of the intensity that usually characterizes factional conflict in Communist parties becomes apparent when the battle is won or can no longer be contained. The denunciation and disgrace visited upon a purged leader or faction is usually extreme, and polemics against banished former allies are uninhibited.

Among the Soviet-sphere party-states a major departure from Stalin's general practice of physical "liquidation" of fallen leaders came after his death. Unsuccessful leaders—with the notable exceptions of Beria and Imre Nagy—no longer suffered death but, depending on the case, political disgrace or demotion. Although after Stalin the Soviet leadership accepted a measure of diversity in the East European party-states, and gave limited recognition to Yugoslavia's "different road to socialism," the basic demand of the Soviet leadership on the East European parties has remained that each preserve its political monopoly in the state, maintain ideological censorship, and keep pluralist tendencies inside or outside the party framework contained.

Oligarchic versus One-Man Leadership

Most Communist party leaderships are oligarchic in formal structure, but at the same time manifest a strong dynamic toward one-man dominance over the leading group. Among the *collective* of leaders—to use the official term—a struggle for primacy recurs. Within the party apparatus and the state structure in parties holding power, a complex battle between the followings of the principal contenders takes place. It is not a struggle for votes among the party rank and file for election of candidates to the Central Committee, or for delegates to party congresses. Rather, it is a co-optation process reaching downward from the key personalities in the leadership circle at the apex of the party. It is a struggle for footing on the bureaucratic pyramids of party and state. It is from the positions they hold on this pyramid that a victorious leader and his following work their will in the party-state as a whole. The formidable veto power of withholding consent through the vote is denied the party rank and file in practice. The Central Committee members and delegates to party congresses proved the strictly pro forma ratification of the results of co-optation politics. The observance of the bare procedure is a kind of respect paid to the theory but not the practice of democratic legitimization. Such co-optation politics resembles struggles within boss-led political machines elsewhere, but applies to entire nations and societies under party state rule.

It is of some use to distinguish—but not too categorically—successive phases of oligarchic or collective and one-man leadership in the history of most Communist parties. Collective leadership is the official term for an oligarchic situation in the leading group where one leader holds a position of limited power with respect to his colleagues. He acts as a kind of first among equals, normally occupying the post of first or general secretary, but the leading group, the Politburo or its equivalent, serves as a genuine stage of policy decision. In this situation the prime figure usually shares to some extent executive functions with a second leader who holds most often the post of prime minister in the state apparatus. The element of collective leadership can weaken, and the element of one-man rulership strengthen, as the prime leader succeeds in expanding his position of strength. The reverse process can also occur, and often during a leader's drive for dominance the balance between the two elements can waver back and forth. Once a leader gains a predominance of power and influence, the focus of factional conflict may then shift to a pattern of struggle among lesser leaders for the predominant leader's favor, and among rival policy groups for his endorsement. While factionalism usually assumes the latter aspect under leaders who win great prestige as founders or consolidators of party-states—here would be included Lenin, Stalin, Tito, Mao, Ho, Castro—even in these cases the leader cannot regard his position as fully secure. A parallel can be drawn to the Machiavellian view of the prince; the prince never ceases his striving to assure his dominance over all the other aristocrats of politics around him who also desire preeminence. Similarly, a Marxist-Leninist "prince" must do the same within the party's leading group. He must always balance his accumulated strength both against the collective counter-weight of the party oligarchy, and simultaneously deflect, restrain, or remove actual or potential rivals for his position.

Perhaps more than any other Communist leader, Stalin succeeded in extricating himself from the restraining influence of the leading group, but only after he had instituted a reign of terror inside as well as outside the party. The great terror of the thirties was initiated by Stalin after a former ally and other Politburo members joined in a move to curb his powers in 1934. Stalin routed all major opponents and installed his own following in key positions in the party and took massive powers to himself. He suppressed any and all autonomous political tendencies in the party. He destroyed the remnants of the Politburo's institutional authority, but even then the specter of the repressed oligarchy lived on in Stalin's suspiciousness of those around him.

Mao Tse-tung's Cultural Revolution sought the same end with somewhat different means. Mao used the Red Guards as the functional equivalent of Stalin's secret police, but as a public and not secret weapon of ideological-political as well as physical coercion against those who resisted. But Mao's chosen ally in the enterprise and presumptive heir, Lin Piao, evidently turned against him. His attempted assassination of Mao, according to official stories, led to his own downfall and subsequent death. Even Khrushchev—under whose aegis intraparty conflicts ceased to be literally a life-and-death affair—relentlessly sought the expulsion from the party of his fallen challengers in the Presidium of 1957, raising the possibility of Stalinesque show trials against them at the Twenty-second Party Congress in 1961. His inability to settle accounts with his own "antiparty" opponents counted against his own power as leader.

The extreme efforts of Stalin and Mao to enforce their total will on the party leadership, though extraordinary, illuminate the problem of authority with which all prime party leaders must grapple. Although the problem has analogies in most political systems, it is aggravated in Communist parties and especially in party-states. The absence in most cases of a genuinely institutionalized seat of executive authority adds a powerful element of insecurity to the prime leader's position. He finds himself surrounded by a leading group which in concept combines both executive and legislative functions. His formal coequals in the Politburo or its equivalent are all presumptively executives and legislators. Under the right circumstances they can exert their prerogative against his personal leadership. This was done, for example, against Khrushchev—first unsuccessfully in 1957 and then successfully in the CPSU Presidium in 1964. At the Politburo level the leader suffers from an institutional insecurity which can prompt even the strongest to magnify his fears and to seek extraordinary measures to secure his primacy.

The characteristic insecurity of the leader's position can be traced back to Lenin's model of the Communist party. Lenin never translated his personal supremacy in the party into a formal seat of executive authority which successors could occupy. Rather, he left only the example of a revolutionary leader-hero. His successors were hard put to rival his achievement and were impelled to build leader "cults" in a kind of imitation of the founding leader. Only on his deathbed did Lenin become acutely aware of the succession problem, and saw with foreboding the rising menace of an internecine struggle for leadership among his heirs. In his "testament" he anticipated the coming conflict between Trotsky and Stalin and belatedly recognized that the latter had built his own illicit seat of power as general secretary, the presumed servant and not master of the Politburo. Ironically, this most realistic of revolutionary politicians was never fully conscious of the practical difficulties inherent in the notion of a collegial or collective executive harmonized solely on the basis of the like-mindedness of its members.

While the prime leader must grapple with the oligarchic group's inherent tendency to counter his power, he is in a better position to manipulate the tradition of ideological monolithism to advantage than is the group. The party is formally committed to the proposition that there can be only one correct policy flowing from one correct interpretation of doctrine at any particular historical juncture. This leads to the notion in the party that one head is better than many in resolving doctrinal issues and undertaking effective political action. Moreover, if he has shown success in policy, he can say it flows from his superior understanding of doctrine and its application, and assert his claim as an unassailable "theoretician" of the party. If he can make his claim hold, his power to determine policy is greatly enhanced. If he has also won organizational command in the party apparatus, he is in a position to assert that the buck logically stops with him on all questions of power and policy. At the same time, he becomes vulnerable to attack if he fails to convey the image of forward movement, or if his key policies fail.

Communist Factional Cleavage

SOURCES OF FACTIONAL CLEAVAGE

Factionalism normally focuses within a rather narrow arena at the apex of the bureaucratic pyramid of the party and the party-state and from there reverberates downward through the structures of party and state. Although factional maneuvering in the party is concentrated in the secretariat and the apparatus of the Central Committee, and in the state within the Council of Ministers, with few exceptions factional issues can be finally resolved only within the Politburo circle itself.

While the struggles for power and primacy turn the leading group inward upon itself, the concurrent and interconnected conflicts over policy turn them toward society and the world outside. How an issue is defined in conflicts over policy is tied to the question of power in the leading group. A leader seeking power tries to define the issues to his advantage so as to galvanize support within the party and state, and once in power he seeks to sustain his definition of the main issues and to prevent conflict around him from destroying that definition and from exposing his leadership to challenge. The party leader must develop his main policy lines within the specific context of the spectrum of policy orientations in the party. While there has been a history of opportunism in the manipulation and exploitation of issues by contending leaders in Communist parties— especially the most eminent —leaders develop in their careers distinctive political identities which put them to one side or the other in the spectrum. Comparing Tito and Mao, Molotov and Khrushchev, Togliatti and Kim Il-song, or Dubček and Ulbricht illustrates the contrasts in orientation.

The cleavages bear some kinship with divisions between conservative and reforming tendencies in other political systems. However, their peculiarities are bound up with the inner nature of the Marxist-Leninist ideocratic party and the party-state. In the party seeking power, the root of the cleavage is located in the conflicting necessities produced by the single-minded drive for total power and the diversity of means required to attain it. The party seeks the overthrow of an existing political system as such. In order to do so, it must operate within that system's sociopolitical, ideological, and national fabric; otherwise the gaining of power cannot become a practical possibility. Once the party gains power and succeeds in establishing the party-state, the dilemma does not disappear but emerges in new forms: in the strains between the imperatives of revolutionary ideology and the pressing practical requirements of ruling and managing all spheres of a complex society and nation-state.

Before 1917 the dilemma between ends and means was expressed in classic form in the Russian Marxist movement. The cleavage between Lenin's militant Bolsheviks and the less immoderate or gradualist Menshevik wing turned on the question of whether Russian conditions necessitated a leap to power as Lenin sought or a stage-by-stage approach to the acquisition of rule as the Mensheviks believed. The same basic cleavage over the ways and means to power afflicts contemporary Communist parties. For Communist party leaderships in modern pluralist political systems, the way to power is strewn with difficulties and is easily lost in the thickets of a highly differentiated and diversified competitive politics. It is no accident that it is in such diversified systems that the "deviation" of "revisionism" seems to abound, and policies of adaptation of Marxist-Leninist ideology to complex circumstances flourish at the cost of the clarity and purity of revolutionary tenents. Allende in Chile, Togliatti in Italy, and Garaudy in France are examples of the adaptive side of Marxism-Leninism in the recent past.

The other side of Marxism-Leninism is typically expressed by parties in societies where the traditional order is dissolving under modernization and no new system has yet replaced it—as exists in various stages in much of the Third World. Here party leaderships are attracted by ideas of direct and violent routes to power. Maoism, with its precepts of politics-out-of-the-barrel-of-a-gun and guerrilla warfare, provides the model of this aspect of Marxism-Leninism. While Maoism and its imitative offshoots seek to arouse maximal revolutionary passion with visions of a royal road to power, they in fact have engaged in various reformulations of doctrine and strategy to fit diverse local circumstances. Their guerrilla strategies contain their own brands of revisionism: the party organization, for example, tends to be superceded in Debrayist or Guevarist guerrilla doctrine by the military leadership.

Above all, the cleavage has found persistent and manifold expression in the party-in-power of the party-state. Again Lenin provides a classic example. In his few years of rule after 1917, Lenin swung from "war-communism" at home and militant revolutionism abroad to the New Economic Policy of economic and political retreat at home and pragmatic accommodations with Western powers abroad. Though muting the militant elements of Communist ideology, Lenin in no way saw himself as departing fundamentally from it. Yet despite his prestige, the swing provoked protests and opposition from "left" Communists inside the Soviet party.

After Lenin's death intraparty struggle swirled around Trotsky's and Stalin's opposing lines of "permanent revolution" versus "socialism-in-one-country." At this point Trotsky stood on the "left" and Stalin on the "right" wing. After Trotsky's defeat, Stalin moved left with his programs of collectivization, forced industrialization and "cultural revolution"; he was unsuccessfully opposed on the right by Bukharin—himself a former left Communist. Though in the succession conflict after Lenin the principals changed in position, the changes were closely tied with winning factional preponderance and leadership within the party-state.

Stalin himself gave a description of the inherent cleavage in the new party-state when he saw a basic conflict between party functionaries who were drawn by "Russian revolutionary sweep" and those attracted to "American efficiency." He warned against going to either extreme, although he made it clear that the efficiency tendency posed the greater danger to the party-state. Toward the end of his despotic reign, efficiency in agriculture and industrialization had lost ground—even though it remained as a theme in the Stalinist slogans to overtake the United States in production.

Stalin's unprecedented system of ideocratic hegemony over a sixth of the world's surface had been won at massive human costs, which were manifest in the failure of agricultural policy and loss of incentive in production among those he ruled. He curbed factionalism as an autonomous political factor within the Soviet and Moscow-led Communist parties. He became the final arbiter of all conflict, but he did not destroy the factional tendency. His despotic monolithism finally provoked a fateful split with Tito's Yugoslav party, which had eluded his direct domination. That split in 1946 and Stalin's death a few years later set the stage for a revival of factionalism as a major and unpredictable factor in the politics of the Soviet party, the new post–World War II party-states, and parties of the Communist movement as a whole.

Out of the Soviet-Yugoslav split arose a broad conflict within and among the party-states and nonruling parties, between "dogmatists" and "revisionists." In the Soviet party-state a conflict emerged between conservative and reformist elements. Khrushchev in his rise to power exploited conservative grievances, yet he soon turned against the conservatives in his bold attack on Stalin and Stalinism at the Twentieth Party Congress in 1956. He became the champion of coexistence in foreign affairs, a loosening of the reins over the East European and other parties, and political relaxation and economic reform at home. As a result, he aroused the opposition of the neo-Stalinists and the ideologue-guardians of the party-state both at home and abroad. The conflict spread to the system of parties as a whole and helped provoke the Sino-Soviet dispute. Khrushchev's downfall produced the more conservative and ideologically orthodox Brezhnev Politburo and the counter-movement against anti-Stalinism in the Soviet and other parties.

In China the conflict between the opposing wings in the party-state was dramatically displayed in Mao's Cultural Revolution. Despite the polemical exaggeration of the invective of the antagonists in the Chinese party-state, there was a core of truth in Mao's depiction of his opponents as revisionists or rightists and their view of his faction as dogmatist and ultrarevolutionists. Mao's Cultural Revolution was at once the outward manifestation of a fierce power struggle between Mao and other leaders of the CCP and an acute expression of the cleavage between the revolutionary-ideologizing and the pragmatic-rationalizing wings of the party-state. The cleavage between the two wings of party leadership can be found, despite manifold variations according to local situations, in the political history of virtually every Communist party.

THE OPPOSING WINGS OF COMMUNIST LEADERSHIPS

It is important not to be deceived by the rhetorical excesses of the contenders in their public polemics. Representations of opponents as entirely beyond the pale of correct doctrine and practice must be taken with a grain of salt. The conflicts move within a broader political and ideological consensus in Communist party politics. Both sides see themselves as devoted to the party as the historically appointed agency for transforming Marxist-Leninist ideology into political reality. But as the extreme ends of each wing of the party are approached, the strain on the Marxist-Leninist consensus increases. This is true of left as well as well as right-wing "deviations." For example, the revolutionary revivalism of Mao's Cultural Revolution was carried to a point where it began to put the very party of the Chinese party state in question. Mao formed his Red Guards as an extraparty instrument designed to free his policy not only from a few party leaders opposing him but from the party apparatus itself.

Although Mao's own control of the Red Guard movement became shaky in the chaotic conditions produced by the Cultural Revolution, the Red Guards' fanatic loyalty was not to a new revolutionary party, but was solely to Mao and Maoism as the quintessence of Marxism-Leninism. There are, of course, notable differences between Mao's Cultural Revolution and Stalin's second Soviet revolution of the thirties—which the latter incidentally also termed a *cultural revolution.* However, Mao followed Stalin's example, with his own variations of the magnified-leader cult, ideological-struggle campaigns, and terror. In both cases, the "revolution" sought to enforce the leader's political will not simply within the party institution but over and against it. With the waning of Mao's Cultural Revolution, the institutions of the party-state reasserted themselves, at least temporarily, under Chou En-lai's stewardship. In the USSR such a countertendency could only emerge into the open after Stalin's death. Under Khrushchev and Brezhnev, the Soviet party regained its institutional supremacy within the party-state. Though the party remained a prime tool, it was no longer the tool of a dictatorial ruler beyond the reach of any direct institutional control.

By contrast, the pragmatic-rationalizing wing of the party and party-state puts less emphasis on ideological militancy and monolithic revolutionism. It is inclined to adjust theory and practice to processes of social and political change not easily conformable to doctrinal expectations, often under the rubric of "creative Marxism-Leninism." It is more inclined to pragmatic and heterogeneous attacks on internal problems in industry and agriculture. It usually places greater reliance on material incentives and recognition of mundane social needs than on coercive or ideological stimuli. This wing of the party-state often condones self-regulating or localized methods of conducting the day-to-day activities of the economic management. It is less tolerant of incipient pluralizing tendencies in society at large. Tito, Khruschev, and Dubček provide examples of this general approach to policy.

This does not mean that ideology is ignored under such leaders. Rather, this wing is disposed to give greater emphasis to the goals of Communist ideology and less to the prospect of protracted class war posited in Marxist-Leninist doctrines. The promises of increasing abundance equitably distributed and decreasing internal political stress are typically made the basis of this wing's formulation of party programs. These general elements of policy orientation, for example, characterized the Yugoslav Communist League's programs under Tito, Khrushchev's New Party Program, and Dubček's Action Program. Notably, in the late years of Tito's rule, Tito himself has sought to counterbalance the reform policies of his regime by reinforcing the orthodox principles of Communist party rule. Khrushchev's fall was followed by a counterswing under Brezhnev against anti-Stalinism and internal relaxation, and, of course, Dubček's liberalizing policy was simply destroyed from without by Soviet armed force and led to Mos-

cow's formulation of the Brezhnev Doctrine, designed to curb reformist forces at work in the East European party-states.

As in the case of Maoism and other expressions of the revolutionary-ideologizing party wing, the tendencies of the pragmatic-rationalizing wing when carried to logical conclusions also depart from the
original model of the party and party state as conceived by Lenin. Few
of this wing's spokesmen intend to produce such departures. Rather,
this wing has been less intolerant toward the presence of a diversity
of ideological or intellectual trends outside the sphere of Marxism-
Leninism, in society at large.

However, in most instances, the spokesmen of the opposing
wings, when the conflict between them intensifies, picture their opponents as apostates. In fact, they are usually speaking only about the
potential heterodoxy inhering in any coherent practical policy. Lenin's
own career of leadership—to which party polemicists constantly refer
as the supremely authoritative example of correct political action—is
many faceted. Each party wing can plausibly validate the claims it
makes for its position by pointing to one or another aspect of Lenin's
practice in one or another phase of his political life. The perfect unity
of theory and practice which the Marxist-Leninist parties proclaim as
the touchstone of correct policy, and of which Lenin is the exemplar,
is far more elusive and equivocal in reality than the doctrinal exegesis
of official party statements would imply.

Nonetheless, the history of the internal politics of the parties and
the party states permits one broad observation. A faction accused of
revisionism suffers a greater disadvantage than one charged with dogmatism. Revisionism has traditionally been deemed the greater sin or
deviation. This follows logically from the ultimately ideocratic character of the party institution itself. Lenin in his most practical of hand-
books on how to win power, *What Is to Be Done?*, is insistent on the
point that the strictest adherence to doctrinal fundamentals is the
essential precondition for the existence of a revolutionary movement.
The innovator or reformer is always acutely vulnerable to the charge
of tampering with the fundamentals. Even Lenin came under attack in
his own party when he seemed to violate his own dictum in his tactical
retreats and accommodations with necessitous realities. Only his great
prestige as the maker of the revolution preserved him from mortal
danger.

It is in this context that the failure of Khrushchev's effort to win
official acceptance of the reverse proposition—that dogmatism and
not revisionism was a greater danger—should be seen. In his struggle
with Mao and with conservative factions in the USSR, Eastern Europe,
and the movement as a whole, Khrushchev sought to reverse the
formula that revisionism was the main danger to correct Communist
strategy; his campaign for a time seemed close to success, as a number

of parties, including the French Communist party, endorsed the new formula. But the campaign foundered and collapsed when Khrushchev encountered insurmountable resistance on the issue. The Brezhnev Politburo retained the standard formula. The suppression of the "Czech Spring" in 1968 confirmed in brutal deed that the old version was still the Soviet party policy.

Historically, therefore, Communist parties as institutions have been skewed in favor of the ideological monolithism issuing from both the Leninist and Stalinist traditions. Especially in the party-states— with the exception of Tito's Yugoslavia—the reform or pragmatic-rationalizing wing has suffered repeated reverses and has gained only tenuous holds at various times on party leaderships. Nagy in Hungary in 1956 and Dubček in Czechoslovakia in 1968 suffered destruction from Soviet armed force. Khrushchev's own reforms and anti-Stalin policies eventually foundered. Kádár's economic reformism in contemporary Hungary won only grudging toleration from the Brezhnev Politburo, and is likely to be withdrawn at the first sign of any sudden unfolding of spontaneous liberalization.

Party-states like Rumania and Albania, which have enjoyed quasi-autonomy for a decade or so, are nonetheless ruled by strict guardians of the party's ideocratic power in their domestic regime. The Soviet Leadership has been more disposed to suffer the existence of party-states asserting a measure of independence in foreign policy than party-states whose leaderships in major ways relax party ideological and political controls over society. Since Khrushchev's fall, revisionist elements in the Soviet-oriented nonruling parties have lost ground, and their spokesmen have been muffled or removed from positions of influence or expelled from party membership.

The Sino-Soviet dispute itself, which began in the form of a conflict between Mao's revolutionary-ideologizing line in the Chinese party and Khrushchev's pragmatic de-Stalinizing line in the Soviet party, has tended to push the Soviet leadership toward more orthodox ideological positions. This became evident after Khrushchev's fall. In the Sino-Soviet movement as a whole, the post-Khrushchev Soviet leadership has sought to display its revolutionary credentials in the face of Maoist attacks on Soviet "Khrushchevism" and revisionism and alleged lack of revolutionary commitment. Again the logic of ideocratic factional politics has favored the more doctrinaire over the more reform-minded element.

Factions in the Communist Party-State

CONTINUITY VERSUS CHANGE IN THE PARTY-STATE

The ideocratic party, according to Lenin's original design, was to be made faction-free and unaffected by pluralizing tendencies from within and without in order to make it an efficient instrument of revolution in the outside world. Moreover, class conflict and hence political conflict was, according to Lenin's expectations, to be liquidated in the USSR as the party-state consolidated the revolution. However, the potentials for alternatives to the party-state within the societies they rule have shown a continuing and lively presence. Periodic eruptions and manifestations of discontent in the East European party-states are not sporadic or isolated phenomena. Among the more notable of these episodes are the Soviet-Yugoslav break of 1948, the East German workers rising of 1953, the Hungarian revolt and the Polish ferment of 1956, the Albanian-Soviet rift of 1961, the rise of Rumanian autonomy in foreign affairs in the early 1960's, the Czechoslovak liberalization of 1968, and the Polish workers' riots of 1970. The rapid emergence of liberalizing, pluralist, and nationalist tendencies that appeared in the few brief months of the "Czech Spring" before it was crushed by the Soviet army was a brief but clear revelation of what lies beneath the monolithic surface of the party-state itself. In the USSR the small and beleaguered Democratic Movement born of the anti-Stalinist trends of the Khrushchev years represents a whole range of familiar Western and indigenous political and philosophical outlooks. Even Mao's Cultural Revolution was stimulated by his fears of the erosion of the Chinese Communist revolution after his death and its submersion by other forces. Instead of fading away under political and social transformations effected by the party-state, as anticipated by its founders, other political spectra within society begin to show through in various ways whenever political and ideological controls weaken or relax.

The experience of limited relaxation in the USSR under Khrushchev led Khrushchev's successors, the Brezhnev Politburo, to expend great energies to contain the pressures of differentiating and pluralizing tendencies in both Eastern Europe and the USSR which began to emerge during the Khrushchev years. The Polish food riots were a major danger signal. The Czech episode showed how economic reform can escalate into political liberalization, but the Polish disturbances demonstrated the danger in a leadership's failure to address rising popular expectations for improved conditions of life. Brezhnev's formula for skirting this dilemma was to seek major injections of science and technology, as well as grain, from the West, principally from the United States and Canada. He thus hoped, it appears, to avoid basic restructuring of the centrally controlled Soviet economy rather than risk fundamental economic and institutional reforms. Such basic reform might offer promise of economic success but also could release forces in Soviet society destabilizing to the party-state itself.

Yet the Brezhnev Politburo also eschewed the alternative of restoring the party-state to the hegemonistic extremes of the Stalin years as a means of suppressing internal pressures for change. Such a choice, though by no means excluded, was fraught with danger for the ruling group as a whole, not to speak of the society at large. Brezhnev's overall policy rather was designed to sustain a pragmatic-orthodox version of the party-state. To a remarkable degree, the design resembled the third stage of pragmatic Communist rule Milovan Djilas projected in his *The New Class* at the end of the 1950s: Djilas's scheme, expected such a stage would follow revolutionary (Leninist) and dogmatic (Stalinist) stages.

The party-state, like a pressure cooker, compresses within itself the diverse, dynamic forces of whole societies striving to break free of confinement. Party leaderships must master these energies and, if possible, exploit them to their own purposes without being mastered by them. Weak points appear in the structural casing of the party-state, worrying its overseers, aggravating divisions among them over appropriate remedial action, and giving vent to the compressed impulses of national societies.

It is the striking revelation of Solzhenitsyn's *Gulag Archipelago*, for example, that even in the most repressive Stalinist phase of the Soviet party-state there yet survived innate a vibrant and original intellectual and national culture beyond the reach of terror. If this was true of the founding Soviet party-state, it is perhaps even truer of its East European counterparts. Not yet fully known, however, is the extent of the survival of intellectual and national traditions and culture of the Chinese nation within the Maoist party-state and its allied party-states of North Korea and North Vietnam. It is probable that here too there are hidden histories yet to be revealed.

From the standpoint of society at large, and even to some degree of the officialdoms of the state as distinguished from the party apparatus itself, the party's leading circle resembles more an extraordinary faction than a rulership arising naturally out of the state and society. To use a metaphor, the party rulership bears some resemblance to a mafia *in* but not *of* state and society. However, it is a mafia with an ideological purpose. All of its history of coercion and terror against society and society's classes has its justification in that purpose.

It is then more accurate to speak of the party-state as an internally antagonistic and dualistic entity. The party-state contains an implicit opposition between the coexistent apparatuses of the party and the state. The party, quite explicitly in its own doctrines, inhabits and controls the state structure, seeing in it a potential counterregime which can rise to challenge party hegemony if allowed an autonomous life. It is an agency through which the spontaneous impulses of society and nation could gain explicit and coherent expression and undermine the party's power. Though the state structure is contorted to conform to the uses of the party rulership, it remains by its character attuned to the interests and needs of society at large. It is an organ which is potentially orderable to the public good of the people of which it is the particular expression. The state as state ultimately finds the ground of its authority in the nation from which it derives. Neither the Soviet nor any other party rulership has risked dispensing with the elaborate facade of a "constitutional" structure of authority based on popular representation. The party institution, on the other hand, must justify its power not from people or God but wholly on the ground of a theory of history and in the name of mankind of the future.

Khrushchev sought to develop a design for a major institutional departure from the Stalin-style direction of the USSR's political economy. His reforms aimed at the absorption of the state's traditional managerial-economic functions into the party apparatus, and he revived the long-dormant Marxist doctrine of the withering-away-of-the-state as the reforms looked toward the "transition to communism." The logic of the reforms pointed toward the conversion of the party institution itself into a kind of substitute for the stage and a resolution of the party-state dualism. Khrushchev's reforms began to founder even while he ruled, and were completely reversed by his successors after his downfall. The reforms aroused the ire of state functionaries fearing loss of status and ultimate displacement by party executives, of regional party leaders opposed to their own conversion from political chiefs ruling territories to executives responsible for an economic sector, and of party ideologue-guardians wedded to the party-state dichotomy as essential to the ideocratic regime. The reconsolidation under Brezhnev of the party's monocratic internal structure, restoration of the ministerial centralism of the state, and return to the traditional approach to ideology as a central function of the party displayed the inertial force in the institutional structure Lenin founded and Stalin perfected. The party-state was placed back on its classic foundations as a dualistic political entity.

Nonetheless, the Brezhnev restoration of the principles of the party-state did not remove the tensions between the political-ideological impulsions of the ideocratic system and the need for institutions that can function effectively and responsively in an intricate, modernizing continental society and empire. The recognition prevailed in the leadership that traditional methods were proving of decreasing effect despite the absence of agreement on remedies. Factional disputes that swirl around countless related issues are broadly reflected in the continuing debate in party circles over politics or economics—which should hold priority in policy and to what degree? Khrushchev promoted the doctrine that economics had irrevocably moved to first place in overall policy. Brezhnev, especially at first, returned to the primacy of politics, but in the 1970s—from about the time of the riots in Poland—has given increased emphasis to economics, science, and technology. Yet he has carefully avoided going to the length of Khrushchev's revisionism in putting economics decisively ahead of politics. Hence the cross-purposes at work are evident in the shifting emphases in Brezhnev's own policy. In the 1960s he concentrated in world politics on the build-up of military, naval, and strategic forces. In the 1970s, his turn to detente sought to discover shortcuts to surmounting the USSR's lag in the Second Industrial Revolution in science and technology. The latter policy in its turn posed dangers for the political-ideological insulation of the party-state from "outside" forces. As a result of his shift, Brezhnev not only gained supporters but has had to cope with opponents in the upper echelons of the party-state. The pattern of reform and counterreform illustrates the contradictory elements in the party-state. A similar dynamic tension, a kind of unresolved dialectic, can be found in virtually every other modern Communist party-state.

INCIPIENT POLITICAL AND INTEREST GROUPS AND LEADERSHIP CLEAVAGE

Factional politics and cleavages at the apex of the party-state register, however indirectly and distortedly, the influences of incipient interest groups and latent political elements in the state officialdom and in society at large. Such elements on the margins of or outside of the inner circle come into play in leadership factional politics.[2] Of course, within the party apparatus itself various protoconstituencies enter into the balance of factional politics within the leadership. For example, Khrushchev in his defeat of his principal rivals, Molotov, Kaganovich, and Malenkov, successfully drew on the broad support he had gained among the middle-level regional party executives, and was able to exploit the long-standing resentments of this new generation of party executives in the provinces against the domination of the Stalinist old guard in Moscow. With the aid of Marshal Zhukov, Khrushchev succeeded in bringing his regional constituency to Moscow and convening the Central Committee, where they held a majority—an unprecedented and so far unrepeated court of judgment of the leadership struggle within the party Presidium (Politburo). Normally the matter would have been settled within the Politburo, and in this case obviously to Khrushchev's detriment, since there was a majority against him in that body. However, even if the affair had been settled within the Politburo, the actual resolution of the crisis would have depended in part on the capacity of the rivals to marshal their forces from the power bases and followings they had built up among various elites of the party-state.

Khrushchev's industrial-decentralization reform held the promise of increased authority for party regional executives, an asset for Khrushchev; it was a liability for him in that it aroused opposition among the state economic managers in the central ministries and caused unease among the officialdom of the military-industrial economy, not to speak of the military itself. It also disturbed elements in the central party apparatus dedicated to economic centralism on political and ideological grounds. However, none of the foregoing elements was unified in like or dislike of the reform; rather, there were various divisions among them, and each element tended more toward one view or another. Khrushchev's 1962 party reform bifurcating the party into industrial and agricultural branches was far more risky politically than the 1957 industrial decentralization. With party reform, he lost much of his earlier support in the regional party apparatus. At the same time, resistance among the elements that resented the 1957 decentralization increased. That resistance even included state economic managers who favored economic reform in principle, like Kosygin, but who saw the party reform as a menace to the economic prerogatives of the state.

Brezhnev made it his first order of business to conciliate those elements and interests in the party and state which Khrushchev's reforms had offended. He avoided actions that directly threatened the traditional balance among such groups. His careful rehabilitation of Stalin's reputation reflected this shift. Anti-Stalinism had won Khrushchev support in the intelligentsia, especially among liberally inclined writers, and had also opened the way for the rise of a spontaneous anti-Stalinist dissenting trend within the literary, scientific, and professional intelligentsia. Under Brezhnev's drive against incipient ideological diversity in Soviet society, the anti-Stalinist impetus formed the Democratic Movement led by such figures as the nuclear scientist Sakharov and the writer Solzhenitsyn.

Both Khrushchev and Brezhnev in contrasting ways looked beyond the confines of the party-state for sources of support in the state and in society at large. There was the unorthodox populist element in Khrushchevian rhetoric, in his grass-roots consumerism and promises to end the coercive practices of Stalinism. The Brezhnev Politburo saw danger to the party-state in this potent combination of general appeals; instead, in thinly veiled ways Brezhnev played upon traditional Russian imperial patriotism as a support for his leadership. This species of patriotism finds its focus in the administrative and military elites of the Soviet state apparatus and taps reservoirs in the people at large. It is exploitable as a counterpoise against those forces in Soviet society—especially in its professional and scientific elites— with the potential for producing a Soviet internal liberalization. Yet, the Brezhnev tactic no less than Khrushchev's was not a wholly safe or predictable expedient in shoring up the foundations of the party-state.

Despite its insulated and secretive inner politics, the leadership of the party-state is not wholly impervious to forces outside itself in the society over which it holds sway. In most party-states in the post-Stalin period similar patterns of factional politics and internal cleavage can be delineated, though with significant variations according to differing circumstances and national cultures ruled by the party-states.

Conclusion: The Ideocratic Party-State versus the Pluralistic Nation-State

In general the political dialect among the parties and party-states stimulated first by Tito's and then Khrushchev's break with the strict Stalinist model of the ideocratic party-state has not produced a one-way movement, deterministically inevitable, toward internal relaxation or a steadily moderating, less ideological relationship with the outside world. Rather, it has proved to be an unpredictable, conflict-ridden, to-and-fro process. Deeply imbedded and basic elements of the ideocracy and entrenched interests of the party-state's core elite counter the pressures of pluralizing tendencies at work in the society and nation at large.

The Communist parties and party-states have kept their outer bulwarks generally intact, but they move over dangerous reefs in their own world. The course of factional and internal politics in and among them has been anything but predictable over the past two decades. Their leaderships know this far more intimately than the outside observer: they need no reminding of the deceptiveness of seemingly unassailable leadership and power. They know how quickly such positions can unravel.

Most of the time Communist leaderships operate on the principle that all internal factional conflict is fraught with dangers of spinning out of control and drawing forces outside the party institution into the conflict. Ideological presuppositions have combined with historical circumstances in producing varying degrees of "siege" mentality. The generally accepted hypothetical proposition, and also a kind of rule of thumb derived from general political experience—namely, that if there are serious divisions within a political association, outside forces are tempted to play on them for their own purposes—in Marxism-Leninism, is converted into a categorical imperative: factional division in the party will inevitably be exploited by the class enemy in order to destroy the party. Though Stalin and Mao raised the principle to bizarre heights in practice, it has remained operative in varying degrees of intensity in Communist parties, and in no ruling party has it lost its force. Attempts to moderate the operation of the principle have occurred, for example, in Tito's Yugoslavia, in Dubček's eight-month rule in Czechoslovakia, and even under Khrushchev. The tenuous or abortive results of such attempts reveal the dilemma faced by Communist leaders seeking major departures from the monolithic traditions of party leadership of Leninism and Stalinism.

While Communist doctrine magnifies the deterministic character of linkages between internal and external political conflict, such linkages nonetheless are present. Dynamic relationships are identifiable between the two spheres. The history and content of factional struggles in Communist party systems fit broadly, if loosely, into the wider settings of the politics of the modern world. Marxism, Leninism, Stalinism, Maoism, and the other variants of the Communist political experience arose out of conflicts which originated in the modern West. Although Communist parties have been most successful in establishing themselves in power in the East, they had their source in the West in Marxism, a militant and messianic secular movement of and for not the East but the West. Marxism consciously rejected the modern parliamentary or republican pluralist nation-state, which it ultimately viewed as no more than the most advanced expression of exploitative class society destined to be abolished by the Communist revolution.

The Russian state, that nation-empire on the divide of West and East, and entering the twentieth century a half modern, half traditional society, was the birthplace of Leninism. An offshoot of Marxism, Leninism gave a categorical and totalist quality to its rejection of the modern pluralist nation-state. Leninist Marxism and its contemporary variants find their ultimate rationale for the party-state in their professed mission as agencies of the worldwide process of disintegration of the nation-state based on classes.

Lenin's concept of the ideocratic party and party-state produced in practice and not only in theory a great divide in the politics of the modern world. On the one hand, Lenin spoke of the party-state as a transitional institution and a dictatorial agency for the purpose of revolution only. At the same time, he tacitly allowed also for its extended historical existence by speaking of the protracted period which he expected the process of revolution to occupy. Stalin, his successor, with the aid of dogma and terror on a far greater scale than Lenin employed, vastly magnified the hegemonistic power structure of the party-state. He produced what his Yugoslav critics ironically called the state-that-does-not-wither. Most of the party-states in the post-Stalin period, at least those of the USSR and East Europe, have by contrast departed from the totalitarian extreme of Stalin but without renouncing their hegemonistic and totalist claims in the societies they control. In practice, the party-states of today show few, if any, signs of their own future withering according to the Marxist expectation.

Beneath the complexities of the East-West relationship, the underlying conflict between the two models of modern organization of man and society, between the basically pluralist, internally differentiated nation-state and the ideocratic party-state, still resonates. This deeper conflict echoes, despite the distortions of polemic and the obscurities of doctrinal formalism, in the factional debates in and among the parties and party-states—whether the issue is expressed in the pejoratives of ideological debate as "revisionism" versus "dogmatism," "adventurism" versus "capitulationism," "anti-imperialist struggle" versus "peaceful coexistence," or "Maoism" versus "Khrushchevism." Moreover, just as recurring campaigns within Communist systems for revivifying ideological élan registers the self-reinforcing impulses of the party-state, so every major attempt at internal relaxation and liberalization reveals the presence of a tendency leading away from the ideocratic party-state and toward the pluralist nation-state. The latter potentiality is the specter which haunts Communist leaders in the party-states and profoundly affects the factional conflict within and among them.

NOTES

1. For a detailed analysis of the modes of indirect communication in leadership politics, see Sidney I. Ploss, "The Language of Conflict," in *The Soviet Political Process* (Toronto: Ginn and Co., 1971), pp. 117–22. Ploss's analysis applies in a general way not just to the Soviet but to most other party-states.

2. The following articles offer useful and comprehensive classifications and typologies of the incipient political elements, interest groups, lobbies, dissenting or dissident tendencies within the party-state: H. Gordon Skilling, "Interest Groups and Communist Politics," *World Politics* 18, no. 3 (Apr. 1966): 435–51; also Skilling, "Opposition in Communist East Europe," in Robert A. Dahl, ed., *Regimes and Oppositions* (New Haven and London: Yale Univ. Press, 1973), pp. 89–120.

16

An Analysis of Factionalism of Chinese Communist Party Politics

ANDREW J. NATHAN

Since the establishment of the People's Republic of China in 1949, a highly centralized political system has been constructed in China. Crucial political battles have been contained within a small—and, until the Cultural Revolution, remarkably stable—elite of party, army, and state officials. Mass movements and upheavals, such as the land reform, the Three-Anti, Five-Anti, and Anti-Confucius–Lin Piao campaigns, the Great Leap Forward, and the Great Proletarian Cultural Revolution, have been important events in Chinese politics, but the final crunch of policy decisions has not come through such exercises of the mass line. It has come in that mysterious location known to the Chinese as the center *(chung-yang)*.

Until 1965, the center kept its doings largely secret and, except for the purges of Kao Kang and Jao Shu-shih in 1954 and P'eng Teh-huai in 1959, kept under wraps whatever factional maneuvers there were. The most influential Western analysis of Chinese intraelite

This is a revised version of an article published in *China Quarterly,* no. 53 (Jan.–Mar. 1973): 34–66; most of the citations in that publication have been omitted here. The theoretical portion also appears in Andrew J. Nathan, *Peking Politics, 1918–1923: Factionalism and the Failure of Constitutionalism* (Berkeley and Los Angeles: Univ. of California Press, 1975). I am grateful to both publishers for permission to use the text as the basis for this chapter.

conflict at that time was that it consisted of "discussion" *(t'ao-lun)* within a basically consensual politburo and among shifting "opinion groups" with no "organized force" behind them.[1]

The purges and accusations which began in late 1965 and still continue on a reduced scale shook this interpretation, and a number of scholars have advanced new analyses which take greater account of central elite conflict. One explanation, which represents the least change from the pre–Cultural Revolution opinion group model, is the "policy making under Mao" interpretation, which sees conflict as essentially a bureaucratic decision-making process dominated by Mao. A similar but less explicit "Mao-in-command" explanation sees Mao as "testing" his colleagues' political loyalty and sometimes decisively beating back efforts to challenge his preeminence.[2] Deviating further from the opinion group model are interpretations which explain political alignments and policy advocacy in terms of leaders' attachments to various bureaucratic interest groups—the various field armies, "commissars" versus "commanders," "the Party" versus "the gun," "the legal specialists" versus "the new cadres," etc.

This chapter suggests still another interpretation of Chinese Communist party (CCP) elite politics: factionalism. Given China's late nineteenth and early twentieth-century history of factionalism, and the precedent of factionalism in other Communist regimes, factionalism seems at least plausible as an explanation for the Chinese case.[3] However, the secrecy of the center's proceedings was only partially breached by the revelations of the Cultural Revolution, and it is still not possible to portray confidently the structure or membership of factions, their styles of operation, or their political bases. Indeed, it is not possible to establish beyond question that factions really exist in China or that, if they do, they constitute the major form of political organization at the center.[4]

In contrast, therefore, to scholars who have palpable factions to study and who can begin by describing them, I proceed here by examining the concept of faction and how politics structured by factions *would* look. I then argue for the applicability of factionalism as a plausible explanation for Chinese elite politics, on the basis of the limited evidence available. Finally, I conclude with some observations on the relevance of the present argument to the study of factionalism generally.[5]

Characteristics of Factions

THE BASIS OF FACTION

One kind of human behavior found in all societies is the "clientelist tie."[6] A clientelist tie is a nonascriptive two-person relationship founded on exchange, in which rights and obligations are established between two parties. A clientelist tie is thus a personal relationship, especially chosen by the partners from their total social networks. It is cultivated by the continuing exchange of gifts or services. This does not mean that the subjective content of the relationship is unfriendly or cynical; indeed, the contrary is normally the case. Since the exchange involves the provision by each partner of goods or services the other partner wants, the parties to the relationship are dissimilar—very often they are unequal in status, wealth, or power. The tie sets up well-understood, although seldom explicit, rights and obligations between the partners; it can be abrogated by either partner at will; and it is not exclusive—in that either partner is free to establish other, similar ties simultaneously, so long as they do not involve contradictory obligations.

Such ties include patron-client relations, godfather-parent relations, some types of trader-customer relations, and so forth. Corporate ties, such as lineage relations, co-membership in association, or co-membership in a group of blood brothers, etc., are not clientelist ties, although shared corporate memberships sometimes provide an initial contact which leads to the establishment of clientelist ties.

The clientelist tie should be distinguished from the generic exchange relationship. Several theorists have suggested that all social processes except those that are irrational or non-goal-oriented or expressive can validly be analyzed in terms of exchange; indeed, any kind of reciprocity, including the negative reciprocity of an eye for an eye, can be usefully classified as exchange. Since the clientelist tie is based on exchange, it must be clear that it is an exchange relationship only of a limited and specific kind. Embedded in different cultures, it is more or less explicitly recognized, spelled out, legitimized, and reinforced in varied forms; but no matter what the context, it is relatively stable and persistent, involves clearly understood rights and obligations, and is purposely cultivated by the participants. The clientelist tie is thus a special, quasi-contractual, subtype of exchange relationship.

The clientelist tie should also be distinguished from the power relationship. If a subordinate has no real choice but obedience, a power relationship exists, and the political behavior of the superior-subordinate parties will be quite different from what they would be if the real possibility of abrogating the tie existed. In many cases the right of abrogation formally exists but in fact cannot be exercised, as with the tie between landlord and tenant in some Latin American haciendas, or between lord and vassal in feudal Europe. These are better regarded as relationships of power than as clientelist ties. In practice, of course, it is often difficult to tell the difference, and there is a gray area in which a real relationship may fall.

Clientelist ties in any society articulate to form complex networks in that a patron with a client or clients may himself become a client of some other patron. Networks may thus come to consist of several layers. Such networks may serve many functions, including social insurance, trade, and, most important for politics, the mobilization and wielding of influence. There are three forms of the consequences of political conflict organized primarily through clientelist ties rather than through formal organizations, corporate units like lineages, or mass or class movements. First, the individual engaging in political conflict may cash in on his personal ties to operate as a power broker, without directly and explicitly involving his partners in any common or sustained endeavor. Examples include influence peddling by lawyers who specialize in arranging access to particular bureaucracies, mediation of political disputes by middlemen, and the bridging of government-village gaps by local "linkage" figures. The second possibility, which occurs in a setting of genuine electoral competition, has been called the "clientelist party," "vertical group," or "machine"— a mass political organization which buys electoral support with particularistic rewards distributed through a leader-follower network of clientelist ties.[7]

The third possible form of clientelist-tie-based political conflict occurs in an oligarchic or relatively small-scale setting when an individual leader mobilizes some portion of his network of primary, secondary, tertiary, etc., ties for political purposes. While a machine or clientelist party consists of a great many layers of personnel, this third type of clientelist political structure consists of only one or a few layers. Such a structure—one mobilized on the basis of clientelist ties to engage in politics, and consisting of only a few, rather than a great many, layers of personnel—is in essence a faction.[8]

Factional configurations include what may be called simple or complex factions, and may control from within or without one or more "supportive structures" or power bases, such as clubs, parties, mobs, newspapers, banks, ministries, armies, businesses, and the like (see Figure 1). What all these configurations have in common is the one-to-one, rather than corporate, pattern of relationship between leaders or subleaders and followers. Structurally, the faction is articulated through one or more nodes or subleaders, and it is recruited and coordinated on the basis of the personal exchange relationships here defined as clientelist ties.

STRUCTURE OF FACTIONS

Factions have certain structural characteristics in common—though each characteristic is not necessarily unique to factions (for example, a guerrilla band may be just as flexible as a faction, and for some of the same reasons), but none of them is universal, and the combination of characteristics is distinctive to factions. Because they are based on personal exchange relations rather than on authority relations, fac-

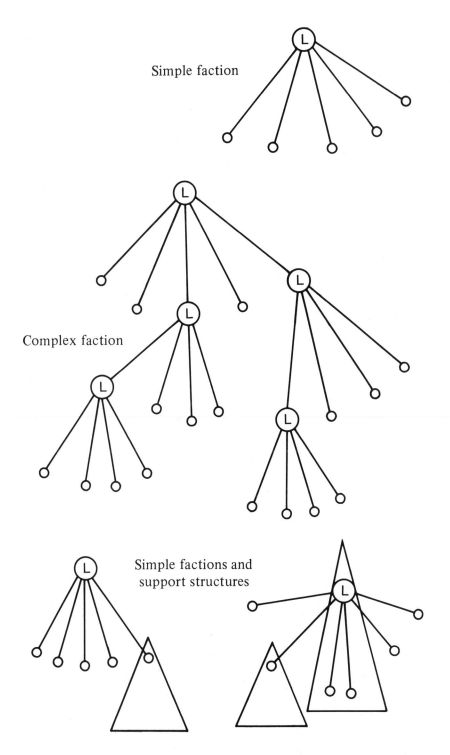

Simple faction

Complex faction

Simple factions and
support structures

Figure 1. Factional Configurations

391

tions do not become "corporatized" after their formation but remain structured by the clientelist ties which formed their basis of recruitment.[9] A leader sees the opportunity for political gain, separately recruits each member into the faction, and directs the activities of each member for the overall good of the faction. Each follower may in turn recruit others as his own followers. The members of the entire faction need never meet, though they may do so. The members' activities in disparate locations and institutions are coordinated through individual communications with the leader which tend to follow the lines of recruitment. Indeed, in routine political situations, regularized coordination can be dispensed with, and the faction as a whole can rely on the members' loyalty to the leader to ensure that each member works to the faction's benefit.

Such a communications pattern, however, has limitations. In complex factions, upward and downward communications are not delivered directly to their recipient, but flow through the series of "nodes" or subleaders. The more steps through which the information flows, the more time it takes and the more distorted it is likely to become. This tends to limit the number of levels to which the faction can extend without becoming corporatized, and the degree to which large and complex factions can engage in finely coordinated activities. Thus, the faction is capable of great flexibility in seizing political opportunities and engaging in general political strategy from scattered positions throughout a political arena; at the same time, it is self-limiting in its extensiveness and in the effectiveness of coordination of its own organization.[10]

A faction depends for its growth and continuity on the ability of the leader to secure and distribute rewards to his followers. It tends to expand and contract with success or failure. It may also be dissolved when removed from power, but the leader can reconstitute it when he regains the capability to reward the members. A faction is thus capable of intermittent but persistent functioning. It takes form out of the broader social network of clientelist ties and in response to an opportunity for political gain, and if it becomes necessary to retire from politics, as during the dominance of the political arena by an enemy, it can become dormant. Its political activities then cease, especially if the members have scattered; or the activities may continue at a low level of occasional contact with other opposition groups to scheme for a return to power. When the enemy is overthrown, the faction may return to full activity unchanged in form and flexibility.

A faction cannot survive its leader. The members may continue in political activity for a time after the leader's death or retirement, and may even continue to be known by the original name of the faction. But since the set of clientelist ties on which it is founded forms a unique configuration centered on the leader, the faction can never be taken over as a whole by a successor. The unique combination of personal and strategic political positions held by the faction cannot be completely reconstructed once the leader is lost.

The more extended a complex faction becomes, the greater the number of subordinate leaders it contains and the farther removed they are from the primary leader. The leader of each simple faction within the complex faction is primarily responsible to his own followers for political spoils. This responsibility may come into contradiction with the loyalty he owes to his own leader—who is pursuing the interests of a different set of persons. This creates the tendency for the leaders of lower segments to betray the interests of the faction as a whole in order to secure greater rewards for their own segments, which are capable of operating as distinct factions if they free themselves from the larger faction.

Because of this tendency toward breakdown, complex factions are most likely to develop to the largest possible size within formal bureaucratic organizations. In formal organizations, first, the personal loyalty of lower-level faction leaders to higher leaders is reinforced by the hierarchical authority patterns of the formal structure. In addition, the faction has the benefit of the formal intraorganizational communications network, to aid in coordinating its activities. Finally, the effort to gain control of or to influence the politics of the organization requires the cooperation of the subleaders at various levels, and tends to bring their interests into harmony. Thus the hierarchy and established communications and authority structures of the contextual organization provide a kind of trellis upon which the complex faction is more able to extend its own informal personal loyalties and relations.

There is a tendency for vertical cleavages to develop within the complex faction, running up to the level directly under the highest leader. Vertical cleavages can also develop at each lower level, but are more likely to remain latent while they are submerged within the greater rivalry between major segments. Because the struggle is for access to and influence over the top leader, there is a tendency for these cleavages to be limited to two. The conflict between the two major entities within a faction will be kept under tight rein by the faction leader; after his retirement or death, however, the two entities are likely to become two new complex factions.

Internal cleavage tends to be increased by the fruits of victory. First, the path to victory inevitably involves reaching opportunistic alliances with factional leaders who are incorporated within the factional network but who are not reliable. Second, the increased scale and numerical force of the faction as it grows enhances the tendency for divergent interests to emerge among component subleaders and subfactions. Even if loyalty prevents an open revolt against the leader, it permits political clashes and struggles among his subordinates.

Third, if the faction comes near to or achieves victory in the general political arena, the unifying factor or a common enemy ceases to exist, while divisive factors such as the struggle over spoils, and efforts by smaller, enemy factions to "buy over" component units, increase in salience. Fourth, the growth of the faction tends to deprive the leader himself of direct control over component units, weakens his position vis-à-vis subordinates, and thus hastens his political retirement and the consequent open split of the faction. In short, division and decline are almost inevitable results of success. The only sure way to avoid such disintegration is to refuse to expand beyond the borders of an internally unified, and easily defended, factional base.

Finally, as a consequence of these structural characteristics, the faction is limited in the amount and kinds of power it can generate and wield. A faction is limited in size, in follower commitment, and in stability by the principles of its own organization. Certain other types of conflict structure—for example, highly organized political parties or armies—can, by virtue of their complex, functionally specialized organization, their clear boundaries, and their high degree of control over participants, engage in feats of mobilization, indoctrination, and coordination which are beyond the capabilities of factions. Factions, however, enjoy less power capability than formal organizations because of the limitations on their extensiveness, coordination, and control of followers, as a result of their basis in the clientelist tie, their one-to-one communications structure, and their tendency toward breakdown. A faction is limited in this way, of course, only so long as it remains a faction; there is nothing inherent in the existence of a faction to prevent its members from organizing themselves in some other way. But as long as people continue to organize themselves on the basis of clientelist ties, the result will be factional structures with built-in limitations on the amount of power they are capable of acquiring.

Characteristics of Factional Politics

FACTIONAL POLITICAL BEHAVIOR

Certain modes of conflict are typical of politics among factions. The following set of characteristics of factional political behavior is a consequence of the power limitations typical of factions. That is, the several factions in any factional arena will tend, over time, to enjoy relative power equality, for no faction will be able to achieve and maintain overwhelmingly superior power. One faction may temporarily enjoy greater power than rival factions, but this power will not be so much greater that the victorious faction is capable of expunging its rivals and assuring its permanent dominance. This is the more so because the flexibility of the weaker factions and their capability for intermittent functioning enhance their ability to evade and survive repression. A faction engaging in conflict with other factions must therefore operate on the assumption that it will not be able decisively and finally to eliminate its rivals.[11]

(1) Since the impulse to crush one's rivals is stymied by the limited nature of factional power, a code of civility arises which circumscribes the nature of conflict. Factions relatively seldom kill, jail, or even confiscate the property of their opponents within the system (however, the killing and jailing of those felt to present a threat to the system is another matter: see point 12). Indeed, factional systems tend toward extremely polite face-to-face conduct among rival politicians.[12]

(2) Since factions are incapable of building sufficient power to rid the political system of rival factions, they have little incentive to try to do so; for any given faction, the most important and usually most immediate concern is to protect its own base of power while opposing accretions of power to rival factions, and incentives to increase its own power are of secondary importance. Defensive political strategies thus predominate over political initiatives, both in frequency and importance.

(3) When a faction does take a political initiative—which it does only on those rare occasions when it feels that its power base is secure and its rivals are relatively off balance—it relies on secret preparations and surprise offensive. This minimizes the ability of rivals to prepare their defensive moves in advance and provides the aggressive faction with a momentum which carries it farther than would otherwise be the case before the defensive moves of rivals stop its progress.

(4) In the face of such an initiative, the defensive orientation of the other factions in the system tends to encourage them to unite against the initiative. Thus factional political systems tend to block the emergence of strong leaders. The strong leader constitutes a threat to the other factions' opportunities for power, and they band together long enough to topple him from power. This may lead to chronic governmental instability. In France, for example, where cabinet governments were dependent on alignments of parliamentary factions, the very fact that a politician was able to organize a cabinet set in motion the jealousies and opposition that soon led to its fall.

(5) Since the political life of a factional system consists of occasional initiatives by constituent factions, followed by defensive alliances against the initiator, any given faction is obliged to enter into a series of constantly shifting defensive alliances. Factional alliances cannot remain stable; today's enemy may have to be tomorrow's ally.

(6) It is virtually impossible for factions to make ideological agreement a primary condition for alliance with other factions. While factions operate within a broad ideological consensus on the legitimacy of the system (see point 13), they exaggerate the small differences that remain among them (see point 10). Because factions must

often cooperate with those with whom they have recently disagreed, factional alignments, although they do not cross major ideological boundaries, within those boundaries are not determined by doctrinal affinities.[13]

(7) When decisions (resolutions of conflict, policy decisions) are made by the factional system as a whole, they are made by consensus among the factions. To attempt to take action without first achieving such a consensus would take a ruling coalition beyond the limits of its power; the decision could never be enforced. Furthermore, the effort to enforce a decision would hasten the formation of an opposition coalition to topple the ruling coalition from power. Decision by consensus is also advantageous in that action is taken in the company of one's rivals, so that responsibility cannot be pinned on any single faction.

(8) There is a typical cycle of formation and decline of consensus. The cycle begins with a political crisis. As the factions contemplate the crisis, it presently becomes clear to each one what every faction is capable of attaining; after a lapse of time the crisis becomes "ripe," and necessity forces the factions to disregard their positions of principle which had blocked consensus, and action becomes possible. Then, as a result of consensus among the factions on the need for action, a faction or factional alliance achieves power and receives a mandate to act. The victorious faction takes culturally appropriate actions to test and solidify the support the other factions have been obliged to give it. The leader may refuse to take office until the other factions have publicly committed themselves to him; he may try to associate the leaders of other factions in the action he proposes to take; he may allow, or encourage, the crisis to worsen. Ultimately, he acts.

The final phase is the decline of the factional consensus. The actions taken by the faction or coalition in power inevitably have implications for the relative strength of all the factions in the system. While the actions carry the system through the crisis which had produced the consensus, they benefit some factions—usually the one in power and its allies—more than others. The other factions act to block efforts of the leading faction to strengthen itself, and the consensus deteriorates. The factions return to mutual squabbling. The period of factional conflict often lasts a long while, as the factions maneuver for political resources, alliances, and a favorable moment and pretext for precipitating a new crisis. Eventually a faction feels it is in a good position to take a political initiative, to precipitate a test of strength with its major opponent. Whatever form it takes, the test of strength initiates a new crisis, which begins another cycle.

(9) A further characteristic of factional political behavior is a consequence of the factions' basis in clientelist ties, and of the fact that the resources with which factions carry out political conflict are not corpo-

rate, shared resources, but are the personal resources of the individual members—their personal prestige, official positions, etc., and their own further clientelist ties. To weaken their rivals, factions try to discredit opposition faction members, to dislodge them from their posts, and to buy away their allies. This leads to a politics of personality, in which rumor, character assassination, bribery, and deception are used. Passions of jealousy and revenge are aroused, opportunism and corruption are fostered, and urgent short-term political goals require the compromise of principles. These, in short, are the "comic opera" politics or "pure politics" so characteristic of factional systems.[14]

(10) One further characteristic of factional political conflict is doctrinalism—i.e., the couching of factional political conflict in terms of abstract issues of ideology, honor, and "face." Factions adopt rigid and minutely defined ideological positions, exaggerate small differences on abstract questions, and stress the purity of their own motives. Yet the issues which arouse such fierce and elaborate debates appear on close examination to be, not issues of principle, but those with strategic implications for factional power. Although the real ideological distances among factions are small, and although no faction is likely to be able to carry out an innovative political program, grand policies and sweeping programs are articulated and debated, with small points attracting the most passionate and lengthy discussion. Such debate serves several purposes. It distinguishes one faction from another, providing a rationale for the continued struggle among such otherwise similar entities. It also provides an opportunity to discredit other politicians and to justify oneself on abstract or ideological grounds. Moreover, the broad programs often include inconspicuous provisions of true strategic political importance.[15]

THE FACTIONAL SYSTEM

A second set of characteristics of factional politics concerns the size and configuration of the factional system as a whole, and the ways in which it relates to its political environment.

(11) Any factional arena will be composed of a rather limited number of factions, because in an arena with a very great number of factions, it would be in the interests of the factions to amalgamate, in order to defend against other factions doing the same thing. The incentives to amalgamate cease to be stronger than the incentives to engage in conflict only when the total number of factions has been reduced to the point where most of the constituent factions enjoy enough strength to launch political initiatives and defend themselves, while further amalgamation would simply bring in more followers to share the rewards of the faction without decisively affecting its ability to survive. It is doubtful whether more than a score or so of factions can exist in a given factional arena.

(12) Besides the unity of a code of civility (point 1) and of dependence on alliance with former enemies (point 5), the factional elite is further united by one overriding shared interest: that the resources for which they are struggling should be allocated among themselves and in accordance with the rules of conflict they are following, rather than to some force outside the system, which pays no attention to those rules and whose victory would end the existence of the factions. The result is a sharp difference between the modes of intraelite conflict described here and the drastic steps which may be taken by the united factional elite to resist external enemies or to destroy counterelites who challenge the legitimacy of the factional system. When, for example, a foreign conquest, rebellion, or military coup threatens to overthrow a factional regime, the factions will unite behind a suitable leader long enough to preserve the system, before returning to politics as usual.[16] If the threat to the system comes from within, from a factional leader attempting to break the rules, the efforts of the other factions will be directed toward defeating that attempt and reestablishing the stability of the system.

(13) Within the factional elite, it is taboo to question the principle of legitimacy on which the factions base their claim to a role in the larger society. Thus, for example, a factional parliament, regime, or party may play the role, in society at large, of a central or local government, on the basis of a constitutional or charismatic claim to legitimacy. No matter how much the vicissitudes of struggle oblige the factions to trample in fact on constitutional principles, or to disobey in fact their symbolic leader, these must never be openly questioned or flouted, since that would encourage other forces in society to "throw the rascals out." Thus politicians in factional systems compete in expressions of fealty to the constitution or leader, and rationalize every action and every position in terms of their fidelity to it or him. Care is taken to assure the constitutional or charismatic continuity of the regime.

(14) Issues which arise within the elite are resolved only slowly and with difficulty. The consensus which is necessary for action is difficult to achieve because every decision is more advantageous to some factions than to others. Only the cycle of crisis and consensus brings action, but it is short-term action to meet the immediate emergency, and may in any case be followed by contradictory decisions after the next cycle of conflict. The resulting failure of policy to move clearly in any one direction is what was called, in the French Third and Fourth republics, *immobilisme.*

(15) The immobilism of factional systems, the lack of extreme sanctions employed in their struggles, and their tendency to defend their existence against rival elites or external threats mean that they are in a certain sense extremely stable. It does not seem to be true, as

some writers have suggested, that factional systems have an inherent tendency to break down.[17] In the absence of outside pressures (including those from forces within the society), no force within the factional system is capable of amassing enough power to overthrow it. Thus, only continued factionalism can be predicted on the basis of the fact that a system is already factional.

Factions in China

To the extent that a factional model is applicable to China, one would expect to find either direct evidence of the existence of factions, such as descriptions of the organization and membership of specific factions, or circumstantial evidence of their existence, such as incidents which display the modes of conflict characteristic of factions. The Cultural Revolution period is a good place to begin the search for such evidence because of the relative openness of political conflict at all levels. The available evidence, I argue, permits the view that Chinese politics at the central government level has been structured largely by factions, especially if the Cultural Revolution is regarded not as a first outbreak of conflict but as an episode in which a long-standing factional system attempted to defend its existence against an attack by outside forces; that political conflict at the intermediate (regional and provincial) levels has been nonfactional, or, at most, intermittently factional; and that the local-level mass movements of the Cultural Revolution were essentially nonfactional.

FACTIONALISM AT THE CENTER

The center is an ill-defined elite of several hundred high officials of the party, army, and state bureaucracies. Almost all the members of this elite have devoted their lives to the revolutionary movement, are party members, and have served extensively in the People's Liberation Army (PLA). Despite differing current affiliations, therefore, it is a single elite whose political ties and concerns cross institutional boundaries. While party Central Committee membership is prestigious, it does not define the central elite, whose composition shifts more rapidly than central committees can be reconstituted. Informal organs such as the "work conference," with flexible membership, are the locus of political conflict within this central elite.[18]

There is some direct evidence of the existence of personal factions in this top elite. Scholars have been able to identify certain figures as followers of, among others, T'ao Chu, Lin Piao, Liu Shao-ch'i, and, of course, Mao Tse-tung. Analysis of the backgrounds of purged leaders suggests that certain shared experiences may have led to the formation of personal ties which help to explain who was purged during the Cultural Revolution. Many purged leaders have been charged with crimes like "fostering personal forces, establishing their personal authority, winning over defectors and renegades, forming private parties. . . ."[19] However, this evidence is not conclusive, and it remains impossible to delineate with confidence who the major factional leaders have been, much less who their followers were and are.

As circumstantial evidence, however, we find that the central political arena during the Cultural Revolution quite clearly displayed most of the fifteen characteristics of factional conflict. Almost all commentators have noted the absence of extreme sanctions against defeated politicians. Most defeated leaders were punished only by reeducation, while even the most severely sanctioned leaders suffered only the humiliation of mass denunciations; few, if any, were executed. Many purged leaders have now returned to office. Also noteworthy was the effort to provide some legal vindication, however flimsy, for the deposition of leaders like Liu Shao-ch'i and P'eng Chen, suggesting a concern for the constitutional continuity of the regime.

Defensive tactics predominated during the Cultural Revolution. One thinks of P'eng Chen's effort through his February 12 directive to turn the brunt of Mao's attack onto the "academic authorities"; the countermobilization of loyalist Red Guards or revolutionary rebels by local officials under attack; the disregarding or distortion of directives from the center; or the "sham" confessions which were actually self-justifications. By contrast, political initiatives such as Yao Wen-yuan's attack on Wu Han, or the launching of the Red Guards, were relatively rare and were apparently prepared in secret and sprung by surprise. Opposition to the emergence of a strong leader was shown by the resistance of other leaders to the accretion of power in Mao's hands. The shifting of factional alliances is reflected in the rise and fall of various propaganda directors, chiefs of staff, and the like; in the purging by 1969 of three-fifths of the pre–Cultural Revolution Central Committee; and in the fall of twenty-three of twenty-eight provincial leaders, of four out of five members of the original Group of Five directing the Cultural Revolution, and of thirteen of eighteen members of the Central Cultural Revolution Group.[20] The irrelevance of doctrine in determining factional alliances is suggested by the fact that many attacked as anti-Mao during this period had records which were utterly pro-Mao, while Chou En-lai, for example, who was not always particularly pro-Mao, managed to retain the title of a Maoist. The purges of Ch'en Po-ta and Lin Piao in 1971 were further validation of this.

That decision-making within the central elite was by consensus and compromise is suggested by the contradictory orders which were often issued simultaneously or even within the same document, such as the famous Sixteen Points, and by the oscillations noted by many analysts between radical and moderate policies emanating from the center. A closer look at these oscillations suggests that they followed the typical factional cycle in which a crisis leads to a policy decision, which itself becomes the focus of renewed conflict leading ultimately to another crisis. For example, the events of July to September 1967 began with a crisis, the Wuhan incident, which temporarily unified the factions at the center against rule-breaking violence by local military commanders against central officials. The call was issued to "pluck out a small handful" in the army. During August, the Red Guards responded by stealing weapons and attacking the PLA. Thus, the July decision which originally represented the joint interests of all the factions at the center in suppressing armed action by military dissidents, began to redound too strongly to the political advantage of the pro–Red Guard factions at the center. This led to renewed policy debate at the center and presumably to a showdown, which brought about a new decision—this time repudiating the concept of attacking a handful in the army, and purging three members of the Central Cultural Revolution Group.

The "comic opera" conflict of personal vilification and imaginative attack was certainly a feature of the Cultural Revolution, and, as we have seen, such tactics are serious and meaningful in factional systems, where the personal prestige, position, and contacts of the politician are his prime resources. Equally evident was doctrinalism, as seen, for example, in the practice of "waving the Red Flag to oppose the Red Flag."

Of the fifteen characteristics of factional politics, then, ten are identifiable in or consistent with the events of the Cultural Revolution. The eleventh—the relatively small number of factions in the system— cannot be confirmed or denied on the basis of our present inadequate information. It is perhaps too early to reach a judgment with respect to two further characteristics—immobilism and stability—although one could argue that no matter how much the Chinese political system seemed to be breaking down during the Cultural Revolution, it did not actually break down; and no matter how much it seemed to be making definite policy decisions, it did not opt for any single consistent foreign policy, development strategy, defense policy, policy on the role of intellectuals, or the like, but wavered between contradictory poles very much like a system composed of constantly shifting factional alliances.

This leaves two characteristics to be looked for—a taboo on discussion of the principle of legitimacy, and solidarity of the factions in the face of outside threats. The episode of the Red Guards seems to contradict these predictions, since members of the elite went outside the elite itself to mobilize a social force—the students (a force which had previously threatened many elites in modern Chinese history)— and encouraged this force to attack the leaders of the party itself. Yet the politics of the central elite was already factional in the early 1960s, and Mao, for reasons discussed below, apparently decided to break the rules of factional politics and directly mobilize a social force to destroy the factional system. The non-Maoist members of the factional elite responded, as the model predicts, with solidarity against the student threat, and took steps to demobilize the Red Guards. In doing so, they scrupulously avoided criticizing Mao, since they had in recent years increasingly based the legitimacy of the regime upon Mao's personal charisma rather than on the claimed historical mission of the party as an institution. I will return to this interpretation of the Cultural Revolution in the next section, after reviewing the evidence on conflict beyond the center.

FACTIONALISM AT THE INTERMEDIATE LEVEL AND LOCAL LEVEL

Data on political conflict at the intermediate levels of the Chinese political system have been scarce. Perhaps the most confident assertion we can make is that relatively independent political subsystems ("independent kingdoms") have existed in the Chinese political system. These include provinces—two famous examples being Inner Mongolia under Ulanfu and Szechwan under Li Ching-ch'üan—and bureaucracies such as the five field army systems of the PLA and the state bureaucracy under Chou En-lai.[21]

There was political conflict within many or all of these subsystems during the Cultural Revolution. There were struggles in every province and region over the composition of the revolutionary committees, and conflict was reported in such bureaucratic units as the PLA Air Force and the Ministry of Foreign Affairs. Although such episodes often displayed signs of factional conflict—e.g., they were long, complex, and indecisive, with a succession of contradictory policy outputs; there seemed to be limits on sanctions imposed on defeated leaders; and they were characterized by personal vituperation and by "waving the Red Flag to oppose the Red Flag"—we know too little about events in most of these arenas to characterize them with confidence.

Even if we tentatively conclude that the Cultural Revolution witnessed some factional conflict in many of the intermediate-level arenas of the Chinese political system, a number of important points remain obscure. We cannot be sure whether political conflict was factional in these arenas in the years before the Cultural Revolution or whether the Cultural Revolution brought out factions by causing the disintegration of institutions like party committees and PLA hierarchies. We don't know how intermediate-level factions during the Cultural Revolution related to factions at the center. Perhaps the best guess is that before the Cultural Revolution such independent kingdoms were institutional power bases dominated by factions whose leaders were participants at the central level. Factions within these outlying arenas were merely latent, and intraprovince or intrabureaucracy conflict was primarily "institutional" (resolved by authoritative institutional decisions arrived at by following legitimate, regular procedures of decision-making). The Cultural Revolution, initiated at the center and necessarily involving the fates of the "independent kings" around the country, weakened these institutions and gave intermediate-level factions the chance to emerge and fight for power.

As for the local levels, the evidence for factionalism seems, at first glance, to be unambiguous: beginning in January 1967, the Chinese press periodically launched attacks on "factionalism, anarchism, and sectarianism" at the local level. However, upon closer inspection, it appears that what the Chinese press called factionalism is not what is under consideration here. In the first place, the Red Guard units did not behave like factions in the sense here defined. They engaged in violent clashes, sometimes killing their enemies, and seemed to stress aggressive initiatives rather than defensive tactics. Rather than entering shifting alliances to block the emergence of strong leadership, Red Guard units tended to amalgamate in each city into two large armed camps, each under a strong leader. While it is often unclear why a Red Guard unit chose to ally with one camp rather than another, there is no evidence that preexisting clientelist ties structured the choice of association; rather, shared class background and ideological position appear to have been the determining factors. Instead of cycles of consensus and conflict, Red Guard organizations seem to have engaged in a downward spiral of increasingly violent confrontation.[22]

Indeed, the few concrete studies of the Red Guards and other units of "mass factionalism" indicate that these units were not structured as factions. The most detailed of such studies shows that the Red Guards in one Canton school at first organized as an elite formal organization consisting of "five-red" students, structured along the same lines as the school itself, so that the lowest unit in the Red Guard organizational hierarchy was a group of students selected from a given class. As this structure crumbled, the movement took on the loose structure of a mass of "friendship groups," each of which was apparently a corporate unit rather than a faction. The Red Guard units then sorted themselves into two stable alliance systems.[23]

The structure and political behavior of Red Guard and other mass factions bear more resemblance to those of certain loosely structured mass social movements than to those of factions as defined here. The coherence of these mass factions of the Cultural Revolution was based not on the mobilization of exchange-based clientelist ties for the pursuit of gain, but on the mobilization of social tensions and resentments which arose because of the differential access to rewards enjoyed by different social categories. People allied themselves with those whom they perceived as belonging to the same category, as disadvantaged in the same way, and as seeking the same type of reparation. The difference between the Cultural Revolution mass factions and most other mass movements was that they were highly responsive to signals from the center and thus lent themselves to manipulation as somewhat clumsy instruments in the factional struggle being waged there.

This does not mean that there was not also factionalism in the present sense in villages and enterprises. It seems likely that the launching of the Red Guards into factories and suburban areas weakened the institutional control and led in at least some places to the mobilization of factions to pay off old scores or otherwise take advantage of the opportunity presented. However, though this has a certain probability, we lack the evidence to show that it did take place.

An Interpretation of Factionalism of CCP History

This survey of the circumstantial evidence suggests that we are justified in delving further into the implications of factionalism as an explanation for Chinese politics. Let us accept as a working hypothesis that during the Cultural Revolution the politics of the center was structured largely by factions; and also that the politics of the Red Guards was nonfactional and that the intermediate-level independent kingdoms were at first internally organized as stable institutions, but suffered outbreaks of factionalism. Let us also assume that if factionalism was present in the Cultural Revolution, it had also been present in earlier periods. Since the purpose of this chapter is to establish the plausibility of factionalism as an explanation for Chinese elite politics, let us examine CCP history from the point of view of an interpretation of that history in terms of factionalism.

PRE-1959

Although factionalism as an explanation applies best to the period after 1959, we can explore the explanation further by assuming factionalism since the earliest days of the party as well. The Chinese Communist party and its army have formed throughout their history a single institutional system with a single elite performing simultaneously the functions of political and military leadership. While the institution as a whole was striving toward power in the Chinese revolution, its elite was from the beginning frequently racked with internal conflict. Studies of intraparty conflict have focused heavily on the explicit content of the ideological and policy issues under debate and have not analyzed the way in which the party/army elite organized itself for intraelite conflict or the way in which such conflict was carried out. The doctrinalism of these debates, the lack of extreme intraparty sanctions, the inability of Mao to exclude his opponents and their views from the party, all hint at the operation of factions; this suspicion is encouraged by the charges aired during the Cultural Revolution that Mao's enemies had built personal followings and opposed him throughout the history of the party.[24]

As the party/army elite grew, I argue, each major leader played upon his personal network of clientelist ties to cultivate a personal faction, seeding his followers in important party and army posts and using them and their resources of office, prestige, and personal connections to further his own standing in the movement and the adoption of the policies he thought it should follow. As it happened, the organization of intraparty debate by factions boded better for the future of the movement than would some other types of intraparty dissension. Through its limitation of sanctions and its shifting alliances, factionalism bound the movement together and prevented its fragmentation into permanently hostile rival movements.[25] Since the CCP as a whole existed in a condition of strong threat from the Kuomintang and the Japanese, it could not have survived if it had not limited its internal rivalries to the factional forms.

With the liberation in 1949, the organizational substructure increased in size and complexity, and the resources of power available for control by elite factions increased. However, the central elite itself, I hypothesize, remained factional in its internal divisions. It is not now possible to identify the factional leaders, but the obvious starting points for further research are such names as Mao Tse-tung, Teng Hsiao-p'ing, Liu Shao-ch'i, Lin Piao, P'eng Teh-huai, and Kao Kang. Factionalism would have been superceded (1) if intraelite conflict had ceased, which it clearly did not; (2) if a member of the elite had mobilized the institutional means (as did Stalin) or had the personal charisma to earn the sole power to resolve conflict, which also clearly did not occur; (3) if the party had split into permanently hostile segments which moved beyond the rules and resources of factional conflict toward the goal of mutual extirpation, which obviously did not occur; or (4) if the party had established procedural rules (e.g., voting in the Central Committee) which all its elite members accepted as the sole legitimate way to resolve controversy, and whose decisions were accepted as binding by all. This final alternative—the institutionalization of the party as a conflict-resolving mechanism—may have seemed for a time to have occurred, but as the 1950s wore on, the evidence accumulated that, on the contrary, factional conflict continued.

The factional conflicts were for the most part deeply hidden. Only occasionally, as in the Kao-Jao purge of 1954 and the P'eng Teh-huai purge of 1959, did factionalism erupt into public view. But the record of the 1950s and early 1960s is full of circumstantial evidence of factional conflict. This evidence includes regularly shifting policy lines (the alternation of radical and moderate policies in agriculture, foreign policy, cultural affairs, and the like), the often simultaneous issuing of contradictory policy signals, and the resulting failure of the system to move consistently in any single policy direction after the initial establishment of order and the destruction of the landlord class and other opposition elements. If, despite factional conflict, the allocation of most of the top posts in the polity remained essentially stable for most of the period, it was perhaps because many positions, such as Central Committee seats, were more honorary than substantive. Real power shifted more rapidly than formal position. Moreover, the struggle for position in the first decade or so after liberation probably centered on control of newly liberated regional and provincial independent kingdoms. It was a phase in which factional efforts were heavily directed at competing to consolidate power within the broad polity. The process which has been discerned in the PLA, in which each field army became the consolidated power base of one or more factions while "observers" from other factions were present in each field army (also serving as "hostages"), was probably widely repeated in other institutions throughout the system. As control of these bases became stabilized, the struggle shifted to new posts higher up in the system.

There is no reason to suppose that Liu Shao-ch'i and Mao were consistently on opposite sides of the issues during these years; quite possibly in the shifting alliances of elite factions they sometimes found themselves on the same side of an issue. But in 1959 in the aftermath of the Great Leap they found themselves opposing one another. Factional rivalries perhaps at this point reached a new stage of intensity, with the subsystems stabilized under factional control and conflict now focused on positions at the very top of the system. Most faction leaders were unified in the wish to subtract from Mao's too-dominant power. The bargain which was struck called for greater power to pass into the hands of Liu Shao-ch'i and his followers and allies, and for Mao to move into a weaker position.

Post-1959

The period from 1959 to 1962 was one of contradictory developments of the sort to be expected in the aftermath of such a factional consensus. Mao's actual power was weak, and within the small world of the elite he was subjected to persistent, damaging attack by followers of one of his rivals, P'eng Chen. At the same time, his charisma was exploited by the regime to strengthen its legitimacy, harmed by the Great Leap; the cult of Mao was launched even while—and perhaps all the more willingly because—Mao himself was in eclipse. The new minister of defense, Lin Piao, in an effort to solidify his own faction's control over the PLA, initiated a program to study the thoughts of Mao within the army. Whether he was already then allied with Mao or simply turned to the Mao-study campaign as a convenient means of consolidating his personal influence against rival factions in the PLA is unclear. In any case, the campaign made Lin a natural ally for Mao in the latter's counterattack on his rivals, which began in 1962.[26]

Mao's counterattack of 1962–1964, carried out with the help of Lin Piao, was still within the rules of factional strife. It included the

Socialist education campaign, the Learn-From-the-PLA campaign, the extension of PLA influence throughout the country, the escalation of the cult of Mao, and the pressure for attacks on intellectual cadres in the party. Mao's strategy was to use his national prestige, which his opponents had been obliged to enhance for the sake of the regime itself, and his alliance with Lin Piao to undermine the personal power of his rivals, founded in the party and cultural apparatuses. The rivals responded in typical factional fashion by stymying, blocking, and evading Mao's initiatives.

If Mao had continued to attack his rivals in the factional tradition of the party, he would eventually have precipitated another of the periodic elite crises, a realignment of the factions, and a redistribution of power which might have improved his position. But Mao decided to break the rules, to mobilize new sources of power from outside the elite. We may speculate that his goal was no longer merely an improved position for his faction within the elite, but an end to factionalism and its associated policy oscillations and an institutionalization of the party as an instrument of Maoist will, capable of outliving Mao himself. Perhaps a sense of impending death aroused at this moment a new urgency.[27] Lacking the organized intraparty power base of Stalin, Mao prepared to mobilize student power to drive his rivals out of office. The students were an attractive choice because of their historical role as official-topplers in modern China, because of Mao's faith in the revolutionary qualities of youth, and because of their suppressed tensions which were capable of exploding into a passionate political movement upon orders from a respected authority. "Perhaps for the first time in the history of a communist state," as one expert has written, "a leadership faction [was to go] outside the party for its main support."[28]

If the essence of the Cultural Revolution was, as I have argued, a student-based Maoist attack on the factional party elite, then its decisive period was the year in which the battle was fought over mobilizing versus demobilizing the students. This year (August 1966 to September 1967) saw a series of efforts by the factional elite to resist Mao's extraparty offensive, demobilize the Red Guards, and restore the factional conflict system, if not the factional alignments, of the first fifteen years of the regime. The ultimate reason for the victory of Mao's rivals was that Mao had no direct organizational link to the Red Guards and was obliged to employ means under the control of the party center (the authority of the party center, the hierarchy of party committees, the official press) to call the Red Guards into existence and to direct their activities. Even as he reached outside the factional system for his instrument of power, he remained dependent on the party for the means of wielding the instrument. In order to achieve his aims, Mao would have had to retain a shifting majority within the party center as he isolated his enemies one by one for attack by the students. This ultimately proved impossible. His efforts to achieve this shifting majority account for the rapid series of typical factional cycles of consensus, conflict, and crisis, each finding its response in the alternately rabid and restrained behavior of the Red Guards, which characterized the central year of the Cultural Revolution. Although the shifting alignments within the party center are invisible to us, the rhythms of the struggle can be perceived.

The first cycle began with the launching of the Red Guards in August 1966 under a compromise document, the Sixteen Points, which ordered the Red Guards to be both radical and restrained; proceeded through the countermobilization of loyalist student and worker-peasant groups by party officials; and moved to a crisis of disorder in September which caused the factions at the center to agree on the Red Guards' returning home and on the focusing of attacks on a small number of high party officials who had already suffered factional reverses in the preceding months. In the second cycle, the Maoists launched new attacks, centered in Peking and Shanghai, on officials in governmental organs, and denunciations were published of some high non-Maoist officers of the PLA; a crisis of disorder in factories, docks, and railways caused a new decision from the center in January 1967 for the intervention of PLA units to restore order. In the third cycle, factions resisting Mao seized the initiative and, in the "February adverse current," took a number of steps further restricting the Red Guard movement; the Maoists countered by publishing new attacks on the "top Party person," signaling a revival of Red Guard activism throughout the country; the resulting disorder finally reached such serious proportions that the center once again reached a decision in late April or early May 1967 for the reimposition of order by the PLA on the local level. In the fourth cycle, the Wuhan incident (July 1967) provided the Maoists with a pretext for demanding an attack on non-Maoist officers in the PLA; the resulting upsurge of the Red Guards led to the stealing of weapons and the outbreak of serious fighting; in response, the center reached the decision once again to clamp down on the masses; and in September Chian Ch'ing gave a speech attacking mass factionalism, and three Maoist members of the Central Cultural Revolution Group were purged.

The defeat of the fourth launching of the Red Guards, I argue, settled the fate of Mao's effort to end factionalism at the party center. Key factions at the center—perhaps an example was the faction of Chou En-lai—had supported Mao long enough to enable him to launch the successive Red Guard outbursts; we may speculate that such factions advanced their own positions as members of other factions became discredited by Red Guard attacks. Now such swing factions feared further Red Guard activism, either because they were ready to consolidate their own positions or because they felt that future attacks would be directed at them. Mao could no longer garner the support he needed within the central elite to give him access to the tools necessary to direct the Red Guards. He could no longer divide and conquer in the party center; on this issue, the other factions of the center were now united against him and his allies. Although the Cultural Revolution was to continue in name and with occasional outbreaks of violence, and although the press was to carry word of struggles between the left and the right until 1969, after September 1967 there was no longer any hope of using the Red Guards to cleanse the party center of factionalism.

But this did not mean that disorder came to a halt. Conflicts at the intermediate and local levels of the system had been called into being by the factional struggle at the top. They now had a momentum of their own. At the mass organization level, there was the problem of putting a stop to the downward spiral of vengeance, resentment, and violence, and of channeling aroused student activism into some controllable organizational framework. At the intermediate levels, many of the formerly secure subsystems had seen outbreaks of internal conflict, possibly of a factional nature, and most of these struggles were still under way. Thus the period from the autumn of 1967 to the autumn of 1968 was spent in trying to organize the masses in "great alliances" and the provincial and regional officials in revolutionary committees. The job of resolving local controversies and restoring order must have been rendered all the more complex by the fact that the interests of the factions of the party center were intimately bound up in each decision made. The shape of the future would be determined by the allocation of power in the regional and provincial revolutionary committees. These would be the new independent kingdoms upon which future factions would base their power.

The decision as to who would control the contested intermediate levels of 1968 was not solely in the hands of the party center (as it had been in the 1950s), but also depended upon the balance of strength of the locally contending groups (whether factions or not). The support of a central faction was not adequate to assure the dominance of an otherwise weak local figure over the revolutionary committee, while a strong figure without central backing could bargain for such legitimation with central factions. The implications of this fact for the personnel makeup of the factional center of the party were enormous. Many of the old factional leaders had already been humiliated and pushed from power. Now leaders on the regional and provincial levels found themselves in a position to bargain with the remaining factions of the center for exchanges of support. The result has been called an expansion of the central-level arena of conflict to include the intermediate-level leaders. I would interpret it as a partial "changing of the guard" in which a new generation of factional leaders was drawn into the central elite to replace those of the old elite who had fallen during the preceding two years. The system of factional conflict, however, remained unchanged.[29]

Since 1968 there have been conflicts over whether the Cultural Revolution was good or bad, the role of students, the constitution of the party, and a host of other issues. These conflicts have been carried out with many echoes of the Cultural Revolution—attacks on Liu Shaoch'i and Lin Piao, exhortations to rebel, and occasional outbreaks of local violence. There have also continued to be changes in personnel at the higher levels of the system—e.g., the purges of Ch'en Po-ta and of Lin Piao and his followers. Although these conflicts have been intricate and significant, they indicate not that the Cultural Revolution remains unsettled but that China remains fundamentally in the pre-Cultural Revolution pattern of factional conflict at the center.

Chinese Factionalism and the Comparative Study of Factions

The most important implication of this chapter for the comparative study of factionalism is that the study of factions can be put on a sound basis only when a satisfactory definition of faction is adopted, and that such a definition must be "structural"—i.e., faction must be defined in terms of a specific set of motives for participation and a specific set of communications patterns, and must be contrasted with other kinds of political organizations—whether parties, mass movements, tribes, armies, or whatever—that have different motivational (or compliance) structures and different communications structures.

The study of factions suffers when factions are defined in a way that brings together structurally and behaviorally diverse political units simply because they are feuding components of larger units or are called factions in their respective cultures. Such a procedure tries to bring into one analytic category units that are public and those that are secret; violent groups and nonviolent groups; the bureaucratically organized and the network-like; the instrumental and the ideological; the exchange-based, the class-based, and the program-based. The problem is that factions in this sense have little in common behaviorally. While organizational or group structure has long been recognized as one of the most powerful predictive variables for behavior in the social sciences, the factor of being simply a subunit of a larger unit is too vague to have much predictive value.

These considerations suggest why it seems desirable to locate the comparative study of factions within the study of clientelist political structures. Clientelist structures are a distinct structural type, characterized by the motivation of participants through dyadic exchange relationships of a specific kind. Moreover, among clientelist structures, subtypes may be discerned. Thus, in the typology distinguishing among brokerage, clientelist parties, and factions, factions are characterizable by their relatively small size and restriction to a small-scale or oligarchic arena, such as the Chinese central elite.

It would also be possible to characterize and compare total political systems in which clientelist political associations play an important role. Thus, for example, we might say that the "Philippine model" consists of homogeneous patron-client chains from top to bottom of the system, with no particular boundaries between levels; the "Indian model" consists of distinct local, provincial, and national factional arenas with factions at each level linked to those at the contiguous levels through shifting faction-to-faction deals and alliances; the "early twentieth century American model" consists of local-level machines permanently linked to a corporate party that has continuity at the national level; the "eighteenth century English model" has local-level machines linked to legislative factions at the national level; and the "Japanese model" is very much like the early English model with the difference that each machine at the local level is run directly by a member of the national-level faction, rather than by an independent local machine leader.

However one subdivides the diversity of clientelistically organized political units or systems, they share many behavioral characteristics: the flow of particularistic benefits, the resistance to change, the abhorrence of violence, and so on. If the field of study is narrowed specifically to factions, the range of common characteristics is increased.

This is not to argue that kinds of so-called factions which do not fit a definition in terms of clientelism ought not to be studied. But the structural basis of such units ought to be carefully scrutinized. If members do not participate for clientelist reasons, do they participate for ideological reasons, program reasons, communal-solidarity reasons? If communication is not primarily dyadic, is it bureaucratic? If decision-making is not concentrated in a leader, is it democratic, collegial, or consensual? Is the unit large or small? How many layers or segments does it contain? In these terms, what are often classed together as factions will be seen to be a diverse set of structures whose differences are most likely more important than their similarities.

Notes

1. Franz Schurmann, *Ideology and Organization in Communist China* (Berkeley and Los Angeles: Univ. of California Press, 1966), pp. 55–57. Opinion groups twice solidified into "organized opinion groups," Schurmann notes, but were quickly rooted out. We may regard as variants of his model those interpretations which classify leaders as "radicals" or "moderates," "dogmatists" or "pragmatists," etc., and view the Chinese political process as a debate among them.

2. See Michael C. Oksenberg, "Policy Making Under Mao, 1949–1968: An Overview," in John M. H. Lindbeck, ed., *China: Management of a Revolutionary Society* (Seattle: Univ. of Washington Press, 1971), pp. 79–115; and Philip Bridgham's three articles on the Cultural Revolution in *China Quarterly*, no. 29 (Jan.–Mar. 1967): 1–35; no. 34 (Apr.–June 1968): 6–37; and no. 41 (Jan.–Mar. 1970): 1–25; and Bridgham, "Factionalism in the Central Committee," in John Wilson Lewis, ed., *Party Leadership and Revolutionary Power in China* (Cambridge: At the Univ. Press, 1970), pp. 203–35.

3. See, for example, Lloyd Eastman, *Throne and Mandarins* (Cambridge: Harvard Univ. Press, 1967); Andrew J. Nathan, *Peking Politics, 1918–1923: Factionalism and the Failure of Constitutionalism* (Berkeley and Los Angeles: Univ. of California Press, 1975); and Hung-mao Tien, *Government and Politics in Kuomintang China, 1927–1937* (Stanford: Stanford Univ. Press, 1972).

4. Thus one study of elite politics in 1956–1957 makes occasional reference to factional alignments as a way of explaining political behavior, but also uses other kinds of explanations: Roderick MacFarquhar, *The Origins of the Cultural Revolution* (New York: Columbia Univ. Press, 1974), vol. 1.

5. It should be noted that this is not intended as a complete explanation for all aspects of CCP elite politics. It seeks to explain the mechanisms of conflict, not the ultimate motives for conflict, which at various times may have encompassed disagreements about the nature of man, the state of the world, the role of the party, the means to economic development, personal concern about the fate of the revolution, or personality clashes.

6. In recent years, studies of clientelist ties have proliferated. Terms vary—*dyadic contract, dyadic alliance, patronage tie, patron-client tie,* etc.—but they refer to the same general phenomenon. See George M. Foster, "The Dyadic Contract: A Model for the Social Structure of a Mexican Peasant Village," in Jack M. Potter, May N. Diaz, and George M. Foster, eds., *Peasant Society: A Reader* (Boston: Little, Brown, 1967), pp. 213–30; James C. Scott, "Patron-Client Politics and Political Change in Southeast Asia," *American Political Science Review* 66, no. 1 (Mar. 1972): 91–113; and Carl H. Landé, "Networks and Groups in Southeast Asia: Some Observations on the Group Theory of Politics," *American Political Science Review* 67, no. 1 (Mar. 1973): 103–27.

7. A distinction can fruitfully be made between clientelist parties defined as integrating all levels of the political system through clientelist ties, and machines, defined as operating strictly on the local level. See James C. Scott, *Comparative Political Corruption* (Englewood Cliffs: Prentice-Hall 1972), chs. 6–9; and John Duncan Powell, "Peasant Society and Clientelist Politics," *American Political Science Review* 64, no. 2 (June 1970): 411–25. For case studies of political systems organized by clientelist parties, see Robert

H. Dix. *Colombia: The Political Dimensions of Change* (New Haven: Yale Univ. Press, 1967), esp. chs. 8, 9; Keith R. Legg, *Politics in Modern Greece* (Stanford: Stanford Univ. Press, 1969), esp chs. 6–8; Myron Weiner, *Party Building in a New Nation: The Indian National Congress* (Chicago: Univ. of Chicago Press, 1967); and William Foote Whyte, *Street Corner Society* (Chicago: Univ. of Chicago Press, 1955), esp. ch. 6.

8. This concept of faction is similar to that offered by Ralph W. Nicholas, "Factions: A Comparative Analysis," in Michael Banton, ed., *Political Systems and the Distribution of Power*, Association of Social Anthropologists, Monograph no. 2 (London: Tavistock Publications, 1965), pp. 27–29; and to Landé's concept of the "dyadic following" in "Networks and Groups in Southeast Asia." It should be stressed that faction is here defined in a technical sense; by faction I do *not* mean an "organized opinion group" (Schurmann, *Ideology and Organization in Communist China*, p. 56), contending warlords, or Red Guards. Although restrictive, the definition advanced here seems to fit a wide range of configurations found in political systems and subsystems including governments, parties, bureaucracies, parliaments, courts, and villages in a number of different geographical areas and historical periods. Some examples are cited in Andrew J. Nathan, "Factionalism in Early Republican China: The Politics of the Peking Government" (Ph.D diss., Harvard Univ. 1970), pp. 372–85.

9. If a faction becomes corporatized, the clientelist relations are submerged in authority relations, and the structure ceases to be a faction in this sense. On the concept of corporate, see Max Weber, *Theory of Social and Economic Organization*, trans. A. M. Henderson and Talcott Parsons (New York: The Free Press, 1964), pp. 145–48.

10. Communications patterns and other structural features discussed here do not necessarily limit the size of clientelist parties as they do the size of factions. Although a clientelist party is founded on patronage dispensed through clientelist ties, it also takes on elements of formal organization (party label, headquarters, officers, rules) to enable it to administer its mass electoral base. It is in this sense not a "pure type" of clientelist structure. Faction and party both represent adaptations to the political environment: the clientelist party is adapted to, and tends to maintain, a mass electoral political system; the faction is adapted to, and tends to maintain, an oligarchic or small-scale system.

11. A major reason for differences in the power of factions is the differing power of their support structures (regional and/or institutional power bases). But opposing power bases cannot be entirely eliminated, nor, given the tendency of large, victorious factions to split, can they be taken over.

12. See Nathan Leites, *On the Game of Politics in France* (Stanford: Stanford Univ. Press, 1959). Also, cf. F. G. Bailey, "Parapolitical Systems," p. 282; Bernard Gallin, "Political Factionalism and Its Impact on Chinese Village School Organization in Taiwan," p. 390; and Melford E. Spiro, "Factionalism and Politics in Village Burma," pp. 410–21, all in Marc J. Swartz, ed., *Local-Level Politics: Social and Cultural Perspectives* (Chicago: Aldine, 1968).

13. In the Chinese context, for example, factional alignments did not cross the ideological boundaries between the late Ch'ing conservatives on the one hand and the constitutionalists and revolutionaries on the other, or between the Kuomintang and the CCP. But within each major ideological current, factional alignments were not determined by ideological compatibilities; ideological stands were developed and revised in the course of politics.

14. Cf. James L. Payne, *Patterns of Conflict in Colombia* (New Haven: Yale Univ. Press, 1968), pp. 3–24. Payne attempts to explain factionalism in Colombian politics on the basis of the prevalence of status incentives rather than program incentives among Colombian politicians. Yet factionalism may occur in the presence of either type of incentive: politicians in factional systems will tend to act as if they were motivated by status incentives because of the importance of personal prestige and personal connections as political resources in factional systems; it is immaterial how high-minded the ultimate motives for conflict are.

15. Myron Weiner, *Party Politics in India: The Development of a Multi-Party System* (Princeton: Princeton Univ. Press, 1957), pp. 237–40. See also Lewis A. Coser, *The Functions of Social Conflict* (New York: The Free Press, 1964), pp. 33–38.

16. Of course, they may not succeed in preserving the system. If the social context of the regime has been changing so that, for example, new problems demand solutions or new groups demand access to the system, immobilism (see point 14) may prevent the

regime from responding successfully. The consequent loss of legitimacy may make it an easy target for a strong rival. An example is the crumbling of the Peking government before the Kuomintang advance in 1928. The Clemenceau and Poincaré ministries in France are well-known instances of resistance by a factional system to external threat. See Phillip M. Williams, *Crisis and Compromise: Politics in the Fourth Republic* (Garden City: Anchor Books, 1966), p. 11.

17. Bernard J. Siegel and Alan R. Beals, "Pervasive Factionalism," *American Anthropologist* 62 (1960): 394–417.

18. Parris H. Chang, "Research Notes on the Changing Loci of Decision in the Chinese Communist Party," *China Quarterly*, no. 44 (Oct.–Dec. 1970): 170–73.

19. Cited in *Hung-ch'i* [Red flag], no. 12 (1967), which is excerpted in "Quarterly Chronicle and Documentation," section of *China Quarterly*, no. 32 (Oct.–Dec. 1967): 198. Cf. Parris H. Chang, "Mao's Great Purge: A Political Balance Sheet," *Problems of Communism* 18, no. 2 (Mar.–Apr. 1969): 8.

20. See Richard Baum, "China: Year of the Mangoes," *Asian Studies* 9, no. 1 (Jan. 1969): 3–4; and Gordon A. Bennett, "China's Continuing Revolution: Will It Be Permanent?" *Asian Studies* 10, no. 1 (Jan. 1970): 3.

21. Frederick C. Teiwes, in *Provincial Party Personnel in Mainland China, 1955–1966* (New York: Columbia Univ., East Asian Institute, 1967), has shown (p. 62) that provincial leadership was mainly stable during the 1956–1966 period, which seems consistent with the independent kingdoms view advanced here, although Teiwes himself concludes that the data do not support the idea of province-level factions (pp. 27–28).

22. This analysis is based on Ezra F. Vogel, *Canton Under Communism: Programs and Politics in a Provincial Capital, 1949–1968* (Cambridge: Harvard Univ. Press, 1969), pp. 323–35; Gordon A. Bennett and Ronald N. Montaperto, *Red Guard: The Political Biography of Dai Hsiao-ai* (Garden City: Doubleday, 1971); and John Israel, "The Red Guards in Historical Perspective: Continuity and Change in the Chinese Youth Movement," *China Quarterly*, no. 30 (Apr.–June 1967): 1–32.

23. See, for example, "Mass Factionalism in Communist China," *Current Scene* 6, no. 8 (May 15, 1968): 1–13.

24. See, for example, Benjamin I. Schwartz, *Chinese Communism and the Rise of Mao* (Cambridge: Harvard Univ. Press, 1952); and John E. Rue, *Mao Tse-tung in Opposition, 1927–1935* (Stanford: Stanford Univ. Press, 1966).

25. This generalization applies best to the history of the party after about 1938. Before that there were several incidents of intraparty military conflict and of permanent splits.

26. See Philip Bridgham, "Mao's 'Cultural Revolution': Origin and Development," *China Quarterly*, no. 29 (Jan.–Mar. 1967): 2–7. Also see Ralph L. Powell, "The Increasing Power of Lin Piao and the Party Soldiers, 1959–1966," *China Quarterly*, no. 34 (Apr.–June 1968): 62–63; and Merle Goldman, "Party Policies Toward the Intellectuals: The Unique Blooming and Contending of 1961–1962," in Lewis, ed., *Party Leadership and Revolutionary Power in China*, pp. 268–303.

27. So Robert Jay Lifton has argued, in *Revolutionary Immortality: Mao Tse-tung and the Chinese Cultural Revolution* (New York: Vintage Books, 1968).

28. John Wilson Lewis, "Leader, Commissar, and Bureaucrat: The Chinese Political System in the Last Days of the Revolution," in Ping-ti Ho and Tang Tsou, eds., *China in Crisis* (Chicago: Univ. of Chicago Press, 1968), vol. 1, bk. 2, p. 474. Note that if one views the Cultural Revolution not as a factional attack on Mao but as a Maoist attack on factions, one disposes of most of the objections to a factional interpretation raised by Frederick C. Teiwes, in "A Review Article: The Evolution of Leadership Purges in Communist China," *China Quarterly*, no. 41 (Jan.–Mar. 1970): 122–35.

29. Cf. Donald W. Klein and Lois B. Hager, "The Ninth Central Committee," *China Quarterly*, no. 45 (Jan.–Mar. 1971): 55–56. This is a new generation in the sense that these men had not previously been operating at the central level. Most or all of them had been high officials of the party or army or both. They had been followers in factions, we assume, but now they emerged as leaders in their own right, in the aftermath of the deterioration of many of the pre–Cultural Revolution factions.

Part Five
CONCLUSION

17

Party and Faction: Modes of Political Competition

Dennis C. Beller
Frank P. Belloni

Defining Faction

Factions in varied forms exist in the politics of numerous countries around the world, a few of which have been described in the preceding chapters. The terms and labels for factions vary according to the languages and country; e.g., *habatsu* in Japanese, *siya* in Hebrew, *tendance* in French, and *correnti* in Italian; and in Spanish, *sub-lema* in Uruguay, *sector* in Bolivia, and a number of terms—*línea, corriente, ala, tendencia,* etc.—in Chile. Perhaps because of the existence of so many expressions for and notions about factions, there is, as Raphael Zariski notes in some detail in Chapter 2, very little agreement on the definition of faction.

Nevertheless, it is possible to clarify the dimensions of the lack of agreement. In general, scholars vary from those preferring a precise and restrictive definition to those preferring a loose and flexible definition. Andrew Nathan, for example, has come out strongly in support of a narrow definition of faction—specifically, the methodologically refined concept of the "clientelist" group. Nathan provides an extensive discussion of the precision in meaning of which that concept is capable. He is insistent that other types of group formation, even if called factions in common parlance, should by definition be some sort

417

of structure other than true factions. In contrast, other authors prefer a broader, more generalized definition. Thus Christopher Mitchell defines faction broadly as any "deep structural division" within a movement or tendency; and K. G. Machado describes factions as variable by "basis, degree, and permanence of organization."

Most often, however, scholars have favored a broad approach, acknowledging that there are different basic types of factions. In their study of American factions, for example, Thomas Roback and Judson James make use of the distinction initiated by William Chambers, suggesting that there are both preparty factions and intraparty factions;[1] however, they add that there may be a further distinct type, postparty factions. In his study of British party cleavages, Arthur Cyr utilizes the distinction originated by Richard Rose, between a faction proper and a tendency.[2] This distinction is also relied upon by Roback and James, but according to them a tendency should be viewed more as a subtype of faction rather than as something which contrasts with faction. A different sort of distinction is made by Peter Merkl in his chapter on West German politics: that between intraparty factions and nonpartisan factions in local politics.

Another basis for distinguishing among factions relies primarily on levels of organizational sophistication. Frank Belloni notes a difference in Italy between factions of notables on the one hand, and more ideological and more organized factions on the other. He describes Italian Christian Democratic party factions as in large part having changed from the former type to the latter type. Similarly, Mitchell describes a difference between informal factions and formal factions in Bolivia's MNR; and Ronald McDonald describes a basic difference between personalistic, ad hoc factions found in Colombian parties and more institutionalized and bureaucratized factions found in Uruguayan parties.

Finally, factional forms are distinguished on yet another criterion: extraparty or cross-party or even multiparty factions, which include all or parts of more than one party. Indeed, among those inclined toward a broader definition of faction, one of the most significant points to emerge from several of the case studies in this book is that the very distinction between party and faction—the distinction taken for granted at least since the early faction studies of V. O. Key, Jr.[3]—may itself be invalid or in need of modification. Several authors have discussed such cross-party factional groups in this volume. Merkl notes that Germany has been characterized by occasional cross-party factions; and Roback and James report a number of cross-party coalition factions. A similar observation is made for France by Bruce Campbell and Sue Ellen Charlton, who note an overlapping of faction and party in that country. The point is made particularly succinctly by Mitchell in his analysis of Bolivian factions: factions "may take the form of organized subunits within a political party, or of many rival parties within a given ideological movement." Mitchell goes on to offer a justification for dropping the party/faction distinction:

> Mutually hostile subunits within a given party may elect to stay within a very loose confederation, or they may set themselves up as formally separate parties. These new parties, in turn, may further subdivide or may recombine into multiparty "fronts" or even into new parties. Thus, rigid distinctions between intraparty and interparty division don't seem helpful. . . .

It is clear that scholars recognize several different types of factional formations, distinguishable by a variety of factors, including basic structural properties, organizational context, and perhaps other factors. One may prefer to reserve the term *faction* for only one of the recognized types, and to search for more suitable names for the other types; or one may regard many or all of them as factions, and consider that the phenomenon of faction has several distinguishable subclassifications. It seems clear to us that the latter is the more desirable course, because of its implications for functional properties of factions—an argument we shall pursue further at the end of this chapter.

We propose therefore that a more valid definition of faction—at least at the present state of our knowledge and our theory—is a flexible and relative one, one which permits classification of types of factions in accordance with various kinds of structural patterns, and in accordance with various organizational contexts within which factions exist. We thus define faction as *any relatively organized group that exists within the context of some other group and which* (as a *political* faction) *competes with rivals for power advantages within the larger group of which it is a part.*

The case studies in this book have described the full range of the varied and distinguishable forms of factional groupings. We find two fundamental characteristics in terms of which the many different concepts of faction vary, and thus in accordance with which different factional types are classifiable. These are organizational characteristics and contextual characteristics. Organizationally, we identify three modal types of factions: (1) factional cliques or tendencies; (2) personal, client-group factions; and (3) institutionalized or organizational factions. The second type, client-group factions, may be further subdivided into small, private followings and larger more routinized machines.

ORGANIZATIONAL CHARACTERISTICS OF FACTION TYPES

The first type, factional cliques or tendencies, includes those group formations composed of individuals who have some interest in common—ideological, policy, material, personal, or other—but who are not at all formally organized in pursuit of that goal or interest. Indeed, cliques may very nearly lack organization altogether, or else whatever organization exists is highly informal and transitory, and is not necessarily a consciously perceived organization on the part of the group's members. Often groups of this type are described with terms like *wings* of a party or organization, *currents* or *tendencies,* or *informal factions.* The model for this type of faction corresponds generally to the ad hoc and tendency groups first described by Rose, although he did not extend his concepts beyond the restricted context of parliamentary parties.

The second type, personal or client-group factions, refers to the model that has been well developed, initially by the social anthropologists, and which has been used by Nathan, Fukui, Nicholson, and Machado in this book. Variously termed *patron-client* groups, *clientelist* groups, etc., personal factions are unlike cliques in that they have true organization, in the specialized form of the unique, personally recruited and maintained bond of leader and follower. The further subclassification of this type of faction recognizes the established distinction between highly personal factions recruited privately and on a small scale, and often in a traditional context—the following; and those personal factions recruited on a more public and slightly larger scale, and often in the context of the mass franchise—the machine. Machines are capable of consisting of more "layers" in their organizational structure, thus slightly depersonalizing the leader for the lower ranks of the membership and making him more of a symbol—such as with the notorious "boss" of a city machine in America. The chapter by Machado illustrates some of these distinctions between a traditional, personal following and a more modernized personal machine. Various published writings that develop the model of the client-group have been mentioned in the preceding chapters,[4] and Nathan's study of factionalism in the Chinese Communist party provides one such construction of the model (see Chapter 16), including the distinction between a following (called by Nathan a true faction) and a machine.

The third type, institutionalized or organizational factions, are those groups that correspond to or approximate the model of a formalized organization—one which has acquired a significant number of the features social scientists consider attributes of a "corporate" group. Factions of this type are frequently described with the terms *formalized* factions, *developed* factions, etc. This type consists of those factions that differ completely not only from the almost organizationless cliques but also from client-groups, in that their organization does not rest on the personal bond of leader-follower recruitment and exchange but consists instead of more impersonal, egalitarian mechanisms of joining an organization, having officials, being subject to formal rules and following regular procedures, and having names or nonpersonal symbols for the group, etc. One model for the institutionalized faction is represented in Roback and James's seven-characteristic version of faction, in Chapter 14; another is in concepts of the corporate group, such as that of M. G. Smith,[5] cited in Chapter 5 by Myron Aronoff.

The other basis on which different types of factions are identifiable is context. The most prominent context of factions in political studies is that of political parties, but in fact political party lumps together several politically significant types of faction contexts. Thus, preparty factions, intraparty factions, cross-party factions, and perhaps post-party factions as Roback and James suggest, all constitute different types of factions—their differences consisting in the context. Moreover, intraparty factions are further subclassifiable: there are major and fundamental differences between intraparty factions of the party elite, the party activists, and the party rank and file; and between intraparty factions of the party's organizational segments—such as the parliamentary party, the party bureaucracy, the local branches, the candidates' campaign organizations, etc.

Additionally, outside of parties altogether, faction types are distinguishable in villages or towns—contexts whose factions have been extensively studied by political anthropologists and more recently by political scientists as well. Contextual classification of factions is hardly exhausted by reference to parties and villages, however, even though those are the two sets of contexts most extensively dealt with by students of politics. While they have not been considered here, this dimension of classification would certainly include factions in government bureaucracies, in military services, and other sectors of government; in private businesses and associations, interest groups, labor unions, churches, clubs, etc. There are a great many contexts, and therefore contextual types, of factions; the point here is to recognize that context, as much as structure, determines faction type.

These types of factions are models, and real factions will correspond to or fit the models well or badly. Real factions may be found to be somewhere between two of the organizational types, or even to have attributes of all three. Moreover, real factions are under no obligations to these models and may change their nature and thus their classification. A group may exist for a time as a clique or as a client-group, but then acquire formal, institutional organization; an institutional faction, likewise, may abandon formal organization to become an almost unorganized clique or tendency or to be reconstituted on the basis of a personalized clientelist recruitment. In the same way, real factions may not correspond perfectly to predetermined contextual types; real factions may thus overlap two or more contextual categories or exist in contexts difficult to classify precisely. Finally, it should also be clear that there is no necessary definitional relationship between factions of a particular organizational type and factions of a particular contextual type. Factional cliques, client-groups, or institutionalized factions may exist as preparty factions, as parliamentary party factions, as cross-party factions, as village factions, etc.; stated the other way around, factions in a village or within a party membership or party elite—or in any context—may be cliques, client-groups, or highly developed factional organizations.

Comparative Faction Structure

As we saw in Chapter 1, analyses of factions have taken three general directions: study of the structural characteristics of factions, of the causes of factions, and of the functional roles and consequences of factionalism. Most structural characteristics—e.g., duration, cognition, internal cleavages, and the many factors of faction organization, such as membership, leadership, hierarchy, communications, etc.—vary according to what structural type of factions are being described. This is the reason precise structural definitions of faction tend to exclude certain types of factions: some are by definition highly structured, some are distinctive because of their relative lack of structure.

CLIQUES AND TENDENCIES

Factional cliques and tendencies have very little structure. They are either almost totally unorganized or else they exhibit a very ephemeral organization, such as a single issue or electoral campaign may generate and which is typically quite informal. For unorganized, ad hoc tendencies, membership is vague at best, usually consisting of self-identification or even externally ascribed identification; there normally is no purposeful recruitment at all. A leader's personality may be prominent, but in a charismatic, not a clientelist, manner. Organizational leadership is ad hoc, and hierarchical chain of command is nonexistent. Such groups usually acquire only nicknames or "tags," sometimes originating with the press or other outside observers; or they have no identifying symbol at all. Cliques generally lack headquarters, scheduled meetings, regularized procedures, organizational specialization, etc.; occasionally a few of these characteristics may exist, but on an ad hoc basis and in an informal and uninstituted fashion.

Duration of life as a group is typically very short for cliques and tendencies. Cliques that come into existence in response to a specific issue or candidate's campaign last as long as that issue or electoral campaign. Cliques that exist as ideological wings or tendencies, however, may last longer, although quite often in a very sporadic fashion. Such ad hoc groups are highly susceptible to internal division into subcliques or subtendencies. Intraparty cliques and tendencies may or may not be associated with some outside organization or interest. With respect to cognition, cliques are frequently composed of members with a minimum of cognizance of their shared membership in a group, except in a vague way, or at the irregular occasions of their common mobilization to action in a conflict over an issue or in an election.

Some of the preparty factions that Chambers first studied were of this cliquish type; and tendencies in contemporary Britain were described by Rose. Several of the case studies in this book deal with clique-type factions. In Chapter 12, Cyr describes the factional cliques in Britain's Conservative parliamentary party. They are, he finds, "ad hoc alliances of MPs gathered together on a particular issue, having at times strong ties to constituency associations and economic interest groups, without the formal organization and continuity over time characteristic of factions." Membership in these groups is very loosely determined and largely dependent upon an individual's self-identification. The groups were mobilized to act as groups only insofar as their members tended to vote or speak out in the same ways when the relevant issue came up. There was also a longer-lasting factional clique of opposition to the abolition of retail price maintenance, and other attempts to develop organized factions on the Conservative party's right, but the basic character of divisions in the Conservative party has remained that of factional cliques. Cyr describes the Labour party as consisting of a well-organized institutional faction on the party's left wing, plus a moderate group, consisting essentially of the remainder of the party, as a counterpart to the Labour left. It might be argued, however, that the moderates of Labour may be more aptly characterized as a large factional tendency than as an organized faction. Its characteristic simply as the amorphous group of those of the parliamentary party *not* in the left faction suggests this: clearly it differs in structure from the more organized left.

Roback and James in Chapter 14 deal with factions different from those described by Cyr, in that their subjects are not parliamentary factions but factions of party mid-elites and activists. They thus describe factions of a different contextual type. In that context, the authors find a contemporary trend—in both the Democratic and Republican parties—of older party machines and organized factions being replaced by cliques and tendencies. These factional cliques, the authors indicate, are of two subtypes: ideological tendencies or wings of parties, and electoral tendencies. Ideological wings "have no continuing structures of communication and mobilization and have no organizational basis. . . ." Some examples they give are the plantation and new right conservatisms in the South, and regional subcultural ideological groups. In electoral tendencies, "like-minded individuals band together in nomination and campaign situations to support particular candidates. . . ." These are not, however, the same thing as institutionalized campaign organizations; rather, they are typified by mass, volunteer amateurs. Examples the authors give are the Goldwater, McCarthy, and McGovern presidential campaign movements, as they refer to them; and although the examples they cite are national in character, electoral tendencies also occur at the state- and local-government levels. These factions may approximate the form of a client-group faction or even an institutionalized faction, in that they may acquire an organizational structure resembling a political machine or professional campaign team; but as long as their organization is essentially temporary, they remain basically factional tendencies.

In Chapter 11, Mitchell describes Bolivian factions that were cliques, especially in the leftist and reformist movement in the 1930s —groups that "were usually small circles of political activists. . . ." He notes that although "personality certainly played an independent role occasionally, more usually ideas or ideological commitments cast personalities in one competing group or another." Some of these groups underwent changes and acquired more organizational characteristics in the 1940s and 1950s, and during the years of the MNR's rule in Bolivia, the political system of the MNR/governmental elite was a mixed collection of factions having some institutionalized characteristics, some clientelist characteristics, and some, as the author describes, were *camarillas* ("cliques").

Factional cliques and tendencies may be identified in various other political systems. It appears that the Gaullist UDR in France is a party of cliques and tendencies. Although groups with some institutionalized organization have from time to time existed within the UDR —such as the UDT—almost all the factions described by Campbell and Charlton, from the old-guard Gaullists to the New Frontier, and to the many personality cliques, ideological wings, and tendencies defined by tactical posture toward the current president of the republic, are classifiable as factional cliques.

Personal, Client-Group Factions

Personal or client-group factions are based on the person of their leader, and the hierarchy of personal subleaders within them; organizationally, client-groups reflect the special circumstances of their personal, leader-follower nature. The specialized clientelist recruitment constitutes the very basis of the formation and continued existence of the faction. This is particularly true for those client-groups which are purely personal followings—groups which are wholly dependent for their existence on individual recruitment of each follower by the leader and which thus consist of faction "members" only in this special sense. The authors whose concern is client-groups of this personal following type all agree that membership size is always small for such groups. In machine-type client-group factions, on the other hand, there are more layers of leaders' followers as subleaders, whose followers are sub-subleaders with followers of their own, etc.; here, membership size can become a good deal larger and tends to acquire a bit more anonymity in the sense that the rank and file are further removed from personal dependence on the top leader.

Hierarchy or chain of command in personal factions is always theoretically limited to the vertical link pattern of relationships which defines all aspects of intrafaction organization and communication. It is in a leader's interest to discourage horizontal links, which will tend to weaken the group's cohesiveness and will tend to compromise the clientelist nature of the faction, inclining it more toward an organizational faction. Other organizational characteristics may vary greatly, except that the pattern of structure by personal, vertical ties is retained. Most often the names for these groups are the name of the leader, which comes to be a symbol for the entire group. Ordinarily only the office or home of the leader comes informally to serve as a headquarters for the faction. Normally meetings are not held on a regular basis; indeed, as Nathan argues, meetings of the entire faction are likely to be unnecessary, and may never be held. If meetings are held, they do not depend upon regularized rules and procedures, but upon the pyramid of personal ties of the members.

Client-group factions are generally of intermediate duration; they tend to last much longer than a single political issue or electoral campaign—the typical duration of cliques—yet they are ordinarily unable to outlast the active political life of the faction leader. When personal factions manage to persist beyond the careers of their leaders, this ordinarily represents a new, successor client-group faction or else the modification of the faction in the direction of a less personal, more institutional faction—perhaps with the original leader taking on symbolic, but not leadership, functions for the group. Subfactions may exist, as several of the preceding chapters have shown, in the form of networks of patron-client relationships within the factions; indeed, client-groups frequently subdivide and split along the lines of their internal leader-follower structure. Personal factions, like cliques and tendencies, may or may not be associated with outside interest groups. Finally, with reference to cognition, client-group factions are generally composed of members aware of their common identity, though not necessarily mobilized by that awareness; that is, awareness will tend to be restricted to the vertical links which structure the group internally.

Most of the preparty factions in Chambers' studies were personal factions of this type, generally personal or family followings; the factions in Key's studies were cliquish personal machines, for the most part, organized by party leaders and by candidates in support of their campaigns. As we have seen, also, it was clientelist followings that were the primary concern of the anthropologists like Nicholas[6] and others, who developed the study of traditional village factions. Several authors have presented studies of personal client-group factions in this book, some concentrating on the analysis of the pure type or model of the client-group and others concentrating on analysis of real factions in particular countries. Nicholson, in his study of policy outcomes of the factional politics at various levels of India's political system in Chapter 7, describes the client-group as a general concept. A most fulsome treatment of the clientist model of faction is offered by Nathan, who uses the model for analyzing not traditional village factions but factions in the Chinese Communist party central elite. A model such as this is particularly apt for a country like China, Nathan finds, because of the Chinese Communist party's absolute prohibition against formal, organized intraparty factionalism. In Chapter 15, Carl Linden finds essentially similar indications in the Soviet elite, where factionalism "focuses within a rather narrow arena at the apex of the bureaucratic pyramid of the party and the party-state and from there reverberates downward through the structure of the party and state."

In Chapter 3, Fukui presents a picture of culturally determined clientelist organizational principles, found extensively throughout Japanese society. In Japanese party factions particularly, however, Fukui finds that there is some tendency for factions to develop beyond the generic client-group type, a change the author characterizes as a move from the informal structure, typical of Japanese tradition, to a more formal mode of structure—a modern development in Japanese society. In Chapter 4, Belloni describes a similar change among Italy's Christian Democratic factions, which were initially groups of devotees of party notables, essentially personalized, informal, and clientelist in organizational structure, and concentrated among the party elite—in party executives, national party assemblies, and the parliamentary party. Examples were the Gronchiani (followers of Giovanni Gronchi) and the Dossettiani (followers of Giuseppe Dossetti) in the late 1940s and early 1950s. Subsequently, through the efforts initially of some DC faction leaders, and eventually as a result of decisions by leaders of the party, all the DC's major factions became more institutionalized—more organized, and more formalized and discrete in structure.

Machado, in his analysis of local factions in Philippine party politics in Chapter 8, finds that client-group factions have been of two subtypes: the older type, essentially a traditional, family-based personal following; and a newer type, essentially an electoral phenomenon and more of a personal political machine. The organizational center of the traditional factional following was a landowning extended family, held together by bonds of kinship and marriage; the faction organization and membership were based on patron-client relationships consisting, for the most part, of kinship dependencies and the relations between landlord and tenant farmer, organized through tenant farm "overseers," who were the electoral organizers, or *liders*. The factional machine was more of a public office-oriented organization; patronage, rather than kinship and tenancy, constituted the basis of the leader-follower tie. These factions consisted less of rural aristocrats and peasant farmers and more of emancipated "new men." The faction leadership depended on a team of followers who were loyal personally to the leader, who were mostly public officeholders (barrio captains and councillors, etc.), and who had their own loyal followers, who constituted the faction *liders* or voter organizers—in a fashion reminiscent of earlier American "ward heelers."

Probably the classic version of the machine is the late nineteenth- and early twentieth-century American city machine, described by Roback and James in Chapter 14. Heavily based on public patronage and fed by the waves of Southern European and other immigrants to American cities at that time, machines were, as the authors say, exceptionally durable and effective, some with internal organizational machinery sufficiently developed so as to approximate a more organizational type of faction. The American machine largely declined by the middle of the twentieth century, though, as the authors indicate, a few machines of the old style continue to exist today.

INSTITUTIONALIZED, ORGANIZATIONAL FACTIONS

Institutionalized factions are distinct as a faction type primarily because of their developed organizational structure and its relative formalization. The personal appeal of a leader may be a part of the basis of cohesiveness of institutional factions, but if organization is more formal than personal, and if the leader's appeal is more public and symbolic than personal and private, then the group is basically an institution and not a personal or client-group faction. Almost any kind of common interest can be the basis for the existence of such a group, from ideological interests to material interests, from a public-spirited interest to a selfish one, and—for the individual—even the mere interest of joining for joining's sake. Structures—including all the organizational factors of name, membership, leadership, procedures, durability, etc.—are sufficiently developed that the faction is or approximates a corporate group.

Membership of institutional factions is relatively formalized, at times taking the form of semiofficial membership lists, even membership cards. The French political scientist, Maurice Duverger, had reported "friends" subscription cards for members of Socialist factions in France in the 1930s;[7] such membership lists and cards are described by Mitchell for more formally organized factions of Bolivia's MNR in the 1960s, and according to Belloni, Italy's Christian Democratic factions had membership lists (although not cards) even at the local level. Recruitment is ordinarily aggressively prosecuted, the goal being not so much to bring new individuals into a personal relationship with a faction leader as to add sheer numbers to the ranks of the faction. Leadership in institutionalized factions can become highly officialized, although the factions in the case studies in this book tended to retain a large measure of informality in leadership roles. Similarly, there is potential for internal hierarchical lines of authority to become extensively and formally developed, but in these case studies they are reported as being only partially developed—except when a faction captures portions of the party executive or party bureaucracy and uses the latter's hierarchy as its own.

Nevertheless, institutional factions develop considerable routinization of rules and procedures, with scheduled meetings, preplanned agendas, formal votes, and sometimes elaborate records of their proceedings, and often with designated meeting places or faction headquarters. They take names—the name of the leader or of a founding or former leader, but often also more formal names implying ideological identification, inspirational symbolism, or functional equivalence to political parties. Some engage in outside organizational activities—such as certain Israeli factions do with their respective kibbutz movements; and some achieve a certain amount of internal specialization—such as having a recognized press staff or public relations staff, or having designated experts on this or that subject. Many maintain their own press, and most keep at least some treasury. Intraparty institutionalized factions, like the other categories of factions, may or may not be associated with extraparty interest groups; when they are, various outside organizational facilities often become available to them—such as the facilities provided by the collateral groups associated with certain factions of Italy's Christian Democratic party.

In durability, institutional factions may be very long-lasting—although this is not necessarily assured to them. Having lasting organizational bonds makes them capable of continued existence beyond issues and elections, and beyond their leaders' careers and lives. Generally, although formal organization also tends to mitigate against it, institutional factions, too, may contain factions within them, especially if they become quite large and diverse in membership. Finally, with respect to cognition, institutional factions are almost always highly self-conscious as groups. To some extent, members' consciousness of their factional identity is one basis of the existence of the faction as a group and, in any case, is fostered by the formalization and symbolization of the group and by its public activities.

Aronoff, in Chapter 5, deals with the institutionalized faction as a conceptual type. He proposes that corporateness and noncorporateness be considered as extremes on a continuum, rather than as exclusive type-classifications which assign a priori identifications to party and faction. To define corporateness, Aronoff borrows from an anthropologist, M. G. Smith, eight discrete properties of corporate group formation: boundedness, determinate membership, identity, organization, procedure, common affairs, autonomy, and presumed perpetuity. Rather than use these as dichotomizing criteria, as Smith did, Aronoff suggests that they each be used as the basis of a scalar measurement of actual factions. The three factions of the Israel Labor party are all to some degree organizationally developed; yet they differ significantly from each other in the degree to which they reflect or do not reflect the eight qualities of corporateness. One, Rafi, is very incompletely developed on all the characteristics and marginally corporate at best, even though for a time it had been a separate party; it comes closest to being a clientist faction, centered on the leadership initially of David Ben-Gurion and later of Moshe Dayan. On the other extreme, one faction—Achdut Haavoda—is quite highly developed on all the characteristics and approximates quite closely the model of a corporate group. The third faction, Mapai, proves to be intermediate in corporateness.

As we have noted, in several countries party factions have undergone a change from (usually semitraditional) clientelist form toward greater institutionalization. Japan's LDP factions changed to some degree, Fukui reports, and in the direction of institutionalization: they have become relatively "more explicit and more precisely defined structurally and functionally." Thus, for example, despite their semiclientelist basis (and their small size), he reports that the factions now have some functional specialization, they have their own treasuries, and they maintain offices and meeting places—and quiet retreats! Fukui cites several writers who also have stressed the institutionalization of LDP factions. Bolivia's MNR, during the period of its dominance in the 1950s, changed both its policies and its internal political arrangements, and, as Mitchell indicates, its informal factions became more organizationally formal. Many of these factions took formalized names—*Sector de Izquierda, Sector Socialista,* and others; several, Mitchell reports, were organizationally quite developed, with membership cards, pictorial symbols, faction press, etc.

Belloni's account of Italy's DC explores factional organization extensively. All the factions are self-consciously named. Their memberships are loosely and variably determined, but extend throughout the party organization, from the national party elite to the rank-and-file members in the local party sections. DC factions recruit actively and continuously. Fairly precise leadership cadres exist in several organizational echelons, and with moderately developed procedures and chains of command. Most have regular headquarters, often as facilities provided by a collateral interest group. Most maintain a newspaper or other press facility for publication of the factions' views on intraparty and other issues. Almost all maintain financial resources of their own. The DC's factions meet fairly regularly, though not necessarily on precise schedules, but in accordance with the volume of party issues requiring factional decisions.

The Labour left faction in Britain's Labour party is described by Cyr. It is well organized and highly ideological, largely held together by its members' devotion to the Socialist program. It has also had some charismatic unity, during the period of its leadership by Aneurin

Bevan, but that has not lasted. The left remains in possession, Cyr indicates, of "an established communications network, and the use of cadres to mobilize support," and of an extensive press. Labour's trade unions faction is less organized and extends beyond the parliamentary party. Institutionalized factions are also described by Merkl in West German parties, particularly the militant youth factions in the major national German parties; and in the French Socialist party, described by Campbell and Charlton. Some of the latter are remnants of former parties; some, like CERES, are study groups and political clubs—CERES, say the authors, is sometimes accused of being "a party within the party."

In American parties, Roback and James indicated, there are not currently many examples of *highly* developed institutionalized factions; however, the authors do report a bewildering variety of intraparty groups, which range from slightly institutionalized tendencies and personal client-groups to cliquish and personalized institutional factions. At the national level, they describe the congressional (i.e., parliamentary) Conservative Coalition, which resembles a slightly organized cross-party tendency; and the House Democratic Study Group and Republican Wednesday Clubs of the House and Senate. In statewide parties, they describe the upstate-downstate factional divisions in some state parties, and a long list of "amateur" clubs, youth and women's auxiliary organizations, etc.—all presumably exhibiting organizational development and formalization. They also cite as factions certain national party bodies, such as the Democratic Policy Council; a long list of Republican societies for liberals and societies for conservatives; and a number of nonpartisan factions possessing contingents within both major parties. Many of these groups, as factions, are probably better understood as slightly institutionalized tendencies, but many are rather cliquish organizational factions.

Causes of Faction

Why do factions vary so greatly? Why do they exist at all? Questions of what causes or contributes to factionalism and to factions' different forms have been explored at great length by several authors in this book and are thoroughly reviewed by Zariski in Chapter 2; an extensive list of suggested causes has been discussed. The many causal factors may be grouped into general classifications: first, societal and cultural causes; second, political causes, in the form of characteristics of the political system; and third, structural causes, in the form of structural properties of the host party or organization.

SOCIETAL CAUSES OF FACTION

Causes of factionalism coming under the classification of social and cultural factors are the least thoroughly analyzed and understood, and the least conclusive, of all types of causes. Causal factors of this type include such things as indigenous cultural norms; various attributes of the socioeconomic structure—class structure, age structure and youth activism, education, level of economic development, etc.; and factors of social change, class mobility, immigration, breakdown of traditional values, development or modernization, etc. Zariski recognizes cultural norms as one of the factors determining the organization, cohesion, and durability of factions. As is evident from his review of cultural factors, the indigenous cultural norms of societies have been used to explain two kinds of things about factionalism: a general factor amounting to proclivities toward divisiveness, fission, or internecine conflict, etc.; and native forms of group formation, especially client-group formation, such as is extensively argued by Fukui about traditional Japanese culture.

Cultural inclination toward divisiveness is cited by several of this book's authors as contributing to political factionalism. Campbell and Charlton describe the degree to which France's unique legacy of social, cultural, and ideological cleavages has been an enduring cause of fragmentation in French politics. Similarly, in Aronoff's analysis of Israeli factionalism, attributes of Jewish culture, including "the tendency of the Jewish people to divide themselves into competing political camps," is part of the explanation for divisiveness in social and political institutions in that country. And, in much the same vein, Roback and James cite regional subcultural divisions in America as affecting both the "intensity and substance" of American factional tendencies.

Zariski reviews studies which explore some questions of socioeconomic causes of factions; as elements contributing to the likelihood that individuals will join factions, he identifies their having a more advanced educational level and their coming from a middle-class background. He also cites studies which suggest that there is no direct relationship between tendencies toward factionalism and a variety of socioeconomic indicators. Merkl identifies another type of social factor of factionalism in Germany: all three of Germany's major parties have long contained major factions in the form of explicitly constituted and highly organized youth movements within the party.

Zariski also points out that there is inconsistent and inconclusive evidence on relationships between socioeconomic change or modernization and tendencies toward political factionalism. As we saw in Chapter 1, anthropologist R. W. Nicholas first suggested that change or breakdown of society and its traditions and values, etc., is likely to result in factionalism in politics—as the most apt form of political structure in such circumstances. Zariski cites studies by Samuel Barnes which tend to corroborate this view; and in this book, McDonald, in

Chapter 9, finds that "factions evolved and were sustained in Uruguay and Colombia largely, if not solely, in response to conditions generated by modernization." On the other hand, several authors have noted that factions tend to hinder modernization and development. Nathan notes factions' resistance to change, and Nicholson describes factional politics as blocking development because of the incapacity of a faction system to operationalize government projects which upset a traditional distribution of wealth within the community.

POLITICAL CAUSES OF FACTION

Many causes of factionalism have in common the element of being aspects of the political system outside the factions' immediate party or host organization. Some are universalistic causes like politics itself, or conflict, and are implicitly accepted as causes of factionalism by everyone; and some are generic causes like patronage, which is mentioned by almost all writers. Besides these, specific causal factors include the social basis of participation in the national political system; characteristics of the electoral system; and, above all, characteristics of the party system, including the number of parties and the relative strengths of parties.

Elitism in the political system can be a systemic cause of factionalism, particularly factionalism of client-groups. Mitchell argues that elitist or nonpopular politics in Bolivia produced factionalism in that country: "Factionalism has engaged primarily the political elite and has tended to intensify when—for one reason or another—a segment of that elite has found itself without firm popular backing." Nef makes the same point for Chile: as long as traditional Chilean politics was "gentlemen's politics," and only society's elites participated in politics, "factionalism within the elite facilitated the maintenance of systemic stability and a modicum of what has been called 'oligarchical pluralism.'" Much the same characterization of factional politics is made by Machado, for the Philippines.

A special type of causal factor is that of the electoral systems for public office. There are two factors here; one is the direct party primary, most analysis of which is confined to American experiences. First examined by Key, the role of the direct primary has long been considered to encourage factionalism, and Zariski reconfirms that view in Chapter 2. Roback and James, however, describe the direct primary as one of the causes of the *decline* of machine factions in America; evidently, primaries may encourage factionalism but may also inhibit specific forms of factional structure. The other factor in electoral systems, and the one much more extensively analyzed, is proportional representation (PR), used in numerous European and other countries. Zariski in 1960 concluded that while PR may still have the effect of strengthening parties' central leaders at the expense of factions, under certain circumstances the effect might be reversed. In Chapter 2 Zariski cites several studies which tend to confirm the view that PR may augment, rather than stifle, factionalism—particularly electoral systems using PR coupled with preference voting, in which voters select not only a party list but also their favored names on the list. (We enter a note of caution here: it is probably a mistake to compare directly, as Zariski has done, PR in public elections and PR used in intraparty elections for party assemblies and executive bodies. The mechanism used in the two contexts functions in wholly noncomparable ways for intraparty factionalism. PR in the intraparty electoral context is reviewed in the following section.)

Several authors have reached conclusions regarding PR in this book and have confirmed the effects PR can have in causing and enhancing factionalism. Fukui describes the Japanese PR system, in which the parties, in effect, do not put up party lists, with the result that the multiple candidates of a single party are competing with each other as much as they are with candidates of rival parties, and must therefore seek campaign organizational and financial support from individual factions. Aronoff describes the unique PR electoral law in Israel, in which the entire country consists of a single multimember district for election of all members of the Knesset—an electoral regime which has mitigated against tight control of the parties and has fostered multiple parties and multiple intraparty factions.

The preference vote mechanism, as Zariski points out, has been most extensively studied and commented upon in the context of its use in Italy, where its effects are pronounced. In Chapter 4 Belloni confirms the role of preference voting in contributing to factionalism by urging voters of a particular party to vote for specific candidates: "Preference voting is manipulated by the factions and by the collateral interest groups which support various factions." McDonald, as well, indicates that PR as used in Uruguay fosters factionalism: the electoral system there is an extended form of preference voting, not for individual candidates but for separate rival *faction (sub-lema)* lists competing for portions of the total party share of the seats in each multimember district. As McDonald states, the effect of the electoral law in Uruguay has been to give legal recognition to the *sub-lemas.* He argues that PR may not necessarily result in the multiplication of parties, as is conventionally supposed; a two-party system may well survive in a PR electoral context when the multiplication of factions becomes the device for absorption of the normal multiplicative tendencies of PR. On balance, a strong case exists for the argument that PR is just as likely, perhaps more likely, to cause factionalism as to inhibit it.

The main political system causes of factionalism are those associated with the party system. Two sets of questions have been raised: first, whether factionalism is caused or encouraged by a party's strength (or recent victory) or by its weakness (or recent defeat); and second, whether factionalism is related to the number of participants in the party system—one (or a dominant party), two, or many. Zariski explores at great length a critical aspect of the first of these sets of questions. Concentrating on the function of intraparty depolarization, he argues that greater party strength induces depolarizing tendencies —i.e., moderation, avoidance of extremes, etc., and thus, in a way, minimization or reduction of factionalism—within the party; and also that success (i.e., a recent electoral victory or electoral gains) induces depolarizing tendencies. The implication of Mitchell's account of Bolivian politics is consistent with this argument; Mitchell holds that factionalism increases when parties decline in strength, at least in the sense of becoming cut off from mass support. Other writers, however, find a relationship between *increased* factionalism and greater party strength (or between increased factionalism and recent electoral success). Nathan declares that factional cleavages increase with "the fruits of victory" and "are almost inevitable results of success." Nef also reports that the decline of the popular electoral strength of parties of the right in Chile resulted in their closing ranks and abandoning factional differences; and that growing electoral support for the centrist parties produced in them growing internal factionalism. Merkl, too, indicates that in West Germany's CDU, internal divisions only appeared once Adenauer had consolidated his (and the CDU's) power. It thus seems that there is reason to conclude that electoral success and party strength are factors tending to contribute to factionalism, just as much as party weakness, in other circumstances, may contribute to factionalism.

The other set of questions are those of the relations between the number of parties in the party system and intraparty factionalism. In discussing the two-party system in Chapter 2, Zariski finds only that there has been no evidence to support his 1960 propositions concerning effects of a two-party system on factionalism. Concerning the relevance of multiparty systems for factionalism, he offers the following hypothesis: the greater the number of parties in the party system, the greater will be the tendency toward miltifactionalism within a party and the less will be the tendency toward interfactional compromise. Campbell and Charlton agree, not only because of the tactical choices before the parties but because of the continuous irritation of old ideological differences: "the multiparty system itself contributed to multifactionalism," they say, "because of tactical competition and because of the ongoing tendency to resurrect and manipulate ideological differences."

The greatest amount of attention to the relevance of the party system for factionalism, however, has been directed at the dominant-party system. The possibility that factionalism in a dominant party is caused by the fact of the dominant-party system is a suggestion going back to the work of Key and those who furthered his inquiries, like Allan Sindler.[8] It was Key's view, in relation to American statewide party systems, that the more dominant a party, the greater its tendency toward extreme multifactionalism; and the less the dominance (i.e., the more there is some party opposition), the less the factionalism and the more likely that factionalism will be *bi*factionalism. Zariski, in his 1965 work based on the Italian Christian Democrats,[9] concluded that a dominant-party system definitely tended to encourage intraparty factionalism. In fact, however, the number of factions has not increased indefinitely in the DC; but in other respects he finds the arguments are still viable that a dominant-party system encourages factionalism—and specifically multifactionalism—within the dominant party. Belloni in Chapter 4 shows that factionalism is an almost inescapable consequence of the DC's spreading itself across the social structure and representing, or seeking to represent, nearly all elements of society. This same factor applies to other dominant parties whose dominance is attributable to the party's actual or hoped-for breadth and panoramic representation of society (as opposed to dominance through a single mass class)—e.g., the Congress party in India, probably Labor in Israel and the Liberal Democrats in Japan, and possibly the UDR in France.

STRUCTURAL CAUSES OF FACTION

A variety of causes of factionalism are associated with structural characteristics of the party or organization of which the factions are a part. Structural causes include sociological complexity of the party; ideological looseness of the party; the origin of the party in a merger of predecessor parties; the party's internal looseness or decentralized structure, especially a caucus-type party structure; and most important, the use of proportional representation for intraparty representation in elective party assemblies and executive bodies.

 We have already alluded to the "polyclassist" nature of mass parties such as Italy's DC as a factor tending to cause and augment factionalism; the existence of multiple and varied constituencies within any party can be a prime cause of factionalism. Looseness or vagueness of party ideology may be an associated conditioning factor of factionalism. Fukui identifies this characteristic as applicable to both the Liberal Democratic party and the Japan Socialist party—the latter despite its ostensible devotion to the doctrine of democratic centralism. In fact, Fukui finds, these parties are "eclectic, tolerant, and inclusive," which "encourages pluralistic tendencies and competition within both the JSP and LDP." This interpretation is applicable to Italy's DC and

Italian Socialist party, to France's UDR and Socialist party, to Israel's Labor party, to India's Congress party, and to the Republican and Democratic parties in America.

One factor commonly causing factionalism is a party's having originated in a union or merger of several predecessor parties, which may continue to maintain some semblance of organization and identity within the newly formed party, as its factions. Thus, the DC was formed out of remnants of prefascist Italian parties, whose leaders became prominent personalities and faction heads of the new party. In West Germany, Merkl reports, two of the major parties—the CDU and the FDP—"strained" under their formation as unifications of predecessor parties. The two major parties in Japan—the LDP and JSP—"came into existence with factionalism already built in," in that both were formed as "federations" of diverse political groups. Aronoff's study, Chapter 5, focuses on the birth of the Israel Labor party through the merger of three groups, each of which had existed as a separate party prior to the merger, and each of which was accorded recognition by the party's formal internal structure for a transitional period of adjustment to their complete unification. Campbell and Charlton describe the setting up of the French Socialist party as a merger of remnants of France's old SFIO plus numerous other leftist parties and groups, and a providing to factions formal recognition and internal representation on a continuing basis.

The nature of party organization is another cause of factionalism; loosely organized parties encourage intraparty factions. This argument originated with Duverger, who found that the looser, caucus-type parties were more given to factionalism than the more rigorously centralized branch-type parties. In the 1960s, Zariski concurred with this finding and added that factions in a looser, caucus-type party would themselves be looser in organization and less cohesive, while those in branch-type parties would have greater organizational cohesion and continuity. In Chapter 2 Zariski finds additional evidence in support of this proposition. In less-structured parties—Zariski describes some of them as catchall parties—a "lack of central control over finances and campaign workers . . . tends to encourage proliferation of factions"—although he also reviews evidence that factionalism may be just as extensive in branch-type parties as in caucus-type parties. Merkl notes that CDU factionalism is attributable to the party's decentralized structure. American parties are often noted for their organizational looseness—they were clearly labeled as caucus parties by Duverger; Roback and James identify decentralized structure of the parties as providing a base for factionalism—although they also argue that party decentralization *prevented* ideological factions such as are commonly found in Europe. The obverse of this causal element is the effective elimination of all but the most cliquish or most private personal followings in parties, such as the Communist parties, which maintain extreme centralization.

Probably the most extensively cited cause of factionalism is that of the use of PR in intraparty election systems—to be distinguished again from the public electoral system for official governmental offices. Zariski, again, explores this area of cause of factions and begins with the view expressed by the Italian political scientist, Giovanni Sartori, that "the use of PR in intraparty elections has a much more significant effect on the multiplication of factions than does the use of PR in general elections."[10] Zariski, however, remains unconvinced and considers the possibility that intraparty PR may be the result, not the cause, of intraparty factionalism; and it was Sartori's argument, ultimately, that intraparty PR determines the *character* of factions more than it does the *number* of factions.

Nevertheless, in this book the same Christian Democratic party that was the basis of Sartori's and Zariski's conclusions provides Belloni with the basis for concluding that intraparty PR does encourage factionalism—it is a "facilitative condition," as he describes it, of DC factions. It was the adoption of its motion-list system in the mid-1960s, and its extension to the local party voting, he finds, that did the most to solidify and institutionalize the factions in the DC. A system of intraparty elections quite close to the DC's motion-list system is described by Campbell and Charlton for the French Socialist party, where its effect is the same; and Aronoff describes a comparable system in Israel's Labor party.

Functional Roles and Consequences of Factionalism

In a general sense, factions structure the processes of intraparty politics and decision-making. Virtually every author agrees, in one way or another, that factions define the struggle for control of the party, its policies, its leadership and offices, its doctrines, its treasury, etc.; factions are devices for the distribution of party patronage—and, for governing parties, of government patronage; and they are instruments for generating and supporting rival candidacies for public office.

FACTIONAL SYSTEMS

There are various typical patterns which we may isolate, patterns of the processes of intraparty competition and the party's choosing among factional alternatives—in short, typical patterns of faction systems. One is a closed, *elitist* factionalism: a narrow, restricted intraelite competition, in which the factions are typically cliques or personal, client-group followings. The participants in factional systems of this type generally attempt to keep their competition within the inner circles of which they are the main constituents—an effort in which they may or may not succeed. Competition may be mild or intense, but is generally played by "rules of the game," and control of the party tends to rotate among shifting coalitions of the factions, in a manner reminiscent of the "balance of power" of pre-nuclear-age world politics. Nathan describes such a system in the Communist party elite in China, which only occasionally has permitted a spillover of political conflict into larger realms of the party and the political system. Linden describes the same basic pattern in Soviet Communist party politics, indicating that it does not always remain restricted to the elite, but "reverberates down" through the structures of the overlapping party and state. When factions are confined to parliamentary parties, as with Britain's Conservatives, they are likely to be factional systems of this type. Also, faction systems of some Latin American parties appear to have been largely of this pattern.

A second pattern is one of *open* factionalism; of choices made by the whole party, from among factions which organize themselves as extensively as they can throughout the entire organizational framework of the party, and beyond, to outside interest groups and to sections of the general voting public. Factions in systems of this type are more often groups which have acquired a good measure of organizational characteristics, either as institutionalized factions or as elaborate clientist machines—or, less likely, as large tendencies. In these faction systems, too, top-level control of the party tends to go to periodic coalitions (e.g., the mainstream described in the LDP by Fukui, the majority described in the DC by Belloni) among the factions, or to amorphous majoritarian tendencies (such as the Labour moderates or the De Gasperian centrists of the early DC); or may remain a longer time with a single majority faction. Participants in these systems seek to broaden their rivalries, to extend their competition and thus the base of the public within the party making the choices among the factions, as far as possible throughout the party and the political system. The faction systems of the Liberal Democratic party of Japan, the Christian Democratic party of Italy, the Labor party of Israel, and possibly the Socialist party of France and the Labour party of Britain, among others, fit this pattern.

A third pattern is one of factional *alliances:* factional competition which proceeds in terms of increasing aggregations or coalitions of factions at successively higher levels of the party or party-state hierarchy. Factions in this factional system pattern typically originate in the form of local groups—they may be cliques, they may be personal followings or personal machines, or they may be institutionalized local clubs, associations, etc. Local factions are grouped or federated into intermediate-level alliances—often at a regional or provincial level of the political system and intermediate faction alliances. The factions may feel free to transfer their loyalties from party to party. In faction systems of this pattern, the participants seek to broaden and extend their rivalry at their immediate level, but seek not to extend it to an adjoining level, which may threaten a coalition or the basis of a coalition at that other level. Some Western caucus-type parties originated in such alliances in the nineteenth century. Today, factional systems reflecting this pattern include those of both major parties in the Philippines, the Congress party factional system in India, and to a limited extent the Democratic and Republican parties in the United States, and perhaps the parties of Uruguay.

Real faction systems vary a great deal and reflect the typical characteristics of these patterns in different degrees. Recognition of their existence, in no matter which pattern, poses the questions of the functions of factionalism, both in the sense of roles factions play for the party and for the political system and in the sense of the impact or consequences factionalism has on its host organization and on the polity. Functional questions, like causal and structural questions, are many and varied but may be grouped into two general headings: functional roles that are specific to the political party or organization within which the factions exist; and functions and consequences for the total political system and for society at large.

FUNCTIONAL ROLES FOR POLITICAL PARTIES

Particularly with reference to the impact of factions on their host party, functional questions touch most closely on the traditional antifaction bias. Thus factions are so often viewed negatively: as the essence of impassioned violence, of particularistic selfishness, and of all the disruptive and schismatic forces within a party—a party which, the implication is, would otherwise be united. The traditional view is basically a presumption of a functional nature about factions. As we saw, the antifaction bias was expressed by most of the early modern writers on faction; Lasswell,[11] who offered the first modern political science definition of faction, reflected the bias, as did nearly all the writers reviewed in Chapter 1. Moreover, such a view is recognized in a somewhat different perspective by the founders of political parties, who frequently attempt to prevent intraparty factions by writing into the party charter and bylaws prohibitions against factions. In particular, as Linden shows in Chapter 15, and as several authors have described, this view is characteristic of Marxist-Leninist parties, which take the greatest trouble to prevent the occurrence of factions on any organized or enduring basis.

Many of these dysfunctional conclusions are reaffirmed by authors of the case studies in this book. Several find factions to be divisive. Fukui and Aronoff both describe factionalism as divisive for the host party—the LDP in Japan and the Labor party in Israel; factional divisions are described as leading to breakaway splits in several parties of the left in Chile, and among the Socialists in Italy, in France, and in Bolivia. Several authors have also found factions to result in corruption, ineffectiveness, and other dysfunctional consequences—particularly from the point of view of the host party. Thus, some reach the conclusion that factional politics weakens and discredits the authority and legitimacy of the host party. In Israel factional splits "called into question the legitimacy of the party institutions." Fukui finds in Japan that "factionalism in the two major parties has considerably weakened the authority and effectiveness of their leaders both as party officers and as public officials." In the same vein, Mitchell finds in Bolivia that "an important long-range effect of MNR factionalism was the discrediting of the party."

A related dysfunctional consequence of factionalism for the party is noted by a number of authors: that factionalism is inconsistent with advancement of leaders on the basis of merit, and that it inhibits open discussion and resolution of intraparty decisions on the basis of rationality. Fukui declares that for advancement, "the premium is on durability (seniority) and amiability rather than on functional skills or competence"; and Aronoff concludes that "to the extent that factional politics concentrated on competition for representation in party institutions, it largely detracted from recruitment on the basis of merit." Similarly, decision-making abandons reason: according to Fukui, "once a policy becomes a symbolic stake in an interfactional dispute, rational arguments become irrelevant and the real issue is buried under empty rhetoric."

A number of authors, however, find that positive, as well as negative, consequences flow from intraparty factional competition. Several find that factions serve to represent and articulate varied interests of portions of a party and/or their supporters. Cyr says of Britain that factions "represent different constituencies within a single party," and Belloni finds that factions "provide organizational channels through which are articulated the varied interests of the broad-ranging constituency" of the party. Factionalism in this regard constitutes a function of especial significance in cases of a large, multiclass dominant party, and of even greater significance in a single-party system, where organized political expression is denied to all societal interests other than through the monopolistic party. And, indeed, Linden finds this function to be characteristic of Communist party elitist regimes, in which the factions "register, however indirectly and distortedly, the influences of incipient interest groups and latent political elements in the state officialdom and in society at large."

The political functions provided by factions for their host parties are more than representation of interests, however. In the intraparty struggles and rivalries among factions, the party is provided alternatives; thus factional competition serves as a mechanism for the party's making choices among policies, ideologies, and leaders. This function is clearly indicated in the analyses of the Soviet and Chinese Communist parties, and of the major parties of dominant-party systems, such as Italy's DC—in which this function is very prominent. Even in the fractionalized, multiparty system of Bolivia, Mitchell reports, the extensive factionalism of the leftist parties, largely excluded from power, "provided a forum in which . . . strategies could be discussed, winnowed, and refined." Sometimes intraparty rivalries and choices are predominantly among ideological groups and their ideologies, as Mitchell finds among parties of the left in Bolivia, and other times they are predominantly among leadership groups and personalities, as he finds in the more centrist MNR. Ultimately, the constant competition among rival sets of alternative positions and personalities may provide accountability to the party, and thus, as Belloni finds, provide a distinct regimen of intraparty democracy. Intraparty democracy is also cited by Campbell and Charlton for the French Socialist party, and by Fukui for the LDP in Japan, although in the latter case the author concludes that it is outweighed by dysfunctional consequences of factionalism.

Despite the presumption in the traditional bias that factions inflame the passions of political violence and divide parties, a few authors have noted that factionalism may serve the host party by moderating and limiting conflict within the party—perhaps in the manner of a safety valve (the term used by Merkl to describe local nonpartisan factions): Zariski refers to such a function, and Nathan finds the elite factionalism of the CCP to be a restraining factor in Chinese politics. Moreover, several authors have concluded that there is a definite functionality of faction systems for providing unity to the parent organization—again despite the traditional bias. In cases of parties formed as mergers of smaller parties, and in cases of parties proving to have internal segments insistent on being heard, parties may rely on factionalism as a means of holding the party together. Several parties have managed to keep together a tenuous union of former parties through explicitly constituted representation of factional constituents on party bodies—e.g., the Labor party in Israel, the Socialist party in France. Other parties have evolved such formalized factional representation systems in intraparty decision-making and elections of party executive bodies, etc.—e.g., the Christian Democrats in Italy. In the case of the French Socialist party, Campbell and Charlton indicate that such formalized internal factionalism not only contributes to continued party unity but may also help the further growth of the party, through absorption of additional small partisan groups which may be offered some guarantee against extinction, by having a continued existence as a recognized faction.

Thus, in several different ways, factionalism is often functional, in a positive fashion, for a political party. Factionalism may be the means for a party's coming together and for a party's staying together; it may serve to represent group interests within a party and to provide the full party with a competitive means of making choices among viewpoints and leaders. It thus may constitute a means to intraparty accountability and democracy. Despite continuing dysfunctional (to the party) effects of faction-inspired disunity, factionalism may also provide unity. Indeed, it can be the case that dysfunctional divisiveness and functional unity may coexist. Several authors described such a coexistence. Campbell and Charlton, again speaking of the French Socialist Party, conclude that while factionalism in the PS does constitute "a potential threat to party unity, or at least an inherent source of weakness," it simultaneously provides a bridging function, binding together diverse elements in the party—part of the very "ambiguity of faction" that was the focus of their study. Such bridging and divisive consequences are seen also by Aronoff as a continuing prospect for the Israel Labor party.

Functional Consequences of Factionalism for the Polity

All writers agree that intraparty politics has important consequences for a political system beyond that party or immediate arena itself. The proportion of the sum total of politics defined by factionalism may be such that the significance of factionalism outweighs or rivals that of the party system—as it did, for example, in Uruguayan politics or in Colombian politics, where governments frequently depended on cross-party factions. In some countries the faction system virtually substitutes for the party system or, in effect, becomes the political system. Such a conclusion is inescapable in a single-party system, where there is only one organization in existence and politics in the form of competition among formally constituted, rival political organizations is foreclosed. Much the same degree of significance of factionalism for the entire polity applies to dominant-party system countries: if one party continues to have an overwhelming and predominating share of government offices and control of government activities, then whatever happens within that party of necessity is a determining factor of government. Thus a dominant party's faction system may be, as some have said, at least a quasi-party system, partially replacing the party system proper. Years ago, Key opened the line of inquiry on whether factional competition might serve as at least a partial substitute for competition among parties. On the basis of American statewide party regimes, he found factions to be functionally inferior to parties and unsatisfactory for adequate functioning of democracy. Subsequently the Indian political scientist, R. Kothari, reached an essentially opposite conclusion, based on the Indian Congress party system.[12] In any case, no matter what the party-system type, the existence of one or more intraparty factional systems is likely to be a factor of great importance to the political system of a country.

In the case studies in this book, a number of those who find intraparty factionalism to have a dysfunctional or functional effect on the host party also find that factionalism to have the same effect on the party *system*. Thus some who find factionalism to result in a weakening of the party also find that this amounts to a weakening of the party system. Insofar as factions are schismatic and divisive for a host party, the consequences may entail divisiveness for the entire political system; and insofar as factionalism tends to discredit or impugn the legitimacy or moral authority of a party, this may mean discrediting of, and popular disaffection from, the party politics system. Or, if the party system is weak, factionalism in the parties may prevent the system's becoming strengthened; such an interpretation was made by Machado of the factionalized Philippine parties, where factionalism forestalled the development of nationwide party loyalties. Factionalism can also weaken parliamentary cabinet governments. This is true particularly for coalition governments, necessitated by the absence of a single party with a parliamentary majority. In this situation, factionalism may be a major cause of instability and fall of governments—as it notoriously was in France's Fourth Republic. In Israel, Aronoff indicates, a Labor coalition government's majority in the parliament is harassed not only by the opposition parties but also by the Labor factions, threatening to break party discipline. Finally, Belloni cites this consequence of factionalism in Italy: "The government's majority is subject to disintegration at any time by virtue of the withdrawal of support of a single faction whose voting strength is equal to the margin of security of the majority."

Moreover, in weakening the party system, factionalism in the end may threaten the established constitutional order itself. Thus, several authors noted that under conditions of the challenges of open, mass political participation in politics, an elitist factionalism may weaken the existing system by resisting changes. An interesting element of this factor of undermining the constituted state is that factionalism may become *inflationary* for politics—a term used by Machado to describe Philippine factionalism. In the last Philippine presidential election prior to the declaration of martial law, the costs of the election were a major factor in the devaluation of the national currency. Machado concludes: "The costs of factional party politics appeared to be reaching the limits imposed by the Philippine economy." Fukui reports a similar situation: he argues that in Japan "the factions have contributed to the vicious circle of the more money available, the more demands for more money, until the whole fabric of Japanese party politics tends to become contaminated." By weakening and discrediting parties and party politics, by tending toward maintenance of elite politics and resistance to populistic changes, and at times by creating an inflationary condition in the economy, factionalism is sometimes credited with leading to the vulnerability of the regime to forceful overthrow. Mitchell finds the vulnerability created by the discrediting of the ruling institution was enough to make Bolivia a tempting target for a coup. Machado blames the inflationary character of faction politics for the coup in the Philippines, McDonald finds that factionalism contributed to military takeovers in Uruguay and Colombia, and Nef blames factionalism for leading to the Chilean coup.

At the same time, however, just as with functions for the party, factions frequently have positive consequences for the political system. Factions may serve to integrate disparate elements in the political system, and in a number of different ways. In certain contexts, and particularly among factions at the local, village level, factions often provide a real measure of integration within the community—crosscutting other lines of social cleavage, such as class, caste, ethnic groups, etc. This function is frequently described by students of factionalism in India, including Nicholson in Chapter 7. In Israel, a country with unusual problems of integration among masses of diverse immigrant groups, Aronoff reports that the factional system provided an institutional loyalty which crosscut ethnic, geographic, and other loyalties, and prevented polarization along those lines.

Even more common, factionalism provides a measure of integration among the leaders, activists, and participants in the national party system, within the Parliament and among the professionals of the parties. In Italy, Belloni reports, the DC's left-wing factions relate closely to Italy's left-wing parties, and DC right-wing factions relate closely to right-wing parties, thus tending to provide avenues of access to the centers of power for political groups on the partisan extremes. This depolarization of the political spectrum is all the more significant in a dominant-party system, as Italy has so long been, and, above all, in the context of Italy's long-standing exclusion of the extreme parties from participation in government coalitions. Integration of this sort within the party system is tantamount to the creation of de facto cross-party factional tendencies, as several authors have indicated—such as on the French left. In Britain, Cyr declares that "intraparty cleavages may undercut very directly the main division between Conservatives and Labour by joining partisans of both parties on specific issues." In Colombia, McDonald shows, this kind of alliance became virtually an institutional part of the political system. There, the two parties each divided internally between a moderate and a radical faction, and government alternated between unity within a single party and unity between the two respective moderate factions, in a cross-party coalition.

When a party is the only party in a single-party system, or is the dominant party in a dominant-party system, the functional aspects of factionalism for the party necessarily carry over into the total political system. Thus to the extent that factions are found to function as the agents of the representation and articulation of discrete interests and constituencies within the single or dominant party, those factions are representing and articulating interests of the polity at large. In a single or dominant party most of society's classes, sectors, major interests, and communities, etc. are normally represented to some degree—a function appertaining not just to that party but to the entire political system. Similarly, functions such as constituting a forum for the experimenting with and debating of issues and ideas are, in a single or dominant party, being performed for the nation's political system as a whole. The provision of policy alternatives, of leadership alternatives, etc., within such parties likewise constitutes the providing of alternatives for the system. That functions of this sort are served by faction systems for the entire political system of a country is a point elaborated on by Belloni: for Italy's coalition governments, "minority factions have been as important in fulfilling the functions of a 'loyal opposition' as the opposition parties themselves." Ultimately, this results in a "built-in check on the power of the government, a restraint on a party continuously in power"—a restraint which the ostensible opposition cannot provide because of the combined factors of its dispersion in a multiplicity of parties and the historic exclusion of parts of it from participation in the national government.

Conclusions

The very idea of faction comes to us with an inheritance whose affective content is a highly negative evaluation seemingly indelibly associated with the term. The "evil" of faction was initially established for modern times by those eighteenth-century gentlemen who liked to consider government to be a stately endeavor and who found the passions of political combat much to their distaste. Factions and parties were equated one with the other then, and were indistinguishably threatening to the people of the times. But with succeeding generations, new forms of political organization developed, to which nineteenth-century statesmen attached the term *party*, and which became respected pillars of the modern political system—especially the Western conception of the *democratic* system. Factions have been left to be the objects of our decision, of our disdain for the baser aspects of political conflict.

The consequences of the antifaction bias tradition are two. First, it leaves many contemporary participants in and observers of politics with a direct negative evaluation applicable to any political object to which the word *faction* may become attached. Negative evaluations of faction—structural, causal, and functional—are still to be found. Thus it is a common approach to the analysis of party factions to view them as by-products or derivatives of parties, and as consequences of parties' malfunctioning. The bias nowadays, moreover, generally is closely associated with a positive bias toward political parties.

Most negative evaluations in the long run are generally the same as or similar to those that once were put upon *faction* and *party* as interchangeable terms. That factions divide, weaken, inflame, corrupt, disrupt, etc.—often enough readily "documentable," to be sure—are complaints which, except for our modern linguistic idiom, would leave eighteenth-century antagonists of parties quite comfortable. In the sense of the bias, there is ultimately no real difference between today's antipathy to factions from the viewpoint of parties and the historical antipathy toward parties.

The second consequence of the antifaction bias is a much subtler one; it amounts to a perspective in our approaches to the analysis and understanding of politics. One of the most enduring themes in the study of factions in contemporary political science has been the contrasting of characteristics of factions with those of political parties; and, recently, faction studies in anthropology have relied on this theme also. This comparison has been the primary basis of analysis in many studies, and an implicit one in most. The comparison has almost always been an invidious one: factions are ever deemed to be less than parties. That is, the comparison, despite the many forms it takes, has always to do with the consideration and weighing of factions *by political party standards*—standards which imply that parties have more of something, or are somehow better, than factions, or that factions in some manner fail to measure up.

For the most part, scholars and commentators have presumed a one-to-one relationship between political competition and political parties. The presumption has been that parties are *the* units of political competition. The notion of political competition, in effect, has long been bound by the notion of party. Thus political scientists have categorized political systems in terms of classificatory devices which rely on attributes of parties as the discriminating variable—most often, simply the number of parties in the national political competition: one, two, or "multi." Conventionally, in other words, we define political systems in terms of their parties—even though logically, it has sometimes been suggested, we *should* define parties by their political competition.[13]

Whatever are commonly described as parties—or whatever parties are by any definition—*may* be the most salient organizations of political competition; so too, however, may other organizations—e.g., intraparty groups commonly described as factions. In Japan, where the LDP is a long-standing majority dominant party, Fukui has concluded that "the saliency of the LDP factions has created in the minds of politicians and voters alike an image of a quasi-multiparty system operating within the LDP and effectively replacing the five-party system as the main arena of competition for power." If the LDP's faction system has replaced the party system for the politicians and the voters, then the political scientists are left the only ones insisting that Japanese politics be analyzed and understood somehow in terms of *parties* and *party systems* when it has long ceased to be that for everyone else. In Italy, where the DC has continuously been not a majority party but a relatively dominant party, the self-contained system of factions in the DC, Belloni concludes, "has acquired a salience in the Italian polity that warrants the kind of attention normally accorded only the party system itself." Because the DC is not a majority party, "the principle unit of power becomes the organized faction," a point Italians themselves recognize when they refer to their politics as *correntocrazia*— loosely translated, "factionocracy." Factionocracy is a concept for which theories of the political system have not thus far found room.

Our point here is that parties do not have a monopoly on valid political competition in reality, no matter what legal or other differences may exist between them and other groups. Actual competition may be among parties, or among intraparty factions, or both; it may be among organizations that defy neat categorization as parties or factions or something else; and above all, competition may exist on several levels simultaneously, in which case no one level may be identified by definition as the only or the most significant one. Parties are not the "norm" of organizations of political competition, and factions are not organizations to be understood in terms of inherent inferiority and inadequacy in political party terms. Rather, we argue, parties (and there are many types of parties) and factions (the many types of factions) are equally to be understood as varieties of organizations of political competition.

The case studies in this book have demonstrated that a great variety of organizational forms may aptly be deemed factions. Parties may have factions, and parties may *be* factions; alignments may have factions; armies, bureaucracies, priesthoods, and villages may have factions; and factions may have factions. Instead of continuing the conventional insistence that factions be viewed from the vantage point of parties, we argue for a perspective which incorporates parties and factions equally—or any other organizational units that may exist—as political competition groups. Thus faction study requires the capacity to apply structural comparisons from the perspective of a single, unified scheme whose basis is the functional commonality of political competition—the suggestion for scalar measurement of corporateness is one such possibility.

Organizations of political competition will vary both by form of organization and by context of organization. There will be some common characteristics of organizations of a particular organizational form, without regard to context—e.g., all client-groups will have certain common features, no matter in what context they exist; and there will be some common characteristics of organizations of a particular organizational context, without regard to form—e.g., all village factions, or all parliamentary party factions, etc., will have certain common features, no matter of what form they are. Moreover, with respect to the latter point—the commonality of groups in a single context—these common characteristics will be determined by the nature of that context: thus, features of the structure, the causes, the functions, etc., of factions will in part reflect characteristics of the organizations of which they are factions.

This approach not only puts organizational form into a single comparative framework, it also requires specification of the immediate context—i.e., the parent organization—in order accurately to describe any specific instance of faction. There is no point whatever in attempting to resolve whether clientist groups in traditional village settings are or are not "true" factions, or whether informal, transitory cliques in Communist parties are or are not "real" factions, etc. Factions in villages, if they exist, will be village factions; in Communist parties, factions will be Communist party factions. Differences between villages factions and elite intraparty factions will inhere in the differences between villages and party elites. In addition, any factions may also be cliques, client-groups, or institutions, which will entail further mutual differences in terms of those structural variations; and parties will have their own structural subclassifications. They may all be compared as organizational units of political competition, and their structural and contextual contrasts analyzed in terms of that plane of reference.

Focus on faction redirects our attention to *organized units of competition* not fixed by definitions of party—or any other organization type. After all, what is significant about factions ultimately is their *activity* and its consequences—not their structural properties. Fitting this into the larger picture, we find that what is significant in political systems is not so much the number of structural characteristics of organizations but the dynamics and consequences of their interactions. Thus, our attention should be directed toward critical types of political activity —one of which is competition for power. The units of competition— be they parties, factions, or whatever—are best understood in terms of analyses within the single framework of political organizations engaged in competitive activity. By redirecting our attention from party politics to *competitive* politics, we may compare organizations of competition in competitive party systems, in one-party systems, and in nonparty systems. Faction politics thus puts all political systems into a single comparative framework. In short, it is a perspective, a way of looking at politics.

NOTES

1. William Nisbet Chambers, *Political Parties in a New Nation: The American Experience, 1776–1809* (New York: Oxford Univ. Press, 1963); Chambers, "Party Development and Party Action: The American Origins," *Journal of History and Theory* 3, no. 1 (1963): 91–120; and Chambers, "Politics and Nation-Building in America," in Joseph LaPalombara and Myron Weiner, eds., *Political Parties and Political Development* (Princeton: Princeton Univ. Press, 1966), pp. 79–106.

2. Richard Rose, "Parties, Factions, and Tendencies in Britain," *Political Studies* 12, no. 1 (Feb. 1964): 33–46.

3. V. O. Key, Jr., *Southern Politics in State and Nation* (New York: Alfred A. Knopf, 1949); Key, *American State Politics: An Introduction* (New York: Alfred A. Knopf, 1956); and Key, *Politics, Parties, and Pressure Groups* (New York: Thomas Y. Crowell, 1942 [2d ed., 1947; 3d ed., 1952; 4th ed., 1958; 5th ed., 1964]). Key's most extensive analysis of factionalism appears in *Politics, Parties, and Pressure Groups*, 3d edition.

4. For example, George M. Foster, "The Dyadic Contract: A Model for the Social Structure of a Mexican Peasant Village," in Jack M. Potter, May N. Diaz, and George M. Foster, eds., *Peasant Society: A Reader* (Boston: Little, Brown, 1967), pp. 213–30; John Duncan Powell, "Peasant Society and Clientelist Politics," *American Political Science Review* 64, no. 2 (June 1970): 411–25; James C. Scott, "Patron-Client Politics and Political Change in Southeast Asia," *American Political Science Review* 66, no. 1 (Mar. 1972): 91–112; and Norman K. Nicholson, "The Factional Model and the Study of Politics," *Comparative Political Studies* 5, no. 3 (Oct. 1972): 291–314.

5. M. G. Smith, "A Structural Approach to Comparative Politics," in David Easton, ed., *Varieties of Political Theory* (Englewood Cliffs: Prentice-Hall, 1966), pp. 113–28.

6. Ralph W. Nicholas, "Factions: A Comparative Analysis," in Michael Banton, ed., *Political Systems and the Distribution of Power*, Association of Social Anthropologists, Monograph no. 2 (London: Tavistock Publications, 1965), pp. 21–61; and Nicholas, "Segmentary Factional Political Systems," in Marc J. Swartz, Victor W. Turner, and Arthur Tuden, eds., *Political Anthropology* (Chicago: Aldine, 1966), pp. 49–59.

7. Maurice Duverger, *Political Parties: Their Organization and Activity in the Modern State*, trans. Barbara and Robert North (New York: John Wiley and Sons, 1954).

8. Allan P. Sindler, "Bifactional Rivalry as an Alternative to Two-Party Competition in Louisiana," *American Political Science Review* 49, no. 3 (Sept. 1955): 641–62; Sindler, *Huey Long's Louisiana: State Politics, 1920–1952* (Baltimore: Johns Hopkins Press, 1956); and Sindler, *Political Parties in the United States* (New York: St. Martin's Press, 1966).

9. Raphael Zariski, "Intra-Party Conflict in a Dominant Party: The Experience of the Italian Christian Democracy," *Journal of Politics* 27 (Feb. 1965): 3–34.

10. Giovanni Sartori, "Tentative Framework for a Typology of Political Parties" (Draft paper for the Conference on Political Parties, Social Science Research Council, Rome, Jan. 1964); and Sartori, "Proporzionalismo, frazionismo, e crisi dei partiti," *Rivista Italiana di Scienza Politica* 1, no. 3 (Dec. 1971): 629–55.

11. "A faction seems to subordinate the public good to private gain." Harold D. Lasswell, "Factions," *Encyclopedia of the Social Sciences*, 5: 51.

449

12. Rajni Kothari, "The Congress Party 'System' in India," *Asian Survey* 4 (Dec. 1964): 1161–74.

13. Harry Eckstein, "Parties, Political—II: Party Systems," *International Encyclopedia of the Social Sciences* 9: 436–53.

Index

Index

453

Faction Politics was compiled and edited by Frank P. Belloni and Dennis C. Beller. Copy editing was done by Paulette Wamego, proofing for the publisher was by Jean Holzinger and Gail Marceaux. Cover art by Jack Swartz, text by Shelly Lowenkopf using optima display and Baskerville text. Composition by Datagraphics, Inc., Phoenix, Arizona on a Videocomp 830. Offset printing and binding by the Crawfordsville, Ind., Manufacturing Division of R. R. Donnelley and Sons Co.